Lecture Notes in Computer Science   10528

Commenced Publication in 1973
Founding and Former Series Editors:
Gerhard Goos, Juris Hartmanis, and Jan van Leeuwen

More information about this series at http://www.springer.com/series/7407

Ming Liu · Haoyao Chen
Markus Vincze (Eds.)

Computer
Vision Systems

11th International Conference, ICVS 2017
Shenzhen, China, July 10–13, 2017
Revised Selected Papers

Springer

Editors
Ming Liu
Hong Kong University of Science
and Technology
Hong Kong
China

Haoyao Chen
Harbin Institute of Technology
Shenzhen
China

Markus Vincze
Technische Universtiät Wien
Vienna
Austria

ISSN 0302-9743 ISSN 1611-3349 (electronic)
Lecture Notes in Computer Science
ISBN 978-3-319-68344-7 ISBN 978-3-319-68345-4 (eBook)
DOI 10.1007/978-3-319-68345-4

Library of Congress Control Number: 2017955722

LNCS Sublibrary: SL1 – Theoretical Computer Science and General Issues

Printed on acid-free paper

This Springer imprint is published by Springer Nature
The registered company is Springer International Publishing AG
The registered company address is: Gewerbestrasse 11, 6330 Cham, Switzerland

Preface

The 11th International Conference on Computer Vision Systems (ICVS 2017) aimed to gather researchers and developers from both academia and industry worldwide and to explore the state of the art and the prospects of vision systems. ICVS 2017 was held in Shenzhen, China, during July 10–13, 2017. The perspective on systems offers a unique opportunity for sharing competence in application development and for identifying application-driven research questions. This 11th ICVS event continued the momentum of the series held in Spain (1999), Canada (2001), Austria (2003), USA (2006), Germany (2007), Greece (2008), Belgium (2009), France (2011), Russia (2013), and Denmark (2015). ICVS 2017 was held for the first time in Asia and was a great event for all participants, with excellent technical and social programs in Shenzhen, China. The objective of this conference is to provide a forum and opportunity for scientists and engineers to meet and assess the latest developments in the fast-growing field of computer vision systems.

The conference received 92 submissions from 13 countries and regions and finally accepted 61 papers for presentation. Each summited paper was reviewed by at least two reviewers and was ranked in a list according to their scores. The acceptance rate was approximately 66%. The Program Committee aimed to balance the program with papers on theoretic development and experimentation. In this volume, the papers are organized into 11 sections: (1) Visual Control, (2) Visual Navigation, (3) Visual Inspection, (4) Image Processing, (5) Human–Robot Interaction, (6) Stereo System, (7) Image Retrieval, (8) Visual Detection, (9) Visual Recognition, (10) System Design, and (11) 3D Vision/Fusion. Special thanks to Prof. Roland Siegwart, Prof. Hesheng Wang, and Prof. Yongchun Fang for their wonderful plenary and keynote talks.

We would like to express our gratitude to every individual who contributed to the success of ICVS 2017. Firstly, we thank all authors for contributing their papers to the conference. We are also indebted to the members of the community who offered their precious time and expertise in performing various roles ranging from organizational to reviewing roles. Your efforts, energy, and degree of professionalism deserve the highest commendations. Special thanks to the Program Committee members and the external reviewers for their support in evaluating the papers submitted to ICVS 2017, thereby ensuring the quality of the scientific program. We also offer thanks to all the colleagues, secretaries, volunteers, and engineers involved in the conference organization, particularly Qinghai Liao, Haoyang Ye, Lei Tai, Yuying Chen, Qing Liang, Sujie Lu, Bin Luo, Yaonan Fei, Jinshuai Liu, Kaiqing Zhou, Zhichen Pan, and Hao Deng as conference secretaries. A special thanks to the members of the Steering Committee, Prof. Henrik Christensen, Prof. James Crowley, and Prof. Bruce Draper, for their guidance and valuable advice.

The conference would not have been possible without the supporters and sponsors: Hong Kong University of Science and Technology, City University of Hong Kong

Shenzhen Research Institute, Harbin Institute of Technology (Shenzhen), TU Wien, and Shenzhen Institutes of Advanced Technology, CAS, with special thanks to IntoRobot Open Source IoT Team and Shenzhen MOLMC Technology. Finally, we thank Springer for publishing the proceedings in the LNCS series.

It is our hope that this fine collection of articles will be a valuable resource for our readers and will stimulate further research into the vibrant area of computer vision systems.

August 2017   Ming Liu
                                                     Haoyao Chen
                                                    Markus Vincze

Organization

Honorary Chairs

Henrik I. Christensen   University of California San Diego, USA
James L. Crowley   Inria, France
Bruce Draper   Colorado State University, USA

Conference Chairs

Markus Vincze   Technische Universität Wien, Austria
Ming Liu   Hong Kong University of Science and Technology, Hong Kong, SAR China

Program Chairs

Haoyao Chen   Harbin Institute of Technology Shenzhen, China
Lazaros Nalpantidis   Aalborg University Copenhagen, Denmark
Ning Sun   Nankai University, China
Zeyang Xia   Shenzhen Institutes of Advanced Technology of CAS, China

Exhibition Chair

Xiaorui Zhu   Harbin Institute of Technology, China

Publicity Chairs

Yantao Shen   University of Nevada, USA
Shixin Mao   Industrial Technology Research Institute, China

Tutorials and Workshops Chairs

Youfu Li   City University of Hong Kong, Hong Kong, SAR China
Lujia Wang   Shenzhen Institute of Advanced Technology of CAS, China

Publication Chairs

Yongsheng Ou   Shenzhen Institute of Advanced Technology of CAS, China
Huaping Liu   Tsinghua University, China

Financial Chair

Xuebo Zhang   Nankai University, China

Registration Chair

Yuqing He   Shenyang Institute of Automation, China

Award Chair

Erbao Dong   University of Science and Technology of China, China

Conference Secretaries

Qinghai Liao   Hong Kong University of Science and Technology,
                                Hong Kong, SAR China
Lei Tai   Hong Kong University of Science and Technology,
                                Hong Kong, SAR China
Haoyang Ye   Hong Kong University of Science and Technology,
                                Hong Kong, SAR China
Qing Liang   Hong Kong University of Science and Technology,
                                Hong Kong, SAR China
Yuying Chen   Hong Kong University of Science and Technology,
                                Hong Kong, SAR China
Sujie Lu   Hong Kong University of Science and Technology,
                                Hong Kong, SAR China
Bin Luo   Harbin Institute of Technology Shenzhen, China
Yaonan Fei   Harbin Institute of Technology Shenzhen, China
Jinshuai Liu   Harbin Institute of Technology Shenzhen, China
Kaiqiang Zhou   Harbin Institute of Technology Shenzhen, China
Zhichen Pan   Harbin Institute of Technology Shenzhen, China
Hao Deng   Shenzhen Institutes of Advanced Technology of CAS,
                                China

Program Committee

Ales Leonardis	Bernt Schiele	Huiyu Zhou
Alexandre Bernardino	Biao Zhang	Ioannis Pratikakis
Anan Suebsomran	Bruce Draper	James Crowley
Antonios Gasteratos	Claudio Pinhanez	Jian Huang
Antonis Argyros	Constantine Kotropoulos	Jian-Gang Wang
Atsushi Mitani	François Bremond	Jindong Tan
Baerbel Mertsching	Genci Capi	Jingchuan Wang
Balasundram Amavasai	Gerald Schaefer	John Tsotsos
Baopu Li	Haoyang Ye	Jong Hyeon Park
Baoquan Li	Haoyao Chen	Jorge Cabrera

Junyan Ma
Kensuke Harada
Lazaros Nalpantidis
Lei Tai
Lucas Paletta
Lujia Wang
Min Tan
Ming Liu
Ming Zhang
Minhua Zheng
Ning Sun
Panos Trahanias
Qieshi Zhang

Qing Liang
Qinghai Liao
Qingsong Xu
Robert Fisher
Sebastian Wrede
Sheng Bi
Srikanth Saripalli
Stübl Gernot
Toshio Tsuji
Wai-Keung Fung
Xiangfei Qian
Xiaorui Zhu
Xin Kang

Xinwu Liang
Xuebo Zhang
Yangmin Li
Yoichi Sato
Youfu Li
Yunjiang Lou
Zeyang Xia
Zhan Song
Zhaozheng Yin
Zhe Liu
Zhuming Bi

Sponsors

 THE HONG KONG UNIVERSITY OF SCIENCE AND TECHNOLOGY

Hong Kong University of
Science and Technology

 Harbin Institute of Technology

Harbin Institute of Technology

香港城市大學
City University
of Hong Kong

City University of Hong Kong
Shenzhen Research Institute

 TECHNISCHE UNIVERSITÄT WIEN

VIENNA UNIVERSITY OF TECHNOLOGY

TU Wien

Shenzhen Institutes
of Advanced Technology, CAS

MOLMC Shenzhen
Technology Co., Ltd.

IntoRobot

IntoRobot Open Source IoT
Research Team

Contents

Visual Inspection

Image Processing

Image Retrieval

Visual Detection

Visual Recognition

System Design

3D Vision/Fusion

Visual Control

Towards a Cloud Robotics Platform
for Distributed Visual SLAM

Peng Yun[1], Jianhao Jiao[2], and Ming Liu[2(⊠)]

[1] Department of Computer Science Engineering,
HKUST, Kowloon, Hong Kong
pyun@ust.hk
[2] Department of Electronic and Computer Engineering,
HKUST, Kowloon, Hong Kong
{jjiao,eelium}@ust.hk

Abstract. Cloud computing allows robots to offload computation and share information as well as skills. Visual SLAM is one of the intensively computational tasks for mobile robots. It can benefit from the cloud. In this paper, we propose a novel cloud robotics platform named RSE-PF for distributed visual SLAM with close attention to the infrastructure of the cloud. We implement it with Amazon Web Services and OpenResty. We demonstrate the feasibility, robustness, and elasticity of the proposed platform with a use case of perspective-n-point solution. In this use case, the average round-trip delay is 153 ms, which meets the near real-time requirement of mobile robots.

Keywords: Cloud robotics · Mobile robots · Visual SLAM · Perspective-n-point

1 Introduction

1.1 Motivation

Visual SLAM is one of the intensively computational tasks for mobile robots [1,2]. It requires powerful processors to estimate the pose from each incoming frame in real time [3]. Cloud computing is a promising method to make up for the deficiency of local computational ability. Traditional robotics, which combined with cloud computing, evolves into cloud robotics in recent years. The cloud allows robots to offload intensively computational tasks and large-scale storage, so that both cost and power consumption of robots get reduced [4]. Besides,

This work was sponsored by the Research Grant Council of Hong Kong SAR Government, China, under project No. 16212815, 21202816 and National Natural Science Foundation of China No. 6140021318 and 61640305; Shenzhen Science, Technology and Innovation Comission (SZSTI) JCYJ20160428154842603 and JCYJ20160401100022706; partially supported by the HKUST Project IGN16EG12. All rewarded to Prof. Ming Liu.

© Springer International Publishing AG 2017
M. Liu et al. (Eds.): ICVS 2017, LNCS 10528, pp. 3–15, 2017.
DOI: 10.1007/978-3-319-68345-4_1

robots have an access to a shared repository on the cloud [5–7]. As a result, data sharing and skills reusing can be achieved. A robot is eventually not only a machine but also a bridge between its user and heterogeneous services.

Although the cloud benefits robots, some drawbacks and challenges still exist and must be further addressed. Existing cloud robotics platforms enable data transmission and executing computation parallelly [4,8] and optimizedly [9,10]. However, few of them pay attention to the infrastructure of the cloud. Similar to other cloud platforms, the platform for distributed visual SLAM is open to the public and required to run stably in a long time. Under a long-term operation, some modules of the cloud tend to crash occasionally. In this paper, we pay close attention to the robustness, security, and elasticity of the cloud. We propose a novel cloud robotics platform named RSE-PF for distributed visual SLAM.

Besides, most of the previous work constructed their cloud platforms with ROS[1]. ROS provides researchers a middleware to design their robot systems in a modular way. The loosely coupled modules can be re-used, which helps researchers implement their robot systems conveniently. However, there are still some shortcomings with ROS, like its huge overhead and platform dependencies. Therefore, different with [5], RSE-PF does not treat ROS as a necessary part.

1.2   Contribution

We stress the following contributions in this paper.

- We clarify the tasks of each cloud service type for distributed visual SLAM and propose a novel cloud robotics platform named RSE-PF.
- We demonstrate the feasibility, robustness, and elasticity of RSE-PF with implementing the perspective-n-point solution for autonomous robots creating point cloud maps in a distributed way.

  The features of RSE-PF are as follows.

Robust: The broken servers are detected and replaced automatically.
Secure: Only authorized users are allowed to send requests to the cloud.
Elastic: The cloud scales outward when it is under huge pressure. It scales inward when it keeps idle for a while.
Multiple programming languages supported: Visual SLAM services could be implemented with C/CPP and Lua scripts. Researchers are allowed to implement their application with/without ROS.

1.3   Organization

In Sect. 2, a brief introduction to cloud computing and previous work is described. In Sect. 3, we clarify the tasks of three cloud service types for distributed visual SLAM. The RSE-PF model is presented in Sect. 4 along with the implementation in Sect. 5. In Sect. 6, we demonstrate the feasibility and features of RSE-PF via implementing the perspective-n-point solution based on proposed cloud platform. Finally, we conclude with a discussion of our future work.

---

[1] http://www.ros.org/.

2 Related Work

2.1 Cloud Computing

NIST defined cloud computing and three service types of it [11], i.e. Software as a Service (SaaS), Platform as a Service (PaaS), and Infrastructure as a Service (IaaS). In brief, SaaS applications are exposed to users. The users have an access to the functional applications via various devices (e.g. mobile phones, laptops, tablets) and do not manage or control hardware resources or runtime environments directly. The users of PaaS are provided a platform which includes programming languages, dependencies, and management tools. They are allowed to deploy their applications on the platform without consideration on the infrastructure of the cloud. As for IaaS, the users are able to manage or control the cloud infrastructure in the way provided by IaaS providers. IaaS, PaaS, and SaaS offer increasing abstraction. The relationship of these three cloud service types is considered as Fig. 1.

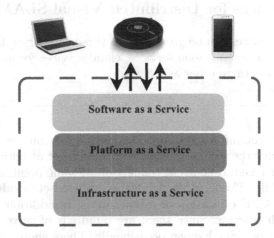

Fig. 1. The relationship of IaaS, PaaS, and SaaS: IaaS provides basic computing, storage as well as network components to the platform. PaaS provides necessary runtime environment to applications. SaaS is the functional applications which are exposed to the users.

2.2 Cloud-Based Visual SLAM

As for visual SLAM, robots are required to compute the camera pose from each incoming frame. Limited by on-board computational ability, robots are hard to locate themselves and map the scene in real time. Enti et al. [4] proposed DAvinCi framework which offloaded intensively computational workload from onboard resources to a backend cluster system. They implemented such a software framework around Hadoop cluster with ROS message. They proved the feasibility of their system and performance gains in execution times through implementing the FastSLAM based on DAvinCi. RoboEarth [6] aims to develop a giant repository and achieve a World Wide Web for robots so that robots are able to share data and reuse skills. As a part of RoboEarth project, Repyuta [5] provided an access to RoboEarth knowledge repository which enables robots to share data and skills. Based on Rapyuta, [7] implemented a dense visual odometry algorithm on a smartphone-class ARM multi-core CPU.

A common feature of previous work is that they built a bridge between clients and servers with ROS message or WebSocket. Clients send data to the cloud, and servers finally send results back. In this way, offloading can be achieved. However, the infrastructure of the cloud does not get a full use. In this paper, we propose a cloud robotics platform for distributed visual SLAM with consideration on robustness, security, and elasticity. Besides, in order to show the feasibility and features of RSE-PF, we demonstrate the use case that multiple robots create point cloud maps simultaneously and distributedly with the PnP solution service based on RSE-PF.

3   Cloud Services for Distributed Visual SLAM

In general, cloud services can be grouped into three categories: IaaS, PaaS, and SaaS [11]. Similar to general cloud services, cloud services for distributed visual SLAM includes these three types as follows.

3.1   IaaS

IaaS provides basic computation, storage, and network resources. Since the cloud is open to the public, the security of the cloud should get attention. Besides, the cloud may be under high concurrent connection at some point, and it may also keep idle for a while. Therefore, it should be adjusted elastically according to some metrics like CPU utilization or robot counts. In addition, the infrastructure must be fault-tolerant. Since there are hundreds of servers in the cloud, some crashes or errors may happen occasionally. There should be a robustness mechanism to handle such situations, like replacing the crashed server with a new one.

3.2   PaaS

PaaS provides prerequisites to SaaS applications, like dependencies, programming language supports, etc. It also provides each robot client with secure and isolated runtime environments. Besides, the communication protocol between robots and the cloud should be well-designed to save bandwidth resources and reduce network delay. In addition, the platform should be with low overhead so that the cloud are able to handle high concurrent connections.

3.3 SaaS

SaaS provides visual SLAM services in a stateless way. The stateless way means the received requests contain all necessary information for SaaS applications, and the cloud does not need to retain information for computation. In Sect. 6, the PnP solution is one of the stateless applications.

As mentioned in IaaS, one robustness mechanism is to replace the crashed server with a new one. With this mechanism, the new server can hardly provide services to the past users if the SaaS application is stateful. It is because the state information has gone with the crashed server. Take ORB-SLAM [3] for an example. ORB-SLAM is classified as a stateful algorithm in this paper, for the keyframes of ORB-SLAM could be considered as the state of this algorithm. When the server running ORB-SLAM crashes, another one can hardly replace it and continue to provide services because the keyframes have gone with that broken server.

Besides, it is important to consider the influence of network delay in some visual SLAM applications which are sensitive to network delay. At $t + \Delta t_1$, the cloud receives the message which was sent at t. The result of this message will be received by the robot at $t + \Delta t_1 + \Delta t_2$. Δt_1 and Δt_2 are the network delay of uploading and downloading respectively.

4   RSE-PF Model

Based on three cloud service types, we propose RSE-PF for distributed visual SLAM. As depicted in Fig. 2, it consists of a firewall, a load balancer, a monitor, a scale modifier, multiple backend servers, and multiple data servers. The main functions of each part are as follows.

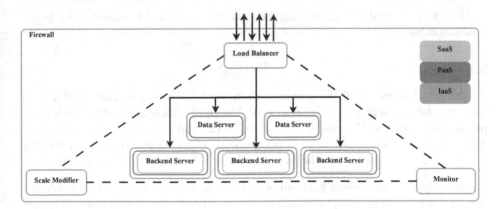

Fig. 2. The architecture of RSE-PF model (Orange: infrastructure, blue: platform, green: software) (Color figure online)

firewall: Since the cloud provides services to the public, a firewall is a necessary part of the cloud. Developers design the security rules, open ports, and access control lists to protect the cloud from unauthorized visits.

load balancer: It distributes requests to backend and data servers. It also executes health detection towards backend and data servers periodically.

monitor: It monitors the states of the cloud, including the result of the health detection, CPU and bandwidth usage of backend server, etc. Once some events get detected, the monitor will inform the scale modifier.

scale modifier: It modifies the scale of the cloud after getting informed by the monitor. It launches servers when the cloud is under big pressure. It also kills servers when the cloud keeps idle for a while. Besides, it replaces the broken server with a new one according to the result of health detection.

backend server: Developers design the transmission method between robots and the cloud. They also implement their visual SLAM applications like PnP, place recognition in a stateless way.

data server: It stores data which needs long-term storage or to be shared among multiple robots. Images, key frames, and maps can be stored in visual SLAM applications.

In Fig. 2, IaaS, PaaS, and SaaS are labeled accordingly. The mechanism of IaaS originates from Amazon Web Services[2], which is as follows. After requests reach the load balancer through a firewall, the load balancer distributes the requests to backend and data servers. Backend servers make computation and exchange data with data servers. In addition, when the monitor detects events like unhealthy servers or some metrics exceeding warning lines, it will inform the scale modifier. Subsequently, the scale modifier will adjust the cloud scale.

5   RSE-PF Implementation

In this part, we will detail the implementation of RSE-PF model from IaaS, PaaS, and SaaS.

5.1   IaaS

As proposed above, RSE-PF consists of a load balancer, a scale modifier, a monitor, data servers and backend servers. Multiple companies provide their IaaS productions, such as Amazon Web Services(AWS) and Google Compute Engine[3]. AWS provides some cloud services infrastructures, covering computing, storing and network. We implement the IaaS of RSE-PF based on AWS as follows.

Computing: We implement backend servers with Amazon EC2 instances. Amazon EC2 allows users to exploit cloud resources on demand. Via Amazon Machine Images or executing pre-prepared scripts, EC2 instances are armed with qualified environments immediately after they get created.

---

[2] https://aws.amazon.com/.
[3] https://cloud.google.com/compute/.

Storage: AWS provides multiple types of storage, including S3, EBS, and Glacier, etc. S3 allows long-time storing, just like network disks. A little difference to network disks is that S3 naturally serves machines instead of human beings. API is provided to help developers manage and develop the cloud automatically. EBS provides high IOPS, just like hard disk, while Glacier provides cheap and permanent storing service, which suits for storing log files and raw data.

Network: Amazon Virtual Private Cloud can be used to construct the cloud architecture and improve the security of the cloud. Besides, main parts can be doubled with VPC to add redundancy and achieve high availability.

Security: Besides VPC, each EC2 instance is protected by a firewall. Users can limit unauthorized visits with secure strategies of this firewall.

Management: Elastic Load Balancer of AWS can be used as a load balancer. It performs request distribution and health detection. In particular, HTTP, HTTPS, and WebSocket protocols are all supported in AWS Elastic Load Balancer. CloudWatch of AWS helps monitor the whole cloud. It alarms when some metrics of the cloud exceeding their thresholds. In addition, AWS Auto Scaling helps modify the scale of cloud system elastically after being alarmed by Cloud-Watch.

5.2   PaaS

The PaaS of RSE-PF is implemented based on $OpenResty^{TM4}$. It is a powerful web platform which integrates Nginx core, Lua libraries and LuaJIT. Researchers are allowed to implement web services on it with Lua scripts, Nginx C modules, and C/CPP programming languages. Compared to huge overhead of ROS, $OpenResty^{TM}$ is capable of handling 10 K to 1000 K connections in a single server.

The flowchart RSE-PF PaaS is shown in Fig. 3. Subsequently, we will define the communication protocol and explain how to build an isolated computing environment for each robot.

Communication Protocol: In general, messages of visual SLAM transmitted between robots and the cloud could be classified as three types: command, data, and result messages. In most applications of visual SLAM, both command and result messages are small-scale, like place recognition and pose estimation. Therefore, we encode command and result messages into JavaScript Object Notation (JSON). JSON is a lightweight data exchange format which is easy for machines to parse and generate. The JSON format string can be easily decoded in the cloud via $OpenResty^{TM}$ cjson Lua model. Typical messages are shown in Fig. 3.

To maintain a bi-directional full duplex connection between robots and the cloud, WebSocket is used to transmit messages, especially command and result messages. WebSocket is built on the top of HTTP. It creates open communication channels between clients and servers. As a consequence, the cloud is able to publish messages actively without robots asking results periodically.

---

[4] https://OpenResty.org/.

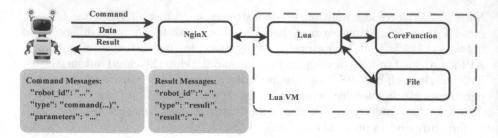

Fig. 3. The flowchart of RSE-PF PaaS (Robots send command and data messages to the cloud, while the cloud publishes results back to robots. In the cloud, when the connection between the robot and the cloud is established, a Lua VM is created. Following computation work will be completely processed in this Lua VM.)

Besides, compared with HTTP, WebSocket-based transmission helps save bandwidth resources hundreds of times under high concurrent connection. It also helps reduce 70% network delay compared with HTTP long polling [12].

Payload length of messages is one of the key metrics because large scale messages consume plenty of bandwidth resources. Some results demonstrated that the delay and packet loss will increase if payload length of messages increases [5]. Therefore, we compress JSON format string with Zip before transmission.

In applications of visual SLAM, robots might need to offload some data like point clouds, maps, and RGB images to the cloud for storage or computation. These data might be larger than 100 Kbytes. Converting images or point clouds to JSON format string would result in an even larger message size. When the payload length goes up, the performance goes down. As a result, we adopt HTTP to post files to data servers instead of encoding them to JSON string so that larger message size caused by converting is avoided.

Isolated Computing Environment: When the connection between the robot and the cloud is established, a Lua VM is created. Further computational tasks will totally be processed in this Lua VM. After loading necessary Lua models or C dynamic link libraries, the computational environment specific for this robot

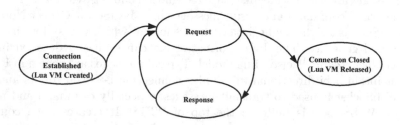

Fig. 4. The state diagram of the cloud (When the connection is established, the Lua VM is created. The robotic services will be provided in a request-response way. Once the connection is closed, the Lua VM will be released)

is prepared. Besides, the memory of each Lua VM is also isolated from others. After the Lua VM having been created, the robotic services start. The robot sends command messages to the cloud, and the cloud will publish result messages actively towards the robot. If the robot does not need services any more, this connection will be closed, and the Lua VM will be released simultaneously. The life length of Lua VM is as the same to the connection, which is shown in Fig. 4.

5.3   SaaS

In RSE-PF, we develop visual SLAM services with Lua and C/CPP. Lua is a lightweight script language, which could help implement some basic processing, like encoding and decoding of JSON format string, recording logs, etc. C/CPP could help implement complicated logics in visual SLAM algorithms. In RSE-PF, developers are allowed to compile their C/CPP codes of robotic services into dynamic link libraries, which will be called by LuaJIT FFI.

As shown in Fig. 3, The message received by Nginx are processed by Lua basically, like file operations, encoding and decoding. It implements complicated logics of visual SLAM by calling core functions which is dynamic link libraries coded by C/CPP. Finally, the returned value from core functions will be published actively to the robot. Furthermore, in order to detail the method to implement SaaS of RSE-PF, we take perspective-n-point as an example in next section.

6   RSE-PF Use Case

In this section, we implement perspective-n-point (PnP) solution [13] based on RSE-PF to demonstrate its feasibility and features. With PnP robotic service, robots create point cloud maps from the NYU Depth V2 dataset [14].

The perspective-n-point is the problem of estimating the position and orientation of the camera given n correspondent points. It originates from camera calibration and is widely used in many fields, especially location and navigation of autonomous robots.

6.1   Implementation

Since both matched key points and transformation matrix are in small scale in PnP solution service, all necessary information are sent by command or result messages via WebSocket. Besides, we compress JSON-format string with libz to reduce bandwidth costs.

The division of computation between robots and the cloud is shown in Fig. 5. In the cloud, Lua modules process requests basically, including encoding, decoding, compressing and decompressing. We implement PnP solution based on the solvePnPRansac function of OpenCV. It makes the final solution more robust to outliers with RANSAC. We encapsulate the PnP solution into a core function. The process is shown in Fig. 6. The robot computes descriptors and matches

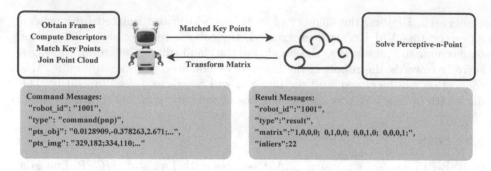

Fig. 5. Computation division between robots and the cloud (PnP)

Lua Scripts   C/CPP core function

```
server_initialization()
while true
{
    data = receive()
    data = uncompress(data)
    if the data contains close command
        close the connection
    else
    {
        result = ffi.pnp_solution(data)
        result = compress(result)
        send(result)
    }
}
```

```
char* pnp_solution(char* data)
{
    parameters = decode_json(data)
    result = solvePnPRansac(parameters)
    result = encode_json(result)
    return result
}
```

Fig. 6. The pseudocode of PnP robotic service.

keypoints locally. After received transform matrix, it will join current frame into the point cloud. Finally, the point cloud of the whole scene will be created.

As proposed in Sect. 5, we implement the infrastructure of RSE-PF with AWS. Data servers are not used in this case because necessary information is in small scale (less than 10 KB) and can be carried in command messages. We choose AWS in Seoul because the delay from our lab in Shenzhen to Seoul EC2 server is the lowest among all AWS regions. AWS ELB, Cloud Watch, and Auto Scaling are used to construct the IaaS of RSE-PF. A hundred Docker containers act as robots and request PnP services. Docker containers run on a Core i7 processor with 16 GB RAM (Fig. 7).

Perspective   Front

Top   Left

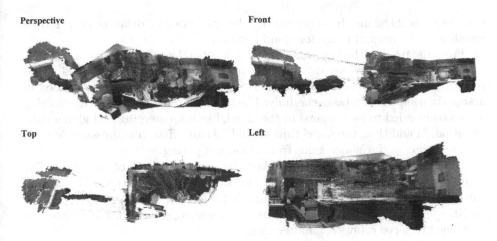

Fig. 7. The point cloud map created by one of Docker containers

6.2 Result

We record the real-time performance of all these robots. Robots perform near 5 fps in this use case, and the average time from sending a command message to receiving a result message is 156.36 ms. Specifically, the average time for server

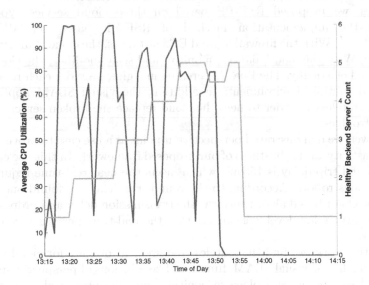

Fig. 8. The average CPU utilization and the healthy server count of the cloud when the cloud faces an increasing number of requests. (Every 20 s, a docker container is launched, so that a hundred docker containers sent requests to the cloud at the same time. Finally, we kill all docker containers after 13:52.)

computing is 29.82 ms. In other words, the transmission delay is near 130 ms which is in the normal range for cloud computing.

From the results, the transmission delay is a bottleneck for real-time distributed visual SLAM services. If better real-time performances are expected, cloud resources close to robots are preferred. Besides, developers are recommended to assign the computation tasks carefully. The tasks which are not sensitive to delay are recommended to be assigned to the cloud, like map merging and global optimization. In addition, the saved time should be more than transmission delay so that real-time performance gains from cloud computing.

Besides, Fig. 8 demonstrates the elasticity and robustness of the cloud. The cloud scales up when the average CPU utilization exceeds the threshold (70% in this case). It scales down when keeping idle for a while (5 min in this case). At 13:50, one backend server crashed. Another backend server took its place and continued to serve robots soon after that.

7 Conclusion and Future Work

In this paper, we firstly defined the tasks of three cloud service types for distributed visual SLAM. IaaS provides basic computation, storage, and network infrastructures. It is also equipped with mechanisms of security, elasticity, and robustness. PaaS defines the transmission protocols between robots and the cloud. It also provides isolated computational environments to each robot. SaaS provides visual SLAM applications for robots in a stateless way.

Besides, we proposed RSE-PF based on three cloud service types and described the implementation method of RSE-PF based on AWS and $OpenResty^{TM}$. With the firewall around EC2 instances, the cloud is under secure protection. With the load balancer, monitor, and scale modifier, the cloud runs robustly and elastically. The Lua VM created in Nginx provides each robot with an isolated runtime environment. In addition, the visual SLAM applications should be stateless in order to help the cloud replace the broken server without shooting troubles.

Moreover, we demonstrated perspective-n-point as a use case to prove the feasibility, elasticity, and robustness of our proposed framework. In this use case, the average round trip delay is 153 ms, which meets the near real-time requirement of autonomous robots. According to the round-trip delay, we found one bottleneck of the cloud-based algorithms was the transmission delay and proposed two recommendations for developers to improve the real-time performance of their algorithms.

From this work, we find the stateless requirement of SaaS for cloud robotics is a little harsh. For visual SLAM, functions like solutions of perspective-n-point, iterative closest point, and place recognition could be processed in a stateless way, but some algorithms like ORB-SLAM are complicated to implement statelessly. In the future, we plan to implement the PaaS part of RSE-PF with Docker to handle such complex robotic services. Besides vision, robots are capable of locating themselves based on WiFi signal strength [15]. It can be implemented as a SaaS application and helps robots locate themselves in indoor scenes.

References

1. Liu, M.: Robotic online path planning on point cloud. IEEE Trans. Cybern. **46**(5), 1217–1228 (2016)
2. Gianni, M., Papadakis, P., Pirri, F., Liu, M., Pomerleau, F., Colas, F., Zimmermann, K., Svoboda, T., Petricek, T., Kruijff, G.J.M.: A unified framework for planning and execution-monitoring of mobile robots. In: AAAI Conference on Automated Action Planning for Autonomous Mobile Robots, pp. 39–44 (2011)
3. Mur-Artal, R., Montiel, J.M.M., Tardos, J.D.: ORB-SLAM: a versatile and accurate monocular slam system. IEEE Trans. Robot. **31**(5), 1147–1163 (2015)
4. Arumugam, R., Enti, V.R., Bingbing, L., Xiaojun, W., Baskaran, K., Kong, F.F., Kumar, A.S., Meng, K.D., Kit, G.W.: DAvinCi: a cloud computing framework for service robots. In: 2010 IEEE International Conference on Robotics and Automation (ICRA), pp. 3084–3089. IEEE (2010)
5. Hunziker, D., Gajamohan, M., Waibel, M., D'Andrea, R.: Rapyuta: the roboearth cloud engine. In: 2013 IEEE International Conference on Robotics and Automation (ICRA), pp. 438–444. IEEE (2013)
6. Waibel, M., Beetz, M., Civera, J., d'Andrea, R., Elfring, J., Galvez-Lopez, D., Häussermann, K., Janssen, R., Montiel, J.M.M., Perzylo, A., et al.: Roboearth. IEEE Robot. Autom. Mag. **18**(2), 69–82 (2011)
7. Mohanarajah, G., Usenko, V., Singh, M., D'Andrea, R., Waibel, M.: Cloud-based collaborative 3D mapping in real-time with low-cost robots. IEEE Trans. Autom. Sci. Eng. **12**(2), 423–431 (2015)
8. Beksi, W.J., Spruth, J., Papanikolopoulos, N.: CORE: a cloud-based object recognition engine for robotics. In: 2015 IEEE/RSJ International Conference on Intelligent Robots and Systems (IROS), pp. 4512–4517. IEEE (2015)
9. Wang, L., Liu, M., Meng, M.Q.-H.: A hierarchical auction-based mechanism for real-time resource allocation in cloud robotic systems. IEEE Trans. Cybern. **47**(2), 473–484 (2017)
10. Rahman, A., Jin, J., Cricenti, A., Rahman, A., Yuan, D.: A cloud robotics framework of optimal task offloading for smart city applications. In: 2016 IEEE Global Communications Conference (GLOBECOM), pp. 1–7. IEEE (2016)
11. Mell, P., Grance, T., et al.: The NIST Definition of Cloud Computing (2011)
12. Lubbers, P., Albers, B., Salim, F., Pye, T.: Pro HTML5 Programming. Springer, Heidelberg (2011). doi:10.1007/978-1-4302-3865-2
13. Gao, X.-S., Hou, X.-R., Tang, J., Cheng, H.-F.: Complete solution classification for the perspective-three-point problem. IEEE Trans. Pattern Anal. Mach. Intell. **25**(8), 930–943 (2003)
14. Silberman, N., Hoiem, D., Kohli, P., Fergus, R.: Indoor segmentation and support inference from RGBD images. In: Fitzgibbon, A., Lazebnik, S., Perona, P., Sato, Y., Schmid, C. (eds.) ECCV 2012. LNCS, vol. 7576, pp. 746–760. Springer, Heidelberg (2012). doi:10.1007/978-3-642-33715-4_54
15. Sun, Y., Liu, M., Meng, Q.H.: WiFi signal strength-based robot indoor localization. In: IEEE International Conference on Information and Automation, pp. 250–256 (2014)

A Practical Visual Positioning Method for Industrial Overhead Crane Systems

Bo He, Yongchun Fang$^{(\boxtimes)}$, and Ning Sun

Institute of Robotics and Automatic Information System,
Nankai University, Tianjin 300350, China
hebowf1990@126.com, {fangyc,sunn}@nankai.edu.cn

Abstract. To solve the problem of information acquisition of an industrial overhead crane, this paper uses an industrial camera to get the information. The information includes the height and the swing angle of the hook and the distance between the hook and the cargo. To obtain the real-time data of the hook's height and swing angle, firstly the whole image captured by the industrial camera is processed and the hook's initial position is obtained by shape matching. As the trolley tracks the hook according to the local information of the image, the height is calculated by the interpolation method according to the number of local pixels. The swing angle is measured by the height of the hook and the distance between the initial and current positions of the upper edge. In addition to the measurement of the height and swing angle, this platform calculates the distance between the hook and the cargo based on a visual method, the cargo is observed by such features as length, width and height input by operators. This method gets the static information of the industrial scene, drives the trolley to the cargo, detects whether the hook's swing is within the proper range, and hoists the hook to the desired position. Experimental results on a 32-ton industrial crane system implies that this algorithm solves the problem of information collection and transfers the hook to a desired position.

Keywords: Industrial crane · Information acquisition · Real-time positioning

1 Introduction

An overhead crane is a transportation equipment widely used in many industrial production situations. Most of the cranes are manually operated, which causes many injury accidents. For this reason, it is important to design an automatic control system for overhead cranes. For this reason, many algorithms are proposed to restrain the swing of the hook or position the cargos precisely. As a

Y. Fang—This work is supported by the National Natural Science Foundation of China (11372144, 61503200) and the Natural Science Foundation of Tianjin (15JCQNJC03800).

© Springer International Publishing AG 2017
M. Liu et al. (Eds.): ICVS 2017, LNCS 10528, pp. 16–25, 2017.
DOI: 10.1007/978-3-319-68345-4_2

basic need to synthesize the algorithms, acquiring the states of the crane system is crucial.

As a frequently used equipment in industry, a lot of works have been done to solve the control problem of overhead cranes, and the proposed algorithms are tested on small scale laboratory cranes [1–11]. Because of the simple mechanical structure and the usage of high accuracy sensors [12], the state variables of the entire system can be obtained for laboratory cranes. In practice, because of the complex industrial situations and the consideration of the costs, we seldom get all the state variables of an industrial crane system, including the height and the swing angle of the hook, the velocity of the trolley, and the distance between the crane and the cargo, which are very important for automatic control of cranes. To be specific, the height of the hook provides the vertical position of the hook, and this information is useful in many control algorithms. The frequently used method to measure the height of the hook is using an absolute encoder, and the rope length can be calculated by the reduction ratio and the data of the absolute encoder. The measurement of the swing angle is necessary in most feedback control methods, which can be measured by some special mechanical structures on small scale laboratory crane platforms. In industrial situations, the swing of the hook is usually observed by workers near the cranes, but the accuracy cannot be guaranteed. The velocity of the trolley is measured by encoders, which is adopted in many practical situations. Positioning is a very important aspect of an automatic crane, the common method to calculate the displacement of the trolley is to accumulate the encoder's data. Another method for position measurement is to divide the ground into different areas, and transport the cargo to the specified grid, but this method highly depends upon on the operating environment.

The collection of system states mentioned above is achieved by contact sensors, but the drawback of most contact sensors is that one sensor can only measure one specific kind of signal. Collecting the information based on the visual method is more flexible and economic, and different system states can be obtained by only one camera. The visual method is applied in many areas in manufacturing [13,14]. Many researchers use cameras as signal collectors on crane platforms. In [15], a ball is installed under the hook to detect the swing angle. Singhose et al. use a stick as a guidance, and make the crane track the trajectory of the stick through a camera installed on the trolley [16], which uses input shaping to optimize the operating process. In [17] , two cameras are installed on the mechanized platform to position the payload and measure the swing angle. Binocular vision is also adopted in [18], and after getting the states of the crane system by two cameras, the sliding-mode control is used in the transportation process.

Compared with the laboratory cranes, the industrial cranes are usually operated in more complex situations, which makes it difficult to collect all states. It is important to pick up the information we really need and easy to get in practice.

For the information collection problem for practical cranes, this paper provides an information collection method based on an industrial camera, the information to be collected includes the rope length, the swing angle and the distance between the hook and the cargo. To be specific, before the movement of the trolley, we first obtain the position of the hook and the distance between the hook and the cargo through static images using feature matching. Then, the trolley transports the hook to the set point right above the cargo. In the transportation process, we use local characteristics to track the hook and measure the swing angle by the images captured by an industrial camera. After the horizontal movement, it is detected whether the positioning error caused by swing is in a reasonable range. Finally, the hook is lowered to the target place according to the height information captured by the camera, which uses the partial information of the image to track the hook and calculate the height by interpolation method.

2   Scenario Analysis

We define one corner of the plant as the origin of the world coordinate. The camera is fixed on the trolley, which is convenient to calculate the extrinsic parameter matrixes M_1.

To get the intrinsic matrix, we lower the hook to a specific position, measure the distance between the camera and the hook, and then obtain the pixel number of the upper edge. The intrinsic matrix M_2 can be calculated by the pixel number and actual distance. The relationship between a point X_w in the world coordinate and the imaging point M can be expressed as:

$$M = M_1 M_2 X_W \tag{1}$$

When transporting the cargo to the target place, we should consider the acceptable offset of the hook and make the error converge to an appropriate range. The error is induced by three factors, which includes the accuracy of the camera, the error caused by hook's swing, and the vibration transmitted from the trolley.

The accuracy of the camera depends on the resolution. It is assumed that the resolution of the camera is $m \times n$. After installing the camera to the fixed place, the corresponding observation size near the ground is $x \times y$, then one pixel can represent the actual distance Δl, satisfying the following equation:

$$\Delta l = l/m \tag{2}$$

In practice, we are interested in the error near the hook instead of the error near the ground. We assume the distance between the hook and the camera is l_0, and the height of the camera is l_1. The distance represented by each pixel near the hook is

$$\Delta l_{hook} = l_0 \Delta l / l_1 \tag{3}$$

In the transportation process, the trolley will vibrate due to the hook's sway or the uneven pathway. We should investigate the vibration during the movement process as a feedback in some algorithms. After the trolley is transported to the target place, we should also observe the hook's sway because it will affect the locating control performance. To obtain the error caused by vibration, the trolley starts to move with its maximal speed, and then we measure the deviation of the camera by observing the change of the image's edge. Assume that the largest deviation of the image near the ground is $\Delta l_{vibration}$.

The sway of the hook will also affect the positioning of the cargo. The maximal error induced by swing is Δl_{sway}, and the total deviation of the measurement Δl_{total} can be expressed as:

$$\Delta l_{total} \leq \Delta l_{sway} + \Delta l + \Delta l_{vibration}. \tag{4}$$

The total deviation, which can be detected by the camera, converges to an appropriate bound as the vibration and sway become more and more slight. Then we can lower the cargo to the ground with an acceptable error. But Δl_{total} calculated by (4) is the deviation near the ground, and we should convert it to the acceptable deviation Δl_1 near the hook through the following equation:

$$\Delta l_1 \leq l_0 \Delta l_{total}/l_1. \tag{5}$$

In this equation, l_0 is the distance between the hook and the camera, and l_1 represents the height of the camera. After the horizontal moving, if the deviation is larger than Δl_1, we should wait until the deviation converges to the proper bound, and then proceed to the next operation.

3   Measurement of the Height and Sway Angle

To obtain the real-time information of the hook, we adopt the partial feature matching method to track the hook and measure the height and the sway angle. The flow chart of the whole process is shown in Fig. 1. First, the states of the trolley should be confirmed. If the trolley is not moving, we detect whether the vibration exists. Otherwise, the camera collects the image of the workplace.

Commonly, the hooks of the heavy-load cranes are extremely large, and the camera's installation place should be kept away from the rope, so it cannot be installed right above the hook. Because of this, the image captured by the camera involves the side information of the hook, which enables the camera to adopt shape matching to find it. The camera is fixed on the trolley, so the hook is operated in the specific area of the camera's field of view. Based on this, we detect the outline of the hook in a specific area, which increases the efficiency of the shape matching process.

The features of the hook will change as the hook is at different heights. The camera should consider all the situations to exactly detect the hook.

After finding the hook, one can get the upper edge through the change of the coordinate values, and then extract the number of pixels of the upper edge. The interpolation method is adopted to calculate the length of the rope according to the length-pixel number relationship measured off-line. The position of the hook at this moment is considered as the initial position.

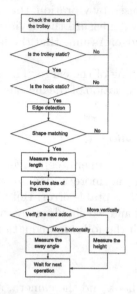

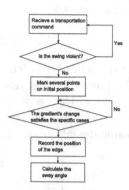

Fig. 1. The total flowchart.   **Fig. 2.** The flowchart of the measurement of sway angle.

According to the industrial standard, the trolley and the hook cannot move at the same time, so when the trolley moves horizontally or stops moving, and we only pay attention to the sway angle. When the sway angle converges to an acceptable range and the hook starts moving vertically, the height of the hook is the only problem we should concern.

The sway angle of the hook is measured by an industrial camera, and the flowchart of the process is shown in Fig. 2. The upper edge of the hook is tracked as the trolley moves horizontally. Then we calculate the distance between the initial position and the last position, which is represented by d_2, The sway angle θ_0 can be calculated by the following equation:

$$\theta_0 = \arctan\left(d_2/l_2\right), \tag{6}$$

where l_2 is the length of the rope at this time.

To measure the rope length, when the hook is at the initial position, we mark several spots on the upper edge of the hook, and the number of spots satisfy the Gaussian distribution because the spots close to the centre of the hook are more effective. Then we should know the next action is hoisting or lowering to decide whether the measurement range should expand or compress. For each spot, we get n_0 pixels along the sway direction of the hook, and detect the gradient variation to get the position of the upper edge. Then the number of pixels of the upper edge can be obtained by edge detection, which will reflect the length of the rope through interpolation. The sway angle is so small that we can assume the number of pixels are the same when the hook is at the lower point and the higher point. Based on this, we can ignore the change of the number caused by sway. So the interpolation method is available whether the hook is swaying or not swaying. To adopt the interpolation method, the relationship between the number of pixels of upper edge and the length of the rope should be built off-line. There are several sets of data:

$$(h_1, x_1), (h_2, x_2), \ldots, (h_n, x_n). \tag{7}$$

In this equation, x_n is the number of pixels when the height of the hook is h_n. Assume that the number of pixels at current time is x_m, we can judge the range of the number is $x_k < x_m < x_{k+1}$, the height of the hook can be expressed as:

$$h_m = h_k \frac{x_m - x_k}{x_{k+1} - x_k}. \tag{8}$$

4   Measurement of the Distance Between the Hook and the Cargo

The distance of the hook and the cargo is measured by the industrial camera to facilitate the design of the online trajectory tracking algorithm. Before capturing the static image, it is confirmed that the trolley and the hook are stable. The worker inputs the length, the width and the height of the cargo, and guarantees that the cargo is on the ground. Then we calculate the range of the length and width on the platform of the height, which satisfies the following inequality:

$$l_{low} < l_{cargo} < l_{high} \tag{9}$$
$$d_{low} < d_{cargo} < d_{high}. \tag{10}$$

Then we can get the range of the total pixel numbers n_{cargo}, which is expressed as:

$$2l_{low} + 2d_{low} < n_{cargo} < 2l_{high} + 2d_{high}. \tag{11}$$

The Canny edge detection algorithm is adopted to count the number of pixels of the edge. If the number satisfies (11), then it is detected whether the shape is a quadrilateral and the range of the included angles satisfies the following condition:

$$\alpha_{min} < \alpha < \alpha_{max}, \tag{12}$$

where α_{min}, α_{max} are calculated by the camera's parameters calibrated before. The rope and the hook may interference the views of the camera. To improve the efficient of the process, this area will not be detected. If the cargo is infected by this, the trolley will change its position automatically to find the cargo.

After finding the edge of the cargo, the coordinate of the corner will be selected to calculate the center of the cargo. Assume that the corner with the minimum x-coordinate and y-coordinate is (x_1, y_1); other corners $(x_2, y_2), (x_3, y_3), (x_4, y_4)$ are acquired clockwise. The coordinates of the cargo's center x_{cargo}, y_{cargo} can be expressed as:

$$x_{cargo} = \frac{(x_2 - x_1) + (x_3 - x_4)}{2} \tag{13}$$

$$y_{cargo} = \frac{(y_3 - y_1) + (y_2 - y_4)}{2}. \tag{14}$$

The coordinate of the midpoint (x_0, y_0) of the hook's upper edge is easy to acquire, and the coordinate of the center of the hook x_{hook}, y_{hook} satisfies:

$$d_x = x_{cargo} - x_{hook} \tag{15}$$

$$d_y = y_{cargo} - y_{hook}. \tag{16}$$

To improve the accuracy and efficiency of the transformation, an online trajectory planning method [19] is adopted to accomplish this process. The distance to the target position, which is estimated by operators in [19], is detected by the camera and substituting into the equations of this algorithm to calculate the proper parameters of the trajectory.

5   Experiment Results

The experimental platform is a standard 32 ton double-girder crane. Considering the space to place the tools and the passway, the main operation area of this crane is 47.5 m × 25 m. In this platform we use a Blackfly camera made by Point Grey company, whose the model in [20] is used to calculate the visual angle, the horizontal and vertical viewing angle as $\theta_h = 68.31°, \theta_v = 56.98°$. The height of the camera is 10 m. We can calculate that the distance of one pixel near the ground is 0.0106 m. Because the view of the camera cannot cover the whole area, the operators should move the overhead crane to the area where the cargo is in view of the camera.

Considering the feature of the hook in this platform, the right side of the hook is used for shape matching, the position of the upper edge is detected according to the variation trend of the pixel. The relationship between the rope's length and the pixel's number is measured outline. The rope's length can be calculated by (8).

To verify the accuracy of the height detection, we fix the laser on the trolley and an reflector on the hook. Table 1 lists the comparison of these two kinds of data, where the error of the laser is 0.002 m. We assume the data measured by the laser is precise. The table implies that when the distance increases, the accuracy decreases. The maximum error of the method proposed in this paper is 0.02 m.

Table 1. The accuracy of height measurement.

Camera	Laser
0.03016	0.03025
0.05083	0.05071
0.07049	0.07067
0.09102	0.09131
0.11064	0.11037

The process of the measurement of the sway angle is shown in Fig. 3. The initial position of the upper edge is the white line, and the position of the upper edge is the blue line during the transit process. The distance of the blue and the white line is 0.3 m, and by using Eq. (6), we can calculate the sway angle as 3.37°.

Fig. 3. Measurement of the sway angle.

Figures 4 and 5 express the deviation caused by sway and tremble, where the trolley is operated at the maximum speed to guarantee that the sway is severe enough. The result is shown in Figs. 4 and 5.

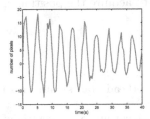

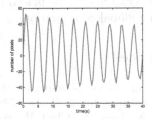

Fig. 4. The deviation induced by vibration. (Color figure online)

Fig. 5. The deviation induced by sway. (Color figure online)

The maximum deviation induced by sway is 50 pixels, one pixel represents 0.0106 m near the ground, so the maximum deviation is $\Delta l_{sway} = 0.53$ m. Similarly, the maximum deviation caused by vibration is $\Delta l_{vibration} = 0.22$ m, and the maximum total deviation is $\Delta l_{total} = 0.75\,\text{m}$. Normally, the hook is not operated close to the ground. The deviation of the hook can be calculated by Eq. (5). In this experiment, the rope's length is 6 m, the height of the camera is 10.5 m, the maximum deviation at that height is 0.43 m. The camera detect the deviation incessantly until it satisfies the acceptable deviation.

After some basic tests, we apply this method on the 32 ton overhead crane produced by Tianjin Hoisting Equipment Company. This technique collects the information exactly and the hook is transported to the target place precisely. Compared with the manual operation, the efficiency is enhanced and the safety is guaranteed.

6   Conclusion

To meet the practical demand of industrial cranes, this paper proposes a method of using an industrial camera to measure the height and the sway angle of the hook. The distance between the hook and the cargo is also acquired by the camera. Firstly, the camera collects the image if the trolley and the hook are static, acquiring the initial position of the hook by the graph matching method. In the process of transporting the hook or the cargo, the camera can realize the real-time object tracking through persistently detecting the upper edge. The height is calculated by the interpolation method according to the number of pixels of the edge. The sway angle of the hook is obtained by comparing the present position and the initial position. After the horizontal transportation, the camera detects whether the hook's deviation induced by sway and vibration is at a proper range to guarantee the accuracy is acceptable before the cargo start lowering. This method is applied on the overhead crane system in a practical industrial situation, where the information of the system is collected by the camera. The hook is located at the target position by cooperating with the motion control system. The next step to improve this system is adapting the information collected by the camera in a more intelligent algorithm. In this paper, the operators should move the trolley to the position close to the cargo, and more cameras will be placed in the workspace to acquire the position of the cargo in a global coordination.

References

1. Lee, H.: Motion planning for three-dimensional overhead cranes with highspeed load hoisting. Int. J. Control **78**(12), 875–886 (2005)
2. Sun, N., Fang, Y., Chen, H., Wu, Y., Lu, B.: Nonlinear antiswing control of off-shore cranes with unknown parameters and persistent ship-induced perturbations: theoretical design and hardware experiments. IEEE Trans. Ind. Electron., to be published
3. Le, T.A., Lee, S.-G., Moon, S.-C.: Partial feedback linearization andsliding mode techniques for 2D crane control. Trans. Inst. Meas. Control **36**(1), 78–87 (2014)
4. Park, H., Chwa, D., Hong, K.-S.: A feedback linearization control of container cranes: varying rope length. Int. J. Control Autom. Syst. **5**(4), 379–387 (2007)

5. Sun, N., Fang, Y., Chen, H., Fu, Y., Lu, B.: Nonlinear stabilizing control for ship-mounted cranes with disturbances induced by ship roll and heave movements: design, analysis, and experiments. IEEE Trans. Syst. Man Cybern.: Syst., to be published. doi:10.1109/TSMC.2017.2700393
6. Zavari, K., Pipeleers, G., Swevers, J.: Gain-scheduled controller design: illustration on an overhead crane. IEEE Trans. Industr. Electron. **61**(7), 3713–3718 (2014)
7. Sun, N., Wu, Y., Fang, Y., Chen, H., Lu, B.: Nonlinear continuous global stabilization control for underactuated RTAC systems: design, analysis, and experimentation. IEEE/ASME Trans. Mechatron. **22**(2), 1104–1115 (2017)
8. Boschetti, G., Caracciolo, R., Richiedei, D., Trevisani, A.: Moving the suspended load of an overhead crane along a pre-specified path: a non-time based approach. Robot. Comput.-Integr. Manuf. **30**(3), 256–264 (2014)
9. Sun, N., Wu, Y., Fang, Y., Chen, H.: Nonlinear antiswing control for crane systems with double pendulum swing effects and uncertain parameters: design and experiments. IEEE Trans. Autom. Sci. Eng., to be published. doi:10.1109/TASE.2017.2723539
10. Sun, N., Fang, Y., Chen, H., Lu, B.: Amplitude-saturated nonlinear output feedback antiswing control for underactuated cranes with double-pendulum cargo dynamics. IEEE Trans. Industr. Electron. **64**(3), 2135–2146 (2017)
11. Sun, N., Wu, Y., Fang, Y., Chen, H.: Nonlinear stabilization control of multiple-RTAC systems subject to amplitude-restricted actuating torques using only angular position feedback. IEEE Trans. Industr. Electron. **64**(4), 3084–3094 (2017)
12. Ma, B., Fang, Y., Wang, P.: Experiment system for automatic control of 3D overhead crane. Control Eng. Chin. **18**(2), 239–243 (2011)
13. Wang, Y., Chen, T., He, Z.: Review on the machine vision measurement and control technology for intelligent manufacturing equipment. Control Theory Appl. **32**(3), 273–286 (2015)
14. Wang, Y., Liu, C., Yang, X.: Online calibration of visual measurement system based on industrial robot. Robot **33**(3), 299–302 (2011)
15. Pan, T., Xu, W.: Detection of rope and ropes swaying angle of overhead crane based on computer vision. Comput. Meas. Control **23**(7), 2263–2269 (2015)
16. Kelvin, C., Singhose, W., Bhaumik, P.: Using machine vision and hand-motion control to improve crane operator performance. IEEE Trans. Syst. Man Cybern. **42**(6), 1496–1503 (2012)
17. Takahiro, I., Yasuo, Y.: Control of a boom crane using installed stereo vision. In: International Conference on Sensing Technology, pp. 189–194 (2012)
18. Lunhui, L., Chunghao, H., Sungchih, K.: Efficient visual feedback method to control a three-dimensional overhead crane. IEEE Trans. Industr. Electron. **61**(8), 4073–4083 (2014)
19. He, B., Fang, Y., Liu, H., Sun, N.: Precise positioning online trajectory planner design and application for overhead cranes. Control Theory Appl. **33**(10), 1352–1358 (2016)
20. Corke, P.: Robotics, Vision and Control. Springer, Berlin (2011). doi:10.1007/978-3-642-20144-8

A Testbed for Vision-Based Networked Control Systems

Christoph Bachhuber(✉) ⓘ, Simon Conrady, Michael Schütz,
and Eckehard Steinbach

Chair of Media Technology, Technical University of Munich, Munich, Germany
christoph.bachhuber@tum.de

Abstract. With the availability of low-latency wireless communication
and low-delay video communication solutions, vision-based networked
control systems (NCS) become feasible. In this paper, we describe an
NCS testbed which is suitable for the evaluation of the interplay of computer vision algorithms, network protocols and control algorithms under
a delay constraint. The system comprises an inverted pendulum which
is monitored by a video camera. The h.264-encoded video is sent over a
network to an image processing computer. This computer extracts the
angle of inclination of the pendulum from the decoded video and sends
it over a wireless link to the pendulum. The pendulum uses the angle
in a control algorithm to keep itself in a vertical position. We provide a
detailed description of the system including the control algorithm and
the image processing algorithms, and analyse the latency contributors
of the system. The build instructions and source code of the testbed
are publicly available. As the testbed is based on standard low-priced
components, it is particularly suitable for educational purposes.

Keywords: Vision-based control · Networked control systems · Computer vision systems · Low delay video communication

1 Introduction

Camera-based control, that is using visual information to control a physical
process, has many benefits compared to sensors which need to be physically
attached to an object such as angle or position sensors. This reduces the cabling
effort and the overall complexity. For example, vision-based control of a robot
arm reduces the number of sensors that need to be installed inside the arm.
A camera can observe the robot arm and its status can be determined using
image processing algorithms. Furthermore, cameras can unify the functionality
of many sensors. Again using the robot arm example, a camera can estimate
the arm's position and the force applied to an object [2]. Finally, cameras are
extremely flexible sensors that can be enabled for novel sensor tasks by simply
updating the computer vision software processing the video stream. NCS increase
the flexibility of the control architecture further, allowing almost unconstrained

© Springer International Publishing AG 2017
M. Liu et al. (Eds.): ICVS 2017, LNCS 10528, pp. 26–36, 2017.
DOI: 10.1007/978-3-319-68345-4_3

spatial positioning of sensors, processing units and actuators relative to each other. When using cameras in NCS, the video output of the camera has to be compressed such that it can be transmitted over communication channels with constrained transmission capacity. Recent research efforts are working on providing appropriate network structures with high reliability and low latency for Machine-to-Machine communication in 5G cellular networks [5].

A key issue of networked control systems is latency. In highly dynamic scenarios, control systems have to react quickly to unforeseen changes. Example use cases are autonomous driving or high-speed assembly lines. Current video communication applications exhibit rather high latencies of 80 ms or more [4]. Therefore, further research needs to be conducted in minimizing the individual delay contributions in NCS. To facilitate such experiments, we describe a test environment (testbed) for the networked control of an inverted pendulum. As depicted in Fig. 1, it combines camera-based control with wired and wireless networking.

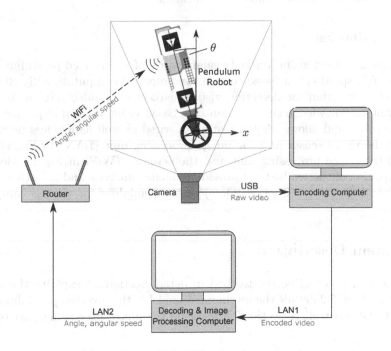

Fig. 1. Hardware setup of the testbed. Above each arrow, the type of connection is specified, and below each arrow the kind of transmitted data. Logging data is not included in this plot.

1.1   Related Work

The inverted pendulum is a classical example of an unstable system and has been studied extensively. Chan et al. [8] provide an excellent overview over the classes of approaches that have been undertaken previously. The mechanical model in Sect. 2.2 is mainly based on the works by Ooi [16] and Bonafilia et al. [6].

Visual control of an inverted pendulum has been extensively studied as well. Usually, the authors use cart-based pendulums in contrast to our wheeled pendulum. We can distinguish three main approaches. First, detecting the pendulum without markers [12,14] and second detecting passive markers [17,19]. Both approaches are performed either via edge detection or pattern matching. The third type of approaches detects active markers such as light sources on the pendulum [13,18], which can be done via thresholding the pixel values. None of the previous works includes a wireless network for communicating the angle of inclination to the pendulum.

The third field of related work covers NCS. Eker et al. [11] control a rotary pendulum using bluetooth transmission, but they do not use visual control. Chen et al. [9] use visual control for a linear tracking problem, in which they use distributed image processing with various time delays and propose a switching control scheme that enables successful tracking.

1.2   Contribution

We provide a testbed for networked visual control of an inverted pendulum[1]. To facilitate high speed vision-based control, we propose a computationally efficient and precise algorithm for detecting visual markers in a video stream. It is to the best of our knowledge the first non-cart based visual control approach with a mobile robot and allows for the testing of wired as well as wireless networks between the visual sensor and the image processing unit (LAN1 in Fig. 1) and between the image processing unit and the actuator (WiFi in Fig. 1). Besides the description of the testbed, we provide a latency analysis and investigate the stability and Quality of Control (QoC) of the pendulum for various sampling periods.

2   System Description

In this section we describe the testbed in detail. Section 2.1 explains the hardware setup, Sect. 2.2 details the mechanical model of the inverted pendulum and the used LQR-controller. Section 2.3 presents the image processing part of the testbed.

2.1   Hardware Setup

The schematic testbed setup is depicted in Fig. 1. The pendulum is in the field of view of a high frame rate camera (Ximea MQ022CG-CM). It records a grayscale image with a resolution of 640×480 pixels at an adjustable frame rate, which

---

[1] The source code and setup instructions are available in the following GitHub repository: https://github.com/cbachhuber/PendulumTestBed.

ranges in our experiments from 70 Hz to 240 Hz. Stable control of the pendulum is with our setup achieved for frame rates above 74 Hz. The raw video is transferred to the Encoding Computer over USB 3.0. The first PC (Encoding Computer) encodes the video using the x264 [1] encoder written in C++. The encoded video is streamed over a wired ethernet network (LAN1) with 1Gbit/s transmission rate to the Decoding & Image Processing Computer. At a frame rate of 100 Hz, the bit rate of the encoded video is 337 kByte/s.

The second PC (Decoding & Image Processing Computer) decodes the video using the h.264 video decoder of the libav library, also written in C++. The visual markers on the pendulum (shown in Fig. 2d) are then detected using shape detection functions of OpenCV [7], as further described in Sect. 2.3. From the marker positions, the pendulum angle is computed and sent to the pendulum robot via wireless LAN (WiFi) using an intermediary router, in our case a TP-Link TD-W8970B. The python implementation of the control algorithm in the robot finally uses the angle alongside its motor speed values and position to compute an actuation value for the motors, with the goal of keeping itself upright. This system is representative for a vision-based NCS: the camera and the Encoding Computer embody a remote visual sensor, which is via a network (in this setup LAN1) connected to a cloud computer (Decoding & Image Processing Computer), which processes the data and sends the extracted information over a network (LAN2 and WiFi) to an actuator (Pendulum Robot).

The pendulum is built from a LEGO® Mindstorms EV3 Kit, see Fig. 2. It consists of the main brick running on top of the robot running a Debian Linux-based operating system named ev3dev[2]. The brick controls the motors connected to the wheels. To add wireless LAN capability, an Edimax EW-7811UN Wireless USB Adapter is plugged into the USB port, as depicted in Fig. 2b. Alternatively, an Ethernet to USB adapter can be used for a wired connection. The pendulum is built for maximum height to minimize the angular acceleration and therefore achieve the maximum possible latency at which it is possible to control the pendulum. Milton et al. [15] show in a numerical analysis that for a pendulum such as the one used in this work, for which the center of mass is at a height of 125 mm, the critical latency is approximately 80 ms. Therefore, the entire chain including camera, processing on the PCs, transmission, processing on the robot and the actuator delays have to sum up to less than 80 ms. A detailed discussion of the delay contributions is given in Sect. 3.2.

In addition, comprehensive logging is implemented. The pendulum reports all its sensor values to the Decoding & Image Processing Computer, where they are written to a comma separated value file alongside the current angle measurements. We also provide python scripts that process this data to provide, among others, the standard deviation of the angle of the pendulum.

The mechanical parameters of the pendulum are given in Table 1. The wheel measurements have been determined by James Wiger[3] in extensive experiments. The motor parameters are reproduced from [6].

---

[2] www.ev3dev.org, accessed on 06.04.2017.
[3] http://jwiger.blogspot.de/2012/09/the-lego-tire-test.html, accessed on 05.04.2017.

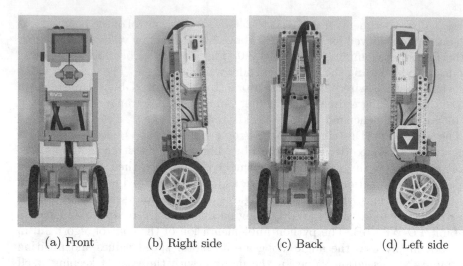

(a) Front   (b) Right side   (c) Back   (d) Left side

Fig. 2. Lego model of the pendulum robot. Note the visual markers in Fig. 2d.

Table 1. Parameters of the pendulum robot

Parameter	Value	Unit
Body mass	0.492	kg
Body inertia moment	$43.46 \cdot 10^{-3}$	kg·m^2
Height of the center of gravity	0.125	m
Mass of one wheel	0.029	kg
Wheel radius	0.0412	m
Wheel inertia moment	$49.34 \cdot 10^{-6}$	kg·m^2
DC motor resistance	6.69	Ω
DC motor electro-motoric force constant	0.468	Vs/rad
DC motor torque constant	0.317	Nm/A

2.2 Mechanical Model and Control Algorithm

The mechanical model of the system is based on the reports by Bonafilia et al. [6]. The state vector $\boldsymbol{x} = [x\ \dot{x}\ \theta\ \dot{\theta}]$ of the system contains the variables x and $\dot{x}$, which denote the position [m], and speed [m/s] of the robot's wheel axis, see Fig. 1. θ and $\dot{\theta}$ are the angle [deg], and angular speed [deg/s] of the robot's body, see Fig. 1. The input u of the system is the motor voltage [V]. Solving and linearising the involved mechanical equations around the working point $\boldsymbol{x} = \boldsymbol{0}$ as in [6] yields the differential equations

$$
\begin{bmatrix} \dot{x} \\ \ddot{x} \\ \dot{\theta} \\ \ddot{\theta} \end{bmatrix} = \begin{bmatrix} 0 & 1 & 0 & 0 \\ 0 & -153.95 & -23.04 & 6.35 \\ 0 & 0 & 0 & 1 \\ 0 & 1250.43 & 242.66 & -51.58 \end{bmatrix} \cdot \begin{bmatrix} x \\ \dot{x} \\ \theta \\ \dot{\theta} \end{bmatrix} + \begin{bmatrix} 0 \\ 15.06 \\ 0 \\ -122.35 \end{bmatrix} \cdot u \quad (1)
$$

for the inverted pendulum with parameters as in Table 1. Second derivatives represent acceleration. We define the control law to be

$$u = -\boldsymbol{kx}. \tag{2}$$

The control gain vector $\boldsymbol{k}$ can be obtained by deriving the solution of the linear quadratic regulator as in the work of Eide et al. [10]. The optimal LQR controller minimizes the quadratic cost function

$$J = \int_{o}^{\infty} \left(\boldsymbol{x}^{\mathrm{T}}(t)\boldsymbol{Q}\boldsymbol{x}(t) + u^2(t)R \right) \mathrm{d}t \tag{3}$$

with the symmetric weighting matrices $\boldsymbol{Q}$ as weight of $\boldsymbol{x}$ and R as weight of u. For the weighting matrix $\boldsymbol{Q}$ we used a unit matrix with the value 200 for the first and third entry of the diagonal. And the second matrix $R = 1$ is just a scalar because of the one-dimensional input u of the system. Applying the solution from [10], this yields the control gain vector

$$\boldsymbol{k} = \begin{bmatrix} 14.14 & 25.29 & 33.13 & 3.35 \end{bmatrix}. \tag{4}$$

The control loop on the pendulum robot works as follows: first, the robot collects position data from the motors and receives the angle data over the WiFi connection. Next, it computes the control gain using Eq. (2). The robot then reads out the voltage of the battery and divides the control gain by the voltage. We take this measure to make the physical power of the motors independent of the battery voltage. This is reasonable because for a lower battery (and therefore motor) voltage, a higher gain value to achieve the same physical motor power is required. Finally, the current control gain is used to update the duty cycles of the motors. Afterwards, the loop starts from the beginning.

2.3   Angle Extraction Using Image Processing

To extract the angle of inclination from the video stream, the Decoding & Image Processing Computer, see Fig. 1, searches for the two visual markers attached along the vertical axis of the pendulum. The markers are depicted on the left side of the pendulum in the Figs. 1 and 2d. A marker consists of a black square containing a white triangle, where the centroids of both shapes are co-located. These markers allow for monochromatic image processing, therefore reducing the computational complexity. Furthermore, they have a very distinctive, yet simple shape, allowing nearly constant processing time for various rotations and backgrounds. Finally, these are passive markers, in contrast to active markers such as light-emitting diodes used e.g. in [13,18], which reduces system complexity.

The image processing algorithm needs to localize the markers. This is done using OpenCV [7] functions exclusively. The marker detection consists of an outer and inner loop. The outer loop first performs blurring of the image to reduce computation time by removing small, complex structures. Afterwards, the pixel values are binarized using simple thresholding. All shapes in the image are then detected with the findContours function of OpenCV. These are used in the inner loop to identify the marker contours by looping through all shapes and rejecting those which are not squares, are not of sufficient size, and do not contain a triangle. If the number of remaining shapes is two, the marker identification was successful. From the marker contours, the outer loop extracts the centroids of the markers and computes the current pendulum angle

$$\theta = \arctan\left(\frac{x_2 - x_1}{y_2 - y_1}\right). \tag{5}$$

The variables $x_{1,2}$ and $y_{1,2}$ are the pixel coordinates of the two marker centroids. The algorithm also computes the angular speed $\dot{\theta}$ as the difference of the current to the previous angle divided by the sampling period.

These values are sent to the robot using the UDP protocol. The sampling period of the angle extraction and the control loop period on the robot are not necessarily the same. Therefore, the robot always uses the latest available angle sample if one or more angle samples arrived via UDP during one control loop cycle. If no sample arrives, the robot predicts the angle and angular speed using Eq. (1).

3 System Evaluation

During setup, we evaluated the precision of the angle measurement and analysed the system latencies. Furthermore, we conducted experiments to determine a correlation between the camera frame rate and the QoC, in this context represented by the standard deviation of the angle.

3.1 Precision of the Angle Extraction

For a given image processing algorithm applied to raw images without any video coding artifacts, the precision of the angle measurement mainly depends on the resolution of the image, and the size and distance of the markers in the 640×480 image. In our test setup the two markers had an edge length of 28 pixels and are at a distance of 191 pixels to each other.

As ground truth, we use paper sheets onto which the markers are printed with various predefined angles, different for each paper sheet. Angle alignment of the camera to the test sheet is done using horizontal and vertical straight lines on the paper sheet, to which the camera pixel rows and columns are subsequently aligned. Using this manual alignment, we can align the camera with an angular precision of approximately $0.1°$ to the sheet of paper. Over a range of ground truth marker angles, we could achieve an average angle error of $0.07°$, and a maximum error of $0.17°$. We therefore estimate the upper bound of the error of the angle estimation to be $0.3°$.

The angle estimation error can be reduced by increasing the image resolution or waiving the blurring at the beginning of the image processing (see Sect. 2.3). But both measures would increase image processing time, which is limited by the camera frame period for real-time capability. In the current setup, image processing takes on average 0.7 ms, not allowing for significantly higher resolutions since we target to use very high frame rate cameras with 1 kHz.

3.2   Latency Analysis

The latency contributors are depicted in Table 2. For each latency, we report the minimum, mean and maximum value. Constant latencies such as the camera processing have the same value for each entry.

Table 2. Latency contributors

Contributor	Min [ms]	Mean [ms]	Max [ms]
Camera frame period	0.00	5.00	10.00
Camera processing	6.02	6.02	6.02
Color conversion (I)	0.40	0.42	0.67
Encoding	0.77	0.83	1.16
Video transmission	0.26	0.26	0.27
Decoding	0.26	0.31	0.81
Color conversion (II)	0.40	0.47	1.04
Image processing	0.60	0.68	1.09
Angle transmission	1.91	4.35	7.52
Control loop	0.02	5.02	10.02
Motor reaction time	25.00	25.00	25.00
Sum	35.64	48.36	63.60

There are two sampling processes, camera frame period and control loop. Both run in this setup at a frequency of 100 Hz, yielding a maximum sampling delay of 10 ms each. On average, a newly appearing event in front of the camera or newly arriving angle data in the control loop have to wait 5 ms before being further processed. Their minimum is a direct processing of the data. This value equals 20 ms for the control loop because operations after the angle reception until the actuation command is sent to the motors take that amount of time.

Camera processing latency is the time difference between when an event occurs in front of the camera and the image is ready for encoding in the Encoding Computer. Using the system by Bachhuber and Steinbach [3], we measured a constant delay of 6.02 ms.

The time for angle transmission over the wireless link (WiFi) was measured indirectly via round-trip latency tests. We measured the round-trip time for the link, and divided it by two to obtain the values for angle transmission in Table 2.

The motor reaction time is the time difference between issuing a command to run the motor and a physical reaction of the motor to that command. To measure this, we light up an LED at the same time as starting the motor. For an LED, the time between the start of an electrical current and the start of light emission is in the domain of nanoseconds, and therefore negligible in this context. We recorded the motor and the LED with a high frame rate camera and computed the time difference between lighting the LED and the start of the motor rotation. The result is approximately 25 ms of motor reaction time. Note that this is only until the initiation of rotation. In the slow motion video we see that it takes another 10 to 20 ms until the motor reaches the target rotational speed.

The remaining latencies were measured using the *chrono* class of C++. Color conversion (I) takes place in the Encoding Computer, color conversion (II) in the Decoding & Image Processing Computer.

With this setup, we have an End-to-End delay of 70 ms to 80 ms. The investigations of Milton et al. [15] show that for our setup the critical latency is approximately 80 ms. Therefore, theory predicts that our system is stable, which is confirmed by the implementation. In Sect. 3.3, we see that for lower camera frame rates, and therefore higher camera frame periods and E2E latencies, the system becomes unstable.

From the delay perspective, the system with video coding, as depicted in Fig. 1, leads to a small delay improvement compared to a previous system in which one PC is connected to the camera and directly applies image processing. For such a setup, the PC's CPU has to perform image retrieval from the camera, color conversion and image processing. As a result, image processing on the highly loaded CPU takes on average 3 ms, 2.32 ms more than in our current setup. In the current setup, the two PCs share processing load of the one-PC setup and can therefore allocate more computational resources to processing the tasks. The mean delay introduced by one additional color conversion, encoding, transmission and decoding adds up to 1.82 ms, giving a 0.5 ms E2E delay reduction of the video coding system compared to a system with one PC.

3.3 How Camera Frame Rate Affects Quality of Control

Camera frame rate affects the QoC and the stability of control. For the inverted pendulum, we measure the QoC by the standard deviation of the angle over time. We record all angle measurement samples and compute their standard deviation. The result from this test is that the QoC remains constant for camera frame rates between 240 Hz and 80 Hz at approximately 0.6°. Between 80 Hz and 74 Hz, the QoC deteriorates to approximately 1°, but the pendulum still successfully balances. For frame rates below 74 Hz, the angle standard deviation further increases, and the pendulum falls over after a few seconds of balancing.

4 Conclusions

We developed a testbed for networked control systems that allow for the testing of computer vision algorithms, network protocols and control algorithms. The testbed consists of an inverted pendulum which is monitored by a camera. The video from the camera is transmitted over a network and analyzed in an image processing algorithm. The image processing extracts the angle of the pendulum and sends it to the pendulum, which uses the angle to stabilize itself in a vertical position.

We analyzed the End-to-End latency of the system and investigated the minimally allowable camera frame rate to be 74 Hz. In future work, we will evaluate angle extraction algorithms in terms of computational complexity and angle precision. In addition we plan to investigate cross-layer optimization exploiting image content characteristics to prioritize packets, packet erasure coding, and real-time network protocols for wired and wireless network setups with multiple pendulums and irregular camera sampling periods.

References

1. x264 - a free open-source h.264 encoder. http://www.videolan.org/developers/x264.html. 30 Jan 2017
2. Alt, N., Steinbach, E.: Visuo-haptic sensor for force measurement and contact shape estimation. In: Proceedings of IEEE International Symposium on Haptic Audio Visual Environments and Games (HAVE), pp. 24–28 (2013)
3. Bachhuber, C., Steinbach, E.: A system for high precision glass-to-glass delay measurements in video communication. In: Proceedings of IEEE International Conference on Image Processing (ICIP), pp. 2132–2136 (2016)
4. Bachhuber, C., Steinbach, E.: Are today's video communication solutions ready for the tactile internet? In: IEEE Wireless Communications and Networking Conference Workshops (WCNCW) (2017)
5. Boccardi, F., et al.: Five disruptive technology directions for 5G. IEEE Commun. Mag. 52(2), 74 80 (2014)
6. Bonafilia, B., et al.: Self-Balancing Two-wheeled Robot (2015)
7. Bradski, G.: Open source CV library. Dr. Dobb's J. Softw. Tools (2000)
8. Chan, R.P.M., Stol, K.A., Halkyard, C.R.: Review of modelling and control of two-wheeled robots. Ann. Rev. Control 37(1), 89–103 (2013)
9. Chen, C.C., Wu, H., Kühnlenz, K., Hirche, S.: Switching control for a networked vision-based control system. Automatisierungstechnik Methoden und Anwendungen der Steuerungs-, Regelungs-und Informationstechnik 59(2), 124–133 (2011)
10. Eide, R., et al.: LQG control design for balancing an inverted pendulum mobile robot. Intell. Control Autom. 2(02), 160 (2011)
11. Eker, J., Cervin, A., Hörjel, A.: Distributed wireless control using bluetooth. In: Proceedings of the IFAC Conference on New Technologies for Computer Control (2001)
12. Espinoza-Quesada, E., Ramos-Velasco, L.: Visual servoing for an inverted pendulum using a digital signal processor. In: 2006 IEEE International Symposium on Signal Processing and Information Technology (2006)
13. Hirata, K., Kimura, Y., Sugimoto, K.: Visual feedback control of cart-pendulum systems with webcam. In: IEEE International Conference on Mechatronics (ICM), pp. 1–6. IEEE (2007)
14. Kizir, S., Ocak, H., Bingul, Z., Oysu, C.: Time delay compensated vision based stabilization control of an inverted pendulum. Int. J. Innov. Comput. Inf. Control 8(12), 8133–8145 (2012)

15. Milton, J., Cabrera, J.L., Ohira, T., Tajima, S., Tonosaki, Y., Eurich, C.W., Campbell, S.A.: The time-delayed inverted pendulum: implications for human balance control. Chaos: Interdisc. J. Nonlinear Sci. **19**(2), 026110 (2009)
16. Ooi, R.C.: Balancing a two-wheeled autonomous robot. University of Western Australia 3 (2003)
17. Tu, Y.W., Ho, M.T.: Design and implementation of robust visual servoing control of an inverted pendulum with an fpga-based image co-processor. Mechatronics **21**(7), 1170–1182 (2011)
18. Wang, H., et al.: Hybrid control for vision based cart-inverted pendulum system. In: American Control Conference, pp. 3845–3850. IEEE (2008)
19. Wenzel, L., Vazquez, N., Nair, D., Jamal, R.: Computer vision based inverted pendulum. In: Proceedings of the 17th IEEE Instrumentation and Measurement Technology Conference, IMTC 2000, vol. 3, pp. 1319–1323. IEEE (2000)

Visual Servoing of Wheeled Mobile Robots Under Dynamic Environment

Chenghao Yin[1], Baoquan Li[1(✉)], Wuxi Shi[1], and Ning Sun[2]

[1] School of Electrical Engineering and Automation, Tianjin Key Laboratory of
Advanced Technology of Electrical Engineering and Energy,
Tianjin Polytechnic University, Tianjin 300387, China
ych_930525@163.com, libq@tjpu.edu.cn, shiwuxi@163.com
[2] Institute of Robotics and Automatic Information System, Nankai University,
Tianjin 300350, China
sunn@nankai.edu.cn

Abstract. In this paper, a novel method is proposed about visual servoing with a monocular wheeled mobile robot system, which can deal with dynamic visual targets. For the existing methods, the mobile robot can reach the desired pose correctly where the feature points are fixed. However, the mobile robot cannot reach the desired pose when the feature points have been moved. By adding a fixed camera in the scene for monitoring the movement of the feature points, the proposed approach can still work well when feature points are moved. From the images of the monitor camera, the POSIT algorithm is utilized to calculate the movement of the feature points. Likewise, we can calculate the relationship between the relevant coordinate systems with respect to the feature points. By coordinate transformation, the translation vector and rotation matrix between the current pose and the desired pose of mobile robot can be obtained by real-time image feedback. Finally, by utilizing the polar coordinate representation, a motion controller is adopted to pilot the mobile robot reach the desired pose. The feasibility of the proposed method is investigated by simulation results.

Keywords: Wheeled mobile robot · Visual servoing · POSIT algorithm · Dynamic feature points

1 Introduction

In daily life, the vast majority of the external information is perceived by human eyes, implying the importance of vision sensors. When the mobile robots are equipped with visual sensors, they become more intelligent and their application fields become more widely [1], such as universe discovery, deep sea exploration, and biology research [2]. Therefore, with the development of computer

B. Li—This work is supported in part by National Natural Science Foundation of China under Grant 61603271, and in part by the Natural Science Foundation of Tianjin under Grant 15JCYBJC47800 and Grant 16JCQNJC03800.

© Springer International Publishing AG 2017
M. Liu et al. (Eds.): ICVS 2017, LNCS 10528, pp. 37–46, 2017.
DOI: 10.1007/978-3-319-68345-4_4

technology and vision equipment, the studies of robot visual servoing systems have attracted the attention of many researchers. For monocular vision systems, the inherent problem is the lack of 3D model of the scene. Moreover, wheeled mobile robots have nonholonomic motion constraints, which has brought great challenges for mobile robots visual servoing task. However, many existing methods those accomplish visual servoing tasks are restricted by utilizing the fixed features in the scene. Since the feature points are required to be static, the application of the mobile robot visual servoing is restricted. As a result, a novel strategy that deals with the movement of feature points is urgently needed for visual servoing, so as to greatly improve the ability of mobile robots for environment adaptation.

In recent years, the research for vision sensor equipped mobile robot system has mainly focused on visual navigation, visual tracking, visual servoing, visual SLAM and so on. The term visual servoing means using image information to steer the mobile robot reach the desired pose. Nowadays, more and more visual servoing control methods are utilized to mobile robots, which can be divided into three categories: image-based visual servoing [3], position-based visual servoing [4], and hybrid visual servoing. The image-based visual servoing strategy defines the error signal directly in the image plane, without the use of image information for three-dimensional reconstruction. The position-based visual servoing strategy uses the image signal to estimate the three-dimensional position of robots. The hybrid visual servoing control system includes both the information in the three-dimensional Cartesian coordinate system and the information in the two-dimensional image plane space.

For wheeled mobile robots, they are underactuated systems [5,6], with nonholonomic motion constraints. There are two basic movements of the mobile robot: the first is the trajectory tracking control; the second is from the initial position to the target position (regulation control). Any continuous time-invariant state feedback controller cannot achieve the stabilization of nonholonomic systems, as well known for Brockett necessary condition [7]. Murrieri et al. [8] bring forward a hybrid control method, and Lyapunov theory is utilized to solve the problem of mobile robots parking, but image feature points must remain unchanged in the entire visual servo process. Unfortunately, in real applications, feature points are moved sometimes due to many reasons such as workspace occupation. Therefore, it is with significant importance to design a method that the mobile robot can be driven to the desired pose although the feature points have been moved.

Owing to the lack of depth information in the visual servoing process, the design of the visual servoing controller should face with a great deal of difficulty. To deal with this problem, Fang et al. utilize the method of adaptive update law [9] to compensate for constant non-measurable depth information. Moreover, in [10], a controller is designed for a visual servoing task of the mobile robot with unified tracking and regulation, where the pose of the robot is obtained by decomposing homographies. However, these methods can only be applied to calibrated cameras [11]. In [12], with an uncalibrated visual servo regulation method, not only the visual servoing task can be completed and the camera intrinsic parameters can also be calculated. Unfortunately, the premise of applying these methods is that the visual targets cannot be moved, which largely limits their applications. An approach for landing on a moving target using an image-based visual servoing controllor is proposed in [13]. According to Liu et al. [14,15], visual homing task is achieved from scale with an uncalibrated omnidirectional camera. A fast outlier rejection approach is discussed in [15]. In contrast, all the feature points can be moved in our method, for that the mobile robot system executes visual servoing tasks by taking into account both the feature points before and after they are moved.

In this paper, an efficient visual servo regulation strategy is designed for monocular mobile robots in the case where the feature points can be moved. The visual servoing scheme of this paper has the following three parts. Firstly, the movement of the feature points is calculated by the fixed camera using the POSIT algorithm [16]. For the second stage, the real-time the translation vector and rotation matrix of the robot current pose and desired pose are obtained. At last, In order to drive the robot to the desired pose, an effective motion controller is adopted which by polar coordinates representation [17]. The simulation results show the feasibility of the visual servoing strategy. The main contribution of the proposed method is it can address the dynamic environment in visual servoing of mobile robot.

2 Problem Formulation

2.1 System Description

Figure 1 shows the coordinate systems in visual servoing, where the camera and mobile robot frames are set to be identical. The current pose of the robot/camera is represented by $\mathcal{F}^c$. The origin of $\mathcal{F}^c$ is located at the optical center of the camera and is also located in the center of the robot wheel axis. z^c-axis of frame $\mathcal{F}^c$ is along the onboard camera optical axis, which is the direction of the robot forward. x^c-axis is parallel to the wheel axis of the robot, and the y^c-axis of $\mathcal{F}^c$ is perpendicular to the plane $z^c x^c$ of motion. $\mathcal{F}^d$ is the desired position of the robot. The frame $\mathcal{F}^s$ denotes the pose of the monitor camera. The purpose of the fixed camera is to monitor the movement of the feature points. M_i is the position of the features before they are move. $\mathcal{F}^o$ represents the visual target coordinate system before the features are moved. M_i^* is defined to denote the features after they are move. $\mathcal{F}^a$ represents the visual target coordinate system after the feature points are moved. In this method, the coordinates of the feature points are known.

The rotation angle between the current pose and the desired pose of the mobile robot is $\theta(t)$. $\alpha(t)$ is the angle between the current robot orientation and the translation vector from $\mathcal{F}^c$ to $\mathcal{F}^d$, and $\phi(t)$ denotes the angle between the desired robot orientation and the translation vector from $\mathcal{F}^c$ to $\mathcal{F}^d$. The directions of $\theta(t), \alpha(t), \phi(t)$ are marked as well, and in the figure their values are all positive.

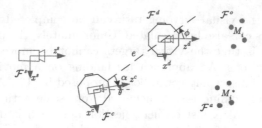

Fig. 1. Coordinate systems relationship.

Many of the existing methods study the robot visual servoing in the premise that the feature points should be fixed, however, the movement of the feature points is rarely involved. In this paper, the mobile robot can still be regulated correctly after the feature points are moved.

2.2   Coordinate Systems Relationship

In this part, we will briefly describe the representation between the coordinate systems. For instance, $\mathcal{F}^d$ is taken as the reference frame. The translation vector and the rotation matrix of $\mathcal{F}^c$ with respect to $\mathcal{F}^d$ are denoted as ${}^{d}T_c(t)$ and ${}^{d}_{c}R(t)$, respectively. Moreover, the translation vector and the rotation matrix of $\mathcal{F}^d$ with respect to $\mathcal{F}^c$ are denoted as ${}^{c}T_d(t)$ and ${}^{c}_{d}R(t)$. Similar with the above instanced representation, we denote relevant relationship between certain frames in the following.

2.3   Control Scheme

The main work of this paper is to design visual servoing scheme for wheeled mobile robots under dynamic environment. The scheme flow diagram presented in this paper is shown in Fig. 2.

Remark. Since there involve many coordinate systems in this method, we use superscript and subscript to distinguish their transformation relationships, as denoted by Craig [18].

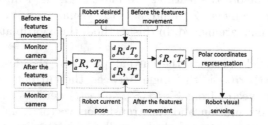

Fig. 2. Scheme of the visual servoing system.

3   Monitor Camera

3.1   POSIT Algorithm

If we know the coordinates of four or more feature points in the environment and know the positions of the feature points on the camera image, the POSIT algorithm [16] can be used to calculate the relationship between these feature points and the camera. The rotation matrix R and the translation vector T can be obtained through the above method.

The POSIT algorithm can provide 6 DOFs relative pose information. However, since the mobile robot is moved on a plane, it is only necessary to know the rotation angle of the y-axis as the rotation axis and the translation vector of the x-axis and z-axis. Therefore, only 3 DOFs is necessary to control the motion of the mobile robots.

3.2   Monitor Camera and Features Relationship Before Movement

The target reference coordinate system is defined as $\{M_1, u, v, w\}$. The first point M_1 in the feature points is employed as the origin. and M_i is the spatial position of the i-th feature point (represented by $[\, U_i\ V_i\ W_i\,]$). The unit vectors with respect to the axes of $\mathcal{F}^s$ (fixed camera coordinate system) are defined by i, j, k, respectively. The rotation matrix ${}_o^s R(t)$ and the translation vector ${}^s T_o(t)$ between the feature points coordinate system before moving and the monitor camera coordinate system can be calculated by the POSIT algorithm [16].

The rotation matrix ${}_o^s R(t)$ and the translation vector ${}^s T_o(t)$ can be expressed as follows:

$$
{}_o^s R = \begin{bmatrix} i_u & i_v & i_w \\ j_u & j_v & j_w \\ k_u & k_v & k_w \end{bmatrix} = \begin{bmatrix} i^T \\ j^T \\ k^T \end{bmatrix}, {}^s T_o = \begin{bmatrix} X_1 \\ Y_1 \\ Z_1 \end{bmatrix}. \tag{1}
$$

3.3   Relationship of Monitor Camera and Features After Movement

The target coordinate system after moving is defined as $\{M_1^*, u^*, v^*, w^*\}$. The origin of the target coordinate system is denoted by the first point M_1^*, and M_i^* is the spatial position of the i-th feature point (represented by $[\, U_i^*\ V_i^*\ W_i^*\,]$).

The rotation matrix ${}_a^s R(t)$ and the translation vector ${}^s T_a(t)$ can be calculated by the POSIT algorithm in the similar way, as shown below:

$$
{}_a^s R = \begin{bmatrix} i_{u^*} & i_{v^*} & i_{w^*} \\ j_{u^*} & j_{v^*} & j_{w^*} \\ k_{u^*} & k_{v^*} & k_{w^*} \end{bmatrix} = \begin{bmatrix} i^{*T} \\ j^{*T} \\ k^{*T} \end{bmatrix}, {}^s T_a = \begin{bmatrix} X_1^* \\ Y_1^* \\ Z_1^* \end{bmatrix}. \tag{2}
$$

3.4   Relationship of Features Before and After Movement

Through the above two steps, we can get the transformation of the feature points before and after moving in the monitor camera coordinate system.

The relationship between the feature points coordinate system before and after movement is shown as follows:

The rotation matrix $_a^oR(t)$ and the translation vector $^oT_a(t)$ are given as

$$
_a^oR = \begin{bmatrix} i'_{u'} & i'_{v'} & i'_{w'} \\ j'_{u'} & j'_{v'} & j'_{w'} \\ k'_{u'} & k'_{v'} & k'_{w'} \end{bmatrix}, \quad ^oT_a = \begin{bmatrix} a \\ b \\ c \end{bmatrix}. \tag{3}
$$

From the formulas (1) and (2), formula (3) can be calculated as follows;

$$
_a^sR = {}_o^sR_a^oR. \tag{4}
$$

The rotation matrix $_a^oR(t)$ can be calculated by (4). The relationship between the feature points after moving and before moving can be expressed as:

$$
\begin{bmatrix} _a^sR & {}^sT_a \\ 0 & 1 \end{bmatrix} = \begin{bmatrix} _o^sR & {}^sT_o \\ 0 & 1 \end{bmatrix} \begin{bmatrix} _a^oR & {}^oT_a \\ 0 & 1 \end{bmatrix}. \tag{5}
$$

Then, the rotation matrix $^oT_a(t)$ can be calculated by (5).

4 The Mobile Robot Control Strategy

4.1 Relationship of Desired Pose and Features Before Moving

The above three processes are done by the monitor camera. The robot desired coordinate system $\mathcal{F}^d$ has been established. The unit vectors with respect to the axes of $\mathcal{F}^d$ are defined by g, e, f, respectively.

Firstly, move the wheeled mobile robot to the desired pose and use the precalibrated camera to capture the feature points before moving. The rotation matrix $_o^dR(t)$ and the translation vector $^dT_o(t)$, which are between the feature points before movement and the mobile robot's desired coordinate system, are denoted as follows

$$
_o^dR = \begin{bmatrix} e_u & e_v & e_w \\ f_u & f_v & f_w \\ g_u & g_v & g_w \end{bmatrix}, \quad ^dT_o = \begin{bmatrix} X_{c1} \\ Y_{c1} \\ Z_{c1} \end{bmatrix} \tag{6}
$$

where (X_{c1}, Y_{c1}, Z_{c1}) is the coordinate value of feature point M_1 in the desired coordinates. The rotation matrix $_o^dR(t)$ and the translation vector $^dT_o(t)$ can be calculated by the POSIT algorithm.

4.2 Relationship of Current Pose and Features Movement

Before executing the visual servoing task, the mobile robot is placed at the initial pose, and the feature points have been moved accordingly. The initial coordinate system of the mobile robot is denoted by $\mathcal{F}^c$. The unit vectors with respect to the axes of $\mathcal{F}^c$ are defined by e', f', g', respectively.

$(X'_{c1}, Y'_{c1}, Z'_{c1})$ denotes the coordinate value of the point M_1^* in the current coordinate system of the mobile robot. Therefore, the rotation matrix $_a^cR(t)$

and the translation vector $^c\boldsymbol{T}_a(t)$ can be calculated by the POSIT algorithm as follows:

$$
{}_a^c R = \begin{bmatrix} e'_{u'} & e'_{v'} & e'_{w'} \\ f'_{u'} & f'_{v'} & f'_{w'} \\ g'_{u'} & g'_{v'} & g'_{w'} \end{bmatrix}, {}^c\boldsymbol{T}_a = \begin{bmatrix} X'_{c1} \\ Y'_{c1} \\ Z'_{c1} \end{bmatrix}. \tag{7}
$$

4.3 Relationship of Current Pose and Desired Pose

By above analysis, it can obtain the relationship between the current pose and the desired pose of the mobile robot. The rotation matrix between the current pose and the desired pose is $_c^d R(t)$ and the relevant translation vector is $^d\boldsymbol{T}_c(t)$.

Utilizing (3), (6), and (7) we obtain

$$
{}_o^d R {}_a^o R = {}_c^d R {}_a^c R. \tag{8}
$$

From (8), the rotation matrix $_c^d R(t)$ can be obtained.

Then, the coordinate systems transformation can be obtained as follows:

$$
\begin{bmatrix} {}_o^d R & {}^d T_o \\ 0 & 1 \end{bmatrix} \begin{bmatrix} {}_a^o R & {}^o T_a \\ 0 & 1 \end{bmatrix} = \begin{bmatrix} {}_c^d R & {}^d T_c \\ 0 & 1 \end{bmatrix} \begin{bmatrix} {}_a^c R & {}^c T_a \\ 0 & 1 \end{bmatrix}. \tag{9}
$$

Therefore, the translation vectors $^d\boldsymbol{T}_c(t)$ can be calculated from the Eq. (9).

4.4 Robot Kinematics

This part introduces the kinematics of the mobile robot under polar coordinates [17].

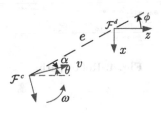

Fig. 3. Polar coordinate of the mobile robot.

As shown in Fig. 3, the mobile robot pose is represented by polar coordinates, which involves the error distance $e > 0$ and robot orientation θ with respect to $\mathcal{F}^d$. Let $\alpha = \phi - \theta$ be the angle between the mobile robot orientation and the distance vector e, the following kinematics can be obtained:

$$
\begin{cases} \dot{e} = -v \cos \alpha, \\ \dot{\alpha} = v \dfrac{\sin \alpha}{e} - w, \\ \dot{\phi} = v \dfrac{\sin \alpha}{e}. \end{cases} \tag{10}
$$

The linear and angular velocity controllers are adopted as follows [17]:

$$v = (\gamma \cos \alpha)e, \quad w = k\alpha + \frac{\gamma \cos \alpha \sin \alpha}{\alpha}(\alpha + h\phi). \tag{11}$$

5 Simulation Results

The simulation tests are provided in this section to validate the performance of this designed scheme. The internal parameters of the virtual camera are set as

$$K = \begin{bmatrix} 998.00 & 0 & 369.42 \\ 0 & 998.00 & 306.44 \\ 0 & 0 & 1 \end{bmatrix}. \tag{12}$$

Set the initial pose of the mobile robot as follows

$$(0.8\text{m}, -2.0\,\text{m}, 35°), \tag{13}$$

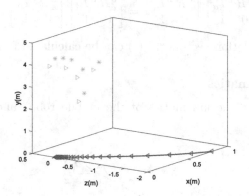

Fig. 4. Robot path.

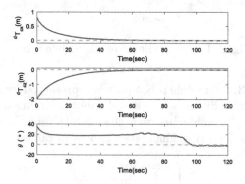

Fig. 5. Evolution of the robot pose [solid line: simulation results; dashed line: desired value (zero)].

and the desired pose of the robot is (0.0 m, 0.0 m, 0°). Image noise is added with standard deviation $\sigma = 0.1$ pixels to test the overall anti-jamming capability. The control gains are chosen as $\gamma = 0.115, k = 0.07, h = -1.66$.

As shown in Fig. 4 is the movement trajectory of the mobile robot in the three-dimensional space, which is smooth in working space in the process of visual servoing. The triangle points indicates the position before the feature points moves, and the star points indicates the position after the feature points moves. The evolution of the mobile robot states $({}^dT_{cz}(t),\, {}^dT_{cx}(t),\, \theta(t))$ is shown in Fig. 5, and it is known that the steady-state errors is small enough. The simulation results show the effectiveness of the proposed method.

6   Conclusion and Future Work

This paper is based on monocular wheeled mobile robots with an onboard camera. In the proposed approach, when the feature points are moved in the scene, the mobile robot can still be driven to the desired pose. In order to acquire the information of the feature points movement, it is necessary to add a monitor camera in the workspace. The POSIT algorithm is used to calculate the relationship between the feature points before and after the movement. Similarly, the POSIT algorithm can be used to obtain each relationship between certain coordinate systems. In this way, we can get the real-time translation vector and the rotation matrix between the current pose and the desired pose of the mobile robot. Then, polar coordinate based controller is adopted. Simulation results verify the feasibility of the proposed strategy.

For future work, we will carry out experimental verification for the provided method. Moreover, the 3D geometry of the landmark should be known for this method, therefore, we will complete the mobile robot visual servoing when the landmark location is unknown.

References

1. Liu, Y., Xiong, R., Wang, Y., Huang, H., Xie, X., Liu, X., Zhang, G.: Stereo visual-inertial odometry with multiple Kalman filters ensemble. IEEE Trans. Ind. Electron. **63**(10), 6205–6216 (2016)
2. Chen, H., Wang, C., Li, X.J., Sun, D.: Transportation of multiple biological cells through saturation-controlled optical teezers in crowded microenvironments. IEEE/ASME Trans. Mechatron. **21**(2), 888–899 (2016)
3. Becerra, H.M., Lopez-Nicolas, G., Sagues, C.: Asliding-mode-control law for mobile robots based on epipolar visual servoing from three views. IEEE Trans. Robot. **27**(1), 175–183 (2011)
4. Zhang, X., Fang, Y., Sun, N.: Visual servoing of mobile robots for posture stabilization: from theory to experiments. Int. J. Robust Nonlinear Control **25**(1), 1–15 (2015)
5. Sun, N., Fang, Y., Chen, H., Lu, B.: Amplitude-saturated nonlinear output feedback antiswing control for underactuated cranes with double-pendulum cargo dynamics. IEEE Trans. Ind. Electron. **64**(3), 2135–2146 (2017)

6. Sun, N., Wu, Y., Fang, Y., Chen, H., Lu, B.: Nonlinear continuous global stabilization control for underactuated RTAC systems: design, analysis, and experimentation. IEEE/ASME Trans. Mechatron., in press. doi:10.1109/TMECH.2016. 2631550

7. Luca, A.D., Oriolo, G.: Trajectory planning and control for planar robots with passive last joint. Int. J. Robot. Res. 21(5), 575–590 (2002)

8. Murrieri, P., Fontanelli, D., Bicchi, A.: A hybrid-control approach to the parking problem of a wheeled vehicle using limited view-angle visual feedback. Int. J. Robot. Res. 23(4–5), 437–448 (2004)

9. Fang, Y., Dixon, W.E., Dawson, D.M., Chawda, P.: Homography-based visual servo regulation of mobile robots. IEEE Trans. Syst. Man. Cybern. Part B 35(5), 1041–1050 (2005)

10. MacKunis, W., Gans, N., Parikh, A., Dixon, W.E.: Unified tracking and regulation visual servo control for wheeled mobile robots. Asian J. Control 16(3), 669–678 (2014)

11. Zhang, Z.: A flexible new technique for camera calibration. IEEE Trans. Pattern Anal. Mach. Intell. 22(11), 1330–1334 (2000)

12. Li, B., Fang, Y., Zhang, X.: Visual servo regulation of wheeled mobile robots with an uncalibrated onboard camera. IEEE/ASME Trans. Mechatron. 21(5), 2330–2342 (2016)

13. Serra, P., Cunha, R., Hamel, T., Cabecinhas, D., Silvestre, C.: Landing on a moving target using image-based visual servo control. IEEE Conference on Decision Control, Los Angeles, CA, USA, pp. 2179–2184, February 2015

14. Liu, M., Pradalier, C., Pomerleau, F., Siegwart, R.: Scale-only visual homing from an omnidirectional camera. In: IEEE International Conference on Robotics and Automation, pp. 3944–3949, May 2012. doi:10.1109/ICRA.2012.6224900

15. Liu, M., Pradalier, C., Siegwart, R.: Visual homing from scale with an uncalibrated omnidirectional camera. IEEE Trans. Robot. 29(6), 1353–1365 (2013)

16. Dementhon, D.F., Davis, L.S.: Model-based object pose in 25 lines of code. Int. J. Comput. Vis. 15(1), 123–141 (1995)

17. Aicardi, M., Casalino, G., Bicchi, A., Balestrino, A.: Closed loop steering of unicycle-like vehicles via Lyapunov techniques. IEEE Robot. Autom. Mag. 2(1), 27–35 (1995)

18. Craig, J.J.: Introduction to Robotics: Mechanics and Control, 3rd edn. Prentice-Hall, Upper Saddle River (2005)

Towards Space Carving with a Hand-Held Camera

Zhirui Wang$^{(\boxtimes)}$ and Laurent Kneip

Australian National University, Canberra, Australia
u5428281@anu.edu.au

Abstract. With the rise of VR applications, dense reconstruction of 3D object models becomes an increasingly important subproblem of computer vision. Most existing methods focus on the reconstruction of the actual object and assume that camera poses are known and the observed object is clearly dominant in the image. The goal of this paper is to extend these technologies to less artificial data, and enable dense 3D object modeling from an ordinary hand-held camera observing an object on top of a structured, unknown planar background. The key of our method consists of recovering highly accurate camera poses from structure from motion based on a planar scene assumption, and modeling the structure on the planar background with implicitly smooth Bezier splines. We present a complete end-to-end pipeline able to produce meaningful dense 3D models from a simple space carving approach in near real-time.

1 Introduction

3D object modeling is a popular subbranch of computer vision. Important fields of application are given by cultural heritage and 3D content generation for virtual reality applications such as immersive computer gaming or education software. At least until now, accurate reconstruction of 3D objects is a technology that mostly relies on expensive hardware, depth cameras, or—in the case of visual information—fixed known camera positions. This often impedes the usage in consumer grade applications, where users expect to use simple hand-held hardware such as their private

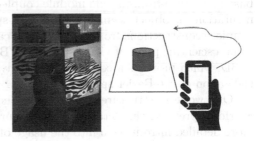

Fig. 1. Dense 3D object mapping with consumer grade hardware. We model the complete structure of the background for highly accurate camera pose computation.

self-phone. Using videos captured by a hand-held device means that the camera poses are unknown and need to be resolved as part of the object reconstruction process, for instance using standard online structure-from-motion or visual

© Springer International Publishing AG 2017
M. Liu et al. (Eds.): ICVS 2017, LNCS 10528, pp. 47–61, 2017.
DOI: 10.1007/978-3-319-68345-4_5

SLAM methods. The latter, however, often do not provide sufficiently high accuracy for accurate 3D modeling. The present paper examines the feasibility of— in the case of small-scale object reconstruction—exploiting and modeling the structure of the planar background below the object in order to achieve highly accurate camera poses. The latter are then fed to a space carving module within which we reconstruct the visual hull of the object. The setup is illustrated in Fig. 1.

The idea of our background modelling consists of mapping complete edges rather than just sparse sets of points as in classical structure-from-motion. This idea has been re-picked up in the recent literature, and proven to provide more accurate camera motion estimation than traditional sparse point-based methods [30]. We model the background in terms of all photometric edges and use smooth continuous free-form 3D curves as a general model for the edges.

We use edges as features and model them in 3D via smooth curves because:

- Compared to the traditional sparse point-based methods, edges in images make up for a significantly larger amount of data points to be registered to a model. Modeling them with a continuous free-form curve model furthermore adds implicit smoothness constraints to the representation. The result is superior signal-to-noise ratio and improved overall accuracy.
- Edges represent a perhaps more natural choice in man-made environments, where objects are often made up of homogeneously colored (i.e. texture-less) piece-wise planar surfaces. We constrain our method to user-picked planar scenes, but it still motivates our research in a wider context.

We present a full pipeline for 3D object model reconstruction with calibrated hand-held monocular cameras. The pipeline is composed of a free-form curve based structure-from-motion module coupled to a user-assisted graph cut implementation for object segmentation and a space-carving back-end for providing simple reconstructions from the obtained camera poses. Our main contribution from a scientific point of view is the use of Bezier splines for modeling the curves in 3D, which provides a combination of advantages in particular during the initialization of the Bezier spline parameters.

Our work is structured as follows: Sect. 2 looks at further related work. Section 3 presents the detailed steps of our pipeline. Section 4 then provides a more detailed introduction into the usage of Bezier splines in curve-based structure from motion. Section 5 finally presents the results we have been able to obtain on real data, before Sect. 6 concludes with a discussion about the feasibility of the proposed idea, and further avenues to go from here.

2   Related Work

Curve-Based Visual Localization and Mapping: Curve-based structure from motion has a long-standing tradition in geometric computer vision. Early work by Porrill and Pollard [32] has discovered how curve and surface tangents can be included into fundamental epipolar geometry for stereo calibration, an idea lateron followed up by Feldmar et al. [13] and Kaminski and Shashua [18]. However, the investigated algebraic constraints for solving multiple view geometry problems are known to be very easily affected by noise. In order to improve the quality of curve-based structure from motion, further works by Faugeras and Mourrain [12] and Kahl and Heyden [17] therefore looked at special types of curves such as straight lines and cones, respectively.

In contrast to those early contributions in algebraic geometry, a different line of research is formed by works that investigate curve-based structure from motion from the point of view of 3D model parametrisation and optimisation. Kahl and August [16] are among the first to show complete, free-form 3D curve reconstruction from registered 2D images. Later works then focus on improving the parametrisation of the 3D curves, presenting sub-division curves [15], non-rational B-splines [35], and implicit representations via 3D probability distributions [34]. These works, however, mostly focus on the reconstruction problem, and do not use the curve measurements in order to refine the camera poses.

Complete structure-from-motion optimisation including general curve models and camera poses has first been shown by Berthilsson et al. [3]. The approach however suffers from a bias that occurs when the model is only partially observed. Nurutdinova and Fitzgibbon [30] illustrate this problem in detail, and present an inverse data-to-model registration concept that transparently handles missing data. Fabbri and Kimia [11] solve the problem by modeling curves as a set of shorter line segments, and Cashman and Fitzgibbon [6] model the occlusions explicitly. The successful inclusion of shorter line segments (i.e. edglets) has furthermore been demonstrated in real-time visual SLAM [8]. Further related work from the visual SLAM community is given by Engel et al. [9,10], who estimate semi-dense depth maps in high-gradient regions of the image, and then register subsequent images based on a photometric error criterion. The work however deviates from curve-based structure from motion in that it depends on depth information in dense sub-regions of the image, and only maintains local depth estimates rather than fully parametrised edges in 3D.

We use a similar representation than Nurutdinova and Fitzgibbon [30], but replace the B-splines by Bezier splines. While maintaining a comparable compactness of representation, Bezier splines have the advantage of more geometrically meaningful parameters, and thus also simplified parameter initialization.

Dense Object Modeling: The perhaps most well-known, large-scale project on 3D object modeling within the computer vision community is given by Stanford's digital Michelangelo project [24]. The project however uses expensive Laser scanners as input information. A 3D shape can also be reconstructed from a set of images that observe the entire scene from multiple viewpoints. An interesting approach for solving this problem is given by the volume intersection algorithm [29]. After extracting and projecting the object silhouettes in each image, the algorithm computes the intersection volume of the resulting cones to approximate the 3D shape. The idea has first been presented in [26] and is widely used in object reconstruction. The theoretical foundation was established by Laurentini [23], who gives a definition of the problem and argues that the visual hull is the best possible shape approximation which can be obtained from the object's silhouettes. More recent reconstruction methods go beyond the idea of silhouettes and also use photometric information to model cavities that otherwise cannot be identified through the visual hull [2,21].

More recently, the availability of vast computational resource even in small-scale format has pushed the development of systems that achieve simultaneous localization and dense mapping real time. These methods, however, either rely on RGB-D sensors [4,27], or do not maintain a global representation of the environment [28]. A global representation of a dense surface for photometric optimization in regular structure from motion has been presented in [7], but the approach is far from real-time capability. Dedicate real-time 3D modeling frameworks for mobile hardware have been presented in [22,31], but they do not produce highly accurate reconstructions since mostly extrapolating the dense surfaces from sparse point estimations.

3   Framework Overview

Let's assume that we have a flat horizontal background with sufficient structured texture on it. The texture does not need to be known in advance, which potentially enables us to apply the method on top of any flat surface that meets the minimum requirements in terms of the available texture. The object to reconstruct is placed on top of the structured background. We then move with a hand-held camera around the object and capture a continuous image stream that is used for solving all tasks: recover camera poses, model the background, and produce our final result, which is a dense 3D model of the object.

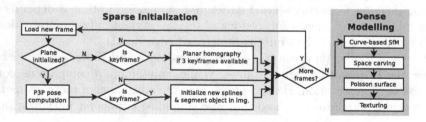

Fig. 2. System overview. Our pipeline consists of an incremental sparse initialization procedure during which camera poses and the relative orientation of the background plane are identified. The sparse part is followed by a sequence of batch optimization algorithms to recover the final 3D model.

An overview of our end-to-end pipeline is indicated in Fig. 2. From a high-level perspective, the framework can be divided into two separate processing stages. The first block is an incremental sparse initialization procedure during which we identify initial camera poses with respect to the background plane. During this sparse computation, the background is simply modelled by 2D points lying on the ground plane. Spare time during the sparse initialization is used to prepare each one of the retained keyframes for the sub-sequent space carving approach. This notably involves the extraction of the object's silhouette in the image using established segmentation techniques. The second block then contains a sequence of batch optimization algorithms for extracting the dense 3D model. This notably includes the curve-based background modelling step, which is discussed in Sect. 4.

The remainder of this section looks at the details of the sparse initialization, image-based object segmentation, and the final dense batch optimization block.

3.1 Incremental Sparse Initialization

The entire sparse initialization part relies on local invariant keypoint extraction and matching in order to compute an initial guess of camera poses as well as the relative positioning of the ground plane. In case of a planar scene, the mapping of points from one image to another can be easily expressed by a homography transformation [14]. We therefore bootstrap the sparse computation by first collecting three frames with sufficient frame-to-frame disparity (called *keyframe*), and then find their relative pose by a robust computation of the *planar homography* between these frames. We use three frames because the subsequent decomposition of the homography into relative rotation, translation and plane normal leads to two possible solutions [25]. In order to resolve the ambiguity, we simply compute two planar homographies for distinct pairs of frames of the first three keyframes, and then compare the similarity of the plane normal vectors after rotating them into one common frame.

Once the first relative poses as well as the normal vector and the depth of the background plane are identified, we can define a world frame such that the normal vector of the ground plane is aligned with the vertical axis e_z, and the height of the plane is $z = 0$. All points that have been identified as inliers during the robust planar homography computation can furthermore—since effectively lying on the ground plane—be initialized by simply intersecting the spatial measurement ray from any of the first three keyframes with the ground plane. Subsequent frames can now be aligned to the existing sparse background model by simple robust camera resectioning. In our work, we use P3P [20] embedded into Ransac [19] followed by nonlinear optimization to align subsequent frames with the existing model.

We keep defining and storing keyframes during tracking whenever the frame-to-frame disparity exceeds a given threshold. We furthermore keep adding new 3D points to the background model as parts of the background may have been occluded in earlier frames. We notably use the result from the silhouette extraction to define whether or not a point belongs to the background. Points keep being added to the background by simply intersecting spatial rays with the background plane. The sparse tracking and mapping part is concluded by a windowed bundle adjustment implementation that optimizes the 6 DoF pose of every keyframe, as well as the 2 DoF position of every point on the background plane.

3.2   Silhouette Extraction

For each key-frame, we use GrabCut [33] to perform image segmentation and extract the object's silhouette. GrabCut executes graph cut in an MRF to segment out a foreground object from the rest. The corresponding data terms rely on Gaussian Mixture Models (GMMs) for the appearance of both foreground and background pixels. They are initialized from a simple user-defined box drawn around the object. The GrabCut algorithm then alternates between performing the segmentation and refining the foreground and background models using the updated segmentations until convergence.

We chose GrabCut because it permits high quality image segmentations from only very little user input. In our implementation, we require the user to manually draw an initial bounding box around the object in the very first keyframe only. In subsequent keyframes, we find the initial bounding box by pyramidal tracking of the image patch defined by the object's bounding box in a previous keyframe.

3.3   Dense 3D Modeling

We use space carving to obtain the 3D model of the object. Space carving is a voxel based 3D reconstruction algorithm that aims at approximating the space occupied by the object by cubic voxels. The idea is simple: Each voxel is projected into each keyframe to determine whether it lies inside or outside the silhouettes. If a voxel lies completely outside the silhouette in one of the keyframes, it can be eliminated from the model. Computation is speeded up by a hierarchical, coarse-to-fine voxelization of space: We first aim at culling bigger voxels, and only split them up into 8 smaller voxels if the voxel potentially intersects with the boundary of the object. The approximation error becomes smaller as the resolution of the original voxel grid is growing. The algorithm is furthermore robust against image under-segmentation errors: even if parts of the background end up inside the object's silhouette in one of the keyframes, it will not remain part of the volume as long as there is at least one keyframe where this part is outside the object region.

To conclude, the boundary surface of the object is extracted by identifying all voxel-corner points that are not fully covered by other voxels, and deriving a Poisson-surface reconstruction from them. The resulting triangular mesh is finally textured by identifying the most fronto-parallel keyframe for every triangle, and identifying the corresponding piece of texture by reprojecting the vertices of the triangle into that keyframe.

4   Curve-Based Structure from Motion with Bezier Splines

As explained in Sect. 3, the sparse initialization is only used for obtaining an initial estimate of the camera poses as well as the relative orientation of the ground plane. Our core scientific contribution consists of modelling the exact structure of the background with free-form curves parametrized in the ground plane, and then performing joint optimization of the background structure as well as the camera poses by running curve-based structure from motion. The present section explains how we represent the structure, how the corresponding parameters are initialized, and how it can be used for global optimization.

4.1 Short Review of Bezier Splines

We represent the background by first detecting all edges in all keyframes that lie on the background, and then model them using free-form curves. Poses and structure can hence be optimized by registering the reprojection of the curve models with the features obtained from an edge detector [5]. The curves are modelled in segments where each segment is represented by a spline. This permits a smooth, continuous parametrization of the curve with a very limited number of control points.

We chose Bezier splines because they are compact and have a clear geometric meaning, thus facilitating parameter initialization. They are furthermore invariant with respect to affine transformations. Our curve segments are small, and perspective transformations within a local neighbourhood can be approximated by affine transformations, which means that any perspective transformation applied to the control points of an entire curve still results in reasonably good approximations of the optimal Bezier spline control points.

The general definition of a Bezier spline is:

$$\mathbf{B}(t) = \sum_{i=0}^{k} b_{i,k}\mathbf{P_i}, \tag{1}$$

where $b_{i,k} = \binom{k}{i} t^i (1-t)^{k-i}$ and $\binom{k}{i} = \frac{k!}{i!(k-i)!}$. As mentioned, we represent each curve with a sequence of Bezier segments rather than one long segment with many control points. We therefore keep k as small as possible and set it to 4. Equation (1) becomes:

$$\mathbf{B}(t) = (1-t)^3\mathbf{P_1} + 3(1-t)^2 t\mathbf{P_2} + 3(1-t)t^2\mathbf{P_3} + t^3\mathbf{P_4} \quad (0 < t < 1). \tag{2}$$

The smoothness of the curve is maintained by sharing some of the parameters between neighboring segments: For each segment, the second and third control point are represented as a function of the first and last control point and the gradient at those points. The first and the last of the control points as well as the gradient at those points are then shared

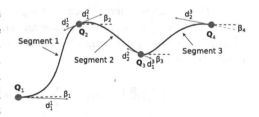

Fig. 3. Example of a smooth curve parametrization with 3 Bezier spline segments.

between subsequent segments. Since—by definition of Bezier splines—the gradient of the curve at the first and the last control point is effectively equal to the direction of the line that connects the first and the last control points to the neighbouring control points, sharing this direction between neighbouring segments implicitly leads to an overall smooth curve representation. An example of a curve with 3 Bezier spline segments and all defining parameters is indicated in Fig. 3. Let us denote the sequence of starting and ending points of the curve segments with $\{\mathbf{Q}_1, \cdots, \mathbf{Q}_n\}$. Let segment i simply be the segment between $\mathbf{Q}_i$ and $\mathbf{Q}_{i+1}$. Let ϕ_i furthermore denote the gradient at $\mathbf{Q}_i$. The control points $\{\mathbf{P}_1^i, \cdots, \mathbf{P}_4^i\}$ of segment i are then given by:

$$\mathbf{P}_1^i = \mathbf{Q}_i, \ \mathbf{P}_2^i = \mathbf{Q}_i + d_1^i \begin{bmatrix} cos\phi_i \\ sin\phi_i \end{bmatrix}, \ \mathbf{P}_3^i = \mathbf{Q}_{i+1} - d_2^i \begin{bmatrix} cos\phi_{i+1} \\ sin\phi_{i+1} \end{bmatrix}, \ \mathbf{P}_4^i = \mathbf{Q}_{i+1} \quad (3)$$

4.2 Bezier Spline Parameter Initialization

The initialization of a Bezier spline segment turns out to be easy. We first initialize them in the image. An edge is defined as a set of pixels $\mathbf{C} = \{\mathbf{p}_1, \cdots, \mathbf{p}_l\}$. The first and last control points of each Bezier spline segment (i.e. the sequence $\{\mathbf{Q}_1, \cdots, \mathbf{Q}_n\}$) are simply initialized by subsampling $\mathbf{C}$ with regularly spaced points. The density of points is defined by considering the local curvature: The higher the curvature, the smaller the distance between $\mathbf{Q}_i$ and $\mathbf{Q}_{i+1}$. The local gradients $\{\phi_i, \cdots, \phi_{i+1}\}$ can also be estimated straight from the data. The only parameters that remain to be initialized are d_1^i and d_2^i. They can be initialized for

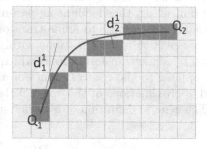

Fig. 4. Example of a spline segment. The spline initialization consists of minimizing the sum of orthogonal distances from each point on the edge to the spline (in red) over d_1^1 and d_2^1. (Color figure online)

each segment individually by searching along the gradient directions near $\mathbf{Q}_i$ and $\mathbf{Q}_{i+1}$.

Substituting (3) in (2) and considering $\mathbf{Q}_i$, $\mathbf{Q}_{i+1}$, ϕ_i, and ϕ_{i+1} to be fixed, each Bezier spline segment $\mathbf{B}_i$ can be regarded as a function of the three scalars d_1^i, d_2^i and t. If $\mathbf{C}_i$ furthermore denotes the subset of p pixels belonging to segment i, the objective for initializing the remaining parameters of each segment can be formulated as

$$\left\{\hat{d}_1^i, \hat{d}_2^i\right\} = \underset{d_1^i, d_2^i}{\operatorname{argmin}} \sum_{j=1}^{p} \min_{t} \|\mathbf{C}_i\,[j] - \mathbf{B}_i(d_1^i, d_2^i, t)\|^2 \quad (4)$$

The energy is also illustrated in Fig. 4. The minimum location for this energy is simply found by applying Gauss-Newton with numerical Jacobian computation. However, the objective is not entirely trivial to compute, as the derivation depends on an internal minimization over the curve parameter t to find the nearest point on the spline. We rederive the values for t before each Gauss-Newton iteration, and notably do so via a simple 1D bisectioning search. It is intuitively clear that—under the assumption of sufficiently small curvature—finding the optimal t is likely a convex problem, which causes the bi-sectioning search to converge very quickly.

The Bezier spline parameters are first computed in a reference frame, and then projected into the ground plane by again intersecting the rays corresponding to the control points in the image with the ground plane itself. As explained above, due to certain transformation invariance properties of Bezier splines, this projection results in sufficiently good initial values for the subsequent global optimization.

4.3 Global Optimization

The poses and the background model are finally optimized in a joint curve-based bundle adjustment implementation. Let us assume that there are in total n Bezier spline segments. We define the vector $\mathbf{b}_i = \begin{bmatrix} \mathbf{Q}_i^T & \mathbf{Q}_{i+1}^T & \phi_i & \phi_{i+1} & d_1^i & d_2^i \end{bmatrix}^T$ as the vector of parameters defining the Bezier spline $\mathbf{B}_i$, which may hence be written as a function $\mathbf{B}(\mathbf{b}_i, t)$. It is clear that many of the parameters are shared among different segments, but we ignore this here for the sake of a simplified notation. Let us furthermore assume that we have m camera poses and that the pose of each camera is parametrized by the 6-vector π_j. The objective of our global optimization may then be formulated as minimizing the distance between reprojected samples of each Bezier spline segment and their closest edge points in each one of the keyframes. If $\mathbf{C}^j$ denotes all pixels along an edge in keyframe j, and $\eta(\mathbf{x}, \mathbf{C}^j)$ a function that returns the nearest neighbour of $\mathbf{x}$ within $\mathbf{C}^j$, the optimization objective may be formulated as

$$\left\{ \hat{\pi}_1, \cdots, \hat{\pi}_m, \hat{\mathbf{b}}_1, \cdots, \hat{\mathbf{b}}_n \right\} =$$

$$\underset{\pi_1, \cdots, \pi_m, \mathbf{b}_1, \cdots, \mathbf{b}_n}{\operatorname{argmin}} \sum_{i=1}^{n} \sum_{j=1}^{m} \sum_{t=0}^{9} \| f_{\pi_j} \left(\mathbf{B}(\mathbf{b}_i, 0.1 \cdot t) \right) - \eta \left(f_{\pi_j} \left(\mathbf{B}(\mathbf{b}_i, 0.1 \cdot t) \right), \mathbf{C}^j \right) \|^2.$$

$$(5)$$

Note that $f_{\pi_j}(\mathbf{x})$ here denotes the transformation from a world frame into the image plane of a camera with pose parameters π_j. Besides the extrinsic pose parameters, this function also makes use of a suitable camera model with known, pre-calibrated intrinsic parameters (omitted again for the sake of the simplicity of the notation). As can be observed, the internal sum iterates over t and—through the multiplication with 0.1—produces 10 homogeneously distributed samples for reprojection error computation on each Bezier spline segment. We keep this number fixed, although—in the future—we plan to investigate an adaptive number of sampling points depending on the length of the spline segment. Missing data and occlusions that potentially cause outlier residuals are handled by adding a robust Huber norm to the computation.

In order to compute the nearest neighbour efficiently, we follow [36] and precompute a nearest-neighbour map for the edges of each keyframe. We fix the nearest neighbour point during the numerical Jacobian matrix computation, because a small change in the reprojected location could otherwise lead to very large residual changes due to an unexpected, significant change of the nearest neighbour if operating at the center between two distinct curves. This furthermore requires a projection of the residual vectors onto the local gradient direction. The interested reader is invited to look at [36] for further details.

5   Experimental Results

We evaluate our work using a self-captured dataset of a real object. We print out a structured texture—a zebra pattern—for use as a ground plane, and put our object—a small elephant—on top of it. We use a consumer grade, hand-held camera to simply capture a continuous sequence of images while moving around the object. We first evaluate our spline-based background model by comparing it against the edges directly extracted from the original image of the background pattern we printed out. We furthermore analyze the residual error and the optimized trajectory before and after spline-based bundle adjustment. To conclude, we present some segmentation results obtained by GrabCut, and show the final reconstructed 3D model and its improvement through the curve-based background modelling step.

5.1   Evaluation of the Spline-Based Background Model

The error of our Bezier-spline based background model is computed by registering it directly with the edges extracted from the original pattern image, and evaluating the residual error. The registration is done by a continuous minimization of the sum of euclidean distances of each point on a Bezier spline to its closest point on an edge extracted from the pattern. The objective is similar to (5), except that we have only one image, optimize only for a 2D similarity transformation, and of course—for the sake of evaluating the quality of the model—keep the Bezier spline coefficients fixed.

Figure 5(a) and (b) show the Bezier splines registered inside the original image of the background pattern before and after curve-based global non-linear refinement, respectively. The left-top part of the splines is missing due to some occlusions. The result shows a clear improvement of the background model, although some of the splines fail to converge. This, however, does not compromise the quality of our camera poses, as we use a robust Huber norm that is able to handle a certain number of outlier residuals. The improvement can also be put into numbers, as we observe an error drop from 3.107844e+03 to 2.073013e+03 throughout the curve-based non-linear refinement.

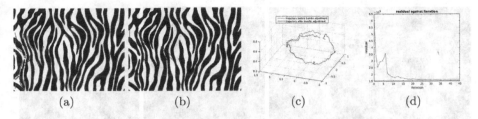

Fig. 5. (a): Bezier splines before optimization, registered to the original pattern. (b): Bezier splines after optimization, registered to the original pattern. (c): Camera poses before and after optimization. (d): Development of the overall residual during the non-linear refinement of the curves.

5.2 Evaluation of the Camera Poses

There is no ground truth pose information, which makes it difficult to evaluate the improvement of the camera poses quantitatively. However, as can be observed in Fig. 5(c), the change in the camera poses is quite substantial. Figure 5(d) furthermore shows the overall residual error during each iteration of the non-linear refinement. As can be observed, the residual generally goes down and converges at the end. From this result, we can conclude that the camera poses are optimized as well.

We solve the non-linear least squares problem (5) using the Levenberg-Marquardt implementation of the Ceres-Solver library [1]. The latter is an open source C++ library that is able to solve large-scale non-linear optimization problems. The performance of the optimizer is stable as long as the initial guess of the camera poses is not too far off.

5.3 Some Segmentation Results

The weakly supervised segmentation can of course easily fail if the similarity between the object and the background appearance is too similar. Depending on the shape of the object, the user-defined bounding box also always contains parts of the background as well, which disturbs the initialization of a clean foreground model. Together with specularity, shadows, and reflections, these problems complicate a robust extraction of the object's silhouette and perhaps makes it the weakest part in our current reconstruction pipeline. However, on the example presented here, the segmentation generally returns good results. A few example segmentations are indicated in Fig. 6.

5.4 Evaluation of the Dense 3D Model

In order to evaluate the importance of the curve-based structure-from-motion part, Fig. 7(b) and (b) show some Poisson surface reconstructions obtained from performing space carving with the optimal poses from the sparse and the curve-based optimization, respectively. As can be observed, the reconstruction from

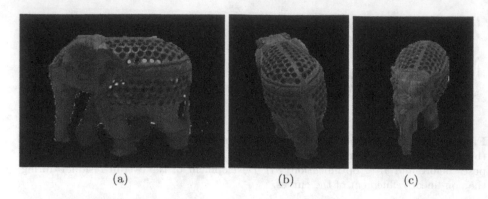

Fig. 6. Example segmentations from various viewpoints.

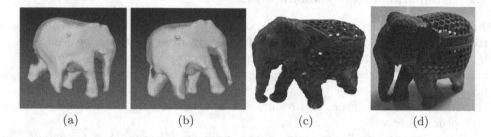

Fig. 7. (a): Poisson surface reconstruction from sparse optimization. (b): Poisson Surface reconstruction from curve-based reconstruction. (c): The final textured model. (d): A picture of the original model from a similar view-point.

sparse poses is losing details such as the tail and part of the foot. This points to bad alignment, as misalignments generally cause the intersection volume of space carving to become smaller. As can be observed, the poses from our curve-based optimization module have improved, thus maintaining those details in the reconstruction. Figure 7(c) and (d) show our final textured model and an image of the original object, respectively.

6   Discussion

The core contribution of our work consists of a successful demonstration of how to use free-form curve models for modeling the environment, and how this can possibly help to increase the accuracy of regular monocular structure from motion. This is demonstrated through the improved dense reconstructions we obtained from our space carving framework. There are many avenues to use this result for further applications. First, we intend to improve several bottlenecks of our dense reconstruction framework and embed it into a real smart-phone application. One important point that would have to be addressed is the compensation of rolling shutter distortions. We furthermore intend to extend the mapping back-end to a hybrid approach that uses a 3D surface representation for the foreground object, and a curve-based representation for the background. The 3D surface will notably be used to enforce joint photometric and silhouette consistency, thus enabling the mapping of cavities with respect to the visual hull, as well as implicit model texturing. As a last point, we intend to use the presented Bezier spline parametrization for refining general non-planar sparse structure-from-motion results and modeling large-scale environments.

References

1. Agarwal, S., Mierle, K., et al.: Ceres solver. http://ceres-solver.org
2. Balzer, J., Soatto, S.: Second-order shape optimization for geometric inverse problems in vision. In: Proceedings of the IEEE Conference on Computer Vision and Pattern Recognition (CVPR) (2014)
3. Berthilsson, R., Astrom, K., Heyden, A.: Reconstruction of general curves, using factorization and bundle adjustment. Int. J. Comput. Vis. (IJCV) **41**(3), 171–182 (2001)
4. Bylow, E., Sturm, J., Kerl, C., Kahl, F., Cremers, D.: Direct camera pose tracking and mapping with signed distance functions. In: Demo Track of the RGB-D Workshop on Advanced Reasoning with Depth Cameras at Robotics: Science and Systems (RSS) (2013)
5. Canny, J.: A computational approach to edge detection. IEEE Trans. Pattern Anal. Mach. Intell. (PAMI) **8**(6), 679–698 (1986)
6. Cashman, T.J., Fitzgibbon, A.W.: What shape are dolphins? Building 3D morphable models from 2D images. IEEE Trans. Pattern Anal. Mach. Intell. (PAMI) **35**(1), 232–244 (2013)
7. Delaunoy, A., Pollefeys, M.: Photometric bundle adjustment for dense multi-view 3D modeling. In: Proceedings of the IEEE Conference on Computer Vision and Pattern Recognition (CVPR) (2014)
8. Eade, E., Drummond, T.: Edge landmarks in monocular SLAM. Image Vis. Comput. (IVC) **27**(5), 588–596 (2009)
9. Engel, J., Schöps, T., Cremers, D.: LSD-SLAM: large-scale direct monocular SLAM. In: Fleet, D., Pajdla, T., Schiele, B., Tuytelaars, T. (eds.) ECCV 2014. LNCS, vol. 8690, pp. 834–849. Springer, Cham (2014). doi:10.1007/978-3-319-10605-2_54
10. Engel, J., Sturm, J., Cremers, D.: Semi-dense visual odometry for a monocular camera. In: Proceedings of the International Conference on Computer Vision (ICCV) (2013)
11. Fabbri, R., Kimia, B.: 3D curve sketch: flexible curve-based stereo reconstruction and calibration. In: Proceedings of the IEEE Conference on Computer Vision and Pattern Recognition (CVPR) (2010)
12. Faugeras, O., Mourrain, B.: On the geometry and algebra of the point and line correspondences between n images. In: Proceedings of the International Conference on Computer Vision (ICCV) (1995)
13. Feldmar, J., Betting, F., Ayache, N.: 3D-2D projective registration of free-form curves and surfaces. In: Proceedings of the International Conference on Computer Vision (ICCV) (1995)
14. Hartley, R., Zisserman, A.: Multiple View Geometry in Computer Vision, 2nd edn. Cambridge University Press, New York (2004)

15. Kaess, M., Zboinski, R., Dellaert, F.: MCMC-based multiview reconstruction of piecewise smooth subdivision curves with a variable number of control points. In: Pajdla, T., Matas, J. (eds.) ECCV 2004 Part III. LNCS, vol. 3023, pp. 329–341. Springer, Heidelberg (2004). doi:10.1007/978-3-540-24672-5_26

16. Kahl, F., August, J.: Multiview reconstruction of space curves. In: Proceedings of the International Conference on Computer Vision (ICCV) (2003)

17. Kahl, F., Heyden, A.: Using conic correspondences in two images to estimate the epipolar geometry. In: Proceedings of the International Conference on Computer Vision (ICCV) (1998)

18. Kaminski, J.Y., Shashua, A.: Multiple view geometry of general algebraic curves. Int. J. Comput. Vis. (IJCV) **56**(3), 195–219 (2004)

19. Kneip, L., Furgale, P.: OpenGV: a unified and generalized approach to real-time calibrated geometric vision. In: Proceedings of the IEEE International Conference on Robotics and Automation (ICRA), Hongkong (2014)

20. Kneip, L., Scaramuzza, D., Siegwart, R.: A novel parametrization of the perspective-three-point problem for a direct computation of absolute camera position and orientation. In: Proceedings of the IEEE Conference on Computer Vision and Pattern Recognition (CVPR), Colorado Springs, USA (2011)

21. Kolev, K., Brox, T., Cremers, D.: Fast joint estimation of silhouettes and dense 3D geometry from multiple images. IEEE Trans. Pattern Anal. Mach. Intell. (PAMI) **34**(3), 493–505 (2012)

22. Kolev, K., Tanskanen, P., Speciale, P., Pollefeys, M.: Turning mobile phones into 3D scanners. In: Proceedings of the IEEE Conference on Computer Vision and Pattern Recognition (CVPR) (2014)

23. Laurentini, A.: The visual hull concept for silhouette-based image understanding. IEEE Trans. Pattern Anal. Mach. Intell. **16**(2), 150–162 (1994)

24. Levoy, M., Pulli, K., Curless, B., Rusinkiewicz, S., Koller, D., Pereira, L., Ginzton, M., Anderson, S., Davis, J., Ginsberg, J., Shade, J., Fulk, D.: The digital michelangelo project: 3D scanning of large statues. In: ACM Transactions on Graphics (SIGGRAPH) (2011)

25. Malis, E., Vargas, M.: Deeper understanding of the homography decomposition for vision-based control. Ph.D. thesis, INRIA (2007)

26. Martin, W.N., Aggarwal, J.K.: Volumetric descriptions of objects from multiple views. IEEE Trans. Pattern Anal. Mach. Intell. **5**(2), 150 (1983)

27. Newcombe, R.A., Izadi, S., Hilliges, O., Molyneaux, D., Kim, D., Davison, A.J., Kohli, P., Shotton, J., Hodges, S., Fitzgibbon, A.: Kinectfusion: real-time dense surface mapping and tracking. In: Proceedings of the International Symposium on Mixed and Augmented Reality (ISMAR) (2011)

28. Newcombe, R.A., Lovegrove, S.J., Davison, A.J.: DTAM: dense tracking and mapping in real-time. In: Proceedings of the International Conference on Computer Vision (ICCV) (2011)

29. Nitschke, C.: A Framework for Realtime 3-D Reconstruction by Space Carving Using Graphics Hardware. diplom. de, Hamburg (2007)

30. Nurutdinova, I., Fitzgibbon, A.: Towards pointless structure from motion: 3D reconstruction and camera parameters from general 3D curves. In: Proceedings of the International Conference on Computer Vision (ICCV) (2015)

31. Pan, Q., Reitmayr, G., Drummond, T.: ProFORMA: probabilistic feature-based on-line rapid model acquisition. In: Proceedings of the British Machine Vision Conference (BMVC), London, UK (2009)

32. Porrill, J., Pollard, S.: Curve matching and stereo calibration. Image Vis. Comput. (IVC) **9**(1), 45–50 (1991)

33. Rother, C., Kolmogorov, V., Blake, A.: Grabcut: interactive foreground extraction using iterated graph cuts. In: ACM transactions on graphics (TOG), vol. 23, pp. 309–314. ACM (2004)

34. Teney, D., Piater, J.: Sampling-based multiview reconstruction without correspondences for 3D edges. In: Proceedings of the International Symposium on 3D Data Processing, Visualization and Transmission (3DPVT) (2012)

35. Xiao, Y.J., Li, Y.: Optimized stereo reconstruction of free-form space curves based on a nonuniform rational B-spline model. J. Opt. Soc. Am. **22**(9), 1746–1762 (2005)

36. Zhou, Y., Kneip, L., Li, H.: Semi-dense visual odometry for RGB-D cameras using approximate nearest neighbour fields. In: Proceedings of the IEEE International Conference on Robotics and Automation (ICRA) (2017)

Monocular Epipolar Constraint for Optical Flow Estimation

Mahmoud A. Mohamed[(✉)], M. Hossein Mirabdollah, and Bärbel Mertsching

GET Lab, University of Paderborn, Pohlweg 47-49, 33098 Paderborn, Germany
{mahmoud,mirabdollah,mertsching}@get.upb.de

Abstract. In this paper, the usage of the monocular epipolar geometry for the calculation of optical flow is investigated. We derive the necessary formulation to use the epipolar constraint for the calculation of differential optical flow using the total variational model in a multi-resolution pyramid scheme. Therefore, we minimize an objective function which contains the epipolar constraint with a residual function based on different types of descriptors (brightness, HOG, CENSUS and MLDP). For the calculation of epipolar lines, the relevant fundamental matrices are calculated based on the 7- and 8- point methods. Moreover, SIFT and Lukas-Kanade methods are used to obtain matched features between two consecutive frames, by which fundamental matrices can be calculated. The effect of using different combination of the feature matching methods, fundamental matrix calculation and descriptors are evaluated based on the KITTI 2012 dataset.

1 Introduction

For realistic scenes captured by a monocular camera, the optical flow is defined as the two-dimensional projection of motions of a three-dimensional world. Although optical flow calculation has been investigated for a long time, it is still known as an open problem especially if the flows are due to the large motions and the scenes are low textured. The main interesting promising approaches for the calculation of optical flow is differential methods using total variational optimization methods, due to the fact that different constraints can be casted as a single cost function resulting into well established elegant methods which take care of all objectives simultaneously. Several differential optical flow approaches have already proposed, which mainly apply the brightness constancy constraint by assuming constant intensity of pixels through a sequence of consecutive images.

Where the optical flow is mostly induced by camera motions, i.e. stationary objects, the epipolar geometry can be applied to obtain another constraint for the flow of a pixel. First, the fundamental matrix which relates the motion of the camera between two consecutive images is estimated. Second, for each point in the first frame, the location of the correspondent point in the next consecutive frame is constrained over an epipolar line. Fundamental matrices in particular can be estimated using the 8-point or 7-point [4] approaches.

© Springer International Publishing AG 2017
M. Liu et al. (Eds.): ICVS 2017, LNCS 10528, pp. 62–71, 2017.
DOI: 10.1007/978-3-319-68345-4_6

The epipolar geometry of a stereo camera has been widely used for the estimation of optical flow [15]. In turn, few methods applied the monocular epipolar geometry for the optical flow estimation. In [17], the correspondent points are found by searching over epipolar lines and used a semi-global block matching technique. The method has three main shortcomings. First, the estimation of the fundamental matrix is not always accurate especially when the base lines are small and the rotations are relatively big. Second, the camera calibration information is used to speed up their epipolar search based on the semi global block matching method and third, the applied approximation of rotation matrix which is valid only for small rotations. In [16], the joint estimation of the fundamental matrix and the optical flow estimation is formulated as a total variation with L2 norm (TV-L2) problem. Such a formulation is badly ill-conditioned and diverges in most of the cases if no initial guesses of the fundamental matrices are available. The reason is that fundamental matrix estimation is sensitive even to minor amount of measurement noise. Additionally, in this work, the formulation of the method is not presented for the multi-resolution pyramid analysis. In turn, [7] used the epipolar constraint for the estimation of sparse optical flows and did not apply a smoothness constraint. In [12], an approach to dense depth estimation from a single monocular camera was proposed. The authors proposed an algorithm that segments the optical flow field into a set of motion models, each with its own epipolar geometry.

In the work which we present in this paper, we have not used any kind of segmentation such as [12,17]. We apply the epipolar constraint directly in the context of a global local optimization process. Moreover, we give appropriate weight to the epipolar constraint benefit from both brightness/texture information and epipolar constraint to tackle with the inaccuracy of fundamental matrices. Additionally, we formulate the usage of the epipolar constraint in the calculation of differential optical flow based on the total variation TV-L1 in a pyramid context to deal with large optical flows. The effect of different parameters is investigated and optimal parameters to reach the best performance is presented. The performance of the proposed formulation is examined by applying different types of descriptors and different methods to estimate fundamental matrices. The method is evaluated by the challenging KITTI 2012 dataset.

2 Dense Optical Flow Estimation

The brightness constraint assumes that the intensity of a pixel stays constant if the object or camera moves. Given two consecutive images $I_1(x, y)$ and $I_2(x, y)$, the optical flow maps each pixel (x, y), in image I_1 to a pixel (x', y'), in image I_2. The brightness constraint has been used in most of sub-pixel approaches for the optical flow estimation. It states that $I_1(x, y) = I_2(x', y')$, where $x'_i = x_i + u_i$ and $y'_i = y_i + v_i$, and $[u \ v]^T$ is a 2D optical flow vector. In the calculation of a differential optical flow model, the brightness constraint can be linearized using Taylor expansion as follows:

$$I_x(x, y)u + I_y(x, y)v = -I_t(x, y) \tag{1}$$

where $I_x(x, y) = \frac{\partial I_1(x,y)}{\partial x}$, $I_y(x, y) = \frac{\partial I_1(x,y)}{\partial y}$ and $I_t(x, y) = I_2(x, y) - I_1(x, y)$. In spite of that, Eq. (1) is under-determined equation. It contains only one equation with two unknowns which can be solved only by assuming other constraint i.e. smoothness constraint to build a system of independent equations. Furthermore, the brightness constraint fails in case of illumination changes. To cope with this problem, many optical flow methods proposed to rely on the gradient constancy. Gradient constancy assumption considers that image gradients does not change with the motion of the object or camera and it is formulated as follow:

$$\nabla_3 I_1(x, y, t) - \nabla_3 I_2(x + u, y + v, t + dt) = 0. \tag{2}$$

Recently, image textures which are robust against illumination changes has been successfully integrated in the estimation of optical flow. Therefore, the modified local directional pattern introduced in [8,10], the histogram of oriented gradient [13], and the census signature [6,11] were used to describe texture features. Afterwards, the total variation TV-L1 model has been modified to utilize the texture constancy assumption based on the extracted features. The texture constraint is formulated as:

$$\sum_{i=0}^{N} [S_1(x, y, t)_i - S_2(x + u, y + v, t + dt)_i] = 0, \tag{3}$$

where S_1 and S_2 are the extracted texture descriptors from I_1 and I_2 respectively, while N is the number of the channel for a descriptor.

3   Epipolar Constraint

For homogeneous and therefore less textured regions, Eq. (1) provides a dependent system of equations and therefore no valid solution can be obtained. However, the epipolar constraint can be applied, if the optical flow between two consecutive images is mostly induced by camera motion [7]. In spite of that, the epipolar constraint can be leveraged to calculate the optical flow even for low textured regions. For two matching points, $q = (x, y)$ and $p = (x', y')$ in two consecutive images captured at two different camera positions, the following equation holds:

$$\mathbf{q}^T F \mathbf{p} = 0 \tag{4}$$

where $\mathbf{p} = [x \ y \ 1]^T$ and $\mathbf{q} = [x' \ y' \ 1]^T$, F is a 3×3 matrix known as the fundamental matrix. As a result, the location of a point in image I_1 is constrained by an epipolar line in the image I_2. Therefore, Eq. (4) can be formulated as follows:

$$ax_i' + by_i' + c = 0 \tag{5}$$

where $[a\ b\ c]^T = \frac{1}{\eta}F\mathbf{q}$. η is a normalization factor such that $a^2 + b^2 = 1$. By substituting $x'_i = x_i + u_i$ and $y'_i = y_i + v_i$ in Eq. (5), an equation in terms of u and v is obtained:

$$au + bv = -ax - by - c \tag{6}$$

The above formulation is valid for the case that the optical flow is calculated on the original image scale. For the calculation of large optical flow, the well-known coarse-to-fine approach [2] is applied. In this approach, the image is subsampled iteratively several times and then the flow is calculated from the coarsest to the finest level:

$$I_l(x, y) = I_{l-1}(sx, sy); \tag{7}$$

where l is level index such that $I_0 = I$. Given the fundamental matrix for the original image, the epipolar line equations at each level have to be determined. In this regard we rewrite the co-planarity constraint as follows:

$$[\alpha x'\ \alpha y'\ \alpha]F[\alpha x\ \alpha y\ \alpha]^T = 0 \tag{8}$$

where $\alpha = s^l$. We can verify that for two matching points on level l such as $[x_l, y_l]^T$, $[x'_l, y'_l]^T$, they can be related to a point in the original image as follows:

$$[x_l, y_l]^T = \alpha[x, y]^T$$
$$[x'_l, y'_l]^T = \alpha[x', y']^T \tag{9}$$

Therefore we have:

$$[x'_l\ y'_l\ \alpha]\ F\ [x_l\ y_l\ \alpha]^T = 0 \tag{10}$$

Consequently, we obtain a new line equation for each point at level l as follows:

$$a_l x'_l + b_l y'_l + c_l = 0 \tag{11}$$

As a result, the line equation containing u_l and v_l will be as follows:

$$a_l u_l + b_l v_l + a_l x_l + b_l y_l + c_l \tag{12}$$

4   Proposed Optical Flow Model

The regularized cost function including the epipolar constraint can be written as follows:

$$\min_{u,v}\ E(u, v) = \sum_{\Omega} \left(\lambda \rho(x, y, u, v)^2 + \gamma \parallel a_l u + b_l v + d \parallel + \eta \left(\parallel \nabla u \parallel + \parallel \nabla v \parallel \right) \right),$$
$$\tag{13}$$

where λ, η and γ are the importance weight of the data term, the smoothness term and the epipolar constraint, respectively. $\rho(x)^2 = x^2$ is a convex function.

We optimize the above cost function Eq. (13) based on the combination of local and global costs using the dual variable optimization as explained in [18]. We apply the TV-L1 smoothness term in [18] to estimate the dual variables $(\hat{u}, \hat{v})$ and we optimize the data term E_d as follows:

$$\min_{u,v} \ E_d(u,v) = \lambda\rho(x,y,u,v)^2 + \gamma(a_l u + b_l v + d)^2 + \frac{1}{2\theta}(u - \hat{u})^2 + \frac{1}{2\theta}(v - \hat{v})^2, \quad (14)$$

Assuming that $\theta = 0.5$, using the dual TV-L1 algorithm, Eq. (14) can be optimized by solving it for (u,v) by doing:

$$\frac{\partial}{\partial u}\left(\lambda\rho(x,y,u,v)^2 + \gamma(a_l u + b_l v + d)^2 + \frac{1}{2\theta}(u - \hat{u})^2\right) = 0,$$

$$\frac{\partial}{\partial v}\left(\lambda\rho(x,y,u,v)^2 + \gamma(a_l u + b_l v + d)^2 + \frac{1}{2\theta}(v - \hat{v})^2\right) = 0. \quad (15)$$

Equation (15) is linear in (u,v) and can be solved as a linear system $Aw = B$ by using the values of the dual variables $\hat{u}$ and $\hat{v}$ from the smoothness part [18]. For every pixel, the residual function is calculated using the differences between two descriptors [9,13]. Assume $S_1(x,y)$ and $S_2(x+u, y+v)$ are the descriptors extracted from the two images $I_1(x,y)$ and $I_2(x+u, y+v)$, respectively. The residual function between the two n-channel descriptors can be represented as:

$$\rho(x,y,u,v)^2 = \sum_{i=1}^{n}\left(S_i'(x+u, y+v) - S_i(x,y)\right)^2$$

$$= \sum_{i=1}^{n}\rho_i(x,y,u,v)^2, \quad (16)$$

where n is the number of channel (number of bits/bins). In practice, the summation over all ρ_i^2 will measure the similarity distance between the two descriptors. The final data term can be extended as follow:

$$\min_{w} \ E_d(w) = \sum_{\Omega}\left(\lambda\sum_{i=1}^{n}\rho(x,y,w)^2 + 2\gamma(a_l u + b_l v + d)A_l + \frac{1}{2\theta}(w - \hat{w})^2\right),$$
$$(17)$$

where $w = [u\,v]^T$, $\hat{w} = [\hat{u}\,\hat{v}]^T$, $A_l = [a_l\,b_l]^T$ Hence, A and B matrices of the linear system described in (15) can be written as:

$$A = \begin{bmatrix} \frac{1}{2\lambda\theta} + \sum S_x'^2 + 2\gamma(a_l)^2 & \sum S_x'S_y' + 2\gamma a_l b_l \\ \sum S_x'S_y' + 2\gamma a_l b_l & \frac{1}{2\lambda\theta} + \sum S_y'^2 + 2\gamma(b_l)^2 \end{bmatrix}. \quad (18)$$

and

$$B = \begin{bmatrix} \left(\frac{1}{2\lambda\theta} + \sum S_x'^2\right)\hat{u} + \sum S_x'\sum S_y'\hat{v} - \sum S_x'\sum S_t + 2\gamma a_l(a_l x + b_l y + d) \\ \left(\frac{1}{2\lambda\theta} + \sum S_y'^2\right)\hat{v} + \sum S_x'\sum S_y'\hat{u} - \sum S_y'\sum S_t + 2\gamma b_l(a_l x + b_l y + d) \end{bmatrix}. \quad (19)$$

For solving for (u,v) and $(\hat{u}, \hat{v})$ we follow the framework explained in [10] and use the same smoothness term.

5   Experimental Results

Based on the training dataset of KITTI 2012 [3] and the general formulation presented in Sect. 4, we would like to investigate how the epipolar constraint works if it is applied along with different data terms and fundamental matrix estimation methods. In this regard, we use different data terms based on BC, MLDP, Census, and HOG. For the estimation of the fundamental matrix, we use the 8-point, and the 7-point methods. Figure 1 shows the outliers (%AEE > 3pixels) which is the average percentage of pixels which have AEE more than 3 pixels. This is the main major in KITTI portal to evaluate methods. Figure 1a depicts the results based on the 7-point method for fundamental matrix estimation and Fig. 1b is based on the 8-point method. As we can see, increasing the epipolar weight γ from zero reduces the errors regardless of the type of data term, feature tracker or fundamental matrix estimation methods.

Looking at both figures, unexpectedly, we can notice that the LK feature tracker outperforms SIFT noticeably, despite the common belief about the high accuracy of SIFT. Actually, it stems from the fact that corner features in outdoor scenes are extracted and localized much better using LK than blob features using SIFT. Additionally, unlike SIFT, the LK does not rely on the repeatability of features. In SIFT, blob features from both images are extracted and then based on their descriptors the matched points are found. This problem increases the ratio of mismatches specially in the case of occluded points and affects the quality of the fundamental matrix significantly. In turn, the LK tracks corner features from one frame using the sparse optical flow technique. As a result, repeatability is not an issue in LK tracker. Concerning the weight of the epipolar constraint, we can see that the best results are obtained for the weight $\gamma = 1.5$. Obviously, for smaller γ, the data term play more important roles in the determination of flow which can result in large errors in homogeneous regions. Moreover, the inaccuracy of the estimated fundamental matrix, degrades the results for increasing values of γ.

To have clear comparison results, the average of the endpoint errors (AEE), the average of the angular errors (AAE) and the outliers (%AEE > 3pixels) are presented in Table 1. We can see that the LK tracker and 7-point method for the estimation of fundamental matrix give the best results for all types of data terms. The best combination is HOG descriptor, Lk tracker and 7-point method. The better performance of the HOG in comparison to other data terms are due to the richer description of each point in the image. Census and MLDP both drop some important information which make them weaker in comparison to HOG. The reason that 7-point method outperforms the 8-point method stems from two facts. First, the 7-point method needs one point less than the 8-point method which makes it more robust against outliers. Second, rank deficiency of the fundamental matrix is directly taken into account during the fundamental matrix calculation process. Whereas, in the 8-point method rank deficiency is enforced later indirectly.

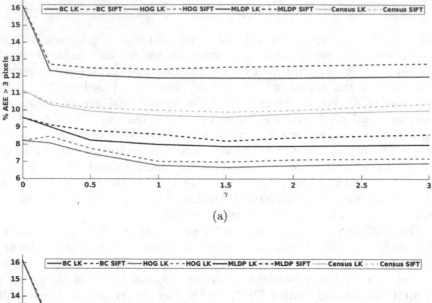

(a)

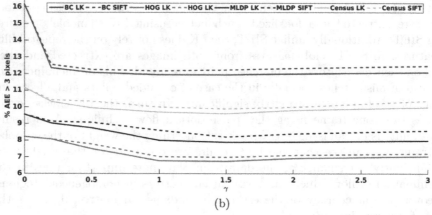

(b)

Fig. 1. The average error for all sequences of the KITTI 2012 training data set as a function of the epipolar wight γ. Outliers (%AEE > 3pixels) using 7-points algorithm (a) and using 8-points algorithm (b).

5.1   Challenging Sequences

In this experiment, we measure the effect of applying the epipolar constraint with a weight $\gamma = 1.5$. We choose challenging sequences from KITTI training data set which have homogeneous regions, texture regions, strongly varying lighting conditions, and many non-Lambertian surfaces. Table 2 shows a comparison between the estimated optical flow base on HOG descriptor and BC. The epipolar line constraint succeed to get better optical flow and the AEE and outliers (%AEE > 3pixels) are significantly reduced.

Table 1. The average errors (see text for details) of the estimated optical flow using 7-point and 8 points fundamental matrix with Lukas Kanade and SIFT.

		LK			SIFT		
		AEE	AAE	Outliers	AEE	AAE	Outliers
BC	7-points	02.45	02.72	11.08 %	02.53	02.76	12.23 %
	8-points	02.50	02.73	11.94 %	02.62	02.90	12.53 %
HOG	7-points	**01.52**	**01.72**	**06.68 %**	01.65	01.84	06.99 %
	8-points	01.56	01.74	06.74 %	01.65	01.84	06.99 %
MLDP	7-points	01.69	01.73	06.68 %	01.71	01.88	08.01 %
	8-points	01.74	01.76	07.89 %	01.75	01.93	08.20 %
Census	7-points	01.95	01.87	09.80 %	02.06	02.03	09.85 %
	8-points	02.06	01.93	09.89 %	02.20	02.17	09.93 %

Table 2. AEE and $AEE > 3$ pixels for BC and HOG applied on challenging sequences from KITTI training data set.

AEE

Sequence number		10	19	39	70	71	84	114	178
BC	$\gamma = 0.0$	18.50	08.03	16.80	15.65	15.26	09.27	15.58	10.48
	$\gamma = 1.5$	04.62	04.98	12.34	03.64	00.60	00.73	02.72	02.76
HOG	$\gamma = 0.0$	01.75	01.14	02.84	01.38	00.50	01.12	00.98	01.53
	$\gamma = 1.5$	01.21	01.07	01.45	01.27	00.48	0.92	00.96	01.32

Outliers (% AEE >3 Pixels)

Sequence number		25	54	74	101	113	135	163	181
BC	$\gamma = 0.0$	38.87 %	15.87 %	84.31 %	57.78 %	12.37 %	55.45 %	14.02 %	54.95 %
	$\gamma = 1.5$	37.81 %	15.86 %	74.94 %	48.74 %	09.67 %	48.05 %	11.80 %	55.70 %
HOG	$\gamma = 0.0$	30.57 %	23.33 %	50.77 %	19.42 %	22.97 %	14.58 %	19.31 %	41.71 %
	$\gamma = 1.5$	13.01 %	14.79 %	42.40 %	11.41 %	16.20 %	07.80 %	12.18 %	31.49 %

Table 3. KITTI 2012 evaluation test in April 2017.

	HOG with epipolar line constraint				HOG without epipolar line constraint			
AEE error	Out-Noc	Out-All	Avg-Noc	Avg-All	Out-Noc	Out-All	Avg-Noc	Avg-All
2 pixels	09.51%	21.00%	01.80 px	06.00 px	13.41%	24.91%	02.90 px	09.10 px
3 pixels	06.95%	17.91%	01.80 px	06.00 px	10.87%	22.44%	02.90 px	09.10 px
4 pixels	05.79 %	16.08 %	01.80 px	06.00 px	09.58 %	21.00%	02.90 px	09.10 px
5 pixels	05.06%	14.73%	01.80 px	06.00 px	08.71%	19.90%	02.90 px	09.10 px

5.2   KITTI Evaluation

At the date of submission in April 2017, the proposed method is evaluated using the KITTI 2012 flow dataset. Meanwhile, we test the proposed method using HOG descriptor and without using the epipolar line constraint and we got the results shown in Table 3. Table 4 shows comparisons with recently published methods. The proposed method has the name MEC-Flow in the KITTI website.

Table 4. Comparison with state-of-the art methods on the KITTI 2012 data set in April 2017.

Method	Out-Noc	Out-All	Avg-Noc	Avg-All
GC-BM-Bino [1]	18.83%	29.30%	5.0 px	12.1 px
TF+OFM [5]	10.22%	18.46%	2.0 px	5.0 px
MLDP-OF [10]	8.67%	18.78%	2.4 px	6.7 px
TVL1-HOG [13]	7.91%	18.90%	2.0 px	6.1 px
EpicFlow [14]	7.88%	17.08%	1.5 px	3.8 px
MEC-Flow (proposed method)	**6.95%**	17.91%	1.8 px	6.0 px

6   Conclusion

In this paper, we derive the necessary formulation to integrate the epipolar constraint for an uncalibrated camera using the variational optical flow estimation. The epipolar constraint is used along with different data terms and different feature tracking and fundamental matrix estimation methods. The optimal combination of different sub algorithms and the optimal weight are found based on the KITTI 2012 training dataset. We also evaluate the results for the test sequences on the KITTI 2012 portal. The iterative enhancement of the fundamental matrix is not investigated in this paper and it is of our interest to evaluate the enhancing of the fundamental matrices in fine levels.

References

1. Bernd, K., Henning, L.: Trinocular optical flow estimation for intelligent vehicle applications. In: 15th International IEEE Conference on Intelligent Transportation Systems (ITSC). IEEE, September 2012
2. Brox, T., Bruhn, A., Papenberg, N., Weickert, J.: High accuracy optical flow estimation based on a theory for warping. In: Pajdla, T., Matas, J. (eds.) ECCV 2004. LNCS, vol. 3024, pp. 25–36. Springer, Heidelberg (2004). doi:10.1007/978-3-540-24673-2_3
3. Geiger, A., Lenz, P., Stiller, C., Urtasun, R.: Vision meets robotics: the KITTI dataset. Int. J. Robot. Res. (IJRR) **32**, 1231–1237 (2013)
4. Hartley, R., Zisserman, A.: Multiple View Geometry in Computer Vision, 2nd edn. Cambridge University Press, New York (2003)

5. Kennedy, R., Taylor, C.J.: Optical flow with geometric occlusion estimation and fusion of multiple frames. In: Tai, X.-C., Bae, E., Chan, T.F., Lysaker, M. (eds.) EMMCVPR 2015. LNCS, vol. 8932, pp. 364–377. Springer, Cham (2015). doi:10.1007/978-3-319-14612-6_27

6. Mohamed, M., Mertsching, B.: TV-L1 optical flow estimation with image details recovering based on modified census transform. Adv. Vis. Comput. **7431**, 482–491 (2012)

7. Mohamed, M.A., Mirabdollah, M.H., Mertsching, B.: Differential optical flow estimation under monocular epipolar line constraint. In: Nalpantidis, L., Krüger, V., Eklundh, J.-O., Gasteratos, A. (eds.) ICVS 2015. LNCS, vol. 9163, pp. 354–363. Springer, Cham (2015). doi:10.1007/978-3-319-20904-3_32

8. Mohamed, M.A., Boddeker, C., Mertsching, B.: Real-time moving objects tracking for mobile-robots using motion information. In: 2014 IEEE International Symposium on Safety, Security, and Rescue Robotics (SSRR), pp. 1–6. IEEE (2014)

9. Mohamed, M.A., Rashwan, H.A., Mertsching, B., Garcia, M.A., Puig, D.: On improving the robustness of variational optical flow against illumination changes. In: Proceedings of the 4th ACM/IEEE International Workshop on Analysis and Retrieval of Tracked Events and Motion in Imagery Stream, pp. 1–8. ACM (2013)

10. Mohamed, M.A., Rashwan, H.A., Mertsching, B., Garcia, M.A., Puig, D.: Illumination-robust optical flow using a local directional pattern. IEEE Trans. Circuits Syst. Video Technol. **24**, 1–9 (2014)

11. Müller, T., Rabe, C., Rannacher, J., Franke, U., Mester, R.: Illumination-robust dense optical flow using census signatures. In: Mester, R., Felsberg, M. (eds.) DAGM 2011. LNCS, vol. 6835, pp. 236–245. Springer, Heidelberg (2011). doi:10.1007/978-3-642-23123-0_24

12. Ranftl, R., Vineet, V., Chen, Q., Koltun, V.: Dense monocular depth estimation in complex dynamic scenes. In: The IEEE Conference on Computer Vision and Pattern Recognition (CVPR), pp. 4058–4066, June 2016

13. Rashwan, H.A., Mohamed, M.A., Garcia, M.A., Mertsching, B., Puig, D.: Illumination robust optical flow model based on histogram of oriented gradients. In: Weickert, J., Hein, M., Schiele, B. (eds.) GCPR 2013. LNCS, vol. 8142, pp. 354–363. Springer, Heidelberg (2013). doi:10.1007/978-3-642-40602-7_38

14. Revaud, J., Weinzaepfel, P., Harchaoui, Z., Schmid, C.: Epicflow: edge-preserving interpolation of correspondences for optical flow. In: The IEEE Conference on Computer Vision and Pattern Recognition, CVPR 2015, Boston, MA, USA, 7–12, June, pp. 1164–1172. IEEE (2015)

15. Taniai, T., Sinha, S., Sato, Y.: Fast multi-frame stereo scene flow with motion segmentation. In: The IEEE Computer Vision and Pattern Recognition (CVPR). IEEE, March 2017

16. Valgaerts, L., Bruhn, A., Weickert, J.: A variational model for the joint recovery of the fundamental matrix and the optical flow. In: Rigoll, G. (ed.) DAGM 2008. LNCS, vol. 5096, pp. 314–324. Springer, Heidelberg (2008). doi:10.1007/978-3-540-69321-5_32

17. Yamaguchi, K., McAllester, D.A., Urtasun, R.: Robust monocular epipolar flow estimation. In: The IEEE Computer Vision and Pattern Recognition (CVPR), pp. 1862–1869. IEEE (2013)

18. Zach, C., Pock, T., Bischof, H.: A duality based approach for realtime TV-L^1 optical flow. In: Hamprecht, F.A., Schnörr, C., Jähne, B. (eds.) DAGM 2007. LNCS, vol. 4713, pp. 214–223. Springer, Heidelberg (2007). doi:10.1007/978-3-540-74936-3_22

Visual Servo Tracking Control of Quadrotor with a Cable Suspended Load

Erping Jia, Haoyao Chen[✉], Yanjie Li, Yunjiang Lou,
and Yunhui Liu

School of Mechanical Engineering and Automation,
Harbin Institute of Technology Shenzhen, Shenzhen, China
1540780335@qq.com, {hychen5,autolyj,
louyj}@hit.edu.cn, yhliu@mae.cuhk.edu.hk

Abstract. To follow a moving target, the visual servo control of a quadrotor with a cable suspended load is proposed. A monocular camera with rotation degree along y axis is equipped on the quadrotor. The dynamic model for the whole system is presented to design target tracking controller. An image based visual servoing controller is proposed to provide position and yaw reference information for the quadrotor control, when the quadrotor is too far away from target. OpenTLD is used to provide the visual feedback information for visual servoing. When the quadrotor is close enough to the target, the AprilTag technology is applied to provide the pose information for position control. Based on the dynamic model and the reference information from the visual servoing or AprilTag, a quadrotor-load PD controller is presented. Finally, simulation results are presented to illustrate the effectiveness of the proposed approaches.

Keywords: Visual servoing · UAV · Suspended load · Target tracking control

1 Introduction

Recently, unmanned aerial vehicles (UAVs) have been widely used in surveillance in hard-to-reach or disaster-stricken areas [1–3]. And there is increasing attention paid in the field of transportation, especially in manipulation of UAVs with a cable-suspended load [2]. Aerial transportation of a cable suspended load has been studied for helicopters and quadrotors [4, 5]. Both small-size single and multiple autonomous vehicles are considered for transporting and deploying loads [6–8]. Because the load's dynamics varies during the transportation, it is challenging to achieve stable control of both the quadrotor and the suspended load. Transportation and deployment of loads with a UAV are especially complex task because of both the dynamics of the load and the target recognition. Stable target tracking and precise control of load are important for safe transportation, and it is challenging to achieve smooth transportation.

There are already many research results in the literature to solve the problem of transportation stability. For slow transportation, the dynamic effects of the load to the quadrotor can be approximated by unstructured disturbances without considering the nontrivial dynamic coupling between the load and the quadrotor. However, the dynamics of the load will be excited significantly for rapid load transportation. Sadr *et al.* [9]

© Springer International Publishing AG 2017
M. Liu et al. (Eds.): ICVS 2017, LNCS 10528, pp. 72–85, 2017.
DOI: 10.1007/978-3-319-68345-4_7

presented a dynamic model, and designed an anti-swing nonlinear controller for the position and attitude control of a quadrotor with a suspended load. Cruz and Fierro [10] developed an adaptive controller by integrating the least-square estimation and the geometric control to transport the load. Alothman et al. [2] utilized the linear quadratic regulator (LQR) to design controller for lifting and transporting the load; the nonlinear dynamic model considered the cable-suspended load, and was linearized at the hovering point. Sreenath et al. [11] presented a nonlinear control technique based on a dynamic model for the swing free stabilization and trajectory tracking of a quadrotor with a suspended load; the dynamic model was deduced based on Lagrange D'Alembert principle. Lee et al. [12] implemented a three stages geometric nonlinear control strategy for trajectory tracking of quadrotor with a suspended load. The quadrotor dynamic model with eight degree of freedom was represented based on the differentially flatness; the hybrid control system stability analysis was presented to guarantee the stabilization and path tracking tasks.

To deploy the suspended load on the moving target successfully, it is important to track the target stably by the quadrotor. Camera is widely-used sensor for visual tracking, and it is usually light enough to be equipped on the UAVs. Thus the tracking control with visual information is considered in the paper to implement transportation tasks. Many approaches to visual tracking, especially the visual servo control, have been developed in the literature. Visual servo control is about the tracking of a static or moving object with a camera; there are two different visual servo control catalogues, including image based visual servo control (IBVS) and position-based visual servo control (PBVS) [13]. The IBVS exhibits better robustness against calibration error. Kendoul et al. [13] developed a nonlinear visual servo controller, and proved of the system stability; the UAV was controlled to track the moving target. Xu et al. [14] utilized a cooperative object and an infrared camera for UAV's pose estimation, but only the yaw angle was computed and used to control the UAV. Herisse et al. [15] developed an approach to hovering and terrain following of a quadrotor; the approach is based on the optical flow captured by an on-board camera in static or textured indoor environment. A nonlinear controller was applied for the motion control without considering the heading control.

In the paper, we aim to develop a control approach to implement visual servo tracking of quadrotor with a cable suspended load. To design the controller, the dynamic model [11] for the quadrotor with a cable suspended load is utilized. Because the load is released from the quadrotor at the end of the transportation task, the quadrotor with a suspended load is treated as a hybrid system with two modes, i.e., taut and loose cable connections to the quadrotor base. The cable is taut and transferring a force between load and quadrotor in the first mode, while there is no tension in the cable and the load is in free fall in the other mode. AprilTag [16] is a technology widely used to provide robust target detection, and provides 6 degree of freedom estimation of the target pose from a single image if an AprilTag is attached on the target. The pose of an AprilTag in the world frame is easily acquired by the rigid body transformation between different frame systems. However, the quadrotor may be sometimes too far away from target, and it is difficult to detect the AprilTag attached on the target. Therefore, the OpenTLD [17] is used to detect the target when the quadrotor is far away. Compared to AprilTag, OpenTLD can track natural image blobs without assigning special pattern but lacking the ability of providing 6-DOF pose estimation. To control the quadrotor system, an OpenTLD-based IBVS controller is presented inspired from the work in [18]. The original work [18] was designed for a quadrotor without a suspended load, and no dynamics variation was considered in the control process. The proposed controller will drive the quadrotor with a suspended load to approach the target until the AprilTag is detected, and then the controller with the Aprilag's pose estimation is applied.

The remainder of this paper is organized as follows. Section 2 presents the dynamic model of the quadrotor with a suspended load. Section 3 proposed the IBVS controller design, quadrotor pose estimation through AprilTag, and the controller of quadrotor with a cable suspended load. Section 4 provides some simulations to illustrate the performance, following with the conclusion of the work in Sect. 5.

2 Dynamic Modeling of a Quadrotor with a Cable Suspended Load

A quadrotor with a cable suspended load is illustrated at Fig. 1. As shown in Fig. 1, the inertial frame is defined by the unit vectors $\vec{e}_1 = [1, 0, 0], \vec{e}_2 = [0, 1, 0]$ and $\vec{e}_3 = [0, 0, 1] \in R$ where $\vec{e}_3$ denotes the gravity direction. The frame $\vec{b}_1, \vec{b}_2, \vec{b}_3$ denotes the body frame located at the mass center of the quadrotor, where $\vec{b}_1$ represents the head direction of quadrotor. R denotes the rotation matrix from the body frame to the inertial frame. $\{f_1, f_2, f_3, f_4\}$ denotes the upward thrusts on the four rotors, respectively. The $l \in R$ denotes the length of cable connecting quadrotor with load. Define $T \in R$ as the tension on the cable. When the cable breaks, the tension value becomes zero. Based on the work in [19], a hybrid model is presented for the cases of nonzero and zero tension force.

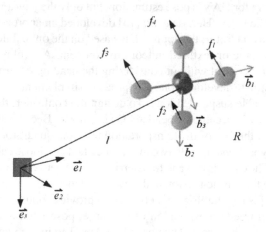

Fig. 1. A quadrotor with a cable suspended load.

2.1 Dynamical Model with Nonzero Cable Tension

The system configuration is defined by the load location w.r.t. the inertial frame, the load attitude and the quadrotor attitude. The configuration has 8 degrees of freedom with space $Q = SE(3) \times S^2$, and four degree underactuation, when the cable is taut. The relationship between quadrotor and load positions is given as

$$x_Q = v_L - l_Q \tag{1}$$

where $x_Q, x_L \in R^3$ are the position vectors of the mass center of the quadrotor and the suspended load in the inertial frame, respectively, $l_Q = lq$, and $q \subset S^2 \subset R^2$ denotes the unit vector from quadrotor to the suspended load. Based on Lagrange D'Alembert principle, the equations of motion for the quadrotor with cable-suspended load are obtained as

$$\dot{x}_L = v_L \tag{2}$$

$$(m_Q + m_L)(\dot{v}_L + ge_3) = (q \cdot f \operatorname{Re}_3 - m_Q l(\dot{q} \cdot \dot{q}))q \tag{3}$$

$$\dot{q} = w \times q \tag{4}$$

$$m_Q l w = -\dot{q} \times f \operatorname{Re}_3 \tag{5}$$

$$\dot{R} = R\hat{\Omega} \tag{6}$$

$$J_Q \dot{\Omega} + \Omega \times J_Q \Omega = M \tag{7}$$

where m_Q and m_L denote the mass of the quadrotor and load, respectively, v_L denotes the velocity of the load, f is the total thrust, $w \in R^3$ is the angular velocity of the suspended load, $\Omega \in R^3$ denotes the angular velocity of the quadrotor in the body-fixed frame and $J_Q \in R^{3 \times 3}$ denotes the inertia matrix of the quadrotor with respect to the body frame, the hat map $\hat{} : R^3 \to SO(3)$ is defined such that $\hat{x}y = x \times y, \forall x, y \in R^3$. The above dynamics is written in a standard form as

$$\dot{X}_n = f_n(X_n) + g_n(X_n)u,$$

where $X_n = \{x_L, q, R, v_L, w, \Omega\}$ and $u = \{f, M\}$ denote the system state and input, receptively.

Note that the quadrotor attitude dynamics (7) is decoupled from the load position and attitude dynamics (3) and (5), while the load attitude dynamics is decoupled from the load position dynamics. And the gravity does not influence the load attitude dynamics. The load attitude dynamics (5) is rewritten directly in terms of the load attitude, $q \in S^2$ and its derivatives, as

$$m_Q l \ddot{q} + m_Q l(\dot{q} \cdot \dot{q}) = q \times (q \times f\operatorname{Re}_3), \tag{8}$$

The above equation for the load attitude dynamics is used for control design.

2.2   Dynamical Model with Zero Cable Tension

When the load is released from the quadrotor, the cable tension becomes zero, the quadrotor and load turn to separate systems, with the load being in free fall. The dynamical model is identical to that in [20], given as

$$\dot{x}_L = v_L, \quad m_L(\dot{v}_L + ge_3) = 0, \tag{9}$$

$$\dot{x}_Q = v_Q, \quad m_Q(\dot{v}_Q + ge_3) = f Re_3, \tag{10}$$

$$\dot{R} = R\hat{\Omega}, \quad J_Q\dot{\Omega} + \Omega \times J_Q\Omega = M. \tag{11}$$

The above dynamics is also written in the standard form

$$\dot{X}_Z = f_Z(X_Z) + g_Z(X_Z)u,$$

where $X_Z = \{x_L, x_Q, R, v_L, v_Q, \Omega\}$ is the state.

3   Controller Design

The task objective is to design a scheme for the autonomous tracking control of a quadrotor with a cable suspended load; the quadrotor is also desired to deploy the load to a moving target autonomously. The control scheme contains three parts, including a IBVS tracking controller, AprilTag-based pose estimation, and the controller of quadrotor with a cable suspended load.

3.1   Image Based Visual Servoing Controller

Figure 2 shows the control framework of the proposed IBVS controller. Object detector plays an important role in efficient IBVS controller. The famous OpenTLD tracker [17] is utilized in our work; its advantage lies in the learning capability and thus no need of any previous knowledge about the tracked object. In the IBVS controller, the location and size of a bounding image blob is used as the feedback as shown in Fig. 2. The references to the controller contains the desired centroid location and size of the bounding box in the image.

The OpenTLD tracker provides the location of the upper-left corner (x_{bb}, y_{bb}) and the blob width w_{bb} and height h_{bb}. With the provided feedback information, we have

$$f_u = \frac{x_{bb} + \left(\frac{w_{bb}}{2}\right)}{w_{im}} \tag{12}$$

$$f_v = \frac{y_{bb} + \left(\frac{h_{bb}}{2}\right)}{h_{im}} \tag{13}$$

$$f_\Delta = \sqrt{\frac{w_{im} \cdot h_{im}}{w_{bb} \cdot h_{bb}}} \& x_{tm} \tag{14}$$

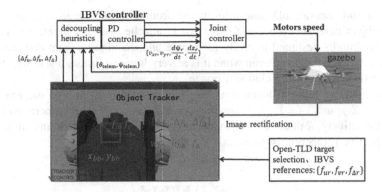

Fig. 2. Flowchart of the control framework including the IBVS controller and quadrotor controller.

where w_{im} and h_{im} are the width and height of image, and x_{tm} denotes the frontal distance from the drone to the target. The distance is approximately proportional to the value of f_Δ.

Because the target's movement on the image plane naturally couples the controlled variables of the quadrotor, the altitude and lateral movement control is then decoupled by providing the following tracking error

$$\Delta f_{u\psi} = \Delta f_u, \tag{15}$$

$$\Delta f_{uy} = \Delta f_u - \frac{\psi_{telemref} - \psi_{telem}}{FOV_u}, \tag{16}$$

$$\Delta f_{vz} = \Delta f_v - \frac{\theta_{centroidref} - \theta_{telem}}{FOV_v}, \tag{17}$$

$$\Delta f_{\Delta\psi} = \Delta f_\Delta, \tag{18}$$

where θ_{telem} and ψ_{telem} are the pitch and yaw angles of the quadrotor respectively obtained from the quadrotor odometry data, FOV_u and FOV_v denote the horizontal and vertical field of view of the camera, $\theta_{telemref}$ is a predefined yaw reference $\theta_{centroidref} = 0$, and θ_{telem} is the command pitch obtained from the drone's telemetry data. By using the PD controller [18], the speed reference commands in the inertia frame $\{v_{xr}, v_{yr}, \frac{d\psi_r}{dt}, \frac{dz_r}{dt}\}$ is then computed; the computed commands are further used as the reference for the controller developed in Sect. 3.3.

3.2 AprilTag-Based Pose Estimation of Quadrotor

If the quadrotor pose with respect to the tracked object is provided, the tracking control of the quadrotor on the moving target can achieve better performance on robustness compared to IBVS controllers. The OpenTLD tracker can provide image blob location and size but lacking of 3D relative pose information, and furthermore the natural features may be lost during the motion. Artificial features, like QR code pattern, can give robust and accurate 6D pose information from a single image, and thus greatly simplify object detection process if a pattern is attached on the target. AprilTag are artificial landmarks designed to easily recognize and distinguish from one another; it can be detected and localized even when it is at very low resolution, unevenly lit, oddly rotated, or tucked away in a cluttered image.

Figure 3 shows the transformations between frames in a pin-hole camera model. The (X_c, Y_c, Z_c) and (X_w, Y_w, Z_w) are the coordinates *w.r.t.* the camera and world frames, respectively, R denotes the rotation matrix and T denotes the translation vector. The perspective projection is given as

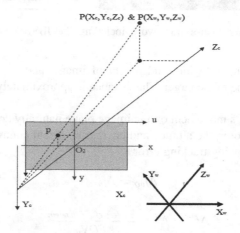

Fig. 3. Frame transformation of pin-hole camera

$$Z_c = \begin{bmatrix} u \\ v \\ 1 \end{bmatrix} = \begin{bmatrix} \alpha_x & 0 & y_0 & 0 \\ 0 & \alpha_y & y_0 & 0 \\ 0 & 0 & 1 & 0 \end{bmatrix} \begin{bmatrix} R & t \\ 0^T & 1 \end{bmatrix} \begin{bmatrix} X_w \\ Y_w \\ Z_w \\ 1 \end{bmatrix} = P \begin{bmatrix} R & t \\ 0^T & 1 \end{bmatrix} \begin{bmatrix} X_w \\ Y_w \\ Z_w \\ 1 \end{bmatrix} \tag{19}$$

where

$$P = \begin{bmatrix} \alpha_x & 0 & y_0 & 0 \\ 0 & \alpha_y & y_0 & 0 \\ 0 & 0 & 1 & 0 \end{bmatrix}$$

denotes the camera's internal parameter matrix.

By defining the AprilTag frame at the center of the tag plane, the 2D image coordinates $\hat{p}_i = (u_i, v_i)$ projected from the point $p_i = (X_i, Y_i, Z_i)$ w.r.t. the tag frame is computed according to (19). The residual error between the measured and projected coordinates is defined as $p_i - \hat{p}_i$. The transformation matrix from tag to camera is calculated by using the Gauss-Newton or Levevberg-Marquardt method

$$T_t^c = \arg\min \frac{1}{2}\Sigma_{i\in R}\|p_i - \hat{p}_1\|^2,$$

where $T_t^c = \begin{bmatrix} R & t \\ 0^T & 1 \end{bmatrix}$. With the transformation matrix, the quadrotor is then controlled to follow target at a predefined relative pose with the following controller.

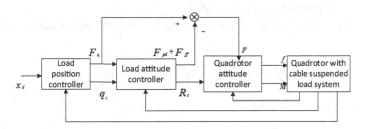

Fig. 4. Controller structure for tracking load position

3.3 Controller Design

Based on the dynamics model, reference commands and visual feedback information, a nonlinear geometric controller design is presented that enables tracking of either the quadrotor attitude, the load attitude or the position of the load. Figure 4 illustrates the inner-outer loop controller structure for the load position tracking. Before proceeding to describe the controller, we will first define configuration error functions on the Manifolds $SO(3)$ and $SO(3)$ [21]. The error functions e_R, e_Ω on $SO(3)$ are given by,

$$e_R = \frac{1}{2}(R_d^T R \quad R^T R_d)^\vee, \tag{20}$$

$$e_\Omega = \Omega - R^T R_d \Omega_d, \tag{21}$$

where R_d and Ω_d are the desired orientation and angular velocity of the quadrotor respectively. Similarly, the error functions e_q, $e_{\dot{q}}$ on TS^2 are given by,

$$e_q = \hat{q}^2 q_d, \tag{22}$$

$$e_q = \dot{q} - (q_d - \dot{q}_d) \times q \tag{23}$$

where q_d, is the desired load orientation. The tracking errors for position and velocity respectively is defined as,

$$e_x = x - x_d, \tag{24}$$

$$e_v = v - v_d, \tag{25}$$

where $x_d(t) \in R^3$ is the desired quadrotor or load position, and $v_d = \dot{x}_d$.

With the above error definitions, the moment torque control law is given as

$$M = -\frac{1}{\varepsilon^2} k_R e_R - \frac{1}{\varepsilon} k_\Omega e_\Omega + \Omega \times J_Q \Omega - J(\hat{\Omega} R^T \Omega_d - R^T R_d \dot{\Omega}_d) \tag{26}$$

where k_R, k_Ω are positive constants, and $0 < \varepsilon < 1$.

Based on the load attitude dynamics in (5), the computed quadrotor attitude is defined as

$$R_c := [b_{1c}; b_{3c} \times b_{1c}; b_{3c}], \hat{\Omega}_c = R_c^T \dot{R}_c \tag{27}$$

where $b_{3c} \in S^2$ is calculated by

$$b_{3c} = F/\|F\| \tag{28}$$

where,

$$F = F_n - F_{pd} - F_{ff} \tag{29}$$

where F_n, F_{pd} and F_{ff} are as defined below

$$F_n = -(q_d \cdot q)q, \tag{30}$$

$$F_{pd} = -k_q e_q - k_w e_{\dot{q}}, \tag{31}$$

$$F_{ff} = m_Q l \langle q, q_d \times \dot{q}_d \rangle (q \times \dot{q}) + m_Q l (q_d \times \ddot{q}_d) \times q. \tag{32}$$

The $b_{1d} \in S^2$ is chosen with the desired heading direction of the quadrotor which is not parallel to b_{3c}, and then the unit vector b_{1c} is defined as

$$b_{1c} = \frac{1}{\|b_{3c} \times b_{1d}\|} (b_{3c} \times (b_{3c} \times b_{3d})) \tag{33}$$

Then the quadrotor thrust f is defined by

$$f = F \cdot R_c e_3 \tag{34}$$

Considering the load position dynamics in (3), the computed load attitude is defined as

$$q_c = -A/\|A\| \tag{39}$$

where,

$$A = -k_{xQ}e_{xQ} - k_{vQ}e_{vQ} - k_{xL}e_{xL} + (m_Q + m_L)(\ddot{x}_L^d + ge_3) + m_Q l(\dot{q} \cdot \dot{q})q \qquad (40)$$

Then F_n in (30) is recalculated as

$$F_n = (A \cdot q)q. \qquad (41)$$

Let the desired quadrotor and load attitude in (26), (29) replaced by the computed values, R_c, and q_c respectively. The quadrotor thrust and moment are calculated by (26) and (34).

4 Simulations

To verify the effectiveness of the proposed approach, several simulations were performed in the simulation environment Gazebo.

4.1 Simulation Setup

Figure 5 illustrates the simulation platform. The Firefly manufactured by Ascending Tech was used in our simulation. The six-rotor uav is controlled the same as a quadrotor. The uav, equipped with a mono camera, is connected with a load by a simulated cable. The mobile robot Guardian was used as the moving target. The properties of the uav were given as m = 0.56779 kg, $J = diag[3.4756.3, 4.58929, 9.77] \times 10^2$ kgm^2, and the gravity g = 9.81. The load was set as m = 0.2 kg, and $l = 0.75$ m. The controller parameters were set as

$$k_x = [2.0, 2.0, 1.5], k_v = [2.5, 2.5, 2.5], k_q = [2.5, 2.5, 1.5],$$

$$k_w = [2.5, 2.5, 2.5], \frac{k_R}{\varepsilon^2} = [0.8, 0.8, 12.0], \frac{k_\Omega}{\varepsilon} = [1.5, 1.5, 2.5].$$

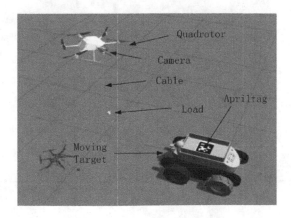

Fig. 5. Simulation platform overview

The desired locations of the uav was calculated from the IBVS controller and AprilTag. The initial uav status was set as

$$x(0) = [0, 0, 2.5], \dot{x}(0) = 0_{3 \times 1}, R(0) = I_{3 \times 3}, \Omega(0) = 0_{3 \times 1}$$

The initial direction of the cable q was set as $[0, 0, 1]$, and its initial angular velocity was set as zero. The load was desired to stay straightly under the uav. And thus the desired cable direction was set as q = $[0, 0, 1]$, and the desired cable angular velocity is zero.

4.2   Simulation Results

A simulation was performed to illustrate the affection of the load control to the stability of the uav. As shown in Fig. 6, the results of using the proposed quadrotor-load PD controller or not were presented. From Fig. 6, it is easy to see that the proposed controller reduced the vibration of the load greatly, and the load control was more stable.

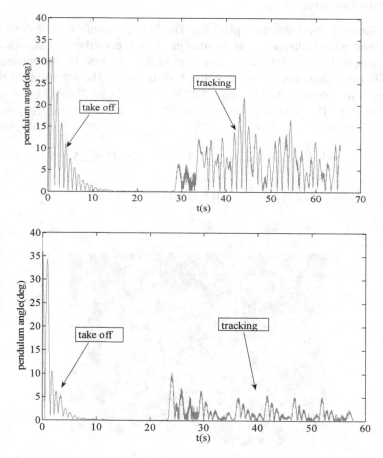

Fig. 6. Control effect of the cable direction.

Figure 7 illustrates the tracking errors of the proposed controller. From Fig. 7, we can see that the quadrotor can tracks the moving target very well. The uav started to track the AprilTag from 20s. Although the tracking errors in y direction based on AprilTag was not very good, the errors in both directions were bounded.

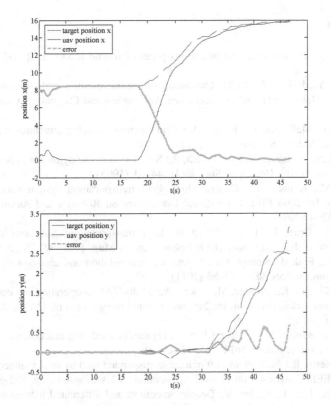

Fig. 7. Tracking error along the x and y directions

5   Conclusions and Future Work

In the paper, a visual servo control framework was developed for autonomously transporting a load with a cable connected to a quadrotor. The dynamic model for quadrotor with a cable suspended load was given to achieve a dynamic control of the target system. An image-based visual servo controller was developed to provide desired flying reference when quadrotor is far away from the target. The OpenTLD tracker was used to provide visual feedback information. In addition, AprilTag was utilized to achieve more robust target estimation when the quadrotor is close to the target. With the quadrotor reference from the OpenTLD and AprilTag trackers, a PD controller was designed based on the dynamic model to control the quadrotor-load system. The simulations by using the dynamics engine in Gazebo, were performed to illustrate the effectiveness of the proposed approach. Our future work includes performing experiments with real quadrotors.

Acknowledgments. This work was supported by a grant from the Shenzhen Science and Innovation Committee [Reference No. JCYJ20160427183958817], a grant from the National Natural Science Foundation of China [Reference No. 61673131], and a grant from the Hong Kong Research Grant Council [Reference No. 14204814].

References

1. Tadokoro, S.: Present state and future prospects of rescue robots. J. IEICE **92**, 203–208 (2009)
2. Alothman, Y., Jasim, W., Gu, D.: Quad-rotor lifting-transporting cable-suspended payloads control. In: 21st International Conference on Automation and Computing, Glasgow, pp 1–6 (2015)
3. Lindsey, Q., Mellinger, D., Kumar, V.: Construction of cubic structures with quadrotor teams. Proc. Robot.: Sci. Syst. VII (2011)
4. Cicolani, L.S., Kanning, G., Synnestvedt, R.: Simulation of the dynamics of helicopter slung load systems. J. Am. Helicopter Soc. **40**(4), 44–61 (1995)
5. Bernard, M., Kondak, K.: Generic slung load transportation system using small size helicopters. In: 2009 IEEE International Conference on Robotics and Automation, Kobe, pp 3258–3264 (2009)
6. Palunko, I., Cruz, P., Fierro, R.: Agile load transportation: Safe and efficient load manipulation with aerial robots. IEEE Robot. Autom. Mag. **19**(3), 69–79 (2012)
7. Michael, N., Fink, J., Kumar, V.: Cooperative manipulation and transportation with aerial robots. Auton. Robots **30**(1), 73–86 (2011)
8. Maza, I., Kondak, K., Bernard, M., Ollero, A.: Multi-UAV cooperation and control for load transportation and deployment. In: 2nd International Symposium on UAVs, Reno, pp 417–449 (2009)
9. Sadr, S., Moosavian, S.A.A., Zarafshan, P.: Dynamics modeling and control of a quadrotor with swing load. J. Robot. **2014**, 265897 (2014)
10. Cruz, P., Fierro, R.: Autonomous lift of a cable-suspended load by an unmanned aerial robot. In: 2014 IEEE Conference on Control Applications, Massachusetts, pp. 802–807 (2014)
11. Sreenath, K., Lee, T., Kumar, V.: Geometric control and differential flatness of a quadrotor UAV with a cable-suspended load. In: 52nd Annual Conference on Decision and Control, Florence, pp 2269–2274 (2013)
12. Lee, T., Sreenath, K., Kumar, V.: Geometric control of cooperating multiple quadrotor UAVs with a suspended payload. In: 52nd Annual Conference on Decision and Control, Florence, pp 5510–5515 (2013)
13. Kendoul, F., Nonami, K., Fantoni, I., Lozano, R.: An adaptive vision-based autopilot for mini flying machines guidance, navigation and control. Auton. Robots **27**(3), 165–188 (2009)
14. Xu, G., Qi, X., Zeng, Q., Tian, Y., Guo, R., Wang, B.: Use of land's cooperative object to estimate UAV's pose for autonomous landing. Chin. J. Aeronaut. **26**(6), 1498–1505 (2013)
15. Herisse, B., Russotto, F.X., Hamel, T., Mahony, R.: Hovering flight and vertical landing control of a VTOL unmanned aerial vehicle using optical flow. In: 2008 IEEE/RSJ International Conference on Intelligent Robots and Systems, Nice, pp. 801–806 (2008)
16. Olson, E.: AprilTag: a robust and flexible visual fiducial system. In: 2011 IEEE International Conference on Robotics and Automation, Shanghai, pp 3400–3407 (2011)
17. Kalal, Z., Mikolajczyk, K., Matas, J.: Tracking-learning-detection. IEEE Trans. Pattern Anal. Mach. Intell. **34**(7), 1409–1422 (2012)

18. Pestana, J., Sanchez-Lopez, J.L., Campoy, P., Saripalli, S.: Vision based GPS-Denied object tracking and following for unmanned aerial vehicles. In: 2013 IEEE international symposium on Safety, security, and rescue robotics, pp 1–6 (2013)
19. Jain, R.P.K.: Transportation of cable suspended load using unmanned aerial vehicles: a real-time model predictive control approach (2015)
20. Lee, T., Leoky, M., McClamroch, N.H.: Geometric tracking control of a quadrotor UAV on SE(3). In: 49th IEEE Conference on Decision and Control, Atlanta, pp 5420–5425 (2010)
21. Lewis, A., Bullo, F.: Geometric Control of Mechanical Systems. Springer Science & Business Media, Berlin (2005)

Global Localization for Future Space Exploration Rovers

Evangelos Boukas[1], Athanasios S. Polydoros[2], Gianfranco Visentin[3],
Lazaros Nalpantidis[1(✉)], and Antonios Gasteratos[4]

[1] Robotics, Vision and Machine Intelligence (RVMI) Laboratory, Department of
Materials and Production, Aalborg University Copenhagen, Copenhagen, Denmark
{eb,lanalpa}@make.aau.dk

[2] Intelligent and Interactive Systems, School of Mathematics, Computer Science and
Physics, University of Innsbruck, Innsbruck, Austria
Athanasios.Polydoros@uibk.ac.at

[3] Automation and Robotics Section (TEC-MMA), European Space Agency,
Noordwijk, The Netherlands
Gianfranco.Visentin@esa.int

[4] Laboratory of Robotics and Automation, School of Engineering, Democritus
University of Thrace, Xanthi, Greece
agaster@pme.duth.gr

Abstract. In the context of robotic space exploration the problem of
autonomous global or absolute localization remains unsolved. Current
rovers require human in the loop approaches to acquire global positioning. In this paper we assess this problem by refining our previous work
in a way that advances the performance of the system while making the
procedure feasible for real implementation on rovers. A map of semantic
landmarks (the Global Network - GN) is extracted on an area that the
rover traverses prior to the mission and, during the exploration, a Local
Network (LN) is built and matched to estimate rover's global location.
We have optimized several aspects of the system: the motion estimation,
the detection and classification –by benchmarking several classifiers– and
we have tested the system in a Mars like scenario. With the aim to achieve
realistic terms in our scenario a custom robotic platform was developed,
bearing operation features similar to ESA's ExoMars. Our results indicate that the proposed system is able to perform global localization and
converges relatively fast to an accurate solution.

1   Introduction

Future space exploration rovers ought to bear autonomy in such a level that
will allow them to perform complex tasks without the need of direct human
guidance (see the Mars Sample Return —MSR— mission [1]). In the core of
these capabilities lays the self-localization of rovers, with the next frontier being
global localization. From the Pathfinder's *Sojourner* [2] to the latest *Curiosity* [3], the methods employed in relative localization advanced vastly, mainly
due to the research concerning Visual Odometry (VO). A bright example of

© Springer International Publishing AG 2017
M. Liu et al. (Eds.): ICVS 2017, LNCS 10528, pp. 86–98, 2017.
DOI: 10.1007/978-3-319-68345-4_8

such advancements is the *ExoMars* rover that will explicitly employ VO to perform self localization [4]. However, so far, no rover has been able to perform accurate self localization on a planetary scale, in the same way that terrestrial field robots employ Global Navigation Satellite Systems (GNSS).

In our previous work [5] we have introduced the first autonomous global localization method employing semantic information of ground landmarks (regions of interest - ROIs), such as rocks and rock flatbeds (outcrops). The paper in hand stands as the description of our latest advancements in the global localization system taking into consideration ESA's requirements and expected capabilities of future exploration rovers. The improvements and noteworthy points of our enhanced system can be summarized as follows: Motion Estimation: We included a windowed Bundle Adjustment (wBA) component that is capable of efficiently adjusting the length of the employed previous information by utilizing accurate Inertial Measurement Unit (IMU) measurements. ROI detection: The previous ellipse fitting-based detection method has been revised to include both the propagation of the size estimation from multiple occurrences and a well established uncertainty connected with each detection. ROI description: We advanced the description of ROIs by involving the shape information by means of face normals, in the two-dimensional azimuth-elevation space. Machine Learning: We have extensively benchmarked a series of classifiers in order to find out which one is most suitable for our scenario. Consequently, alternatively to the computationally expensive k-NN classifier it emerged that *Gaussian Processes* should be employed. Robotics testbed: We constructed a novel robotics testbed and setup a Mars representative real scenario to fulfill the needs of this work.

2   Method Outline

The proposed system (Fig. 1) is partitioned in an offline and an onboard procedure. In the offline one a georeference (or aeroreferenced) image is provided and the system outputs labeled regions of interest (ROIs) in the form of a GN. The onboard one comprises the localization and the online detection and classification of boulders and creates a LN which is matched with the GN. The detection

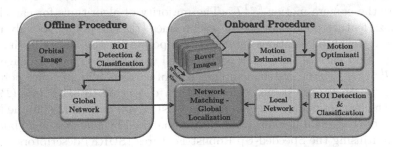

Fig. 1. The system comprises two procedures; an offline and an online one. The offline is a pre-mission one and the online is executed onboard as part of the GNC system.

(Sect. 4) of the ROIs provides candidate boulders which are not necessarily correct. The machine learning subsystem efficiently labels the ROIs ensuring that little or no false positives are inserted into the system. The selection of the appropriate machine learning technique is also discussed in Sect. 5. The output of the classification are correct boulders that form a GN which is fed to the rover as prior information.

The navigation system on the rover is able to efficiently localize itself on the relative starting frame. The rover utilizes a stereo camera as the sole sensor for motion estimation, as it is the most common case in rovers. We follow a feature based approach in the relative localization, which employs a variable windowed BA, in order to avoid the accumulation of drift (Sect. 3). The path planing is assumed as being a black box, since it falls out of the scope of this work. At each new stereo acquisition the detection of ROIs is employed, followed by a classification step. The output labeled ROIs are concatenated by properly assigning them the estimated position, size and their respective uncertainties. The classified rover ROIs form the LN, which is matched onboard to the GN to provide global localization.

3   Rover Relative Localization

In the current work, the relative localization system requires solely a pair of stereo frames and consists of two parts; an initial motion estimation and a motion estimation refinement. The first part is a frame to frame motion estimation from "3D to 2D" correspondences achieved by employing the Efficient PnP (EPnP) method [6]. The second is performed by means of a wBA. As mentioned in our previous work [5] the current state of the art on space exploration rovers and, consequently, their computational capabilities, does not allow the implementation of full BA. In order to overcome this issue we use wBA with an online adjustment of the window size. The main parts of our system include: "3D reconstruction", "Feature Extraction", "Initial Motion Estimation", and "Motion Optimization".

Initial Motion Estimation. Assuming two camera frames k, $k-1$ we seek to calculate the camera motion ${}^{k-1}T_k^c$. The majority of algorithms for calculating VO utilize feature points tracked on eachframes [7]. The points, usually represent static world 3D locations serving as tie points for the motion estimation. Assuming that each of the frames is connected with a stereo pair of images (I_k^l, I_k^r and I_{k-1}^l, I_{k-1}^r), the system computes sets of corresponding feature points p_k and p_{k-1} on the image plane, which are then converted to 3D points (P_k and P_{k-1}). The feature points we employ in our system are detected using the Maximally Stable Extremal Regions (MSER) and matched by a nearest neighborhood criterion utilising the Speeded-Up Robust Features (SURF) descriptors.

Two main approaches are used to project those feature matches to 3D points. The first is the dense case, where a disparity map is created form stereo calibrated/rectified images. In the second case, namely the sparse one, the points are the 3D representation of features matched on a stereo pair. Usually for computational reasons the latter is selected. However, in the case of space exploration rovers and according to our previous work [8] the dense stereo correspondence algorithm has been completely removed from the computational pipeline by implementing it on FPGAs. Let us assume a calibrated camera (frame k) with parameters $\{f_u, f_v$ the horizontal and vertical focal lengths (in pixels), c_u, c_v the principal point coordinates$\}$ and the disparity map D_k. A 2D point $p_k = \{u_l, v_l\}^T$ in the image I_k^l, with image coordinates u,v is projected to the 3D P_k using:

$$P_k = \left[\frac{(u - c_u) \cdot b}{D_k(u,v)}, \frac{(v - c_v) \cdot b}{D_k(u,v)}, \frac{b \cdot f_u}{D_k(u,v)} \right]^T \tag{1}$$

Following the extraction of corresponding 3D points, the motion $^{k-1}T_k^c$ must be computed. Most of the algorithms for stereo visual odometry employ the so called "3D to 3D" where the $^{k-1}T_k^c$ is the one that minimizes the criterion:

$$^{k-1}T_k^c = \arg\min_T (\sum_i^N ||P_k - {^{k-1}T_k^c} \times P_{k-1,i}^c||^2) \tag{2}$$

Another approach is the one of the 2D-2D motion estimation where there is no need for 3D projection. However, this approach leads to an unknown scale for the translation vector, which is usually solved with the inclusion of an IMU. In our case the $^{k-1}T_k^c$ is computed by utilising the "3D to 2D" approach, which ends in the computation of the transformation that minimizes the reprojection $\tilde{p}_{k-1}$ of the 3D reconstructed points of the frame $k-1$ to the frame k:

$$^{k-1}T_k^c = \arg\min_T (\sum_i^N ||p_{k-1} - \tilde{p}_{k-1}||^2), \tag{3}$$

In the core of our system lays the non-iterative EPnP method [6]. EPnP does not employ the minimization of all the $\{P_k, P_{k-1}\}$ matches but, rather, generates four virtual points vp and expresses all the 3D points as a linear combination of these vp. The minimization is performed on the virtual points. It is obvious that the points will include outliers. However, since we make use of the EPnP we are able to perform RANSAC without adding to much copmutational cost to the system. At each iteration of the RANSAC, seven points are utilized to produce a motion using EPnP. The inliers produced by RANSAC are utilized to provide the final frame to frame $^{k-1}T_k^c$.

Motion Estimation Optimization. Despite the efficiency of the motion estimation, the case of space exploration rovers is a massively demanding. At several cases great alterations occur in the yaw, pitch and roll and, moreover, the rover has to stay or pivot in place in order to conduct accurate scientific experiments. Even though in our previous work [5] we stated that BA is not an option for rovers, we revisited the subject and implemented BA in a way that will not introduce an onerous computational burden. In particular, we have implemented a variable wBA. Let us assume a set of m camera poses $\{\mu_1, ..., \mu_m\}$, a set of n 3D points $\{P_1, ..., P_n\}$ and a set $S = \{p_{i,j}\}$ of their measured projection on the cameras, where $p_{i,j}$ represents the projection of the ith point P on the jth camera pose. Then the BA is expressed as the minimization over all the points and camera coordinates:

$$\left\{\mu'_j, P'_i\right\} = \arg\min_{\mu_j, P_i}(\sum_{p_{i,j} \in S} v \times (p_{i,j} - \tilde{p}_{i,j})^2), \tag{4}$$

where $\tilde{p}_{i,j}$ is the reprojection of the 3D point P_i to the jth camera pose and v is the binary observability indication. The case of wBA is the one where the camera pose set $\{\mu_1, ..., \mu_m\}$ is altered to contain only a subset of the whole pose graph. In our work the window is defined so that the camera pose set becomes $\{\mu_k - w, ..., \mu_k\}$, where the w can vary in the range $\{3, 10\}$ according to the difficulty of the terrain traversed; initially $w = 3$. As the rover moves the system decides wether to extend, slide or decrease the window based on the IMU readings. We employ range $th^{var} = [th^{var}_{min}, th^{var}_{max}]$ on the variance of the hectometers (roll, pitch) on board the rover as follows: In the case that the latest N_{IMU} inclinometer readings produce any variance $\sigma_{IMU} \in th^{var}$ then the window is sliding. On the other hand, if $\sigma_{IMU} > th^{var}_{max}$ the windows is extended to the next frame. Finally, when $\sigma_{IMU} < th^{var}_{min}$ the window is sliding while the while its size is reduced by one. It must be noted that the first camera pose of each window set at each time is considered stationary and that the system is solved by utilizing the SBA with Levenberg Marquardt minimization [9]. The relative localization system we employed presents several realistic aspects making it appropriate for implementation on rovers. Firstly, by utilizing the points from an FPGA we remove the necessity to extract intra-stereo feature points. The employment of an non-iterative PnP solution as well as the online selection of the window for the BA pulls out a sizable load from the, usually, limited rover's computational capacity.

4   Detection of ROIs on Orbital and Rover Images

In this work we have separated the detection and the classification for the ROIs; for the specific dataset only boulders are considered (see Sect. 7). The reader should refer to [5] for more details on the system, as here we describe briefly the detection on the orbital and rover images and analyze mostly the new additions to the system. Two main metrics are employed in the detection of the rocks in the orbital images; the Hessian analysis [10] and the weighted Entropy [11], both of which are statistically assessed with an adaptive threshold. The extreme values in the distribution of the eigenvalues of $H(x, y)$ ($|H(x, y)| > 2 \cdot \sigma$) create blobs that are considered detections. The second metric measures the randomness in a local area. The weighted entropy LE^w is based on the Shannon entropy but fused with a Gaussian weight to incorporate the intensity variance as well:

$$LE^w = - \sum_{i=0}^{255} w(i) \cdot p(i) \cdot log_2(p(i)), \tag{5}$$

where $w(i) = 1 - G\,(\mu, \sigma_e)$, μ is the mean of the neighborhood and $\sigma_e^2 = 8$.

Considering the detection on the rover side, since we include only boulders, the aforementioned metrics are complimented by a 3D filter that extracts the protruding features in the field of view (FOV) of the camera. In order to do so v-disparity was employed to extract the ground plane, which appears as a prominent line. In each line of the v-disparity, values larger than the value coinciding with the detected line, are considered to represent 3D points that protrude from the ground. Inevitably, the detection includes same false areas which are, nevertheless removed by the classification procedure as described in Sect. 5.

An interesting part of the detection on the rover side is the accumulation of a newly detected ROI in the LN, once it has been classified (see Sect. 5) as a boulder. In our previous work [5] we the authors accumulated the ROIs by performing ellipse fitting and region growing. Here, we enhance this part by properly assessing the position and the size of the uncertainty. Concerning the location of the boulder in the relative localization frame it is straightforward that, since the two estimations are independent, the fine position of the ROI can be calculated as:

$$\left\{ X_{roi}^{LF}, C_{roi}^{LF} \right\} = \left\{ X_{rov}^{LF} + X_{roi}^{RF}, C_{rov^{LF} + roi^{RF}} \right\}, \tag{6}$$

where $\left\{ X_{roi}^{LF}, C_{roi}^{LF} \right\}$ are the mean and covariance of the detected ROI in the relative localization frame, LF is the localization frame and RF is the rover frame. On the other hand the estimation of the size of each boulder is calculated as the weighted mean of each measurement assuring that highly uncertain measurements will not contribute as much:

$$\left\{ S_{ROI} = \frac{\sum_{i=1}^{} \frac{S_i}{\sigma_i^2}}{\sum_{i=1}^{} \frac{1}{\sigma_i^2}}, \sigma_S^2 = \sqrt{\frac{1}{\sum_{i=1}^{} \sigma_i^2}} \right\} \tag{7}$$

5 Machine Learning for ROI Classification

In this section we present the methodology that was applied to perform classification on the orbital and rover images. The candidate ROIs are labeled by the classifier and the false detections are removed.

Feature Space. The feature space upon which the classification is applied is different in the orbital and rover cases. This is due to the fact that on the rover side 3D information is available. In the case of orbital images the HSV colorspace has been selected as the feature. Even though this is a simplistic descriptor, it can perform adequately and its repeatability helps in the benchmarking of different classifiers. On the rover side the HSV colorspace is accompanied by the 3D representation of the ROI, by means of face normals. We selected to represent the face normals in their minimal and most condense form; i.e. azimuth and elevation. The reconstructed ROI in the rover's FOV is converted in a triangular mesh providing faces upon which the normals are calculated.

Classification Definition. In order to select the appropriate classifier we benchmarked a series of classifiers. The classification is performed independently on the orbital and the rover images. This results into two different datasets samples **x** of which are the detected ROIs and each ROI is described by a set of attributes **d**. Given a new sample $\mathbf{x}^\star$ the algorithms provide $p(C_j|\mathbf{x}^\star)$, the probability of that sample to belong in the class C_j.

Pre-processing of Data. Previously to applying the machine leaning algorithms to the datasets, the data are processed in order to map them into a common interval, decorrelate the attributes and reduce the dimensionally. The attributes are mapped into the interval $[-1, 1]$, then they are decorrelated and reduced using Principal Components Analysis (PCA) which applies a linear transformation to the original dataset. The derivation of the principal components is performed by employing eigen-decomposition on the covariance matrix of the original data which provides a set of eigenvectors with their corresponding eigenvalues. The transformed data derive from the inner product between the original data and the eigenvectors. Since the number of the attributes –as they extracted from the ROIs– is large, we employ dimensionality reduction based on the PCA algorithm. Thus, principal components whose data-variance, represented by the eigenvalues, is not significant are removed while the subset's data variance is almost equal to a given portion of the total variance.

5.1   Classifier Evaluation Results

The processed datasets are used for the benchmarking of machine learning algorithms on ROI recognition. The evaluation includes the following classifiers: k Nearest Neighbour (kNN), naive Bayes (NB), Logistic Regression (LR), Classification Tree (CTree) Support Vector Machine (SVM) and Gaussian Process (GP).

The ML algorithms are evaluated both on rover and orbital datasets (Table 1). The main challenges are the small number of samples in training sets, the small rate of rocks in the orbital frames and the high number of attributes. In

Table 1. Description of the evaluation datasets

Dataset	Training samples	Testing samples	# of attributes	Rate of rocks
Orbital	89	2366	1200	10%
Rover	1391	9777	2000	60%

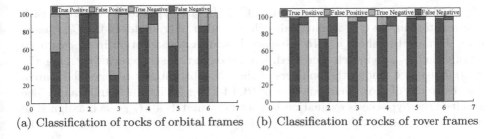

(a) Classification of rocks of orbital frames   (b) Classification of rocks of rover frames

Fig. 2. Classification results.

general ML algorithms should have a good portion of training samples in order to effectively classify novel ones (generalization ability). This is not the case in both datasets, especially for the orbital frames which also includes a small number of rocks. The low rate of instances that belong to a particular class can also lead to a model which does not generalize well. Furthermore, the large number of attributes is also problematic and hence the algorithm should scale well to high-dimensions. The benchmarking results for each case are depicted in Fig. 2(a) and (b).

According to the aforementioned evaluation we employed the GP for both the rover and orbital cases. Following the automated classification the system creates the two networks that contain the semantic/spatial information of the boulders. The classified boulders on the orbital images form the GN, which represents the area in which the rover will be absolutely localized, and the rover ones form the LN as described in the last paragraph of Sect. 4. The classification subsystem is realistic for implementation in actual missions as the most computational expensive part is performed offline and the rover is fed only with a rich but low footprint representation containing the list of boulders with their position and label.

6   Rover and Orbital Network Matching

The matching is performed under the assumption that the rover has received a GN calculated beforehand and has created a LN by exploring its surrounding area. The method employed here for the matching of the LN and GN is a modified 2D version of the DARCES algorithm [12]. Such an approach has been followed also in [13] but with long range $(1+\mathrm{km})$ features detected with high power LIDARs which is not applicable, so far, on rovers. The idea of DARCES is the identification of common constellations (triangles) in the GN and LN. It is described in two parts: (i) the hypothesis generation and (ii) the hypothesis evaluation. During the hypothesis generation the triangles formed by all the points of the LN and GN are constructed and considered as possible matches. The total number of triangles can be calculated as: $G^k = \frac{G}{(G-3)!}$, where G is the number of ROIs in the GN. Let as assume the set of triangles in the LN,

C_{Gn} and the set of triangles in the LN, C_{Gn}. In the hypothesis evaluation each constellation in the C_{Ln} is matched with a number of triangles in the C_{Gn} based on a distance threshold d_D. In the case that for a constellation in C_{Gl} with no triangle in C_{Gn}, no match is created. Even though this space seems extreme, the spatial distance among the boulders in the LN substantially reduces the search. The existence of more than one type of ROI further limits the search range. The result of the hypothesis evaluation is a set of m matches $M_{L,G}$ each assigned to a weight w^D being calculated as $w_i^D = \frac{1}{D_i}$, where $i \in [1, ..., m]$ and D_i is the distance of the ith match. Each match is associated to a transformation $^G_{LF}T_i$ from the local frame LF to the global frame GF. Similar transformations are concatenated in g groups Tr containing t matches each. Each of the groups is assigned with a probability as follows:

$$p_j^{Tr} = \frac{\sum_t w_t^D}{\sum_m w_m^D}, \qquad (8)$$

with $j \in [1, ..., g]$. The system selects the group Tr_j with the highest probability based on a uniqueness ratio. The final transformation that aligns the LN to the GN is derived from the constellation in the selected group that covers the larger area. This matching algorithm is not performed at each detection, but rather at a predefined interval of detections or at the end of a long route (for example) the end of a sol.

7   Experimental Results Using HDPR

This section serves as the description of the experimental procedure and results. Firstly the experimental setup, including a custom built rover, and the produced dataset are introduced. Moreover, the results of our subsystems are clearly presented and discussed.

7.1   Dataset

In the context of global localization [5] it is crucial to benchmark our algorithms in representative scenarios. Such scenarios, should be long range (i.e. >1 km). Since each algorithm exploits different characteristics of the environment [14], there is no single available dataset suitable for all algorithms. The most complete dataset, so far, is the one produced by the ESA Seeker activity [15]. No matter the verisimilitude of the area this dataset was collected, there is always some deviation from an actual Mars mission area. Therefore, we constructed a custom rover, namely the *Heavy Duty Planetary Rover* (HDPR) to create a scenario that will closely resemble an actual Martian area, in the sense of boulder distribution. The HDPR rover, depicted in Fig. 3, is capable of traversing different types of terrain with a speed of up to 1 m/s. The decisions concerning the rover setup targeted the close resemblance to the ExoMars rover mission. The camera system is based on the ExoMars rover, by placing the localization cameras (LocCam) in the same configuration (height and tilt) and by creating an analog for the *Wide Angle Camera* (WAC) on the HDPR PanCam. Along with the rover we have developed an infrastructure that allows prompt and easy deployment on the field. A completely power-autonomous ground control station (GCS) was developed, including a long range Wi-Fi antenna capable of communicating with the rover at a distance of 1.5–2 km.

Fig. 3. A closeup look of the HDPR rover that was constructed in the context of this work.

In order to achieve global localization the rovers shall detect landmarks along their route. These landmarks can be any type of prominent characteristics of the terrain, for example rocks, craters, flatbeds (outcrops), etc. In the case of our experiment we decided to utilize only boulders as the creation of other landmarks, such as craters, was unfeasible. We employed a known distribution of an actual location on Mars; namely the near Gale Crater area, which was the landing position of the MSL rover (Curiosity). The research of Golombek et al. [16], concerning the rock distribution on possible rover landing locations, was crucial to our decisions. As shown in Table 2, there exist several area types concerning rock abundance, ranging from "Very Low" to "High". The density of rocks of a diameter larger than 1.1 m per m^2 is 0.0047. Moreover, the density of rocks of a diameter larger than 1.5 m^2 is $\frac{57+170}{450\cdot450} = 0.00056$. We decided to create two rock types, namely $\oslash = 1.1$ m and $\oslash = 1.5$ m. Rocks with $\oslash < 1$ m cannot be viewed or properly detected from current orthophotos available for Mars.

Table 2. Rock distribution on the gale crater landing site [16]

Rock density	Total number of 1.5–2.25 m diameter rocks in 450 m bin	Cumulative number/m^2 of rocks >1.1 m in diameter
High	669 > 321	0.015
Medium-high	171–320	0.0081
Medium-low	57–170	0.0047
Low	4–65	0.0019
Very low	1–3	0.000198

However, for the shake of realism, and as an extra challenge to our algorithm, we included some 0.8 m diameter rocks with the same distribution as the medium ones (1.1 m) leading to 3 different types of rock in total.

(a)   (b)

Fig. 4. 3D reconstruction and orthophoto of the test area at the Noordwijk coast, The Netherlands.

The rover's route was 1412.39 m, as reported by the RTK GPS employed as a groundtruth device. The orbital image, acquired by a UAV, namely the Sensefly eBee, covered an area of 2 km × 0.2 km and was sub-sampled in 0.25 m × 0.25 m resolution (Fig. 4). However, following the detection and classification on the "orbital" image, a surrounding area, equal to 3 km × 3 km was virtually populated with landmarks, following the aforementioned distribution. This dataset is scheduled to be published formally in a separate publication later this year.

Two separate routes of the rover, accompanied by the respective "orbital imagery" were created, one for training (see Sect. 5) and one for the actual testing. We should note here that the dataset involves inherent difficulties: (i) the non-smooth trajectory of the rover; the rover performs steep turns, a usual behavior in actual missions, and (ii) the difference in lighting conditions amongst the training and testing parts. The realistic characteristics of the dataset are apparent. As a first point, the distribution of the boulders are emulating an actual area on Mars. Moreover, the rover bears the similar sensory as the ones available on actual rovers. Finally, the whole dataset was designed to simulate a rover traversing long distances as in the case of an MSR mission.

7.2   Evaluation

The stereo pairs stemming from the LocCam of the HDPR were processed by the relative localization algorithm in a wBA manner, as described in Sect. 3, in order to assess its accuracy. For the sake of the evaluation, we manually aligned the first few meters of the dataset with the groundtruth. The total error of the relative localization subsystem was found to be 12.31 m (1.16%) after a route of 1412.39 m, while the error was continuously kept below 2%. Figure 5 depicts the output of the relative localization compared to the uncorrected VO and the groundtruth trajectory versus the groundtruth in a 3D perspective. The performance of the relative localization is of great importance to the system as it affects the input of the global localization submodule.

The boulders that have been detected and classified by our system on the rover side along with their respective uncertainty are depicted in Fig. 5(b). The extraction of boulders (detection and classification) is performed off-line on the orbital images and online on the rover ones.

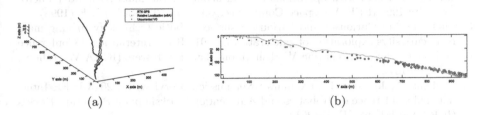

(a)   (b)

Fig. 5. (a) The accuracy of the relative localization subsystem 12.31 m (1.16%) after a route of 1412.39 m. With blue, black, red, we depict our algorithm's relative localization, the uncorrected VO and the groundtruth, respectively. (b) The Local ROI network and the boulder uncertainty (position only) associated with each one. The rover's relative localization is depicted as the blue line. (Color figure online)

Initially the rover possess no information about its global position and orientation. Once executed, the system is able to provide possible positions in the global frame. In the experimental test described here, the rover was able to find the correct global position after the detection of 27 boulders, 273.3 m away from its starting point. The position error calculated in comparison with the groundtruth was 13.34 m and, more significantly, the rover achieved global localization.

8   Conclusions

In this paper we presented an enhanced global localization system, suitable for integration on space exploration rovers. Such a rover will be able to localize itself on an absolute frame, given that the area it traverses includes some landmarks observable from satellite imagery. The system utilizes landmarks detected by the rover (LN) and matches them in pre-computed networks (GN) to achieve global localization. An accurate relative localization system was developed and several machine learning approaches were benchmarked to classify boulders. We proved that the system provides adequate results in a Mars like scenario and a representative robotic system. As future work we target the correction of not only the final position of the rover but all the intermediate poses in the trajectory.

References

1. Mattingly, R., May, L.: Mars sample return as a campaign. In: 2011 IEEE Aerospace Conference, pp. 1–13. IEEE (2011)
2. Mishkin, A.H., Morrison, J.C., Nguyen, T.T., Stone, H.W., Cooper, B.K., Wilcox, B.H.: Experiences with operations and autonomy of the mars pathfinder microrover. In: 1998 IEEE Aerospace Conference, vol. 2, pp. 337–351. IEEE (1998)
3. Maimone, M.: Curiouser and curiouser: surface robotic technology driving mars rover curiositys exploration of gale crater. In: 2013 IEEE International Conference on Robotics and Automation Workshop: on Planetary Rovers (ICRA Workshop). IEEE (2013)
4. Baglioni, P., Joudrier, L.: Exomars rover mission overview. In: 2013 IEEE International Conference on Robotics and Automation Workshop: on Planetary Rovers (ICRA Workshop). IEEE (2013)
5. Boukas, E., Gasteratos, A., Visentin, G.: Towards orbital based global rover localization. In: 2015 IEEE International Conference on Robotics and Automation (ICRA), pp. 2874–2881, May 2015
6. Lepetit, V., Moreno-Noguer, F., Fua, P.: EPnP: an accurate O(n) solution to the PnP problem. Int. J. Comput. Vis. **81**(2), 155–166 (2009)
7. Scaramuzza, D., Fraundorfer, F.: Visual odometry: Part I: the first 30 years and fundamentals. IEEE Robot. Autom. Mag. **18**(4), 80–92 (2011)
8. Kostavelis, I., Nalpantidis, L., Boukas, E., Rodrigalvarez, M.A., Stamoulias, I., Lentaris, G., Diamantopoulos, D., Siozios, K., Soudris, D., Gasteratos, A.: Spartan: developing a vision system for future autonomous space exploration robots. J. Field Robot. **31**(1), 107–140 (2014)
9. Lourakis, M.I., Argyros, A.A.: SBA: a software package for generic sparse bundle adjustment. ACM Trans. Math. Softw. (TOMS) **36**(1), 2 (2009)
10. Lakemond, R., Sridharan, S., Fookes, C.: Hessian-based affine adaptation of salient local image features. J. Math. Imaging Vis. **44**(2), 150–167 (2012)
11. Shapira, L., Oicherman, B.: Black is green: adaptive color transformation for reduced ink usage. In: Computer Graphics Forum, vol. 31, pp. 365–372. Wiley Online Library (2012)
12. Chen, C.S., Hung, Y.P., Cheng, J.B.: Ransac-based darces: a new approach to fast automatic registration of partially overlapping range images. IEEE Trans. Pattern Anal. Mach. Intell. **21**(11), 1229–1234 (1999)
13. Carle, P.J., Barfoot, T.D.: Global rover localization by matching Lidar and orbital 3D maps. In: 2010 IEEE International Conference on Robotics and Automation (ICRA), pp. 881–886. IEEE (2010)
14. Boukas, E., Gasteratos, A., Visentin, G.: Localization of planetary exploration rovers with orbital imaging: a survey of approache. In: 2014 IEEE International Conference on Workshop on Modelling, Estimation, Perception and Control of All Terrain Mobile Robots (ICRA Workshop). IEEE (2014)
15. Woods, M., Shaw, A., Tidey, E., Van Pham, B., Artan, U., Maddison, B., Cross, G.: Seeker-autonomous long range rover navigation for remote exploration. In: International Symposiumon Artificial Intelligence, Robotics and Automation in Space (i-SAIRAS) (2012)
16. Golombek, M., Huertas, A., Kipp, D., Calef, F.: Detection and characterization of rocks and rock size-frequency distributions at the final four mars science laboratory landing sites. Int. J. Mars Sci. Explor. **7**, 1–22 (2012)

Visual Navigation

Vision-Based Robot Path Planning
with Deep Learning

Ping Wu[1,2], Yang Cao[1], Yuqing He[2(✉)], and Decai Li[2]

[1] Shenyang Jianzhu University, Shenyang, China
caoyang@sjzu.edu.cn
[2] Shenyang Institute of Automation Chinese Academy of Sciences,
Shenyang, China
{wuping,heyuqing,lidecai}@sia.cn

Abstract. In this paper, a new method based on deep convolutional neural network (CNN) for path planning of robot is proposed, the aim of which is to transform the mission of path planning into a task of environment classification. Firstly, the images of road are collected from cameras installed as required, and then the comprehensive features are abstracted directly from original images through the CNN. Finally, according to the results of classification, the moving direction of robots is exported. In this way, we build an end-to-end recognition system which maps from raw data to motion behavior of robot. Furthermore, experiment has been provided to demonstrate the performance of the proposed method on different roads.

Keywords: Path planning · Convolutional neural network (CNN) · Classification

1 Introduction

Path planning system is one of important researches of intelligent robot and the system is based on environmental information to adjust the moving direction of robot. With the improvement of computer technology and artificial intelligence (AI), the plentiful research achievements have been obtained on robot path planning increasingly. Generally, the common algorithms can be summarized as: the method based on map-building [8], the method based on artificial potential field (APF) [9], the method based on artificial intelligence [1].

(1) **map-building:** A lot of methods based on map-building, such as visibility graph [10], grid method [11] and topology algorithm [12], have been developed on path planning in order to turn the environment information into a two-dimensional model. Map-building method displays its excellent performance, which has been applied in [2, 13, 14]. The model theory of map-building is simple, but the grid map of obstacle information is difficult to calculate under the limitation of robot sensor information resources. Besides, the map-building method is a static-environment planning. In fact, the robots need to dynamically and quickly update the map data leading to difficultly ensure the real-time path planning.

© Springer International Publishing AG 2017
M. Liu et al. (Eds.): ICVS 2017, LNCS 10528, pp. 101–111, 2017.
DOI: 10.1007/978-3-319-68345-4_9

(2) **artificial potential field:** To solve the real-time problem, a potential field with fuzzy control method is proposed in [3], to satisfy the requirements of real-time mobile robot path planning in dynamic environment through taking the advantage of velocity vector, modifying potential field force function, and integrating with the fuzzy control method. And an improved APF method is applied in mobile robot navigation, which makes possible controllability in complex real-world sceneries with dynamic obstacles if a reachable configuration set exists [4]. For simple principle and easy control of the real-time obstacle avoidance, the APF method has been extensively studied in robot path planning, but there is a serious problem of local minima.

(3) **artificial intelligence:** To improve the minimum, the method based on AI is a powerful approach for path planning, such as a fuzzy logic theory, a genetic algorithm and artificial neural networks and so on. In [15], a fuzzy logic controller has been designed to improve the movement of mobile robot, and the navigation system has to avoid obstacles efficiently. Moreover, the improved genetic algorithm for dynamic motion planning problem is introduced to improve path planning efficiency in [16]. And a novel hybrid method is proposed for the globally optimal path planning in literature [5] based on an artificial neural network. The AI method produces an optimal solution of dynamic environment, but there is a complex image process including image capture, image pretreatment, minutia extraction, etc.

The path planning is a complicated process starting with the perception of environment. The above-mentioned methods all need a complex feature processing in environmental perception. Extracting environmental information from natural images is a challenging problem with many practical applications. To solve the issue, this paper aims to design a multi-layer CNN to solve robot path planning problem and an end-to-end system is built without express specific feature mapping.

Some related works that are similar to solve the exploration problem in a corridor environment [17], to solve obstacle avoidance in real-world indoor environments [6], or to perceive forest trials on a quad-rotor vehicle [7] based on a deep neural network. But in the paper, a CNN model is used to convert path planning as environment classification, the aim of which is to solve the planning problem in different environment roads.

2 Related Algorithm

As mentioned above, the map-building is easy to build environment model, but the grid map of obstacle information is hard to calculate. And the APF approach is adopted in dynamic environment with a problem of local minima. However, artificial intelligence provides a lot of new ideas for path planning, but the image process is difficult. Each method has merits and demerits, but all the methods above have a tedious process of environmental information. To solve the problem, this paper provides an end-to-end model based on CNN to focuses on path recognition in path planning with cameras observing the environment.

CNN is one of algorithms for image processing in deep learning technology and has realized excellent performance for owning a unique processing of two-dimensional data and a powerful learning ability. For example, in October 2012, Hinton built a deep CNN for famous ImageNet recognition which has achieved an eye-catching result. In the same year, Google Brain project has also made a major breakthrough in image recognition, which gets an auto-clustering algorithm on image by training image data form a video selected on YouTube with unsupervised training methods. The CNN model trains original image directly and does not use any artificial extraction feature, all of which enrich the end-to-end learning ability. So CNN can be regarded as a good image processing model in robot path planning.

CNN is a multi-layer artificial neural network and adopts end-to-end supervised feature learning and adjusts parameters through back propagation. The basic network structure consists of some parts: input layer, convolution layer, pooling layer, fully-connected layer and output layer, and some other layers interspersed between convolution layers. The basic structure is shown in Fig. 1. CNN extracts the pixel features from natural image directly by using two-dimensional convolution. The end-to-end behavior changes the process of image preprocessing and feature extraction of traditional image classification into a black box, in this way to directly get features instead of spending a lot of time to extract the image features.

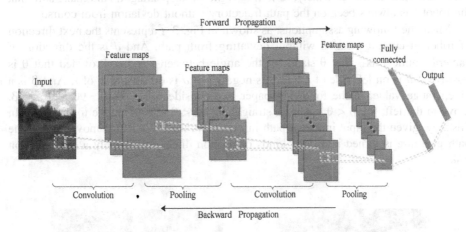

Fig. 1. The CNN structure

3 Proposed Approach

3.1 The System Framework

The basic idea of this paper is to label the environmental information firstly, use CNN to classify environmental information, and finally decide which direction to move for robot according to the prediction result. The system framework is shown in Fig. 2. Here is how the specific process works: First, use cameras to take information of path. Next, convert the information into color pictures that are subsequently labeled. Then, enter the images information into the appropriate CNN network for training directly, and then get prediction of accuracy rate. Finally, obtain the probability of each image belonging to a certain class, and decide the next direction of robot according to the highest probability of image classification of the current state.

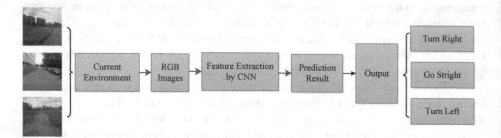

Fig. 2. The system of path planning

In the paper, the description of path planning into classification is as follows: the adjustment of robot's movement is based on current location information to choose which direction to move, namely, to left, to right, or keep straight. And make sure that the robot has always been on the path trajectory without deviation from course.

Make the following assumptions: as shown in Fig. 3, $\vec{t}$ represents the next direction of robot in current location without deviating from path. And $\vec{a}$ is the direction of camera's optical axis. Let θ stand for the angle between $\vec{t}$ and $\vec{a}$. Provided that θ is positive if $\vec{a}$ is on left side of $\vec{t}$, and θ is negative if $\vec{a}$ is on right side of $\vec{t}$. And β is a given range value, in the following paper, we consider $\beta = 20°$. If $-90° < \theta < -\beta$, move to the left; if $-\beta < \theta < +\beta$, go straight; if $+\beta < \theta < +90°$, move to the right. In this way, given the input image of path information, the robot's next movement of the path planning is turned into three kinds of motion directions, namely a classification task.

 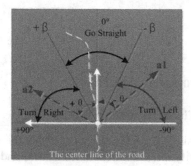

Fig. 3. The model of path planning

3.2   The Proposed CNN Structure

Four overlapping iterative convolution layers and pooling layers, non-linear layer, Dropout layers and Softmax layers are stacked into a deep CNN in this paper. The use of multiple convolution and pooling layers is to extract more useful feature information from the image.

In CNN network structure, the size of original picture is 101×101 in input layer, and there are 32 neurons in first hidden layer, 200 neurons in last hidden layer, 3 neurons in the output layer. Softmax function is used as loss function, while Sigmoid is to be the activation function in each layer. At the same time, adopt the maximum pooling method with all convolution kernels size of 4×4 and the pooling kernels size of 2×2. The specific parameters are shown in Table 1.

Table 1. The parameters of propsed CNN

No.	Layers	No. of features	Feature_Size	Kernel_ Size	Step
1	Input	3	101×101	-	-
2	CNN-1	32	98×98	4×4	1
3	Pool-1	32	49×49	2×2	2
4	CNN-2	32	46×46	4×4	1
5	Pool-2	32	23×23	2×2	2
6	CNN-3	32	20×20	4×4	1
7	Pool-3	32	10×10	2×2	2
8	CNN-4	32	8×8	3×3	1
9	Pool-4	32	4×4	2×2	2
10	Fully	200	-	-	-
11	Output	3	-	-	-

The algorithm is trained and predicted as follows: as RGB images input, the neuron parameters on all layers are initialized firstly. Subsequently, feature extraction is performed using multiple convolutions and pooling layers. After the feature extraction, the features are fed to the fully-connected layer by forward propagation algorithm. And then the fully-connected layer computes data information and provides the result to output layer. Finally the test results are produced in output layer after weights and deviations are adjusted by back propagation algorithm.

3.3   The Training of CNN

Process of network training is made up of forward and back propagation. Forward propagation includes feature extraction and classification calculation: input a sample to the network, and calculate the corresponding actual output. The back propagation mainly contains feedback of error and update calculation of weight: calculate the error between actual output and expected output, and minimizing the error and adjust weights by backward propagation. The specific training process is as follows:

(1) Initialize parameters of the network such as weights and biases.

(2) Select a sample from training dataset into the network and get an actual output vector. In this process, we input a batch sample, in other words, input a certain number of samples in one epoch and get an output matrix, which each column is an actual output-vector of the sample.

(3) Calculate the error between actual output and predetermined output.

(4) Propagate back the error obtained by (3) layer by layer and obtain gradients of the error cost function by stochastic gradient descent method so that weight parameters are updated.

(5) Enter remaining training samples into the network, and complete the steps from (2) to (4) until all training samples are completed. Thus one iteration progress is end.

(6) Stop the iteration if expected recognition rate or iteration termination condition is satisfied.

(7) Put test sample into the trained network to get a correct rate of classification, and then gain the classification probability of each class.

4 Experiment

In this section, we will first introduce collection of environmental data, including the database establishment and data samples. And then, experimental results and related analysis will be provided for the path planning. The details will be adopted with the corresponding experiments in the following.

4.1 Data Collection

The experimental data is respectively collected on cement and natural soil road by three cameras installed on the mobile robot, and the tracks of road are shown in Fig. 4. The installed orientations of camera are $-30°$, $0°$, $+30°$, as shown in Fig. 5. Meanwhile 3 types of datasets are labeled into 3 labels, namely, a total of two path datasets with six video sets, and each video set is about 10 min with 30 frames per second. To convert the video into pictures with an interval for every 3 frames, and get a RGB image dataset to process into 101×101 size.

Fig. 4. The path trajectory

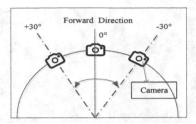

Fig. 5. Cameras installation

Fig. 6. Cement road samples

The adopted network structure is composed of several parts: (**1**) Input images are only of size $101 \times 101 \times 3$ (101 wide, 101 high, 3 color channels). (**2**) CNN layers (CNN-1, CNN-2, etc.) will result in volume such as $[98 \times 98 \times 32]$ if we decided to use 32 filters. (**3**) RELU layers will apply an activation function of the max(0,x) thresholding at zero, which leaves the size of the volume unchanged ($[98 \times 98 \times 32]$). (**4**) Pool layers (Pool-1, Pool-2, etc.) will perform a downsampling operation along the spatial dimensions (width, height), resulting in volume such as $[49 \times 49 \times 12]$. (**5**) FC (fully-connected) layer will compute the class scores, resulting in volume of size $[1 \times 1 \times 3]$, where each of the 3 numbers correspond to a class score. Besides, the number of neurons is given by $(W - F + 2P)/S + 1$, in case of the input volume size (W), the receptive field size of the CNN layer neurons (F), the stride sizes are applied (S), and the amount of zero padding used (P) on the border. For example, we would get a 46×46 output for a 49×49 input and a 4×4 filter with stride 1 and pad 0. The parameters are given above in Table 1.

Providing that LC is the label of images collected by left camera, SC is the label of images collected by middle camera, RC is the label of images collected by right camera. Some environmental samples are shown in Figs. 6 and 7. The dataset includes 2 subsets: the training set, the test set, seen in Table 2. The training set contains all the image types and is used to adjust weights of network during the training phase. The test set is used to test classification performance of network for the absence of training data during training process. Finally, by depending on the performance of test set, the network structure is needed to make some adjustments, or increase the number of training iterations.

(a) Soil path samples-1   (b) Soil path samples-2

Fig. 7. Soil path samples (the same path in different seasons)

Table 2. The dataset

Environment	Training data (pieces)			Test data (pieces)			Total
	LC	SC	RC	LC	SC	RC	-
Cement Road	4500	4500	4500	1500	1500	1500	1,8000
Soil Path-1	4000	4000	4000	1000	1000	1000	1,5000
Soil Path-2	3000	3000	3000	1000	1000	1000	1,2000

4.2   Results and Analysis

Generally, multi-convolution layers can improve CNN generalization, so this paper adopts a four-layer convolution according to some experience and obtains a good result. From the result, we can see that the test accuracy is generally increased with the growth of time, while the training loss is decreased with the increase of iterations.

The experimental data is trained and predicted, and the relationship between training iterations and predicted accuracy is shown in Table 3. Through judging the accuracy of classification, we can conclude from Table 3: the accuracy of the cement pavement and soil pavement are gradually stable when the iteration is about 1000 times. The up to 99% accuracy rate indicates that the experimental results are relatively excellent.

In addition, each input image has three predicted probability of corresponding to the three labels, and then to decide the next direction of movement according to the maximum probability of the label. Some results are shown in Figs. 8, 9 and 10. Take Fig. 8 as an example, the probability of picture (a) respectively predicted as LC, SC, RC is 0.8125, 0.1823, 0.0052, and the picture is judged as class LC, so the next step of robot is to turn right.

From Table 3, we can see that the CNN method can classify path information and the prediction result is quite good. According to Figs. 8, 9 and 10, the next direction of robot can be predicted. Besides, the experimental results show that CNN has a good sense of perception for environment whether on cement roads or natural soil roads. This proves that CNN can preferably solve the problem of environmental perception and provide a new method for path planning as mentioned in this literature.

Table 3. Experimental results of accuracy

Iterations	100	300	500	700	900	1000
Cement road	0.9747	0.9800	0.9946	0.9973	0.9987	0.9987
Soil path-1	0.9642	0.9847	0.9912	0.9831	0.9836	0.9836
Soil path-1	0.8321	0.9880	0.9933	0.9960	0.9973	0.9973

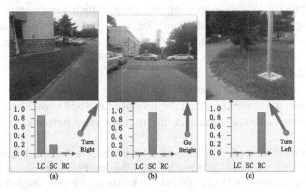

Fig. 8. The results of cement road

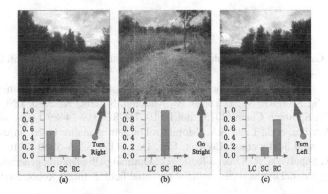

Fig. 9. The results of soil path-1

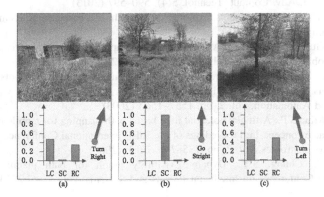

Fig. 10. The results of soil path-2

5 Conclusion

According to deep CNN, we present a new method for path planning. The method learns road information automatically from raw data rather than hand-engineered data without intervention of human and influence of environmental uncertainty. Moreover, compared with traditional approaches, the method is skilled in mapping raw pixels from cameras directly to decide moving direction, which implements an end-to-end process avoiding the calculation difficulty of vast grid information and the design difficulty of gravitational field and repulsive force field. In addition, experimental results show that our method has a strong adaptability on different roads, such as cement road and soil path.

In the future, our next work is guided by adopting more complicated paths to judge the robustness, and we also expect that the proposed method shows better results if we combine with other methods to enhance the robustness of network.

Acknowledgements. This work was supported by the Nature Science Foundation of China (Grant Nos. U1608253 and 61473282) and by the Liaoning Provincial Social Planning Found (L15BGL017). The authors would like to thank the reviewers for their insightful comments and suggestions.

References

1. Gigras, Y., Gupta, K.: Artificial intelligence in robot path planning. Int. J. Soft Comput. Eng. 2(2), 471–474 (2012)
2. Yakovlev, K., Baskin, E., Hramoin, I.: Grid-based angle-constrained path planning. In: Hölldobler, S., Krötzsch, M., Peñaloza, R., Rudolph, S. (eds.) KI 2015. LNCS, vol. 9324, pp. 208–221. Springer, Cham (2015). doi:10.1007/978-3-319-24489-1_16
3. Rui, M., Wei-Jun, S.U., Lian, X.F.: Mobile robot path planning based on dynamic fuzzy artificial potential field method. Comput. Eng. Des. 9(17), 5233–5240 (2010)
4. Montiel, O., Sepúlveda, R., Orozco-Rosas, U.: Optimal path planning generation for mobile robots using parallel evolutionary artificial potential field. J. Intell. Robot. Syst. 79(2), 1–21 (2015)
5. Wei, X.: Efficient robot path planning based on simulated annealing artificial neural networks. Int. J. Adv. Comput. Technol. 5(4), 590–597 (2013)
6. Tai, L., Liu, M.: Mobile robots exploration through cnn-based reinforcement learning. Robot. Biomim. 3(1), 24 (2016)
7. Giusti, A., Guzzi, J., Dan, C.C.: A machine learning approach to visual perception of forest trails for mobile robots. IEEE Robot. Autom. Lett. 1(2), 661–667 (2016)
8. Hahnel, D., Triebel, R., Burgard, W.: Map building with mobile robots in dynamic environments. In: ICRA 2003 Proceedings of the IEEE International Conference on Robotics and Automation, vol. 2, pp. 1557–1563 (2003)
9. Min, C.L., Min, G.P.: Artificial potential field based path planning for mobile robots using a virtual obstacle concept. In: Proceedings of the IEEE International Conference on Advanced Intelligent Mechatronics, vol. 2, pp. 735–740. IEEE (2003)
10. Huang, H.P., Chung, S.Y.: Dynamic visibility graph for path planning. In: IEEE International Conference on Intelligent Robots and Systems, vol. 3, pp. 2813–2818. IEEE (2004)

11. Kanehara, M., Kagami, S., Kuffner, J.J., Thompson, S.: Path shortening and smoothing of grid-based path planning with consideration of obstacles. In: IEEE International Conference on Systems, Man and Cybernetics, pp. 991–996. IEEE (2007)

12. Kim, S., Likhachev, M.: Path planning for a tethered robot using Multi-Heuristic A* with topology-based heuristics. In: IEEE International Conference on Intelligent Robots and Systems, pp. 4656–4663. IEEE (2015)

13. Contreras, J.D., Fernando, M.S., Fredy, H.M.S.: Path planning for mobile robots based on visibility graphs and A* algorithm. In: International Conference on Digital Image Processing (2015)

14. Ha, J.S., Choi, H.L.: A topology-guided path integral approach for stochastic optimal control. In: IEEE International Conference on Robotics and Automation. IEEE (2016)

15. Pandey, A., Sonkar, R.K., Pandey, K.K.: Path planning navigation of mobile robot with obstacles avoidance using fuzzy logic controller. In: IEEE International Conference on Intelligent Systems and Control, pp. 39–41. IEEE (2014)

16. Panda, R.K., Choudhury, B.B.: An effective path planning of mobile robot using genetic algorithm. In: IEEE International Conference on Computational Intelligence & Communication Technology, pp. 287–291 (2015)

17. Tai, L., Li, S., Liu, M.: A deep-network solution towards model-less obstacle avoidance. In: IEEE International Conference on Intelligent Robots and Systems, pp. 2759–2764. IEEE (2016)

A Method for Improving Target Tracking Accuracy of Vehicle Radar

Yue Guan, Shanshan Feng, Haibo Huang[(⊠)], and Liguo Chen[(⊠)]

School of Mechanical and Electric Engineering and Collaborative Innovation
Center of Suzhou Nano Science and Technology, Soochow University,
178 Gan-Jiang Road(East), Gu-Su District, Suzhou, China
{hbhuang, chenliguo}@suda.edu.cn

Abstract. Compared with other vehicle sensors, the vehicle radar has strong
adaptability and it can detect targets in the harsh environment, which make the
vehicle radar technology become popular in the field of vehicle sensors.
However, there will be a big error in target tracking while detecting targets on
the road through vehicle radar. In order to solve this problem, this paper has
present a method which uses Elman neural network to study historical trajectory
of the target and then predicts the next coordinates of this target. At last the
improved nearest neighbor method is used to remove false alarms by combining
information of the predicted coordinates and the measurement coordinates, so
the target tracking can be finished. The Matlab simulation results prove that the
method can improve the target tracking accuracy of vehicle radar.

Keywords: Vehicle radar · Target tracking · Neural network · Improved
nearest neighbor method

1 Introduction

With the development of automobile industry, automobile safety has become the focus
of people's attention. Compared with other vehicle sensors, vehicle radar has advantages in detection accuracy and environmental adaptability. So vehicle radar can still
perform well under harsh environment such as low visibility and some unexpected
situations. Therefore, vehicle radar is usually used to detect the road targets to prevent
traffic accidents. Now the vehicle radar can detect and track the target. However, there
is a big error in tracking due to the large number of road targets and complex environment. At present, there are several main methods for target tracking including
Kalman filtering method [1], particle filter algorithm [2, 3], correlation gate method [4]
and so on. Kalman filter is a linear unbiased estimation with minimum mean squared
error, but its computational complexity is large and the model is difficult to establish
which make it difficult to use [5]. There are many problems in practical application with
particle filter algorithm because it needs a lot of data and its convergence rate is
uncertain [6]. About correlation gate method, determining parameters of the correlation
gate is difficult. Different shapes and sizes of the correlation gate have great influence
on target tracking.

© Springer International Publishing AG 2017
M. Liu et al. (Eds.): ICVS 2017, LNCS 10528, pp. 112–119, 2017.
DOI: 10.1007/978-3-319-68345-4_10

In the study on improving the target tracking accuracy of vehicle radar, some scholars use the SNR model to evaluate fixed parameters during the detection, and then the target trajectory and target tracking strength can be obtained to help improve the target tracking accuracy and stability [7]. Also there is a research using compressed sensing theory to improve the target tracking accuracy. The research makes sparse representation of radar signal to finish the design of sparse transform matrix and observation matrix. And then the measured signal can be rebuilt under the condition of lower sampling rate. At the receiver, optimized particle filter is used to estimate the target state. The tracking performance of radar is improved and the needed radar data is reduced with this method [8].

For vehicle radar, there are two difficulties in target tracking: (1) the complexity of the road environment causes a lot of false targets in each radar echo, which makes it difficult to distinguish from the actual targets; (2) for actual targets, the distance between each target is very close, which means the spectral value of each target in the echo spectrum is also close and it is easy causing the tracking error. To solve these problems, this paper converts the coordinates of detected coordinates from different times into the same coordinate system. And then Elman neural network is used to study historical trajectory of the target to predict the next coordinates. At last the improved nearest neighbor method is used to tracking targets. Matlab is used to simulate this method and the results prove that the method can improve the target tracking accuracy of vehicle radar.

2 Coordinate Transformation

Different from the way of fixed radar detection, information coming from the vehicle radar is in different coordinate systems because the vehicle radar and the target are in high speed motion, which means that when tracking targets we need to convert the information detected at previous time into the same coordinate system. And then we can process the target trajectory. Figure 1 is a schematic diagram of coordinate compensation.

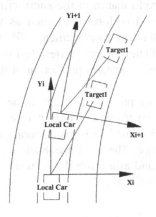

Fig. 1. Schematic diagram of coordinates compensation

This figure shows us that compared with the coordinates of the car at the last moment, the change of the car's coordinates at the next moment can be described by means of rotation transformation and translation transformation. Therefore, the compensation of coordinates can be divided into rotation and translation transformation.

At time i, coordinates of the target in the local coordinate system can be expressed as (x_i, y_i). If the target's speed is v and the sampling period is T, the moving distance of the target during the sampling period is $L = v \cdot T$. Considering the assumption that any line or curve can be considered to be an arc, this paper regards the contour of the lane in the short distance as an arc. Therefore, the distance L is the arc length the local car driving through during the sampling period. At time i, the arc radius r can be obtained from the other sensors in the local car. So the rotation angle of the local car can be obtained by the arc length formula:

$$\varphi = \frac{L}{r} \tag{1}$$

Coordinates after rotation can be expressed as:

$$\begin{cases} x'_i = -x \cos \varphi + y \sin \varphi \\ y'_i = x \sin \varphi + y \cos \varphi \end{cases} \tag{2}$$

Coordinates after translation can be expressed as:

$$\begin{cases} x_{i+1} = x'_i + L \cos \varphi \\ y_{i+1} = y'_i + L \sin \varphi \end{cases} \tag{3}$$

3 Coordinates Prediction

Elman neural network is a kind of feedback neural network. It can directly reflect the dynamic characteristics of the system as it can store the internal state. Elman neural network usually has a good performance in the short-term prediction. It is applied to lots of aspects and has a good performance, such as the prediction of the stock market [9], the prediction of the dam displacement [10] and so on, which proves that it is very suitable for the prediction in time series. Just because of this, Elman neural network can be used to achieve short-term prediction of the target with high accuracy in real-time.

Elman neural network is a typical local recurrent network, including input layer, hidden layer, the connection layer and the output layer. Compared with BP neural network, a connection layer is added to Elman neural network and this comes into being a local feedback structure. The local feedback structure is highly sensitive to historical data for each event and as a result the network has the function of dynamic modeling. Its structure is shown in Fig. 2.

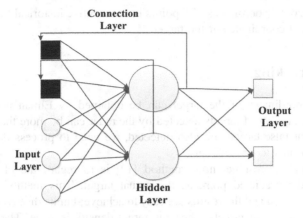

Fig. 2. Structure of Elman neural network

The mathematical model of Elman neural network displays as follows:

$$x(k) = f(W^{I1}x_C(k) + W^{I2}u(k-1)) \tag{4}$$

$$x_C(k) = \alpha x_C(k-1) + x(k-1) \tag{5}$$

$$y(k) = g(W^{I3}x(k)) \tag{6}$$

In these formulas, W^{I1} is the connection weight between the hidden layer and the connection layer; W^{I2} is the connection weight between the input layer and the hidden layer; W^{I2} is the connection weight between the hidden layer and the output layer; $u(k-1)$ is input; $x(k)$ is output of the hidden layer; $x_C(k)$ is the output of the connection layer; $y(k)$ is the output of the output layer; $0 \leq \alpha < 1$ is self connected feedback gain factor. Usually $f(x)$ is set to sigmoid function:

$$f(x) = \frac{1}{1 + e^{-x}} \tag{7}$$

Some of the values in the input layer are very different from each other and we need to normalize the data, such as limiting these data to a certain range to prevent some low value of the characteristics being submerged. What's more, it can also provide convenience for the later data processing and ensure convergence speed when computing.

The structure of Elman neural network has great influence on the performance of the whole system. The most important part is to figure out the number of neurons in the hidden layer. The hidden layer neuron is used to extract the feature of the input vectors in the network learning period, and the number of the hidden layer neurons affects the training results and generalization ability of the network. The method to determine the number of hidden layer neurons is not clear up to now [11]. At present, most people use trial and error method to determine the number of hidden layer neurons. This paper also uses this method to determine the structure of the network. Input of this network is the vertical and horizontal coordinates of 5 points in consecutive historical trajectories, and output is predicted coordinates of the target.

4 Target Tracking

The predicted coordinates of the target can be obtained by Elman neural network. Considering that number of targets detected by the radar can be more than actual ones, which means that false targets are also detected, we need to process detected results with predicted results to track targets.

The traditional nearest neighbor method [12] is to regard the closest point of observation to the predicted point as the actual target. This method carries small amount of computation and the results are easy to achieve; but its disadvantage is that it can be easy to track error targets when the target density is large. Therefore, on the basis of the nearest neighbor method, this paper improves the method by combining the actual target point at last time and the predicted point at this moment to track the actual target.

We make a hypothesis that the actual coordinate of the target at last moment is $P_0(x_0, y_0)$, and the predicted coordinate at this moment is $P_Y(x_Y, y_Y)$, and the observed coordinates at this moment are $P_1(x_1, y_1)$, $P_2(x_2, y_2)$, $\cdots$, $P_n(x_n, y_n)$, and the moving distance of the target during the sampling period is $L = v \cdot T$. So We can make sure that the actual target should be nearest to both predicted point and the distance L. We define a new distance to help track targets as following:

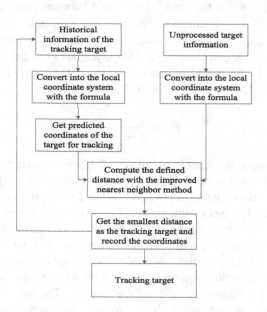

Fig. 3. Flow chart of this paper's target tracking method

$$R_n = \left| \sqrt{(x_n - x_0)^2 + (y_n - y_0)^2} - vT \right| + \sqrt{(x_n - x_Y)^2 + (y_n - y_Y)^2} \qquad (8)$$

In sequence $\{R_1, R_2, \cdots, R_n\}$, the smallest R_n can be considered as coming from the actual target. So we can track target with R_n. The flow chart of this paper's target tracking method is shown in Fig. 3.

5   Simulation

In this paper, Matlab is used to simulate the target tracking method. The vehicle radar works at 24 GHz and the bandwidth is 250 MHz. The simulation studies on a single target. Information known is the historical coordinates of the target. In consideration of the time used by detecting a target with a vehicle radar is about 20 ms, which means for a single target, the vehicle radar can output 50 coordinates in a second, so ensure the real-time and accuracy of tracking we use 35 coordinates of the target to study, and another 35 coordinates to compare with the prediction rather than more coordinates. The predicted results by Elman neural network are shown in Figs. 4 and 5.

The error of distance between the predicted points and the actual points shows in Fig. 6.

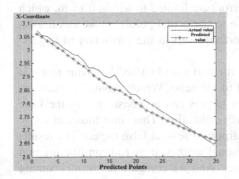

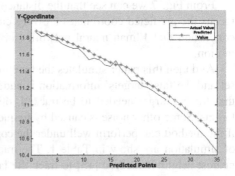

Fig. 4. Prediction of X coordinates   **Fig. 5.** Prediction of Y coordinates

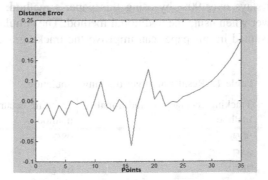

Fig. 6. Distance error between predicted points and actual points

Learned by the neural network, which keeps the predicting continuous. Then 10 sets of data including 10000 coordinates are set to simulate the paper method to prove if the paper method can perform well in long time work. Each group includes 1000 coordinates and the results are presented with average distance errors which are shown in Fig. 7.

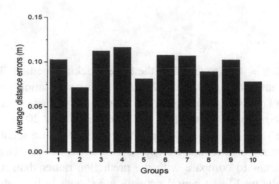

Fig. 7. Average distance error between predicted points and actual points of 10 groups

From Fig. 7 we can see that the distance errors are limited to within 0.15 m, which means the predicted coordinates are very close to the actual points, so we can draw a conclusion that Elman neural network can perform well in the prediction of targets' motion.

And then this paper simulates the tracking method with Matlab. A moving target is set and the false targets' information is added to the echo. Which should be known is that for the target needed to be tracked, other targets can be considered as the false targets. Some other noise is caused by frequency estimation. This simulation can verify if the method can perform well under the condition of several false targets. The results of simulation are show in Table 1. The traditional method uses Kalman filtering and nearest neighbor method [13] to track the target. And we compare the results coming from the traditional method and the paper method.

The table says that with more and more false targets the tracking accuracy will decrease but it still stays over 90% by using this paper's method. And the tracking accuracy will be lower when using the traditional method. The simulation results prove that the method presented in this paper can improve the tracking accuracy.

Table 1. Results of target tracking simulation.

Numbers of false targets	Tracking accuracy of traditional method	Tracking accuracy of improved method
4	90%	98%
8	84%	96%
10	76%	93%

6   Conclusion

In order to improve the tracking accuracy in the complex road environment, this paper uses Elman neural network to predict coordinates of the target and improves the nearest neighbor method to track targets. At last Matlab is used to simulate the tracking method and the simulation results prove the high accuracy of coordinates prediction and the effectiveness of the tracking method.

Acknowledgment. This research was financially supported by the Project of the National Natural Science Foundation of China (No. 61327802) and Program for New Century Excellent Talents (NCET-13-0923).

References

1. Gustafsson, F., Hendeby, G.: Some relations between extended and unscented Kalman filters. IEEE Trans. Sig. Process. **60**, 545–555 (2012)
2. Zhang, R.H., Lei, M.: Review of state of the art of particle filter technique. Noise Vibr. Control **2**, 1–4 (2010)
3. Cao, L., Li, Y., Huang, Y.: Study of target tracking in underwater acoustic sensor networks based on time delay modified particle filter. Tech. Acoust. **31**, 67–71 (2012)
4. Wu, S.J., Mei, X.C.: Radar Signal Processing and Data Processing Technology. Publishing House of Electronics Industry, Beijing (2008)
5. Wang, B.: Adaptive radar parameter selection and waveform design for target tracking. Tsinghua University, Beijing (2011)
6. Yan, Y.H.: The research and realization of improved particle filter algorithm on FPGA platform. Beijing Jiaotong University, Beijing (2009)
7. Wang, Y., Lei, B.: Research on object tracking algorithms based on a model to radar noise-signal ratio. Foreign Electron. Meas. Technol. **34**(1), 28–35 (2015)
8. Yang, J., Zhang, Q., Luo, Y., et al.: Method for multiple targets tracking in cognitive radar based on compressed sensing. J. Radars. http://www.cnki.net/kcms/doi/10.3724/SP.J.1300. 2014.14107.html. Accessed 24 Nov 2014
9. Yu, J., Guo, P.: Stock price forecasting model based on improved Elman neural network. Comput. Technol. Dev. **18**(3), 43–45 (2008)
10. Wang, H.J., Jiang, J.Q., Li, F.Q.: Application of Elman neural network and Matlab to dam displacement prediction. Water Power **31**(1), 31–37 (2005)
11. Zhang, Y.L.: Modeling and application of neural network in stock market prediction. Dalian University of Technology, Dalian (2004)
12. Aubrey, B.: Multidimensional assignment formulation of data association problems arising from multi-target and multi-sensor tracking. Comput. Optim. Appl. **3**(1), 27–57 (1994)
13. Macaveiu, A., Campeanu, A.: Automotive radar target tracking by Kalman filtering. In: International Conference on Telecommunication in Modern Satellite, vol. 2, pp. 553–556 (2014)

A Robust RGB-D Image-Based SLAM System

Liangliang Pan[1,2,3], Jun Cheng[1,3]([✉]), Wei Feng[1,3],
and Xiaopeng Ji[1,2,3]

[1] Guangdong Provincial Key Laboratory of Robotics and Intelligent System,
Shenzhen Institutes of Advanced Technology, Chinese Academy of Sciences,
Shenzhen, China
{ll.pan,jun.cheng,wei.feng,xp.ji}@siat.ac.cn
[2] Shenzhen College of Advanced Technology,
University of Chinese Academy of Sciences, Shenzhen, China
[3] The Chinese University of Hong Kong, Hong Kong, China

Abstract. Visual SLAM is widely used in robotics and computer vision. Although there have been many excellent achievements over the past few decades, there are still some challenges. 2D feature-based SLAM algorithm has been suffering from the inaccurate or insufficient correspondences while dealing with the case of textureless or frequently repeating regions. Furthermore, most of the SLAM systems cannot be used for long-term localization in a wide range of environment because of the heavy burden of calculating and memory. In this paper, we propose a robust RGB-D keyframe-based SLAM algorithm. The novelty of proposed approach lies in using both 2D and 3D features for tracking, pose estimation and bundle adjustment. By using 2D and 3D features, the SLAM system can achieve high accuracy and robustness in some challenging environments. The experimental results on TUM RGB-D dataset [1] and ICL-NUIM dataset [2] verify the effectiveness of our algorithm.

Keywords: RGB-D · SLAM · Visual feature · Mapping

1 Introduction

Visual Simultaneous Localization and Mapping (Visual SLAM) widely used in many fields, including unmanned aerial vehicle (UAV), automated guided vehicle (AGV), augmented reality & virtual reality (AR & VR) etc. Cameras have been widely used to collect information from the environment, due to their low cost, richness of the sensor data provided and the availability of general computers. Visual SLAM technology relies mainly on the bordered camera(s), for solving mobile robot's pose estimation while reconstructing unknown environment.

In recent years, some RGB-D cameras like Microsoft Kinect, Asus Xtion live pro, have been widely applied to SLAM system because of their low cost and strong ability of getting both color and depth images. RGB-D camera has been successfully applied to many robust visual SLAM systems [3–6]. A RGB-D SLAM system typically includes front-end and back-end. The front-end also named visual odometer, mainly performs feature extraction and data association, which includes feature tracking and loop closure. Visual odometry is the process of determining the position and orientation

M. Liu et al. (Eds.): ICVS 2017, LNCS 10528, pp. 120–130, 2017.
DOI: 10.1007/978-3-319-68345-4_11

of a robot by analyzing the associated images, which can provide an initial value for back-end optimization. The back-end uses the measurements provided by the visual odometry for global optimization, and reducing the accumulated error. Visual odometry is divided into feature-based method and directed method according to whether the visual feature is necessary for matching [7]. Compared with directed method, feature-based visual odometry is more mainstream due to its advantage of illumination invariance, insensitive to dynamic object by far [7]. In order to achieve a stable tracking and get a more accurate motion estimation, those visual features have the characteristics of repeatability, distinctiveness, and invariance to illumination, rotation, position, viewpoint, scale and so on. The common visual features including point, line and plane, in which point features are widely used in the visual SLAM system. There are some popular feature points like Harris, SIFT, SURF, FAST and ORB, etc. Compared with the line and plane, the point features are easier to obtain, more stable, and have better invariance to illumination and viewpoint in most environments. But plane features have better property to rotation invariance, and stable performance in the textureless region.

In our work, both 2D point features and 3D normal vector of plane features are used to register the RGB-D frames which make the system more robust than conventional vision-based RGB-D SLAM system. Figure 1 shows a motivating example of our system outputs of the *fr1_room sequence* from the TUM RGB-D benchmark. The contributions of this paper are summarized as follows.

Fig. 1. Result of the 3D reconstruction of the *fr1_room sequence* from the TUM RGB-D Benchmark [1], performed in real-time by our RGB-D algorithm on the standard laptop.

- Our proposed algorithm both uses 2D and 3D features for estimating the camera pose and bundle adjustment.
- Our system is keyframe-based, which is effective for long-term localization in a wide range of environments.
- We show a detailed experiment on open datasets to prove our system is more accurate than conventional RGB-D SLAM system in pose estimation.

The remainder of our paper is organized as follows: in the Sect. 2, we introduce some related works about current featured-based RGB-D SLAM researches. Section 3 presents a detailed description of our system architecture. The experimental results on several popular open datasets are presented in Sect. 4. And in the Sect. 5, we make a briefly conclusion and point out our future work.

2   Related Work

Visual SLAM is a system that uses the camera as the main sensor to construct the trajectory of the robot and maps of the environment [8]. Excellent results have been reported by many researchers. But there are still many challenging questions needed to be explored, such as robust feature detection, data association, and computationally efficient large-scale state estimation [9].

Feature Section: There are numerous visual features successfully applied to visual SLAM system as the landmarks. Bevington et al. [10] proposed a Harris's 3D vision system named DROID, which used the motion of harries corner for 3D reconstruction. DROID can determine both the camera motion and the 3D position of the feature in the short term. Se et al. [11] proposed a vision-based mobile robot SLAM algorithm based on SIFT features. However, both time and memory efficiency are seriously affected by the complex detection and extraction process of SIFT.

RGBD-SLAM System: In terms of RGB-D SLAM, Henry et al. [12] proposed a RGB-D SLAM system, which utilized a joint optimization algorithm to combine visual features and shape-based alignment, which both combined the visual and depth information for view-based loop-closure detection. Based on Henry's work, Endres et al. [3] proposed a 3D SLAM system, which extracted visual keypoints from the color image and utilized the depth image to provide the 3D position, which used RANSAC to estimate the transformations between association keypoints and optimize the pose estimate used g2o. But it's limited by a small environment because of the heavy burden of caculating and memory. In parallel, there are also some RGB-D SLAM systems equipped with GPU, like the KinectFusion presented by Newcombe et al. [4], which is a RGB-D SLAM system for accurate real-time mapping in the complex indoor scenes. And the camera pose is simultaneously obtained by tracking the live depth frame relative to the global model using a coarse-to-fine ICP algorithm. The system is also limited by small environment because of the memory consumption and easily fails in tracking under textureless environment. Moreover, KinectFusion requires additional GPU, which is limited on most mobile platforms. Di et al. [13] presented an extended BA-based SLAM method using a RGB-D camera to decrease the drift and refine the camera pose parameters for motion estimation.

SLAM Using High-Level Primitives: Related works based on the plane can be traced back to the works done by Weingarten and Siegwart [14], they used 3D laser scanner to delivering dense 3D point cloud, which could be converted into a plane representation composed of polygons and infinite place parameters, and then performed plane-to-plane registration with ICP algorithm. Trevor et al. [15] proposed a SLAM system which combined a RGB-D camera and a 2D laser to detect the planar surfaces for pose estimation. Taguchi et al. [16] is related with our proposed system, which utilized the minimal set of primitives (composed of points and planes) in a RANSAC framework to robustly compute correspondence and estimate the camera pose. But it's also limited to the small environment, and it can't provide the accuracy of pose estimation with the groundtruth in any dataset.

3 Proposed Approach

3.1 System Architecture

The architecture of our proposed system shown in Fig. 2, which takes a set of RGB-D frames as the system input. Our system is a keyframe-based SLAM system, where we select some representative frames as keyframes and store them in a global map. In the remainder of this section, we will focus on introducing main modules of the system: feature extraction, pose estimation, bundle adjustment, and loop closure.

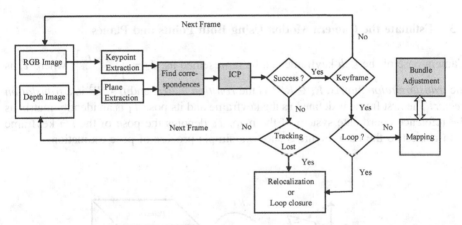

Fig. 2. Schematic overview of our approach. Our system is a keyframe-based RGB-D SLAM system which extracts keypoints and plane primitives as the *measurements* from each frame. Subsequently, we compute the transformation matrix and register some *measurements* from the keyframes into the map as the *landmarks*. Finally, we run bundle adjustment to refine the poses of keyframe and coordinate of landmarks in the map in an asynchronous thread. Meantime, a thread is set for relocalization and loop closure in the case of tracking lost or encountered a loop. Our main work contributes on the gray area.

3.2 Extract Points and Planes

As analyzed in the Second 2, a robust visual feature plays an important role in the feature detection and match. Here we use the ORB [17] as the 2D feature. ORB is a binary feature descriptor with 256 dimensions, which is invariance to rotation and illumination. Normal vector of the plane is used the 3D feature. The normal vector of the planes and the distance between planes have proven to be effective and accurate for rotation and translation estimation [18]. We detect and extract plane primitives from the 3D point cloud according to multi-stage RANSAC algorithm [16].

Each keypoint is represented as: $Po_i = (p_i, D_i)$, where $p_i = (x_i, y_i, z_i)$ is the 3D coordinates, and D_i is the ORB descriptor. Denote $\pi_j = (n_j, d_j, N_j)$ as the plane primitive, where $n_j = (a_j, b_j, c_j)^T$ denotes the normal vector of the plane, d_j is the distance from coordinate origin to the plane and N_j is the number of keypoints contained on the plane.

After obtaining the 2D keypoints and 3D plane primitives, we can find the correspondence between point-to-point and plane-to-plane. As for point, we utilize the nearest neighbor descriptor matching to find the point correspondence between points in the current frame and map implemented by OpenCV library. As for plane, there are limited planes every frame in most indoor scenes due to the limited viewing angle (<120°) and limited range (0.3 m–5 m) of RGB-D cameras [19]. We use brute force algorithm to search all of the potential correspondence between adjacent keyframes. After obtained initial correspondence, we utilize these correspondence for pose estimation and bundle adjustment, which will be detailed in the Sects. 3.3 and 3.4. In the Sect. 3.5, we make a brief description of the relocalization module.

3.3   Estimate the Camera Motion Using Both Points and Planes

Camera pose of the *k-th* keyframe can be represented as: $T_k = \begin{bmatrix} R_k & t_k \\ 0^T & 1 \end{bmatrix}$, where T_k is the *transformation matrix*, $R_k \in R^{3*3}$ is the *rotation matrix* and $t_k \in R^3$ is a *translation vector*. The first frame is defined as the keyframe and its pose T_1 is an identity matrix as the reference coordinate system of the map. T_k denotes the pose of the *kth* keyframe with respect to the map. Figure 3 shows a simple process of pose estimation.

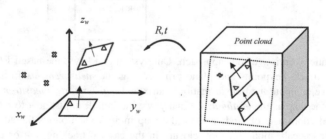

Fig. 3. The transformation between the world and camera coordinate frames. Where the triangle represent the keypoints on the planes, and the cross represented the keypoints outside the planes, dashed box represented the current frame, the cube represented the pointcloud generated by the current RGB and depth image.

Suppose a pair of matching 3D points and a pair of planes:

$$\begin{cases} Po = \{p_1,\ldots,p_n\}, & Po' = \{p'_1,\ldots,p'_n\} \\ Pl = \{\pi_1,\ldots,\pi_m\}, & Pl' = \{\pi'_1,\ldots,\pi'_m\} \end{cases} \tag{1}$$

Let $Po = \{p_1,\ldots,p_n\}$ and $Pl = \{\pi_1,\ldots,\pi_m\}$ respectively denote a set of 3D points and planes in the map, $Po' = \{p'_1,\ldots,p'_n\}$ and $Pl' = \{\pi'_1,\ldots,\pi'_m\}$ denote their correspondence in the current frame. We need to find a transformation $T = \{R,t\}$ to make:

$$\forall i,j \quad p'_i = Rp_i + t \quad \& \quad n'_j = Rn_j + t \tag{2}$$

Define the error term for the *i-th* point pair, and the error term for the *j-th* plane:

$$e_i = (p'_i - (Rp_i + t)), \quad e_j = w_j\left(n'_j - (Rn_j + t)\right) \tag{3}$$

In experiments, we used $w_j = \max\{1, N_j\}$ as the weight of the *jth* planes for estimating the pose of camera. Then we begin to construct the least squares problem to get $\{R,t\}$ to make the square sum of the errors is minimized:

$$J = \underset{\{R,t\}}{\arg\min} \sum_{i=1}^{n} ||(p'_i - (Rp_i + t))||_2^2 + \sum_{j=1}^{m} w_j||(n'_j - (Rn_j + t))||_2^2 \tag{4}$$

Three Steps to Solve the Optimization Problem:

(1) *Calculate the centroid positions of two sets of point p, p', then coordinates of each keypoint subtracted the centroid:*

$$p = \frac{1}{n}\sum_{i=1}^{n}(p_i), \quad p' = \frac{1}{n}\sum_{i=1}^{n}(p'_i)$$
$$q_i = p_i - p, \quad q'_i = p'_i - p' \tag{5}$$

(2) *The rotation matrix R is calculated using the following optimization problem:*

$$R^* = \underset{R}{\arg\min} \sum_{i=1}^{n} ||q'_i - Rq_i||^2 + \sum_{j=1}^{m} w_j||n'_j - Rn_j||^2 \tag{6}$$

(3) *The translation vector t is calculated from the rotation matrix R obtained in the previous step.*

$$t^* = \underset{t}{\arg\min} ||t - (p' - R^*p)||^2 + \sum_{j=1}^{m} w_j||n'^T_j \cdot t - (d_j - d'_j)||^2 \tag{7}$$

where d_j and d'_j is the distance from plane π_j, π'_j to the coordinate origin. Then we use the Levenberg-Marquadt implementation in g2o [20] to get R^* and t^*.

After obtaining the pose of current frame. The selection mechanism in our experiments is used to determine whether the current frame is a new keyframe. To insert a new keyframe, all the following conditions need to be met.

(1) *More than 10 frames in our experiment (related with the frame rate of camera) must have passed from the last keyframe.*
(2) *The rotation matrix R and translation vector t are valid.*
(3) *Current frame tracks at least 100 points or at least 50 points and 1 plane.*

3.4 Bundle Adjustment

Initial pose estimate is obtained by matching the correspondence between map and the current frame. The pose estimation of every frame exits some errors because of the noise and inaccurate correspondence. After more keyframes are inserted into the map, the cumulative error will increase. So we need to introduce a global optimization for eliminating cumulative error to make the pose estimation more accurate. Conventional bundle adjustment approaches simultaneously optimize the pose of keyframes and map points using the keypoints obtained from every keyframe. In our system, we use both points and planes for global optimization to camera pose as well as points coordinates in the map.

Suppose the points set and planes set are $\bar{P}_o$ and $\bar{P}_l$:

$$\bar{P}_o = \{p_1, p_2, \ldots, p_n\}, \quad \bar{P}_l = \{\pi_1, \pi_2, \ldots, \pi_m\} \tag{8}$$

Where $p_i = (x_i, y_i, z_i)^T$, and $\pi_j = (n_j, d_j, N_j)$ represent the coordinates of point and planes landmark in the map respectively. Using the $\{(R^1, t^1), (R^2, t^2), \ldots, (R^s, t^s)\}$ to represent all the poses of keyframes. We introduce this optimization problem:

$$\{p_i, \pi_j, R^k, t^k | i \in p_i^k; j \in p_j^k; k = 1, \ldots, s\}$$
$$= \underset{p_i, \pi_j, R^k, t^k}{\operatorname{argmin}} \sum_{k=1}^{s} \{\sum_{i \in p_i^k} \|p_i^k - (R^k p_i + t^k)\|^2 + \sum_{j \in p_j^k} w_j \|n_j^k - (R^k n_j + t^k)\|^2\} \tag{9}$$

And we also use the Levenberg-Marquadt implementation in g2o [20] to solve this problem. Then we can obtain the final pose estimation and the parameters of landmarks (including planes and points landmark).

3.5 Loop Closure and Relocalization

Loop detection is the module used to check whether the current scenes have been already described. The importance of loop closure lie in that it can eliminate the drift accumulated caused by visual odometry, resulting in a globally consistent map. Relocalization refers to a process by which a mobile robot performs self-positioning and restores its own motion state when tracking lost caused by occlusion, blocking or pure rotation happens. In order to achieve accurate relocalization and loop detection, we use the DBOW2 [21], which has been proven its accuracy and robustness of loop detection in large environment [22, 23]. Tracking may be lost due to insufficient or incorrect correspondence. On one hand, once we tracking lost, we start the relocalization module to relocate the camera pose. On the other hand, a loop detection is set for every new keyframe. If a loop is detected, we compute a similarity transformation and eliminate the drift accumulated in the loop. At last, we align two sides of the loop and fuse duplicated points.

4 Experimental Evaluation

Due to KITTI dataset doesn't provide the depth frame of the sequences. We have evaluated our system in two popular datasets [1, 2] and compare with state-of-art RGB-D SLAM, and always using results published by the original authors and dataset. We run our system in an Intel Core i7-6400 laptop with 8 GB RAM.

4.1 TUM RGB-D Dataset

TUM RGB-D dataset [1] contains RGB-D data and ground-truth data for evaluating RGB-D system. The ground-truth trajectory is obtained from a high-accuracy motion-capture system. It contains indoor sequences from RGB-D sensors grouped in several categories by different texture, illumination and structure conditions. We show results of parts of these sequences where most RGB-D methods are usually evaluated. In Table 1, we compare the accuracy of our approach with other state-of-the-art SLAM methods. Figure 4 shows some sequences of computed trajectories compared with the ground-truth. We use the absolute translation RMSE tabs proposed in [1] as the metrics in our experiments for indicating the accuracy of the algorithm.

Table 1. TUM RGB-D dataset parts of sequences comparison translation RMSE (m)

Sequences	Proposed approach	Kintinuous [5]	RGB-D SLAM [3]	DVO-SLAM [24]	ORB-SLAM2 [23]
fr1_desk	**0.015**	0.037	0.026	0.021	0.016
fr1_desk2	0.032	0.075	0.087	0.046	**0.022**
fr1_room	0.063	0.071	–	**0.043**	0.047
fr2_desk	**0.006**	0.034	0.057	0.017	0.009
fr2_xyz	**0.003**	0.029	–	0.018	0.004
fr3_stn	**0.005**	0.030	–	0.018	0.010

4.2 CL-NUIM Dataset

The ICL-NUIM is a popular RGB-D dataset for evaluation of visual odometry, 3D reconstruction and SLAM algorithms. It contains two different scenes (the living room and the office room scene) with groundtruth which produced by Kintinuous SLAM [4]. We show the result of our algorithm in all those 8 sequences. Table 2 show the comparison of pose estimation accuracy of ours with some state-of-the-art methods. Considering the ICP and ICP + RGB-D in the dataset are all improved versions of the

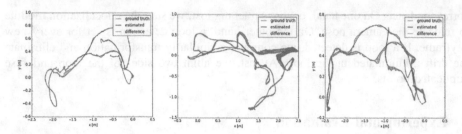

Fig. 4. The estimate trajectory (*black*) and groundtruth (*read*) in TUM dataset sequences of fr1_desk(left), fr1_room(middle), r1_desk2 (right), and the red line segment represents the difference between the estimated trajectory and the groundtruth. (Color figure online)

Table 2. CL-NUIM RGB-D dataset parts of sequences comparison translation RMSE (m)

Sequences	Proposed approach	RGB-D [25]	DVO [24]	ORB-SLAM2 [23]
live_room0	0.010	0.456	0.114	**0.008**
live_room1	0.872	0.629	**0.106**	0.141
live_room2	**0.099**	0.161	0.107	0.210
live_room3	**0.016**	1.029	0.188	0.031
office_room0	**0.024**	0.270	0.398	0.050
office_room1	0.047	0.617	0.446	**0.035**
office_room2	**0.012**	0.266	0.327	0.018
office_room3	**0.064**	0.475	0.207	0.126

Kintinuous SLAM, we just compare our experimental result with other three SLAM systems provided by the dataset.

5 Conclusions and Future Work

In this paper, we present a novel 3D SLAM system which fully use both texture features (2D keypoint) and geometric features (3D normal vector) for pose estimation and bundle adjustment. Our algorithm extracts 2D keypoints from color images and 3D normal vector of planes from point cloud. It is able to perform relocalization and loop closing relying on DBOW2 module in real-time in standard laptop with Core i7 and 4 core. We focus on using both texture and geometric features for robust pose estimation in challenging sequences. The experimental results show the effectiveness and accuracy in pose estimation. In this research, we just utilize the points and planes for pose estimation and bundle adjustment. In the future work, we would incorporate the plane features into the final map, which will make the map more compact than the point-based map, In addition, incorporating the plane features into the map can increase the semantic information of the map which is help for navigation and relocalization.

Acknowledgement. This work supported by CAS Key Technology Talent Program Shenzhen Technology Project (JSGG20160331185256983, JSGG20160229115709109), Guangdong

Technology Project(2016B010108010, 2016B010125003), State Joint Engineering Laboratory for Robotics and Intelligent Manufacturing funded by National Development and Reform Commission (No. 2015581), Key Laboratory of Human-Machine Intelligence-Synergy Systems, Shenzhen Institutes of Advanced Technology, Chinese Academy of Sciences (2014DP173025).

References

1. Sturm, J., Engelhard, N., Endres, F., Burgard, W., Cremers, D.: A benchmark for the evaluation of RGB-D SLAM systems. In: IROS, pp. 573–580 (2012)
2. Handa, A., Whelan, T., McDonald, J., Davison, A.J.: A benchmark for RGB-D visual odometry, 3D reconstruction and SLAM. In: ICRA, pp. 1524–1531 (2014)
3. Endres, F., Hess, J., Sturm, J., Cremers, D., Burgard, W.: 3-D mapping with an RGB-D camera. IEEE Trans. Robot. 1(30), 177–187 (2014)
4. Newcombe, R., et al.: KinectFusion: real-time dense surface mapping and tracking. In: ISMAR, pp. 127–136 (2011)
5. Whelan, T., Kaess, M., Johannsson, H., et al.: Real-time large-scale dense RGB-D SLAM with volumetric fusion. IJRR 34, 598–626 (2015)
6. Whelan, T., Leutenegger, S., Salasmoreno, R.F., et al.: ElasticFusion: dense SLAM without a pose graph. In: RSS 2015 (2015)
7. Xiang, G., et al.: 14 Lectures on Visual SLAM: From Theory to Practice. Publishing House of Electronics Industry (2017)
8. Chen, Z., Samarabandu, J., Rodrigo, R.: Recent advances in simultaneous localization and map-building using computer vision. J. Adv. Robot. 21(3–4), 233–265 (2007)
9. Neira, J., Davison, A.J., Leonard, J.J.: Guest editorial special issue on visual SLAM. IEEE Trans. Robot. 5(24), 929–931 (2008)
10. Bevington, P.R., Robinson, D.K., et al.: Data reduction and error analysis for the physical sciences. J. Comput. Phys. 4(7), 415–416 (1993)
11. Se, S., Lowe, D., Little, J.: Mobile robot localization and mapping with uncertainty using scale-invariant visual landmarks. IJRR 8(21), 735–758 (2002)
12. Henry, P., Krainin, M., Herbst, E., Ren, X., Fox, D.: RGB-D mapping: using Kinect-style depth cameras for dense 3D modeling of indoor environments. IJRR 5(31), 647–663 (2012)
13. Di, K., Zhao, Q., Wan, W., et al.: RGB-D SLAM based on extended bundle adjustment with 2D and 3D information. Sensors 8(16), 1285 (2016)
14. Weingarten, J., Siegwart, R.: 3D SLAM using planar segments. In: IROS, pp. 3062–3067 (2006)
15. Trevor, A.J.B, Rogers, J.G, Christensen, H.I.: Planar surface SLAM with 3D and 2D sensors. In: ICRA, pp. 3041–3048 (2012)
16. Taguchi, Y., Jian, Y.D., Ramalingam, S., Feng, C.: Point-plane SLAM for hand-held 3D sensors. In: ICRA, pp. 5182–5189 (2013)
17. Rublee, E., Rabaud, V., Konolige, K., Bradski, G.: ORB: an efficient alternative to SIFT or SURF. In: ICCV, pp. 2564–2571 (2011)
18. Walker, M.W., Shao, L., Volz, R.A.: Estimating 3-D location parameters using dual number quaternions. CVGIP: Image Underst. 3(54), 358–367 (1991)
19. Ataer-Cansizoglu, E., Taguchi, Y., Ramalingam, S., Garaas, T.: Tracking an RGB-D camera using points and planes. In: ICCV Workshops, pp. 51–58 (2013)
20. Kümmerle, R., Grisetti, G., Strasdat, H., et al.: g2o: a general framework for graph optimization. In: ICRA, pp. 3607–3613 (2011)

21. Galvez-López, D., Tardos, J.D.: Bags of binary words for fast place recognition in image sequences. IEEE Trans. Robot. 5(28), 1188–1197 (2012)
22. Mur-Artal, R., Montiel, J.M.M., Tardós, J.D.: ORB-SLAM: a versatile and accurate monocular SLAM system. IEEE Trans. Robot. 5(31), 1147–1163 (2015)
23. Mur-Artal, R., Tardós, J.D.: ORB-SLAM2: an open-source SLAM system for monocular, stereo and RGB-D cameras. arXiv preprint arXiv:1610.06475 (2016)
24. Kerl, C., Sturm, J., Cremers, D.: Dense visual SLAM for RGB-D cameras. In: IROS, pp. 2100–2106 (2013)
25. Steinbrücker, F., Sturm, J., Cremers, D.: Real-time visual odometry from dense RGB-D images. In: ICCV Workshops, pp. 719–722 (2011)

Robust Relocalization Based on Active Loop Closure for Real-Time Monocular SLAM

Xieyuanli Chen, Huimin Lu[(⊠)], Junhao Xiao, Hui Zhang,
and Pan Wang

College of Mechatronics and Automation,
National University of Defense Technology, Changsha 410073, Hunan, China
chenxieyuanli@hotmail.com, lhmnew@nudt.edu.cn

Abstract. Remarkable performance has been achieved using the state-of-the-art monocular Simultaneous Localization and Mapping (SLAM) algorithms. However, tracking failure is still a challenging problem during the monocular SLAM process, and it seems to be even inevitable when carrying out long-term SLAM in large-scale environments. In this paper, we propose an *active loop closure* based relocalization system, which enables the monocular SLAM to detect and recover from tracking failures automatically even in previously unvisited areas where no keyframe exists. We test our system by extensive experiments including using the most popular KITTI dataset, and our own dataset acquired by a hand-held camera in outdoor large-scale and indoor small-scale real-world environments where man-made shakes and interruptions were added. The experimental results show that the least recovery time (within 5 ms) and the longest success distance (up to 46 m) were achieved comparing to other relocalization systems. Furthermore, our system is more robust than others, as it can be used in different kinds of situations, i.e., tracking failures caused by the blur, sudden motion and occlusion. Besides robots or autonomous vehicles, our system can also be employed in other applications, like mobile phones, drones, etc.

Keywords: Relocalization · Monocular SLAM · Active loop closure · Robots

1 Introduction

SLAM is a key component of autonomous navigation system for robots in GPS-denied environments. It is normally described as the problem of estimating the robot pose, and at the same time reconstructing the environment incrementally. Considering that cameras are very cheap and easy to use, monocular SLAM has been developed rapidly.

The state-of-the-art monocular SLAM systems perform well in rich featured, static or lowly dynamic environments. However, since it is difficult to calculate the accurate

Electronic supplementary material The online version of this chapter (doi:10.1007/978-3-319-68345-4_12) contains supplementary material, which is available to authorized users.
The video of the experimental results can be found on our website: http://www.trustie.net/organizations/23/videos

© Springer International Publishing AG 2017
M. Liu et al. (Eds.): ICVS 2017, LNCS 10528, pp. 131–143, 2017.
DOI: 10.1007/978-3-319-68345-4_12

depth of observed features using only one camera, most existing monocular SLAM systems are less robust than those based on stereo and RGB-D cameras. For example, the localization or the robot pose tracking is easy to fail during the monocular SLAM process, especially when performing long-term SLAM in large-scale environments.

When tracking failure happens, the most effective solution is to add an image-to-map relocalization module, since a large amount of measurements in the map can be used to mitigate the side-effect of outliers and higher accuracy can be achieved in pose estimation [26]. However, most of image-to-map approaches are resource-consuming and normally designed for small workplace or indoor scenarios [7, 24, 26]. They are obviously inapplicable for mobile robots to perform long-term tasks. Inspired by Stradat et al. [23] and Mur-Artal and Tardós [14], our system only performs feature matching in a local map when the tracking fails, so the calculation burden in pose estimation is limited, and real-time relocalization can be realized in large-scale environments.

After the relocalization, the drift of SLAM system may become larger, since during the tracking failure period, the robot is not able to collect enough information to accurately localize itself and build the map. It is well-known that loop closure can efficiently eliminate the accumulated error. However, most current research only focus on how to detect and close a loop passively, but not to control robots to actively create loop closures to correct the SLAM drift. In this paper, we propose a novel approach about active loop closure, which uses the information of the robot/camera pose obtained from the relocalization to navigate robots finding a loop actively, and therefore eliminate the accumulated drift. The major contributions of this paper are as follows:

- An image-to-map relocalization method based on local map is proposed, which limits the calculation burden and realizes a real-time relocalization in large-scale scenes.
- A robust relocalization system based on active loop closure is proposed, where the pose information obtained from the latest relocalization is utilized to navigate robots to find a loop actively and in turn eliminate the drift caused by the tracking failure.

2 Related Work

2.1 Relocalization

The relocalization problem can be traced back to robot global self-localization in given maps and was first realized by Dellaert et al. [4]. With robots gradually applied to real scenes, the relocalization became a tracking recovery problem, and three types of approaches were proposed [25]: map-to-map, image-to-image and image-to-map.

Map-to-Map. It was first implemented by Clemente et al. [2]. They found matches between landmarks in two submaps, which is very complex and time-consuming. Also, because the sparse map built by monocular SLAM does not always provide enough mappoints, this method is less accurate and unreliable for monocular SLAM.

Image-to-Image. With the development of the monocular SLAM from the initial filtering approaches to current keyframe-based SLAM, the image-to-image method has been explored rapidly. It was first realized by Reitmayr [18] and Klein [11]. Then, Sivic and Zisserman [21] proposed Bag of Words (BoW) using visual words for place recognition, which was widely used in the relocalization and loop closure for its high accuracy. For example, Eade and Drummond [5] used BoW with SIFT [13] to determine the current submap. Cummins and Newman [3] used it with SURF [1] to achieve high robustness to perceptual aliasing. Mur-Artal and Tardós [15] used it with ORB [19], and built the well-known ORB-SLAM [14]. Although it has become popular to use image-to-image method in the relocalization problem, this method is only effective when robots run in the previously visited places where keyframes exist. This assumption does not hold for mobile robots when running in large-scale environments exploring unvisited places.

Image-to-Map. This problem can be solved by image-to-map approaches which were first proposed by Pupilli and Calway [16]. They built a short-distance tracking recovery system by exploring multiple hypotheses with a particle filter. To realize a global image-to-map approach, Lowe and Little [20] used SIFT features in 2D scenario. Williams et al. proposed a 3D relocalization based on a filter approach and feature recognition [26]. They made great contribution to this problem by first publishing a survey comparing different types of relocalization and loop closing approaches [25]. According to the survey, to deal with relocalization problem in the monocular SLAM, image-to-map approaches perform best for their higher accuracy, speed and robustness. After Williams et al., Straub et al. [24] used Locality Sensitive Hashing (LSH) [9] to speed up nearest neighbor searching. Feng et al. [7] improved this work using online learning process to construct the hash key, which made the relocalization more robust.

2.2 Active Loop Closure

Loop closure is another important problem in the SLAM system, which can correct the accumulated error of the map and the robot trajectory. Traditional loop closure methods are passive and normally performed by human or on the preplanned trajectories. However, robots' motions can strongly affect the SLAM performance, and it has become a hot topic named "Active SLAM" coined by Feder [6]. Active SLAM can be described as controlling the robot's motion to minimize the uncertainty of its map and localization. Our system introduces this idea into the relocalization using active loop closure, which aims to correct the drift and finally achieves higher accuracy and robustness.

Our work is similar to [7, 24, 26] for using the image-to-map relocalization method. However, their works are based on pre-trained classifiers or hash methods, which need extra time to train the classifiers and can only be used in small workplaces or indoor scenarios, while our method, based on a local map, can be used in larger-scale environments with higher accuracy and efficiency. The local map we used is similar to that of [14, 23], but they used it for image-to-image methods which are only valid in previously visited places. Stachniss et al. [22] and Rahimi et al. [17] also used active loop closure to reduce the drift. [22] realized it using a laser scanner, while [17] realized it by relaxing the loop closure requirements to increase the chances of loop closing. To the best of our knowledge, it is first proposed by us to combine the relocalization and active loop closure, which can simultaneously overcome the shortcomings of these two methods and achieve a good performance as an integrated system.

3 Proposed System

The proposed system is based on the state-of-the-art real-time Monocular SLAM, ORB-SLAM [14], but the system is of strong generalization and can be integrated into any appearance-based SLAM system.

3.1 The Overview of the System

Figure 1 demonstrates the structure of the proposed system, which is composed of five parts: Tracking, Loop Closing, Local Mapping, Relocalization and Active Loop Closure. Following the original ORB-SLAM, we use the same tracking thread in charge of localizing the camera in every frame and deciding when to insert a new keyframe, the same local mapping thread in charge of processing new keyframes and maintaining the local map, and the same loop closing thread in charge of searching loops and correcting the accumulated drift if closing the loop successfully. We also make several improvements on the original ORB-SLAM, which are explained in Sect. 3.2. When the tracking fails, the proposed system will employ the relocalization module on each incoming frame, and it is explained in detail in Sect. 3.3. To solve the drift problem during the tracking failure, the proposed system can actively create loop closure to reduce the drift through path planning and robot movements, which is explained in Sect. 3.4.

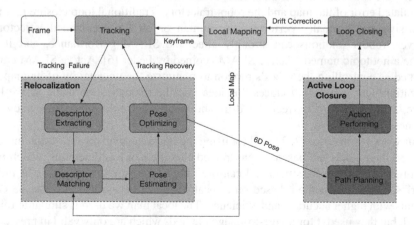

Fig. 1. The overview of the proposed robust relocalization system based on active loop closure. It includes five main parts: tracking, local mapping, loop closing, relocalization and active loop closure.

3.2   SLAM Implementation

The original ORB-SLAM system includes three main threads: tracking, local mapping, and loop closing. In order to better implement our system, we made several improvements on the original ORB-SLAM system as follows:

The Tracking. Thanks to the ORB features, which are fast, robust, rotation invariant and scale invariant in a certain level, we can extract a larger number of features in each frame to improve the accuracy and success rate of the relocalization. The resolution of the image we used is 640×480, and we found that it is suitable to extract 2000 corners for indoor environments, and 4000 corners for outdoor environments.

The Local Map. The local map in ORB-SLAM contains two sets of keyframes K1 and K2. The keyframes in K1 share the same mappoints with the current frame, while the keyframes in K2 are the neighbors of those in K1. Different to tracking the whole local map, we only employs K1 as a map for image-to-map relocalization, which can reduce the searching time and will not affect the accuracy and successful rate.

The Loop Closure. Since the system will try to detect loops within every incoming frame after the relocalization, it is vital to design a good keyframe selection policy, which will not ignore any potential match, but also not be too open to raise computation burden. This policy in original ORB-SLAM includes four conditions [14]. To keep the localization accuracy, we use a more strict policy which requires the tracked points doubled from 50 to 100, since we increase the number of extracted features. Meanwhile, we raise the similarity rate from 90% to 95% to keep the same inserting threshold, which in fact makes it easier to realize the active loop closure.

3.3   Relocalization Module

In our relocalization module, image-to-map method is used based on the local map. Similar to most image-to-map approaches, we estimate a 6D pose from 2D image to 3D world coordinate correspondences, but the difference is that our method only uses the simplest exhaustive nearest neighbor searching method to establish the associations between the descriptors extracted from the current frame and the mappoints stored in the local map, while most other methods are classifier-based, which are time-consuming and sometimes inaccurate. Our method benefits from the ORB features and the local map, for ORB features allow us directly compute the Hamming distance between the respective binary descriptors very efficiently using low-level hardware operations, and the local map helps us reduce the searching space in an efficient way. Once the tracking fails, the proposed relocalization method will try to recover tracking by finding the robot/camera pose in every incoming frame which is summarized in the Algorithm 1 from line 1 to 9. The steps of the proposed relocalization method are described as follows:

- **Feature Extracting:** The first step is to extract ORB features in the current frame (line 2). Like ORB-SLAM, we use the image pyramid and detect FAST keypoints in each level to make it more accurate.

- **Descriptor Matching:** The second step is to find the matches between the extracted features and mappoints stored in the local map (line 3). Instead of using complex classifier-based methods, we employ the simplest exhaustive nearest neighbor searching to establish the associations based on the local map, which is fast and accurate.
- **Pose Estimating:** The third step is to estimate the robot/camera pose from the set of 2D to 3D matches by solving a PnP problem [12] using a RANSAC scheme (line 5).
- **Pose Optimizing:** Finally, we use the Levenberg-Marquadt method implemented in g2o [10] to refine the pose (line 6).

Comparing to the image-to-image approaches, e.g. the method employed by original ORB-SLAM, ours can work in previously unvisited places (verified in experiment 4.1) and is faster than other relocalization approaches (shown in Table 1). In addition, our method is more accurate and robust benefiting from the active loop closure, which will be described in the following part.

Algorithm 1: Robust relocalization based on active loop closure for real-time monocular SLAM

Require: Current frame: f, local map: map_l,
      Pose before the tracking failure: $pose^*$.

Ensure: The updated map and the keyframe of the robot.

1: **If** $tracking_{lost}$ = $true$ **then**
2:      $descriptors \leftarrow$ Extraction(f)
3:      (matches, N) $\leftarrow$ Matching($descriptors$, map_l)
4: **If** $N > th_N$ **then**
5:         $pose_{raw} \leftarrow$ RANSAC(PnP($matches$))
6:         $pose \leftarrow$ g2o($pose_{raw}$)
7:         $relocalization \leftarrow true$
8:      **End If**
9: **End If**
10: **If** $relocalization$ = $true$ **then**
11:      $direction \leftarrow$ Calculate($pose^*$, $pose$)
12:      **While** $loop_{closing}$ = $false$ **do**
13:         $path \leftarrow$ Plan($direction$)
14:         Action($path$)
15:      **End While**
16: **End If**

3.4 Active Loop Closure Module

As discussed above, fast and long-distance tracking recovery can be achieved using the proposed relocalization module. However, because of information missing during the tracking failure, it is inevitable to have a larger drift after the relocalization. We therefore employ an active loop closure module to reduce the drift after the relocalization and acquire more accurate maps, which is summarized in the Algorithm 1 from

Table 1. The computation time needed in the relocalization process

Steps	Different methods (Number of features)[b]				
	Ours (2000)	Ours (4000)	ORB-SLAM (1000) [15]	Williams (145) [26]	LSH-based (216) [24]
Feature extraction[a]	18.2 ms	29.0 ms	14.4 ms	14.0 ms	122.9 ms
Matching	2.1 ms	4.7 ms	6.4 ms	0.3 ms	50.0 ms
Pose estimation	2.1 ms	2.5 ms	14.9 ms	0.7 ms	10.0 ms
Pose optimiziton	0.8 ms	1.3 ms	/	4.0 ms	0.5 ms
Total	23.2 ms	37.5 ms	35.7 ms	19 ms	183.4 ms

[a]Including Classification
[b]We quoted the data of other methods from publications [15, 24, 26]

line 10 to 16. Once recovering the tracking process successfully, the system will enable the active loop closure module which includes three steps:

- **Direction Computing:** We first calculate the robot's motion direction (line 12). After the relocalization, we get an optimized *pose* and a camera *pose*[*] stored in the last keyframe before the tracking failure. Their absolute transformations in **SE**(3) are:

$$pose : \mathbf{T_w} = \begin{pmatrix} \mathbf{R} & \mathbf{t} \\ 0 & 1 \end{pmatrix}, pose^* : \mathbf{T_w^*} = \begin{pmatrix} \mathbf{R}^* & \mathbf{t}^* \\ 0 & 1 \end{pmatrix} \qquad (1)$$

where for simplicity, we assume the scale factor to be 1, which does not affect the calculation of the direction. We then compute the relative transformation $\Delta \mathbf{T}$ between the current pose and the last *pose*[*]:

$$\Delta \mathbf{T} = \begin{pmatrix} \Delta \mathbf{R} & \Delta \mathbf{t} \\ 0 & 1 \end{pmatrix} = \mathbf{T_w} \bullet \mathbf{T_w^*} \qquad (2)$$

In this paper, we only consider the case that robots conduct the relocalization when travelling forwards into unvisited environments, so the camera's orientation is almost constant. We therefore only take the translation into consideration and compute the *direction* as follows:

$$direction : \mathbf{d} = \Delta \mathbf{t} \qquad (3)$$

- **Path Planning:** The second step is to plan a path using the computed direction to realize a loop closure (line 14). According to [22], it is not the best solution for the robot to just move backwards a few meters to revisit previously seen areas, because the mappoints and the camera poses stored in each node/keyframe are consistent. In the proposed system, this conclusion is also right, which is verified in experiment 4.1. Rather than just moving backwards a few meters, we use the calculated direction and the tracking failure distance to find a loop. Assuming the robot moving forwards into unvisited environments with a constant speed V_{robot} during the tracking failure time $T_{failure}$, we can compute the tracking failure distance $D_{failure}$ as follows:

$$D_{failure} = V_{robot} \times T_{failure} \qquad (4)$$

Taking the $D_{failure}$ as the radius and the computed *direction* as the initial normal vector, we can plan a semicircle path for the robot to realize loop closure. In fact, any algorithm which can plan a path between current *pose* and the last *pose*[*] based on the calculated *direction* can be used in our system.

- **Action Performing:** The third step is to control the robot moving along the planned path. The active loop closure module will be performed by repeating step 2 and 3 until a loop closure is detected successfully.

4   Experiments

We conducted two groups of experiments to test the proposed system. The first group were carried out using a hand-held camera in large-scale outdoor environments and small-scale indoor environments with man-made shakes and interruptions. The second group were conducted using the KITTI datasets [8], and we took out frames in a certain interval from each sequence to simulate tracking failures. All the experiments were run on a laptop computer equipped with a 2.4 GHz i7 CPU and 4 GB memory.

4.1   The Experiments on Sequences Acquired by a Hand-Held Camera

We conducted three experiments using a hand-held camera to test the performance of the proposed system on tracking recovery, drift correction with active loop closure and dealing with strong shaking. The former two experiments were performed in the large-scale NUDT campus, while the third experiment was conducted in an indoor lab scenario. We use a hand-held camera to simulate the robot, which is actually more challenging because of strong shakes and high varying speeds. The real-time performance was also tested and compared with other relocalization methods.

Tracking Recovery. As illustrated in Fig. 2, the tracking can be recovered using the proposed system after a long distance failure (25 m) in previously unvisited environments, where no keyframe exists. After the relocalization, robots can continue the SLAM. However, because of the missing data during the tracking failure, the drift becomes larger and the accuracy of pose estimation reduced greatly.

Drift Correction by Active Loop Closure. We perform active loop closure after each relocalization, and stop it when finding a loop closure. We also conducted the test of moving backwards a few meters to revisit previous areas. From the experimental results (shown in Fig. 3), we can conclude that active loop closure performs much better in correcting the drift than just moving backwards a few meters.

Fig. 2. The proposed relocalization system running in NUDT campus. While conducting SLAM ①, we introduced a tracking failure manually by suspending the tracking thread and keeping on moving for 15 s (25 m). After that, we resumed the tracking thread and the tracking failure happened ②. The proposed system enable the relocalization module automatically and recovered the tracking successfully ③, where a pose was computed and a keyframe was inserted. However, due to the missing data, the scale drift became larger (the space between keyframes became smaller) and the accuracy of pose estimation reduced greatly (there was an obvious deviation between the newly computed camera pose and the previous trajectory) ④.

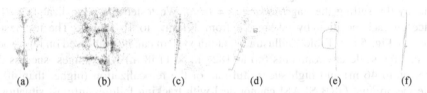

Fig. 3. Drift correction results by active loop closure. After the relocalization (a), we can see an error of the camera's pose estimation, zoomed in (d), where there is an obvious deviation between the newly computed camera pose and the previous trajectory. Then, we compared active loop closure (b) and moving backwards a few meters (c). (e) shows the camera's trajectory after active loop closure, which is straight and corrected without any deviation, while (f) shows the camera's trajectory after just moving backwards a few meters and the deviation still exists.

Dealing with Strong Shaking and High Speed. In this experiment, we moved the camera with a high speed and shook it greatly to make the tracking fail during the SLAM process in an indoor lab environment. The experimental results (in Fig. 4) show that after combining the relocalization module and active loop closure module, the proposed system works well even when there are strong shakes in the camera's motion.

Real-Time Performance. We evaluate the real-time performance of the proposed system and other systems by comparing the computation time needed in each steps of the relocalization process. As shown in Table 1, our system (23.2 ms) is faster than

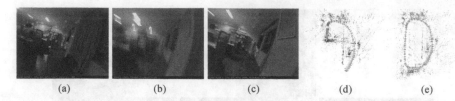

| (a) | (b) | (c) | (d) | (e) |

Fig. 4. The SLAM results when there are strong shakes in the camera's high-speed motion. While conducting SLAM (a), tracking failure happened because of a strong shake in the camera's high-speed motion (b). Our system can rapidly recover the tracking (c), which illustrates that our system has a strong robustness even in such challenging situations. (d) shows the result without loop closure, while (e) shows the result with a loop closure. The better performance shown in (e) verifies again that our system can perform better after integrating active loop closure module.

those in [24] (183.4 ms) and [15] (35.7 ms), and is lightly slower than that in [26]. Furthermore, considering that 2000 features were extracted in our system while only 145 features were extracted in [26], the real time performance of our system is quite good. Apart from feature extraction, our system only needs 5.0 ms (the same as [26]) for the relocalization, which is the best among all relocalization methods.

4.2   The Experimental Results on the KITTI Dataset

We used the image sequence 00 to 05 from the popular KITTI dataset to test the proposed system. To simulate tracking failures, we randomly chose 50 positions in each sequence, took out image frames close to them, and then set the tracking failure manually (by setting the flag $tracking_{lost} = true$). We tested the relocalization performance on each position by taking out from 1 frame to 10 frames. The test results (shown in Fig. 5 and Table 2) illustrate that our system can be employed on high-speed cars in large scale environments (up to 1828 m × 1158 m) with longest success distance (up to 46 m) and high successful rate of the relocalization (higher than 40%), while the original ORB-SLAM cannot deal with tracking failures in most situations.

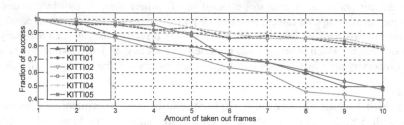

Fig. 5. Successful rates of the relocalization on the KITTI dataset. The solid lines represent the results in larger scale environments with a lot of bends, while the dotted lines represent the results in the environments without many bends.

In addition, following the ORB-SLAM, we used the relative position error (putting errors in the context of space scales) comparing to the given ground truth to evaluate

Table 2. Results on the KITTI dataset

Sequence	Space scale (m × m)	The maximum number of taken out frames (distance m)[a]
KITTI00	564 × 496	61 (29 m)
KITTI01	1828 × 1158	90 (240 m)[b]
KITTI02	599 × 946	28 (37 m)
KITTI03	471 × 199	46 (38 m)
KITTI04	0.5 × 394	31 (46 m)
KITTI05	479 × 426	104 (9 m)[c]

[a]The distance means the length of the trajectory during the tracking failures computed from ground truth
[b]Running on a highway environment with small changes
[c]Stop in one position for a long time

the relocalization accuracy of the proposed system, which is shown in Fig. 6. We can see that the errors on the KITTI sequence 00 and 05 are obviously smaller than those on sequence 03 and 04, because there are many loops in the former two sequences. We are surprised to find that with loop closure, our system has the same accuracy (within 6%) as the original ORB-SLAM, even when hundreds of frames were taken out from the image sequence. It verifies again that by combining active loop closure, our system can achieve more robust and accurate relocalization for the monocular visual SLAM.

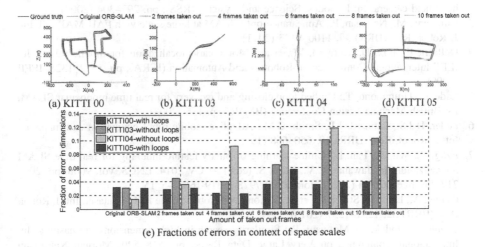

(a) KITTI 00   (b) KITTI 03   (c) KITTI 04   (d) KITTI 05

(e) Fractions of errors in context of space scales

Fig. 6. (a), (b), (c) and (d) show the experimental results of our system conducted on the KITTI sequence 00, 03, 04 and 05 when different number of frames from 1 to 10 were taken out respectively. (e) shows the comparison of the fraction of their errors (the estimated position error comparing to the given ground truth) in the context of space scales.

5   Conclusion and Future Work

In this work, we proposed an integrated system combining image-to-map relocalization and active loop closure to solve the well-known tracking failure problem in the visual SLAM system. The experimental results show that better robustness can be achieved by our system than other relocalization systems, and our system can be employed in challenging situations even in previously unvisited places. By combining the active loop closure with the relocalization, high accuracy and efficiency can be achieved simultaneously in our system, which also provides a good example to answer the "when to use" problem in active SLAM.

In the future, it would be desirable to run our system in real robots with advanced path planning and robot controlling algorithms. We are also interested in applying our system in the multi-robot SLAM.

Acknowledgment. This work was supported by National Science Foundation of China (No. 61403409, No. 61503401).

References

1. Bay, H., Tuytelaars, T., Van Gool, L.: SURF: speeded up robust features. In: Leonardis, A., Bischof, H., Pinz, A. (eds.) ECCV 2006. LNCS, vol. 3951, pp. 404–417. Springer, Heidelberg (2006). doi:10.1007/11744023_32
2. Clemente, L.A., Davison, A.J., Reid, I.D., et al.: Mapping large loops with a single hand-held camera. In: Robotics: Science and Systems (RSS), pp. 297–304 (2007)
3. Cummins, M., Newman, P.: Appearance-only SLAM at large scale with FAB-MAP 2.0. Int. J. Robot. Res. (IJRR) **30**, 1100–1123 (2011)
4. Dellaert, F., Fox, D., Burgard, W., et al.: Monte carlo localization for mobile robots. In: IEEE International Conference on Robotics and Automation (ICRA), pp. 1322–1328. IEEE (1999)
5. Eade, E., Drummond, T.: Unified loop closing and recovery for real time monocular SLAM. In: British Machine Vision Conference (BMVC), p. 136 (2008)
6. Feder, H.J.S., Leonard, J.J., Smith, C.M.: Adaptive mobile robot navigation and mapping. Int. J. Robot. Res. (IJRR) **18**, 650–668 (1999)
7. Feng, Y., Wu, Y., Fan, L.: Online learning of binary feature indexing for real-time SLAM relocalization. In: Jawahar, C.V., Shan, S. (eds.) ACCV 2014. LNCS, vol. 9008, pp. 206–217. Springer, Cham (2015). doi:10.1007/978-3-319-16628-5_15
8. Geiger, A., Lenz, P., Stiller, C., et al.: Vision meets robotics: the KITTI dataset. Int. J. Robot. Res. (IJRR) **32**, 1231–1237 (2013)
9. Gionis, A., Indyk, P., Motwani, R.: Similarity search in high dimensions via hashing. In: International Conference on Very Large Data Bases, pp. 518–529. Morgan Kaufmann Publishers Inc. (1999)
10. Kümmerle, R., Grisetti, G., Strasdat, H., et al.: g2o: a general framework for graph optimization. In: IEEE International Conference on Robotics and Automation (ICRA), pp. 3607–3613 (2011)
11. Klein, G., Murray, D.: Improving the agility of keyframe-based SLAM. In: Forsyth, D., Torr, P., Zisserman, A. (eds.) ECCV 2008. LNCS, vol. 5303, pp. 802–815. Springer, Heidelberg (2008). doi:10.1007/978-3-540-88688-4_59

12. Lepetit, V., Moreno-Noguer, F., Fua, P.: Epnp: an accurate o (n) solution to the pnp problem. Int. J. Comput. Vis. (IJCV) **81**, 155 (2009)
13. Lowe, D.G.: Distinctive image features from scale-invariant keypoints. Int. J. Comput. Vis. (IJCV) **60**, 91–110 (2004)
14. Mur-Artal, R., Montiel, J.M.M., Tardós, J.D.: ORB-SLAM: a versatile and accurate monocular SLAM system. IEEE Trans. Robot. (ITRO) **31**, 1147–1163 (2015)
15. Mur-Artal, R., Tardós, J.D.: Fast relocalisation and loop closing in keyframe-based SLAM. In: International Conference on Robotics and Automation (ICRA), pp. 846–853 (2014)
16. Pupilli, M., Calway, A.: Real-time camera tracking using a particle filter. In: British Machine Vision Conference (BMVC) (2005)
17. Rahimi, A., Morency, L.P., Darrell, T.: Reducing drift in parametric motion tracking. In: IEEE International Conference on Computer Vision (ICCV), vol. 311, pp. 315–322 (2001)
18. Reitmayr, G., Drummond, T.: Going out: robust model-based tracking for outdoor augmented reality. In: IEEE and ACM International Symposium on Mixed and Augmented Reality (ISMAR), pp. 109–118. IEEE Computer Society (2006)
19. Rublee, E., Rabaud, V., Konolige, K., et al.: ORB: an efficient alternative to SIFT or SURF. In: International Conference on Computer Vision (ICCV), pp. 2564–2571. IEEE (2011)
20. Se, S., Lowe, D.G., Little, J.J.: Vision-based global localization and mapping for mobile robots. IEEE Trans. Robot. (ITRO) **21**, 364–375 (2005)
21. Sivic, J., Zisserman, A.: Video Google: a text retrieval approach to object matching in videos. In: IEEE International Conference on Computer Vision (ICCV), pp. 1470–1477. IEEE (2003)
22. Stachniss, C., Hahnel, D., Burgard, W.: Exploration with active loop-closing for FastSLAM. In: IEEE/RSJ International Conference on Intelligent Robots and Systems (IROS), pp. 1505–1510. IEEE (2004)
23. Strasdat, H., Davison, A.J., Montiel, J.M.M., et al.: Double window optimisation for constant time visual SLAM. In: International Conference on Computer Vision (ICCV), pp. 2352–2359 (2011)
24. Straub, J., Hilsenbeck, S., Schroth, G., et al.: Fast relocalization for visual odometry using binary features. In: IEEE International Conference on Image Processing (ICIP), pp. 2548–2552 (2013)
25. Williams, B., Cummins, M., Neira, J., et al.: A comparison of loop closing techniques in monocular SLAM. Robot. Auton. Syst. (RAS) **57**, 1188–1197 (2009)
26. Williams, B., Klein, G., Reid, I.: Automatic relocalization and loop closing for real-time monocular SLAM. IEEE Trans. Pattern Anal. Mach. Intell. (TPAMI) **33**, 1699–1712 (2011)

On Scale Initialization in Non-overlapping Multi-perspective Visual Odometry

Yifu Wang$^{(\boxtimes)}$ and Laurent Kneip

Australian National University, Canberra, Australia
u5434194@anu.edu.au, laurent.kneip@anu.edu.au

Abstract. Multi-perspective camera systems pointing into all directions represent an increasingly interesting solution for visual localization and mapping. They combine the benefits of omni-directional measurements with a sufficient baseline for producing measurements in metric scale. However, the observability of metric scale suffers from degenerate cases if the cameras do not share any overlap in their field of view. This problem is of particular importance in many relevant practical applications, and it impacts most heavily on the difficulty of bootstrapping the structure-from-motion process. The present paper introduces a complete real-time pipeline for visual odometry with non-overlapping, multi-perspective camera systems, and in particular presents a solution to the scale initialization problem. We evaluate our method on both simulated and real data, thus proving robust initialization capacity as well as best-in-class performance regarding the overall motion estimation accuracy.

1 Introduction

Over the past decade, automated real-time visual localization and mapping has often been proclaimed as a mature computer vision technology. However, it is only with the emerge of novel, billion-dollar industries such as autonomous driving, robotics, and mixed reality consumer products that this technology gets now put to a serious test. While single camera solutions [4,10,19,20,22,28] are certainly the most interesting from a more scientific point of view, they are also challenged by many potential bottlenecks such as a limited field of view, moderate sampling rates, and a low ability to deal with texture-poor environments or agile motion. In addition to fast sensors such as inertial measurement units, the engineering standpoint therefore envisages the use of stereo [17], depth [21,25,29,30], or even light-field cameras that simplify or robustify the solution of the structure-from-motion problem by providing direct 3D depth-of-scene measurements.

The present paper is focusing on yet another type of sensor system that aims at combining benefits from different directions, namely *Multi-Perspective Cameras (MPCs)*. If pointing the cameras into different, opposite directions, the flow fields caused by translational and rotational motion become very distinctive [15], meaning that MPC solutions are strong at avoiding motion degeneracies. Furthermore, omni-directional observation of the environment makes failures due to texture-poor situations much more unlikely. In contrast to regular

M. Liu et al. (Eds.): ICVS 2017, LNCS 10528, pp. 144–157, 2017.
DOI: 10.1007/978-3-319-68345-4_13

omni-directional cameras, MPCs maintain the advantage of not introducing any significant lens distortions in the perceived visual information. Just like plain monocular cameras, MPCs also remain kinetic depth sensors. This means that they have no inherent limitations like stereo or depth cameras, which have limited range, or—in the latter case—cannot be used outdoors. As a final benefit, MPC systems are able to produce measurements in metric scale even if there is no internal overlap in the cameras' field of view.

MPCs are becoming increasingly important from an economic point of view. Looking at the most recent designs from the automotive or the consumer electronics industry, it is not uncommon to find a large number of affordable visual onboard sensors looking into various directions to provide complete capturing of the surrounding environment. An example of the fields of view of a modern car's visual sensors is shown in Fig. 1. The drawback with many such arrangements, however, is that the sensors do not share any significant overlap in their field of view. We call those camera arrays *non-overlapping MPCs*.

Fig. 1. Example fields of view of a multi-perspective camera mounted on a modern car.

The proper handling of non-overlapping MPCs requires the solution of two fundamental problems:

- As discussed in [3], non-overlapping MPCs are easily affected by motion degeneracies that cause scale unobservabilities, such as straight or Ackermann motion. This is a severe problem especially in automotive applications or in general during the bootstrapping phase, where no scale information can be propagated from prior processing.
- In order to truly benefit from the omni-directional measurements of MPCs, the measurements need to be processed jointly in each step of the computation. This is challenging as classical formulations of space resectioning and bundle adjustment all rely on a simple perspective camera model.

The present paper notably provides solutions to these two problems. The paper is organized as follows. Section 2 introduces further related work. Section 3 then provides an overview of our complete non-overlapping MPC motion estimation pipeline as well as the joint bootstrapping and global optimization modules. Section 4 finally presents the promising results we have obtained on both simulated and real data.

2   Motivation and Further Background

The motion estimation problem with MPCs can be approached in two fundamentally different ways. The first one consists of a loosely-coupled scheme where the information in each camera is used to solve individual monocular structure-from-motion problems, and the results from every camera are then fused in a subsequent pose averaging module. Kazik et al. [9] apply this solution strategy to a stereo camera rig with two cameras pointing into opposite directions. The inherent difficulty of this approach results from the scale invariance of the individual monocular structure-from-motion results. Individual visual scales first have to be resolved through an application of the hand-eye calibration constraint [8] before the individual pose results can be fused. Furthermore, the fact that the measurements of each camera are processed independently means that the benefit of having omni-directional measurements remains effectively unexploited during the geometric computations.

The second solution strategy assumes that the frames captured by each camera are synchronized, and hence can be bundled in a multi-frame measurement that contains one image of each camera from the same instant in time. Relying on the idea of *Using many cameras as one* [24], the fundamental problems of structure from motion can now be solved jointly for the entire MPC system, rather than for each camera individually. The measurements captured by the entire MPC can notably be described using a generalized camera, a model that envisages the description of measured image points via spatial rays that intersect with the corresponding camera's center, all expressed in a common frame for the entire MPC. By relying on the generalized camera model, the problems of joint absolute and relative camera pose estimation for the entire MPC rig have been successfully solved [12–14,18,23,24,27]. An excellent summary of the state-of-the-art in generalized camera pose computation is provided by the OpenGV library [11], a relatively complete collection of algorithms for solving related problems.

Despite the fact that closed-form solutions for the underlying algebraic geometry problems of generalized absolute and relative camera pose computation have already been presented, a full end-to-end pipeline for visual odometry with a non-overlapping MPC system that relies exclusively on the generalized camera paradigm remains an open problem. The problem mostly lies in the bootstrapping phase. As explained in [3], the relative pose for a multi-camera system can only be computed if the motion does not suffer from the degenerate case of Ackermann-like motion (which includes the case of purely straight motion). Unfortunately, in a visual odometry scenario, the images often originate from a smooth trajectory with only moderate dynamics, hence causing the motion between two sufficiently close frames to be almost always very close to the degenerate case. Kneip and Li [13] claim that the rotation can still be found, but we confirmed through our experiments that even the quality of the relative rotation is not sufficiently good to reliably bootstrap MPC visual odometry. A robust initialization procedure, as well as a complete, real-time end-to-end pipeline, notably, are the main contributions of this work.

3   Joint Motion Estimation with Non-overlapping Multi-perspective Cameras

This section outlines our complete MPC motion estimation pipeline. We start with an overview of the entire framework, explaining the state machine and resulting sequence of operations especially during the initialization procedure. We then look at two important sub-problems of the initialization, namely the robust retrieval of absolute orientations for the first frames of a sequence, as well as a joint linear recovery of the corresponding relative translations and 3D points. We conclude with an insight into the final bundle adjustment back-end that is entered once the initialization is completed.

3.1 Notations and Prior Assumptions

The MPC frames of a video sequence are denoted by VP_j, where $j = \{1, \cdots, m\}$. Their poses are expressed by transformation matrices $\mathbf{T}_j = \begin{bmatrix} \mathbf{R}_j \ \mathbf{t}_j \\ \mathbf{0} \ 1 \end{bmatrix}$ such that $\mathbf{T}_j \mathbf{x}$ transforms $\mathbf{x}$ from the MPC to the world frame (denoted W). Let us now assume that our MPC has k cameras. This leads to the definition of transformation matrices $\mathbf{T}_c = \begin{bmatrix} \mathbf{R}_c \ \mathbf{t}_c \\ \mathbf{0} \ 1 \end{bmatrix}$, where $c \in \{1, \cdots, k\}$. They permit the transformation of points from the

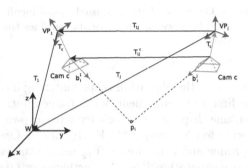

Fig. 2. Notations used throughout this paper (best viewed in color). Please see text for detailed explanations.

respective camera frame c to the MPC frame. Assuming that the MPC rig is static, these transformations are constant and determined through a prior extrinsic calibration process. We also define the relative transformation $\mathbf{T}_{1j} = \begin{bmatrix} \mathbf{R}_{1j} \ \mathbf{t}_{1j} \\ \mathbf{0} \ 1 \end{bmatrix}$ that allows us to transform points from VP_j back to VP_1. We furthermore assume that—given that we are in a visual odometry scenario and that the cameras have no overlap in their fields of view—the cameras do not share any point observations. We therefore can associate each one of our points $\mathbf{p}_i, i \in \{1, \cdots, n\}$ to one specific camera within the rig, denoted by the index c_i. To conclude, we also assume that the intrinsic camera parameters are known, which is why we can always transform 2D points into spatial unit vectors pointing from the individual camera centers to the respective world points. We denote these measurements $\mathbf{b}_i^j$, meaning the measurement of point $\mathbf{p}_i$ (with camera c_i) in the MPC frame VP_j. Our derivations furthermore utilize the transformation $\mathbf{T}_{1j}^c$, which permits the direct transformation of points from the camera frame c in VP_j to the camera frame c in VP_1. All variables are indicated in Fig. 2.

3.2 Framework Overview

A flowchart of our proposed method detailing all steps including the initialization procedure is illustrated in Fig. 3. After the definition of a first (multi-perspective)

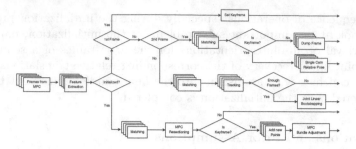

Fig. 3. Overview of the proposed visual localization and mapping pipeline for MPC systems. The flowchart in particular outlines the detailed idea behind the initialization procedure.

keyframe[1], the algorithm keeps matching inter-camera correspondences between the first and subsequent MPC frames until the average of the median frame-to-frame disparity for each camera surpasses a predefined threshold (verified in the decision nodes "Is Keyframe?"). Once this happens, we add a second keyframe and compute all $\mathbf{T}_{12}^c$ using classical single camera calibrated relative pose computation [26]. We furthermore triangulate an individual point cloud for every camera in the MPC array. Subsequent frames from the individual cameras are then aligned with respect to these maps using classical single camera calibrated absolute pose computation [16]. Once enough frames are collected, the initialization is completed by the joint, linear MPC pose initialization module outlined in Sects. 3.3 and 3.4. Note that individual single camera tracking is only performed in order to eliminate outlier measurements and obtain prior knowledge about relative rotations. It bypasses the weakness of methods such as [13] of not being able to deliver robust generalized relative pose results in most practically relevant cases. The actual final initialization step and all subsequent modules then perform joint MPC measurement processing.

After the initialization is completed, the frames of each new MPC pose are matched individually to the frames of the most recent MPC keyframe, but the alignment is solved jointly using generalized camera absolute pose computation [12]. We keep checking the local distinctiveness of every MPC frame by evaluating the frame-to-frame disparities in the above outlined manner, and add new keyframes everytime the threshold is surpassed. To conclude, we add new 3D points everytime a new keyframe is added, and perform generalized windowed bundle adjustment to jointly optimize over several recent MPC poses and the 3D landmark positions. This back-end optimization procedure is outlined in Sect. 3.5.

---

[1] *Keyframes* are simply frames that are retained in a buffer of frames due to sufficient local distinctiveness [10].

3.3 Initial Estimation of Relative Rotations

The very first part of our computation executes visual odometry in each camera individually. In order to make use of the relative orientations, we propose to first eliminate the redundancy in the information. This is done by first combining the computed orientations with the camera-to-MPC transformations $\mathbf{T}_c$ in order to obtain relative orientation estimates for the entire MPC rig. We now have k samples for the MPC frame-to-frame orientations in the frame buffer. We apply L_1 rotation averaging based on the Weiszfeld algorithm as outlined in [6] in order to obtain an accurate, unique representation.

3.4 Joint Linear Bootstrapping

The computation steps until here provide sets of inlier inter-camera correspondences and reasonable relative rotations between subsequent MPC frames. The missing variables towards a successful bootstrapping of the computation are given by MPC positions and point depths. Translations and point depths can also be taken from the prior individual visual odometry computations [9], but they may be unreliable, and—more importantly—have different unknown visual scale factors that would first have to be resolved.

We propose a new solution to this problem which solves for all scaled variables (i.e. positions and point depths) through one joint, closed-form, linear initialization procedure. What we are exploiting here is the known fact that structure from motion can be formulated as a linear problem once the relative rotations are subtracted from the computation (although results will not minimize a geometrically meaningful error anymore).

Let us assume that we have two MPC view-points VP_1 and VP_j. We start by formulating the hand-eye calibration constraint for a camera c inside the MPC.

$$\begin{cases} \mathbf{t}_c = \mathbf{t}_{1j} + \mathbf{R}_{1j} \cdot \mathbf{t}_c + \mathbf{R}_{1j} \cdot \mathbf{R}_c \cdot \mathbf{t}_{j1}^c \\ \mathbf{R}_c = \mathbf{R}_{1j} \cdot \mathbf{R}_c \cdot \mathbf{R}_{j1}^c \end{cases} \tag{1}$$

Let us now assume that there is one observed world point $\mathbf{p}_i$ giving rise to the measurements $\mathbf{b}_i^1$ and $\mathbf{b}_i^j$ inside the camera. The latter now has the index c_i. The point inside the first camera is simply given as $\lambda_i \cdot \mathbf{b}_i^1$, where λ_i denotes the depth of $\mathbf{p}_i$ seen from camera c_i in VP_1. We now apply $\mathbf{T}_{j1}^{c_i}$ and transform this point into camera c_i of VP_j. In here, the point obviously needs to align with the direction $\mathbf{b}_i^j$, which leads us to the constraint

$$(\mathbf{R}_{j1}^{c_i} \cdot \lambda_i \cdot \mathbf{b}_i^1 + \mathbf{t}_{j1}^{c_i}) \times \mathbf{b}_i^j = 0. \tag{2}$$

By replacing (1) in (2), we finally arrive at

$$(\mathbf{R}_{c_i}^T \cdot \mathbf{R}_{1j}^T \cdot \mathbf{R}_{c_i} \cdot \lambda_i \cdot \mathbf{b}_i^1) \times \mathbf{b}_i^j - (\mathbf{R}_{c_i}^T \cdot \mathbf{R}_{1j}^T \cdot \mathbf{t}_{1j}) \times \mathbf{b}_i^j = -\mathbf{R}_{c_i}^T \cdot \mathbf{R}_{1j}^T (\mathbf{t}_{c_i} - \mathbf{R}_{1j} \cdot \mathbf{t}_{c_i}) \times \mathbf{b}_i^j. \tag{3}$$

Let us now assume that we have n points and m MPC frames. The unknowns are hence given by λ_i, where $i \in \{1, \cdots, n\}$, and $\mathbf{t}_{1j}$, where $j \in \{2, \cdots, m\}$. We only use fully observed points, meaning that each point $\mathbf{p}_i$ is observed by camera c_i in each MPC frame, thus generating the measurement sequence $\{\mathbf{b}_i^1, \cdots, \mathbf{b}_i^m\}$. All pair-wise constraints in the form of (3) can now be grouped in one large linear problem $\mathbf{Ax} = \mathbf{b}$, where

$$
\mathbf{A} = \begin{bmatrix} (\mathbf{R}_{c_1}^T \mathbf{R}_{12}^T \mathbf{R}_{c_1} \mathbf{b}_1^1) \times \mathbf{b}_1^2 & & [\mathbf{b}_1^2]_\times \mathbf{R}_{c_1}^T \mathbf{R}_{12}^T \\ & \cdots & \\ & (\mathbf{R}_{c_n}^T \mathbf{R}_{12}^T \mathbf{R}_{c_n} \mathbf{b}_n^1) \times \mathbf{b}_n^2 & [\mathbf{b}_n^2]_\times \mathbf{R}_{c_n}^T \mathbf{R}_{12}^T \\ \cdots & \cdots & \cdots \\ (\mathbf{R}_{c_1}^T \mathbf{R}_{1m}^T \mathbf{R}_{c_1} \mathbf{b}_1^1) \times \mathbf{b}_1^m & & [\mathbf{b}_1^m]_\times \mathbf{R}_{c_1}^T \mathbf{R}_{1m}^T \\ & \cdots & \cdots \\ & (\mathbf{R}_{c_n}^T \mathbf{R}_{1m}^T \mathbf{R}_{c_n} \mathbf{b}_n^1) \times \mathbf{b}_n^m & [\mathbf{b}_n^m]_\times \mathbf{R}_{c_n}^T \mathbf{R}_{1m}^T \end{bmatrix}
$$
(4)

$$
\mathbf{x} = \begin{bmatrix} \lambda_1 \\ \cdots \\ \lambda_n \\ \mathbf{t}_{12} \\ \cdots \\ \mathbf{t}_{1m} \end{bmatrix} \quad \mathbf{b} = \begin{bmatrix} -\mathbf{R}_{c_1}^T \mathbf{R}_{12}^T (\mathbf{t}_{c_1} - \mathbf{R}_{12}\mathbf{t}_{c_1}) \times \mathbf{b}_1^2 \\ \cdots \\ -\mathbf{R}_{c_n}^T \mathbf{R}_{12}^T (\mathbf{t}_{c_n} - \mathbf{R}_{12}\mathbf{t}_{c_n}) \times \mathbf{b}_n^2 \\ \cdots \\ -\mathbf{R}_{c_1}^T \mathbf{R}_{1m}^T (\mathbf{t}_{c_1} - \mathbf{R}_{1m}\mathbf{t}_{c_1}) \times \mathbf{b}_1^m \\ \cdots \\ -\mathbf{R}_{c_n}^T \mathbf{R}_{1m}^T (\mathbf{t}_{c_n} - \mathbf{R}_{1m}\mathbf{t}_{c_n}) \times \mathbf{b}_n^m \end{bmatrix}
$$
(5)

$\mathbf{A}$ and $\mathbf{b}$ can be computed from the known extrinsics, inlier measurements, and relative rotations, whereas $\mathbf{x}$ contains all unknowns.

The non-homogeneous linear problem $\mathbf{Ax} = \mathbf{b}$ could be solved by a standard technique such as QR decomposition, thus resulting in $\mathbf{x} = (\mathbf{A}^T\mathbf{A})^{-1}\mathbf{A}^T\mathbf{b}$. However, in order to improve the efficiency, we utilize the Schur-complement trick and exploit the sparsity pattern of the matrix. Matrix $\mathbf{A}^T\mathbf{A}$ is divided into four smaller sub-blocks $\mathbf{A}^T\mathbf{A} = \begin{bmatrix} \mathbf{P} & \mathbf{Q} \\ \mathbf{R} & \mathbf{S} \end{bmatrix}$, and our two vectors $\mathbf{x}$ and $\mathbf{b}$ are decomposed accordingly thus resulting in $\mathbf{x} = [\mathbf{x}_1^T, \mathbf{x}_2^T]^T$ and $\mathbf{A}^T\mathbf{b} = [(\mathbf{A}^T\mathbf{b}_1)^T, (\mathbf{A}^T\mathbf{b}_2)^T]^T$. Substituted into the original equation $\mathbf{A}^T\mathbf{Ax} = \mathbf{A}^T\mathbf{b}$, and after variable elimination, we obtain

$$
\begin{cases} \mathbf{Px}_1 = \mathbf{A}^T\mathbf{b}_1 - \mathbf{Qx}_2 \\ (\mathbf{S} - \mathbf{RP}^{-1}\mathbf{Q})\mathbf{x}_2 = \mathbf{A}^T\mathbf{b}_2 - \mathbf{RP}^{-1}\mathbf{A}^T\mathbf{b}_1 \end{cases}
$$
(6)

This form permits us to first solve for $\mathbf{x}_2$ individually, a much smaller problem due to the relatively small number of MPC frames. $\mathbf{x}_1$ is subsequently retrieved by simple variable back-substitution.

3.5   Multi-perspective Windowed Bundle Adjustment

After bootstrapping, we can continuously use multi-perspective absolute camera pose computation [23] in order to align subsequent MPC frames with respect to the local point cloud. Furthermore, we keep buffering keyframes each time the average frame-to-frame disparity exceeds a given threshold. This in fact already constitutes a complete procedure for MPC visual odometry. In order to improve the accuracy of the solution, we add a windowed bundle adjustment back-end to our pipeline [7]. The goal of windowed bundle adjustment (BA) is to optimize 3D point positions and estimated MPC poses over all correspondences observed in a certain number of most recent keyframes. The key idea here is that points are generally observed in more than just two keyframes. By minimizing the reprojection error of every point into every observation frame, we implicitly take multi-view constraints into account, thus improving the final accuracy of both structure and camera poses. The computation is restricted to a bounded window of keyframes not to compromise computational efficiency. This form of non-linear optimization is also known as *sliding window bundle adjustment*.

Let us define the set $\mathcal{J}_i = \{j_1, \cdots, j_k\}$ as the set of MPC keyframe indices for which camera c_i observes the point $\mathbf{p}_i$. Let us furthermore assume that the size of the optimization window is s, and the set of points is already limited to points that have at least two observations within the s most recent keyframes. The objective of windowed bundle adjustment can now be formulated as

$$\left\{\hat{\mathbf{T}}_{m-s+1}, \cdots, \hat{\mathbf{T}}_m, \hat{\mathbf{p}}_1, \cdots, \hat{\mathbf{p}}_n\right\} =$$
$$\underset{\mathbf{T}_{m-s+1}, \cdots, \mathbf{T}_m, \mathbf{p}_1, \cdots, \mathbf{p}_n}{\operatorname{argmin}} \sum_{i=1}^{n} \sum_{j \in \mathcal{J}_i} \|\pi_{c_i}(\tilde{\mathbf{b}}_i^j) - \pi_{c_i}(\mathbf{T}_{c_i}^{-1}\mathbf{T}_j^{-1}\tilde{\mathbf{p}}_i)\|^2. \quad (7)$$

where

- $\mathbf{T}_j$ is parametrized minimally as a function of 6 variables.
- $j \in \{m - s + 1, \cdots, m\}$.
- π_{c_i} is the known (precalibrated) camera-to-world function of camera c_i. It transforms 3D points in homogeneous form into 2D Euclidean points.
- $\bar{\mathbf{x}} =$ takes the homogeneous form of $\mathbf{x}$ by appending a 1.
- $\pi_{c_i}(\tilde{\mathbf{b}}_i^j)$ is the original, measured image location of the spatial direction $\mathbf{b}_i^j$.

4   Experimental Results

We test our algorithm on both simulated and real data. The simulation experiments analyze the noise resilience of our linear bootstrapping algorithm. The real data experiment then evaluates the performance of the complete pipeline by comparing the obtained results against ground truth data collected with an external motion tracking system, as well as a loosely-coupled alternative.

4.1   Results on Simulated Data

We perform experiments on synthetic data to analyze the performance of our linear MPC pose initialization module in the presence of varying levels of noise. In all our simulation experiments, we simply use 2 cameras pointing into opposite directions, and generate 10 random points in front of each camera. We furthermore generate 10 homogeneously distributed camera poses generating near fronto-parallel motion for both cameras. To conclude, we add an oscillating rotation about the main direction of motion. The maximum amplitude of this rotation is set to either $5°, 7.5°, 10°, 15°$ or $20°$, which creates an increasing distance

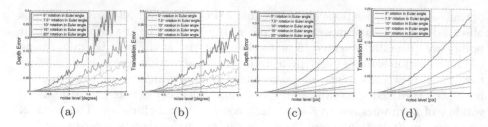

(a)   (b)   (c)   (d)

Fig. 4. Benchmark of our linear bootstrapping algorithm showing relative translation and 3D point depths error for different levels of noise in the relative rotation and 2D landmark observations. The experiment is repeated for different "out-of-plane" dynamics, which causes significant differences in the scale observability of the problem. Note that each value in the figures is averaged over 1000 random experiments.

to the degenerate case of Ackerman motion. We perform two separate experiments in which we add noise to either the relative rotations or the 2D bearing vector measurements pointing from the camera centers to the landmarks. The error for each noise level is averaged over 1000 random experiments.

In our first experiment, we add noise to the relative rotations by multiplying them with another random rotation matrix that is derived from uniformly sampled Euler angles with a maximum value reaching from zero to 2.5°. The reported errors are the relative depth error of the 3D points $\frac{\|\lambda_{est}\|}{\|\lambda_{true}\|}$, and the relative translation magnitude error $\frac{\|t_{est}\|}{\|t_{true}\|}$. The errors are indicated in Figs. 4(a) and (b), respectively.

In our second experiment, we simulate noise on the bearing vectors by adding a random angular deviation θ_{rand} such that $\tan \theta_{rand} < \frac{\sigma}{f}$, where f is a virtual focal length of 500 pixels, and σ is a virtual maximum pixel noise level reaching from 0 to 5 pixels. We analyze the same errors and the results are reported in Figs. 4(c) and (d), respectively.

As can be concluded from the results, a reasonable amount of noise in both the point observations as well as the relative rotations can be tolerated. However, the correct functionality of the linear solver depends critically on the observability of the metric scale. Limiting the maximum amplitude of the out-of-plane rotation to a low angle (e.g. below 5°) can quickly compromise the stability of the solver and cause very large errors. In practice, this means that accurate results can only be expected if we add sufficiently many frames with sufficiently rich dynamics to our solver.

4.2   Results on Real Data

We have been given access to the data already used in [9], which allows us to compare our method against accurate ground truth measurements obtained by an external tracking device, a loosely-coupled alternative [9], and a more traditional approach from the literature [3]. The data consists of two different sequences captured with a synchronized, non-overlapping stereo rig that contains two cameras facing opposite directions. For further details about the hardware including intrinsic parameter values as well as the extrinsic calibration procedure, the reader is kindly referred to [9]. The sequences are henceforth referred to as the *circular* and *straight* motion sequences. In the circular motion sequence, the rig moves with significant out-of-plane rotation along a large loop. In the straight motion sequence, the rig simply moves forward with significantly reduced out-of-plane rotation. Both *circular* and *straight* datasets run at 10FPS. All experiments are conducted on a regular desktop computer with 8 GB RAM and

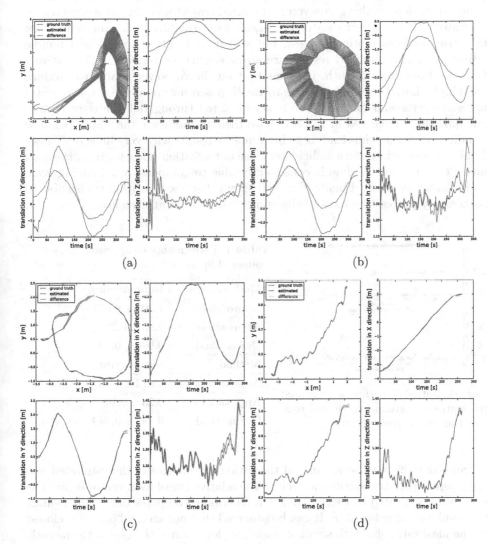

Fig. 5. Bottom row: results obtained on the circular and straight motion sequences from [9]. Top row: results obtained for different algorithm configurations that do not fully exploit the modules presented in this paper.

an Intel Core i7 2.8 GHz CPU. Our C++ implementation runs in real-time, and uses OpenCV [2], Eigen [5], OpenGV [11] and the Ceres Solver library [1]. op In order to assess the impact of our proposed linear bootstrapping and generalized sliding window bundle adjustment modules, we analyze three different algorithm configurations on the circular motion sequence. In our first test—indicated in Fig. 5(a)—we do not use our proposed initialization procedure, but simply rely on the method presented in [13] to bootstrap the algorithm from a pair of sufficiently separated frames in the beginning of the sequence. We tested numerous entry points, but the algorithm consistently fails to produce a good initial relative translation, thus resulting in severely distorted trajectories. In our second test—indicated in Fig. 5(b)—we rely on our linear bootstrapping algorithm to initialize the structure-from-motion process, but still do not activate windowed bundle adjustment. The obtained results are already much better, but still relatively far away from ground truth. It seems that our linear solver is able to produce meaningful initial values, but—due to the ill-posed nature of the problem—still has some error and further error is accumulated throughout the sequence. In our final test—indicated in Fig. 5(c)—we then also activate the sliding window bundle adjustment, thus leading to high-quality results with very little drift away from ground truth. Once a sufficiently close initialization point is given, the non-linear optimization module is consistently able to compensate remaining scale and orientation errors. Finally, Fig. 5(d) shows that the algorithm is also able to successfully process the more challenging straight motion sequence.

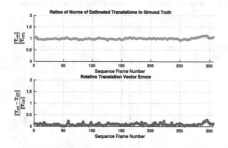

Fig. 6. Ratios of norms of estimated translations to ground truth and relative translation vector errors

Table 1. Performance comparison against [3,9]

Method	Ratio of norms
Approach by [3]	1.005 ± 0.071
Approach by [9]	0.90 ± 0.28
Our method	0.996 ± 0.038
Method	Vector error
Approach by [3]	0.079 ± 0.061
Approach by [9]	0.23 ± 0.19
Our method	0.092 ± 0.049

Similar to [9] we also calculated the ratio of the norms of the estimated and the ground truth translations as well as the relative translation vector error. The results are indicated in Fig. 6. Table 1 furthermore compares our result against the results obtained in [3,9]. It can be observed that our method operates closest to the ideal ratio of 1 with smallest standard deviation with respect to the ratio of norms of the estimated and ground truth translations. Looking at the relative translation vector error ratio, our result is very close to the one obtained in [9], and again achieves smaller standard deviation. The better standard deviation makes us believe that part of the reason for the slightly worse mean may be biases originating from an imperfect alignment with ground truth.

As a final test, we consider it important to verify the performance of our linear bootstrapping algorithm on real data. Rather than applying it just in the very beginning of the dataset, we therefore test if the initialization method can work for arbitrary starting positions across the entire circular motion sequence. The test result of the ratio of norms of estimated and ground truth translations is indicated in Fig. 7. The mean value of the ratio equals to 0.956 and the standard deviation is 0.075. We can conclude that, at least on this sequence, the linear initialization module performs consistently well.

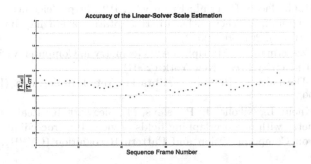

Fig. 7. Accuracy of the linear bootstrapping technique for various starting points across the entire circular motion sequence.

5   Discussion

This paper introduces a complete pipeline for motion estimation with non-overlapping multi-perspective camera systems. The main novelty lies in the fact that nearly all processing stages including bootstrapping, pose tracking, and mapping use the measurements from all cameras simultaneously. The approach is compared against a loosely coupled alternative, thus proving that the joint exploitation of the omni-directional measurements leads to superior motion estimation accuracy.

While our result represents an unprecedented integration of the paradigm of *Using many cameras as one* into a full end-to-end real-time visual odometry pipeline, there still remains space for further improvements. For example, one remaining problem is that the success of our approach still depends on sufficiently good relative rotations estimated from each camera individually at the very beginning. Future research therefore consists of pushing generalized relative pose methods towards a robust recovery of relative rotations even in the case of motion degeneracies. A further point consists of parameterizing poses with similarity transformations, which would simplify drift compensation in the case of extended periods of scale unobservability.

References

1. Agarwal, S., Mierle, K., et al.: Ceres solver. http://ceres-solver.org
2. Bradski, G.: The OpenCV library. Dr. Dobb's J. Softw. Tools (2000)
3. Clipp, B., Kim, J.H., Frahm, J.M., Pollefeys, M., Hartley, R.: Robust 6DOF motion estimation for non-overlapping, multi-camera systems. In: Proceedings of the IEEE Workshop on Applications of Computer Vision, Washington, DC, USA, pp. 1–8 (2008)
4. Engel, J., Schöps, T., Cremers, D.: LSD-SLAM: large-scale direct monocular SLAM. In: Fleet, D., Pajdla, T., Schiele, B., Tuytelaars, T. (eds.) ECCV 2014. LNCS, vol. 8690, pp. 834–849. Springer, Cham (2014). doi:10.1007/978-3-319-10605-2_54
5. Guennebaud, G., Jacob, B., et al.: Eigen v3 (2010). http://eigen.tuxfamily.org
6. Hartley, R., Trumpf, J., Yuchao, D., Li, H.: Rotation averaging. Int. J. Comput. Vis. (IJCV) **103**(3), 267–305 (2013)
7. Hartley, R., Zisserman, A.: Multiple View Geometry in Computer Vision, 2nd edn. Cambridge University Press, New York (2004)
8. Horaud, R., Dornaika, F.: Hand-eye calibration. Int. J. Robot. Res. (IJRR) **14**(3), 195–210 (1995)
9. Kazik, T., Kneip, L., Nikolic, J., Pollefeys, M., Siegwart, R.: Real-time 6D stereo visual odometry with non-overlapping fields of view. In: Proceedings of the IEEE Conference on Computer Vision and Pattern Recognition (CVPR), Providence, USA (2012)
10. Klein, G., Murray, D.: Parallel tracking and mapping for small AR workspaces. In: Proceedings of the International Symposium on Mixed and Augmented Reality (ISMAR), Nara, Japan (2007)
11. Kneip, L., Furgale, P.: OpenGV: a unified and generalized approach to real-time calibrated geometric vision. In: Proceedings of the IEEE International Conference on Robotics and Automation (ICRA), Hongkong (2014)
12. Kneip, L., Furgale, P., Siegwart, R.: Using multi-camera systems in robotics: efficient solutions to the NPnP problem. In: Proceedings of the IEEE International Conference on Robotics and Automation (ICRA), Karlsruhe, Germany (2013)
13. Kneip, L., Li, H.: Efficient computation of relative pose for multi-camera systems. In: Proceedings of the IEEE Conference on Computer Vision and Pattern Recognition (CVPR), Columbus, USA (2014)
14. Kneip, L., Li, H., Seo, Y.: UPnP: an optimal $O(n)$ solution to the absolute pose problem with universal applicability. In: Fleet, D., Pajdla, T., Schiele, B., Tuytelaars, T. (eds.) ECCV 2014. LNCS, vol. 8689, pp. 127–142. Springer, Cham (2014). doi:10.1007/978-3-319-10590-1_9
15. Kneip, L., Lynen, S.: Direct optimization of frame-to-frame rotation. In: Proceedings of the International Conference on Computer Vision (ICCV), Sydney, Australia (2013)
16. Kneip, L., Scaramuzza, D., Siegwart, R.: A novel parametrization of the perspective-three-point problem for a direct computation of absolute camera position and orientation. In: Proceedings of the IEEE Conference on Computer Vision and Pattern Recognition (CVPR), Colorado Springs, USA (2011)
17. Konolige, K., Agrawal, M., Solà, J.: Large scale visual odometry for rough terrain. In: Proceedings of the International Symposium on Robotics Research (ISRR), Hiroshima, Japan (2007)

18. Li, H., Hartley, R., Kim, J.H.: A linear approach to motion estimation using generalized camera models. In: Proceedings of the IEEE Conference on Computer Vision and Pattern Recognition (CVPR), Anchorage, Alaska, USA, pp. 1–8 (2008)
19. Mur-Artal, R., Montiel, J.M.M., Tardós, J.D.: ORB-SLAM: a versatile and accurate monocular SLAM system. IEEE Trans. Robot. (T-RO) **31**(5), 1147–1163 (2015)
20. Newcombe, R., Lovegrove, S., Davison, A.: DTAM: dense tracking and mapping in real-time. In: Proceedings of the International Conference on Computer Vision (ICCV), Barcelona, Spain (2011)
21. Newcombe, R.A., Izadi, S., Hilliges, O., Molyneaux, D., Kim, D., Davison, A.J., Kohli, P., Shotton, J., Hodges, S., Fitzgibbon, A.: Kinectfusion: real-time dense surface mapping and tracking. In: Proceedings of the International Symposium on Mixed and Augmented Reality (ISMAR) (2011)
22. Nistér, D., Naroditsky, O., Bergen, J.: Visual odometry. In: Proceedings of the IEEE Conference on Computer Vision and Pattern Recognition (CVPR), Washington, DC, USA, pp. 652–659 (2004)
23. Nistér, D., Stewénius, H.: A minimal solution to the generalized 3-point pose problem. J. Math. Imaging Vis. (JMIV) **27**(1), 67–79 (2006)
24. Pless, R.: Using many cameras as one. In: Proceedings of the IEEE Conference on Computer Vision and Pattern Recognition (CVPR), Madison, WI, USA, pp. 587–593 (2003)
25. Steinbrücker, F., Sturm, J., Cremers, D.: Real-time visual odometry from dense RGB-D images. In: IEEE International Conference on Computer Vision Workshops (ICCV Workshops) (2011)
26. Stewénius, H., Engels, C., Nistér, D.: Recent developments on direct relative orientation. ISPRS J. Photogramm. Remote Sens. **60**(4), 284–294 (2006)
27. Stewénius, H., Nistér, D.: Solutions to minimal generalized relative pose problems. In: Workshop on Omnidirectional Vision (ICCV), Beijing, China (2005)
28. Strasdat, H., Davison, A.: Scale drift-aware large scale monocular SLAM. In: Proceedings of Robotics: Science and Systems (RSS), Zaragoza, Spain (2010)
29. Tykkälä, T., Audras, C., Comport, A.I.: Direct iterative closest point for real-time visual odometry. In: IEEE International Conference on Computer Vision Workshops (ICCV Workshops) (2011)
30. Whelan, T., Johannsson, H., Kaess, M., Leonard, J.J., McDonald, J.: Robust real-time visual odometry for dense RGB-D mapping. In: Proceedings of the IEEE International Conference on Robotics and Automation (ICRA) (2013)

Visual Inspection

A Vision Inspection System for the Defects of Resistance Spot Welding Based on Neural Network

Shaofeng Ye, Zhiye Guo, Peng Zheng, Lei Wang, and Chun Lin[✉]

School of Aerospace, Xiamen University, Xiamen, China
linchun@xmu.edu.cn

Abstract. The appearance of spot welding reflects the quality of welding to a large extent. In this study, we developed a vision inspection system, which recognizes the defects of weld in electronic components based on neural network. First, the images of weld are acquired by color camera. Then, we extracted 15 features from the welding images that had been corrected and enhanced. Finally, we used 1800 training samples to train the neural network. And then we got a accuracy of 95.82% under 407 testing samples by the neural network classifier, which had 15 input nodes, 4 hidden nodes and 2 output nodes.

Keywords: RSW · Neural network · Machine vision · Defect detection

1 Introduction

The resistance spot welding is widely used in electronics industries [1]. The process is easily influenced by voltage, electric current and action time. It is necessary to detect the quality of the weld in electronic components.

Researchers have present various methods for weld quality. Destructive test was the most common method that widely used to inspect the quality of welding [2, 3]. Cho and Rhee developed a system to measure dynamic resistance and estimate the weld quality [4]. Ultrasonic testing as a nondestructive test method also has been used to evaluate the quality of weld [5, 6]. Ruisz et al. introduced a nondestructive on-line real-time processing system for quality evaluation in resistance spot by analyzing the weld fingerprint on metal bands [7]. Wang et al. detected the line weld defects based on multiple thresholds from X-ray images [8]. Zhang et al. used neural network to recognize the defect from radiographic weld images [9].

In this study, we developed a vision inspection system based on neural network. The weld images are acquired first. After image correction, we preprocessed the images and extracted features. The neural network has been trained with training samples. Finally, we used the neural network classifier to test the testing images.

M. Liu et al. (Eds.): ICVS 2017, LNCS 10528, pp. 161–168, 2017.
DOI: 10.1007/978-3-319-68345-4_14

2 Image Preprocessing

The weld images are acquired by Basler daA1280-54uc color camera with the resolution 1280 * 960. The non-defect is shown in Fig. 1, also some typical defects such as too long, serious offset, partial missing and solder skips.

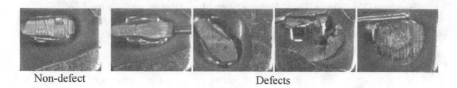

Non-defect   Defects

Fig. 1. The images of weld

2.1 Position Correction

In order to make sure the bottom workpiece are all in the same absolute position, we use the method of model matching to get a model from a standard image and use the model to find a best matches in new images. After matching, we can get a relative position between the new image and the standard image.

2.2 Image Enhancing

The images are decomposed to three single channel gray images that used to extract the region of weld from background. In order to reduce the noise and improve the contrast of weld to its background, we use red channel image subtract blue channel image. Then enhance the image that is get from subtraction. The enhancement image is shown in Fig. 2.

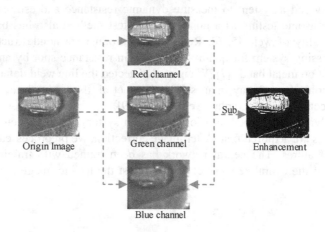

Fig. 2. Image enhancement

The region of weld has high contract to its background and easily to be extracted by simple threshold segment.

The experiment results show that the enhance method robust to difference color and difference light condition, as the Fig. 3 shows.

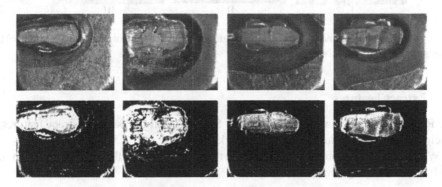

Fig. 3. The image enhance result of difference color and light (Color figure online)

3 Feature Extraction

3.1 Segment Image

The dynamic threshold that is a local threshold segmentation is used to segment the enhancement image [10]. First, use mean filter to smooth the enhancement image. Then, segment the region (Region A) of weld with the smooth image. For some defect images, the segmentation can't able to segment full region of weld shown in Fig. 5II.

In order to segment the weld region completely, we try to use the method of neural network. We select six regions shown in Fig. 4 to train neural network and then get a classifier. The six regions contains the weld, the background, the shadow that is different from background, the missing weld area and so on, so that we can segment the image to six specific region. The region of spot weld (Region B) segmented by neural network classifier is shown in Fig. 5III.

Fig. 4. 6 regions for color training

I   II   III

Fig. 5. Segmentation of the weld area: I. Origin image, II. Segment image with threshold, III. Segment image with ANN.

3.2   Extract Features

The Region A and Region B segmented in Sect. 3.1 will be used to extract features, which are the input vector of neural network.

We extract some geometrical parameters that directly reflect the size and position of welding from the segmented weld region.

- The area, row coordinate, column coordinate and direction of the Region A.
- The area, convexity of the Region B.
- The mean value *Mean(HorProjection(r))*, derivative *Deviation(HorProjection(r))* of the vector *HorProjection(r)* that is the gray horizontal projection of the blue channel image within the Region B.

$$HorProjection(r) = \frac{1}{n(r+r')} + \sum_{(r+r',c+c')\in Region} Image(r+r',c+c') \quad (1)$$

where (r',c') denotes the upper left corner of the smallest enclosing axis-parallel rectangle of the input region. $n(x)$ denotes the number of region points in the corresponding row $r+r'$ or column $c+c'$.

For some partial lack welding samples, the right side of the weld region has a black region (Region C) that is shown in Fig. 6.

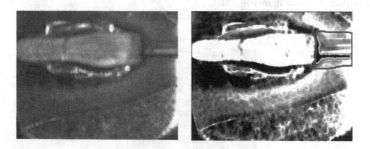

Fig. 6. Features of the over length weld

- The Region C's area and coordinate also be added to features vector.

In brief, there are 15 features that we extracted from weld image. But we can't use hard-threshold to decide whether the weld is a defect. So, we use neural network classifier to estimate the quality of weld.

4 Neural Network Classifier

Neural network is an information processing paradigm that is inspired by the way biological nervous systems, process information [11]. Just like a human being, learns by means of training [12]. The system is composed of a large number of highly interconnected processing elements (neurones) working in unison. The neural network model is shown in Fig. 7.

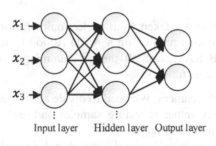

Input layer   Hidden layer Output layer

Fig. 7. Neural network model

There are three layers in the neural network we used and the activation function is Sigmod function.

$$f(x) = \frac{2}{1+e^{-ax}} - 1 \quad (-1 < f(x) < 1) \tag{2}$$

With the defined of activation, we can calculate the result of activation of the unit i in layer l.

$$a_i^{(l)} = f\left(\sum_{j=0}^{n} W_{ij}^{(l-1)} x_j + b_i^{l-1}\right) \tag{3}$$

where l denotes the current layer in the network, x_j is the input of the unit j in the layer $l - 1$. We write $W_{ij}^{(l-1)}$ to denote the weight of the connection between unit i in layer l and unit j in layer $l - 1$. And b_i^{l-1} is the bias associated with unit i in layer l. So $a_i^{(l)}$ is the result of activation of unit i in layer l. The procedure of training and classifying is shown in Fig. 8.

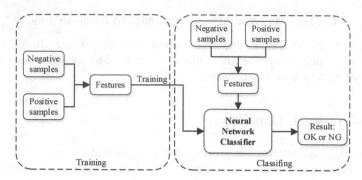

Fig. 8. The procedure of training and classifying

5   Experiment and Results

The images of welding spot are taken from a electronics factory using a color CCD camera. The implementation is running on a AMD Athlon II personal computer with 2.7-GHz CPU and 4 GB RAM, and all the programming is done in Halcon. The experiment and results are as follows:

- Acquire images by color camera. We need to divide all images into two groups that one is training samples anther is testing samples and each group has two class, defect images and non-defect images.
- Select a typical image, training a neural network color classifier.
- Extract features from all training images.
- Set the number of input layer units as 15, and the number of output layer units as 2. The number of hidden layer units should be confirmed by training a neural network with different number. So initialize a number of hidden layer units as 3, then training the network and get a classifier. The Training samples is shown in Table 1.
- Use the classifier to test testing samples and repeat the training process with changing the number of hidden layer units, so that we can get a group results shown in Table 2. The best number of hidden layer units is 4.
- We also need to detect the defect with normal approach that is only using image processing. The comparison results between neural network classifier and normal approach are shown in Table 3.

Table 1. Train samples

	Non-defect	Defect
Neural network classifier	1002	798

Table 2. The results of different number of hidden units

Hidden units number	Accuracy	Hidden units number	Accuracy
3	94.35%	8	94.10%
4	95.82%	9	93.37%
5	94.84%	10	93.61%
6	92.87%	11	90.91%
7	94.35%		

Table 3. The results of two methods

	Testing samples		Correct result		Accuracy
	Non-defect	Defect	Non-defect	Defect	
Neural network classifier	300	107	295	95	95.82%
Normal approach	300	107	297	74	91.15%

6 Conclusions

The quality of the weld in electronic component is very important for it directly affects the quality of products and its performance. We developed a vision system to detect the defects of weld based on neural network. A neural network classifier has been trained by the features that extracted from weld images. We used the testing samples to test the performance of the neural network and compared with normal approach that is only using image processing. The results showed that the neural network classifier had a higher accuracy than normal approach. But the neural network classifier would recognized the defect sample as non-defect and this is intolerance in factory. So, in the next work, we need to develop a more effective method to improve the performance of the neural network classifier to meet the requirement in the factory.

Acknowledgement. This work has been supported in part by the National Natural Science Foundation of China (21373173).

References

1. Zhang, Y., Chen, G., Lin, Z.: Study on weld quality control of resistance spot welding using a neuro-fuzzy algorithm. In: Negoita, M.G., Howlett, R.J., Jain, L.C. (eds.) KES 2004. LNCS, vol. 3215, pp. 544–550. Springer, Heidelberg (2004). doi:10.1007/978-3-540-30134-9_73
2. Khodabakhshi, F., Kazeminezhad, M., Kokabi, A.H.: Metallurgical characteristics and failure mode transition for dissimilar resistance spot welds between ultra-fine grained and coarse-grained low carbon steel sheets. Mater. Sci. Eng., A **637**, 12–22 (2015)
3. Khodabakhshi, F., Kazeminezhad, M., Kokabi, A.H.: On the failure behavior of highly cold worked low carbon steel resistance spot welds. Metall. Mater. Trans. A **45**, 1376–1389 (2014)

4. Cho, Y., Rhee, S.: New technology for measuring dynamic resistance and estimating strength in resistance spot welding. Meas. Sci. Technol. **11**, 1173–1178 (2000)
5. Chen, Z.H., Shi, Y.W., Jiao, B.Q., Zhao, H.Y.: Ultrasonic nondestructive evaluation of spot welds for bzinc-coated high strength steel sheet based on wavelet packet analysis. J. Mater. Process. Technol. **209**, 2329–2337 (2009)
6. Liu, J., Xu, G.C., Xu, D.S., Zhou, G.H., Fan, Q.Y.: Ultrasonic C-scan detection for stainless steel spot welding based on wavelet package analysis. J. Wuhan Univ. Technol. **30**, 580–585 (2015)
7. Ruisz, J., Biber, J., Loipetsberger, M.: Quality evaluation in resistance spot welding by analyzing the weld fingerprint on metal bands by computer vision. Int. J. Adv. Manuf. Technol. **33**, 952–960 (2007)
8. Wang, Y., Sun, Y., Lv, P., Wang, H.: Detection of line weld defects based on multiple thresholds and support vector machine. NDT&E Int. **41**, 517–524 (2008)
9. Zhang, X.G., Xu, J.J., Li, Y.: The research of defect recognition for radiographic weld image based on fuzzy neural network. In: Fifth World Congress on Intelligent Control and Automation, WCICA 2004 (2004)
10. Zhang, A.H., Yu, S.S., Zhou, J.L.: A local-threshold segment algorithm based on edge-detection. Mini-micro Systems 2003-04 (2003)
11. Neural Network: What is a Neural Network. http://www.doc.ic.ac.uk/~nd/surprise_96/journal/vol4/cs11/report.html#
12. Martín, Ó., López, M., Martín, F.: Artificial neural networks for quality control by ultrasonic testing in resistance spot welding. J. Mater. Process. Technol. **183**, 226–233 (2006)

Resistance Welding Spot Defect Detection with Convolutional Neural Networks

Zhiye Guo, Shaofeng Ye, Yiju Wang, and Chun Lin[✉]

School of Aerospace Engineering of Xiamen University, Xiamen 361005, China
linchun@xmu.edu.cn

Abstract. A convolutional neural network based method is proposed in this paper to classify the images of resistance welding spot. The features of resistance wielding spots are very complex and diverse, which made it difficult to separate the good ones and the bad ones using hard threshold. Several types of convolutional neural networks with different depths and layer nodes are built to learn the features of welding spot. 10 thousand labeled images are used for training and 3 hundred images are used to test the network. As a result, we get a 99.01% accuracy on test images, which is 97.70% better than human inspection.

Keywords: Welding spot · Defect detection · Convolutional neural networks

1 Introduction

In modern industry area, the visual inspection systems which are based on machine vision and machine learning algorithm have played a more important role than ever before, especially in the products defect detection. Machine vision has become faster and more precise along with the development of small and cost-effective hardware and has become widely used in various industrial fields. And image processing algorithms is a very important part of inspection systems which is based on machine vision. However, there are some complex problems that traditional image processing algorithms can-not deal with. The resistance welding spot defect detection is one of the tough problems. There are several essential factors acting on the quality of welding spot, such as shape, colors, position, texture, surface undulation and so on. And on the industrial pipeline, these factors are very sensitive to the welding equipment related parameters. Unfortunately, the parameters of welding equipment on the industrial pipeline is usually unstable, and it's responsible for an infinite variety of fantastic welding spot features. Artificial detection can really work exactly in some strange situations, but it is inefficient and may cause errors due to the tiredness of works when they work all day long in high speed state. It's necessary to build an automated machine not only on the basis of traditional machine vision technology but also includes machine learning algorithms.

A standard inspection system is coarsely divided in three main stages: image acquisition, feature extraction, and classification. In this paper, we use convolutional neural networks [1] to classify the welding spot. There are some typical images of welding spot shown in Fig. 1. The first row of Fig. 1 is normal welding spot and the

© Springer International Publishing AG 2017
M. Liu et al. (Eds.): ICVS 2017, LNCS 10528, pp. 169–174, 2017.
DOI: 10.1007/978-3-319-68345-4_15

second row of Fig. 1 is abnormal, from left to right the defect is spot too long, spot skewed, spot wrong position, spot crack. Though there are several different types of defects, in this paper we propose to use the convolutional neural network to divide all welding spot into two categories. There are two reasons for this kind of classification. First one is if dividing welding spot into multi-classification there are not enough samples of abnormal spot for each class. The other one is the inspection systems on the industrial pipeline needless to do the multi-classification but only can output which one is good and which one is not.

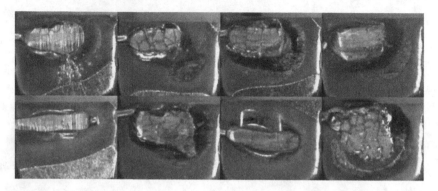

Fig. 1. Resistance welding spot sample image

2 Related Research

In 1980, convolutional neural network was proposed for Necognitron [2]. As the development of GPU-based parallel processing and the improvement of neural network algorithm, the CNN has already show its powerful ability not only in image classification but also in other fields such as language processing [3], speech recognition [4], and financial analysis. The mainly work of this paper is to build an industrial inspection systems which contain CNN algorithm. So we summarize some typical CNN applicate in defect detection and surface inspection systems.

- The paper [5] has built and tested different depth and layer nodes to select adequate structure for surface defect detection. The experiment shows that a single convolution neural network is enough to test several types of defects on textured and non-textured surfaces. And CNN shows higher performance than manual inspection both in time and cost saving.
- The paper [6] proposed a Max-Pooling Convolutional Neural Network to implement a classification task with 7 defects on a steel surface. And it performs supervised feature extraction directly from the pixel representation.
- The paper [7] has worked out an approach in visual defect detection using CNN. The experiment shows that the CNN shows well performance in 12 different classification categories and do not need much prior knowledge on the problem.

3   Construction of CNN

A neural network commonly includes nodes, layers, activate function, input and output, of course, training method and some algorithms that stop neural network from over fitting. For the selection of activate function, normally, we usually use ReLU (Rectified Linear Unit) [8] as activate function between two convolution layers. In this paper, we use ReLU which formula is in Eq. (1) as a convolutional layer activate function and use sigmoid which formula is in Eq. (2) as a fully connected layer activate function.

$$f(x) = \begin{cases} 0, & x < 0 \\ x, & x \geq 0 \end{cases} \tag{1}$$

$$f(x) = \frac{1}{1 + e^{-x}} \tag{2}$$

This is common structure of CNN as shown in Fig. (2). Input layer is the one for data to input, and the output layer can output the result of network, which is the class type in this paper. And we just want to divide the image samples into two categories, so there is only one output node. Result 1 means the good product, 0 map to the bad one. The hidden layers usually consist of some convolution layers, some pooling layers and some fully connected layers. In this paper, we compared three different kinds of depth of convolution layers and pooling layers, but we only use two fully connected layers because two full-connection layers are enough to perform well.

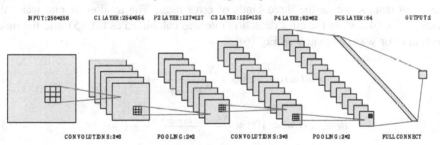

Fig. 2. The structure of CNN

For the CNN training, the training samples will contain images and labels. Label is a mark of image which can indicate that the image belongs to which category. At the training time, there are two steps for training a CNN. First one is forward propagation. However, the most important step is the second one which is called back propagation. The results output from forward propagation will be compared to the actual results. And this method is called the loss function. In this paper, we use cross entropy as the loss function. Where the formula is shown at Eq. (3). The function shows how different between the predict result and the actual one. And we generally use batch gradient decent to train neural network to make the error reverse back from last layer to the first layer. Therefore, all the weight of network will be adjusted according to the error. This progress is called optimization. And in this paper, we use ADADELTA (An Adaptive Learning Rate Method) as optimization algorithm [9].

$$C = -\frac{1}{n}\sum_x [ylna + (1 - y)ln(1 - a)] \tag{3}$$

4   Experimental Result

We use python as the programming language. And training CNN on the Intel i7 desktop with GTX1070 GPU to accelerate. The training image is three channel. Origin image size is 1280 * 960, and we resize it into 256 * 256 for speeding up. Although we use CNN to divide the dataset into two categories, there are several kinds of defects in the actual production process. In addition, the number of negative sample images is far less than the positive one. So we divide the sample image into several classes according to defect types with the help of skilled workers. The result of it as the labels of sample images. And then we use the random algorithm to pick up fixed number of images from these different defect types as test sample images. The number of test sample images of each different defect types we chose depends on the total number of the defect samples. Too many images in the training dataset may lead to an overfitting, and too little images could make CNN learn nothing. And finally there are 11026 images for training and 304 images for testing. We use iterator to read in training set batch by batch, of cause, training set will be shuffle. The loss function is cross entropy and the optimization algorithm is ADADELTA. We use add dropout layer to the construct of CNN to prevent CNN from over fitting [10]. In order to evaluate the experiment results, we define three kinds of error rates. The total error rate was calculated as Eq. (4), while the error detection rate was calculated as Eq. (5), and the miss detection error was calculated as Eq. (6).

$$total\, error = 100 \times \frac{N_{incorrect\, class}}{N_{test\, samples}}(\%) \tag{4}$$

$$detect\, error = 100 \times \frac{N_{positive\, as\, negetive\, class}}{N_{test\, samples}}(\%) \tag{5}$$

$$omission\, error = 100 \times \frac{N_{negetive\, as\, positive\, class}}{N_{test\, samples}}(\%) \tag{6}$$

In this paper, we test three kinds of structures of CNN. The first architecture has 6 hidden layers, a convolutional layer with 32 maps and filters of size 3 * 3, a max-pooling layer of size 2 * 2, a dropout layer of 0.25%, a convolutional layer with 64 maps and filters of size 3 * 3, a max-pooling layer of size 2 * 2, a dropout layer of 0.25%, a fully connected layer with 64 neurons, a fully connected layer with 1 output which would be one or zero (5HL-CNN). In the second one we add a convolution layer with 128 maps and filters of size 3 * 3, a max-pooling layer of size 2 * 2 after the four layer of 5HL-CNN, and we abbreviate it as 7HL-CNN. The last one has 13 hidden layers. The construction of 13HL-CNN is shown at Table 1.

Table 1. Structure of 13HL-CNN

Layer (type)	Output shape	Parament num.
convolution2d_1 (Convolution2D)	(None, 32, 254, 254)	896
maxpooling2d_1 (MaxPooling2D)	(None, 32, 127, 127)	0
convolution2d_2 (Convolution2D)	(None, 32, 125, 125)	9248
maxpooling2d_2 (MaxPooling2D)	(None, 32, 62, 62)	0
convolution2d_3 (Convolution2D)	(None, 64, 60, 60)	18496
maxpooling2d_3 (MaxPooling2D)	(None, 64, 30, 30)	0
convolution2d_4 (Convolution2D)	(None, 64, 28, 28)	36928
maxpooling2d_4 (MaxPooling2D)	(None, 64, 14, 14)	0
convolution2d_5 (Convolution2D)	(None, 128, 12, 12)	73856
maxpooling2d_5 (MaxPooling2D)	(None, 128, 6, 6)	0
convolution2d_6 (Convolution2D)	(None, 128, 4, 4)	147584
maxpooling2d_6 (MaxPooling2D)	(None, 128, 2, 2)	0
dense_1 (Fully connected)	(None, 64)	32832
dense_2 (Fully connected)	(None, 1)	65

We train each kind of structure of CNN about 50 epochs. The error rates of different kind CNN structure was shown at Table 2. The result shows that 13HL-CNN get the best result on the defect detection. We run three types of CNN at the same time. And the average time per epoch do not show that the deeper one CNN cost a more training time but nearly. Although 13HL-CNN is deeper than the others, the parament of 13HL-CNN is less than 7HL-CNN due to the more convolutional layers which have a sharing paraments characteristics. Result in Table 2 shows that 13HL-CNN is better than human inspection. The man who took this detection experiment was trained several hours in the way of watching positive and negative image samples. Then finally arrived a 97.70% accuracy.

Table 2. Experiment result of different structure CNN

Detect method	Total error	Detect error	Omission error	Average time per epoch
5HL-CNN	7.89%	2.63%	5.26%	261.68 s
7HL-CNN	4.93%	2.63%	2.3%	266.24 s
13HL-CNN	0.99%	0.32%	0.63%	267.26 s
Human	2.30%	1.64%	0.66%	–

5 Conclusion

This paper proposes a new defect detection method of resistance welding spot, which is called CNN. And the results of experiment show that CNN has a great advantage than traditional inspection neither manual inspection nor machine vision inspection based on image processing. Through several different types of experiment, we finally get a structure of CNN which makes the total error of resistance welding spot defect detection at 99.01%. It is also clearly that CNN do not need a lot of prior knowledge and human intervention. Once a CNN is trained fully, it will perform well.

Acknowledgments. This work has been supported in part by the National Natural Science Foundation of China (21373173).

References

1. LeCun, Y., Bottou, L., Bengio, Y., Haffner, P.: Gradient-based learning applied to document recognition. Proc. IEEE **86**(11), 2278–2324 (1998)
2. Fukushima, K.: Neocognitron: a self-organizing neural network model for a mechanism of pattern recognition unaffected by shift in position. Biol. Cybern. **36**(4), 193–202 (1980)
3. Collobert, R., Weston, J.: A unified architecture for natural language processing: deep neural networks with multitask learning. In: Proceedings of the 25th ICML, vol. 25, pp. 160–167 (2008)
4. Hinton, G., Deng, L., Yu, D., Dahl, G.E., Mohamed, A.-R., et al.: Deep neural networks for acoustic modeling in speech recognition: the shared views of four research groups. IEEE Sig. Process. Mag. **29**(6), 82–97 (2012)
5. Park, J.-K., Kwon, B.-K., Park, J.-H., Kang, D.-J.: Machine learning-based imaging system for surface defect inspection. Int. J. Precis. Eng. Manuf.-Green Tech. **3**, 303–310 (2016)
6. Masci, J., Meier, U., Ciresan, D., Schmihuber, J.: Steel defect classification with max-pooling convolutional neural networks. In: WCCI 2012 IEEE World Congress on Computational Intelligence, June 2012
7. Weimer, D., Scholz-Reiter, B., Shpitalni, M.: Design of deep convolutional neural network architectures for automated feature extraction in industrial inspection. CIRP Ann.-Manuf. Techonol. **65**, 417–420 (2016)
8. Glorot, X., Bordes, A., Bengio, Y.: Deep sparse rectifier neural networks. J. Mach. Learn. Res. (2010)
9. Zeiler, M.D.: ADADELTA: an adaptive learning rate method, 22 December 2012. arXiv:1212.5701v1 [cs.LG]
10. Srivastava, N., Hinton, G., Krizhevsky, A., et al.: Dropout: a simple way to prevent neural networks from overfitting. J. Mach. Learn. Res. **15**(1), 1929–1958 (2014)

Semi-automatic Training of an Object Recognition System in Scene Camera Data Using Gaze Tracking and Accelerometers

Matteo Cognolato[1,2]([✉]), Mara Graziani[3], Francesca Giordaniello[3],
Gianluca Saetta[4], Franco Bassetto[5], Peter Brugger[4], Barbara Caputo[3],
Henning Müller[1], and Manfredo Atzori[1]

[1] University of Applied Sciences Western Switzerland (HES-SO), Sierre, Switzerland
matteo.cognolato@hevs.ch
[2] Rehabilitation Engineering Laboratory, ETH Zurich, Zurich, Switzerland
[3] University of Rome "La Sapienza", Rome, Italy
[4] Department of Neurology, University Hospital of Zurich, Zurich, Switzerland
[5] Clinic of Plastic Surgery, Padova University Hospital, Padova, Italy

Abstract. Object detection and recognition algorithms usually require large, annotated training sets. The creation of such datasets requires expensive manual annotation. Eye tracking can help in the annotation procedure. Humans use vision constantly to explore the environment and plan motor actions, such as grasping an object.

In this paper we investigate the possibility to semi-automatically train object recognition with eye tracking, accelerometer in scene camera data, learning from the natural hand-eye coordination of humans. Our approach involves three steps. First, sensor data are recorded using eye tracking glasses that are used in combination with accelerometers and surface electromyography that are usually applied when controlling prosthetic hands. Second, a set of patches are extracted automatically from the scene camera data while grasping an object. Third, a convolutional neural network is trained and tested using the extracted patches.

Results show that the parameters of eye-hand coordination can be used to train an object recognition system semi-automatically. These can be exploited with proper sensors to fine-tune a convolutional neural network for object detection and recognition. This approach opens interesting options to train computer vision and multi-modal data integration systems and lays the foundations for future applications in robotics. In particular, this work targets the improvement of prosthetic hands by recognizing the objects that a person may wish to use. However, the approach can easily be generalized.

Keywords: Semi-automatic training · Object recognition · Eye tracking

---

M. Cognolato and M. Graziani have contributed equally to this work.

© Springer International Publishing AG 2017
M. Liu et al. (Eds.): ICVS 2017, LNCS 10528, pp. 175–184, 2017.
DOI: 10.1007/978-3-319-68345-4_16

1   Introduction

Grasping an object is a complex task with several senses being involved. Vision provides the information needed to precisely control the hand and perform the task. Vision precedes the grasping action according to precise schemes called "hand-eye coordination" [4,8]. Thus, the parameters related to eye-hand coordination can be used to provide information about the object that the subject is aiming to grasp. Object recognition and detection have been strongly improved during the last years, also thanks to the application of deep learning and Convolutional Neural Networks (CNNs) [20] that require much training data for optimal results. The creation of annotated datasets is most often done manually, which is expensive and time consuming. It was recently shown that eye tracking can simplify the annotation procedure [19,22].

Human gaze interacts with the surrounding reality in several ways. Gaze alternates between fixations (when the subject's gaze is stable on a portion of the scene) and saccades (when eyes and/or the body are moved to look somewhere else). The advancement of eye/gaze tracking devices allowed to identify where a subject is looking in real-time and in many scenarios. Thanks to these devices, it was shown that the gaze precedes and guides the hand also when performing grasps in routine tasks [12,17]. In the robotic literature the challenge of grasping various objects while regulating the control with visual information has been covered extensively. The object to be grasped is looked at 40–100 ms before the movement [2,9,16] and the fixation lasts for 350–450 ms [5,14]. During the fixation, the subjects attempts to detect the affordance of an object (the physical possibility of an action on the object). As Böhme and Heinke described in [3], the gaze naturally converges to the grasping point of tools [6]. Eye tracking and gaze information have already been introduced successfully in the control of manual prehension and object detection/recognition [19,22]. In Mishra et al. [18], the authors propose active segmentation methods using the fixation points in the image. Papadopoulos et al. [19] present a gaze-based method to annotate training sets for object detection. In Toyama et al. [22] the gaze information provided by a head-mounted eye tracker is used to perform real-time object recognition.

However, the parameters related to the natural hand-eye coordination have never been used to train an object recognition system. In this paper we investigate if this approach can be used to create a training dataset for object classification semi-automatically. The approach is tested on data acquired to investigate both vision and kinematic aspects of grasping, with the aim of improving the control of a myoelectric hand prosthesis. The test consisted of intact subjects grasping various objects with several grasps [11]. The data are acquired using head-mounted eye tracking with a scene camera and sEMG electrodes containing accelerometers. The dataset is then used to fine-tune and test a CNN to perform object recognition. Currently, the approach is designed and tested to be used to improve the control of a myoelectric hand prosthesis. Object recognition can make the prosthesis capable to autonomously understand the required grasp. Thus, it can improve control robustness. On the other hand, the same approach can easily be extended to create a dataset for object detection by annotating the position of the objects in the scene with a bounding-box.

2   Data Acquisition

2.1   Acquisition Setup

The acquisition setup is designed to support the experiment investigating the grasp of several objects. The setup is composed of acquisition hardware and software. The acquisition hardware is composed of a set of surface electromyography electrodes (Delsys Trigno Wireless EMG); a pair of eye tracking glasses with scene camera (Tobii Pro Glasses 2) and a laptop (Dell Latitude E5520). The acquisition software simultaneously records and stores all the data provided by the sensors.

The Delsys Trigno Wireless System consists of 14 electrodes, each equipped with a triaxial accelerometer. It records the surface EMG signal at 2 kHz and the accelerometers at 148 Hz with a baseline noise lower than 0.5 mV RMS (Root Mean Square). The electrodes are placed around the forearm of the subject using a dense sampling approach to record the activity of the muscles controlling the hand. Eight electrodes are placed around the forearm starting from the radio-humeral joint, forming a circular array. The other six electrodes are placed after the first eight, creating a second array in a more distal position, as shown in (Fig. 1). Those electrodes are placed in correspondence to the gap between the electrodes of the first array, starting from the gap between the first and second electrodes. A latex-free elastic band is used to maintain the electrodes in contact with the skin. The Tobii Pro Glasses 2 are a mobile lightweight gaze tracker recording both point-of-regard and scene in front of the subject. The gaze point data are sampled at 100 Hz with a theoretical accuracy and RMS precision of 0.5° and 0.3° respectively. The scene in front of the subject is recorded with a scene camera embedded in the frame in full HD resolution at 25 fps (frames per second). Finally, the laptop manages hardware connections and runs the acquisition software that guides the subjects during the exercise, while recording and storing the data from all the devices.

The acquisition software is a multithreaded application based on the producer-consumer pattern and developed in C++. To synchronize the data from the various sensors, a high resolution timestamp is assigned to each sampled datum. A Graphical User Interface (GUI) developed with Qt is used to guide the subject with vocal instructions.

2.2   Acquisition Protocol

The test was designed to investigate both kinematic and visual aspects of grasping. The aim is to robustly identify the grasp that the subject wants to perform. Each grasp is performed on several objects and, if appliable, several grasps are performed on the same object. Therefore, it mainly consists of grasping

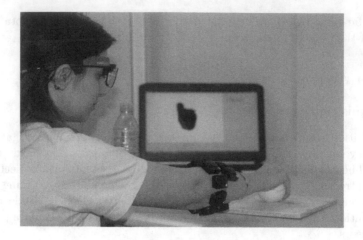

Fig. 1. Overview of the acquisition setup.

Grasp	1	2	3	4	5&6	7	8	9	10	11	12	13	14	15
Description	large diameter	small diameter	index finger extension	medium wrap	prismatic 4 fingers & writing tripod	power sphere	precision sphere	lateral	parallel extension	tripod grasp	power disk	using scissors	palmar pinch	adducted thumb
Objects														

Fig. 2. Overview of the objects and the grasps performed.

30 objects with 15 types of grasps. Grasps and objects are selected based on a grasp taxonomy [10] and their importance in Activities of Daily Living (ADL). The considered grasps together with the used objects are reported in the columns of Fig. 2.

The subject is asked to sit comfortably in front of a desk where the acquisition laptop and the objects to be grasped are positioned. Before each set of grasp repetitions two videos from lateral and first person points of view explain to the subject how to perform the grasp. During this phase, the subject can try the grasp the objects in order to get confident with them. Afterwards, a fixed image of the grasp is shown on screen in order to minimize the distractions during the exercise. The subject is guided by two vocal instructions: the first asking to grasp the object and the second to release it and to return to the rest position. The instructions have the same duration (four seconds) for both grasping and resting and they are recorded as stimulus signal. The exercise can be viewed as composed of five phases: (1) rest (arm comfortably leaning on the desk); (2) movement to reach an object; (3) grasp of an object; (4) release; (5) return to rest. Each grasp is repeated 12 times, while the number of repetitions performed on each object depends on the number of objects used for the specific grasp.

In order to avoid staring at objects between grasps, the subjects were asked to look at the eye tracker calibration target during the resting phase. The acquisition protocol was tested on 6 healthy subjects: 4 males, 2 females, average age 26.6 ± 5.3, all right handed.

3   Data Analysis

In this section we present the approach used to train a computer vision system semi-automatically with eye tracking and accelerometers using the scene camera data. Learning is based on the natural parameters of hand-eye coordination. The section is divided into two parts: the first describes the creation of the training dataset for object classification; the second describes the fine-tuning of the CNN using the created training dataset and the evaluation on the test data.

3.1   Creation of the Training Dataset

Several papers have already investigated the parameters of the coordination between gaze and grasping within eye-hand coordination [2,5,14,17]. They provide information that can be used to localize objects in the scene by detecting the beginning of the movement and the gaze fixations. Thus, we investigated and evaluated the feasibility of using these parameters to automatically extract video patches containing the object that the subject is aiming to grasp. These patches are then used to fine-tune a CNN and test it on the object recognition task.

The video patches containing the object that the subject is aiming to grasp are identified by first detecting the beginning of the movement that the subject performs to reach the object. Based on this, the gaze fixations related to the object to be grasped are used. We investigated two approaches to identify the beginning of the movement: the movement of the arm towards the object, identified with the accelerometer or when the hand started to be pre-shaped for grasping, identified as finger movement with the sEMG signals. However, preliminary analysis showed that the accelerometer performed better than the sEMG. Thus, it was decided to use the movement of the arm towards the object using the accelerometer signals. First, the data acquired are preprocessed and synchronized following the procedure described in [1].

In order to detect the beginning of the movement to reach the object, the forearm was considered as a rigid body to which all the sensors are firmly attached. The magnitude of the 3-axis acceleration vector is calculated for each sensor.

The signals obtained are averaged and the results denoised using a db2 wavelet of level 9. The beginning of the movement is identified as the maximum value of the signal obtained right after the resting of each repetition (identified thanks to the stimulus signal).

The eye fixation on the object to be grasped can be identified based on the parameters describing the eye-hand coordination. Following the results presented in the literature, the fixations are identified between 50 ms before and 450 ms after the beginning of the movement using the EyeMMV Toolbox [15]. A fixation cluster is identified when the gaze of the subject is remaining within a radius of 250 px for more than 70 ms. The fixation coordinates are calculated taking into account only the points with a fixed distance regarding the mean point of the cluster lower than 3 s, with $s = (s_x + s_y)^{1/2}$, s_x and s_y standard deviation of horizontal and vertical coordinates.

The identification of the fixation allows the automatic extraction of patches, centered around the fixation point and with a size of 512 by 512 pixels. The patches are extracted from the first two frames of the scene camera video after the beginning of the identified fixation. The labels of the patches, indicating which object the subject was asked to grasp, are assigned using the information provided by the stimulus signal. These patches are then used to fine-tune a CNN to recognize the object that the subject is aiming to grasp. A flow diagram of the proposed method is shown in Fig. 3.

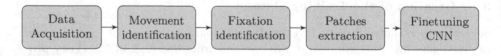

Fig. 3. Flow diagram of the proposed method.

3.2   Evaluation of the Training Dataset for Object Recognition

As reported in Sect. 1, CNNs are currently obtaining good results in many recognition tasks, including object recognition. The training data extracted are tested using one of the CNN architectures that has shown the best results on both image classification and single object localization: the GoogLeNet network [20]. The 2158 patches extracted (Subsect. 3.1) were divided into 30 classes representing the objects. The object recognition was performed using the Berkeley Vision and Learning Center (BVLC) GoogleNet model [21] pre-trained on the ImageNet Large Scale Visual Recognition Competition (ILSVRC) 2012 [7] using the deep learning framework caffe 1.0.0-rc3 [13] together with the framework NVIDIA Deep Learning GPU Training System (DIGITS). To evaluate the performance, a leave-one-person-out approach was used. The fine-tuning of the network is performed with the patches of 5 subjects and tested on the patches of the subject left out. The training and validation datasets are composed of 1438 and 360 (20%) patches on average resized to 256 px respectively. The test datasets contained the patches extracted from a single subject (360 patches on average).

4   Results

The top 1 object classification accuracy is $71.97\% \pm 2.67\%$, considering the 30 classes (range between 68.33% and 75.56%). The probability of having the correct class in the first 5 results (indicated as top 5 accuracy in Table 1) is, $82.53\% \pm 1.77\%$, with a range of 3.33% (81.39%–84.72%). The detailed results of the classification for each subject are reported in Table 1.

The average per-class accuracy (accuracy achieved on each object class) highlights how various objects can be more easily and robustly recognized by the detector. As shown in Table 2, the *remote control* is the object recognized with the best accuracy ($91.67\% \pm 12.91\%$), while *sunglasses* is the one with the lowest

Table 1. Top 1 and Top 5 accuracy on object identification for each subject.

	Top 1 accuracy [%]	Top 5 accuracy [%]
Sbj 1	70.00	80.56
Sbj 2	72.78	81.94
Sbj 3	68.33	81.39
Sbj 4	74.02	81.84
Sbj 5	75.56	84.72
Sbj 6	71.11	84.72
Average accuracy	71.97	82.53

Table 2. Average per-class object classification accuracies.

Object	Per-class accuracy [%]	Object	Per-class accuracy [%]
Belt	68.75 ± 4.19	Razor	55.56 ± 27.22
Book	69.45 ± 24.53	Remote control	91.67 ± 12.91
Fork	74.82 ± 17.94	Scissor	78.46 ± 16.21
Cardboard cup	63.89 ± 37.14	Screwdriver	78.94 ± 10.74
Hairbrush	68.10 ± 37.05	Shoe	45.00 ± 20.74
Key	65.65 ± 22.22	Cell phone	81.25 ± 15.31
Knife	79.17 ± 24.58	Torch	72.92 ± 16.61
Button	58.33 ± 49.16	Zip	61.90 ± 26.60
Mug	68.06 ± 26.04	Measuring tape	87.92 ± 6.74
Mouse	75.00 ± 29.35	Can	80.56 ± 12.54
Peeler	66.67 ± 40.83	Cup	60.00 ± 21.91
Pen	74.00 ± 16.00	Disk	56.25 ± 24.69
Bottle	80.00 ± 25.30	Handle	70.83 ± 29.23
Pencil	77.65 ± 10.89	Ball	76.25 ± 33.68
Plate	75.00 ± 22.36	Sunglasses	43.61 ± 15.00

per-class accuracy ($43.61\% \pm 15.00\%$). The *button* is the object with the highest classification uncertainty ($\pm 49.16\%$ of standard deviation) while the *belt* is the one classified with highest confidence ($\pm 4.19\%$ of standard deviation).

The per-class accuracies for all subjects (30 objects for 6 subjects) range from 0% to 100%. In 4 cases ($\sim 2\%$) the object is recognized in none of the tested images, so with a per-class accuracy of 0%. This happened for classes: *button* for Subject 1, *cardboard cup* for Subject 2, and *button* and *peeler* for Subject 3. On the other hand, in 44 cases ($\sim 24\%$) the object is recognized in all tested patches, so a per-class accuracy of 100%.

5   Discussion and Conclusion

The results show that the parameters of hand-eye coordination can be used to semi-automatically create a training dataset for object recognition from eye tracking, accelerometer and scene camera data. Several approaches can be applied to obtain further improvements.

The application of the eye-hand coordination parameters to gaze and accelerometer data allows the identification of the time interval during which the subject is looking at the object to grasp. This information allows to automatically identify the object within a video or image of the scene. The described procedure can be applied to semi-automatically create a training dataset, in particular in applications involving the eye-hand coordination, such as myoelectric hand prosthesis. A trained system can then be used to perform object recognition, for example to automatically identify the object that the subject is aiming to grasp. This can be useful in several applications and fields such as in robotics and prosthetics where movements can be adapted to objects to be grasped. The same approach can also be used to train or fine-tune object detectors by automatically drawing a bounding-box around the objects to annotate their position in the scene. It can be used to create a training set for object detection or recognition in a real world scenario, with the objects represented in various orientations and positions. Moreover, it can be also extended in an unsupervised scenario in which the ground truth is given by saying the object class and then transcribed by speech recognition.

A few aspects negatively influenced the results, in particular the quality of the patches and the small size of the dataset. The main limitation of the automatic extraction of the patches is related to object representation. Many external factors such as distraction or adaptation to the task (decreasing the level of visual attention) may have an influence on patch extraction. In some cases, the patches can contain: small parts of the object; the object being occluded by the subject's hand; the object to be grasped and parts of the other objects in the scene and background. In the worst case a patch does not contain any object (Fig. 4). From visual inspection we noticed that approximately one third of the patches extracted are not containing the object or just a small portion of it. Increasing the quality of the patches can most likely increase the performance of the classification. This can be done by segmenting the objects in the scene

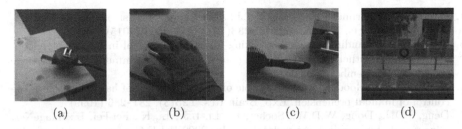

(a)   (b)   (c)   (d)

Fig. 4. (a) Objects correctly represented in the patch. (b) Object being occluded by the subject's hand. (c) Two objects partially represented in the patch. (d) The patch does not contain the object.

(for example, using an objectiveness filter or a region proposal network). The gaze information may then be used to select the object that the subject seems to be interested in, i.e. selecting the region of the object containing the gaze or the closest one. This can lead to a more robust and precise patch extraction, avoiding the mentioned problems. The acquisitions were made in the same location using the same setup and objects. This aspect that can influence the classification accuracy as well as limit the portability of the approach. On the other hand, it does not reduce the importance of the presented techniques. Increasing both size and variability of the dataset can also help to recognize a larger number of objects in various conditions, such as changing light. Moreover this method can easily be applied in a semi-supervised manner, setting a threshold for the classification accuracy below which the system requires human intervention to define the correct object in the scene.

The information provided by the eye-hand coordination was successfully used to semi-automatically create a training dataset for object detection and classification starting from eye tracking, accelerometer and scene video data.

Acknowledgments. The authors would like to thank A. Gigli, A. Gijsberts and V. Gregori from the University of Rome "La Sapienza" for their help on pre-processing the data, the Swiss National Science Foundation and the Hasler Foundation that partially supported this work via the Sinergia project # 160837 Megane Pro and the Elgar Pro project respectively.

References

1. Atzori, M., Gijsberts, A., Castellini, C., Caputo, B., Hager, A.G.M., Elsig, S., Giatsidis, G., Bassetto, F., Müller, H.: Electromyography data for non-invasive naturally-controlled robotic hand prostheses. Sci. Data **1**, 140053 (2014)
2. Biguer, B., Jeannerod, M., Prablanc, C.: The coordination of eye, head, and arm movements during reaching at a single visual target. Exp. Brain Res. **46**(2), 301–304 (1982)
3. Böhme, C., Heinke, D.: Where do we grasp objects? – an experimental verification of the selective attention for action model (SAAM). In: Paletta, L., Tsotsos, J.K. (eds.) WAPCV 2008. LNCS, vol. 5395, pp. 41–53. Springer, Heidelberg (2009). doi:10.1007/978-3-642-00582-4_4

4. Bulloch, M.C., Prime, S.L., Marotta, J.J.: Anticipatory gaze strategies when grasping moving objects. Exp. Brain Res. **233**(12), 3413–3423 (2015)
5. Castellini, C., Sandini, G.: Gaze tracking for robotic control in intelligent teleoperation and prosthetics. In: Proceedings of COGAIN - Communication via Gaze Interaction, November 2014 (2006)
6. Connolly, J.D., Goodale, M.A.: The role of visual feedback of hand position in the control of manual prehension. Exp. Brain Res. **125**(3), 281–286 (1999)
7. Deng, J.D.J., Dong, W.D.W., Socher, R., Li, L.J., Li, K., Fei-Fei, L.: ImageNet: a large-scale hierarchical image database. In: 2009 IEEE Conference on Computer Vision and Pattern Recognition (2009)
8. Desanghere, L., Marotta, J.J.: "Graspability" of objects affects gaze patterns during perception and action tasks. Exp. Brain Res. **212**, 177–187 (2011)
9. Desanghere, L., Marotta, J.J.: The influence of object shape and center of mass on grasp and gaze. Front. Psychol. **6**, 1537 (2015)
10. Feix, T., Pawlik, R., Schmiedmayer, H.B., Romero, J., Kragi, D.: A comprehensive grasp taxonomy. In: Robotics, Science and Systems Conference: Workshop on Understanding the Human Hand for Advancing Robotic Manipulation (2009)
11. Giordaniello, F., Cognolato, M., Graziani, M., Gijsberts, A., Gregori, V., Saetta, G., Hager, A.g.M., Tiengo, C., Bassetto, F., Brugger, P., Müller, H., Atzori, M.: Megane Pro: myo-electricity, visual and gaze tracking data acquisitions to improve hand prosthetics. In: ICORR. IEEE (2017)
12. Hayhoe, M.: Vision using routines: a functional account of vision. Vis. Cogn. **7**(1–3), 43–64 (2000)
13. Jia, Y., Shelhamer, E., Donahue, J., Karayev, S., Long, J., Girshick, R., Guadarrama, S., Darrell, T.: Caffe: convolutional architecture for fast feature embedding. In: Proceedings of the ACM International Conference on Multimedia (2014)
14. Johansson, R.S., Westling, G., Bäckström, A., Flanagan, J.R.: Eye-hand coordination in object manipulation. J. Neurosci. **21**(17), 6917–6932 (2001)
15. Krassanakis, V., Filippakopoulou, V., Nakos, B.: EyeMMV toolbox: an eye movement post-analysis tool based on a two-step spatial dispersion threshold for fixation identification. J. Eye Mov. Res. **7**(1), 1–10 (2014)
16. Land, M., Mennie, N., Rusted, J.: The roles of vision and eye movements in the control of activities of daily living. Perception **28**(11), 1311–1328 (1999)
17. Land, M.F.: Eye movements and the control of actions in everyday life. Prog. Retin. Eye Res. **25**(3), 296–324 (2006)
18. Mishra, A., Aloimonos, Y., Fah, C.L.: Active segmentation with fixation. In: IEEE 12th International Conference on Computer Vision (2009)
19. Papadopoulos, D.P., Clarke, A.D.F., Keller, F., Ferrari, V.: Training object class detectors from eye tracking data. In: European Conference on Computer Vision, pp. 361–376 (2014)
20. Russakovsky, O., Deng, J., Su, H., Krause, J., Satheesh, S., Ma, S., Huang, Z., Karpathy, A., Khosla, A., Bernstein, M., Berg, A.C., Fei-Fei, L.: ImageNet large scale visual recognition challenge. Int. J. Comput. Vis. **115**(3), 211–252 (2015)
21. Szegedy, C., Liu, W., Jia, Y., Sermanet, P., Reed, S., Anguelov, D., Erhan, D., Vanhoucke, V., Rabinovich, A.: Going deeper with convolutions. In: Proceedings of the IEEE Computer Society Conference on Computer Vision and Pattern Recognition (2015)
22. Toyama, T., Kieninger, T., Shafait, F., Dengel, A.: Gaze guided object recognition using a head-mounted eye tracker. In: Proceedings of the Symposium on Eye Tracking Research and Applications, ETRA 2012, vol. 1, no. 212 (2012)

A Surface Defect Detection Based on Convolutional Neural Network

Xiaojun Wu[1,2(✉)], Kai Cao[1], and Xiaodong Gu[1]

[1] Harbin Institute of Technology, Shenzhen 518055, Guangdong, China
wuxj@hit.edu.cn
[2] Shenzhen Key Laboratory for Advanced Motion Control and Modern
Automation Equipment, Shenzhen, Guangdong, China

Abstract. Surface defect detection is a common task in industry production. Generally, designer has to find out a suitable feature to separate defects in the image. The hand-designed feature always changes with different surface properties which lead to weak ability in other datasets. In this paper, we firstly present a general detecting method based on convolutional neural network (CNN) to overcome the common shortcoming. CNN is used to complete image patch classification. And features are automatically exacted in this part. Then, we build a voting mechanism to do a final classification and location. The good performances obtained in both arbitrary textured images and special structure images prove that our algorithm is better than traditional case-by-case detection one. Subsequently, we accelerate algorithm in order to achieve real-time requirements. Finally, multiple scale detection is proposed to get a more detailed locating boundary and a higher accuracy.

Keywords: CNN · Defect inspection

1 Introduction

Visual analysis for product surface is a common computer vision application. Current detection algorithm relies on human-designed features, which are always special and not comprehensive. So it is very difficult to have good portability and often limited by designer's experience. In some high structural texture image and special structure image, it seems difficult to distinguish background and target region. Although feature becomes more and more complex, detection effect is not significantly improved. On the other hand, Deep learning method becomes more and more popular, due to its strong ability in exacting feature. Defect detection is a specific application in industrial detection. In this paper, we introduce an easy surface detection method based on convolutional neutral network (CNN). In the second part of this paper, we briefly introduce the related work. In the third part, we introduce algorithm process, including the single scale detection algorithm, algorithm acceleration and the realization of multi-scale detection algorithm. In the fourth part, we verify the effectiveness of our algorithm on five different data sets, and give the corresponding analysis.

© Springer International Publishing AG 2017
M. Liu et al. (Eds.): ICVS 2017, LNCS 10528, pp. 185–194, 2017.
DOI: 10.1007/978-3-319-68345-4_17

2   Related Work

Generally, texture defect detection method can be divided into four main types: statistical, structural, filter based and model based. These algorithms choose hand-designed features as the core. Statistical methods include such as well-known techniques based on histogram [1] and co-occurrence matrices [2], structural approach [3] include such as texture elements extracted method. Filter based approach [4] include such as spatial domain and frequency domain filtering design. And there are also some model based approaches [5–7]. Although feature becomes more and more complex, designer's subjective experience and cognition still impact the effect of algorithm. A more obvious drawback is that almost all methods are only suitable for similar datasets and get bad results when little change occurred in datasets. In recent few years, deep learning has led to very good performance in several areas, such as visual recognition, speech recognition and natural language processing. Le Cun et al. establishing the modern framework of CNN called LeNet-5 [8]. Since 2006, many methods have been developed. AlexNet [9] is similar to LeNet-5 but with a deeper structure. Then several works are proposed to improve its performance such as ZFNet [10], VGGNet [11], GoogleNet [12] and ResNet [13]. All these networks have been proved to receive a decent object detection results on ILSVRC challenge. One of the most famous objects proposal based CNN detector is region-based CNN(R-CNN) [14]. CNN is proved more effective for different image sets than traditional method.

In this paper, we introduce an easy surface detection method based on CNN. Image features are automatic extracted. In the training stage, all we need to do is to prepare training data and labels. CNN extracts feature according to input characteristics and the labels. After that a voting mechanism is introduced for location. Then, we accelerate algorithm by using sliding window on feature map. When running time is cut down, we propose a multi-scale detection method by using two networks to obtain a more elaborate boundary and a higher accuracy. The follow-up experiment proves our algorithm has good detection performance on some texture image and some special structural image such as metallic gasket and screw image.

3   Methodology

This section presents all the works we have done, including three parts. Firstly, we explain the basic detecting scheme including how to build a convolution neural network (CNN) for image block classification and then how to locate the defect region. The algorithm can be divided into two parts: off-line training and on-line detection. An obvious drawback of CNN is that it needs a lot of time to compute. So referring to R-CNN method, we introduce a method to speed up the algorithm. And in the third part, we use two different networks to refine the results.

3.1   Detection Scheme

We use image blocks as input and design a CNN to classify image blocks. After this step, most background regions are excluded. Then, we use voting mechanism to exclude the interference of the background image blocks which are difficult to separate, realizing classification and location.

Network Structure Design. In this part, we design a network to extract feature and classify each image block. Figure 1 illustrates our CNN structure, it takes image blocks as input (the block size is 64 × 64). Firstly, network processes the block with several convolution and pooling layers to automatically extracted features. Then, inception layer raised from GoogLeNet [12] is used to rich network performance. Inception layer is composed by four branches, three of them are convolution kernels with size 1 × 1, 3 × 3, 5 × 5 and the rest branch is a 3 × 3 pooling kernel (shown in Fig. 1b). Each branch extracts features from the upper layer. Then features are concatenated together for the next layer. Compared with single layer, four branches make feature information richer for classification. Our specific parameters of CNN are shown in Table 1.

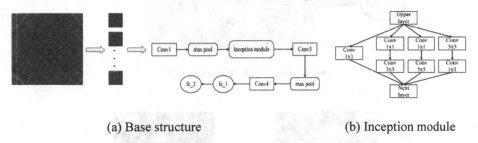

(a) Base structure   (b) Inception module

Fig. 1. CNN structure

Table 1. CNN parameters of layers

Layer ID	Layer type	Output (C × W × H)	Parameter (#kernel number × output size #stride #padding)
0	Input	3 × 64 × 64	
1	Convolution	16 × 32 × 32	16 × 5 × 5 #2 #2
2	Pooling	16 × 16 × 16	2 × 2 MAX
3	Inception	64 × 16 × 16	
4	Convolution	128 × 8 × 8	128 × 5 × 5 #2 #2
5	Pooling	128 × 4 × 4	2 × 2 AVE
6	Convolution	256 × 2 × 2	256 × 3 × 3 #1 #2
7	Full connection	384	
8	Full connection (softmax)	2	

Voting Mechanism. During the stage of patch-classification by CNN, we excluded most of the background regions. As whole image can often be divided into hundreds of patches, false detection is inevitable. In the detection process, an image block misclassification will lead to misclassification and location error in the whole image, as

Fig. 2 shows. Here, we propose a voting mechanism to solve this problem. In the process of image segmentation, the stride of sliding window is equal to half of the size of image block, so that two adjacent image blocks have 50% overlapped area and each pixel in the image is included in four image blocks. Four image blocks generate four CNN voting results. In the positioning process, when the defect votes exceed a certain threshold, the pixel is regarded as defect pixel, just as Fig. 3 shows.

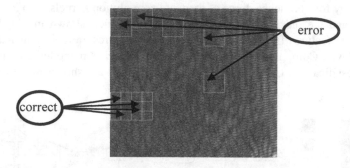

Fig. 2. Misclassification after CNN

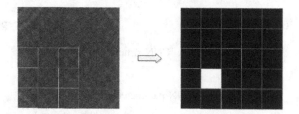

Fig. 3. Voting process

3.2   Algorithm Acceleration

Through the classification and voting mechanism of CNN, the algorithm can effectively realize the defect detection. In the other hand, a large number of data often means slow speed. Large computation is a disadvantage of convolutional neural network. Here, we take some acceleration method to improve the training speed and detection speed. Training speed and detecting speed is about 10 times faster through improvement.

Training Acceleration. Training time of CNN is affected by single iteration time and the number of iterations. When network structure is relatively fixed, single iteration time is relatively fixed. So we accelerate the convergence speed by adding a network branch. The structure of the branch is shown in Fig. 4. This branch is only used in training to avoid impact on detection results. After adding second branch (loss2 branch), the time required for a single iteration is slightly increased. While the total number of iterations drops rapidly, which lead to a nearly 8 times acceleration.

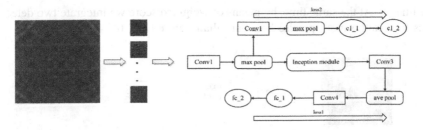

Fig. 4. CNN training mode

Detection Acceleration. Detection speed is important for a defect detection algorithm, however, it is a weakness of CNN. Inspired by fast R-CNN, we adjust the algorithm in order to obtain faster speed without affecting detection results. Whole image is used to replace image block when detecting. When the network spread to the last convolution layer, we get a larger feature map. Each 2×2 window on feature map corresponds to each original image block. So we make sliding windows on the feature map, the window size is 2×2. Then image blocks are predicted based on the judgment of each sliding window. With this method, we exclude redundant computation (shown in Fig. 5) and get an about 17 times acceleration. It takes almost 0.5 s with the input size 512×512 on GPU GT640M.

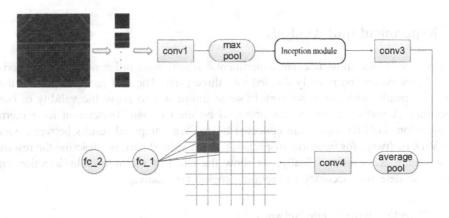

Fig. 5. Detecting process with acceleration

3.3 Multiple Scale Detection

We add more content for the algorithm to achieve a better detection results. Single block size is difficult to fully extract all defect features. So we put two different networks to get a new prediction. We choose the size of input image 64×64 and 32×32 to train two detection network separately. Score coming from the CNN trained with 64×64 images is multiplied by 0.6 and the score of CNN trained with 32×32 is multiplied by 0.4. With the weight score of the two CNN, we achieve better results on some images. At the same time, by means of weighted score we integrate two detection results to obtain a more precise boundary than before (Fig. 6).

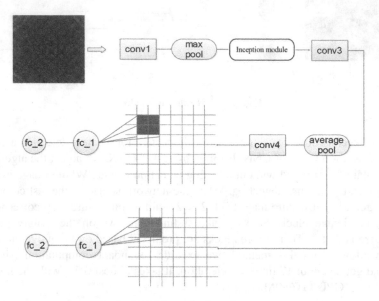

Fig. 6. Multiple scale detection process

4 Experiment and Analysis

In this section, we show relevant experimental results with different dataset. Experimental process can be roughly divided into three parts: The first part, we present the detection results with single network in some image sets to prove the validity of our algorithm. A part of these sets are provided by the German Association for Pattern Recognition (GAPR), others are collected by us. We compared results between ours and ViDi (software for industrial inspection). In the second part, we describe the results of algorithm acceleration. Finally, we show the effect of multiple scale detection on improving detection accuracy and refining region boundaries.

4.1 Detection with Single Network

In this part, we show the detection effect based on single network. We test on 3 different defect types. We train and test our framework on the dataset of DAGM 2007 [15], which representing regional defects, linear defects and point defects and the rest two image sets are collected by us which represent the defects of special structure. We train by SGD with momentum. We use a minibatch size of 128 patches which size is 64 × 64 and fixed learning rates of 10–4, the ratio of training defect patches and non-defect patches is 1:1. We use momentum 0.9, weight decay of 10–5. Detailed results are shown in Fig. 7 and Table 2. It is proved that our single network algorithm has strong detection capability and high applicability on all these image sets.

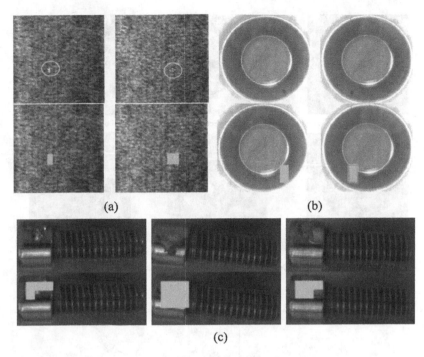

Fig. 7. Result images (a) DAGM defects (b) metallic gasket (c) screw image

Table 2. Detection result in different image sets

Data sets	Truth positive	Truth negative	False positive	False negative	Accuracy
Regional defects	985	150	0	15	98.6%
Linear defects	949	150	0	51	95.6%
Point defects	996	133	17	4	98.2%
Metallic gasket	13	24	2	2	89.1%
Screw image	18	27	3	2	90.0%

As shown in Fig. 8, we compare detection results between our algorithm and ViDi software. ViDi is the first industrial image analysis software based on deep learning. Using the same dataset, thanks to the voting mechanism, when ViDi algorithm fails to detect, we get a good result. Overall, our algorithm has an accuracy of 98.6% better than ViDi (94%).

4.2 Results of Algorithm Acceleration

Figure 9 shows acceleration in training process. From DAGM datasets, it is the iterations curve in training process. Before acceleration, CNN takes about 40000 iterations to make loss equal to 0.1. However, CNN only need 4000 iterations after adding loss2 to do the same work, almost 10 times faster. The weight of loss 1 and loss 2 are equal and result do not degrade.

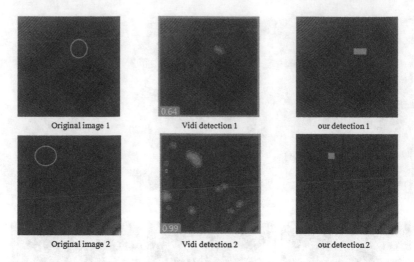

Fig. 8. Detection results compared with ViDi

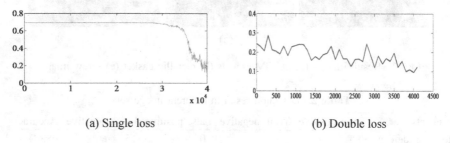

(a) Single loss   (b) Double loss

Fig. 9. The number of iterations with single loss structure

Table 3 shows (GPU GT640M) acceleration in detection process. We use sliding window on feature map to replace cutting image. Finally, we get a speed up about 17 times. Data in Table 3 is counted from the first image set.

Table 3. Time consumption comparison

Method	Time-consuming per image (s)
Cutting image	10.21
Feature map sliding method	0.5856
Speedup ratio	17.435

4.3 Detection with Multiple Network

After detection acceleration, we use two networks to enhance the detection effect. As shown in Fig. 10, the merged detection gets a better detection result. When both networks hit defect region, bagging CNN shows a more detailed region boundary. And

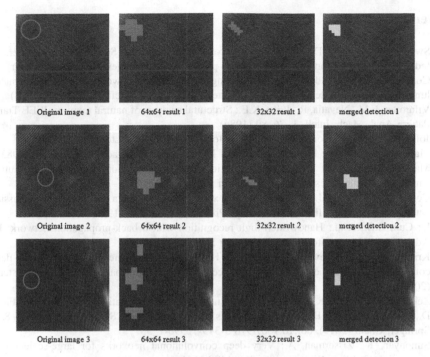

Fig. 10. Merged detections with multiple network

if one or two of the networks fails, merged detection can still get good locating effect. A region detected by two CNNs at the same time is an effective measure to reduce the risk of error detection and for a more detailed boundary. Just like Fig. 10 shown.

5   Conclusions

In this paper, we design a feature extraction method by using convolutional neural networks. Solve the problem of weak adaptability caused by artificial interference in the traditional method. At the same time, we use voting mechanism to avoid false detection in the image and realize defect localization. And we get good test results in five different type image sets. By adding a new branch, the training process is about 8 times faster. Then we improve the detection speed almost 17 times by sliding window on the feature map. In order to solve detecting failure in single network, we using two different networks to get higher detection accuracy and more detailed regional boundaries. As to solve rough boundary contour in our algorithm, more researches is needed in the future.

194	X. Wu et al.

References

1. Swain, M.J., Ballard, D.H.: Indexing via color histograms. In: Sood, A.K., Wechsler, H. (eds.) Active Perception and Robot Vision, pp. 261–273. Springer, Heidelberg (1992)
2. Conners, R.W., et al.: Identifying and locating surface defects in wood: part of an automated lumber processing system. IEEE Trans. Pattern Anal. Mach. Intell. **6**, 573–583 (1983)
3. Vilnrotter, F.M., Nevatia, R., Price, K.E.: Structural analysis of natural textures. IEEE Trans. Pattern Anal. Mach. Intell. **1**, 76–89 (1986)
4. Jolliffe, I.: Principal Component Analysis. John Wiley & Sons Ltd, Hoboken (2002)
5. Mandelbrot, B.B.: The Fractal Geometry of Nature, vol. 173. Macmillan, London (1983)
6. Mao, J., Jain, A.K.: Texture classification and segmentation using multiresolution simultaneous autoregressive models. Pattern Recogn. **25**(2), 173–188 (1992)
7. Comer, M.L., Delp, E.J.: Segmentation of textured images using a multiresolution Gaussian autoregressive model. IEEE Trans. Image Proc. **8**(3), 408–420 (1999)
8. Le Cun, B.B., et al.: Handwritten digit recognition with a back-propagation network. In: Advances in Neural Information Processing Systems (1990)
9. Krizhevsky, A., Sutskever, I., Geoffrey, E., Hinton, G.E.: Imagenet classification with deep convolutional neural networks. In: Advances in Neural Information Processing Systems (2012)
10. Zeiler, M.D., Fergus, R.: Visualizing and understanding convolutional networks. In: Fleet, D., Pajdla, T., Schiele, B., Tuytelaars, T. (eds.) ECCV 2014. LNCS, vol. 8689, pp. 818–833. Springer, Cham (2014). doi:10.1007/978-3-319-10590-1_53
11. Simonyan, K., Zisserman, A.: Very deep convolutional networks for large-scale image recognition (2014). arXiv preprint arXiv:1409.1556
12. Szegedy, C., et al.: Going deeper with convolutions. In: Proceedings of the IEEE Conference on Computer Vision and Pattern Recognition (2015)
13. He, K., et al.: Deep residual learning for image recognition (2015). arXiv preprint arXiv:1512.03385
14. Girshick, R., et al.: Rich feature hierarchies for accurate object detection and semantic segmentation. In: Proceedings of the IEEE Conference on Computer Vision and Pattern Recognition (2014)
15. DAGM 2007 Datasets. https://hci.iwr.uni-heidelberg.de/node/3616. Accessed 10 Apr 2017

A Computer Vision System to Localize and Classify Wastes on the Streets

Mohammad Saeed Rad[1(✉)], Andreas von Kaenel[2], Andre Droux[2],
Francois Tieche[3], Nabil Ouerhani[3], Hazım Kemal Ekenel[4],
and Jean-Philippe Thiran[1]

[1] Signal Processing Laboratory 5, Ecole Polytechnique Federale de Lausanne,
Lausanne, Switzerland
saeed.rad@epfl.ch
[2] Cortexia SA, Chatel-Saint-Denis, Switzerland
[3] Haute Ecole Arc, St-imier, Switzerland
[4] Istanbul Technical University, Istanbul, Turkey

Abstract. Littering quantification is an important step for improving
cleanliness of cities. When human interpretation is too cumbersome or in
some cases impossible, an objective index of cleanliness could reduce the
littering by awareness actions. In this paper, we present a fully automated
computer vision application for littering quantification based on images
taken from the streets and sidewalks. We have employed a deep learning based framework to localize and classify different types of wastes.
Since there was no waste dataset available, we built our acquisition system mounted on a vehicle. Collected images containing different types of
wastes. These images are then annotated for training and benchmarking
the developed system. Our results on real case scenarios show accurate
detection of littering on variant backgrounds.

1 Introduction

Urban littering, defined as the waste products disposed improperly in cities,
has recently become a major concern for our modern cities. Major European
cities place urban cleanliness as a top priority for the authorities, as it directly
impacts the concern and satisfaction of their citizens and the attractiveness of
their economy and tourism. At a recent Clean Europe Network summit[1], the
lack of data has been pointed out as one of the major difficulty in addressing
properly this environmental issue.

The key to properly manage urban cleanliness is to implement a continuous
improvement management system. The measurement of urban litter is manda-
tory for such a process. Anti-littering organizations such as AVPU[2] and cities
worldwide are assessing urban cleanliness by means of human audits. Zurich -
ranked third over 83 European cities for the satisfaction of its citizens regarding

---

[1] http://www.cleaneuropenetwork.eu/de/measuring-litter/aus/.
[2] http://www.avpu.fr/pdf%20AVPU/formation%20grille%20IOP-2014.pdf.

© Springer International Publishing AG 2017
M. Liu et al. (Eds.): ICVS 2017, LNCS 10528, pp. 195–204, 2017.
DOI: 10.1007/978-3-319-68345-4_18

cleanliness[3]- is conducting 14000 audits a year to assess and manage its cleanliness. To provide such a measurement, as an index of cleanliness, a key step is to be able to recognize different types of wastes on urban places, to quantify and to classify them by their type.

In this study, we propose and develop a computer vision application based on deep CNN algorithms to localize and classify urban wastes such as bottles, leaves, etc. in an automated manner in RGB images. This measurement is realized by an image acquisition system consisting of a high-resolution camera, mounted on the top of a vehicle, facing the ground. The front surface of the vehicle are covered by the camera view. The system must be able to detect the smallest defined waste -a cigarette butt, seen from a camera placed at a height of two to three meters. The output of this application is a geo-localized density of different categories of urban wastes. An overview of the system is shown in Fig. 1.

The remainder of this paper is structured as follows. Section 2 presents related works. Then, in Sect. 3, the deep neural network used for detection -including its implementation details- is explained. In Sect. 4, we present the data collection setup and use it to obtain a waste dataset. In Sect. 5 we test our application on a real case scenario and present results. Finally, Sect. 6 summarizes our work and discusses about future work.

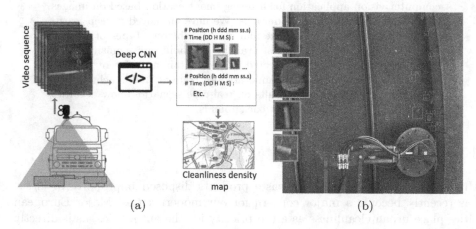

(a)   (b)

Fig. 1. (a) The system overview: the application focuses on detecting different types of urban wastes in RGB images taken by a high-resolution camera, mounted on a vehicle and facing the ground. Its results could be merged in order to produce a waste density map. (b) A visual representation of results obtained by the application: some detected objects are cropped and highlighted.

---

[3] http://ec.europa.eu/regional_policy/sources/docgener/studies/pdf/urban/ survey2015_en.pdf.

2   Related Work

Different methodologies have been developed worldwide to obtain an index of cleanliness for a city. These approaches are mostly focused on human interpretations of cleanliness. However, an automated approach has not yet been developed.

The closest work to this study is a trash related project designed to coarsely segment a pile of garbage in an image [2]. They also provide an Android application, which allows citizens to track and report garbage in their neighborhoods. Bing Image Search API[4] was used to create their dataset. They have labeled images as containing garbage or not. The authors utilize a pre-trained AlexNet [3] model and obtain 83.96% of sensitivity with 90.06% specificity. Their approach focuses on segmenting a pile of garbage in an image and provides no details about types of wastes in that segment.

There exist approaches that classify garbage into recycling categories; [4] proposes an automated recognition system using deep learning algorithm which classifies objects as biodegradable and non-biodegradable. They propose a model and have its implementation done in Caffe [11]. However, there are no experimental results presented. In [5], they propose a system to classify waste in high schools. They design a box containing a camera inside it. In order to do the classification, objects are required to be placed inside the box. Their image processing module is based on finding correlation between the image of the object in the box and 50 different images, then choosing the best one as the right category. The developed system classifies three kinds of waste: PET bottle, soda cans and cartoon box, with a classification performance over 70%.

An automatic waste sorting approach is presented in [6]. They use two different methods: Convolution Neural Networks and Support Vector Machines. Their input is 256 × 256 pixel resolution image of the waste. For their CNN architecture, they use AlexNet [3] model. Their SVM utilizes a bag of features obtained by passing a 8 × 8 window over the whole image. Each algorithm creates a different classifier that separates waste into three main categories: plastic, paper, and metal. They achieved a classification accuracy of 94.8% with SVM, while CNN had an accuracy of 83%. As they have mentioned in their paper, the main reason of not having better results with CNN is the insufficient number of images in their training set. Their approach focuses on classifying a specific object and not to localize it from a far distance.

3   Methodology

In this section, we describe each step of our approach. We explain how we localize and classify the wastes on given input images, then we discuss about the implementation details.

---

[4] https://www.microsoft.com/cognitive-services/en-us/bing-image-search-api.

3.1   Waste Localization and Classification

The proposed system must take care of two main tasks: The first task is to localize all objects in the image. The second task is to classify all detected objects on their right littering category. In this section, all tasks are addressed using a single framework and a shared feature learning base.

The fact that CNNs are trained end-to-end, from raw pixels to final classes, makes them much more advantageous for many tasks than manually designing a suitable feature extractor. Our approach is similar to OverFeat model [1] which proposes a multi-scale deep learning approach that can be used for classification, localization and detection. We replace its classification architecture by GoogLeNet [8]. For localization, as OverFeat put forward, starting from the classification-trained network, the classifier layers are replaced by a regression network and trained to predict object bounding boxes at each spatial location and scale. Then the regression predictions with the classification results are combined at each location to obtain detection results. Object bounding box predictions are generated by running the classifier and regressor networks for all locations and scales. Considering that these two networks are sharing the same feature extraction layers; after computing the classification net, only the final regression layers must be recomputed. The final output layer of regression network has 4 units which correspond to coordinates for the bounding box of the detected object.

We use OverFeat-GoogLeNet model presented in [7]. The original version of OverFeat relies on image representation based on AlexNet [3]. In [7], they were able to directly substitute the GoogLeNet architecture into the OverFeat model and denoted the new model as OverFeat-GoogLeNet. They show that Overfeat-GoogLeNet performs significantly better than OverFeat-AlexNet. GoogLeNet is initially trained on 1.2 million images for 1000-classes object recognition. Overfeat-GoogLeNet uses expressive image features from GoogLeNet that in our implementation are fine-tuned as part of our system. The size of the input layer is fixed to 640×480 pixels. The model is constructed to encode the input image into a 15×20 grid where each cell contains 1024-dimensional top level GoogLeNet features and has a receptive field of size 139×139. Cells are trained to produce the set of all bounding boxes intersecting the central 32×32 region. The convolutional layers are followed by two fully connected layers containing 3092 and 4096 neurons, respectively. At the end, the output layer contains 25 neurons corresponding to different categories of waste.

3.2   Implementation

An open source implementation of OverFeat on Tensorflow [9] was used as a starting point. Then, some modifications were done to perform multi-classification. The image of a cigarette butt must contain at least same number of pixels as the smallest possible bounding box for the network. To fulfill this last criterion, and also regarding to the height of the camera, the resolution is fixed to 1920×1480 pixels. During training, these images occupy a considerable amount of memory while loading their batches. Due to this and the challenge of having a cheaper system capable of processing and detecting wastes onboard on an embedded system, we decided to pass a 640 × 480 pixels sliding window with an overlapping factor over the input image and keep the network input size same as the window size. The final result is produced by converting the detection coordinates with respect to initial full image. Detections within the same category are merged in case of having an overlapping factor of more than 60%. The model is fine-tuned on Tensorflow [9] using Nvidia K40 GPUs for 350,000 iterations with a batch size of 16. Validation is performed every 2,000 iterations.

4   The Dataset

Convolutional Neural Networks have lots of advantages over methods requiring to design a suitable feature extractor. However, one of their drawbacks is the need for a large amount of labeled training samples.

There is no waste image dataset currently available, which differentiates different types of litters/wastes. Our initial idea was to gather a diverse set of images, for example using image search by entering the category names as the keywords or using ImageNet [10], to train our system. However, the final decision was to not use them for training as their conditions like camera view, illumination, etc. were too different from what our system captures. To collect our own dataset, we have built our own acquisition system, mounted on a vehicle and drove several hours in Geneva area, Switzerland. We have obtained 18,676 images. To avoid overlapping between training images we have decreased number of images from 2 to 0.4 frame per second and among them we have annotated 469 full images, which corresponds to 4338, 640 × 480 pixel resolution images. Because of the time and season of our acquisition process, most of wastes found in images were leaves and cigarette butts.

4.1   Categories

Another important step is to define what the waste is and needs to be considered for a cleanliness measure, and also how the categories should be defined in order to cover most of litters. Different organisations use different waste classifications. The OFEV[5] approach, for example, does not take into account gums or excrement, which nevertheless play an important role in the perception of cleanliness and urban pollution. To give an example, in Roma, 5.54 million gums are discarded every year that take about 5 years to degrade. In this work, after some discussion with different cities we have decided to classify different wastes into one of the 25 general categories. Here we mention some important ones: 1. Beverage and meal packages, 2. Cigarettes and derivatives, 3. Leaves, 4. Newspapers and papers, 5. Vegetable waste, etc.

---

[5] http://www.bafu.admin.ch/publikationen/publikation/01604/index.html?lang=fr.

4.2 Setup

We equipped an automatic street sweeper car with a camera and an embedded system to obtain and store our dataset. As it is shown in Fig. 2, the camera was installed on a metallic arm, on top and coming out of the vehicle, having a flat view of the ground. The camera has a rolling shutter with a 1/2.3 in. CMOS sensor and 4K resolution, however after tuning the input image size of the network, the camera was configured to an output of 1920 × 1480 pixel resolution images. The camera was set to get two frames per second and the average speed of the vehicle was twelve kilometers per hour.

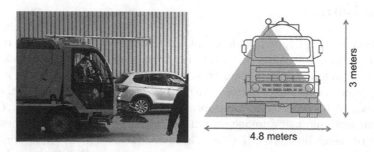

Fig. 2. Our dataset is obtained by a high resolution camera mounted on top of a street sweeper and having a flat view of the ground. The camera is in a distance of approximately three meters from the ground.

4.3 Annotations

Similar to other object recognition problems, our model also requires considerable amount of labeled training samples. We have developed an annotation tool to label a sequence of images by putting a bounding box around each waste and assigning an integer number to it showing its class number. A screenshot of this tool is shown in Fig. 3. This approach is based on the hypothesis that each object is well-separated, countable and has its particular shape, which is not the case for all categories. For example during autumn, the ground is covered by leaves where each individual leaf will not appear the same way that it appears alone. A significant improvement was observed in the correct classification accuracy once two different classes were introduced for leaves: a class for single leaves and another class for piles of leaves. However, for the cleanliness measurement both classes are considered as one category. This approach helped the network to have a better generalization for each type, separately. An example of these two classes is shown in Fig. 4.

5   Results and Discussion

The proposed application was validated using a test set consisting of 62 non-overlapping full-size images collected from our setup, equal to 558 640 × 480

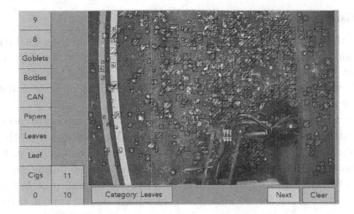

Fig. 3. A screenshot of our annotation tool. This image shows existing challenges to label collected images.

images that are fed to the network. Rectangular ground-truth bounding boxes were defined on each image. In total, they consist of 69 cigarettes, 958 leaves and 394 bounding boxes on piles of leaves. Although other types of waste had been annotated and were used during training, they were not considered for the evaluation. Their number was not sufficient and could not provide a reliable training/testing. For example, in total we have: 8 bottles, 5 cans, 6 goblets in training set.

Fig. 4. The red detections are done by the network only trained with a single category for leaves. A significant improvement was seen when two different classes were defined for leaves: 1- Class leaf, 2- Class leaves. (Color figure online)

We have reached to process images at 2 frames (1920 × 1480) per seconds. This could be interpreted as: with a camera mounted at a height of 3 m, we can detect a cigarette butt with a speed up to 12 km per hour (this number of frame per second enables us to have 15% of overlap between two consecutive images). Both training and testing processes were done on a Nvidia K40 GPU.

5.1   Precision-Recall Analysis

To evaluate the performance of the proposed application in a quantitative manner, a precision-recall analysis was performed [12]. The precision (P) and recall (R) rates of the system are simply defined as: $P = CD/(CD + FP)$ and $R = CD/N$ where CD, FP and N are the total number of correct detections, false positive and ground truth objects respectively.

In order to calculate these parameters, first, each detection needs to be labeled as either correct detection or false positive by reference to the ground truth. For cigarette butts category, a detection is marked as correct when the overlap between its detected bounding boxes and the corresponding ground truth is at least 50%. In Fig. 5(a) the precision and recall of cigarette butts is illustrated. Different values for P and R are obtained by varying a threshold on final detection score for this category. We have reached 63.2% of precision while having 61.02% of recall for the cigarette butts class.

This method of defining correct detection and false positive could pose a problem while evaluating the application for some categories like leaves. Let's imagine a scene covered by leaves. As explained previously, our ground-truth is defined by different overlapping bounding boxes, with different sizes, on some random position, covering leaves. In this case, the algorithm would correctly return different detections on top of leaves' regions, but not exactly the same position that was defined in the ground-truth. To avoid this issue, only for this category, a binary image of detection/ground-truth was produced for each image. Pixels set to 0 indicate background and pixels set to 1 show ground-truth/detection. Comparing these two binary images pixel by pixel gives CD and FP parameters. Figure 5(b) shows precision-recall curve for leaves category. We have obtained 77.35% of precision while having 60% of recall for the leaves class.

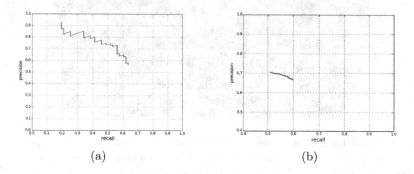

(a)   (b)

Fig. 5. Precision-recall curves for: (a) cigarettes class, (b) leaves class

Although the quantitative results may not seem to be too high, it should also be taken into account that the system is designed to localize very small objects such as cigarette butts in relatively large images, covering five meters of a street. Considering this challenge, these results are promising for waste localization and classification even if they are seen from a distance.

5.2 Qualitative Assessment

Some localization and classification results obtained on sample representative images are shown in Fig. 6. The proposed approach performs well for small objects like a cigarette butt from a three meters height on a clear background as well as in backgrounds crowded by other types of waste. Also, the method is able to detect multiple/overlapped wastes. It should be noted that some leaves/cigarettes were missed on some images, which could be due to our limited training-set. Examples of a false positive detection and a missed detection are shown in Fig. 7.

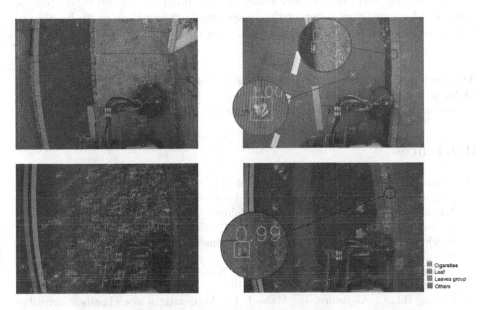

Fig. 6. Example of leaves and cigarettes detections. Orange boxes correspond to cigarettes, green boxes to leaves and blue boxes to piles of leaves. (Color figure online)

Fig. 7. Example of: (a) a false detection (b) a missed detection.

6   Summary and Future Work

In this paper, a novel application for measuring cleanliness of a place, using a deep learning framework was proposed. The application localizes and classifies wastes in RGB images taken by a camera facing ground from three meters of height. Since there was no waste dataset available, we used our proposed acquisition setup to obtain images. We have also developed an annotation tool to label objects in our dataset for 25 different types of waste. Experimental results on a real case scenario -on a test-set obtained by our proposed acquisition setup- show promising performance on variant backgrounds.

As a future work, our dataset could be expanded by adding more images, especially for categories different than cigarette butts and leaves, to be able to detect all existing classes of wastes, and also to increase the accuracy of the current system.

Acknowledgment. The authors would like to thank Mr. Niels Michel, Manager of Dialog & Service at City of Zurich for sharing his in-depth experience on cleanliness measurement thus significantly contributing to this project.

References

1. Sermanet, P., Eigen, D., Zhang, X., et al.: Overfeat: integrated recognition, localization and detection using convolutional networks. In: ICLR (2014)
2. Mittal, G., Yagnik, K.B., Garg, M., Krishnan, N.: Spotgarbage: smartphone app to detect garbage using deep learning. In: UbiComp (2016)
3. Krizhevsky, A., Sutskever, I., Hinton, G.E.: Imagenet classification with deep convolutional neural networks. In: NIPS (2012)
4. Sudha, S., Vidhyalakshmi, M., Pavithra, K., et al.: An automatic classification method for environment. In: TIAR (2016)
5. Carlos, B.L.J., Alejandro, R., Manuel, E.: Automatic waste classification using computer vision as an application in colombian high schools. In: LACNEM (2015)
6. Sakr, G., Mokbel, M., Darwich, A.: Comparing deep learning and support vector machines for autonomous waste sorting. In: IMCIT (2016)
7. Stewart, R., Andriluka, M.: End-to-end people detection in crowded scenes. In: CVPR (2015)
8. Szegedy, C., Liu, W., Jia, Y., et al.: Going deeper with convolutions. CoRR, abs/1409.4842 (2014)
9. Abadi, M., Agarwal, A., Barham, P., et al.: TensorFlow: large-scale machine learning on heterogeneous systems (2015). https://www.tensorflow.org/
10. Deng, J., Dong, W., Socher, R., et al.: ImageNet: a large-scale hierarchical image database. In: CVPR (2009)
11. Jia, Y., Caffe, S., et al.: Convolutional architecture for fast feature embedding. arXiv:1408.5093'14
12. Everingham, M., Van Gool, L., Williams, C.K.I., et al.: The pascal visual object classes (VOC) challenge. In: IJCV (2010)

Image Processing

Two Effective Algorithms for Color Image Denoising

Jian-jun Zhang$^{(\boxtimes)}$, Jian-li Zhang, and Meng Gao

Department of Mathematics, Shanghai University, Shanghai 200444, China
jjzhang@staff.shu.edu.cn

Abstract. We present two effective algorithms for removing impulse noise from color images. Our proposed algorithms take a two-step approach: in the first step, noise color pixel candidates are identified by an impulse detector, and in the second step, only those identified noise candidates in the image are restored by using a modified weighted vector median filter. Extensive experiments indicate that our proposed algorithms have good performance, and are more effective than most of the existing algorithms in removing impulse noise from color images.

Keywords: Color image · Denoising · Impulse noise · Vector median filter

1 Introduction

Removing impulse noise is an import and challenging problem in image processing. A lot of researches have been done for this problem. For example, nonlinear filters such as median filter are successfully applied to impulse noise removal in scalar valued images [6]. For a color image, its pixel has three scalar values. Suppose it is encoded by red, green and blue values in RGB color space. Then it is natural to apply the traditional nonlinear filtering techniques to each channel separately [2]. However, such technique does not use the correlation exists among the three different color channels, and therefore may lead to problems that are not present in scalar valued images [1]. Therefore vector processing techniques for color image denoising are desirable.

To our knowledge, vector median filter (VMF) [1] may be the first and the best-known vector filtering technique for its simplicity, robustness and impulse noise removing ability [13]. Since the development of VMF, many vector filtering techniques are proposed. For example, the vector directional filters (VDF) which consider the vectors' direction is proposed [17]. In [10], the directional-distance filters (DDF) is developed. In [7], a hybrid directional filter (HDF) is proposed by using the output of the VDF and the VMF. Similar to the scalar median filter, the above mentioned vector filters have some undesirable side effects that tend to smear sharp edges and fine details of an image [8]. In order to eliminate such defects, some new vector processing techniques have been developed, see for

© Springer International Publishing AG 2017
M. Liu et al. (Eds.): ICVS 2017, LNCS 10528, pp. 207–217, 2017.
DOI: 10.1007/978-3-319-68345-4_19

example [11,12] and references therein. We remark here that, relaxation Labeling [4] may also be applied to solving color image denoising problem.

Recently, a two-step approach for removing impulse noise from scalar valued images was developed [3,5]. In this work, we present two effective algorithms for removing impulse noise from color images. Our proposed algorithms take a two-step approach. In the first step, noise color pixel candidates are identified by an impulse detector, and then in the second step, only those identified noise candidates in the image are restored by using a modified weighted vector median filter. Extensive experiments indicate that our proposed algorithms have good performance, and are more effective than most of the existing algorithms in removing impulsive noise from color images.

The remainder of the paper is organized as follows. In Sect. 2, we clarify the problems we are considered. In Sect. 3, we present our denoising algorithms. Experimental results are presented in Sect. 4 and Sect. 5 concludes the paper.

2   Problem Setting

The problem we are considered is the impulse noise removal in color images. Given an M by N noisy image, let x_{ij} be the vector of the given image, let v_{ij} be the impulse noise vector, and let z_{ij} be the noise-free color pixel, for $(i,j) \in \mathcal{I} \equiv \{1, \cdots, M\} \times \{1, \cdots, N\}$, and let p be impulse noise probability. Then impulse noise model is described as,

$$x_{ij} = \begin{cases} v_{ij} \text{ with probability } p \\ z_{ij} \text{ with probability } 1 - p \end{cases} \tag{1}$$

The model (1) gives many kinds of impulse noise for color images. Depending on the type of vector v_{ij}, we consider two impulse noise models, called salt-and-pepper noise model, and random-valued impulse noise model. See [9] for example.

For salt-and-pepper noise model, v_{ij} is characterized by the following expression,

$$v_{ij} = \begin{cases} (d_1, v_{ij}^G, v_{ij}^B) \text{ with probability } p_1 \\ (v_{ij}^R, d_2, v_{ij}^B) \text{ with probability } p_2 \\ (v_{ij}^R, v_{ij}^G, d_3) \text{ with probability } p_3 \\ (d_4, d_5, d_6) \text{ with probability } p_4 \end{cases} \tag{2}$$

where d_k takes an extreme value for $k = 1, 2, \cdots, 6$, and $p_1 + p_2 + p_3 + p_4 = 1$. In the remainder of the paper, the two extreme values are denoted by $x_{\min}$ and $x_{\max}$, respectively.

In the case of random-valued impulse noise model, we define v_{ij} by using the following model:

$$v_{ij} = \begin{cases} (r_1, v_{ij}^G, v_{ij}^B) \text{ with probability } p_1 \\ (v_{ij}^R, r_2, v_{ij}^B) \text{ with probability } p_2 \\ (v_{ij}^R, v_{ij}^G, r_3) \text{ with probability } p_3 \\ (r_4, r_5, r_6) \text{ with probability } p_4 \end{cases} \tag{3}$$

where r_k is independent uniformly distributed random numbers for $k = 1, 2, \cdots, 6$, and $p_1 + p_2 + p_3 + p_4 = 1$.

In the following, we will design two denoising algorithms based on the presented noise models.

3 Our Proposed Method

As we have known, it should consider the correlations that exists among the different color channels in the processing of color image data [1,8,14]. However, this correlation property does not need to be considered when detecting impulses in color images. Since for a color vector $X_i = (X_i^R, X_i^G, X_i^B)$, if one of its components is corrupted by impulse, then the whole vector would be contaminated by the impulse. Therefore we can detect impulses in color images by using impulse detection algorithms for scalar valued images.

In the following, we first present the adaptive median filter (AMF) [6], which will be used to identify salt-and-pepper noise in scalar valued images. Then we present our denoising algorithm.

Let W_{ij}^s be a window of size $(2s + 1) \times (2s + 1)$ centered at location (i, j). More definitely, $W_{ij}^s = \{(k, l)|\ (k, l) \in \mathcal{I}, |k - i| \leq s \text{ and } |l - j| \leq s\}$. The observed color image vectors in this window consisting of samples denoted by $X = \{X_1, X_2, \cdots, X_S\}$, with $x_{ij} = X_{(S+1)/2}$, and $S = (2s+1)^2$. The corresponding three individual color channel are denoted as $X^R = \{X_1^R, X_2^R, \cdots, X_S^R\}$, $X^G = \{X_1^G, X_2^G, \cdots, X_S^G\}$ and $X^B = \{X_1^B, X_2^B, \cdots, X_S^B\}$, respectively. We use X^C to represent either of the X^R, X^G, X^B.

Algorithm 1 *(AMF for scalar valued images)*

Initialize $s = 1$, and set the maximum window size be $s_{\max}$. For all pixel location (i, j), do

1. *Compute $x_{\max}^C$, x_{med}^C, $x_{\min}^C$, which are respectively the maximum, median and minimum of the pixel values in W_{ij}^s.*
2. *If $x_{med}^C = x_{\max}^C$ or $x_{med}^C = x_{\min}^C$, set $s = s + 1$; otherwise, go to step 4.*
3. *If $s > s_{\max}$, replace x_{ij}^C by x_{med}^C; otherwise, go to step 1.*
4. *If $x_{\min}^C < x_{ij}^C < x_{\max}^C$, then x_{ij}^C is noise-free; replace x_{ij}^C by x_{med}^C, otherwise.*

Based on the color image noise model (1)(2), we can identify salt-and-pepper noise in color images by using Algorithm 1.

Algorithm 2 *(Noise identification)*

Let y^C be the image obtained by applying Algorithm 1 to the channel x^C. Since noisy pixels take only extreme values $x_{\min}$ or $x_{\max}$, the noise candidate set can be obtained by

$$\mathcal{N} = \{(i, j)|\ (i, j) \in \mathcal{I}, y_{ij}^C \neq x_{ij}^C \text{ and } x_{ij}^C = x_{min}, \text{ or } x_{ij}^C = x_{max}\}.$$

We use

$$\mathcal{N}^c = \{(i, j)|\ (i, j) \in \mathcal{I}, \text{ and } (i, j) \notin \mathcal{N}\},$$

to denote the set of noise-free pixels.

By using Algorithm 2, we now present our denoising algorithm for removing salt-and-pepper noise from color images.

Algorithm 3 *(Denoising algorithm for color images corrupted by salt-and-pepper noise)*

1. (Noise identification): Dividing the image vectors into noise-free set $\mathcal{N}^c$ and noise corrupted set $\mathcal{N}$ by using Algorithm 2.

2. (Restoration): Let the observed image vectors in S_{ij}^w consisting of samples denoted by $X = \{X_1, X_2, \cdots, X_S\}$, with $x_{ij} = X_{(S+1)/2}$. If $x_{ij} \in \mathcal{N}^c$, the output is x_{ij} itself. Otherwise, the output is defined as,

$$X_{(1)} = \arg\min_{X_k \in X} \sum_{\substack{l=1 \\ l \in \mathcal{N}^c}}^{W} \|X_k - X_l\|_2,$$

where $l \in \mathcal{N}^c$ denotes that $(i,j) \in \mathcal{N}^c$ for some $x_{i,j} = X_l$,

$$\|X_k - X_l\|_2 = \sqrt{(X_k^R - X_l^R)^2 + (X_k^G - X_l^G)^2 + (X_k^B - X_l^B)^2},$$

and $\arg\min$ is argument of the minimum, that is,

$$\sum_{\substack{l=1 \\ l \in \mathcal{N}^c}}^{S} \|X_{(1)} - X_l\|_2 = \min_{X_k \in X} \sum_{\substack{l=1 \\ l \in \mathcal{N}^c}}^{S} \|X_k - X_l\|_2.$$

We can easily see that our proposed algorithm (Algorithm 3) is easy to implement. In the used distance measure, we give zeros weights on the noise color pixels. This strategy ensures more effective impulse removal than other methods in the literature such as VMF.

We now consider to remove random-valued impulse noise from color images. Here we use the rank-ordered logarithmic difference (ROLD) algorithm developed in [5] to identify noise color pixels.

Algorithm 4 *(ROLD algorithm)*

Let the observed color image vectors in W_{ij}^s consisting of samples denoted by $X = \{X_1, X_2, \cdots, X_S\}$, with $x_{ij} = X_{(S+1)/2}$. Let $D_j(X_{(S+1)/2}^C) = 1 + \max\{\log_2 |X_j^C - X_{(S+1)/2}^C|, -5\}/5$, for $j = 1, 2, \cdots, S, j \neq (S+1)/2$. Arrange all D_j in an increasing order,

$$D_{(1)} \leq D_{(2)} \leq \cdots \leq D_{(S-1)}.$$

Define local image order statistics as

$$ROLD_l(X_{(S+1)/2}^C) = \sum_{k=1}^{l} D_{(k)}(X_{(S+1)/2}^C).$$

We then identify random-valued impulse noise candidates by using ROLD with threshold T^C: a color vector $X_{(S+1)/2}$ or equivalently, x_{ij} is corrupted with impulse noise if one of its component $X_{(S+1)/2}^C$ satisfies $ROLD_l(X_{(W+1)/2}^C) > T^C$, and it is noise free otherwise.

Now we present our denoising algorithm for color images contaminated by random-valued impulse noise.

Algorithm 5 *(Denoising algorithm for color images contaminated by random valued impulse noise.)*

1. *(Noise identification)*: Dividing the image vectors into noise free set $\mathcal{N}^c$ and noise corrupted set $\mathcal{N}$ by using Algorithm 4.

2. *(Restoration)*: Let the observed image vectors in W_{ij}^s consisting of samples denoted by $X = \{X_1, X_2, \cdots, X_S\}$, with $x_{ij} = X_{(S+1)/2}$. If $x_{ij} \in \mathcal{N}^c$, the output is x_{ij} itself. Otherwise, the output is given by,

$$X_{(1)} = \arg \min_{X_k \in X} \sum_{\substack{l=1 \\ l \in \mathcal{N}^c}}^{S} \|X_k - X_l\|_2.$$

4   Experimental Results

We conduct two experiments in this section, to exam the noise removal ability of our proposed algorithms. Three 512×512 color images are used in our experiments. These three images are "Lena", "Mandril", and "Lake", which are shown in Fig. 1. We also compared performance of our algorithms with many other algorithms in the literature, including VMF [1], AVMF [12], MAVMF [12], quaternion based algorithm, denoted by QVMF [8], VDF [17], AVDF [15], DDF [10] and HDF [7].

In the experiments, 3×3 filter window is used for all above-mentioned techniques. For AVMF, we set $\lambda_1 = 4$, and for MAVMF, we set $\lambda_2 = 12$ [12]. For QVMF, we set the parameter Tol to be 22 as it was set in [8]. For DDF, we set $p = 0.75$ [10]. For AVDF, we use AVDF2, since it performances best in all AVDFs proposed in [15].

We use AMF of maximum size 13 to identify salt-and-pepper noise for Algorithm 3,.

For Algorithm 5, we use ROLD algorithm to identify noise as described. We set $l = 4$ and set the window size to be 3×3, and the threshold is set to be $T = s \cdot q$ with $s = 1.9$ if noise ratio is equal or less than 25%; we set $l = 12$, and set the window size to be 5×5, and the threshold is set to be $T = s \cdot q$ with $s = 5.4$ if noise ratio is greater than 25%. Where q is the fraction of the pixels in each color channel whose ROLD values are less than s.

To get quantitative measure for the noise removal ability of above mentioned algorithms, the normalized color difference (NCD) and the normalized mean square error (NMSE) are used in this section. Let M, N be the image dimensions, and x_{ij} and $\tilde{x}_{ij}$ be the original image vector and its filtered image vector at location (i, j), respectively. Let L^* and (u^*, v^*) be lightness values and chrominance values corresponding to x_{ij} and $\tilde{x}_{ij}$ samples encoded in CIE $L^*u^*v^*$ color

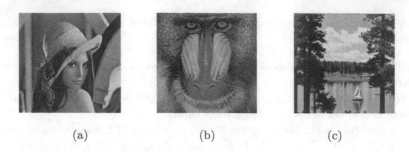

(a)   (b)   (c)

Fig. 1. Original images. (a) Lena, (b) Mandril, (c) Lake.

space, respectively. Then NCD is defined as [16],

$$
\text{NCD} = \frac{\sum_{i=1}^{M}\sum_{j=1}^{N}\sqrt{(L^*_{x_{ij}} - L^*_{\tilde{x}_{ij}})^2 + (u^*_{x_{ij}} - u^*_{\tilde{x}_{ij}})^2 + (v^*_{x_{ij}} - v^*_{\tilde{x}_{ij}})^2}}{\sum_{i=1}^{M}\sum_{j=1}^{N}\sqrt{(L^*_{x_{ij}})^2 + (u^*_{x_{ij}})^2 + (v^*_{x_{ij}})^2}},
$$

and NMSE is defined as

$$
\text{NMSE} = \frac{\sum_{i=1}^{M}\sum_{j=1}^{N}\|x_{ij} - \tilde{x}_{ij}\|_2^2}{\sum_{i=1}^{M}\sum_{j=1}^{N}\|x_{ij}\|_2^2}.
$$

Experiment 1. In this experiment, we test the salt-and-pepper noise removal ability of the above mentioned algorithms. To this end, we use the noise model (1)(2) to corrupt the three original test images by salt-and-pepper noise. In the corruption, different noise levels ranging from 5% to 35% with increments of 10% are carried out. Tables 1, 2 and 3 show respectively, the values of NCD and NMSE for the restored images "Lena", "Mandril" and "Lake". Where "Alg3" denotes our proposed algorithm (Algorithm 3). In Fig. 2, we show the restored images by applying VMF, AVMF and Alg5 to the 25% noise corrupted Lena image.

From the Tables 1, 2 and 3 and Fig. 2, we see that Algorithm 3, has lowest NCD and NMSE values and good subjective performance. Moreover, our algorithm is easy to implement. Based on the given results, we draw a conclusion that our proposed algorithm, Algorithm 3, is competitive with most existing algorithms when applied to salt-and-pepper noise removal.

Experiment 2. In this experiment, we test the random-valued impulse noise removal ability of the above mentioned algorithms. To this end, we use the noise

Table 1. Values of NCD and NMSE obtained by different algorithms applied to salt-and-pepper noise corrupted Lena image.

Noise level	5%		15%		25%		35%	
Algorithm	NCD	NMSE	NCD	NMSE	NCD	NMSE	NCD	NMSE
VMF	0.0301	0.0016	0.0326	0.0019	0.0359	0.0024	0.0401	0.0036
AVMF	0.0065	0.0005	0.0101	0.0011	0.0210	0.0046	0.0424	0.0136
MAVMF	0.0272	0.0015	0.0310	0.0018	0.0351	0.0024	0.0398	0.0035
QVMF	0.0029	0.0003	0.0091	0.0012	0.0176	0.0026	0.0281	0.0048
VDF	0.0410	0.0091	0.0705	0.0299	0.1068	0.0565	0.1525	0.0901
AVDF	0.0851	0.0550	0.1862	0.1579	0.2781	0.2487	0.3653	0.3335
DDF	0.0428	0.0093	0.0687	0.0296	0.1046	0.0558	0.1492	0.0882
HDF	0.0393	0.0083	0.0633	0.0248	0.0942	0.0445	0.1318	0.0676
Alg3	**0.0021**	**0.0001**	**0.0065**	**0.0004**	**0.0114**	**0.0008**	**0.0172**	**0.0017**

Table 2. Values of NCD and NMSE obtained by different algorithms applied to salt-and-pepper noise corrupted Lena image.

Noise level	5%		15%		25%		35%	
Algorithm	NCD	NMSE	NCD	NMSE	NCD	NMSE	NCD	NMSE
VMF	0.1185	0.0228	0.1268	0.0246	0.1322	0.0269	0.1388	0.0302
AVMF	0.0484	0.0085	0.0557	0.0110	0.0738	0.0189	0.1035	0.0341
MAVMF	0.1163	0.0228	0.1267	0.0246	0.1321	0.0269	0.1388	0.0302
QVMF	0.0603	0.0150	0.0866	0.0304	0.1116	0.0435	0.1349	0.0551
VDF	0.1650	0.0551	0.1954	0.0845	0.2339	0.1210	0.2787	0.1643
AVDF	0.1771	0.0767	0.2681	0.1765	0.3545	0.2713	0.4348	0.3565
DDF	0.1418	0.0380	0.1701	0.0616	0.2075	0.0936	0.2499	0.1305
HDF	0.1309	0.0291	0.1544	0.0468	0.1843	0.0689	0.2178	0.0930
Alg3	**0.0076**	**0.0016**	**0.0399**	**0.0049**	**0.0544**	**0.0088**	**0.0702**	**0.0135**

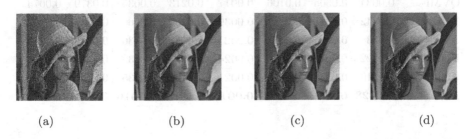

| (a) | (b) | (c) | (d) |

Fig. 2. Restored images by using different algorithms. (a) 25% salt-and-pepper noise corrupted Lena image, (b) VMF, (c) AVMF, (d) Alg3.

Table 3. Values of NCD and NMSE obtained by different algorithms applied to salt-and-pepper noise corrupted Lena image.

Noise level	5%		15%		25%		35%	
Algorithm	NCD	NMSE	NCD	NMSE	NCD	NMSE	NCD	NMSE
VMF	0.0611	0.0051	0.0714	0.0058	0.0753	0.0069	0.0799	0.0085
AVMF	0.0334	0.0015	0.0387	0.0030	0.0521	0.0076	0.0749	0.0175
MAVMF	0.0602	0.0051	0.0711	0.0058	0.0751	0.0069	0.0799	0.0085
QVMF	0.0380	0.0054	0.0522	0.0136	0.0677	0.0222	0.0844	0.0315
VDF	0.0865	0.0165	0.1146	0.0396	0.1518	0.0705	0.1977	0.1091
AVDF	0.1155	0.0589	0.2125	0.1581	0.3063	0.2562	0.3883	0.3382
DDF	0.0808	0.0140	0.1077	0.0352	0.1435	0.0641	0.1859	0.0982
HDF	0.0767	0.0118	0.0990	0.0279	0.1284	0.0484	0.1610	0.0695
Alg3	**0.0042**	**0.0005**	**0.0331**	**0.0014**	**0.0402**	**0.0025**	**0.0481**	**0.0041**

model (1)(3) to contaminate the three original test images by random-valued impulse noise. In the corruption, different noise levels ranging from 5% to 35% with increments of 10% are carried out. Tables 4, 5 and 6 show the values of NCD and NMSE for the restored images "Lena", "Mandril" and "Lake", respectively. Where "Alg5" denotes our proposed algorithm, Algorithm 5. In Fig. 3, we show the restored image by applying VMF, AVMF and Alg5 to the 25% noise corrupted Lena image.

Table 4. Values of NCD and NMSE obtained by different algorithms applied to random-valued impulse noise corrupted Lena image.

Noise level	5%		15%		25%		35%	
Algorithm	NCD	NMSE	NCD	NMSE	NCD	NMSE	NCD	NMSE
VMF	0.0303	0.0016	0.0341	0.0021	0.0398	0.0034	0.0511	0.0071
AVMF	0.0066	0.0005	0.0111	0.0017	0.0254	0.0070	0.0573	0.0213
MAVMF	0.0274	0.0015	0.0325	0.0021	0.0390	0.0034	0.0508	0.0071
QVMF	0.0034	0.0006	0.0106	0.0017	0.0213	0.0035	0.0379	0.0074
VDF	0.0342	0.0021	0.0381	0.0030	0.0457	0.0060	0.0637	0.0152
AVDF	0.0334	0.0016	0.0371	0.0021	0.0453	0.0036	0.0636	0.0080
DDF	0.0322	0.0018	0.0355	0.0024	0.0413	0.0039	0.0540	0.0089
HDF	0.0316	0.0016	0.0355	0.0021	0.0422	0.0035	0.0566	0.0077
Alg5	**0.0028**	**0.0003**	**0.0085**	**0.0010**	**0.0142**	**0.0016**	**0.0205**	**0.0024**

From the Tables 4, 5 and 6 and Fig. 3, we see that Algorithm 5, has lowest NCD and NMSE values and good subjective performance. Moreover, our algorithm is easy to implement. Based on the above results, we conclude that our

Table 5. Values of NCD and NMSE obtained by different algorithms applied to random-valued impulse noise corrupted Lena image.

Noise level	5%		15%		25%		35%	
Algorithm	NCD	NMSE	NCD	NMSE	NCD	NMSE	NCD	NMSE
VMF	0.1170	0.0226	0.1230	0.0242	0.1285	0.0266	0.1371	0.0302
AVMF	0.0331	0.0087	0.0580	0.0112	0.0693	0.0164	0.0934	0.0260
MAVMF	0.1159	0.0226	0.1218	0.0242	0.1284	0.0266	0.1371	0.0302
QVMF	0.0578	0.0135	0.0811	0.0276	0.1051	0.0421	0.1297	0.0569
VDF	0.1571	0.0483	0.1698	0.0630	0.1867	0.0825	0.2138	0.1135
AVDF	0.1295	0.0227	0.1408	0.0281	0.1554	0.0364	0.1779	0.0499
DDF	0.1273	0.0292	0.1328	0.0318	0.1411	0.0367	0.1544	0.0459
HDF	0.1183	0.0218	0.1244	0.0235	0.1332	0.0261	0.1438	0.0302
Alg5	**0.0161**	**0.0053**	**0.0522**	**0.0104**	**0.0596**	**0.0176**	**0.0818**	**0.0228**

Table 6. Values of NCD and NMSE obtained by different algorithms applied to random-valued impulse noise corrupted Lena image.

Noise level	5%		15%		25%		35%	
Algorithm	NCD	NMSE	NCD	NMSE	NCD	NMSE	NCD	NMSE
VMF	0.0613	0.0052	0.0705	0.0064	0.0832	0.0090	0.0973	0.0154
AVMF	0.0334	0.0015	0.0405	0.0039	0.0598	0.0123	0.0971	0.0318
MAVMF	0.0604	0.0052	0.0701	0.0064	0.0830	0.0090	0.0972	0.0154
QVMF	0.0360	0.0028	0.0478	0.0056	0.0633	0.0093	0.0854	0.0160
VDF	0.0776	0.0083	0.0826	0.0106	0.0924	0.0165	0.1116	0.0298
AVDF	0.0639	0.0048	0.0713	0.0062	0.0819	0.0096	0.1026	0.0170
DDF	0.0636	0.0063	0.0730	0.0075	0.0822	0.0103	0.0975	0.0167
HDF	0.0611	0.0051	0.0710	0.0063	0.0835	0.0088	0.0996	0.0146
Alg5	**0.0282**	**0.0010**	**0.0371**	**0.0028**	**0.0459**	**0.0061**	**0.0566**	**0.0087**

(a)   (b)   (c)   (d)

Fig. 3. Restored images by using different methods. (a) 25% random-valued impulse noise corrupted Lena image, (b) VMF, (c) AVMF, (d) Alg5.

proposed algorithm, Algorithm 5, is competitive with the most of other existing algorithms in removing random-valued impulse noise.

5   Conclusions

We present two classes of effective approaches for removing impulse noise from color images. Our proposed algorithms are effective and performance good. Experimental results show that our proposed algorithms have improvements in NCD and NMSE over most of the existing algorithms.

References

1. Astola, J., Haavisto, P., Neuvo, Y.: Vector median filters. Proc. IEEE **78**, 678–689 (1990)
2. Astola, J., Kuosmanen, P.: Fundamentals of Nonlinear Digital Filtering. CRC, Boca Raton (1997)
3. Chan, R.H., Ho, C.W., Nikolova, M.: Salt-and-pepper noise removal by median-type noise detectors and detail-preserving regularization. IEEE Trans. Image Process. **14**, 1479–1485 (2005)
4. Cheng, L., Hou, Z.-G., Tan, M.: Relaxation labeling using an improved hopfield neural network. In: Huang, D.-S., Li, K., Irwin, G.W. (eds.) Intelligent Computing in Signal Processing and Pattern Recognition. LNCIS, vol. 345, pp. 430–439. Springer, Heidelberg (2006)
5. Dong, Y., Chan, R.H., Xu, S.: A detection statistic for random-valued impulse noise. IEEE Trans. Image Process. **16**, 1112–1120 (2007)
6. Gonzalez, R., Woods, R.: Digital Image Processing, 3rd edn. Addison-Wesley, Boston (1993)
7. Gabbouj, M., Cheickh, F.A.: Vector median-vector directional hybrid filter for color image restoration. In: Proceedings of EUSIPCO-96, pp. 879–881 (1996)
8. Jin, L., Li, D.: An efficient color-impulse detector and its application to color images. IEEE Signal Process. Lett. **14**, 397–400 (2007)
9. Khryashchev, V., Kuykin, D., Studenova, A.: Vector median filter with directional detector for color image denoising. In: Proceedings of the World Congress on Engineering (London), vol. 2 (2011)
10. Karakos, D.G., Trahanias, P.E.: Generalized multichannel image-filtering structures. IEEE Trans. Image Process. **6**, 1038–1045 (1997)
11. Lukac, R.: Adaptive vector median filtering. Pattern Recognit. Lett. **24**, 1889–1899 (2003)
12. Lukac, R., Plataniotis, K.N., Venetsanopoulos, A.N., Smolka, B.: A statistically-switched adaptive vector median filter. J. Intell. Robot. Syst. Theory Appl. **42**, 361–391 (2005)
13. Lukac, R., Smolk, B., Plataniotis, K.N.: Sharpening vector median filters. Signal Process. **87**, 2085–2099 (2007)
14. Lukac, R., Smolka, B., Martin, K., Plataniotis, K.N., Venetsanopoulos, A.N.: Vector filtering for color imaging. IEEE Signal Process. Mag. **22**, 74–86 (2005)
15. Plataniotis, K.N., Androutsos, D., Venetsanopoulos, A.N.: Color image processing using adaptive vector directional filters. IEEE Trans. Circ. Syst. **II**(45), 1414–1419 (1998)

16. Plataniotis, K.N., Venetsanopoulos, A.N.: Color Image Processing and Applications. Springer, Berlin (2000)
17. Trahanias, P.E., Karakos, D.G., Venetsanopoulos, A.N.: Directional processing of color images: theory and experimental results. IEEE Trans. Image Process. **5**, 868–880 (1996)

An Image Mosaic Method Based on Deviation Splitting and Transferring for Vehicle Panoramic System

Shanshan Feng, Ting Wang, Haibo Huang$^{(\boxtimes)}$, and Liguo Chen$^{(\boxtimes)}$

School of Mechanical and Electric Engineering & Collaborative Innovation
Center of Suzhou Nano Science and Technology, Soochow University,
178 Gan-Jiang Road (East), Gu-Su District, Suzhou, China
{hbhuang, chenliguo}@suda.edu.cn

Abstract. A method for look-around image mosaic is proposed, in order to solve the problem that dislocation distortion still exists in overlap region in terms of panoramic system. Firstly, the principal and construction difficulties of panoramic system are analyzed. On this basis, combined with the common panoramic image stitching method, the cause for poor image stitching is analyzed. Afterwards, with the purpose of reducing distortion in overlap region, a method for panoramic image mosaic by dividing left and right images to transfer and split original stitching deviation is proposed. In addition, the detailed implementation plan is given. The proposed stitching method is realized by MATLAB programming, and the experiment shows that the dislocation distortion is less than conventional method. The proposed panoramic image mosaic method is small-dislocation and non-blind, thus it can satisfy the requirement of human vision and contribute to panoramic system's realization.

Keywords: Panoramic system · Image stitching · Stitching dislocation

1 Introduction

With the development of economic globalization, the world's car ownership has exceeded 10 billion vehicles. However, at the same time, the frequency of traffic accidents is increasing year by year. In recent years, "pilotless automobile", "new energy", "around view" and other technologies have become the research boom in the automotive industry. Automobile safety technology is developing towards the direction of intelligence and systematization. Among them, the car panorama system can avoid a series of road safety hidden trouble caused by the obstruction of sight and improve the safety of driving. The key to the application of the system is the stitching technology of fisheye image.

At present, there are many R & D institutions for panoramic system technology. For example: In order to achieve the full coverage of small cars, buses and construction vehicles, Chery Automobile Co., Ltd. and Microelectronics Institute of Chinese Academy of Sciences are working together to carry out the research of "vehicle 360 degree environmental reconstruction system" [1–3]. In the market, the main products

© Springer International Publishing AG 2017
M. Liu et al. (Eds.): ICVS 2017, LNCS 10528, pp. 218–227, 2017.
DOI: 10.1007/978-3-319-68345-4_20

are the following categories: Land Rover as a representative of the four-bit image split-screen display system; Nissan AVM (Around View Monitor) based on seamed stitching system; Micron, Delphi and Volkswagen as the representative of the Seamless stitching, which can eliminate the blind seam region, but the existence of splice marks and distortion dislocation is obvious. The panoramic system of Nissan X-Trail and Delphi BEV Gen1.1 as shown in Fig. 1.

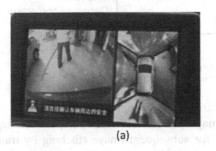 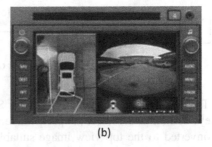

(a)   (b)

Fig. 1. The panoramic system of Nissan X-Trail and Delphi BEV Gen1.1, (a) Nissan X-Trail (2012), (b) Delphi BEV Gen1.1

Presently, in consideration of problems such as distortion in the overlapping area of the panoramic image, there are two solutions:

(1) "Avoidance" strategy. Taking the highest market share of Nissan AVM system as an example. In order to avoid the problem of poor display of the system caused by the dislocation distortion of the overlapping area, the Nissan AVM system had set the gap in the overlapping area, and the blind spot was introduced at the same time.
(2) "Distortion" strategy. The typical method is to use a large number of distortions in the fourth images to achieve the effect of the image in the overlap area without dislocation, such as the three spline interpolation method is used as the distortion of the calculation of the fourth images.

However, all of the above methods are Sequential splicing methods, such as: left and right images are spliced with the front image respectively, then the rear image is spliced with the left image. In the process of image mosaic and the image preprocessing stage, the deviation will cause the distortion of the fourth image splicing. In this paper, a new method is proposed to realize the image stitching by dividing the left and right images, and the experimental results are compared with the conventional stitching method.

2 Image Preprocessing

The process of image preprocessing is shown in Fig. 2. The panoramic system collects the images through the 4 fisheye cameras installed in the car's front, rear, left and right. With image preprocessing, image mosaic and image fusion [4, 5], panoramic image can be displayed. The main purpose of image preprocessing is to restore it to ordinary perspective image and transform the ordinary perspective image into a top view image according to the splicing requirements of the 2D panoramic system.

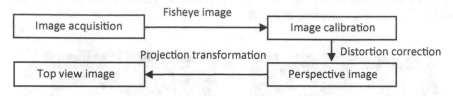

Fig. 2. The process of image preprocessing

The hyperboloid model proposed by Scaramuzz is adopted here to calibrate the fisheye camera and correct the perspective image [6]. The corrected perspective image is converted to the top view image suitable for subsequent image stitching by transformation matrix. In this paper, the projection transformation scheme based on two transformations [7] is adopted, the results are shown in Fig. 3.

Fig. 3. Image preprocessing process diagram, (a) Fisheye distortion image, (b) General perspective image, (c) Top view image

3 Image Mosaic Based on Deviation Splitting and Transferring

With the purpose of reducing distortion in overlap region, a method for panoramic image mosaic by dividing left and right images to transfer and split original stitching deviation is proposed. The following is the whole process of panoramic image mosaic, including image preprocessing, image registration, image stitching and image fusion.

3.1 Extraction of Feature Points in Image Overlap Region

In this paper, Harris corner detection [8] is used to extract the corner points of the grid plate in sequence. It is shown in Fig. 4.

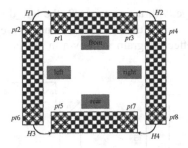

Fig. 4. Feature points extraction of overlap regions diagram (Color figure online)

The red dots in the figure are the feature points detected by corner points. The pt1 and pt2 are set as the pixel coordinate matrices of the front image corner points and the left image corner points respectively. The characteristic corner pair is (pt1, pt2). The feature points of the overlap regions in the four images can be extracted by using this method, and get the characteristic corner pairs of the overlap regions: (pt3, pt4), (pt5, pt6), (pt7, pt8).

3.2 Image Segmentation and Registration

According to the formula (1), the registration matrices can be calculated separately. Its formula can be expressed as:

$$
\begin{cases}
pt1 = H1 \times pt2 \\
pt3 = H2 \times pt4 \\
pt5 = H3 \times pt6 \\
pt7 = H4 \times pt8
\end{cases}
\tag{1}
$$

Here, $H1 \sim H4$ represent the registration matrices between images; $pt1 \sim pt8$ represent pixel coordinate matrices.

As the four-way overlooking image requires a wide range of vision coverage, so there is a strong blooming in the image boundary of the four-way overlooking image. This phenomenon limited the automatic extraction of corners, in order to solve the problem, manual extraction is adopted in this paper. An initial corner is determined by clicking the mouse, and then the corner points in the preset range are detected by the method of Harris corner detection. The experimental results show that the proposed method is suitable for fuzzy region. In this paper, the RANSAC method is used to purify the extracted corner points after corner extraction. The corner points with large deviation are eliminated, and the calculation precision of the registration matrix is improved effectively.

The left and right images are divided into two parts respectively after the completion of the registration matrix calculation, which are recorded as left_up, left_down, right_up and right_down. The registration of the upper and lower two parts can be realized according to the calculation of the corresponding registration matrix. The left_up image is registered to the front image by matrix H1, the right_up image is registered to the front image with the matrix H2, the left_down image is registered to the rear image with the matrix H3, the right_down image is registered to the rear image with the matrix H4. The effect diagram is shown in the Fig. 5(a).

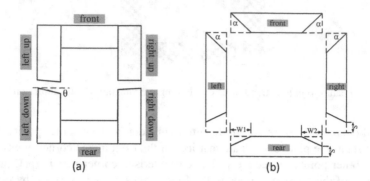

(a)   (b)

Fig. 5. The effect diagram of image segmentation and registration, (a) The schematic diagram of registration, (b) The schematic diagram of cutting seams

The seam diagram is shown in Fig. 5(b). The seams are formed by cutting the overlap regions of the registration images. The diagonals of the overlap regions are set as seams for the registration of left_up, right_up and front images. It sets the rear image height at 1/2 of the overlap region as seams for the registration of left_down, right_down and rear images, which takes into account that the left and right fisheye cameras are far away from the rear of the car, the overlap region of the left, right and rear images is fuzzy seriously. In the figure, W1 and W2 are the width of left_down and right_down images. S represents half of the height for the rear image. It sets the height and width of front, left_up, left_down, right_up, right_down, rear images as (h1,w1),(h2,w2),(h3,w3),(h4, w4),(h5,w5),(h6,w6) respectively after cutting. In addition, the pixel coordinates of the top left corner point of each cropped image are (1, 1). After cutting and image registration, the registration effect is shown in the Fig. 6(a).

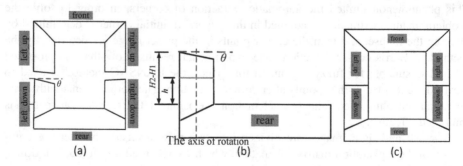

(a)   (b)   (c)

Fig. 6. The schematic of inclination level adjustment and image mosaic, (a) Schematic diagram of image registration, (b) The schematic of inclination level adjustment, (c) Ideal segmentation effect of image mosaic

Thus, the seam of the front and left_up images can be expressed as:

$$\begin{cases} front : v = \frac{w_2-1}{h_1-1} \times u + \frac{h_1-w_2}{h_1-1} \\ left\_up : v = \frac{w_2-1}{h_1-1} \times u + \frac{h_1-w_2}{h_1-1} \end{cases} \tag{2}$$

The seam of the front and right_up images can be expressed as:

$$\begin{cases} front : v = -\frac{w_4}{h_1-1} \times u + \frac{w_4-w_2}{h_1-1} + w_1 \\ right\_up : v = \frac{1-w_4}{h_1-1} \times u + \frac{h_1 \times w_4-1}{H_1-1} \end{cases} \tag{3}$$

The seam of the rear and left_up images can be expressed as:

$$\begin{cases} rear : v = \frac{2 \times (w_3-1)}{2-h_6} \times u + \frac{2-w_3 \times h_6}{2-h_6} \\ left\_down : v = \frac{2 \times (1-w_3)}{h_6-2} \times u + 1 - \frac{(1-w_3)(2 \times H_3-H_6)}{h_6-2} \end{cases} \tag{4}$$

The seam of the rear and left_down images can be expressed as:

$$\begin{cases} rear : v = \frac{2 \times w_5}{h_6-2} \times u + w_6 - \frac{w_5 \times h_6}{h_6-2} \\ right\_down : v = \frac{2 \times (w_5-1)}{h_6-2} \times u + 1 - \frac{(w_5-1)(h_5-h_6+1)}{h_6-2} \end{cases} \tag{5}$$

3.3 Horizontal Adjustment of the Inclination Angle

It can be seen from Fig. 6(a) that the cumulative deviation transfers from the fourth image of the seam to the split sections of the left and right images after division, which is mainly reflected in the tilt angle of image segmentation line relative to the horizontal line. This paper presents a method of horizontally adjusting the segmented image by decreasing the angle of rotation line by line. This technique not only enables the split image to be adjusted horizontally, but also minimizes the pixel voids caused by the rotation.

In this paper, we take the level adjustment of left_down image as an example to illustrate this problem. The principle is shown in Fig. 6(b). The steps are as follows. Firstly, the declination of the upper edge of the left_down image and the horizontal line is calculated, which is set to θ. The height of left_down and rear images are set to H2 and H1 respectively, and the vertical center line of the left_down image is the center of rotation for every line. Finally, the non-overlapping part of the left_down image with the rear image will be adjusted line by line. Taking the line of the left_down image as an example, the height of which distances from the top edge of the rear image is h. The rotation angle β is shown in formula (6).

$$\beta = \frac{\theta}{H2 - H1} \times h \tag{6}$$

3.4   The Mosaic of the Registration Image

The inclined edge will be close to the horizontal line after the horizontal adjustment of the image, which can make it easily for the image mosaic. The translation distance of the upper and lower two images in vertical and horizontal directions can be calculated through the relevant image coordinates of the upper and lower two parts of the image after the horizontal adjustment of deflection angle. The ideal effect is shown in Fig. 6(c).

4   Comparative Analysis of Experiments

In this paper, the commonly used sequential splicing method and the segmentation and splicing method which based on the deviation transfer and split are realized by MATLAB programming. The ideal pixel size of a single grid in the image is 20 × 20 pixels after image preprocessing. The implementation process is as shown in Fig. 7.

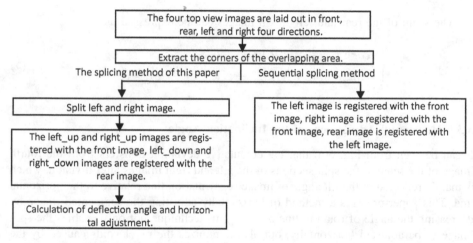

Fig. 7. The algorithm process of the comparison experiment

Figure 8(a) and (b) represent the inclination of the image before and after the horizontal adjustment respectively. It is obvious that the inclination of the right_down image is well adjusted horizontally. Figure 8(c) and (d) represent the effect diagrams of sequential stitching and image splicing method based on the deviation splitting and transferring.

In this paper, the deviation of the pixels between the feature points in the red rectangle region in Fig. 8(c) and the variation of the relevant division points in Fig. 8 (d) before and after the image stitching are compared. The results are shown in Table 1. It can be found that the method proposed in this paper realizes the use of the small deviation at the left and right partitions instead of the large deviations in the seam.

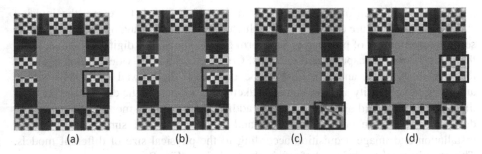

Fig. 8. The effect of stitching results comparison, (a) Before horizontal adjustment, (b) After horizontal adjustment, (c) The sequential stitching, (d) Segmentation and splicing method (Color figure online)

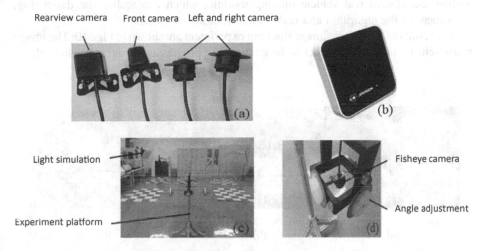

Fig. 9. Hardware platform of experiment, (a) Four way super wide angle fisheye camera for vehicle, (b) Video capture card, (c) Platform analog system, (d) Tilt angle adjusting mechanism

Table 1. Comparison of pixel deviation of two splicing methods

Stitching method	Sample feature points (piece)	Total deviation of pixels (pixel)	Average deviation pixels (pixel)
Sequence	16	148	9.25
Segmentation	8	49	6.1

5 Experimental Results and Conclusions

Before the experiment, a simulation experiment platform of panoramic system is constructed. Guangzhou Zhiyuan electronic development of large wide-angle fisheye cameras are used on the platform, whose working voltage is DC 3.3 V, the image resolution is 480 × 640, the working level angle of view is 185 ± 5 degrees and the vertical is 148 ± 5 degrees.

As the acquisition of the fisheye camera is analog signal, therefore, the jovision audio and video capture card JVS-C301 which supports NTSC analog video signal and second development of program to transform analog signal into digital signal are used, the frame rate of the capture card is 25 fps. Considering that the video analog signal of the camera is weak, and it is easy to be disturbed, the coaxial cable with strong anti-interference ability and low signal weakening is adopted in the connection between the video capture card and the camera. In addition, four camera mounting brackets are designed, which can adjust the height and angle freely and simulate the camera installation and image acquisition according to the physical size of different models. The experimental hardware platform is shown below (Fig. 9).

In this experiment, we use C# programming to construct the software experiment system. In the image processing section, OpenCV is used to carry on the realization of the correlation algorithm. The software system is mainly divided into algorithm test module and system real vehicle running module, which can realize the debugging, experiment of the algorithm and real vehicle running of system.

The results of panoramic image stitching experiment are shown in Fig. 10. The image fusion scheme used in this paper is the gradual and progressive weighted fusion [9].

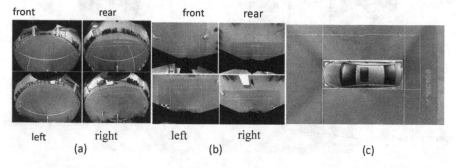

Fig. 10. The impression images of panoramic image stitching experimental results, (a) Fisheye distortion image in real scene, (b) Transformation diagram of overhead view, (c) The effect image of panoramic image

It can be seen from Fig. 11 that compared with the Mercedes-Benz panoramic system, the splitting method based on the deviation transferring and splitting proposed in this paper have achieved the expected target of reducing the dislocation distortion and have better visual effect.

In this paper, the results of the experiment show that the method of image mosaic based on deviation shift and split can effectively eliminate the dislocation and distortion in the panoramic image mosaic. In this method, the dislocation of the fourth image stitching is separated and transferred to the left and right images, and large distortion of the left and right images is avoided through the horizontal adjustment of the inclination. The scheme proposed in this paper achieves a better panoramic image mosaic effect.

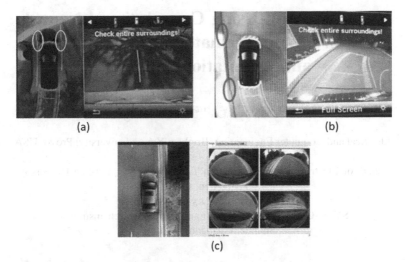

(a)   (b)

(c)

Fig. 11. Comparison of visual effects of panoramic system, (a) Benz 2013 annual panorama system GL, (b) Benz 2014 annual panorama system ML350, (c) The panorama system of this paper

Acknowledgment. This research was financially supported by the Project of the National Natural Science Foundation of China (No. 61327802) and Program for New Century Excellent Talents (NCET-13-0923).

References

1. Lu, B., Qin, R., Li, Q., et al.: Study of vehicle-surrounding image stitch algorithm. Comput. Sci. J. **09**, 293–295 (2013)
2. Liang, Y.J., Li, Q., Chen, D.P., et al.: Wide-view image system based on Internet of cars. Appl. Res. Comput. J. **29**(6), 2145–2147 (2012)
3. Fang, C.Y., Den, J., Tan, Y.X.: Panoramic parking system and image splicing technological study. Automob. Parts J. **11**, 103–105 (2012)
4. Wang, X.D.: Autonomous Parking System Research and Design on Bird's Eye View. Shanghai Jiao Tong University for the Degree of Master, Shanghai (2013)
5. Cancare, F., Bhandari, S., Bartolini, D.B., et al.: A bird's eye view of FPGA-based evolvable hardware. In: Proceedings of AHS, pp. 169–175 (2011)
6. Scaramuzza, D., Martinelli, A., Siegwart, R.: A flexible technique for accurate omnidirectional camera calibration and structure from motion. In: IEEE International Conference on Computer Vision Systems 2006, vol. 1, p. 45. IEEE, New York (2006)
7. Wang, T., Chen, L.: Image preprocessing for vehicle panoramic system. In: SPIE/COS Photonics Asia 2016. International Society for Optics and Photonics, Beijing (2016)
8. Zhang, W., Zhang, J.J.: Research on image mosaic technology based on harris corner. Electron. Qual. **7**, 12–14 (2016)
9. Guo, J.: Multiple Image Stitching Technique Research Based on the Feature Points. Xi'an University of Science and Technology, Xi'an (2012)

Edge Detection Using Convolutional Neural Networks for Nematode Development and Adaptation Analysis

Yao Chou[1], Dah Jye Lee[1(✉)], and Dong Zhang[2,3]

[1] Electrical and Computer Engineering, Brigham Young University, Provo, USA
{yaochou, djlee}@byu.edu
[2] School of Electronics and Information Technology, Sun Yat-Sen University,
Guangzhou, China
zhangd@mail.sysu.edu.cn
[3] SYSU-CMU Shunde International Joint Research Institute,
Shunde, Guangdong, China

Abstract. The Antarctic nematode Plectus Murrayi is an excellent model organism for the study of stress and molecular mechanisms. Biologists analyze its development and adaptation by measuring the body length and volume. This work proposes an edge detection algorithm to automate this labor-intensive task. Traditional edge detection techniques use predefined filters to calculate the edge strength and apply a threshold to it to identify edge pixels. These classic edge detection techniques work independently of the image data and their results are sometimes inconsistent when edge contrast varies. Convolutional Neural Networks (CNNs) are regarded as powerful visual models that yield hierarchies of features learned from image data, and perform well for edge detection. Most CNNs based edge detection methods rely on classification networks to determine if an edge point exists at the center of a small image patch. This patch-by-patch classification approach is slow and inconsistent. In this paper, we propose an efficient CNN-based regression network that is able to produce accurate edge detection result. This network learns a direct end-to-end mapping between the original image and the desired edge image. This image-to-edge mapping is represented as a CNN that takes the original image as the input and outputs its edge map. The feature-based mapping rules of the network are learned directly from the training images and their accompanying ground truth. Experimental results show that this architecture achieves accurate edge detection and is faster than other CNN-based methods.

Keywords: Edge detection · Convolutional Neural Networks · Deep learning · Regression

1 Introduction

In biology, nematodes have now attained the 'model organism' status, which makes them an ideal model for the study of biological systems [1]. Morphological structure analysis is needed for studying their populations and evolution [2]. Currently, a

© Springer International Publishing AG 2017
M. Liu et al. (Eds.): ICVS 2017, LNCS 10528, pp. 228–238, 2017.
DOI: 10.1007/978-3-319-68345-4_21

high-resolution camera is used to collect high-quality nematode image data for analysis. Biologists manually draw the edge of nematodes and estimate their body length and volume. Researches have routinely used the Andrassy's formula [3] as a means to estimate body weight, especially from Plectus Murrayi images. The Andrassy's formula is expressed as

$$W = \frac{lw^2}{k},$$ (1)

where W is the weight in μg, l is the body length of the nematode in μm, w is the widest body width of the nematode, and k is a constant that ranges between 1.6×10^6 and 1.7×10^6. Figure 1 illustrates the technique used to measure the body widths for volume estimation using the Andrassy's formula.

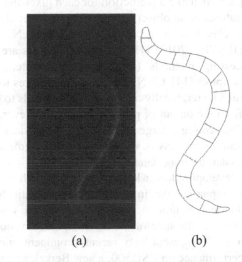

(a)   (b)

Fig. 1. Illustration of the technique used to estimate body volume.

Ecologists interested in estimating nematode biomass generally average the weights calculated from a relatively large number of specimens [4]. However, nematodes are constantly moving and their body and medium are nearly transparent making the boundary between the nematode and the medium blurry and the image contrast sensitive to lighting variation. These challenges make it very difficult to extract a good outline of the nematode. Manually segmenting them from the background to obtain a good outline of the sample remains a labor-intensive task. An efficient and robust image analysis tool is needed to automatically segment and detect the body outline of the nematode from the background. We have developed a unique edge detection method to automate this labor-intensive task.

Traditionally, the boundary of an object in an image can be detected via filter-based algorithms. Some early and popular works in this category are gradient-based algorithms such as Sobel [5], Prewitt, Laplacian of Gaussian (LOG), and Roberts [6]. These methods apply 2D spatial gradient convolution operations to an image and look for local maxima to locate edge points. The Canny edge detection was developed by John F. Canny in the late 1980's. The original Canny algorithm computes the higher and lower thresholds for edge detection based on the statistics of the entire image which prevents the processing of the image blocks independent of each other [7]. These gradient-based approaches are simple and effective but sensitive to noise [8].

In recent years, deep learning has shown remarkable results for high-level vision tasks in various image processing fields for most benchmark image datasets such as MNIST [9], CIFAR-10 [10], SVHN [11], etc. CNN, as a milestone model of deep learning, are driving advances in image analysis. CNNs not only improve the performance of whole-image classification [12], but also make significant progress in extracting features [13]. CNNs make a prediction for each pixel and are able to take the advantage of detailed features of an object image. Krizhevsky et al. made a substantial improvement in image classification accuracy on the ImageNet large-scale visual recognition challenge (ILSVRC 2012) [12]. These approaches are different from the traditional image processing methods (e.g. HOG, SIFT etc.), which involve a hand-crafted feature descriptors [14]. CNNs are deep architectures for learning features. All the features are learned hierarchically all the way from pixels to classifier, and each layer extracts features from the output of previous layers. However, to obtain superior performance, these CNNs require a large amount of training data and a complicated training process. The training process is slow and requires tremendous manpower to manually generate annotated training datasets.

Recently, efforts of developing lower-level vision tasks such as edge detection and contour detection, that emphasize the importance of automatic hierarchical feature learning using Convolutional Neural Networks have started vigorous discussions. These approaches currently are the state-of-the-art in low-level vision tasks. DeepEdge [15] and DeepContour [16] represent two recent prominent successes. DeepEdge demonstrates superior performance on BSD500, a new Berkeley Segmentation Dataset. Their method runs Canny edge detector to extract candidate contour points, extracts the surrounding patches in four different scales and then simultaneously runs them through a pre-trained CNN. The output features of CNN are connected to two separately-trained network branches. During the training, however, the weights in the convolutional layers are fixed and only the weights in the fully connected layers of the two branches are learned. Due to the lack of supervised learning, the features extracted at the hidden layers are not always meaningful. DeepContour can achieve top performance on BSDS500 and NYUD dataset. It customizes the training strategy by partitioning contour (positive) data into subclasses and fitting each subclass by different model parameters. The challenges are the complexity of the algorithm and the use of many label classes which significantly increases the number of parameters.

All the aforementioned CNN-based edge detection methods treat CNN as a classifier. For a small image patch extracted from the original image, the task is to predict if the patch includes an edge point. Each individual patch detection requires one CNN forward pass. The reconstruction is computationally expensive, requiring minutes of computation using a personal computer.

As mentioned above, traditional filter-based algorithms are fast but are not able to take the advantage of the detailed features of the nematode object which leads to unsatisfactory result. On the other hand, current CNN-based edge detection algorithms perform well but slow. In order to build an efficient and robust system for nematode image, we propose a novel fully convolutional neural network for edge detection for specific objects with implicit features. The network learns a direct end-to-end mapping between the original image and its edge map. Since our focus is on improving the network processing speed, the proposed CNN structure is intentionally designed with simplicity. Experiments show our method is as fast as the simple threshold-based methods and much faster than the existing CNN classification approaches. The quality of the network can be further improved when larger and more diverse datasets are available and a larger and deeper model is used. Figure 2 presents an overview of our method.

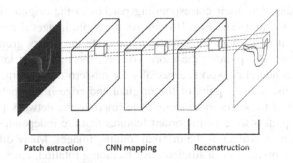

Patch extraction   CNN mapping   Reconstruction

Fig. 2. An overview of our method

This paper is organized as follows: The problem formulation along with the data generation is provided in Sect. 2. In Sect. 3, we present the details of our CNN architecture for this work and show experimental results and discuss our findings. Finally, the paper is summarized and concluded with future research directions in Sect. 4.

2 Model Formulation

Criteria for edge detection are expected to be different for specific applications. Detection of the boundary pixels based on the features obtained from the image data is a reasonable strategy. The main highlight of a deep learning algorithm is that all features are learned from the image data directly. Consider a single original image, denoted as X. Our goal is to map from X to an edge image Y. We wish the network to learn a mapping F which maps X to Y as $Y = F(X)$. Our edge detection method consists of the following steps:

1. Patch extraction and augmentation: extracts (overlapping) patches from the edge image X, selects certain patches as training data, finds their corresponding patches from original image X, and then augments all the patch pairs.
2. CNN Non-linear mapping: this operation nonlinearly maps each patch onto the edge map by the CNN.
3. Result generation: this operation aggregates the above patch-wise processing to generate the final edge map which is expected to be similar to the ground truth Y.

2.1 Patch Extraction and Augmentation

As shown in Fig. 1(a), the body of a nematode is nearly transparent, and its shape varies. Differentiating the body of nematodes from the background consistently with high accuracy is a much more challenging task than many edge detection applications. A sliding window is applied to split the whole ground truth image Y into small overlapping patches. For the nematodes edge detection application, less than 1% of the image pixels in the image are edge points. To avoid using unbalanced data (much more negative than positive) for training, we extract only patches that contain at least one edge pixel. We then find their corresponding patches in the original image X as the input images for training. The Fig. 1(a) shows a sample image of a nematode taken from our dataset. It is segmented manually to generate the binary ground-truth image shown in Fig. 1(b). The phrase "the more you see, the more you know" works for humans as well as neural networks, especially for modern deep neural networks [17]. After generating the training pairs of the original and edge image patches, data augmentation is applied to obtain more samples to improve the network performance.

The network prefers to learn important features that are independent of the object classes, rather than an artifact of the original training images. Many different methods for data augmentation have been studied [18], including rotation, crop, flip, scale, tone change or JPEG compression, etc. Analyzing the characteristic of our data, we choose 2 flips (horizontal and vertical) and 3 rotations (90°, 180°, 270°). This step increases the number of training examples by a factor of 5.

2.2 CNN Non-linear Mapping

Our fully convolutional network architecture excludes pooling and fully connected layers. This is equivalent to convolving the image by a set of filters and bias coefficients. In our formulation, our first layer is expressed as an operation $F1$:

$$F1(x) = max(0, \ W1 * x + B1), \tag{2}$$

where $W1$ and $B1$ represent the filters and bias coefficients respectively, and '$*$' denotes the convolution operation. We apply the Rectified Linear Unit [19] (ReLU, $max(0, x)$) on the filter responses.

Similarly, we add three more convolutional layers after the first layer, each followed by a ReLU layer except the last layer. In order to retain the negative information, we remove the last ReLU layer, and add a Sigmoid layer to map the output value to between 0 and 1. These layers are shown in Eqs. (3)–(6).

$$F2(x) = max(0, \ W2 * x + B2), \tag{3}$$

$$F3(x) = max(0, \ W3 * x + B3), \tag{4}$$

$$F4(x) = W4 * x + B4, \tag{5}$$

$$F(x) = \frac{1}{1 + exp(F4(x))}. \tag{6}$$

Learning the end-to-end mapping function F requires the estimation of network parameters $\Theta = \{W1, W2, W3, W4, B1, B2, B3, B4\}$. This is achieved through minimizing the loss between the reconstructed images $F(X, \Theta)$ and the corresponding ground truth edge map Y. Given a set of original image patches $\{x_i\}$ and their corresponding ground truth patches $\{y_i\}$, we use Mean Squared Error (MSE) as the loss function:

$$L(\Theta) = \frac{1}{n} \sum_{i=1}^{n} \|F(x_i \ ; \ \Theta) - y_i\|^2. \tag{7}$$

where n is the number of training samples. The loss is minimized using stochastic gradient descent (SGD) with the standard backpropagation. The CNN portion of our experiments used the Caffe framework [20] running on an NVIDIA TITAN-X.

2.3   Edge Map Generation

The training process produces a set of convolutional filters and bias coefficients learned from the training data. Contrasting to the training process in which input patches are sent through the network without padding, the prediction network inputs the whole nematode image into the network with padding to retain the same image size as X, and removes the last sigmoid layer to speed up the prediction process. This design allows us to obtain the edge map in one single forward pass. Then the final edge map is obtained by binarizing the output of the CNN.

3   Experiment and Evaluation

The nematode image database we used for this paper was prepared by the Biology Department at Brigham Young University. The proposed approach successfully detected nematode body outlines. Compared with other classic methods, it detected more true edge pixels and much fewer noise pixels.

3.1   Training Data

As shown in the literature, deep learning generally benefits from big data training. We collected 44 nematode images with ground truth that was generated manually. We randomly selected 33 images for training and 11 images for validation. The size of training patches is $37 \times 37 \times 3$, while the corresponding ground truth patches is

21×21. Thus, this 33-image training dataset and 11-image validation dataset can be decomposed into 388136 patches and 115982 patches with stride 2.

3.2　Layers and Filters

In theory, the performance would improve if we increased the network width, i.e., adding more filters, at the cost of execution time. We chose a simple 4-layer network as our model. The detailed settings are presented in Fig. 3. *Padding* $= 0$ and *stride* $= 1$ are fixed in training.

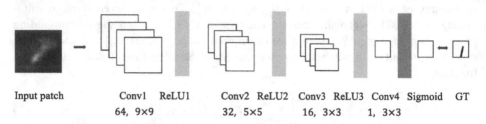

Input patch　　　Conv1　ReLU1　　Conv2　ReLU2　Conv3　ReLU3　Conv4　Sigmoid　GT
　　　　　　　　64, 9×9　　　　　32, 5×5　　16, 3×3　　1, 3×3

Fig. 3. Illustration of Convolutional Neural Network (CNN) architecture.

3.3　Discussion

Although our model was trained from only 33 images, it was able to detect edges of other nematode images within this dataset very well. We believe if trained with more images, the proposed method would perform even better. Results from the proposed method look very close to the ground truth compared with the other traditional edge detection methods that are sensitive to image noise. Our results were compared with classic methods such as Sobel, Canny, LOG, Prewitt, and Roberts, as shown in Fig. 4.

Precision and recall curve is often used for evaluating edge detection algorithms. In our case, the width of the manually annotated nematode edge is only one pixel. Because the edge of nematode is blurry, it sometimes can occupy more than one pixel. All nematode images used for our experiments were taken with a 1360×1024 high-resolution camera. This high resolution allows us to select a window of 11×11 pixels to calculate the recall and precision as shown in Eqs. (8) and (9).

$$Recall = \frac{\#\text{True edge pixels found in edge map}}{\#\text{Positive pixels in ground truth}}, \tag{8}$$

For every edge pixel in the ground truth, if the edge map has at least one positive pixel in its surrounding area of 11×11 pixels, we will count this edge pixel as founded.

$$Precision = \frac{\#\text{True edge pixels found in edge map}}{\#\text{Positive pixels in edge map}}. \tag{9}$$

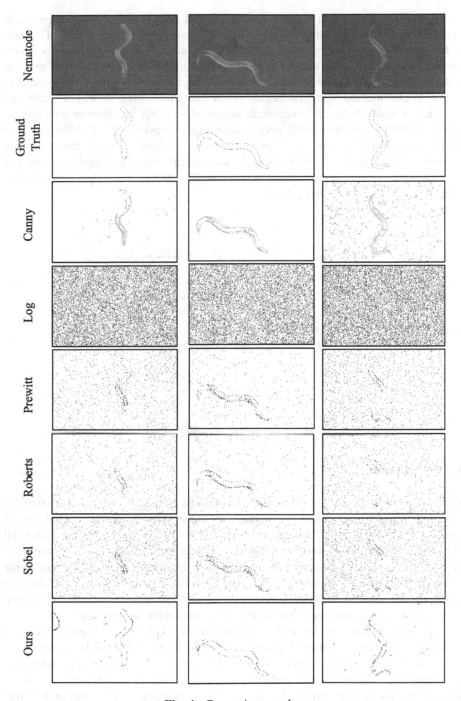

Fig. 4. Comparison results

For every positive pixel in the edge map, it will be counted as a true edge pixels found in edge map, if it locates an edge pixel in the surrounding area of 11×11 pixels in the ground truth. This modified recall and precision evaluate edge detention performance in our nematode images very well. Leading contour detection methods are ranked according to their best F-measure with respect to human ground truth contours in Fig. 5. Our method achieves the top result and shows both improved recall and precision at most of the precision-recall regime. Our CNN architecture was able to handle challenging datasets with very competitive processing speed. After the edge points are detected, we can apply post-processing methods to erode the noise and reconstruct some missing edge points in the subsequent steps. The length and width of the nematode can then be estimated accurately from the refined edge map. At last, volume will be estimated using Eq. (1).

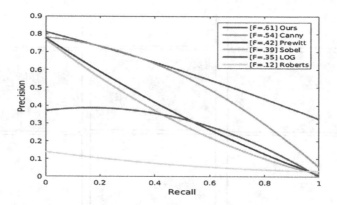

Fig. 5. Recall and precision curve

4   Conclusion

In this paper, we propose an efficient Convolutional Neural Network architecture for edge detection. Our motivation is to achieve the same or more accurate edge detection result by state-of-the-art CNN-based methods and yet process as fast as the traditional filter-based methods. This work proposes an interesting concept that could be improved further. We train a CNN as a regression tool to filter the image patches to be close to the ground truth. With a lightweight structure, our CNN has achieved superior performance efficiently and robustly. It outputs much cleaner and less noisy edge map, which is a foundation in our system for calculate the nematode length and volume later.

The performance can be further improved by exploring different filters and including more training images. Pre/post-processing can be investigated to optimize the edge detection result in our system. Additionally, with the efficiency and robustness of our proposed structure, we believe it is feasible to implement it on a field-programmable gate array (FPGA) to build an embedded vision sensor for edge detection.

Acknowledgment. We would like to thank Ms. Xia Xue and the Biology Department at Brigham Young University for preparing and allowing us to use the nematode images for our experiments and NVIDIA for supporting our research by donating GPU.

References

1. Eyualem-Abebe, J.G.B., Adams, B., Hope, D., Gardner, S., Huettel, R., Mullin, P., Powers, T., Sharma, J., Ye, W., Thomas, W.K.: A position paper on the electronic publication of nematode taxonomic manuscripts. J. Nematol. **38**(3), 305 (2006)
2. Grillo, V., Jackson, F., Cabaret, J., Gilleard, J.S.: Population genetic analysis of the ovine parasitic nematode Teladorsagia circumcincta and evidence for a cryptic species. Int. J. Parasitol. **37**(3), 435–447 (2007)
3. Andrassy, I.: Die rauminhalts-und gewichtsbestimmung der fadenwürmer (Nematoden). Acta Zoologica Hungarica **2**(1), 1–5 (1965)
4. de Tomasel, C.M., Adams, B.J., Tomasel, F.G., Wall, D.H.: The life cycle of the Antarctic nematode under laboratory conditions. J. Nematol. **45**(1), 39–42 (2013)
5. Vairalkar, M.K., Nimbhorkar, S.U.: Edge detection of images using Sobel operator. Int. J. Emerg. Technol. Adv. Eng. **2**(1), 291–293 (2012)
6. Bhardwaj, S., Mittal, A.: A survey on various edge detector techniques. Procedia Technol. **4**, 220–226 (2012)
7. Deokar, P.S., Kaushik, A.R.: Review on distributed canny edge detector using FPGA. Int. J. Innov. Res. Electron. Comm. **1**, 37–45 (2014)
8. Machuca, R., Gilbert, A.L.: Finding edges in noisy scenes. IEEE Trans. Pattern Anal. Mach. Intell. **1**, 103–111 (1981)
9. Wan, L., Zeiler, M., Zhang, S., Cun, Y.L., Fergus, R.: Regularization of neural networks using dropconnect. In: Proceedings of International Conference on Machine Learning, pp. 1058–1066 (2013)
10. Graham, B.: Fractional max-pooling. arXiv preprint arXiv:1412.6071 (2014)
11. Clevert, D.A., Unterthiner, T., Hochreiter, S.: Fast and accurate deep network learning by exponential linear units (ELUs). arXiv preprint arXiv:1511.07289 (2015)
12. Krizhevsky, A., Sutskever, I., Hinton, G.E.: ImageNet classification with deep convolutional neural networks. In: Advances in Neural Information Processing Systems, pp. 1097–1105 (2012)
13. Sharif Razavian, A., Azizpour, H., Sullivan, J., Carlsson, S.: CNN features off-the-shelf: an astounding baseline for recognition. In: Proceedings of IEEE Conference on Computer Vision and Pattern Recognition Workshops, pp. 806–813 (2104)
14. Sargano, A.B., Angelov, P., Habib, Z.: A comprehensive review on handcrafted and learning-based action representation approaches for human activity recognition. Appl. Sci. **7**(1), 110 (2017)
15. Bertasius, G., Shi, J., Torresani, L.: DeepEdge: A multi-scale bifurcated deep network for top-down contour detection. In: Proceedings of IEEE Conference on Computer Vision and Pattern Recognition, pp. 4380–4389 (2015)
16. Shen, W., Wang, X., Wang, Y., Bai, X., Zhang, Z.: DeepContour: a deep convolutional feature learned by positive-sharing loss for contour detection. In: Proceedings of IEEE Conference on Computer Vision and Pattern Recognition, pp. 3982–3991 (2015)
17. Wu, R., Yan, S., Shan, Y., Dang, Q., Sun, G.: Deep image: scaling up image recognition. arXiv preprint arXiv:1501.02876 **7**(8) (2015)

18. Paulin, M., Revaud, J., Harchaoui, Z., Perronnin, F., Schmid, C.: Transformation pursuit for image classification. In: Proceedings of IEEE Conference on Computer Vision and Pattern Recognition, pp. 3646–3653 (2014)
19. Nair, V., Hinton, G.E.: Rectified linear units improve restricted boltzmann machines. In: Proceedings of 27th International Conference on Machine Learning, pp. 807–814 (2010)
20. Jia, Y., Shelhamer, E., Donahue, J., Karayev, S., Long, J., Girshick, R., Guadarrama, S., Darrell, T.: Caffe: convolutional architecture for fast feature embedding. In: Proceedings of 22nd ACM International Conference on Multimedia, 3 November 2014, pp. 675–678 (2014)

Dynamic Environments Localization
via Dimensions Reduction
of Deep Learning Features

Hui Zhang[1]([✉]), Xiangwei Wang[1], Xiaoguo Du[1], Ming Liu[2], and Qijun Chen[1]

[1] RAI-LAB, Tongji University, Shanghai, China
huizhang629@gmail.com
[2] RAM-LAB, Robotics Insititute, HKUST, Hongkong, China

Abstract. How to autonomous locate a robot quickly and accurately in dynamic environments is a primary problem for reliable robot navigation. Monocular visual localization combined with deep learning has gained incredible results. However, the features extracted from deep learning are of huge dimensions and the matching algorithm is complex. How to reduce dimensions with precise localization is one of the difficulties. This paper presents a novel approach for robot localization by training in dynamic environments in a large scale. We extracted features from AlexNet and reduced dimensions of features with IPCA, and what's more, we reduced ambiguities with kernel method, normalization and morphology processing to matching matrix. Finally, we detected best matching sequence online in dynamic environments across seasons. Our localization algorithm can locate robots quickly with high accuracy.

1 Introduction

Where am I? It's the primary problem in reliable robot navigation to locate quickly and accurately in changing environments. Such changes come from many sources including dynamic objects, varying weather and season shifts. An intelligent robot must be equipped with the ability to adapt to these changes. It doesn't conform to reality that automatic driving cars can only run in the trained scenes. So it's essential to express the scene images without the influence of substantial changes. Over the past few years, various types of features have been investigate for localization [2,7,20,27]. Image descriptors can be divided into feature_based and holistic image descriptor. Features_based descriptors play an important role in Computer Vision. Up to now, several hand-crafted features have gained some success [3,16,23,30]. However, the robots often fail to locate themselves in dynamic environments with these hand-crafted feature descriptors.

Holistic images descriptor express one image according to invariant features. Deep-learning has dramatically changed the overnight. It greatly boosted the development of visual perception, object detection and speech recognition [29]. Recent results indicated that the generic descriptors extracted from the convolutional neural networks are very powerful [26].

© Springer International Publishing AG 2017
M. Liu et al. (Eds.): ICVS 2017, LNCS 10528, pp. 239–253, 2017.
DOI: 10.1007/978-3-319-68345-4_22

In 2012, CNNs got incredible accuracy on the AlexNet Large Scale Visual Recognition Challenge (ILSVRC) [10]. It suggested that features extracted from CNNs significantly outperformed hand-crafted features on classification. They trained a large CNN named AlexNet with 1.2 million labeled images. Because the images are classified according to the features extracted from AlexNet, we can also locate robots based on these features. [8] indicated that features from mid-layer of CNNs can remove dataset bias more efficiently. [28] compared the performance of features from different layers. Their results showed that features from the middle layers in the ConvNet hierarchy exhibited robustness against appearance changes induced by the time of day, seasons, or weather conditions. Features from Conv3 layer performs reasonably well in terms of appearance changes.

Nevertheless, the main obstacle of CNNs features is expensive computational costs and memory resources, which is a big challenge for real-time performance. [1] compressed the redundant data of CNN features into a tractable number of bits. The final descriptor is reduced by applying simple compression and binarization techniques for fast matching using the Hamming distance. It's necessary to reduce the dimensions of these vectors. Compression means losing some information. However, we can keep important relationship among data as much as possible. We realize this purpose through Incremental PCA (Principal Component Analysis) that used widely in data analysis [31].

In this paper, we present a novel algorithm to locate a robot in dynamic environments across seasons. The main contributions of this paper are: (1) We proposed a novel localization system in dynamic environments via dimensions reduction of deep learning features. (2) We reduced the dimensions of features extracted from AlexNet. It can not only quicken computing speed but also reduce confusing matching from datasets. (3) Instead of complex data association graph, we found best matching sequence online with morphology processing to matching matrix.

2 Related Work

2.1 Feature Extraction

It's a big challenge to express a scene that changing significantly, shown in Fig. 1. The recent literature proposed a variety of approaches to address the challenge of this field [5,6,18–22]. As we all know, CNNs got incredible accuracy on the AlexNet Large Scale Visual Recognition Challenge (ILSVRC) in 2012 [10]. [8–10,25,26] proved that ConvNets have been demonstrated outperforms traditional hand-crafted features [3,3,16,23]. This network consists of five convolutional layers followed by three fully connected layers and a soft-max layer. It was pretrained with 1.2 million labeled images. The images are classified according to the features extracted from AlexNet. The output of each individual layer can be used as a global image descriptor. We can also match images based on these features and then locate robots. [8] indicated that features from mid-layer of CNNs can remove dataset bias more efficiently. [28] compared the performance of different layers features. Their results showed that features from the middle layers in the ConvNet hierarchy exhibit robustness against appearance changes induced by the time of day, seasons, or weather conditions. Features from Conv3 layer performed reasonably well in terms of extream appearance changes. The vector dimensions of different layers in AlexNet ConvNets are listed in Table 1.

(a) Rainy night   (b) Rainy daytime (c) Shadows of trees and buildings and others

(d) Moving objects   (e) Dusk   (f) Light outsides

Fig. 1. Dynamic environments including dynamic objects, varying weather and season shifts.

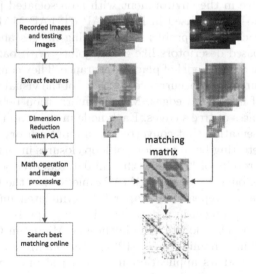

Fig. 2. Outline illustration of dynamic environments localization via dimensions reduction of deep learning features. Features of training images and online images are all extracted from AlexNet.

[28] proved that features from Conv3 layer performed reasonably well in terms of extream appearance changes. Besides, [28] also pointed that fc6 and fc7 outperform the rest layer in terms of viewpoint changes. However, fc6 and fc7 fail completely when appearance changes.

The dimensions of Conv3 are 64896, which means that one image is shown as a 64896 dimensions vector. Online localization will receive images from camera continuously. There is no doubt that a large number of vectors math operation is time-consuming. The different features contained in DCNN are initially returned in a float format. With the aim of facilitating a subsequent binarization, [1] cast these features into a normalized 8-bit integer format. Then a matching matrix is computed by matching all the binary features using the Hamming distance. Their results showed that compression of features can reduce the 99.59% redundancy of their descriptors, while precision is only decreased in about 2%. Besides, their binarization of features allowed using the Hamming distance, that also represented a speedup to match locations.

2.2   Image Matching

Image matching is another challenge after features extraction. By the way, image matching means place recognition in robot localization domain. There is no doubt that the robot's knowledge of the world must be stored as a map, to which the current observation is compared. [17] pointed out that the map framework differs depending on visual sensors and what type of place recognition is being performed. They can be divided into pure image retrieval, topological maps, and topological-metric maps. Pure image retrieval only stores appearance information about each place in the environment with no associated position information, just like Chow-Liu tree used in FAB-MAP [7]. FAB-MAP [7] described a probabilistic approach to the problem of matching images and map augment. They used vector-based descriptors like SURF jointly with bags-of-words. This paper learned a generative model of place appearance. They constructed a Chow-Liu tree [4] to capture the co-occurrence statistics of the visual words. Chow-Liu tree is composed of nodes and edges. Mutual information between variables is shown by the thickness of tree's edges. Each node in the graph corresponds to a bag-of-words representation that converted from input sensory data. FAB-MAP was successful in detecting large portions of loop closures in challenging outdoor environments. But results of [21] show that in datasets over seasons only a few correct matches are found by OpenFABMAP2 due to that the hand-crafted feature descriptors are not repeatable. Paper [21] formulated image matching as a minimum cost flow problem in a data association graph to effectively exploit sequence information. They locate vehicle through Minimum Cost Flow. Their method worked well in dynamic scenes. [12] presented a Markov semi-supervised clustering approach and its application in topological map extraction. As for incremental mapping, slam, and navigation tasks, the approach can be adapted accordingly.

SeqSLAM [20] framed the image recognition problem as one of finding all the templates within local neighborhoods that are the best matching for the current image. It is easy to implement. However, the algorithm of [20] can easily be affected by robot speed. This constraint limits the applications for long-time localization. [24] proved that place recognition performance improves if only the most informative features from each image are used. [14] described a lightweight novel scene recognition method using an adaptive descriptor, which is based on color features and geometric information. [13] presented a scene recognition approach with omnidirectional vision for topological map using lightweight adaptive descriptors. [11] improved place recognition with a reduced feature set. [15] proposed a generic framework for recognition and clustering problem using a non-parametric Dirichlet hierarchical model, named DP-Fusion.

The paper proceeds as follows. In Sect. 3, we describe details of our methodology. Section 4 gives out the experiment results of online localization in dynamic environments on Norland datasets. In Sect. 5, we have a discussion about the results and future work.

3   Approach and Methodology

In this paper, we contribute a new proposal that exploits the advantages of powerful feature representations via CNNs in order to perform a robust vision-based localization across the seasons of the year, as introduced in the graphical explanation of our approach given in Fig. 2. Our work proceeds as follows.

(1) Extract features from Conv3 of AlexNet. Consider dimensions reduction via IPCA.
(2) Vectors of online images will match with datasets vectors one by one through cosine distance. Normalize matching matrix through kernel method to reduce ambiguities caused by confusing datasets. Save matching matrix as a gray image.
(3) Image processing to the gray matching image including image binarization.
(4) Set parameters and find best matching sequence online through RANSAC (random sample consensus).

3.1   Algorithm Framework

The algorithm framework of our method is described in Algorithm 1. About the map framework, we used pure image retrieval but the datasets were stored in order according to the images' incoming time. If so, we can not only ensure accuracy but also compute efficiently. We chose features from Conv3 of AlexNet as our holistic image descriptor. The dimensions of Conv3 are 64896, which means that one image is shown as a 64896 dimensions vector $\mathbf{f}$. We build visual map $\{[\mathbf{f}, \mathbf{l}]\}_{i=1}^{n}$ with location of each image. So the current image sequences are expressed as $\{\mathbf{I}\}_{j=t-m+1}^{t}$. High-dimensional vectors result in time-consuming. We consider dimensions reduction via IPCA. Although image descriptors are somewhat losing information, it reduces the ambiguous matching causing from the confusing datasets like sky, ground and trees. Vectors of online images will

---

Algorithm 1. Algorithm: visual localization

Input: Visual Map $\{[\mathbf{f},l]\}_{i=1}^{n}$, where $\mathbf{f}$ is the feature vector of image on location extracted from AlexNet; l is location of corresponding image; n is the size of visual map; Current image sequences $\{\mathbf{I}\}_{j=t-m+1}^{t}$, where m is the sequence size; last robot location $\hat{l}_{t-1}$

Initialize: $\hat{l}_t = \hat{l}_{t-1}$ **Output**: Robot current location l_t

for $t = 2$ *to* n **do**

 Calculate $\{\hat{\mathbf{f}}\}_{j=t-m+1}^{t}$ the feature of $\{\mathbf{I}\}_{j=t-m+1}^{t}$

 Calculate matching matrix $\mathbf{M}$ and $\mathbf{M}_{ij} = \mathcal{F}(\mathbf{f}_i, \hat{\mathbf{f}}_j)$

 Kernel process to every element of the matching matrix $\hat{\mathbf{m}}_{ij} = e^{1 - \cos \mathbf{m}_{ij}}$

 Normalize the matching matrix $\mathbf{M}_{ij} = \frac{255(\mathbf{M}_{ij} - \mathbf{M}_{min})}{\mathbf{M}_{max} - \mathbf{M}_{min}}$ take $\mathbf{M}$ as a gray image $\mathbf{I}_g$

 Change $\mathbf{I}_g$ to binary image $\mathbf{I}_b$ using suitable thresholding.

 Deal $\mathbf{I}_b$ with morphology method and get image $\mathbf{I}_m$

 Using RANSAC method to find the best matching line $y = kx + b$ on $\mathbf{I}_m$

 The current image's best matching feature in the visual map is $\mathbf{f}_{km+b}$

 Set $\hat{l}_t = l_{km+b}$

end

return $\hat{l}_t$

---

be compared with datasets vectors one by one through cosine distance. We then get matching matrix $\mathbf{S}$ whose elements float in range $(0, 1]$. Normalize matching matrix through kernel method to reduce ambiguities caused by confusing datasets that match against most of the online images. Then it is converted to a binary gray image by a suitable thresholding. We tried to adjust parameters and then find the best matching sequence online through RANSAC. The current image's best matching feature in matching matrix is $\mathbf{f}_{km+b}$. Then the current image's best matching image in the visual map is $\mathbf{l}_{km+b}$.

3.2 Feature Extraction from Deep Learning

We extracted features from Conv3 of AlexNet as our image holistic descriptor provided by Caffe. The dimensions of Conv3 are 64896, which means that one image is expressed by a 64896 dimensions vector. The vector dimensions of different layer in AlexNet ConvNets are listed in Table 1 [10]. [28] gave us the conclusion that the layers higher in the hierarchy are more semantically meaningful but therefore lose their ability to discriminate between individual places within the same semantic type of scene. It's important to decide which layer we use. Features from Conv3 layer performs reasonably well in terms of extream appearance changes.

3.3 Dimensions Reduction

We tested on Norland datasets to determine how many dimensions fit best for time consuming and accuracy. We chose 300 images sequence in the spring season

Table 1. Dimensions of different layer of AlexNet

Layer	Dimensions	Layer	Dimensions
Conv1	$96 \times 55 \times 55$	Conv4	$384 \times 13 \times 13$
pool1	$96 \times 27 \times 27$	Conv5	$256 \times 13 \times 13$
Conv2	$256 \times 27 \times 27$	fc6	$4096 \times 1 \times 1$
pool2	$256 \times 13 \times 13$	fc7	$4096 \times 1 \times 1$
Conv3	$384 \times 13 \times 13$	fc8	$1000 \times 1 \times 1$

Table 2. Relationship between percent of main information and n_components

n_components	Information ratio	n_components	Information ratio
316	99%	51	93%
187	98%	44	92%
136	97%	38	91%
99	96%	33	90%
76	95%	29	89%
62	94%	25	88%

as recorded and 500 images sequence in fall as a test. We used Incremental PCA in scikit-learn for a large number of images matching. IPCA is one of the essential high-dimensional data analysis. IPCA transforms high-dimensional data to low dimensions through the linear transformation. The dimensions of the different layers of AlexNet are shown in Table 1. It is easy to understand that more dimensions we keep more information we will attain, but also time consuming. So the primary task is to determine how many dimensions we keep for each vector.

The relationships between the parameter n_components and main information Ratio are listed in Table 2. In general, we had better keep at least 90% main information ratio in case of influence on accuracy. We also compared matching result among different dimensions. The comparison results are shown in Fig. 3. The best matching line cannot be detected with less than 20 dimensions. 33 dimensions is clear enough and also save computation consuming. In short, we chose 33 dimensions vectors as image descriptors.

3.4 Kernel Transform and Normalization of Matching Matrix

Our task is to find the best matching line precisely. We have to use math transform to make this line clearer. We choose kernel method including inverse the elements of matching matrix and exponentiation. The reasons for choosing this method are listed as follows.

(1) Cosine distance between 2 images cannot stand for the positive proportion between the similarity and the matching matrix elements.

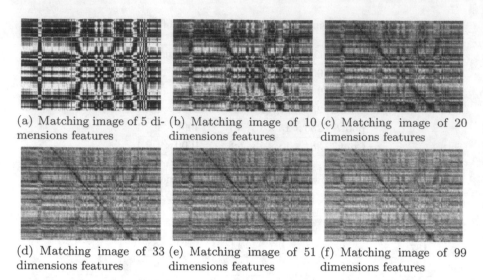

(a) Matching image of 5 dimensions features

(b) Matching image of 10 dimensions features

(c) Matching image of 20 dimensions features

(d) Matching image of 33 dimensions features

(e) Matching image of 51 dimensions features

(f) Matching image of 99 dimensions features

Fig. 3. Comparision matching image among different dimensions including 5, 10, 20, 33, 51, 99 dimensions. The best matching line turns clear with dimensions increasing.

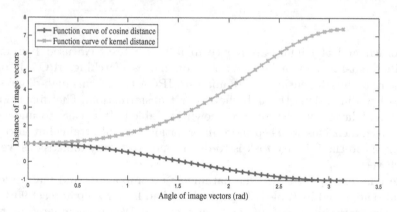

Fig. 4. Function curves of cosine and kernel method distance.

(2) Kernel method will widen the distance between false negative and true positive places.

Figure 4 is function curves comparison computed from cosine distance, shown in Eq. (1), and kernel method distance, shown in Eq. (2). The blue line stands for the cosine distance of two image vectors. The brown line stands for the kernel method distance. We can see that kernel method can augment the difference between totally different and similar places. The color of the best matching line appeared as black and the different places appeared as white, shown in Fig. 5. What's more, normalize matching matrix through kernel method reduced ambiguities that caused by confusing datasets that match against most of the online images. Save matching matrix as a gray image for the following processing including morphology transformation and binarization.

What's more, we normalized the matching matrix with the range of 0 to 255 with Eq. (3). It turned evident after kernel method. It's of great help for the morphology processing and visualization.

(a) Matching matrix of cosine distance

(b) matching matrix after kernel method

Fig. 5. We chose a sequence of 3000 images in spring Norland datasets as trained features and 3000 images in winter Norland datasets as online images. (a) Cosine distance matching matrix. (b) Kernel method distance matching matrix.

We tested kernel method on spring and winter seasons in Norland datasets. There are 3000 spring images and 3000 winter images captured in the same place. Besides, the beginning of two images sequence is the same image. Thus, one line appears on the diagonal for it's the best matching sequence. The matching result is shown in Fig. 5. We matched online images with recorded datasets images one by one through cosine distance with $cos <f_i, f_j>$. However, the matching image shown in Fig. 5(a) appeared confusion between terrible matching and perfect matching. However, the diagonal line becomes evident through kernel method of Eq. (2) and normalization method of Eq. (3). The matching image is shown in Fig. 5(b). At last but not the least, save the matching matrix as a gray image, which will be converted to binary one by suitable threshold.

$$cos <f_i, f_j> = \frac{\sum_{i=1}^{33} a_i b_i}{\sum_{j=1}^{33} a_j^2 \sum_{k=1}^{33} b_k^2} \tag{1}$$

$f_i = \{a_1\ a_2\ \ldots\ a_{33}\}$, $i \in D$, D is set of datasets images, $f_j = \{b_1\ b_2\ \ldots\ b_{33}\}$, $j \in O$, O is set of online images

$$\hat{m}_{ij} = e^{1-\cos m_{ij}} \tag{2}$$

$$M_{ij} = \frac{255\,(M_{ij} - M_{min})}{M_{max} - M_{min}} \tag{3}$$

4   Experiments

Our experiments are designed to show the capabilities of our method with reduced features and image processing. Our approach is able to (i) localization in scenes across seasons ignoring dynamic objects, varying weather and season shifts. (ii) save time and computation consuming. We perform the evaluations on public available Norland datasets used in SeqSLAM [20]. The gray images were captured in 1 frame every second and the size have been cropped into 64×32. If our approach still works in such unclear and tiny images, then it can save a lot of time and computation consuming. Examples of matching images are shown in Fig. 3.

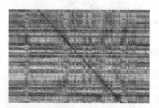
(a) Matching matrix after kernel method and normalization

(b) Binarization image

(c) Best matching line in matching image

Fig. 6. We chose a sequence of 300 images in fall season trained as map and locate online in spring season. (a) Matching image after kernel method and normalization. (b) Binarization image of (a) with suitable thresholding. (c) Detecting line with RANSAC algorithm and the green line is just the best matching line. (Color figure online)

We can see that in Fig. 5(b) the best matching line became obvious. Our task is to find its mathematical model to find the corresponding index in datasets. We decided to use classical RANSAC algorithm.

4.1   Online Search in Dynamic Environments

In Fig. 6, we chose a sequence of 300 images in fall season trained as the map and locate online in the spring season. We can see that the features extracted from Conv3 of AlexNet didn't affect the matching result. On the opposite, reduce the influence of background information, shown in Fig. 6(a). Figure 6(b) is the binarization result of the matching image. You see that most of the interfere information has been wiped off. The capacity of restraining distractor has more important effect during robots localization. We can see that in Fig. 6(c) the green line is just the best matching in this period. The current image's best matching feature in matching matrix is f_{km+b}. Then the current image's best matching image in the visual map is l_{km+b}.

In Fig. 8, we plot 3 lines to assess the error of our approach. The blue line stands for the index of ground truth. Red line means the index of matched images with our approach. The yellow one is index error between ground truth and matching images. The search index in the range [1872, 2026] in x coordinate axes cannot be updated. We will discuss this problem in Sect. 5 (Fig. 7).

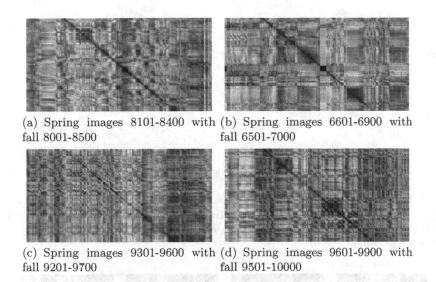

(a) Spring images 8101-8400 with fall 8001-8500

(b) Spring images 6601-6900 with fall 6501-7000

(c) Spring images 9301-9600 with fall 9201-9700

(d) Spring images 9601-9900 with fall 9501-10000

Fig. 7. Examples of some matching images. The number, take '8101–8400' for example, means index of images sequence.

4.2   Results

Our paper present a novel and time-consuming algorithm to locate a robot in dynamic environments across seasons. It's a rapid localization system. We extracted features from Conv3 of AlexNet and it did outperform hand-crafted features in robots localization domain. Dimensions reduction via IPCA is a novel try. Each layer of AlexNet develops advantages in the different domain. It's proved that Conv3 is the best choice for robots localization. Luckily it helped a lot to quicken computing speed and reduce confusing matching from datasets caused by images match against most of the online images. We compared vectors of online images with datasets vectors one by one through kernel method distance. This process widens the difference between similar and totally different places. What's more, image processing to the gray matching image, including converting to binary one by suitable thresholding, turned complex data association graph into simple image processing. As for sequence matching, we used classical RANSAC algorithm to find the best matching line. Our experiments results show that dimensions reduction is a great idea to quicken computing speed and reduce confusing matching. And our algorithm is robust to season shifts, dynamic environments, changing weathers and so on. Examples of some matched images are shown in Fig. 10.

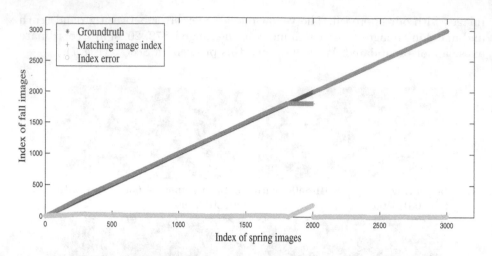

Fig. 8. Experiments result tested on 3000 images. The function of ground truth index line is y = x, shown in blue line. The brown line is matched images index with sequence of 300 images each time. The yellow line is error between real position and matched. (Color figure online)

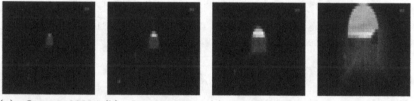

(a)   Images-02204 (b)   Images-02205 (c)   Images-02206 (d)   Images-02207
in spring datasets   in spring datasets   in spring datasets   in spring datasets

Fig. 9. Captured images when the train went through a tunnel in Norland datasets.

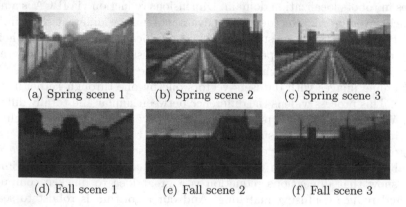

(a) Spring scene 1   (b) Spring scene 2   (c) Spring scene 3

(d) Fall scene 1   (e) Fall scene 2   (f) Fall scene 3

Fig. 10. Examples of some matched images.

Fig. 11. Matching image that covers totally dark images in spring image 1872 to 2026.

5   Discussion and Future Works

The limitation of our system is from the image capture equipment. The images are hard to express in totally dark surroundings. The matching matrix that covers dark images sequence is shown in Fig. 11. Actually in Fig. 8 there is no matching line for images 1872 to 2026, so we cannot detect the matching line at all. Examples of dark images are shown in Fig. 9. The matching image is shown as a black block. We will consider about adding assist of the laser. Besides, the concrete relationship between features dimensions and the localization accuracy will be studied. We want to find out the most suitable dimensions of CNNs features to ensure precision and operation speed. It needs iterative testing. Besides, we will train a generic holistic image descriptor ignoring the influence of season shift, weather changes, dynamic environments and so on. However, it needs a large number of images captured over years to train CNN.

Acknowledgment. This research is a cooperation work between RAM-LAB of HKUST and RAI-LAB of Tongji University. Our work is supported by National Natural Science Foundation (61573260), Natural Science Foundation of Shanghai (16JC1401200); Shenzhen Science, Technology and Innovation Commission (SZSTI) (JCYJ20160428154842603 and JCYJ20160401100022706); partially supported by the HKUST Project (IGN16EG12).

References

1. Arroyo, R., Alcantarilla, P.F., Bergasa, L.M., Romera, E.: Fusion and binarization of CNN features for robust topological localization across seasons. In: 2016 IEEE/RSJ International Conference on Intelligent Robots and Systems (IROS), pp. 4656–4663. IEEE (2016)
2. Arroyo, R., Alcantarilla, P.F., Bergasa, L.M., Yebes, J.J., Bronte, S.: Fast and effective visual place recognition using binary codes and disparity information. In: 2014 IEEE/RSJ International Conference on Intelligent Robots and Systems (IROS 2014), pp. 3089–3094. IEEE (2014)
3. Bay, H., Tuytelaars, T., Van Gool, L.: SURF: Speeded up robust features. In: Leonardis, A., Bischof, H., Pinz, A. (eds.) ECCV 2006. LNCS, vol. 3951, pp. 404–417. Springer, Heidelberg (2006). doi:10.1007/11744023_32
4. Chow, C., Liu, C.: Approximating discrete probability distributions with dependence trees. IEEE Trans. Inf. Theory **14**(3), 462–467 (1968)

5. Churchill, W., Newman, P.: Practice makes perfect? Managing and leveraging visual experiences for lifelong navigation. In: 2012 IEEE International Conference on Robotics and Automation (ICRA), pp. 4525–4532. IEEE (2012)
6. Corke, P., Paul, R., Churchill, W., Newman, P.: Dealing with shadows: capturing intrinsic scene appearance for image-based outdoor localisation. In: 2013 IEEE/RSJ International Conference on Intelligent Robots and Systems (IROS), pp. 2085–2092. IEEE (2013)
7. Cummins, M., Newman, P.: FAB-MAP: probabilistic localization and mapping in the space of appearance. Int. J. Robot. Res. **27**(6), 647–665 (2008)
8. Donahue, J., Jia, Y., Vinyals, O., Hoffman, J., Zhang, N., Tzeng, E., Darrell, T.: DECAF: a deep convolutional activation feature for generic visual recognition. In: ICML, vol. 32, pp. 647–655 (2014)
9. Girshick, R., Donahue, J., Darrell, T., Malik, J.: Rich feature hierarchies for accurate object detection and semantic segmentation. In: Proceedings of IEEE Conference on Computer Vision and Pattern Recognition, pp. 580–587 (2014)
10. Krizhevsky, A., Sutskever, I., Hinton, G.E.: Imagenet classification with deep convolutional neural networks. In: Advances in Neural Information Processing Systems, pp. 1097–1105 (2012)
11. Li, F., Kosecka, J.: Probabilistic location recognition using reduced feature set. In: Proceedings of 2006 IEEE International Conference on Robotics and Automation, ICRA 2006, pp. 3405–3410. IEEE (2006)
12. Liu, M., Colas, F., Pomerleau, F., Siegwart, R.: A Markov semi-supervised clustering approach and its application in topological map extraction. In: 2012 IEEE/RSJ International Conference on Intelligent Robots and Systems (IROS), pp. 4743–4748. IEEE (2012)
13. Liu, M., Scaramuzza, D., Pradalier, C., Siegwart, R., Chen, Q.: Scene recognition with omnidirectional vision for topological map using lightweight adaptive descriptors. In: IEEE/RSJ International Conference on Intelligent Robots and Systems, IROS 2009, pp. 116–121. IEEE (2009)
14. Liu, M., Siegwart, R.: Topological mapping and scene recognition with lightweight color descriptors for an omnidirectional camera. IEEE Trans. Robot. **30**(2), 310–324 (2014)
15. Liu, M., Wang, L., Siegwart, R.: DP-fusion: a generic framework for online multi sensor recognition. In: 2012 IEEE Conference on Multisensor Fusion and Integration for Intelligent Systems (MFI), pp. 7–12. IEEE (2012)
16. Lowe, D.G.: Distinctive image features from scale-invariant keypoints. Int. J. Comput. Vis. **60**(2), 91–110 (2004)
17. Lowry, S., Sünderhauf, N., Newman, P., Leonard, J.J., Cox, D., Corke, P., Milford, M.J.: Visual place recognition: a survey. IEEE Trans. Robot. **32**(1), 1–19 (2016)
18. Lowry, S.M., Milford, M.J., Wyeth, G.F.: Transforming morning to afternoon using linear regression techniques. In: 2014 IEEE International Conference on Robotics and Automation (ICRA), pp. 3950–3955. IEEE (2014)
19. McManus, C., Upcroft, B., Newman, P.: Learning place-dependant features for long-term vision-based localisation. Auton. Rob. **39**(3), 363–387 (2015)
20. Milford, M.J., Wyeth, G.F.: SeqSLAM: visual route-based navigation for sunny summer days and stormy winter nights. In: 2012 IEEE International Conference on Robotics and Automation (ICRA), pp. 1643–1649. IEEE (2012)
21. Naseer, T., Spinello, L., Burgard, W., Stachniss, C.: Robust visual robot localization across seasons using network flows. In: AAAI, pp. 2564–2570 (2014)

22. Neubert, P., Sünderhauf, N., Protzel, P.: Superpixel-based appearance change prediction for long-term navigation across seasons. Robot. Auton. Syst. **69**, 15–27 (2015)
23. Rublee, E., Rabaud, V., Konolige, K., Bradski, G.: ORB: an efficient alternative to SIFT or SURF. In: 2011 IEEE International Conference on Computer Vision (ICCV), pp. 2564–2571. IEEE (2011)
24. Schindler, G., Brown, M., Szeliski, R.: City-scale location recognition. In: IEEE Computer Society Conference on Computer Vision and Pattern Recognition, pp. 1–7 (2007)
25. Sermanet, P., Eigen, D., Zhang, X., Mathieu, M., Fergus, R., LeCun, Y.: Overfeat: integrated recognition, localization and detection using convolutional networks. arXiv preprint arXiv:1312.6229 (2013)
26. Sharif Razavian, A., Azizpour, H., Sullivan, J., Carlsson, S.: CNN features off-the-shelf: an astounding baseline for recognition. In: Proceedings of IEEE Conference on Computer Vision and Pattern Recognition Workshops, pp. 806–813 (2014)
27. Sünderhauf, N., Protzel, P.: BRIEF-Gist-Closing the loop by simple means. In: 2011 IEEE/RSJ International Conference on Intelligent Robots and Systems (IROS), pp. 1234–1241. IEEE (2011)
28. Sünderhauf, N., Shirazi, S., Dayoub, F., Upcroft, B., Milford, M.: On the performance of convnet features for place recognition. In: 2015 IEEE/RSJ International Conference on Intelligent Robots and Systems (IROS), pp. 4297–4304. IEEE (2015)
29. Tai, L., Liu, M., Deep-learning in mobile robotics-from perception to control systems: a survey on why and why not. arXiv preprint arXiv:1612.07139 (2016)
30. Tola, E., Lepetit, V., Fua, P.: A fast local descriptor for dense matching. In: IEEE Conference on Computer Vision and Pattern Recognition, CVPR 2008, pp. 1–8. IEEE (2008)
31. Weng, J., Zhang, Y., Hwang, W. S.: Candid covariance-free incremental principal component analysis. IEEE Trans. Pattern Anal. Mach. Intell. **25**(8), 1034–1040 (2003)

Human Robot Interaction

A Gesture Recognition Method Based on Binocular Vision System

Liqian Feng, Sheng Bi$^{(\boxtimes)}$, Min Dong, and Yunda Liu

School of Computer Science and Engineering,
South China University of Technology, Guangzhou, China
fengliqianflq@gmail.com, {picy,hollymin}@scut.edu.cn

Abstract. This paper demonstrates a gesture recognition approach based on binocular camera. The binocular vision system can deal with stereo imaging problem using disparity map. After the cameras are calibrated, the approach uses skin color model and depth information to separate the hand from the environment in the image. And the features of the gestures are extracted by feature extraction algorithm. These gestures as well as their features constitute a set of training examples in machine learning. The Support Vector Machine (SVM), which is supervised learning models, are used to classify these gestures that are labeled with their meaning, such as digits gesture. In training and classification processes, we use the same feature extraction algorithm handling the gesture image and SVM can recognize the meaning of a gesture. The gesture recognition method mentioned in this paper represents a high accuracy in recognizing number gestures.

Keywords: Gesture recognition · Binocular cameras · Support Vector Machine

1 Introduction

With the development of science and technology, the technique of gesture recognition plays an increasingly essential role in human-computer interaction attracting attention of researchers. While a number of wearable devices for gesture recognition have been produced [1], the computer vision systems based on camera are more widely used because cameras are a fundamental device in terminal, such as computer and smart cell phone. There are a variety of approaches proposed by former researchers in not only static gesture recognition [2, 3] but also dynamic one [4, 5]. In this paper, we propose a static gesture recognition approach based on binocular vision system that consists of two cameras. The binocular cameras can reconstruct the 3D stereo image by the disparity map in order to create the depth map of the environment. A successful depth-camera system Kinect obtain depth information by IR monochrome camera. Both Kinect and the normal binocular cameras system in this paper depend on triangulation method [6]. Another key point in hand and gesture recognition is to construct the skin color model, which is to separate the hand from the environment. So the skin color and the non-skin color constitute a skin-color binary image. Combined with depth image, we use the histogram to eliminate the interference of skin color apart from the hand. And then the contour of the hand in binary image can be located and intercepted.

M. Liu et al. (Eds.): ICVS 2017, LNCS 10528, pp. 257–267, 2017.
DOI: 10.1007/978-3-319-68345-4_23

The feature extraction algorithm is applied to extract the features of a gesture. For example, we defined 10 gestures of numbers from 0 to 9. The features of each gesture with its label number can be seen as the training example in machine learning. We used SVM to train these gestures. After a large number of gestures' features trained in SVM, we use the same algorithm to extract the features of gesture in real-time, then it can be recognized currently.

In Sect. 2, we introduce the principle of binocular vision system as well as the calibration process, which is to obtain the undistorted and rectified image. As a result, the depth image is built. The Sect. 3 indicates the skin color model used in the gesture recognition method to locate the hand in the image. The way to obtain and train the features of the gesture in SVM is shown in Sect. 4. We display a number of experimental results in Sect. 5 and finally the conclusion is made in Sect. 6.

2   Binocular Vision System Background

2.1   Stereo Imaging

In practice, stereo imaging requires four stages using two cameras [7]. First of all, the camera should be calibrated; radial and tangential lens distortion should be removed mathematically [7]. To obtain the camera intrinsic matrix [8], we use chessboard. This calibration algorithm is called Zhang method in his paper [9]. It uses at least ten orientations of chessboard to solve for the locations of those images in global coordinates. As is shown in Fig. 1, the left picture is an undistorted image captured from the camera, while the right one is the original image. We can see that the distortion has been eliminated.

Fig. 1. The undistorted image and the original image

The second stage is called rectification. The outputs of this stage are images that are row-aligned and rectified [7]. As is shown in Fig. 2, mathematically, the rectified binocular vision system suppose that optical axes are parallel, which is shown as Fig. 2 right. Meanwhile in practice, optical axes may not be exactly parallel shown as Fig. 2 left. The rectification stage is to figure out a rotation and translation matrix.

And the third stage is to find the same features in the two camera views. Combining with the second and third stages, we can obtain the disparity map, where a same feature

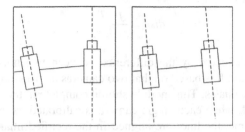

Fig. 2. The optical axes before and after rectification

in the environment would locate in the different pixel in the two cameras. And we can apply the triangulation method to figure out the depth information, which is the final stage in stereo imaging.

2.2 Triangulation Method

Triangulation method is a basic approach in range measurement. In Fig. 3, it is a schematic diagram about this method using two cameras.

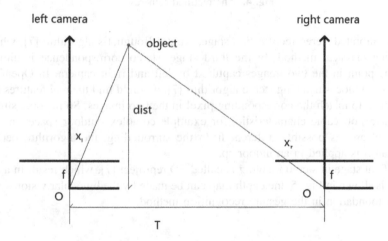

Fig. 3. Triangulation method in binocular system

The distance can be figured out by similar triangles, which is shown in (1). Here, f is used to stand for focal length and the distance between the center of left and right cameras is defined as T below. In Fig. 3, we assume the cameras are row-aligned [7], which means that every pixel row of a camera aligns with the corresponding row in the other camera [7]. So the object in the real world is projected in the two cameras, in which it has horizontal coordinates x_l and x_r respectively with same vertical coordinates. As a result, the meaning of *dist* in (1) is the distance from cameras to the object as well as the depth information.

$$dist = \frac{f \cdot T}{x_l - x_r} \tag{1}$$

And the depth is affected by the difference between two horizontal coordinates, which is called disparity. It is based on that two cameras are row-aligned and the object has same vertical coordinates. This module should complete in the second stage above. As is shown in Fig. 4, when each single camera is calibrated, combined with the two images at the same time, the lines are aligned in the rectified images.

Fig. 4. The rectified cameras

This calibrated stereo rectification stage, we use Bouguet's algorithm [7], which is an existing classical method. In the third stage, stereo correspondence is aimed to match the point in the two images captured by left and right camera. In OpenCV, it implements a block-matching stereo algorithm [7]. It would find the real features in the environment to match the corresponding pixel in the two images. So in some situation which have noticeable characteristic, for example complex outdoor space, in which small pixel area is possibly different from the surrounding, the algorithm performs better than it is applied in an indoor space.

The final stage in stereo imaging is called 3D reproject [7], which result in a depth map. As is shown in Fig. 5, the depth map can be made by the binocular vision system, which is foundation in the gesture recognition method.

Fig. 5. The depth map of the environment.

3 Skin Color Model

Many human body recognition methods [10, 11] in computer vision and artificial intelligence area use skin color model to detect the part of the human body and the surrounding environment. In this paper, the gesture recognition method also adopts the skin color model.

On the whole, we should transform the color space from RGB space to YCbCr space, because in YCbCr color space, the luminance is an independent element Y, and the Cb and Cr value would be affected insignificantly by the light in the environment. And the formula is described as (2)

$$\begin{bmatrix} Y \\ Cb \\ Cr \end{bmatrix} = \begin{bmatrix} 16 \\ 128 \\ 128 \end{bmatrix} + \begin{bmatrix} 64.481 & 128.553 & 24.966 \\ -37.797 & -74.203 & 112.0 \\ 112.0 & -97.786 & -18.214 \end{bmatrix} \begin{bmatrix} R \\ G \\ B \end{bmatrix} \tag{2}$$

In paper [12], the author considered many different types of skin color and come up with the ranges of Cr and Cb values, which should be seen as the skin color, shown in (3).

$$Cr \in [133, 173] \cap Cb \in [77, 127] \tag{3}$$

It is a simple method to define the skin color model, but the model also has disadvantages such as mistaken identification. So it should adopt an improved model to obtain higher accuracy.

For example, in paper [13, 14], the Gaussian model is widely used in skin color modeling.

In practice, these Gaussian Models in skin recognition distinguish the hand from the environment, which constitute the skin-color binary image shown in Fig. 6.

Fig. 6. The skin-color binary image

As is seen in the above binary image, only the area of tester's hand and face was labeled white, while other pixels that represented the surrounding environment was labeled black. It achieved the goal that the gesture had been separated from the background.

4 Training and Recognizing the Gesture

4.1 An Adaptive Threshold to Separate the Gesture

In gesture recognition method, we only need to locate the hand rather than the face or other skin area. So in skin-color binary image above, the pixels of face should be removed. And as a result, only the pixels of hand is white.

The skin color model should combine with depth information. In depth map, every pixel has a depth value in metric. Normally, hands and face are not coplanar. So the pixel of the gesture and the pixel of face have different depth value.

The histogram plot can be used to record the depth map as well as skin-color binary image, which is shown in Fig. 7.

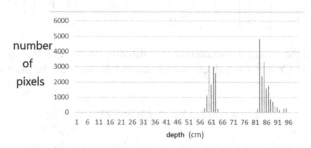

Fig. 7. The histogram of depth in skin-color binary image.

The Fig. 7 indicates the statistics of the pixels number among different depth values in the skin-color binary image Fig. 6. Obviously, there are two significant peaks in the Fig. 7, which means that pixels of hand and face convergent at different depth range. And according to the experience, hands should be closer to the cameras than the face, so in Fig. 7, the intensive pixels in the range from 55 cm to 66 cm is made up of the hand, and the pixel in 80 cm to 95 cm is made up of the face.

So we can come up with a strategy that separate the histogram into two parts. The white pixels in skin-color binary image that is located in the part of lower depth would be reserved, while the other white pixels located in the part of higher depth should be change to black. That means the face would be removed from the skin-color binary image due to its higher depth. In other words, we should set an adaptive threshold that is a gap in depth to reserve the pixels of hand and remove the face in skin-color binary image.

In experiment and practice, sometimes the face and the gesture might appear in image at the same time, while sometimes users may show one hand without the face in front of the cameras. So we cannot set a ratio to distinguish the pixel. Eventually, we count the number of pixels in every continuous interval which has 10 cm length. It starts from the lowest depth in original skin-color binary image until an interval show up with less than 50 pixels, which means a gap in histogram. We record that depth as the threshold and change the white pixels in original skin-color binary image, which has depth higher than it, into black. As is shown in Fig. 8, there is only a hand in the skin-color binary image, which is the gesture we need to train and recognize.

Fig. 8. The face removed in skin-color binary image according to depth

4.2 Features of Gesture Extraction

For a binary image that only has a gesture, we can use a minimum square bounding boxes to set a region of interest. And for a variety of sizes of gesture, we define a standard size of square box so that different size of gesture would resized into the standard size. Furthermore, there are some noise in processed binary image above. So we can use contour finder components and erode the internal contour in vision algorithm.

And then we can define ten standard number gestures, which is shown in Fig. 9.

We use the same procedure in generating these standard gestures and dealing with the real-time image in practice. Before recognizing the gesture in machine learning, a wide range of training set are required. And given a large number of training images, the features of every image should be extracted so that an efficient machine learning algorithm can process them and recognize a real-time gesture in practice.

Fig. 9. Ten standard number gestures from 0 to 9

We adopt the Histogram of Oriented Gradient (HOG) descriptors method that was introduced in [15]. The normalization process in that method has been completed because we would import the binary image directly. And in summary, the HOG descriptors method extracts the features of the binary image into a vector. As a result, vectors, which represent of a gesture, are sent to a SVM for classification. The paper [15] demonstrated the feature extraction process in detail. In training and recognizing the gestures, classifying the vector of gesture image's feature in SVM is a feasible approach.

5　Experiments and Results

To obtain higher accuracy, the cameras need to be fixed, so we construct a box model by a 3D printer shown in Fig. 10, which is easy to rectify.

Fig. 10. A fixed cameras box to obtain stable hardware environment

As experiments, we had trained 100 gestures image as training set to balance the accuracy and efficiency.

To begin with, we tried to calibrate the cameras using checkerboard, which is shown in Fig. 11.

Fig. 11. Checkerboard to calibrate and rectify the cameras.

Not only can it calibrate the singe camera, eliminate radial and tangential lens distortion, but also the rectification process would complete at the same time. After 10 successful calibration. We can recognize the gesture in cameras.

We demonstrate every stage on the screen, which is shown in Fig. 12.

In Fig. 12, the upper left window shows the real-time frame and the captured gesture; and the upper middle one indicates the camera intrinsic matrix as well as the result number of the gesture. To simplify the question, we just output the result into the terminal window. In other application, this gesture recognition method can control other functions for human-computer interaction. The upper right window demonstrates the depth map; the lower left and middle windows show the result of rectification stage; the lower right window indicates the skin-color binary image after it adopted the adaptive threshold algorithm to remove the face region.

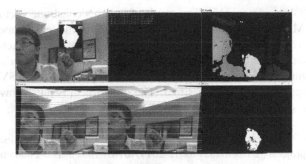

Fig. 12. Result windows

Considering the accuracy rating, in Fig. 12, we demonstrate 20 times experiment from number gestures 0 to 9 and 9 to 0 again. As a result, there is 1 mistake, which is the eighth one, in 20 experiments. It should be recognized as 7, but the result is 0. Meanwhile, the accuracy rating reaches 95%. For random sequence, we tried the first 100 number of π, which is shown in Fig. 13.

Fig. 13. 100 number of Pi result

In Fig. 14, there are 12 error digits in 100 number gestures, which means the accuracy rating is about 88%. And other results is shown in Fig. 14.

category	total experiment	correct	error	accuracy rating
sequential sequence	20	19	1	95%
sequential sequence	100	91	9	91%
random sequence	100	88	12	88%
random sequence	100	90	10	90%

Fig. 14. The experiment results

6 Conclusion

In conclusion, we come up with an associative method in gesture recognition, combined with skin color model and 3D reprojection using binocular vision system. These two models result in a binary image, in which it only has a hand. Although both hands and face can be seen as a component of skin, in 3D depth map, the face and hand can be distinguished by range information. So we use an adaptive depth threshold to separate the gesture. Furthermore, the features of the gesture binary image can be extracted by HOG descriptors [15]. The result of features constitute vectors, which can be sent into SVM. SVM is an effective machine leaning model in supervised classification. Before recognizing in real-time, we train a set of labeled gesture made by features extraction algorithm. And in recognition process, we use the same procedure to generate the gesture binary image and the features vector. As a result, SVM can output the meaning of real-time gesture classified. The experiment results show the accuracy rating, which satisfy the reliability and efficiency.

Acknowledgment. This research work is supported by Guangdong province science and technology plan projects (2015A020219001, 2017A010101031). The Fundamental Research Funds for the Central Universities (2015ZM140, 2017MS048). Guangzhou Key Laboratory of Robotics and Intelligent Software (15180007). Shenzhen peacock project (KQTD201406 30154026047). Shenzhen basic research projects (JCYJ20160429161539298). Guangdong Ministry of Education Foundation (2013B090500093).

References

1. Shin, S., Sung, W.: Dynamic hand gesture recognition for wearable devices with low complexity recurrent neural networks. In: International Symposium on Circuits and Systems (2016)
2. Hasan, H.S., Abdulkareem, S.: Static hand gesture recognition using neural networks. Artif. Intell. Rev. **41**(2), 147–181 (2014)
3. Gupta, S., Jaafar, J., Ahmad, W.F.: Static hand gesture recognition using local gabor filter. Procedia Eng. **41**(41), 827–832 (2012)
4. Wang, X., Xia, M., Cai, H., Gao, Y., Cattani, C.: Hidden-Markov-models-based dynamic hand gesture recognition. In: Mathematical Problems in Engineering, pp. 1–11 (2012)
5. Shen, X., Hua, G., Williams, L., Wu, Y.: Dynamic hand gesture recognition: an exemplar-based approach from motion divergence fields. Image Vis. Comput. **30**(3), 227–235 (2012)
6. Zhang, H., Yan, R.J., Zhou, W.S., Sheng, L.: Binocular vision sensor (Kinect)-based pedestrian following mobile robot. In: Applied Mechanics and Materials, pp. 1326–1329 (2014)
7. Bradski, G., Kaehler, A.: Learning OpenCV: Computer Vision with the OpenCV Library. O'Reilly Media Inc, Sebastopol (2008)
8. Heikkila, J., Silven, O.: A four-step camera calibration procedure with implicit image correction. In: Computer Vision and Pattern Recognition (1997)
9. Zhang, Z.: A flexible new technique for camera calibration. IEEE Trans. Pattern Anal. Mach. Intell. **22**(11), 1330–1334 (2000)
10. Zhang, J., Gu, R., Ye, Q., Ji, Y.: Monocular human action recognition utilizing silhouette feature extraction and skin color detection. In: Parallel and Distributed Computing: Applications and Technologies (2012)
11. Hsu, R., Abdelmottaleb, M., Jain, A.: Face detection in color images. IEEE Trans. Pattern Anal. Mach. Intell. **24**(5), 696–706 (2002)
12. Chai, D., Ngan, K.N.: Locating facial region of a head-and-shoulders color image. In: IEEE International Conference on Automatic Face and Gesture Recognition (1998)
13. Bergasa, L.M., Mazo, M., Gardel, A., Sotelo, M.A., Boquete, L.: Unsupervised and adaptive Gaussian skin-color model. Image Vis. Comput. **18**(12), 987–1003 (2000). Lucky, R.W.: Automatic equalization for digital communication. Bell Syst. Tech. J. **44**(4), 547–588 (1965)

14. Hassanpour, R., Shahbahrami, A., Wong, S.: Adaptive Gaussian mixture model for skin color segmentation. In: Proceedings of World Academy of Science Engineering & Technology, no. 4, p. 1 (2011)
15. Dalal, N., Triggs, B.: Histograms of oriented gradients for human detection. In: Computer Vision and Pattern Recognition (2005)

A Body Emotion-Based Human-Robot Interaction

Tehao Zhu[1,2], Qunfei Zhao[1], and Jing Xiong[3(✉)]

[1] Department of Automation, Shanghai Jiao Tong University, Shanghai, China
{zthjoe, zhaoqf}@sjtu.edu.cn
[2] Nanjing Research Institute of Electronics Technology, Nanjing, China
[3] Shenzhen Institutes of Advanced Technology,
Chinese Academy of Sciences, Shenzhen, China
jing.xiong@siat.ac.cn

Abstract. In order to achieve reasonable and natural interaction when facing vague human actions, a body emotion-based human-robot interaction (BEHRI) algorithm was developed in this paper. Laban movement analysis and fuzzy logic inference was used to extract the movement emotion and torso pose emotion. A finite state machine model was constructed to describe the paradigm of the robot emotion, and then the interactive strategy was designed to generate suitable interactive behaviors. The algorithm was evaluated on UTD-MHAD, and the overall system was tested via questionnaire. The experimental results indicated that the proposed BEHRI algorithm was able to analyze the body emotion precisely, and the interactive behaviors were accessible and satisfying. BEHRI was shown to have good application potentials.

Keywords: Human-robot interaction · Body emotion · Laban movement analysis · Fuzzy logic inference · Finite state machine

1 Introduction

Human-robot interaction (HRI) is one of the most popular research fields. Robots in HRI have similar profile with humans (partially or integrally). With the rapid development of the robot technology, the HRI robots are expected to have nicer social and interactive skills.

Much research has been studied around various key technologies of HRI. In the field of human behavior perception, there are data capturing and processing of multimodal information, e.g., image [1], sound [2], and depth [3]. In the field of action recognition, there are movement [4], expression [5], speech [6], and intonation [7] recognition. In the field of intention inference and interaction strategy, there are multi-agent [8], neural network [9], fuzzy logic [10], and deep learning [11].

Vision-based HRI can achieve the recognition of human action. Once an action is recognized, the appropriate interactive behavior can be selected or generated. However, the action recognition algorithm might fail for many reasons, e.g., the action is performed vaguely, or the class of the performed action is not included in the training samples. To the best of our knowledge, the study of the interaction strategy in this case

© Springer International Publishing AG 2017
M. Liu et al. (Eds.): ICVS 2017, LNCS 10528, pp. 268–278, 2017.
DOI: 10.1007/978-3-319-68345-4_24

is inadequate. In fact, solving this issue will be a principal complement to the integrity of the interaction logic, and will make the interactive behavior of the robot friendlier and more natural.

Previous studies have tried to tackle this problem. Bohus and Horvitz [12] used linguistic hesitation actions to signal the system's state of confusion, which can generate additional time for collecting evidence and resolving uncertainties. Aly and Tapus [13] developed an adapted customized verbal-nonverbal robot's behavior based on the personality dimensions. They proposed the Behavior Expression Animation Toolkit by using linguistic and contextual information to generate a corresponding synchronized set of gestures. The gestures conflict and priority threshold filters were used to selected the most appropriate set of gestures. Liu et al. [14] modeled the communication atmosphere based on emotional states of humans and robots. They estimated the human motion from the speech and gesture using weighted fusion and fuzzy logic. Dautenhahn [15] gave the evaluation criteria to identify requirements on social skills for robots in different application domains. He also concluded three categories of HRI (robot-centered, human-centered, and robot cognition-centered).

In this work, we developed a body emotion-based HRI (BEHRI) algorithm to achieve reasonable and natural interaction when facing vague human actions. The main contribution of this work was to introduce the Laban movement analysis (LMA) form dance science into HRI. LMA and the fuzzy logical inference are used to extract the emotions from the movement and torso pose of people. A finite state machine model was constructed to describe the paradigm of the robot emotion, and then the interactive strategy was designed to generate suitable interactive behaviors. The proposed BEHRI algorithm was shown to be a powerful assistant for the action recognition algorithm, thus be able to promote the interaction procedure effectively.

2   Body Emotion Analysis

Laban movement analysis (LMA) theory was presented by Rudolf Laban, a Hungarian dancer, in 1974 [16]. It is a method for describing and interpreting various human movements. The main components of LMA are Effort, Shape, Space Harmony, etc. [17]. Space Harmony estimates the human movement on three orthogonal planes. In each plane, a pair of opposite emotions is evaluated based on the direction and extent of the movement. We use Space Harmony as one of the measures for analyzing body emotion in our work.

In addition, the torso pose emotion analysis is another component of LMA [18]. Torso is the root of the human skeleton. The appearance of torso largely determines the state of the whole body. We estimate the deformation of the "I" type structure of the torso, and give an emotion label to the current torso pose.

2.1   Movement Emotion Analysis

Movement Projection and Emotion Matching. We use Kinect [19], a popular human motion capture device, to perceive the joint positions in the form of 3D data.

The coordinate system of Kinect is shown in Fig. 1(a). The Space Harmony of LMA makes the human movement be projected into three orthogonal planes, which are defined as the Horizontal Plane, the Wheel Plane, and the Vertical Plane [17]. They are pairwise orthogonal. As the names suggest, the three planes correspond to the XOZ, XOY, and YOZ plane in the Kinect coordinate, respectively (shown in Fig. 1(b)–(d)). According to LMA, the projected movements are matched with a pair of opposite emotions in each plane. Their relationships are summarized in Table 1 [17].

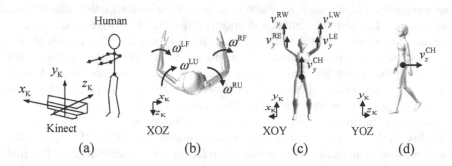

Fig. 1. The Kinect coordinate system (a) and the three projection planes for movement emotion analysis, (b) horizontal plane, (c) vertical plane, and (d) wheel plane.

Table 1. Movements and emotions in each projection plane

Horizontal Plane		Vertical Plane		Wheel Plane	
Movement	Emotion	Movement	Emotion	Movement	Emotion
Spreading	Hospitable	Ascending	Encouraged	Advancing	Active
Enclosing	Impassive	Descending	Distressed	Retreating	Scared

Emotion Estimation. We define E_H, E_V, and E_W as the emotion values of the movements in the Horizontal Plane, the Vertical Plane, and the Wheel Plane, respectively. The range of them are all in $[-1, 1]$. The emotion values of the positive *Spreading*, *Ascending*, and *Advancing* are greater than 0, while those of the negative *Enclosing*, *Descending*, and *Retreating* are less than 0. The formulations of E_H, E_V, and E_W are as follows:

$$E_H = S_H\left[(\omega^{RU} + \omega^{RF}) - (\omega^{LU} + \omega^{LF})\right],\tag{1}$$

$$E_V = S_V\left[\rho v_y^{CH} + (1 - \rho)(v_y^{LE} + v_y^{LW} + v_y^{RE} + v_y^{RW} - 4v_y^{CH})\right],\tag{2}$$

$$E_W = S_W\left(-v_z^{CH}\right),\tag{3}$$

where

$$S_*(x) = \frac{2}{1 + e^{-a_* x}} - 1\tag{4}$$

is the activation function. In (1) ω^* represents the rotational angular velocities of the upper and lower arms in the Horizontal Plane (shown in Fig. 1(b)). The positive values of them mean the rotation directions are clockwise in the top view, and negative values represent anticlockwise rotations.

The velocities in (2) are illustrated in Fig. 1(c). $\rho \in [0, 1]$ is a factor to determine the influence of the torso velocity. Here we set $\rho = 0.5$.

In (3) v_z^{CH} is the torso velocity along z axis, which is shown in Fig. 1(d). Please note that moving forward results in the reduction of v_z^{CH} due to the definition of Kinect coordinate. This is a little bit different from the usual habits.

According to our experiment, the parameters of the activation functions are: $a_H = 0.6\ (\text{rad/s})^{-1}$, $a_V = 7.2\ (\text{m/s})^{-1}$, and $a_W = 3.8\ (\text{m/s})^{-1}$.

2.2 Torso Pose Emotion Analysis

The human body is often simplified as a stick figure model, in which the torso is represented by an "I" type structure, like Fig. 2(a) shows. The poses of spine I_0 and shoulder I_1 dominate the performance of the torso emotion. The torso poses and their emotion performances can be summarized like Table 2 shows [18].

The slant angle of I_1 is the angle θ_{S_1} between I_1 and the horizontal plane. The tilt angle of I_0 is related to the torso rotation. It can be calculated according to the following procedures (also illustrated in Fig. 2(b)):

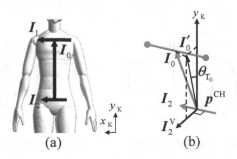

Fig. 2. The stick figure model of the torso. (a) The "I" type structure. (b) The spine tilt angle θ_{T_0}.

Table 2. Torso poses and emotion labels

Lean	Upright ($\phi^1_{T_0} \leq \theta_{T_0} \leq \phi^2_{T_0}$)		Lean Forward ($\theta_{T_0} > \phi^2_{T_0}$)		Lean Backward ($\theta_{T_0} < \phi^1_{T_0}$)	
	Normal	Slant	Normal	Slant	Normal	Slant
Slant	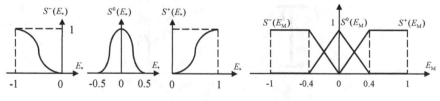					
L_T	*Formal*	*Relaxed*	*Sad*	*Negligent*	*Optimistic*	*Provocative*

*Normal: $|\theta_{S_1}| \leq \phi_{S_1}$, Slant: $|\theta_{S_1}| > \phi_{S_1}$

1. Get the orientation of the body. Here use the vertical vector of the projection of hipline I_2 in the horizontal plane to represent, which is named by I_2^V.
2. Project I_0 into the plane formed by I_2^V and axis y_K, where the projection is I'_0.
3. The angle θ_{T_0} between I'_0 and y_K is the tilt angle of I_0. θ_{T_0} is positive when the person leans forward, and is negative when he/she leans backward.

Define L_T as the label of the torso pose emotion. Table 2 shows the labels of different combinations of θ_{T_0} and θ_{S_1}, where $\phi^1_{T_0} = -0.035$ rad, $\phi^2_{T_0} = 0.35$ rad, and $\phi_{S_1} = 0.1$ rad are the given threshold.

3 Interaction Strategy

3.1 Fuzzy Logic Inference for Global Movement Emotion

A fuzzy logic system is designed to generate the global movement emotion based on the emotions in the three planes. The inputs of the fuzzy logic system are E_H, E_V, and E_W. Their values are categorized into three groups: *Positive* (+), *Normal* (0), and *Negative* (−). The fuzzy membership functions for them are based on S-shape and Bell-shape (Fig. 3(a)). The output is the global movement emotion E_M, the value of which is also categorized into the above three groups. The membership functions of E_M are based on Sigma-shape and Triangular-shape (Fig. 3(b)).

(a) input movement emotion membership   (b) output global emotion membership

Fig. 3. Membership functions for global movement emotion

As the output of the fuzzy logic system, E_M is formalized in the form of the following fuzzy IF-THEN rules:

- IF E_H is (+) OR E_V is (+) OR E_W is (+), THEN E_M is (+).
  OR
- IF E_H is (0) OR E_V is (0) OR E_W is (0), THEN E_M is (0).
  OR
- IF E_H is (−) OR E_V is (−) OR E_W is (−), THEN E_M is (−).

Each individual rule is inferred by the OR operation, and the three rules are also associated by the OR operation. The defuzzification is done by the centroid method.

3.2   Finite State Machine for Interactive Behavior Decision

The interaction strategy is constructed based on the combination of the global movement emotion E_M and the torso pose emotion label L_T. The interactive behavior includes two parts, speech and movement. Speech (SP) is prepared for different conditions, and is selected by the current E_M and L_T directly. Movements are selected according to current emotion state. We suppose the change of the robot's emotion relies on the current emotion state and the external impulse. A finite state machine (FSM) model is constructed to describe the paradigm of the robot emotion:

$$\mathbf{FSM}_{RE} = (\mathbf{RE}, \Sigma_M, \mathbf{F}_M, RE_0) \tag{5}$$

where $\mathbf{RE} = \{RE_p \,|\, p = 1, \cdots, 4\}$ is the set of robot emotion states, representing *Negative (Neg)*, *Normal (Nor)*, *Positive (Pos)*, and *Very Positive (Pos +)*, respectively, and RE_0 is the initial emotion state specified as *Nor*. The movement in each state is generated by the algorithm proposed in [20], where the available poses can be obtained with an Activation-Valence value, and the movements can be planned by Markov model.

$\Sigma_M = \{e_q \,|\, q = 1, \cdots, 5\}$ is the input alphabet, which determines the orientation of state transition. e_q relies on the external impulses E_M and L_T, which is given as ET in Table 3. ETs in three conditions are e_-. We consider the three combinations of E_M and L_T are inconsistent. They appear rarely in daily life. If they really happen, the current emotion state keeps. $\mathbf{F}_M$ is the state-transition functions. The overall $\mathbf{F}_M : \mathbf{RE} \times \Sigma_M \rightarrow \mathbf{RE}$ in this FSM are illustrated in Fig. 4.

Table 3. Interaction strategy based on E_M and L_T

L_T	$E_M < -E_M^T$	$|E_M| \leq E_M^T$	$E_M > E_M^T$
Sad & Negligent	SP: encourage ET: e_5	SP: caring, enthusiastic ET: e_3	SP: (none) ET: e_-
Formal	SP: caring, encourage ET: e_3	SP: polite, hospitable ET: e_1	SP: happy ET: e_2
Relaxed	SP: "Do you feel any discomfort?" ET: e_1	SP: "Do you need to take a rest?" ET: e_1	SP: happy, remind keeping safety ET: e_2
Optimistic	SP: (none) ET: e_-	SP: happy ET: e_2	SP: laugh, witty ET: e_4
Provocative	SP: (none) ET: e_-	SP: laugh, witty ET: e_4	SP: joke, witty, remind keeping safety ET: e_4

*SP: interactive SPeech, ET: Emotion state Transition.

4 Experimental Results

4.1 Evaluation of the Body Emotion Analysis

We use the public dataset UTD-MHAD [21] to evaluate the quantification result of body emotion analysis. The primary reason for using this dataset is that many types of the included actions can match certain emotion types: e.g., "forward lunge" expresses a positive emotion, whereas "sit" expresses a negative one.

UTD-MHAD contains 27 actions performed by eight subjects. Each subject repeated each action four times. According to our assessment, we give 12 actions the positive (+) or negative (−) emotion label as the ground truth manually. We assume that these actions are not recognized, and the proposed BEHRI algorithm is implemented to analyze the global movement emotion and torso pose emotion label of the skeleton joint position sequence.

The results are shown in Table 4, where $\bar{E}_M$ is the average global movement emotion of one type of action in the dataset, and L_T is the ratio of the torso pose emotion labels of the result. The signs of all $\bar{E}_M$ values correspond to the ground truths, and the values are reasonable. As the actions in UTD-MHAD do not contain exaggerated leaning backward, there are no actions labeled "optimistic" or "provocative". Most actions are "formal" or "relaxed", but L_T of the "stand", "sit", and "squat" actions have a large ratio of "sad". Understandably, the subjects bow forward during these actions. In conclusion, BEHRI algorithm quantifies the global movement emotion and the torso pose emotion label of each action type precisely.

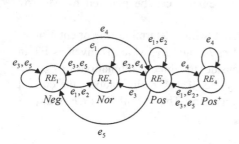

Fig. 4. State-transition functions in the FSM of the robot emotion.

Fig. 5. Visual interface of BEHRI system.

4.2 Evaluation of the Overall BEHRI System

We test the overall BEHRI system by writing an interaction program. The visual interface of the program is like Fig. 5 shows. The robot we used to perform the interactive behaviors is a humanoid robot NAO [22]. We use a questionnaire to give a subjective evaluation. The questionnaire is given in Fig. 6, which is designed based on

Table 4. Body emotion analysis on UTD-MHAD

Action	Ground truth	$\bar{E}_M$	L_T (%)			
			Formal	Relaxed	Sad	Negligent
Right arm swipe to the left	−	−0.2354	87.50%	12.50%	0%	0%
Right arm swipe to the right	+	0.2238	90.63%	9.37%	0%	0%
Right hand wave	+	0.1934	75.00%	25.00%	0%	0%
Clap hands	+	0.1711	100.00%	0%	0%	0%
Two arms curl	+	0.3107	100.00%	0%	0%	0%
Two hands push	+	0.3657	93.75%	6.25%	0%	0%
Hand catch	−	−0.3526	78.13%	21.87%	0%	0%
Jogging	+	0.2745	100.00%	0%	0%	0%
Stand	+	0.2706	50.00%	0%	50.00%	0%
Sit	−	−0.2788	12.50%	0%	87.50%	0%
Forward lunge	+	0.3344	81.25%	0%	18.75%	0%
Squat	−	−0.3237	0%	0%	90.63%	9.37%

BEHRI Questionnaire

Your role: □Participant   □Spectator

Q1. The participant can perform movements with different emotions:
Stiffly 1 2 3 4 5 6 7 Naturally
Q2. The state transitions of the robot match your expectation:
Not at all 1 2 3 4 5 6 7 Very much
Q3. The interactive movements of the robot match your expectation:
Not at all 1 2 3 4 5 6 7 Very much
Q4. The interactive speech of the robot matches your expectation:
Not at all 1 2 3 4 5 6 7 Very much
Q5. You are interested in this human-robot interaction:
Not at all 1 2 3 4 5 6 7 Very much
Q6. Your age: _____
Q7. Your gender: □Male   □Female

Fig. 6. Questionnaire for evaluating BEHRI system.

that in [13]. The main questions are the first five, which are presented on a 7-point Likert scale. Besides the participants completed the questionnaire after their experiments, we organized some of them to watch others' experiment replays and completed the questionnaires again. They evaluated the system as the spectators.

The participants included 11 students (eight males, three females; seven 18–25 years old, four 26–30 years old; three undergraduate students, eight graduate students), and the spectators included six students (five males, one females; four 18–25 years old, two 26–30 years old; all graduate students).

All the 11 participants used BEHRI for the first time. We show them the questionnaire before the experiment in order to let them know what they need to observe and evaluate, then they freely make daily life movements without any cuing or limiting. During the experiment, the participant can see the robot's emotion state, movement, and speech text, and also hear the robot's voice.

Evaluation from the Participants. The results from the participants are illustrated by the dark blue bars in Fig. 7. Most participants satisfied their performances. They gave themselves 5.64/7 in average. The evaluation on emotion state transitions and interactive movements are fairly well, which are 5.18/7 and 4.91/7, respectively. In addition, the standard deviation line of the interactive movement shows that different participants have quite inconsistent opinions. The interactive speeches got 5.55/7, a relatively nice score. Except one participant gave 6 for Q5, other 10 participants gave 7. Accordingly, the participants show great interests in this novel HRI system, and at the same time, hold very high expectations.

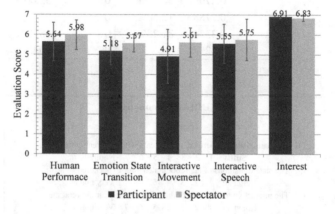

Fig. 7. Questionnaire result from participant and spectator. Red line: standard deviation. (Color figure online)

Evaluation from the Spectators. The scores from the spectators are represented by the orange bars in Fig. 7. The performance of the participants is evaluated 5.98/7 by themselves in average. The state transitions and interactive movements got 5.57/7 and 5.61/7, respectively. The speeches still won a high score (5.75/7), and the interest in BEHRI also almost got a full mark.

Discussion. Considering the evaluations from the above two respects, our BEHRI analyzes the body emotion effectively, and the robot reactions are reasonable. The interactive behaviors of the robot satisfy the users.

The evaluations of the emotion state transition and interactive movement from the participants are relatively lower than others. This issue may be caused by many reasons. The first-try participants are not very clear about the definition of each state. The interactive movements are generated automatically, some of which have limitations in naturalness and do not meet people's habit. Furthermore, the interactive speech is outstanding, so the interactive movement looks even worse.

The evaluations from the spectators are higher than those from the participants in general. This fact suggests the users can gradually understand the BEHRI system after they interact with the robot many times or for a long time.

5 Conclusion

In this work, a body emotion-based human-robot interaction (BEHRI) algorithm was developed to achieve reasonable and natural interaction when facing vague human actions. The body emotions, including movement emotion and torso pose emotion, were quantified by Laban movement analysis and fuzzy logic inference. The emotion paradigm of the robot emotion was defined by four emotion states, and a finite state machine model was used to transfer the emotion states according to the body emotions. Finally, appropriate interactive movement and speech were generated, and then performed by the robot. The quantification effect of BEHRI was verified on UTD-MHAD. The overall system was tested via the questionnaire from the participants and spectators. The experimental results have shown that the analysis of BEHRI was precise, and the system was accessible and satisfying.

Some measures can improve the interaction performance of BEHRI, like: design a tutorial to guide the user "warms up" with the robot quickly; record some human movements and make the robot play for a better performance; and customize interaction scheme for individual users.

Acknowledgements. This work has received funding from the Major Research plan of the National Natural Science Foundation of China (91646205), and the National Natural Science Foundation of China (61403368).

References

1. Reddy, K.K., Shah, M.: Recognizing 50 human action categories of web videos. Mach. Vis. Appl. **24**(5), 971–981 (2013)
2. Alonso Martín, F., Ramey, A., Salichs, M.A.: Speaker identification using three signal voice domains during human-robot interaction. In: Proceedings of 2014 ACM/IEEE International Conference on Human-Robot Interaction, pp. 114–115. ACM (2014)
3. Chaaraoui, A.A., Padilla-López, J.R., Climent-Pérez, P., Flórez-Revuelta, F.: Evolutionary joint selection to improve human action recognition with RGB-D devices. Expert Syst. Appl. **41**(3), 786–794 (2014)
4. Venkataraman, V., Turaga, P., Lehrer, N., Baran, M., Rikakis, T., Wolf, S.L.: Attractor-shape for dynamical analysis of human movement: applications in stroke rehabilitation and action recognition. In: 2013 IEEE Conference on Computer Vision and Pattern Recognition Workshops, pp. 514–520. IEEE Press (2013)
5. Siddiqi, M.H., Ali, R., Khan, A.M., Park, Y.-T., Lee, S.: Human facial expression recognition using stepwise linear discriminant analysis and hidden conditional random fields. IEEE T Image Process **24**(4), 1386–1398 (2015)

6. Yildiz, I.B., von Kriegstein, K., Kiebel, S.J.: From birdsong to human speech recognition: Bayesian inference on a hierarchy of nonlinear dynamical systems. PLoS Comput. Biol. **9** (9), 1–16 (2013)

7. Chatterjee, M., Peng, S.-C.: Processing F0 with cochlear implants: modulation frequency discrimination and speech intonation recognition. Hear. Res. **235**(1), 143–156 (2008)

8. Lichtenstern, M., Frassl, M., Perun, B., Angermann, M.: A prototyping environment for interaction between a human and a robotic multi-agent system. In: 2012 7th ACM/IEEE International Conference on Human-Robot Interaction (HRI), pp. 185–186. IEEE Press (2012)

9. Yamada, T., Murata, S., Arie, H., Ogata, T.: Dynamical integration of language and behavior in a recurrent neural network for human-robot interaction. Front. Neurorobot. **10**(5), 1–17 (2016)

10. Palm, R., Chadalavada, R., Lilienthal, A.: Fuzzy modeling and control for intention recognition in human-robot systems. In: 8th International Conference on Computational Intelligence (IJCCI), Porto, Portugal, pp. 67–74. SciTePress (2016)

11. Liu, P., Glas, D.F., Kanda, T., Ishiguro, H.: Data-driven HRI: learning social behaviors by example from human-human interaction. IEEE Trans. Robot. **32**(4), 988–1008 (2016)

12. Bohus, D., Horvitz, E.: Managing human-robot engagement with forecasts and... um... hesitations. In: Proceedings of 16th International Conference on Multimodal Interaction, pp. 2–9. ACM (2014)

13. Aly, A., Tapus, A.: A model for synthesizing a combined verbal and nonverbal behavior based on personality traits in human-robot interaction. In: Proceedings of 8th ACM/IEEE International Conference on Human-Robot Interaction, pp. 325–332. IEEE Press (2013)

14. Liu, Z., Wu, M., Li, D., Chen, L., Dong, F., Yamazaki, Y., Hirota, K.: Communication atmosphere in humans and robots interaction based on the concept of fuzzy atmosfield generated by emotional states of humans and robots. J. Automat. Mob. Robot. Intell. Syst. **7** (2), 52–63 (2013)

15. Dautenhahn, K.: Socially intelligent robots: dimensions of human–robot interaction. Philos. Trans. Roy. Soc. Lond. B **362**(1480), 679–704 (2007)

16. Laban, R.: The Language of Movement: A Guidebook to Choreutics. Plays, Boston (1974)

17. Hsieh, C., Wang, Y.: Digitalize emotions to improve the quality life-analyzing movement for emotion application. J. Aesthet. Educ. **168**, 64–69 (2009)

18. Ku, M.-S., Chen, Y.: From movement to emotion - a basic research of upper body (analysis foundation of body movement in the digital world 3 of 3). J. Aesthet. Educ. **164**, 38–43 (2008)

19. Kinect - Windows App Development. https://developer.microsoft.com/en-us/windows/kinect

20. Xia, G., Tay, J., Dannenberg, R., Veloso, M.: Autonomous robot dancing driven by beats and emotions of music. In: Proceedings of 11th International Conference on Autonomous Agents and Multiagent Systems, vol. 1, pp. 205–212. International Foundation for Autonomous Agents and Multiagent Systems (2012)

21. Chen, C., Jafari, R., Kehtarnavaz, N.: UTD-MHAD: a multimodal dataset for human action recognition utilizing a depth camera and a wearable inertial sensor. In: 2015 IEEE International Conference on Image Processing (ICIP), pp. 168–172. IEEE Press (2015)

22. Nao Robot: Characteristics - Aldebaran. https://www.ald.softbankrobotics.com/en/cool-robots/nao/find-out-more-about-nao

Robot's Workspace Enhancement with Dynamic Human Presence for Socially-Aware Navigation

Ioannis Kostavelis$^{(\boxtimes)}$, Andreas Kargakos, Dimitrios Giakoumis, and Dimitrios Tzovaras

Centre for Research & Technology Hellas, Information Technologies Institute, 6th Km Charilaou-Thermi Road, 57001 Thermi-Thessaloniki, Greece
{gkostave,akargakos,dgiakoum,Dimitrios.Tzovaras}@iti.gr

Abstract. The incorporation of service robots in human populated environments gives rise to the adaptation of cruise strategies that allow robots to move in a natural, secure and ordinary manner among their cohabitants. Therefore, robots should firstly apprehend their space similarly with the people and, secondly, should adopt human motion anticipation strategies in their planning mechanism. The paper at hand introduces a closed-loop human oriented robot navigation strategy, where on-board a moving robot, multimodal human detection and tracking methods are deployed to predict human motion intention in the shared workspace. The human occupied space is probabilistically constrained following the proxemics theory. The impact of human presence in the commonly shared space is imprinted to the robot's navigation behaviour after undergoing a social filtering step based on the inferred walking pattern. The proposed method has been integrated with a robotic platform and extensively evaluated in terms of socially acceptable behaviour in real-life experiments exhibiting increased navigation capacity in human populated environments.

Keywords: Robot navigation · Leg and human skeleton tracker · Social costmap · Human motion intension prediction · Robot path planning

1 Introduction

The interest of the film industry in making movies such as the *WALL-E* [2008], *Robot & Frank* [2012] and many others reveals the potential for broad acceptance, as well as comprehension of people for domestic and service robots in near future communities. An in-depth study of these movies discloses the human's expectations about the characteristics that the forthcoming artificial agents should retain so as to be broadly acceptable, while someone can infer that naturalness of robots' motion is the main attribute that renders their presence intimate to the humans. This challenge is broadly recognized by the respective scientific community which has already conducted a laborious research on robot motion planning [11]. Yet, the demand for mobile robots to operate in dynamic changing environments where humans are also involved, emerged the development

© Springer International Publishing AG 2017
M. Liu et al. (Eds.): ICVS 2017, LNCS 10528, pp. 279–288, 2017.
DOI: 10.1007/978-3-319-68345-4_25

of more sophisticated motion planning strategies where human factors should be considered [6], integrating contextual representations of the individual's presence [2]. Following this aspect, human-robot co-navigation strategies are foreseen when designing a service robot targeted to operate in human-centric environments [17]. Human aware navigation and planning include a significant variety of implementations and, therefore, we attempt to provide a categorization based on the methodologies utilized for the human space modelling and the navigation methods that consider human presence. The motivation behind this taxonomy it that these well known issues constitute the basic components of the proposed methodology.

Human Space Modelling: Proxemics theory early introduced by Hall [5] comprised the cornerstone of human space apprehension by establishing the theory on how individuals' placement in space affects the quality of their interaction. This theory has been broadly accepted by the roboticists during last decades and embodied in various ways in the human space modelling mechanisms with robots. The work in [12] represents the social zones in terms of isocontours of an implicit function capable of describing complex social interaction. In more recent work, the authors in [15] marked the human space with a single Gaussian kernel parameterized with respect to human calculated velocity differentiating thus, in the modeled space the human presence from the obstacles; yet, this implementation was appropriate only for short term robot motion calculations. A relevant work which capitalizes on the proxemics theory for modelling the human personal space is the one described in [7], where used joint oriented Gaussian functions to model human presence targeting to be incorporated in global path planning level. Contrary to the aforementioned works, the human space modelling follows the notion of the proxemics theory, yet by considering a sequence of Gaussian kernels -instead of a single one- formulated along the estimated human paths, the amplitudes of which degrades considering the human's velocity allowing thus predictive long-term global path planning. Moreover, the proposed method can be extended to multiple human tracking and, hence, to their personal space modelling as well.

Path Planning with Human Presence: Considering dynamic path planning, the work in [13] introduces a path planner that considers the presence of humans in terms of their vision field, their accessibility and their personal choices regarding the human-robot placement. However, this system considers solely static persons but the fast computation time of this module allows online path replanning. Dynamic human presence during path planning is considered in [14], where the location and movement of humans is modeled as potential fields and the most feasible trajectory is calculated using *Rapidly-exploring Random Tree* (RRT). The authors in [8] employ velocity obstacles to infer trajectories ample to avoid humans, while a probabilistic extension of RRT based on predictive Gaussian processes is employed in [4] and proved adequate for path planning in dynamic environments. Similar, yet more contemporary methods are also presented in [16]. Luber et al. [10] proposed a machine learning strategy that employs the measurements of walking people to solve an unsupervised learning problem. Specifically, the authors define the relative motion prototypes and cluster them hierarchically, by exploiting a distance function that relies on a modified *Dynamic Time Warping* (DTW) module. Afterwards, relative motion prototypes are used in a model selection to extract social context, which is further used for the formulation of the cost map. The authors in [17] introduced walking motion anticipatory features that when integrated with a learning scheme proved adequate navigation capacity to maneuver a robot around humans in dynamic environment. The paper at hand, Fig. 1 anticipates the walking motion of the human by inserting the concept of frequently visited areas in a well defined environment. The estimated human workspace is modeled as costmap ample to operate in real-time applications as it is integrated both in global and local planner level.

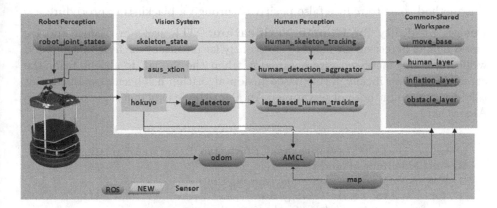

Fig. 1. Block diagram describing the software components involved in the proposed method

2 Human Presence Anticipation

2.1 Human Detection and Tracking

A basic prerequisite for human-aware autonomous robot navigation is that the robot should to detect the people present in its surroundings. For that reason two different human tracking algorithms have been adopted and fused in the present worked, based on LIDAR and RGB-D data obtaining this way constant human awareness during the robot operation, i.e. if the user is out of the field of view (FoV) of the RGB-D sensor it will be tracked with adequate confidence from the laser readings.

Nite Skeleton Tracker: Constant human detection with stationary robotic platform is addressed with the NiTE skeleton tracker. To keep track of the existing persons, which remain in the FoV of the robot's depth camera, the detected human IDs are shorted with respect to the returned confidence value.

This information will be later used for the fusion with leg tracker. The advantage of this modality is that it performs reliable detection with increased confidence, but it cannot be used with moving robot.

Leg Detector: Laser based human tracking is employed herein using the methodology introduced in [9], allowing human tracking while robot is moving. To shortly explain this method, the laser scans are clustered according to distance and a feature vector is extracted for each cluster using specific geometrical features. Next, a random forest classifier is trained, where negative examples are obtained by moving the robot in an environment devoid of people and positive examples are obtained by setting up the laser in an open area with significant people traffic. During inference procedure, all the detected pairs of legs that produce a high probability score are considered as potential humans. This method produces many false positive observations and, therefore, herein we extended this method so as to reduce false positives through a blacklisting procedure.

Fusion Modality for Human Verification: NiTE skeleton tracker and leg based human detection are fused to constantly keep track of the human's location while retaining increased awareness also when the human is absent from the camera FoV. Specifically, a rule based fusion algorithm has been developed that takes in to account both observations. An algorithmic explanation is outlined in Algorithm 1.

Data: LegTracks[ ], SkeletonTracks[ ], StaticMap, RobotTransformation
Result: FinalHumanPoses[ ]
if *RobotIsNotMoving(RobotTranformation)* then
   for $i = 0$ to *LegTracks.size()* do
      for $j = 0$ to *SkeletonTracks.size()* do
         if *isCloseToObStacles(LegTracks[i] , StaticMap)* then
            Blacklist ← LegTracks[i].ID ;
            Break;
         end
         if $Dist(SkeletonTracks[j], LegTracks[i]) < DistThreshold$ then
            LegTracks[i].conf *= (1+ SkeletonTracks[j].conf);
         end
      end
   end
else
   FinalHumanPoses = getHumanPoses(LegTracks , Blacklist);
end
Algorithm 1. Nite human detection and leg detector fusion algorithm

2.2 Short-Term Walking Paths Prediction

In accordance to the theory of the human spatial experience [1], people tend to frequently revisit regions -indoors or outdoors- that stimulate them either with social experience or are related with specific interaction activities. Such regions can be spots with increased human traffic, e.g. doorways, or places with semantic meaning associated with the activities, e.g. a fridge in a kitchen. Based on this theory we identified such frequently visited human positions in a domestic environment and associated them with the target human locations. Then, we formulated the prediction about the human motion intention based on the rationale that when a person is moving s/he will probably approach one of the pre-defined frequently visited areas. By assuming this, the cases of random wandering are considered less probable since they constitute the less frequent walking patterns of people with normal behaviour [3]. Having said that, the next step comprises the modelling of the human motion intention on the robot's workspace. Firstly, we compute the pose deviation vector $\mathbf{D} = [D_i, D_{i+1}, D_N]$ as derived from the current human position $P_H = (x_h, y_h)$ and the N frequently visited positions $\mathbf{P} = [P_{i=1}, P_{i=2}, ..., P_{i=N}]$ in the environment. Note that $P_i = (x, y)$ where x, y comprise the explicit coordinates in the map, and $D_i = (t, r)$ where t, r corresponds to the computed Euclidean translational and rotational deviation respectively. To determine the most probable frequently visited position that the human will move towards to, we minimize the $argmin(\alpha \mathbf{d_r}_{i=1}^{N} + \beta \mathbf{d_l}_{i=1}^{N})$ criterion where α and β are regularization parameters that control situations where the modelled environment is congested, i.e. with many furniture where the user has to follow curved paths to reach a standing position. Moreover, $\mathbf{d_r}$ and $\mathbf{d_l}$ are the vectors that retain the computed Euclidean distance and the rotational deviation of the humans's current position from the pre-defined frequently visited positions, respectively. The minimized values of the criterion are sorted from the most probable to the less probable one. Relying on the assumption that when a human walks towards a target location subconsciously selects the most shortest path, we adopted the D* Lite path planning algorithm in order to model the candidate human paths among the human's current position and the N frequently visited standing positions. The reason of the selection of the D*Lite is mainly due to the fact that this approach repeatedly determines shortest paths between the current position of the human and his/her goal position as the edge costs of a graph change while the human moves towards the goal position, allowing thus fast replanning ample to capture the unexpected changes in human's course. For each point that belongs to human path, an oriented Gaussian kernel is centered therein, the parameters σ_x and σ_y of which, model the personal space of the human in accordance with the proxemics theory; this results in a sequence of partial overlapping kernels. The amplitude A of the first Gaussian kernel in the sequence is reverse proportional to the values of the minimization criterion, indicating that the paths with less probability to be followed by the human have diminished weights. Additionally, the amplitude A of each kernel in the path decreases as the points in the path fend off the human current position and the degradation step is normalized to the total number of the calculated points in the path. This cycle is repeated anytime a human observation is received and due to the simplicity of the calculations and the fast execution rate of the D* algorithm, instantaneous estimations about the human motion are obtained anticipating thus the person's presence in the robot's workspace. To avoid unnecessary computational burden, in cases that human is standing still for a specific time i.e. 2 s, his/her presence is modelled with a sole Gaussian kernel (Fig. 2).

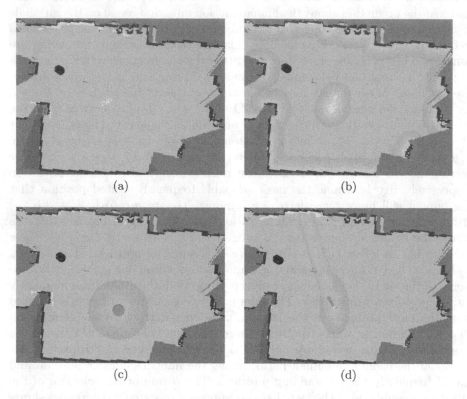

(a)   (b)

(c)   (d)

Fig. 2. (a) Static map with obstacle layer where the human is detected in the middle of room and treated as obstacle, (b) inflation layer, (c) human layer with static human detected and (d) human layer with moving human and predicted path

2.3   Human Anticipation Cost-Map Modelling

Following the aforemention methodology the anticipation of the human's presence within the robot's workspace, in terms of ROS infrastructure has been represented as separate costmap layer. Therefore, the existing costmap layers considered in our method are outlined as follows:

Static Map Layer: Represents the metric map, separating the obstacles from the free space and defines the width and the height of other layers.

Obstacle Layer: Tracks the obstacles as observations obtained by the sensor data and marks them or clears the space by raytracing.

Inflation Layer: Inflation is the process where the cost values decay while moving from obstacle cells to free cells. In this layer, the costmap is quantized with specific symbolic zones, i.e. lethal (actual obstacle), inscribed (robot footprint in collision), freespace and unknown. All the costs are assigned depending on the distance from a lethal cell and decays to the free space cost.

Human Layer: Depending on the observations of the human tracking module and the values of the above layers, extra costs are computed and formulated as final layer to the total costmap. The human layer retains the lower priority comparing to any other layer, since the robot firstly needs to avoid collisions, then to produce paths, and if possible to be also aware of the social cost of these paths. Initially, the human layer is inferred given the position, orientation and velocity of the human in space. If no human is detected, then no layer is generated. If the velocity of the detected human is low, then static human is assumed, and, thus static Gaussian kernel of costs is computed and superimposed to other costmap layers, centered in the detection coordinates. In situations where human velocity is above a threshold (i.e. 2 m/sec experimentaly defined herein compensating the glittering effect of laser measurements) then short-term walking path prediction is enabled as described in Sect. 2.

3 Methodology Evaluation

3.1 Implementation Details

To facilitate autonomous robot navigation, specific components are required to be present, each of which is briefly discussed herein aiming to provide the means to the reader to reproduce the proposed method. For the metric mapping which is responsible to provide the geometrical representation of the robot's surroundings, a Gmapping implementation has been selected, since map construction slightly impacts on the method. To keep track of the robot's pose within the explored environment an AMCL localization method based on LIDAR scans has been adopted. The last required component is the path planning implementation which is responsible to navigate the robot from a current pose to a target location. The utilized global planning implementation is D* Lite algorithm, while for the local planner the default Dynamic Window Approach suitable for short-wheel-axis differential platforms has been utilized. A diagram illustrating the connectivity among the aforementioned modules and the novel human presence anticipation one is exhibited in Fig. 1. The hardware setup on which the proposed method has been implemented and evaluated comprises a Turtlebot2 differential robotic platform equipped with an Asus Xtion PRO LIVE RGB-D sensor and a Hokuyo URG-04LX scanning laser rangefinder. The laser is placed on the top plate of the platform in a front facing orientation taking advantage of its 270ø FoV. The Asus Xtion is placed in the middle of the top plate of the platform yet, slightly lifted in the vertical axis to obtain better human view. The onboard computational unit is a notebook equipped with an $Intel^R$ $Core^{TM}$ i7-3632QM CPU operating at 2.20 GHz with 8 GB RAM.

3.2   Social Acceptable Behavior Assessment

For the evaluation of the robot's ability to retain socially acceptable behaviour, four different metrics already established in the community [15] have been utilized. However, these metrics have been extended to consider also moving human instead of a static one and the referenced time duration T corresponds to the time interval that the robot needs to navigate from its current pose to the target one:

- M_1: The mean distance D_{mean} among the moving human and robot which is computed in the the entire navigation process.
- M_2: The time spent in areas associated with the human personal zone.
- M_3: The social cost which indirectly models the human discomfort by computing $m_3 = \sum_{t=1}^{T} Cs_t \dot{d}_t$, where Cs is the social cost of the cell where the robot's footprint is located and d_t is the duration that the robot operated in that cell. The sum of this product declares the overall time the robot spent within the human personal space during its navigation and indirectly models the human discomfort factor.
- M_4: Total navigation time needed for the robot to reach the desired goal.

3.3   Experimental Results

The method evaluated in three different test cases namely, crossing, parallel and opposing direction movements among human and robot, while has also been compared with two other methods, no human aware navigation (ROS native implementation) and modeling of human presence with static Gaussian kernel model [15]. Each method underwent 30 repetitions for each scenario, totaling to 270 experiments. The indoor area where the experiments have been conducted corresponds to $35\,\mathrm{m}^2$ approximately, ensuring enough space for robot and human co-navigation. The area consists of three doors which have declared as the frequently visited regions of the space and were considered for the human motion intention prediction. The results of the experiments are illustrated in Fig. 3 for each scenario, indicating superior performance of the proposed method when compared to the rest two methods. In general, our dynamic approach in the M_1 mean human-robot distance achieved in total 2.21 m, while static human model and pure navigation achieved 1.92 m and 1.71 m. This result is directly association with the fact that the time the robot spent in the humans personal zone, our dynamic model scored a mean of 0.7 s, while the static human model and the pure navigation approaches scored 2.49 s and 4.17 s respectively. In M_3 metric, social cost calculated from the previous measurements, the dynamic model scored 0.139 units, whereas static human model 0.393 and pure navigation achieved 2.029 units, respectively. Finally, the last metric M_4 does not measure the social behavior of the robot, however is a navigation performance indicator of the robot, where the dynamic human model achieved 31.4 s, the static human model and pure navigation scored 33.9 s and 34.2 s, respectively exhibiting thus, that the proposed method retains better social behavior and minimum robot

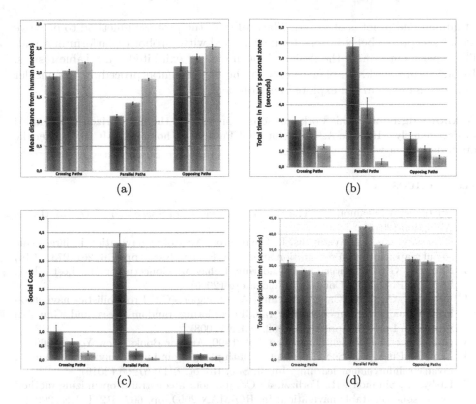

Fig. 3. (a) M_1 mead distance from humans in meters, (b) M_2 total time spent in human's personal zone, (c) M_3 social cost and (d) M_4 total navigation time

travel time as well. This occurs due to the prediction of human motion and the earlier selection of the correct path that the robot needs to follow. The best results were achieved in the scenario where human and robot followed parallel with same direction paths, where both the competitive models had achieved high social scores. That was expected since there is a lot of overlap between human and robot path, however the proposed method successfully maintained better social behavior.

4   Conclusions and Discussion

In this work a human motion anticipation strategy has been introduced suitable for real-time robot navigation in human populated environments. The human presence in the robot's workspace is perceived by fusing multimodal perception modules, while the human walking intention is modeled based on the theory of the human frequently visited areas and the computation of probabilistic human-like paths. The predicted human presence in the robot's workspace is facilitated by adding a separate human-layer in the navigation framework which is parameterized so as to operate in real time scenarios where mutual or unilateral motion of human and robot is observed. The ability of the proposed method to preserve social acceptable behavior has been evaluated with a robotic platform in a real-life experiments where the designed methodology exhibited remarkable results. In our future work, we plan to extend the experimental procedure to consider multiple humans in the explored environment.

Acknowledgments. This work has been supported by the EU Horizon 2020 funded project namely: "Robotic Assistant for MCI Patients at home (RAMCIP)" under the grant agreement with no: 643433.

References

1. Buttimer, A., Seamon, D.: The Human Experience of Space and Place. Routledge, Abingdon (2015)
2. Charalampous, K., Kostavelis, I., Gasteratos, A.: Robot navigation in large-scale social maps: an action recognition approach. Expert Syst. Appl. **66**, 261–273 (2016)
3. Flaherty, G.: Dementia and Wandering Behavior: Concern for the Lost Elder. Springer Publishing Company, Heidelberg (2006)
4. Fulgenzi, C., Tay, C., Spalanzani, A., Laugier, C.: Probabilistic navigation in dynamic environment using rapidly-exploring random trees and Gaussian processes. In: IROS, pp. 1056–1062. IEEE (2008)
5. Hall, E.T.: The Hidden Dimension, vol. 1990. Anchor Books, New York (1969)
6. Kim, B., Pineau, J.: Socially adaptive path planning in human environments using inverse reinforcement learning. Int. J. Soc. Robot. **8**(1), 51–66 (2016)
7. Kirby, R., Simmons, R., Forlizzi, J.: Companion: a constraint-optimizing method for person-acceptable navigation. In: RO-MAN 2009, pp. 607–612. IEEE (2009)
8. Large, F., Vasquez, D., Fraichard, T., Laugier, C.: Avoiding cars and pedestrians using velocity obstacles and motion prediction. In: Intelligent Vehicles Symposium, pp. 375–379. IEEE (2004)
9. Leigh, A., Pineau, J.: Laser-based person tracking for clinical locomotion analysis. In: IROS-Rehabilitation and Assistive Robotics (2014)
10. Luber, M., Spinello, L., Silva, J., Arras, K.O.: Socially-aware robot navigation: a learning approach. In: IROS, pp. 902–907. IEEE (2012)
11. Mac, T.T., Copot, C., Tran, D.T., De Keyser, R.: Heuristic approaches in robot path planning: a survey. RAS **86**, 13–28 (2016)
12. Papadakis, P., Spalanzani, A., Laugier, C.: Social mapping of human-populated environments by implicit function learning. In: IROS, pp. 1701–1706. IEEE (2013)
13. Sisbot, E.A., Marin-Urias, L.F., Alami, R., Simeon, T.: A human aware mobile robot motion planner. IEEE TRO **23**(5), 874–883 (2007)
14. Svenstrup, M., Bak, T., Andersen, H.J.: Trajectory planning for robots in dynamic human environments. In: IROS, pp. 4293–4298. IEEE (2010)
15. Talebpour, Z., Navarro, I., Martinoli, A.: On-board human-aware navigation for indoor resource-constrained robots: a case-study with the ranger. In: Symposium System Integration, pp. 63–68. IEEE (2015)
16. Trautman, P., Ma, J., Murray, R.M., Krause, A.: Robot navigation in dense human crowds: statistical models and experimental studies of human-robot cooperation. IJRR **34**(3), 335–356 (2015)
17. Unhelkar, V.V., Pérez-D'Arpino, C., Stirling, L., Shah, J.A.: Human-robot co-navigation using anticipatory indicators of human walking motion. In: ICRA, pp. 6183–6190. IEEE (2015)

Speaker Identification System Based on Lip-Motion Feature

Xinjun Ma, Chenchen Wu[✉], Yuanyuan Li, and Qianyuan Zhong

School of Mechanical Engineering and Automation,
Harbin Institute of Technology Shenzhen Graduate School, Shenzhen, China
870715761@qq.com

Abstract. Traditional lip features have been used in speech recognition, but lately they have also been found useful as a new biometric identifier in computer vision applications. Firstly, we locate lips according to geometric distribution of human faces. Then, we propose an algorithm for extracting representative frame pictures based on gray changes during speech. Scale-invariant feature transform (SIFT) feature is introduced into speaker identification system. Based on Sift algorithm, we extract lip feature including texture and motion information, which can well describe lip deformation progress during speech. Finally, this paper presents a simple classification algorithm by comparing the ratio of eigenvalue to the reference value. Compared with local binary model (LBP) feature and histogram of oriented gradients (HOG) feature, experimental results show that the improved algorithm of feature extraction and classification can work effectively and achieve a satisfactory performance.

Keywords: Speaker identification · Representative frame pictures · Scale-invarient feature transform (SIFT) · Feature extraction

1 Introduction

The rapid development of network technology has brought us into a new era of network information. The technology makes our life more convenient, but it also brings us a lot of security problems. Traditional security measures, such as personal passwords and keys, have been unable to meet the needs of our life because they can be easily stolen and deciphered. Therefore, we need a new technology which has high security and is difficult to imitate. Now, the rapid development of biometric technology is gaining more popularity. The so-called biometric technology [1] is using inherent physiological and behavior characteristics of human to judge a person through combining computer and optics, acoustics, biological sensors.

At the beginning, the study of lip motion feature is devoted to lip reading [2, 3], namely, understanding what you are talking about by visual rather than listening. Now, lip feature can also be used for recognition [4, 5]. We can build our own lip passwords. Once we have determined the speaking content, it will be the only key. You won't be permitted if you are not the owner or you didn't say the right code. It's only when the sole owner speaks the correct code that we determine the recognition is successful. And the owner can change his password whenever possible.

© Springer International Publishing AG 2017
M. Liu et al. (Eds.): ICVS 2017, LNCS 10528, pp. 289–299, 2017.
DOI: 10.1007/978-3-319-68345-4_26

Lip features are classified into static and dynamic features. Static features include the shape of the lips, gray scale, and texture information. Dynamic features include lip changes during speech, that is, personal behavior habits. They are both difficult to imitate. This paper aims to establish a complete speaker recognition system based on lip motion. To perform a recognition task, we need to build a database including own and others. Representative frame pictures extracted by judging difference of pixel gray value between frames are our research base. After locating lip, we use SIFT to extract feature and adopt Principal Components Analysis (PCA) [6] to reduce dimension. This paper presents a new method to recognize identity by setting double threshold values of the feature vector.

The rest of the paper is organized as follows. We will introduce how to build a database and locate lip, extract several typical pictures from hundreds of pictures in Sect. 2. In Sect. 3, the whole feature extraction process and experimental results are shown. In Sect. 4, we make a summary.

2 Database and Lip Location

2.1 Database

The subject of this study is the entry permission problem, only allowing the owner to enter. For the establishment of the database, we need the host's video and other videos for testing. The recording environment of the database is shown in Fig. 1. The specific process is as follows:

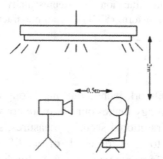

Fig. 1. Schematic diagram of database recording environment

1. Basic parameters of database
   Video format: MP4;
   Color space: YUY2;
   Output size: 480 * 480;
   Video output: frame rate: 30 fps;
   Recording software: AMCap.

2. Database construction
   Sample number: 20 (10 boys, 10 girls);
   Sampling environment: uniform illumination, relatively fixed position of the face, no complex background decoration, no large angle rotation, no beard.
3. Sampling process: Repeat the phrase "nihao" at normal speed, as well as the number of 1 to 9 for each of the four times. Then, repeat the above process at a speed of two times.
4. Sampling results: After getting the video, we can get static images via the command 'videoreader' in MATLAB.

2.2   Face and Lip Location

We adopt Adaboost algorithm whose core is learning theory [7] based on Probably Approximately Correct (PAC) [8] to locate human face [9, 10]. This technology has been developing very mature, whose main process is to use Haar-like feature [11–13] to represent face, and use Adaboost to train weak classifier into a strong classifier. The lip position is to be located further based on the position of face, as shown in Fig. 2.

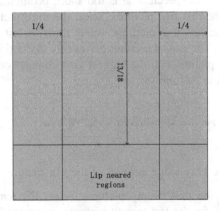

Fig. 2. Lip position of human face

Based on the structure of human face, this paper uses a certain proportion of the face to divide lip. This method has the advantages of small amount of calculation, good real-time performance, as well as preserving the texture features near the lip. Figure 3 shows one example of lip location.

2.3   Extraction of Representative Pictures

Converting a video into static images directly will produce a large number of redundant data. It will obviously increase the amount of calculation and affect the robustness and real-time performance of the system. This paper presents an image extraction algorithm based on time sequence. It means extracting several pictures as representative image with the biggest gray change in each range. Specific steps are as follows:

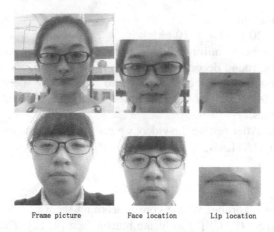

Frame picture   Face location   Lip location

Fig. 3. Lip location example

- The number of images we get is X;
- If $X < 12$, suggesting that speech time is too short, prompting input error.
- If $20 \leq X \leq 60$, for the first five pictures, select the third picture as the first typical frame images, for the last five pictures, select third to last picture as the twelfth typical frame picture. The rest of pictures are evenly divided into ten parts. In every ten pictures, find the picture with the biggest gray changes compared with adjacent picture. The formula is as follows:

$$Pic = \left\{ \sum_{i=1}^{M} \sum_{j=1}^{N} \left| I^t(i,j) - I^{t-1}(i,j) \right| + \sum_{i=1}^{M} \sum_{j=1}^{N} \left| I^t(i,j) - I^{t+1}(i,j) \right| \right\}_{max} \quad (1)$$

where $I^t(i,j)$ denotes the gray value at (x,y) of the t-th picture.

- If $60 < X \leq 480$, for the first twenty pictures, select the tenth picture as the first typical frame images, for the last twenty pictures, select tenth to last picture as the twelfth typical frame picture. The rest of pictures are evenly divided into ten parts. We still use the formula to find representative pictures.
- If $480 > X$, suggesting that the amount of video images is too much, prompting input error.

Using the above algorithm to deal with two videos, we can get results shown in Fig. 4. The two videos are from one person saying 'nihao'. One is recorded at normal speed; the other is at 2 times speed. We can see frame images obtained from the two videos are very similar. This algorithm can not only simplify database and can increase the robustness for speed and scale changes.

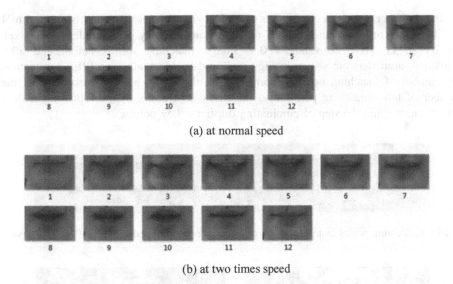

(a) at normal speed

(b) at two times speed

Fig. 4. Representative images extracted from 2 videos with different speed

3 Sift Feature Extraction and Matching Model

3.1 Matching Based on SIFT

SIFT algorithm [14] is a widely used algorithm in image processing. It has good scale invariance and resistance to rotation, and is not sensitive to illumination changes. Key point description proposed in SIFT algorithm, as a kind of local feature, isn't sensitive to light, rotation, noise and scale changes. Generally speaking, this algorithm is to get descriptor of key points in different scale space, and match the corresponding points. SIFT algorithm flow chart is shown in Fig. 5. Bakshi [15] used SIFT in authentication and comparison of lipstick and achieved good results. Lowe [16] proposed surf algorithm based on SIFT.

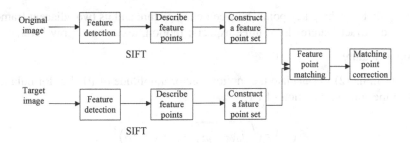

Fig. 5. Flow chart of SIFT algorithm

In this paper, the number of layers of each tower in Gauss Pyramid is reduced to 4 or 5 layers. In order to increase SIFT matching rate and key points under lower pixel, we set $|D(x)| \leq 0.01$, *threshold* $= 0.4$. Image matching results before and after adjusting parameters are shown in Figs. 6, 7 and 8. After adjusting SIFT parameters, the number of matching points becomes more obviously, but at the same time, the number of false matching points also increases. Therefore, in the following feature extraction, we add the step of eliminating duplicate key points.

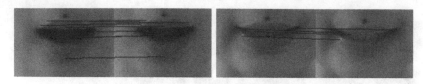

Fig. 6. Feature points matching graph of one person without adjusting SIFT parameters

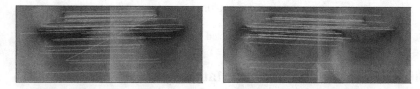

Fig. 7. Feature points matching graph of one person after adjusting SIFT parameters

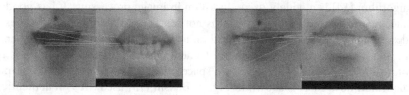

Fig. 8. Feature points matching graph of 2 persons after adjusting SIFT parameters

3.2   Improved Feature Extraction Scheme Based on SIFT

Assuming that matching key points between each picture and its two adjacent frames is P1, P2, we extract features from three aspects: motion, texture and gray level.

1. Motion feature

We use formula (2) to calculate the motion vector amplitude of P1, P2, formula (3) to calculate the motion direction of P1, P2.

$$f_1(i,j) = \sqrt{\left(i_{p1} - i_{p2}\right)^2 + \left(j_{p1} - j_{p2}\right)^2} \qquad (2)$$

$$f_2 = \tan^{-1}\left[\frac{\left(j_{p1} - j_{p2}\right)}{\left(i_{p1} - i_{p2}\right)}\right] \qquad (3)$$

where (i_{p1}, j_{p1}) represents the coordinate position of P1, (i_{p2}, j_{p2}) represents the coordinate position of P2.

For each pair of matching points, we can get a two dimensional feature vector $F = \{f_1, f_2\}$.

2. Texture feature

For each key point, select a 4 * 4 window, as shown in Fig. 9.

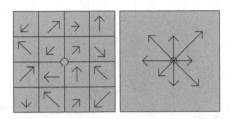

Fig. 9. Feature extraction of motion vectors around key points

Each square represents a pixel point and dot represents the location of the obtained key point. Amplitude and direction of the arrow represent feature vector of the corresponding pixel. The calculated 16 vectors are classified into 8 main directions, namely, a 8-dimension feature vector R. The specific calculation method is given by Eqs. (4) and (5).

Gradient magnitude:

$$m(x, y) = \sqrt{(L(x+1, y) - L(x-1, y))^2 + (L(x, y+1) - L(x, y-1))^2} \quad (4)$$

Gradient direction:

$$\theta(x, y) = \tan^{-1}\left[\frac{L(x, y+1) - L(x, y-1)}{L(x+1, y) - L(x-1, y)}\right] \quad (5)$$

where $L(x, y)$ represents the gray value at (x, y).

3. Gray feature

Extract gray value between the 4 * 4 windows in adjacent pictures. Get absolute value of these 16 numbers and sum them.

$$G = \sum_{k=1}^{16} |I^1(i, j) - I^2(i, j)| \quad (6)$$

where I^1, I^2 represent gray value of 2 adjacent images in corresponding position.

To sum up, for each matching key point, we can obtain a 11-dimension feature vector $T = \{F, R, G\}$. Assuming that the total number of matching key points is n, we can get a feature matrix (n * 11). By reducing dimension through PCA, we can get a feature vector Z (1 * 11).

As can be seen from Fig. 10, for the same person, the value and trend of feature curve are similar. But for different person, they are obviously different. Lip deformation of one person speaking fixed words is basically the same. Featured extracted through the proposed algorithm can be a good representation and reference for us to judge whether it's the owner said the preset words.

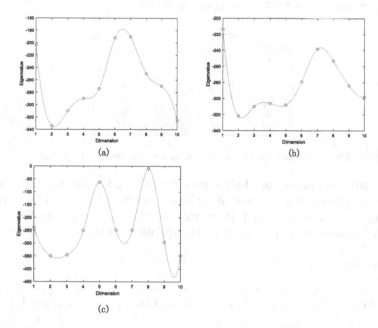

(a)

(b)

(c)

Fig. 10. Feature curve of speaking 'nihao'. (a) and (b) are from one person, (c) is from the other person.

3.3   Classification

Classification Based on Matching Points

From Fig. 8, we can find the number of matching points from 2 persons is less than that from one person. In this paper, the ratio of the number of matching points from test samples to that from database is adopted to judge identity of test sample.

The specific process is as follows:

Assuming that one person repeats a sentence 3 times (Video1, Video2, Video3), we can get 12 representative pictures from every video. Name them 1, 2...12 and use SIFT to deal with every 2 pictures with the same sequence number. We can get 3 sets of matching data, each group of 12. The average value of the corresponding values in 3 sets of data is $A_1, A_2, A_3, \cdots, A_{12}$. The number of matching points between test videos and database videos are $B_1, B_2, B_3, \cdots, B_{12}$, as shown in Fig. 11. Set threshold $\theta = 0.4$, $flag = 0$, if $B_i/A_i < 0.4$, $flag + 1$. Finally, if $flag > 2$, we determine that test sample isn't the owner.

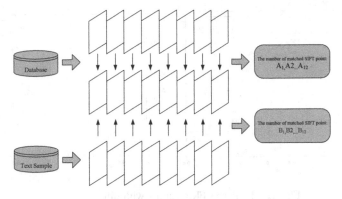

Fig. 11. SIFT matching

Classification Based on Feature Extracted

Commonly used Support Vector Machine (SVM), neural networks, Hidden Markov Model (HMM) and other classification algorithms require a larger database to train, whose calculation is very complex. Based on feature vector extracted, we build a simple and effective classification algorithm. Specific implementation methods are as follows:

1. Extract average value of feature vector in database

$$Z_{mean} = (\sum_{i=1}^{n} Z_i)/n \qquad (7)$$

2. Extract average value of test sample's feature vector Z.
3. Set threshold θ_1, θ_2. $\theta_1 \in (0, 1]$, $\theta_2 = \frac{1}{\theta_1}$, $\theta_1 = 0.7$ in this paper.
4. $t = Z/Z_{mean}$, if $t < \theta_1$ or $t > \theta_2$, $flag + 1$, if $flag > 2$, we determine recognition failed.

Only the two identification methods are adopted, we believe that certification is successful.

3.4 Experimental Results

False match rate (FAR) means output matching success that should have been failed. False Non-Match Rate (FRR) means output matching failed that should have been successful. Figure 12 shows curves of FAR and FRR with thresholds changing. LBP is an operator used to describe local texture feature, with remarkable advantages such as rotation invariance and gray level invariance. HOG is a feature descriptor for object detection in computer vision and image processing. It represents feature by computing and calculating the gradient histogram of local area of images. Table 1 shows FAR and FRR of the 3 kinds of feature. For feature Z, the minimum of FAR and FRR can reach 0.5% and 4.89%. Compared with Z, FAR and FRR of LBP, HOG feature are higher obviously, proving the proposed feature extraction algorithm and classification algorithm are effective.

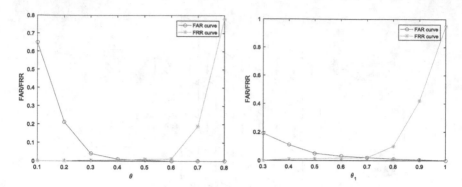

Fig. 12. FAR and FRR curves with different θ, θ_1

Table 1. Experimental results of FAR, FRR

Speech content	FAR			FRR		
	Z	LBP	HOG	Z	LBP	HOG
1	0.85%	11.4%	16.33%	5.65%	23.40%	34.70%
2	0.93%	22.13%	26.60%	5.88%	27.30%	23.60%
3	0.74%	15.00%	17.62%	5.23%	32.00%	42.00%
5	0.50%	11.30%	21.70%	4.89%	17.73%	21.46%
9	0.94%	10.14%	18.50%	5.15%	31.40%	25.50%
nihao	1.20%	20.3%	32.60%	5.96%	29.80%	31.67%

4 Conclusion

Firstly, we establish a database and determine the position of lip according to the law of face organs distribution. Then, this paper shows an algorithm which is robust to changes of speech rate and illumination for extracting typical pictures to simplify calculation. We introduce how to extract lip feature including motion feature, texture feature, gray feature based on matching points got through adjusting SIFT parameter. Finally, we present a two-threshold comparison classification algorithm. The experimental results show that the whole lip motion identification system has good performance and adaptability.

Acknowledgments. This work was supported by the National Nature Science Foundation of China (51677035), the Fundamental Research Projects of Shenzhen (JCYJ20150513151706580), the Science and Technology Plan Project of Shenzhen (GRCK2016082611021550).

References

1. Unar, J.A., Seng, W.C., Abbasi, A.: A review of biometric rechnology along with trends and prospects. J. Pattern Articl. **47**(8), 2673–2688 (2014)

2. Chung, J.S., Zisserman, A.: Lip reading in the wild. In: Lai, S.-H., Lepetit, V., Nishino, K., Sato, Y. (eds.) ACCV 2016. LNCS, vol. 10112, pp. 87–103. Springer, Cham (2017). doi:10. 1007/978-3-319-54184-6_6
3. Chitu, A.G., Driel, K., Rothkrantz, L.J.M.: Automatic lip reading in the Dutch language using active appearance models on high speed recodings. In: Sojka, P., Horák, A., Kopeček, I., Pala, K. (eds.) Text, Speech and Dialogue. TSD 2010. LNCS, vol. 6231, pp. 259–266. Springer, Berlin (2010)
4. Kanak, A., Erzin, E., Yemez, Y., Tekalp, A.M.: Joint audio-video processing for biometric speaker identification. In: IEEE International Conference on Acoustics, Speech and Signal Processing, pp. 561–564. IEEE Press, Hong Kong (2003). doi:10.1109/ICASSP.2003. 1202376
5. Cetingul, H.E., Yemez, Y., Erzin, E., Tskalp, A.M.: Discriminative analysis of lip motion features for speaker identification and speech-reading. J. IEEE Trans. Image Process. 15(10), 2879–2891 (2006). doi:10.1109/TIP.2006.877528
6. Giordani, P.: Principal component analysis. In: Encyclopedia of Social Network Analysis and Mining, pp. 1319–1331. Springer, Heidelberg (2014). doi:10.1007/978-1-4614-6170-8-_154
7. Schapire, R.E.: The strength of weak learnablity. In: Foundations of Computer Science, pp. 197–227. IEEE Press, Research Triangle Park (1989)
8. Valiant, L.G.: A theory of the learnable. In: 16th Annual ACM Symposium on Theory of Computing, pp. 436–445. ACM (1997)
9. Han, P., Liao, J.M.: Face detection based on adaboost. In: Computational Intelligence and Industrial Engineering, pp. 337–240. IEEE Press, Chengdu (2009)
10. Lang, L.Y., Gu, W.W.: Improved face dection algorithm baed on adaboost. In: Electronic Computer Technology, pp. 183–186. IEEE Press, Macau (2009)
11. Oren, M., Pagageorgiou, C., Sinha, P., Osuna, E., Poggio, T.: Pedestrian detection using templates. In: Computer Vision & Pattern Recognition. IEEE Press, San Juan (1997)
12. Xue, Z., Li, S.Z., Teoh, E.K.: Facial feature extraction and image wraping using PCA based ststistic model. In: International Conference on image processing, pp. 689–692. IEEE Press, Thessaloniki (2001)
13. Girshick, R., Donahue, J., Darreell, T., Malik, J.: Rich feature hierarchies for accurate object detection and semantic segmentation. In: IEEE Conference on Computer Vision and Pattern Recognition, pp. 580–587. IEEE Press, Columbus (2014)
14. Lowe, D.G.: Distinctive image features from scale-invariant keypoints. J. Int. J. Comput. Vis. 60(2), 91–110 (2004)
15. Bakshi, S., Raman, R., Sa, P.K.: Lip pattern recognition based on local feature extraction. In: Annual IEEE India Conference. IEEE Press, Hyderabad (2011). doi:10.1109/INDCON. 2011.6139357
16. Turcot, P., Lowe, D.G.: Better matching with fewer features: the selection of useful features in large database recognition problems. In: 12th International Conference on Computer Vision Workshops, pp. 2019–2116. IEEE Press, Kyoto (2009). doi:10.1109/iccvw.2009. 5457541

Integrating Stereo Vision with a CNN Tracker for a Person-Following Robot

Bao Xin Chen, Raghavender Sahdev[(✉)], and John K. Tsotsos

Department of Electrical Engineering and Computer Science and Centre for Vision
Research, York University, Toronto, Canada
{baoxchen,sahdev,tsotsos}@cse.yorku.ca

Abstract. In this paper, we introduce a stereo vision based CNN tracker for a person following robot. The tracker is able to track a person in real-time using an online convolutional neural network. Our approach enables the robot to follow a target under challenging situations such as occlusions, appearance changes, pose changes, crouching, illumination changes or people wearing the same clothes in different environments. The robot follows the target around corners even when it is momentarily unseen by estimating and replicating the local path of the target. We build an extensive dataset for person following robots under challenging situations. We evaluate the proposed system quantitatively by comparing our tracking approach with existing real-time tracking algorithms.

Keywords: CNN tracker · Person following robot · Tracking · Stereo vision

1 Introduction

Person following robots have many applications such as autonomous carts in grocery stores [26], personal guides in hospitals, or airports for autonomous suitcases [1]. Person following robots in dynamic environments need to address the tracking problem under different challenging situations (appearance changes, varying illumination, occlusions, pose changes such as crouching, exchanging jackets etc.). An online convolutional neural network (CNN) is used to track the given target under different situations. The target being tracked might move around corners making it disappear from the field of view of the robot. We address this problem by computing the recent poses of the target and have the robot replicate the local path of the target when the target is not visible in the current frame. The robot being used is a Pioneer 3AT robot which is equipped with a stereo camera. We tested our approach with two stereo cameras namely the Point Grey Bumblebee2[1] and the ZED stereo camera[2].

B.X. Chen and R. Sahdev—*Denotes equal contribution.*

[1] http://www.ptgrey.com/stereo-vision-cameras-systems.

[2] https://www.stereolabs.com.

© Springer International Publishing AG 2017
M. Liu et al. (Eds.): ICVS 2017, LNCS 10528, pp. 300–313, 2017.
DOI: 10.1007/978-3-319-68345-4_27

The main contributions of this paper are: (*i*) A Person Following Robot application using a CNN trained online in real-time ($\approx$20 fps) making use of RGB images and a stereo depth image for tracking, (*ii*) a robot following behaviour which can follow the person even when the person is transiently not in the field of view of the camera, (*iii*) a novel stereo dataset for the task of person following. First, we describe the relevant work for human following robots and tracking using CNNs in Sect. 2. In Sect. 3, we describe our proposed CNN model and the navigation system of the robot. We describe the dataset and experimental results of our approach in Sect. 4. Finally, Sect. 5 concludes the paper and provides possible future work.

2   Related Works

Person Following Robots: Person Following robots have been researched as early as 1998 [31] where the authors used color and contour information of the target for tracking. Similar color based tracking was done in [34] and using an H-S Histogram in hue saturation value (HSV space) in [33]. These approaches could not handle appearance changes or occlusions very well. Some early optical flow based works include that of [8,36]. Optical flow requires the target motion to be different from background motion which limits its usability. Simple feature based works were presented by using edges, corners with color and texture information by Yoshimi et al. [37]. Pre-trained appearance models were used in [4]. Some other feature based methods include Lucas-Kanade features [7], SIFT features [30], HOG features [2] and height and gait with appearance based features in [25]. Recently in 2017 [6] used Selected Online Ada-Boosting to do online learning using depth as a filter to restrict the search for the target. People have been using various other sensors for person following robots like laser based approaches [24] and RGBD camera based approaches, e.g., Kinect [9,12]. Kinect has the drawback of only working indoors. Laser based approaches might not be suitable for places like hospitals, schools, or retail stores which might have a restriction on the usage of laser. Our approach uses a stereo camera which can be used both indoors and outdoors.

Object Tracking: Real-time object tracking is an important task for a person-following robot. Many state of the art algorithms exist that can achieve high accuracy (robustness), e.g., [29] (MGbSA), [17] (CNN as features), [22] (Proposal Selection), [38] (deep learning), [28] (Locally Orderless tracking), etc. However, these approaches do not target real-time performance. Some other works that focus on computation speed include [20] (Struck SVM with GPU), [41] (Structure preserving), [39] (Online Discrimination Feature Selection), [18] (Online Ada-Boosting), etc. Recent work from Camplani et al. [5] (DS-KCF) used RGBD image sequences from a Kinect sensor to track objects under severe occlusions and rank highly on the Princeton Tracking Benchmark [32] with real-time performance (40 fps). One of the earliest works using convolutional neural networks (CNNs) for tracking appeared in 2010 by Fan et al. [14]. They considered tracking as a learning task by using spatial and temporal features to estimate location and scale of the target. Hong et al. [21] used a pre-trained CNN to generate features to train an SVM classifier. Zhai et al. [38] also used a pre-trained CNN, but added a Naive Bayes classifier after the last layer of the CNN. Zhang and Suganthan [40] used one single convolutional layer with 50 4-by-4 filters in the CNN structure. The network was trained from scratch and updated every 5 frames. Gao et al. [17] used pre-trained CNN as feature generator to enhance the ELDA Tracker [16].

CNN Using RGBD Images: Training a CNN model with RGB and stereo depth images is another focus of this paper. Previous work used RGBD CNNs on object detection [19] and object recognition [13]. Couprie et al. [10] used RGBD images to train a single stream CNN classifier to handle semantic segmentation. Eitel et al. [13] trained RGB layers and D layer separately in two CNN streams. These two streams were combined in the fully connected layer.

3   Approach

Here we describe our proposed CNN models and the learning process. The input to the CNN is the RGB channel and the computed depth from the stereo images, we call this as RGBSD (RGB-Stereo Depth). Stereo Depth (SD) is computed using the ZED SDK[3]. The CNN Tracker outputs the depth and the centroid of the target. The depth and centroid are then used by the navigation module of the robot to follow the target and replicate the path when required.

3.1   CNN Models with RGBSD Images

We develop three different CNN models and use each of them separately to validate our approach. The first model (CNN_v1) uses RGBSD layers as a single image to feed the ConvNet. Similar to conventional CNN architectures, the network contains convolutional layers, fully-connected layers, and an output layer (see Fig. 1). The second model (CNN_v2) uses 2 convolutional streams and the input is RGB channels for one stream and just the stereo depth image for the other (see Fig. 1). In the fully connected layer, the input is a combination of the flattened output from those two convolutional streams. The third ConvNet (CNN_v3) is a regular RGB image based CNN. It has a similar structure as that of the first model. Now we describe our approach to initialize and update the CNN tracker.

Initial Training Set Selection: In order to use the CNN model to track a person, we must initialize the CNN classifier. The initialization is done from scratch using random weights. A pre-defined rectangular bounding box is placed in the center of the first frame. To activate the robot following behaviour, a person must stand inside the bounding box at a certain distance from the robot or the target to be tracked can be manually selected. Once the CNN is activated, the

---

[3] https://github.com/stereolabs/zed-opencv.

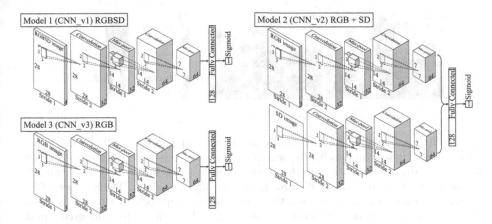

Fig. 1. Three CNN models: Model 1 takes a 4-channel RGBSD image as input; Model 2 takes an RGB image and an SD image as input; Model 3 takes an RGB image only as the input. The parameters of the CNN in each of the layers are chosen empirically for real-time performance.

patch in the bounding box is labeled as class-1. The patches around the bounding box are labeled as class-0. Since these two classes are highly unbalanced, we uniformly select n patches from class-0, and copy the class-1 patch n times to form the training set ($n = 40$ in our experiment). This initial training set is used to train a CNN classifier until it has a very high accuracy on the training set. This might make the classifier overfit the training set. To handle this strong over-fitting, we assume that the target pose and appearance should not change dramatically in the first 50 frames (about 2–3 s).

Test Set Selection: Once the CNN classifier is initialized or updated, we use it to detect the target in the next frame. When a new frame is available along with the stereo depth layer, we search the test patches in a local image region as shown in Fig. 2(a). We also restrict the search space with respect to the depth as shown in Fig. 2(b). If the patches in the image do not have the depth within *previous_depth* $\pm \alpha$, we do not consider them (Fig. 2(c)), where α is the search region in depth direction (we use $\alpha = 0.25$ m). By doing this, most of the patches belonging to the background will be filtered out before passing to the CNN classier. Only the highest responses on class-1 will be considered as the target in the current frame. If no target is detected (e.g., highest responses on class-1 < 0.5) after 0.5 s, it will enter the target missing mode. Then, the whole image is scanned to create a test set.

Update CNN Tracker: To update the classier, a new training set needs to be selected. The update step is performed only if the detection step finds the target (class-1) in the test set. In order to maintain robustness, the most recent 50 class-1 patches are retained from the previous frames to form the class-1 patch pool which is implemented as a First-In-First-Out queue. The patches around the target form the class-0 patch pool. In this new training set, we again uniformly

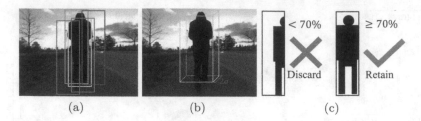

Fig. 2. 3D search region for test set (a) candidate test patches in 2D region (based on a sliding window approach), (b) search region with respect to depth, (c) pixels in black are within $\pm\alpha$ *meters* from the previous depth. If black pixels are less than 70% of the patch, the patch will be discarded, else, it will be retained. The number 70% is chosen experimentally as this covers the human body completely in most of the cases. According to (c), the red and blue patches in (a) will be discarded, the green, pink, and yellow patches will be retained. (Color figure online)

select n patches from class-0 patch pool. For selecting n patches from class-1 patch pool, we sample the patches based on a Poisson distribution with $\lambda = 1.0$ and $k = \lfloor \frac{queue\_index}{10} \rfloor$ (see Eq. 1 and Fig. 3). This gives a higher probability of selecting patches from the recent history rather than selecting older patches. This training set is used to update the classifier. The Poisson distribution based sampling of class-1 patches avoids overfitting and provide a chance to recover from bad detection in the previous frame(s).

$$P(k) = e^{-\lambda}\frac{\lambda^k}{k!} \tag{1}$$

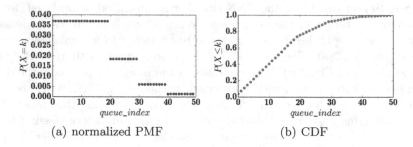

(a) normalized PMF   (b) CDF

Fig. 3. Poisson distribution with $\lambda = 1.0$ and $k = \lfloor \frac{queue\_index}{10} \rfloor$, where *queue_index* is the patch index in First-In-First-Out queue. To select an index, just randomly generate a real number from 0 to 1.0. Then, base on (b) the CDF graph, an index is selected.

3.2   Navigation of the Robot

In this section, we describe the navigation aspect of the robot. There are 2 cases: (i) when the robot can see the target (human) in the image; (ii) when the robot cannot see the target. A proportional integral derivative (PID) controller [27] is used in the former case while the path of the target is replicated in the latter. A local history of the target poses is maintained to compute the local path of the robot. The robot moves to the last observed pose of the target to find the target and continue the following behaviour. There are 4 basic components involved here: Localization of the robot, Target Pose Estimation, Robot following using a PID based controller, and a local path planner (trajectory replication).

Robot Following Using PID Controller: In this section we describe the robot following behavior for the case when the human can be seen in the image. A pre-specified distance, D is maintained between the robot and the target. The linear velocity, v of the robot is directly proportional to the error in current depth, $(d-D)$, where d is the current depth of the target. The angular velocity, ω is proportional to the error in the x coordinate of the target $(x - X\_mid)$. X_mid is the centre of the image in the horizontal direction. Only the Proportional and Integral components of the PID controller are used. We use $D = 1.0\,\text{m}$. Following equations detail the velocities as a function of the error terms.

$$v = K_p * (d - D) + K_i * \int_T (d - D)dt; \qquad (2)$$

$$\omega = K_p' * (x - X\_mid) + K_i' * \int_T (x - X\_mid)dt; \qquad (3)$$

where K_p, K_i, K_p', K_i' are the PI constants, $(d - D)$, $(x - X\_mid)$ are the error terms for the linear and angular velocities and dt is the time difference between successive frames.

Localization: Localization of the robot requires estimating the robot pose with respect to a global coordinate frame. In the 2D case, this is x,y coordinates and the orientation, θ of the robot. The robot must maintain an estimate of its pose as it moves in the presence of dynamic obstacles. Here we address localization using wheel odometry. Wheel odometry is reliable for short distances with an error of less than 4% for environments with a smooth surface (e.g., indoor flooring, outdoor pavement, sidewalk, etc.) for our robot (Pioneer3AT). For this work, the robot is tested in university hallways/corridors which often have minimal features or are featureless (blank walls), hence Visual Odometry based approaches [15] do not give accurate localization. Moreover, the environment is dynamic (has humans walking) which makes Visual odometry even less reliable.

For our work, it is only important that the pose of the robot is accurate for any short time (e.g., 5 s). This is the time we require localization information of the robot to compute the local path of the target and previously accumulated errors due to dead reckoning [3] do not matter.

Target Pose Estimation: The pose (World coordinates) of the target with respect to the camera frame is estimated using the depth and the focal length of the camera [23]. Knowing the pose of the robot and target pose with respect

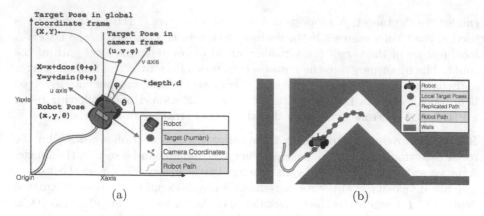

Fig. 4. (a)Estimation of the target pose in the global frame (top view) (b) Local Trajectory of the target poses is stored, when the robot cannot see the target in the image the robot simply replicates the latest local history of target poses stored to find the target. In this work, local history of 100 poses is stored.

to the camera frame, the 2D pose of the target can be estimated accurately in a global frame. Figure 4(a) shows the top view for computing target pose.

Trajectory Replication/Path Planner: Here we describe the navigation algorithm used to follow the human when the robot cannot see the human. This part is used when the person is turning around a corner or around a tree in an outdoor context. The robot always keeps a local history of the recent p poses of the target with respect to the global coordinate frame, this is called the recent trajectory of the target (See Fig. 4(b)). We use $p = 100$ here. If the robot cannot see the target transiently for 0.5 s, it implies that the human turned around a corner or is blocked by something else, so the robot replicates the recent trajectory of the target. By doing so, the robot reaches the last observed pose of the target. After reaching this position, the robot should be able to find the target and resume the following behaviour using the PID based controller. If for some reason the robot cannot find the target after replicating the path, the robot turns on the spot to see if it can find the target, if not the robot stops there and the following behaviour terminates. On the other hand, if the robot finds the target while replicating the local path, the robot shifts to the PID based following behavior. Some of the cases when the target might not be found include when target runs away after the turn or turns somewhere else unexpectedly or vanishes due to some reason. In all these cases it is reasonable to assume that the robot would not be able to find the target. A similar behaviour is expected if a human is following another human.

The overview of our proposed approach is described in Fig. 5. The input to our system is an RGB image and a computed stereo depth image. These images are then run through an online CNN which runs at a frame rate of 20 fps. The CNN returns the depth, the centroid coordinates of the target being tracked and a flag which indicates the presence/absence of the target. If the target is

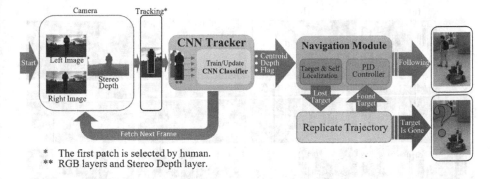

* The first patch is selected by human.
** RGB layers and Stereo Depth layer.

Fig. 5. Overview of the system design of our approach.

present in the scene a PID based controller is used to steer in such a way so as to keep the target in the center of the image; in case of absence of the target, the local path of the target is replicated by the robot to continue the following process. We run our robot at speeds up to 1.0 m/s. The Robot Operating System (ROS) was used for integrating the different components in this work. We tested our approach on a Dell Alienware Laptop with Intel core i7, 7th Gen, 2.8 GHz processor and a GTX 1070 mobile graphics card.

4   Dataset and Experiments

Dataset: Several Datasets exist for pedestrian detection and tracking[4]. In particular, the Princeton Tracking Benchmark [32] provides a unified RGBD dataset for object tracking which includes various occlusions and some appearance changes. But, each sequence is very short (maximum 900 frames, most of them are under 300 frames). Many other works exist that aim at solving the person following problem, but there is a lack of a standardized dataset which could be used to validate the tracking algorithm used for person following robots. In this work, we built an extensive stereo dataset (left, right, and depth images) of 9 indoor and 2 outdoor sequences. Each sequence has more than 2000 frames and up to approximately 12000 frames. The dataset has challenging sequences which have pose changes, intense illumination changes, appearance changes (target removing/wearing a jacket, exchanging jacket with another person, removing/wearing a backpack or picking-up/putting-down an object), crouching and walking, sitting on a chair and getting up, partial and complete occlusions, occlusions by another person wearing same clothes and some other different situations. The dataset also has image sequences when the target is not visible transiently in the image and reappears after some time. The dataset is built in different indoor and outdoor environments in a university context. Some of the samples from the dataset can be seen in Fig. 6. The images are captured at a frame rate of 20 Hz

---

[4] http://homepages.inf.ed.ac.uk/rbf/CVonline/Imagedbase.htm#people.

Fig. 6. Compare some tracking algorithms on our dataset. (1): Hallway 2; (2): Walking Outdoor; (3): Sidewalk; (4): Corridor Corners; (5): Lab & Seminar; (6): Same Clothes 1; (7): Long Corridor; (8): Hallway 1; (9): Lecture Hall. (SOAB [6], OAB [18], ASE [11], DS-KCF [5])

and the resolution is standard VGA (640×480) for bumblebee2 and (672×376) for ZED. We also provide with ground truth of the image sequences[5]. The ground truth contains the bounding box labeled for the target (human) which is manually labeled by human annotators for each frame.

Evaluation Metric: The interest of person following task is to follow a person, so the size of the bounding box is not important for the robot. However, the centroid of the target plays an important role. The evaluation of tracking algorithms has been done in numerous ways. Wu et al. [35] provide details about various existing evaluation metrics that have been used for tracking. For our dataset we use the *precision-plot* as defined in [35] as the metric to evaluate the performance of our approach. We report the percentage of frames in which center of the detected bounding box is within a specific range of pixels from the ground truth (See Fig. 8). Since the initial bounding box size is about (100×350) for all the video sequences, we compute the average precision of all sequences using location error threshold 50 pixels to evaluate tracker performance(see Fig. 9(a)). Figure 9(b) shows the average precision plot over all sequences from Fig. 8.

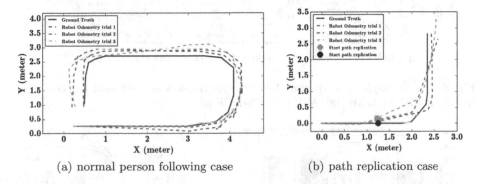

(a) normal person following case   (b) path replication case

Fig. 7. Overall performance of our robot system. (a) *Ground truth* is the path the robot should have taken ideally maintaining a 1-m distance from the target. *Robot Odometry trials* are the robot paths based on wheel odometry. (b) *Ground truth* is the same as the human path we are testing the path replication behaviour here. We have a maximum error (includes tracking, control, and wheel odometry errors) of roughly 30 cm which is not high for our task.

Experiments: We validated our proposed approach in different indoor and outdoor environments. We achieved a frame rate of approx. 20 fps depending on the search window size that we use for the depth range and the local image search region. For evaluation, we compare 3 versions of our tracking algorithm with 4 other existing stereo vision based trackers (for which the code is publicly available). We used the *precision-plot* evaluation metric as defined in [35] to report

---

[5] demo videos and dataset available at http://jtl.lassonde.yorku.ca/2017/05/person-following-cnn/.

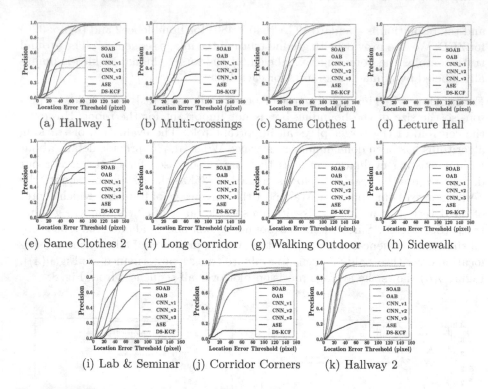

Fig. 8. *Precision-plots*: comparison between our trackers and different tracking algorithms, SOAB [6], OAB [18], ASE [11], DS-KCF [5]

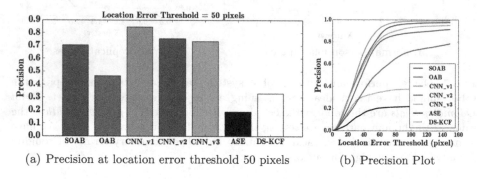

Fig. 9. Comparison over 11 sequences (SOAB [6], OAB [18], ASE [11], DS-KCF [5])

the performance of our system. The performance can be seen in Figs. 6, 8, and 9. We evaluated the performance of our approach on 11 challenging sequences which exhibit varying situations as described in the previous section. It was found that the RGBSD based CNN (CNN_v1) outperformed all other existing approaches. The RGB based CNN (CNN_v3) could not perform better than SOAB [6] in some sequences. We also compare our approach with Danelljan et al. [11] (ASE with monocular images) and Camplani et al. [5] (DS-KCF with RGBD images). We show the performance of our overall robot system in Fig. 7. A demo video of our approach on the robot under different situations can be found at the link (See footnote 5).

5 Conclusion and Future Work

In this paper, we described a robust person following robot system using an online real-time Convolutional Neural Network in the context of robotics. The proposed system could perform very well in dynamic environments under challenging situations. The presented approach could find the person even when the robot could not see it by replicating the local trajectory of the target being followed. Possible future work includes incorporating dynamic obstacle avoidance techniques with the person following robot to give it more intelligence. Person following could also be addressed for places with known maps like using a social robot to follow people in a specific house, malls, retail stores and other places.

Acknowledgement. We acknowledge the financial support of the Natural Sciences and Engineering Research Council of Canada (NSERC), the NSERC Strategic Network for Field Robotics (NCFRN), and the Canada Research Chairs Program through grants to John K. Tsotsos. The authors would like to thank Sidharth Sahdev for helping in the process of dataset generation and making the video for this work.

References

1. Ferreira, B.Q., Karipidou, K., Rosa, F., Petisca, S., Alves-Oliveira, P., Paiva, A.: A study on trust in a robotic suitcase. In: Agah, A., Cabibihan, J.-J., Howard, A.M., Salichs, M.A., He, H. (eds.) ICSR 2016. LNCS, vol. 9979, pp. 179–189. Springer, Cham (2016). doi:10.1007/978-3-319-47437-3_18
2. Awai, M., Shimizu, T., Kaneko, T., Yamashita, A., Asama, H.: Hog-based person following and autonomous returning using generated map by mobile robot equipped with camera and laser range finder. In: Lee, S., Cho, H., Yoon, KJ., Lee J. (eds.) Intelligent Autonomous Systems 12, Advances in Intelligent Systems and Computing, vol. 194, pp. 51–60. Springer, Heidelberg (2013). doi:10.1007/978-3-642-33932-5_6
3. Borenstein, J., Feng, L.: Umbmark: a benchmark test for measuring odometry errors in mobile robots. In: Photonics East 1995, pp. 113–124. International Society for Optics and Photonics (1995)
4. Calisi, D., Iocchi, L., Leone, R.: Person following through appearance models and stereo vision using a mobile robot. In: VISApp Workshop on Robot Vision, pp. 46–56 (2007)
5. Camplani, M., Hannuna, S.L., Mirmehdi, M., Damen, D., Paiement, A., Tao, L., Burghardt, T.: Real-time RGB-D tracking with depth scaling kernelised correlation filters and occlusion handling. In: British Machine Vision Conference, Swansea, UK, 7–10 September 2015. BMVA Press (2015)
6. Chen, B.X., Sahdev, R., Tsotsos, J.K.: Person following robot using selected online Ada-boosting with stereo camera. In: 2017 14th Conference on Computer and Robot Vision (CRV), pp. 48–55. IEEE (2017)

7. Chen, Z., Birchfield, S.T.: Person following with a mobile robot using binocular feature-based tracking. In: IROS 2007. IEEE/RSJ International Conference on Intelligent Robots and Systems, pp. 815–820. IEEE (2007)

8. Chivilò, G., Mezzaro, F., Sgorbissa, A., Zaccaria, R.: Follow-the-leader behaviour through optical flow minimization. In: Proceedings of 2004 IEEE/RSJ International Conference on Intelligent Robots and Systems, IROS 2004, vol. 4, pp. 3182–3187. IEEE (2004)

9. Cosgun, A., Florencio, D.A., Christensen, H.I.: Autonomous person following for telepresence robots. In: 2013 IEEE International Conference on Robotics and Automation (ICRA), pp. 4335–4342. IEEE (2013)

10. Couprie, C., Farabet, C., Najman, L., Lecun, Y.: Indoor semantic segmentation using depth information. In: International Conference on Learning Representations (ICLR 2013), April 2013 (2013)

11. Danelljan, M., Häger, G., Khan, F., Felsberg, M.: Accurate scale estimation for robust visual tracking. In: British Machine Vision Conference, Nottingham, 1–5 September 2014. BMVA Press (2014)

12. Doisy, G., Jevtic, A., Lucet, E., Edan, Y.: Adaptive person-following algorithm based on depth images and mapping. In: Proceedings of the IROS Workshop on Robot Motion Planning (2012)

13. Eitel, A., Springenberg, J.T., Spinello, L., Riedmiller, M., Burgard, W.: Multi-modal deep learning for robust RGB-D object recognition. In: 2015 IEEE/RSJ International Conference on Intelligent Robots and Systems (IROS), pp. 681–687. IEEE (2015)

14. Fan, J., Xu, W., Wu, Y., Gong, Y.: Human tracking using convolutional neural networks. IEEE Trans. Neural Netw. 21(10), 1610–1623 (2010)

15. Fuentes-Pacheco, J., Ruiz-Ascencio, J., Rendón-Mancha, J.M.: Visual simultaneous localization and mapping: a survey. Artif. Intell. Rev. 43(1), 55–81 (2015)

16. Gao, C., Chen, F., Yu, J.G., Huang, R., Sang, N.: Robust visual tracking using exemplar-based detectors. IEEE Trans. Circuits Syst. Video Technol. 27(2), 300–312 (2015)

17. Gao, C., Shi, H., Yu, J.G., Sang, N.: Enhancement of elda tracker based on cnn features and adaptive model update. Sensors 16(4), 545 (2016)

18. Grabner, H., Grabner, M., Bischof, H.: Real-time tracking via on-line boosting. In: Proceedings of the British Machine Vision Conference 2006, Edinburgh, pp. 47–56 (2006)

19. Gupta, S., Girshick, R., Arbeláez, P., Malik, J.: Learning rich features from RGB-D images for object detection and segmentation. In: Fleet, D., Pajdla, T., Schiele, B., Tuytelaars, T. (eds.) ECCV 2014. LNCS, vol. 8695, pp. 345–360. Springer, Cham (2014). doi:10.1007/978-3-319-10584-0_23

20. Hare, S., Golodetz, S., Saffari, A., Vineet, V., Cheng, M.M., Hicks, S.L., Torr, P.H.: Struck: structured output tracking with kernels. IEEE Trans. Pattern Anal. Mach. Intell. 38(10), 2096–2109 (2016)

21. Hong, S., You, T., Kwak, S., Han, B.: Online tracking by learning discriminative saliency map with convolutional neural network. In: ICML, pp. 597–606 (2015)

22. Hua, Y., Alahari, K., Schmid, C.: Online object tracking with proposal selection. In: The IEEE International Conference on Computer Vision (ICCV), December 2015

23. Kanbara, M., Okuma, T., Takemura, H., Yokoya, N.: A stereoscopic video see-through augmented reality system based on real-time vision-based registration. In: Proceedings of IEEE Virtual Reality, pp. 255–262. IEEE (2000)

24. Kobilarov, M., Sukhatme, G., Hyams, J., Batavia, P.: People tracking and following with mobile robot using an omnidirectional camera and a laser. In: Proceedings 2006 IEEE International Conference on Robotics and Automation, ICRA 2006, pp. 557–562. IEEE (2006)
25. Koide, K., Miura, J.: Identification of a specific person using color, height, and gait features for a person following robot. Robot. Auton. Syst. **84**, 76–87 (2016)
26. Nishimura, S., Itou, K., Kikuchi, T., Takemura, H., Mizoguchi, H.: A study of robotizing daily items for an autonomous carrying system-development of person following shopping cart robot. In: 9th International Conference on Control, Automation, Robotics and Vision, ICARCV 2006, pp. 1–6. IEEE (2006)
27. O'Dwyer, A.: Handbook of PI and PID Controller Tuning Rules. World Scientific, Singapore (2009)
28. Oron, S., Bar-Hillel, A., Levi, D., Avidan, S.: Locally orderless tracking. Int. J. Comput. Vis. **111**(2), 213–228 (2015)
29. Sardari, F., Moghaddam, M.E.: A hybrid occlusion free object tracking method using particle filter and modified galaxy based search meta-heuristic algorithm. Appl. Soft Comput. **50**, 280–299 (2017)
30. Satake, J., Chiba, M., Miura, J.: A sift-based person identification using a distance-dependent appearance model for a person following robot. In: 2012 IEEE International Conference on Robotics and Biomimetics (ROBIO), pp. 962–967. IEEE (2012)
31. Schlegel, C., Jaberg, H., Schuster, M.: Vision based person tracking with a mobile robot. In: Proceedings of British Machine Vision Conference. Citeseer (1998)
32. Song, S., Xiao, J.: Tracking revisited using RGBD camera: unified benchmark and baselines. In: Proceedings of the IEEE International Conference on Computer Vision, pp. 233–240 (2013)
33. Takemura, H., Ito, K., Mizoguchi, H.: Person following mobile robot under varying illumination based on distance and color information. In: IEEE International Conference on Robotics and Biomimetics, ROBIO 2007, pp. 1500–1505. IEEE (2007)
34. Tarokh, M., Ferrari, P.: Case study: robotic person following using fuzzy control and image segmentation. J. Field Robot. **20**(9), 557–568 (2003)
35. Wu, Y., Lim, J., Yang, M.H.: Object tracking benchmark. IEEE Trans. Pattern Anal. Mach. Intell. **37**(9), 1834–1848 (2015)
36. Yamane, T., Shirai, Y., Miura, J.: Person tracking by integrating optical flow and uniform brightness regions. In: Proceedings of 1998 IEEE International Conference on Robotics and Automation, vol. 4, pp. 3267–3272. IEEE (1998)
37. Yoshimi, T., Nishiyama, M., Sonoura, T., Nakamoto, H., Tokura, S., Sato, H., Ozaki, F., Matsuhira, N., Mizoguchi, H.: Development of a person following robot with vision based target detection. In: 2006 IEEE/RSJ International Conference on Intelligent Robots and Systems, pp. 5286–5291. IEEE (2006)
38. Zhai, M., Roshtkhari, M.J., Mori, G.: Deep learning of appearance models for online object tracking. arXiv preprint arXiv:1607.02568 (2016)
39. Zhang, K., Zhang, L., Yang, M.H.: Real-time object tracking via online discriminative feature selection. IEEE Trans. Image Process. **22**(12), 4664–4677 (2013)
40. Zhang, L., Suganthan, P.N.: Visual tracking with convolutional neural network. In: 2015 IEEE International Conference on Systems, Man, and Cybernetics (SMC), pp. 2072–2077. IEEE (2015)
41. Zhang, L., van der Maaten, L.: Structure preserving object tracking. In: Proceedings of the IEEE Conference on Computer Vision and Pattern Recognition, pp. 1838–1845 (2013)

Recognition of Human Continuous Action with 3D CNN

Gang Yu[✉] and Ting Li

Harbin Institute of Technology (HIT) Shenzhen Graduate School,
Shenzhen 518055, Guangdong, People's Republic of China
969083604@qq.com

Abstract. Under the boom of the service robot, the human continuous action recognition becomes an indispensable research. In this paper, we propose a continuous action recognition method based on multi-channel 3D CNN for extracting multiple features, which are classified with KNN. First, we use fragmentary action as training samples which can be identified in the process of action. Then the training samples are processed through the gray scale, improved L-K optical flow and Gabor filter, to extract the characteristics of diversification using a priori knowledge. Then the 3D CNN is constructed to process multi-channel features that are formed into 128-dimension feature maps. Finally, we use KNN to classify those samples. We find that the fragmentary action in continuous action of the identification showed a good robustness. And the proposed method is verified in HMDB-51 and UCF-101 to be more accurate than Gaussian Bayes or the single 3D CNN in action recognition.

Keywords: Human continuous action recognition · 3D CNN · KNN · Improved L-K optical flow · Gabor filter

1 Introduction

With the aging of the population increasing, service robots will play an important role in our lives. At the same time in the boom of artificial intelligence, the current service robot research is very hot [1]. In the study of service robots, it is essential to identify the continuous action of the human body, and action recognition is critical and challenging in many research fields and applications [2], such as video surveillance [3] and human-computer interaction. In the action recognition, most of the research is to identify a complete action based on a single background and a single individual [4]. In human continuous action recognition, the action is smooth transition and the boundaries are blurred, while the daily life of the human body movements are always changing frequently, which is also greatly increased the difficulty of action recognition. Also people can recognize action with fragments, but the research using traditional machine learning in the fragmentary action recognition based on the extracted features is limited.

In recent years the rise of the deep learning has brought new opportunities for the action recognition. In this paper, 3D CNN is constructed to extract the features of the fragmented actions. In order to show the characteristics of diversification, at the

© Springer International Publishing AG 2017
M. Liu et al. (Eds.): ICVS 2017, LNCS 10528, pp. 314–322, 2017.
DOI: 10.1007/978-3-319-68345-4_28

beginning of the training, gray scale, improved L-K optical flow and multi-directional Gabor filters of channels are setting using a priori knowledge. After extracting the features with 3D CNN, 128 dimensional feature maps of each sample are obtained. The features are highly concentrated, the same kind of inter-action association is enhanced, the similarity between different actions is weakened.

The remainder of the paper is organized as follows: Sect. 2 reviews the related work about human action recognition briefly. Section 3 explains the technique details of our method. In Sect. 4, evaluations of the proposed method are conducted on challenging dataset. At last, Sect. 5 gives the conclusions and suggests future work.

2 Related Work

At present, most of the researches on action recognition are about recognizing single actions, and the research of human action feature extraction is focused on human geometry, motion information or space-time interest points. Faria et al. [5] extracted spatio-temporal 3D skeleton-based features from RGB-D sensor data that are modeled in order to characterize daily activities, including risk situations. Vemulapalli et al. [6] proposed a new skeletal representation that explicitly models the 3D geometric relationships between various body parts using rotations and translations in 3D space. Wang et al. [7] proposed to characterize the human actions with a novel actionlet ensemble model, which represents the interaction of a subset of human joints. Chen et al. [8] presents a human action recognition method by using depth motion maps (DMMs). Each depth frame in a depth video sequence is projected onto three orthogonal Cartesian planes. Chaaraoui et al. [9] used an evolutionary algorithm is to determine the optimal subset of skeleton joints, taking into account the topological structure of the skeleton, in order to improve the final success rate.

There are few studies on continuous action recognition, Zhu et al. [10] proposed an online Continuous human action recognition (CHAR) algorithm based on skeletal data extracted from RGB-D images captured by Kinect sensors. However, the proposed algorithm still extracts features of the whole human body, and trains the models based on whole body features. Guo et al. [11] proposed a continuous action recognition framework which is based on the bag of words representation. A visual local pattern is regarded as a word and the action is modeled by the distribution of words. But it aims to identify the action category and detect the start and end key frame of each action. It is a challenging task due to the frequent changes of human actions and the ambiguity of action boundaries. Eum et al. [12] proposed a new method for spotting and recognizing continuous human actions using a vision sensor. The method is comprised of depth-MHI-HOG (DMH), action modeling, action spotting, and recognition. But the proposed method recognizes actions also based on start and end points.

The rise of deep learning also promotes the study of action recognition. Ji et al. [13] developed a novel 3D CNN model for action recognition which extracts features from both the spatial and the temporal dimensions by performing 3D convolutions, thereby capturing the motion information encoded in multiple adjacent frames. Karpathy et al. [14] study multiple approaches for extending the connectivity of a CNN in time domain to take advantage of local spatio-temporal information and suggest a multi-resolution, foveated architecture as a promising way of speeding up the training. Simonyan et al. [15] proposed a two-stream ConvNet architecture which incorporates spatial and temporal networks and demonstrated that a ConvNet trained on multi-frame dense optical flow is able to achieve very good performance in spite of limited training data.

In this paper, we construct the 3D CNN structure, and use the gray-scale graph, the improved L-K optical channel and the Gabor filter channel to extract the features. After merging the multi-features, KNN is used to classify the action. And we find that the fragmentary action training model can be directly used for continuous action recognition, in the video of the continuous action of the identification also showed a better robustness. For benchmarking datasets, HMDB-51 [16] and UCF-101 [17] are chosen because they are the largest and most challenging annotated action recognition datasets.

3 Technical Approach

In this section, the overview of the proposed algorithm is displayed in Fig. 1. Ji et al. [13] developed a novel 3D CNN model which sets gray, optical flow and gradient channels. The gray channel is set that gray scale retains the original information. However, we find that the gradient channel has large error when background moved, the gradient is combined with the optical flow that uses the Prewitt operator to convolute images to improve the L-K optical flow for extracting motion features. Since the sample size is required before the model training, the uniformity of the resolution in gray and optical flow channels can make image edge blur that cause information loss. We increase Gabor channels that using Gabor filter to extract the edge characteristics and then unified resolution is performed. Using seven channels of gray, improved L-K optical flow (x, y) and Gabor filter (four orientation), the 3D CNN are constructed that extracted and merge features to get 128 dimensions feature maps. Finally, the KNN is used to classify feature maps to get action classes. Here we use Lanczos interpolation for unified resolution.

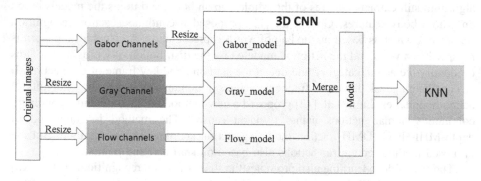

Fig. 1. Overview of the proposed algorithm

3.1   Motion Feature Extraction

The optical flow is the most widely used method in the action feature extraction which is the instantaneous velocity of the pixel motion of the space moving object on the observed imaging surface. It is used to study the change of the image gray scale in time and the object structure in the scene and relationship of movement.

Here we used improved L-K method without pyramid. It is implemented with convolution. First we get the derivatives with f_x, f_y, f_t from $f(x, y, t)$. And the derivate can achieve by convolution,

$$I_x = I * D_x, I_y = I * D_y, I_t = I * D_t \tag{1}$$

For D_x and D_y selected Prewitt filter,

$$D_x = \begin{bmatrix} -1 & 0 & 1 \\ -1 & 0 & 1 \\ -1 & 0 & 1 \end{bmatrix}, D_y = \begin{bmatrix} -1 & -1 & -1 \\ 0 & 0 & 0 \\ 1 & 1 & 1 \end{bmatrix}, D_x = \begin{bmatrix} 1/4 & 1/4 & 1/4 \\ 1/4 & 1/4 & 1/4 \\ 1/4 & 1/4 & 1/4 \end{bmatrix} \tag{2}$$

We seek the velocity that minimizes the squared error in each constraint (called the least-squares (LS) velocity estimate) [18],

$$E(u_1, u_2) = \sum_{x,y} g(x, y) \left[u_1 f_x(x, y, t) + u_2 f_y(x, y, t) + f_t(x, y, t) \right]^2 \tag{3}$$

In matrix notation, these normal equations and their solution are

$$M\vec{u} + \vec{b} = 0, \vec{u} = -M^{-1}\vec{b} \tag{4}$$

(Assuming M exists), where

$$M = \sum g \begin{pmatrix} f_x \\ f_y \end{pmatrix} (f_x \quad f_y) = \begin{bmatrix} \sum g f_x^2 & \sum g f_x f_y \\ \sum g f_x f_y & \sum g f_y^2 \end{bmatrix} \tag{5}$$

$$\vec{b} = \sum g f_t \begin{pmatrix} f_x \\ f_y \end{pmatrix} = \begin{pmatrix} \sum g f_x f_t \\ \sum g f_y f_t \end{pmatrix} \tag{6}$$

So we get u_1, u_2. This method can detect the motion characteristics well in the fixed background. When the background changes or the camera moves, the background is opposite to the moving direction of the target, and the velocity component is different from the positive and negative values, and the motion characteristics can be extracted well.

3.2   Edge Feature Extraction

In image processing, the Gabor function is a linear filter for edge detection. Frequency and orientation representations of Gabor filters are similar to those of the human visual system, and they have been found to be particularly appropriate for texture representation and discrimination. The filter has a real and an imaginary component representing orthogonal directions. The two components may be formed into a complex number or used individually.

Complex:

$$g(x, y; \lambda, \theta, \sigma, \gamma) = \exp\left(-\frac{x'^2 + \gamma'^2 y'^2}{2\sigma^2}\right) \exp\left(i\left(2\pi\frac{x'}{\lambda} + \psi\right)\right) \qquad (7)$$

Real:

$$g(x, y; \lambda, \theta, \sigma, \gamma) = \exp\left(-\frac{x'^2 + \gamma^2 y'^2}{2\sigma^2}\right) \cos\left(i\left(2\pi\frac{x'}{\lambda} + \psi\right)\right) \qquad (8)$$

Imaginary:

$$g(x, y; \lambda, \theta, \sigma, \gamma) = \exp\left(-\frac{x'^2 + \gamma^2 y'^2}{2\sigma^2}\right) \sin\left(i\left(2\pi\frac{x'}{\lambda} + \psi\right)\right) \qquad (9)$$

Where,

$$x' = x\cos\theta + y\sin\theta \qquad (10)$$

And

$$y' = -x\sin\theta + y\cos\theta \qquad (11)$$

In this equation, λ represents the wavelength of the sinusoidal factor, θ represents the orientation of the normal to the parallel stripes of a Gabor function, ψ is the phase offset, σ is the standard deviation of Gaussian envelope and γ is the spatial aspect ratio, and specifies the ellipticity of the support of the Gabor function. Here we choose 3 * 3 Gabor window and $\lambda = \frac{\pi}{2}$, $\theta = 0, \frac{\pi}{4}, \frac{\pi}{2}, \frac{3\pi}{4}$.

3.3   Model Training and Classification with KNN

Before constructing the 3D CNN, the training sample is processed by gray scale, improved optical flow and Gabor filter to generate 7 channels, as shown in the Fig. 2.

After the down-sampling process, the image size becomes 150 * 100. Tran D et al. [19] find small 3 * 3 * 3 convolution kernels in all layers is among the best performing architecture. With current GPU memory, we design our 3D CNN to have 5 convolution layers, 3 pooling layers, followed by one fully connected layer, then merge 7 channels with merge layer that connect those features with fully connected layer. The architecture is the same as each channel. The Fig. 3 is 3D CNN architecture of one channel. All kernels of 3D convolution filters are 3 * 3 * 3 with stride 1 * 1 * 1 expect conv1 which has kernel size of 5 * 5 * 5. And the pooling layer use 3D maxpooling that

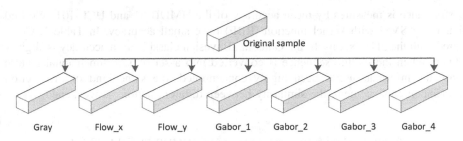

Fig. 2. Seven channels

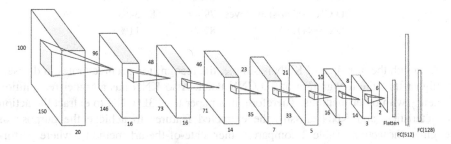

Fig. 3. 3D CNN architecture of one channel

kernel sizes are 2 * 2 * 1 and 2 * 2 * 2. The first fully connected layer is 512 feature maps and the last has 128 output units.

4   Experimental Results

In this section, we evaluate the proposed skeletal representation using two different datasets: HMDB-51 [16] and UCF-101 [17] which are the largest and most challenging annotated action recognition datasets.

HMDB-51 [16] has a total of 6766 videos organized as 51 distinct action categories, which are collected from a wide range of sources. This dataset is more challenging than others because it has more complex backgrounds and context environments. What is more, there are many similar scenes in different categories. Since the number of training video is small in this dataset, it is more challenging to learn representative features.

UCF-101 [17] is an action recognition data set of realistic action videos, collected from YouTube, having 101 action categories. This data set is an extension of UCF50 data set which has 50 action categories.

In the experiments, we will take a complete action from each video, in the selection of every 20 frames for a training sample, the training sample processing to extract a gray channel, two optical flow channels, four Gabor channels. Then we build the 3D CNN model to merge the feature map of each channel to get a set of 128-dimensional feature maps. Finally, we tried CNN itself, Gaussian Bayes and KNN classifying the features to achieve recognition of the action. Table 1 compares those methods, where performance is measures by mean accuracy of the HMDB-51 and UCF-101. We find that using SVM with kernel function (RBF) have small accuracy. In Table 1, Compared with the 3D CNN itself, the Gaussian Bayesian classification accuracy is slightly lower. When the picture sequence is converted into a set of 128-dimensional feature map, the information has been highly concentrated, the same kind of inter-action association enhancement, the similarity between different actions is weakened.

Table 1. Classification mean accuracy on HMDB-51 and UCF-101

Method	HMDB-51	UCF-101
3D CNN	83.05%	90.33%
3D CNN+Gaussian Bayes	79.49	85.34%
3D CNN+KNN	82.71%	91.11%

Although the principle of KNN is simple, the recognition accuracy rates in datasets are higher than the recognition of 3D CNN itself. Also KNN has a higher recognition efficiency with other methods. Therefore, this paper uses 3D CNN to extract the action characteristics, and KNN classify the extracted features to achieve the purpose of recognize the action. Table 2 compares other state-of-the-art methods, where performance is measured by mean accuracy of the HMDB-51 and UCF-101 datasets.

Table 2. Compared accuracy with other methods

Method	HMDB-51	UCF-101
IDT higher-dimensional encodings [20]	61.1%	87.9%
FSTCN (SCI fusion) [20]	59.1%	88.1%
SP-CNN [21]	74.7%	91.6%
3D CNN+KNN	82.71%	91.11%

5 Conclusion

In this paper, an improved 3D CNN architecture is proposed. As a result of the use of fragmented action training, the identification process does not need to detect the starting point and the end point of the action, which can be better applied to the continuous action recognition. And the proposed method is verified in HMDB-51 and UCF-101 to be more accurate than other methods. However, the action recognition is not only concerned about the target itself, but also with the exchange of objects recognition. After all, two similar actions will lead to misidentification without the help of objects recognition. So the human-object interaction features should also be taken into consideration. These will be our future work.

References

1. Wang, J., Zheng, J., Zhang, S., et al.: A face recognition system based on local binary patterns and support vector machine for home security service robot. In: 2016 9th International Symposium on Computational Intelligence and Design (ISCID), vol. 2, pp. 303–307. IEEE (2016)
2. Poppe, R.: A survey on vision-based human action recognition. Image Vis. Comput. **28**(6), 976–990 (2010)
3. Wagner, A., Bartolein, C., Badreddin, E.: Multi-level human-machine-interaction monitoring and system reconfiguration. In: Rodić, A., Borangiu, T. (eds.) RAAD 2016, pp. 370–377. Springer International Publishing, Heidelberg (2016). doi:10.1007/978-3-319-49058-8_40
4. Li, W., Zhang, Z., Liu, Z.: Action recognition based on a bag of 3D points. In: 2010 IEEE Computer Society Conference on Computer Vision and Pattern Recognition Workshops (CVPRW), pp. 9–14. IEEE (2010)
5. Faria, D.R., Vieira, M., Premebida, C., et al.: Probabilistic human daily activity recognition towards robot-assisted living. In: 2015 24th IEEE International Symposium on IEEE Robot and Human Interactive Communication (RO-MAN), pp. 582–587 (2015)
6. Vemulapalli, R., Arrate, F., Chellappa, R.: Human action recognition by representing 3D skeletons as points in a lie group. In: Proceedings of the IEEE Conference on Computer Vision and Pattern Recognition, pp. 588–595 (2014)
7. Wang, J., Liu, Z., Wu, Y.: Learning actionlet ensemble for 3D human action recognition. In: Human Action Recognition with Depth Cameras, pp. 11–40. Springer International Publishing, Heidelberg (2014). doi:10.1007/978-3-319-04561-0_2
8. Chen, C., Liu, K., Kehtarnavaz, N.: Real-time human action recognition based on depth motion maps. J. Real-time Image Process. **12**(1), 155–163 (2016)
9. Chaaraoui, A.A., Padilla-López, J.R., Climent-Pérez, P., et al.: Evolutionary joint selection to improve human action recognition with RGB-D devices. Expert Syst. Appl. **41**(3), 786–794 (2014)
10. Zhu, G., Zhang, L., Shen, P., et al.: An online continuous human action recognition algorithm based on the kinect sensor. Sensors **16**(2), 161 (2016)
11. Guo, P., Miao, Z., Shen, Y., et al.: Continuous human action recognition in real time. Multimedia Tools Appl. **68**(3), 827–844 (2014)
12. Eum, H., Yoon, C., Lee, H., et al.: Continuous human action recognition using depth-MHI-HOG and a spotter model. Sensors **15**(3), 5197–5227 (2015)
13. Ji, S., Xu, W., Yang, M., et al.: 3D convolutional neural networks for human action recognition. IEEE Trans. Pattern Anal. Mach. Intell. **35**(1), 221–231 (2013)
14. Karpathy, A., Toderici, G., Shetty, S., et al.: Large-scale video classification with convolutional neural networks. In: Proceedings of the IEEE Conference on Computer Vision and Pattern Recognition, pp. 1725–1732 (2014)
15. Simonyan, K., Zisserman, A.: Two-stream convolutional networks for action recognition in videos. In: Advances in Neural Information Processing Systems, pp. 568–576 (2014)
16. Kuehne, H., Jhuang, H., Garrote, E., Poggio, T., Serre, T.: HMDB: a large video database for human motion recognition. In: ICCV (2011)
17. Soomro, K., Zamir, A.R., Shah, M.: UCF101: A Dataset of 101 Human Action Classes From Videos in The Wild, CRCV-TR-12-01, November 2012
18. Simoncelli, E.P., Adelson, E.H., Heeger, D.J.: Probability distributions of optical flow. In: IEEE Computer Society Conference on Computer Vision and Pattern Recognition CVPR 1991, pp. 310–315. IEEE (1991)

19. Tran, D., Bourdev, L., Fergus, R., et al.: Learning spatiotemporal features with 3D convolutional networks. In: Proceedings of the IEEE International Conference on Computer Vision, pp. 4489–4497 (2015)
20. Peng, X., Wang, L., Wang, X., et al.: Bag of visual words and fusion methods for action recognition: comprehensive study and good practice. Comput. Vis. Image Underst. **150**, 109–125 (2016)
21. Yu, S., Cheng, Y., Su, S., et al.: Stratified pooling based deep convolutional neural networks for human action recognition. Multimedia Tools Appl. 1–16 (2016)

Stereo System

Multi-view Shape from Shading Constrained by Stereo Image Analysis

Malte Lenoch$^{(\boxtimes)}$, Pia Biebrach, Arne Grumpe, and Christian Wöhler

Image Analysis Group, Faculty of Electrical Engineering and Information
Technology, TU Dortmund University, 44227 Dortmund, Germany
{malte.lenoch,pia.biebrach,arne.grumpe,christian.woehler}@udo.edu

Abstract. In this paper we present the combination of Shape from Shading and stereo vision based on a fully integrated approach. The surface gradients of two camera views of an object are employed to refine an initial disparity map subject to the constraint of integrability of the resulting surface. The gradient field of the object's surface is computed using Photometric Stereo and analytical reflectance models with spatially varying parameters. We evaluate the proposed algorithm on three data sets including a metallic object and objects with depth discontinuities and small details. We achieve compelling results on all data sets including the cast iron where our method is less noise-sensitive than the reference 3D scanner. However, since the scanner exhibits high-frequency noise, we use its low-passed depth data as reference. The mean error of all data sets is 1 mm and below with a low-cost acquisition setup, consisting of two cameras and 18 light sources only. Furthermore, a new method to calibrate the lighting of a multi-view Photometric Stereo setup is briefly introduced.

1 Introduction

High-quality visual inspection of surfaces is a topic of great interest to many fields of study, ranging from industrial quality inspection to medical image analysis. State-of-the-art applications oftentimes rely on active range scanners to acquire depth information of a scene at micron resolution. In general these approaches yield very accurate general structures of objects in the scene while the high-frequency component tends to be noise-afflicted. Furthermore, since active projection is required the applicability is limited to controlled laboratory setups and even more importantly highly influenced by the object shape and its reflective properties, since shadowing of the projected pattern prevents meaningful information. Image-based 3D reconstruction methods yield the great advantage that (under ideal circumstances) a depth value or structural information can be obtained for every pixel of the image.

Combining traditional stereo with shape from shading should be a natural choice since both procedures exhibit complementary shortcomings. Finding correspondences in a robust fashion relies on window-based features that favour

M. Liu et al. (Eds.): ICVS 2017, LNCS 10528, pp. 325–335, 2017.
DOI: 10.1007/978-3-319-68345-4_29

approximately integer-valued disparity values, thus neglecting details in the surface structure. Photometric methods on the other hand acquire gradient information locally at high precision. Yet, small errors in the estimation add up during integration, resulting in depth maps that are distorted. Additionally, non-Lambertian reflectance functions are a difficult setting for stereo matching, while there are many photometric algorithms that have been designed to explicitly handle various types of bidirectional reflectance distribution functions (BRDF). Thus using coarse stereo depth data in conjunction with gradient information is a self-evident solution.

1.1 Related Work

There has been extensive research in the fields of multi-view stereo (MVS) and shape from shading (SfS) in the last decades. However, commonly both fields of research that ultimately aim for the same goal have been treated individually. SfS approaches have overcome the limitation of strictly Lambertian surfaces, e.g. [2,7,13], while the assumption of view-independent intensity (i.e. a Lambertian BRDF) is the foundation for feature matching in traditional stereo scenarios [18]. [23] proposed an architecture that unifies both approaches including structure-from-motion, yet is still limited to diffuse surfaces. [10] replace parametric BRDF models with reference materials of known geometry to estimate normals on surfaces with arbitrary reflectance properties. This idea is extended to a multi-view setting by [1], thus proposing a multi-view photometric stereo (MVPS). [22] improve MVS meshes based on shading cues under arbitrary lighting for Lambertian surfaces. Their drawback of constant albedo has been overcome recently by [14,16] who can handle abruptly changing albedos. [14] use spherical harmonics to estimate the lighting and minimise an energy function that is independent of the surface albedo. [16] use a variational framework that has no need for an initialization and combine stereo and shading subject to strong regularizations. Still, these proposals are limited to Lambertian surfaces and fail if there are gradual changes of the surface albedo that are mistaken for changes of the surface geometry.

In contrast to these methods and the idea of reflectance mixing, we rely on the analytical BRDF models of Blinn [4,9] and Cook-Torrance [8,21] to model uniform or spatially varying reflectance properties of non-Lambertian surfaces. We present a fully integrated equation that defines the process of retrieving an integrable surface from gradient data in conjunction with the disparity offset of this gradient for two camera views. However, since we apply an update equation for the depth map, we need to rely on iterative optimization and thus require an initialization. Since we need a two-camera setup, a stereo disparity map is used for initialization.

2 Preliminary Computations

The main contribution of this paper is the combination of Horn's Shape from Shading [12] with stereo information, namely the disparity map, based on a fully

integrated approach. In the proposed procedure we estimate the initial disparity map by matching the DAISY descriptor [19,20] computed on each pair of
images based on the minimal sum of squared differences. The descriptor matching is refined with semi-global matching (SGM) [11]. We do left-right consistency
checking and eliminate every disparity value for a difference that is larger than
5 pixels. Since a disparity map can be obtained for each pair of images, we take
the median value for each pixel that yields at least 5 valid disparities. Note in
Fig. 3 that this combination enables robust stereo estimation even on metallic
surfaces and those that exhibit spatially varying reflectance properties.

Apart from the initial disparity map, we need to know an initial gradient
field $(p(u,v), q(u,v))^T$ for both left and right camera view of the stereo rig. We
employ a two-camera Photometric Stereo (PS) setup to estimate the surface gradient field. The stereo cameras are calibrated with Bouguet's Matlab toolbox [5]
and the light source positions are estimated as described in Sect. 2.1. The parameters of the BRDF models are estimated based on the depth data computed
from the stereo setup. Except for the cast iron we consider spatially varying
reflectance parameters and take a 9×9 patch surrounding the central pixel into
account during the estimation process. This ensures sufficient data to compute
the reflectance parameters even in the presence of noisy or roughly estimated
depth data, which is likely due to stereo vision artefacts. The surrounding intensities are weighted by a 2D Gaussian $\mathcal{N}(0, 4)$ centred at the current pixel with
a variance of 4 pixels.

2.1   Light Source Calibration

Light Source Direction. The accurate calibration of the light source position
and strength is substantial in PS to compute high-fidelity normal fields. We
calibrate our illumination setup with a diffuse sphere with a manufactured albedo
of $\rho = 0.99$. Images of the sphere in different positions are captured with a
calibrated stereo rig. Sphere centre and radius in image coordinates $(u, v)^T$ have
been estimated with a linear circle fit and projection rays of the sphere surface
can be estimated by inversion of the projection matrices. Since the radius of the
sphere is known ($R = 15\,\mathrm{mm}$), we can estimate the sphere centre position in
3D space by determining the plane where the spread of projection rays forms a
circle with radius R. Based on this initial guess of the sphere parameters and
assuming a Lambertian surface, the directions of the incident light s_i can be
computed from the measured intensity I_n and the surface normal directions n_k.

Light Source Position. However, as we assume non-distant light sources the
actual position of each light source is of interest. Theoretically, the light directions corresponding to the same light source and different sphere positions should
intersect in one point. However, due to measurement noise and numerical uncertainties we rather face a problem of skew lines that we resolve in a linear least
squares fashion. Each light position $l = [l_x, l_y, l_z]^T$ is subject to the following
minimization problem

$$\arg\min_{\alpha_i, l} E = \sum_i \frac{1}{2} \|l - x_i - \alpha_i s_i\|^2 \tag{1}$$

where x_i is a point on the sphere surface and α_i a scaling constant referring to the distance from the surface to the light source. Minimization of (1) can be transformed into a linear matrix - vector problem of the form $Ax = b$ and thus be solved easily.

The resulting light source position, light source intensity and sphere position are then introduced into a global gradient descent framework where the error between rendered images R and measured images I is minimised. Experiments have shown that the image reproduction quality increases when we considered a weak physically plausible Phong lobe [15, 17] in addition to the diffuse term, since the assumption of perfectly diffuse reflectance does not hold in practice. The parameters of the Phong model are $\theta = (0.95, 0.04, 1.42)$ for diffuse weight, specular weight and specular exponent, respectively.

3   Forming the Error Equation

The variational Shape from Shading described by Horn [12] solves the problem of finding the surface $z(x, y)$ that minimizes a function F dependent on z and two of its partial derivatives $z_x = \frac{\partial z}{\partial x} = p, z_y = \frac{\partial z}{\partial y} = q$ in a least squares sense

$$\min_z \iint F(z, z_x, z_y) \mathrm{d}x\mathrm{d}y. \tag{2}$$

The Euler equation used to solve this variational problem is

$$F_z - \frac{\partial}{\partial x} F_{z_x} - \frac{\partial}{\partial y} F_{z_y} = 0. \tag{3}$$

The complete error function presented in this work is composed of two parts. First there is the integrability term that was already defined by [12]

$$E_{\text{int}} = \iint \frac{1}{2} \Big[(z_x - p)^2 + (z_y - q)^2 \Big] \mathrm{d}x\mathrm{d}y, \tag{4}$$

considering the observed gradient field (p, q). The second part and our contribution is the disparity error comparing the gradient fields computed from two scene views based on the disparity δ defined by the depth estimate z

$$E_\delta = \iint \frac{\gamma}{2} \Big[(p_R(\delta(z)) - p_L)^2 + (q_R(\delta(z)) - q_L)^2 \Big] \mathrm{d}x\mathrm{d}y. \tag{5}$$

Therefore the entire error function can be expressed by

$$E_{\text{total}} = \iint \Big(\frac{1}{2} \Big[(z_x - p)^2 + (z_y - q)^2 \Big] +$$
$$\frac{\gamma}{2} \Big[(p_R(\delta(z)) - p_L)^2 + (q_R(\delta(z)) - q_L)^2 \Big] \Big) \mathrm{d}x\mathrm{d}y. \tag{6}$$

Inserting (6) into the Euler equation $F = E_{\text{total}}$ separates both error terms again, because E_{int} is independent of z and E_δ is independent of z_x and z_y.

$$\underbrace{F_z}_{E_\delta} \underbrace{- \frac{\partial}{\partial x} F_{z_x} - \frac{\partial}{\partial y} F_{z_y}}_{E_{\text{int}}} = 0 \qquad (7)$$

3.1 Disparity Term

The following will refer to pixelwise estimates in the discrete case and therefore skip the integration component of the equation. However, the pixel indices (u, v) will be omitted as well for the sake of readability. The first part of the Euler equation is given by the disparity error term (5):

$$F_z = \gamma\Big(p_R(\delta(z)) - p_L\Big) \frac{\partial p_R}{\partial \delta} \frac{\partial \delta}{\partial z} + \gamma\Big(q_R(\delta(z)) - q_L\Big) \frac{\partial q_R}{\partial \delta} \frac{\partial \delta}{\partial z}. \qquad (8)$$

Disparity and depth are related by camera constant f and baselength b of the stereo setup by $\delta = \frac{fb}{z}$ and the disparity can thus be regarded as a function $\delta(z)$, which implies

$$\frac{\partial \delta}{\partial z} = -\frac{fb}{z^2}. \qquad (9)$$

The gradients (p_L, q_L) and (p_R, q_R), respectively are known at discrete pixel values (u, v) only and have to be interpolated to match the continuous projection $(\hat{u}, \hat{v})$ of the current depth estimate $\hat{z}(x, y)$ onto the camera plane. We assume a linear interpolation to be sufficient and thus

$$p_R(\hat{u} - \delta, \hat{v}) = p_R(u, v) + m_p(\hat{u} - \delta - u, v), \quad u = \lfloor \hat{u} - \delta \rfloor.$$

Note that rectified images in our setup yield $\hat{v} = v$ and the same concept applies to q_R. The slope of the linear interpolation is given by $m_p = \frac{\partial p_R}{\partial \delta}$ and $m_q = \frac{\partial q_R}{\partial \delta}$, and can be replaced in (8) yielding the final form of the disparity error based on the current depth estimate $\hat{z}(x, y)$:

$$F_z = -\gamma \frac{fb}{z^2} \Big[\Big(p_R(\delta(\hat{z})) - p_L\Big) m_p + \Big(q_R(\delta(\hat{z})) - q_L\Big) m_q \Big]. \qquad (10)$$

3.2 Integrability Term

The partial derivatives of the integrability error term are given by

$$F_{z_x} = \frac{\partial}{\partial x}(z_x - p) = \frac{\partial^2 z}{\partial x^2} - \frac{\partial p}{\partial x}, \qquad F_{z_y} = \frac{\partial}{\partial y}(z_y - q) = \frac{\partial^2 z}{\partial y^2} - \frac{\partial q}{\partial y}. \qquad (11)$$

The first and second derivative can be approximated by finite differences from the current estimate of the depth data $\hat{z}$. With respect to a centre pixel p_c, the surrounding pixels will be denoted upper p_u, lower p_l, left p_l and right p_r pixel. For example if $p_c = p(u, v)$ then $p_r = p(u + 1, v)$. Let the spatial extent of a pixel be given by Δx and Δy, respectively. The derivatives in (11) can thus be substituted as follows (the relation for q is implicit):

$$\frac{\partial p}{\partial x} \approx \frac{p_r - p_l}{2\Delta x}, \qquad \frac{\partial^2 z}{\partial x^2} \approx \frac{z_r - 2z_c + z_l}{\Delta x^2}. \tag{12}$$

Introducing this relation into (11) we can write the integrability error based on the current depth estimate $z_c = \hat{z}(u, v)$ as

$$-\frac{\partial}{\partial x} F_{z_x} - \frac{\partial}{\partial y} F_{z_y} = \frac{-z_r + 2z_c - z_l}{\Delta x^2} + \frac{p_r - p_l}{2\Delta x} + \frac{-z_d + 2z_c - z_u}{\Delta y^2} + \frac{q_d - q_u}{2\Delta y}. \tag{13}$$

Isolating z_c with the abbreviations $p_x = \frac{p_r - p_l}{2\Delta x}$ and $q_y = \frac{q_r - q_l}{2\Delta y}$ yields

$$2z_c \left(\frac{\Delta x^2 + \Delta y^2}{\Delta x^2 \Delta y^2} \right) - \frac{z_r + z_l}{\Delta x^2} - \frac{z_d + z_u}{\Delta y^2} + p_x + q_y = 0. \tag{14}$$

3.3   Combined Error Function

Let us now introduce all these findings into the Euler equation (3). The result is the combined error term

$$2z_c \left(\frac{\Delta x^2 + \Delta y^2}{\Delta x^2 \Delta y^2} \right) - \frac{z_r + z_l}{\Delta x^2} - \frac{z_d + z_u}{\Delta y^2} + p_x + q_y$$
$$- \gamma \frac{fb}{z_c^2} \left[\left(p_R(\delta(\hat{z})) - p_L \right) m_p + \left(q_R(\delta(\hat{z})) - q_L \right) m_q \right] = 0. \tag{15}$$

Isolating the highest power of z_c yields a cubic equation of the form

$$a_3 z^3 + a_2 z^2 + a_1 z + a_0 = 0 \tag{16}$$

the analytical solution of which is given in the literature, e.g. [6]. Since the solution is one of the three potentially complex roots of (16), we have to choose a solution to continue the next iteration with. Here, we accept the solution for z_c that is closest to the current estimate $\hat{z}(u, v)$ in terms of Euclidean distance in the complex plane.

4   Experiments

In the following, we will present the results obtained with our algorithm on the test data sets. The test data contains a figurine manufactured by a laser sinter 3D printer, a painted plaster mass and a cast iron object. The plaster mass has been partially painted with white acrylic paint and satin varnish to create spatially varying reflectance functions with nearly identical albedos but different specular characteristics. Reference 3D data have been obtained with an industrial quality fringe projection scanner[1]. We apply a Gaussian low-pass filter (size 13×13

---

[1] Vialux zSnapper Vario with AVT Pike F-421 (CCD Sensor), res. 2048×2048 pixels.

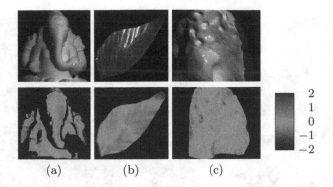

Fig. 1. Example images of the three data sets (a) Ganesh, (b) Leaf, and (c) Plaster (first row) and pixelwise differences between lowpass-filtered range scanner depth data and our method (second row). Scaling is mm.

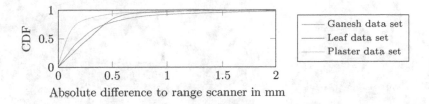

Fig. 2. Cumulative distribution function (CDF) of pixelwise depth differences.

pixels and width 4 pixels) to the 3D scanner data to reduce the high-frequency noise and match the different view points of reference scans and our results with the Iterative Closest Points (ICP) algorithm [3].

We acquire 18 pairs of stereo images of each object with two fixed Lumenera Lu165M cameras under varying incident light directions. For the PS surface normal estimation we employ the BRDF model of Cook-Torrance [8,21] for the cast-iron object[2] and the physically plausible Blinn BRDF model [4,9] for all other data sets. Exemplary images of the data sets are displayed in Fig. 1.

The second row of Fig. 1 depicts the absolute pixelwise differences of the depth data estimated with our method and the 3D range scanner. Since stereo rig and range scanner exhibit different sensor pixel extents we had to interpolate the data onto the coarser grid to make pixelwise comparison feasible. The difference is below 1 mm for most parts of all surfaces. Edges yield the highest errors, where it is important to state that the fringe projection system tends to be inaccurate in these regions as well and there is no real ground truth available.

A statistical assessment of the pixelwise differences is given in Fig. 2 by the cumulative distribution of the distances. The Leaf and Plaster data sets show very high similarity to the range scanner data with 95% of the estimates deviating less than 0.7 mm. In fact, 50% of the error is lower than 0.1 mm for the

---

[2] Modelling the surface as a collection of micro-facets suits metallic objects very well.

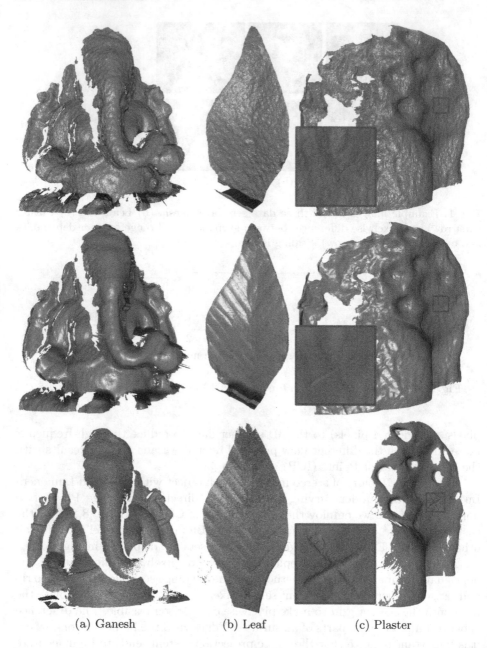

(a) Ganesh   (b) Leaf   (c) Plaster

Fig. 3. Shaded views of depth data obtained from stereo matching (first row), our method (second row), and 3D range scanner (third row). The stereo matching results provide a coarse estimate of the surface. Our method yields dense 3D surfaces that are smooth and still exhibit significant detail (blue box and especially Leaf data set). The range scanner lacks data due to shadowing in concave regions where the image based methods recover depth information and high-frequency noise is apparent for (a) and (b). (Color figure online)

Plaster and 0.3 mm for the metallic Leaf. The high amount of shadowing of the incident light and between the matching views makes both stereo and photometric stereo estimation difficult on the Ganesh data set. This corresponds to the higher differences to the range scanner. Yet, still 85% of the recovered depth data is closer than 0.65 mm to the reference.

Further, it is important to point out that especially the Ganesh data set is sparsely recovered by the 3D scanner as the self-shadowing affects the projected pattern as well. In contrast, the image based methods (stereo matching and our method) obtain dense depth information with respect to the view of the left camera. This is evident in the shaded views of the recovered surfaces in Fig. 3. The stereo matching results provide a coarse estimate of the surface but suffer from preferentially near-integer disparity values, resulting in an artificial large-scale roughness of the surfaces. In contrast to that, the proposed algorithm produces accurate overall estimates of the surface while maintaining small details like the "X" scratch mark on the plaster data (blue box). The cast iron leaf is a challenging object for the fringe projection scanner and the reference yields severe high-frequency noise artefacts. However, our result is smooth and still shows the leaf structure of the object.

Limitations. The optimization relies on the computation of a disparity map from corresponding gradient fields. Thus, a good estimate of the gradient field is essential to recover a meaningful disparity map. Further, we initialize the algorithm with the stereo disparity map and the optimization can get stuck in local minima as can be seen on the Leaf data set at the lower edge (Fig. 3(b)). The algorithm is unable to correct the wrong stereo estimate. A possible cause is our choice of the solution to (15) that is closest to the current depth estimate. However, edges are boundaries to the differential equations and as such in general vulnerable to diverge if not constrained correctly.

5 Conclusion

We have presented a solution to the Multi-view Shape from Shading problem and a method for the light calibration of a corresponding acquisition setup. We achieve a dense reconstruction of all test objects, including areas where the fringe projection scanner can not estimate data due to shadowing. Our acquisition setup is about an order of magnitude less expensive than the reference 3D scanner, consisting only of two cameras and 18 light sources, yet we still achieve reasonable 3D measurements. Furthermore, the reconstructed surfaces are smooth without high-frequency noise and still preserve fine details of the structure. Especially the Leaf poses a problem to the fringe projection scanner but is well reconstructed by our method. Since the 3D shape of metal-like objects is difficult to reconstruct for many state-of-the-art methods, we consider this an important aspect of the contribution. The convergence of our method could be improved with a different selection criterion of the subsequent depth estimate.

References

1. Ackermann, J., Langguth, F., Fuhrmann, S., Kuijper, A., Goesele, M.: Multi-view photometric stereo by example. In: International Conference on 3D Vision, pp. 259–266 (2014)
2. Alldrin, N.G., Kriegman, D.J.: Toward reconstructing surfaces with arbitrary isotropic reflectance: a stratified photometric stereo approach. In: ICCV (2007)
3. Besl, P.J., McKay, N.D.: A method for registration of 3-D shapes. IEEE Trans. Pattern Anal. Mach. Intell. **14**(2), 239–256 (1992)
4. Blinn, J.F.: Models of light reflection for computer synthesized pictures. ACM SIGGRAPH **11**(2), 192–198 (1977)
5. Bouguet, J.Y.: Camera Calibration Toolbox for Matlab (2008). http://www.vision.caltech.edu/bouguetj/calib_doc/index.html
6. Bronstein, I.N., Semendjajew, K., Musiol, G., Mühlig, H.: Taschenbuch der Mathematik, vol. 10. Europa-Lehrmittel, Haan (2016)
7. Chung, H.S., Jia, J.: Efficient photometric stereo on glossy surfaces with wide specular lobes. In: CVPR, pp. 1–8 (2008)
8. Cook, R.L., Torrance, K.E.: A reflectance model for computer graphics. ACM SIGGRAPH **15**(3), 307–316 (1981)
9. Giesen, F.: Phong and Blinn-Phong Normalization Factors, vol. 1, pp. 1–2 (2009). http://www.farbrausch.de/~fg/stuff/phong.pdf
10. Hertzmann, A., Seitz, S.M.: Example-based photometric stereo: shape reconstruction with general, varying BRDFs. PAMI **27**(8), 1254–1264 (2005)
11. Hirschmüller, H.: Accurate and efficient stereo processing by semi-global matching and mutual information. In: CVPR, vol. 2, pp. 807–814 (2005)
12. Horn, B.K.P., Brooks, M.J.: The variational approach to shape from shading. Comput. Vis. Graph. Image Process. **33**, 174–208 (1986)
13. Hui, Z., Sankaranarayanan, A.C.: A dictionary-based approach for estimating shape and spatially-varying reflectance. In: ICCP (2015)
14. Langguth, F., Sunkavalli, K., Hadap, S., Goesele, M.: Shading-aware multi-view stereo. In: Leibe, B., Matas, J., Sebe, N., Welling, M. (eds.) ECCV 2016. LNCS, vol. 9907, pp. 469–485. Springer, Cham (2016). doi:10.1007/978-3-319-46487-9_29
15. Lewis, R.R.: Making shaders more physically plausible. In: Fourth Eurographics Workshop on Rendering, pp. 47–62 (1994)
16. Maurer, D., Ju, Y.C., Breuß, M., Bruhn, A.: Combining shape from shading and stereo: a variational approach for the joint estimation of depth, illumination and albedo. In: BMVC, pp. 76.1–76.14 (2016)
17. Phong, B.T.: Illumination for computer generated pictures. Commun. ACM **18**(6), 311–317 (1975)
18. Seitz, S.M., Curless, B., Diebel, J., Scharstein, D., Szeliski, R.: A comparison and evaluation of multi-view stereo reconstruction algorithms. In: CVPR, vol. 1, pp. 519–526 (2006)
19. Tola, E., Lepetit, V., Fua, P.: A fast local descriptor for dense matching. In: CVPR (2008)
20. Tola, E., Lepetit, V., Fua, P.: DAISY: an efficient dense descriptor applied to wide baseline stereo. PAMI **32**(5), 815–830 (2010)

21. Torrance, K.E., Sparrow, E.M.: Theory for off-specular reflection from roughened surfaces. JOSA **57**(9), 1105–1114 (1967)
22. Wu, C., Wilburn, B., Matsushita, Y., Theobalt, C.: High-quality shape from multi-view stereo and shading under general illumination. In: CVPR (2011)
23. Zhang, L., Curless, B., Hertzmann, A., Seitz, S.M.: Shape and motion under varying illumination: unifying structure from motion, photometric stereo, and multi-view stereo. In: ICCV, vol. 1, pp. 618–626 (2003)

A Wi-Fi Indoor Positioning Modeling Based on Location Fingerprint and Cluster Analysis

Zhili Long[⊠], Xuanyu Men, Jin Niu, Xing Zhou, and Kuanhong Ma

Harbin Institute of Technology Shenzhen, Shenzhen, China
longworking@163.com

Abstract. Wi-Fi indoor positioning modeling based on location fingerprint and cluster analysis is studied. Specific locations are calculated by using RSSI nearest neighbor estimation method, and the positioning accuracies of different terminals are compared. The RSSI signal intensity is used to make clustering process for the fingerprint database. The noise signal in the fingerprint database is filtered. The traditional location fingerprint database, probability estimation fingerprint database and improved clustering algorithm fingerprint database are established. By comparing the positioning error of the testing data in three different fingerprint databases, the accuracy of indoor positioning is improved. Finally, the Wi-Fi data receiving module, the positioning server module and the positioning display module of positioning terminal are established, and the positioning APP is tested in the actual environment.

Keywords: Indoor positioning · Wi-Fi · Location fingerprint · Cluster analysis

1 Introduction

Location-based Service (LBS) has become one of the development and competition in the field of robots, smart home and large shopping malls. To provide more efficient services for people's life and travel, the location information and service demand data can be fed back to the server, and the original data can be further calculated through emerging technologies such as cloud computing and big data [1, 2].

Because of the importance and role of indoor positioning, the domestic and international business circles and academic circles have carried out on the theory and application of indoor positioning. Livetti developed Active Badge applied to indoor positioning system based on infrared technology [3]. iBeacon is the first system of Apple achieving accurate indoor positioning by using Bluetooth technology [4]. Tsingoal Technology developed indoor positioning system by the new technology UWB [5]. In 2000, Microsoft put forward and developed a set of RADAR system based on Wi-Fi positioning, which can realize the continuous tracking of the position [1]. University of California put forward a new Bayesian probability algorithm of positioning model [6]. Haeberlen used the Gaussian method to model the position space of Wi-Fi signal [7].

Although indoor positioning has been researched in research and industry, there are still some problems to be solved. There has not a very stable and reliable product used

© Springer International Publishing AG 2017
M. Liu et al. (Eds.): ICVS 2017, LNCS 10528, pp. 336–345, 2017.
DOI: 10.1007/978-3-319-68345-4_30

in our real life. Wi-Fi is the most widely used technology in indoor wireless network, which brings great convenience to the research of indoor positioning.

2 Wi-Fi Position Estimation Algorithm

Near neighbor estimation algorithm based on signal intensity is an algorithm that can perceive near objects. When signals emitted by the surrounding wireless AP points are measured by mobile devices, the signal intensity RSSI and the physical address MAC are recorded. By comparing RSSI and MAC of different wireless signals with offline database, several fingerprint points which are the nearest to the unknown point are calculated. Then specific location is obtained though the algorithm. The basic principle is that the signal intensities of real-time signals and matched fingerprint points are calculated, and K fingerprint points which are the nearest to the unknown point are selected. The detected signal intensities are recorded as vector $[rssi_1, rssi_2, ..., rssi_m]$, where $1 \leq m \leq n$. The fingerprint signal intensity database is established as shown in formula as followed [8].

$$\text{RSSI} = \begin{bmatrix} (x_1, y_1) rssi_{11} rssi_{12} ... rssi_{1n} \\ (x_2, y_2) rssi_{21} rssi_{22} ... rssi_{2n} \\ ... \\ (x_p, y_p) rssi_{p1} rssi_{p2} ... rssi_{pn} \end{bmatrix} \tag{1}$$

In the formula, each row vector represents a fingerprint point, so there are p fingerprint points. Each point contains the signal intensities of n different AP points.

The distance of signal intensity is calculated as shown as [5].

$$D_m = \left(\sum\nolimits_{j=1}^{m} \left| rssi_j - RSSI_{pm} \right|^q \right)^{\frac{1}{q}}, j = 1, 2, ..., m, 1 \leq m \leq n \tag{2}$$

where

$rssi_{pm}$ represents fingerprint signal intensity in fingerprint database;
$rssi_j$ represents measured signal intensity;
D_m represents the distance of signal intensity;
q represents a natural number which is usually chosen as 2.

The Euclidean distance between the measured signal intensity rss_{ij} and the fingerprint point in database $rssi_{pn}$ is calculated. The calculated distance D_m is rearranged. The minimum K distances away from D_m is chosen as the nearest K fingerprint points. Because the Wi-Fi signal intensity in the indoor space has the characteristic of large floating, so the selected fingerprint points may be the inaccurate fingerprint points generated by the change of the signal, which will cause a larger error in the location estimation. Therefore, the positions are distinguished according to the proportion of different fingerprints, which is shown as [9],

$$(\hat{x}, \hat{y}) = \sum_{i=1}^{K} \frac{\frac{1}{D_i + \varepsilon}}{\sum_{i=1}^{K} \frac{1}{D_i + \varepsilon}} \times (x_i, y_i) \tag{3}$$

where

D_i represents the Euclidean distance,

ε is generally taken as 0.000001 to avoid the special case $D_i + \varepsilon = 0$,

(x_i, y_i) represents the coordinates of the K selected fingerprint points.

3 Improvement of Fingerprint Database

To divide fingerprint points with similar Wi-Fi signal intensities into one class and maximize the difference between adjacent classes, K-mean clustering algorithm [10, 11] is used to classify Wi-Fi signal intensities. The characteristic function of similarity has a great influence on the clustering effect. Euclidean distance function is chosen as the standard to measure the similarity of Wi-Fi signals, as (4),

$$d(rssi_i) = \sqrt[2]{\sum_{i=1}^{n} (rssi_i - rssi_j)^2} \tag{4}$$

The specific steps of K-mean clustering algorithm applied to Wi-Fi signal classification are as follows.

(1) The target sample data that are the classified fingerprint point data n is selected as 14.

(2) The number of divided cluster subsets K is determined. The samples selected are two laboratories and a part of the corridor in the indoor environment, so K is selected as 3.

(3) The initial sample clustering center is selected. The center is selected randomly in the subset. To conform to the actual indoor environment, Wi-Fi signal data from each laboratory and the corridor are selected randomly as the initial cluster head $rssi_j$.

(4) The cluster head $rssi_i$ is taken as the center, and all the data of fingerprint points except other cluster head is traversed. Formula (4) is used to calculate the distances between all fingerprint points data and the three cluster heads. Then the points nearing the cluster head are divided into one class, which is used for the initial classification, as shown in Fig. 1.

(5) The formula (4) is used to calculate in each classification subset until the cluster head position does not change. Then the average of all objects within the subset is updated to the new cluster head. Convergence condition of iterative calculation is shown as followed,

$$E = \sum_{i=1}^{j} \sum_{rssi_i \in C_k} |rssi_i - RSSI_i|^2 \tag{5}$$

where

RSSI$_i$ represents each Wi-Fi signal intensity of fingerprint point,
rssi$_i$ represents cluster head value in divided subset,
j represents the number of Wi-Fi in fingerprint points.

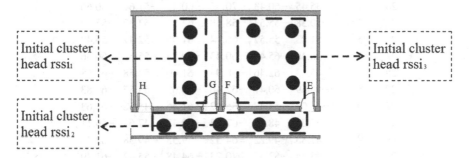

Fig. 1. Division of all fingerprint points

Since each fingerprint point has 3–6 pieces of Wi-Fi signal information, the new cluster head will vary due to different Wi-Fi signals. The Wi-Fi signal fingerprint library should have the following characteristics after the division: the difference between the fingerprint points in the classified subset is the smallest, and the difference between fingerprints in different classified subsets is the largest. This method can not only reduce the complexity of algorithm to improve operational efficiency, but also improve the positioning accuracy when fingerprint points are selected in real-time positioning.

3.1 Establishment of Fingerprint Database Based on K-Mean Clustering

After the collected Wi-Fi signals were filtered by Gaussian filter and average value of each signal was calculated, original fingerprint database is established. After the preliminary classification, the type of signal within the class is determined. Six Wi-Fi signals are contained in the class. The formed fingerprint library is shown as Table 1.

K-mean clustering algorithm is used to calculate the selected original signal fingerprint database. The classification number K is selected as 3. The initial seed cluster heads are selected in each cluster subset. The initial cluster heads are (24, 3) in subset 1, (28, 3) in subset 2 and (26, 9) in subset 3. By MATLAB program, the Euclidean distances between the signal intensities of the remaining points and the signal intensities of the 3 cluster heads are calculated, and the results of the Euclidean distances are shown in Table 2.

According to the Euclidean distances, the fingerprints are reclassified. The minimum Euclidean distance of each row shows the highest similarity to the corresponding cluster head. The fingerprint point and the cluster head are divided into one class. It can be seen from Table 2 that the fingerprints after reclassification are matched with actual indoor environment, and the classification results are shown in Table 3.

Table 1. Original fingerprint database

X(m)	Y(m)	1	2	3	4	5	6
22	1	−54.23	−54.42	−65.24	−53.45	−54.34	−52.86
22	3	−52.86	−55.27	−55.78	−63.58	−59.72	−55.74
22	5	−58.58	−53.67	−62.96	−52.61	−50.65	−54.64
24	1	−55.45	−60.43	−70.46	−60.47	−51.67	−60.66
24	3	−50.38	−55.53	−58.48	−62.37	−53.32	−55.39
24	5	−51.03	−55.57	−66.74	−61.95	−52.47	−56.48
28	1	−48.46	−65.48	−60.43	−59.54	−55.68	−66.36
28	3	−45.33	−62.46	−58.94	−61.40	−52.58	−63.68
28	5	−49.69	−60.47	−62.46	−66.63	−53.57	−69.83
22	9	−48.07	−54.47	−65.32	−61.46	−45.52	−63.63
24	9	−52.21	−48.53	−67.53	−62.47	−47.63	−59.11
26	9	−47.83	−49.22	−64.52	−59.53	−49.38	−62.38
28	9	−53.34	−53.37	−70.23	−64.48	−55.42	−61.49
30	9	−61.42	−58.42	−74.37	−63.63	−59.52	−58.53

Table 2. Euclidean distances

Subset 1	Subset 2	Subset 3
12.1967167713283	19.1550019577133	14.4728573543720
7.48696200070496	15.3999415583307	18.5113397678288
13.9182973096568	20.7773338039316	14.6356516766422
15.0778214606753	15.8132570964998	17.5431384841181
0	11.9979831638488	13.4341319034763
8.41063017853002	13.8908855009319	9.06592521478089
15.5051862291299	6.43345941154524	21.8569188130441
11.9979831638488	0	19.0184042443103
16.3537090594152	10.0754950250596	18.4966618609953
13.5207618128566	12.7240638162499	9.12194606430010
13.4341319034763	19.0184042443103	0
12.4599157300521	15.1033406900593	7.14979719992113
14.0556678959059	17.2220904654458	10.1183546093226
20.7993509514119	24.3506385953223	19.2996347115690

Table 3. Cluster fingerprints

Class	X(m)	Y(m)	Class	X(m)	Y(m)	Class	X(m)	Y(m)
1	22	1	2	28	1	3	22	9
1	22	3	2	28	3	3	24	9
1	22	4	2	28	5	3	26	9
1	24	1	0	0	0	3	28	9
1	24	3	0	0	0	3	30	9
1	24	5	0	0	0	0	0	0

The Fingerprint library is divided into three subsets. The new cluster heads in each subset are calculated and the new cluster head signal value is updated to the new cluster head fingerprint point by MATLAB program. The new cluster head is represented by vector M, as shown in formula (6).

$$
M = \begin{bmatrix} -55.2233 & -54.4533 & -61.3267 & -56.5467 & -54.9033 & -54.4133 \\ -50.0567 & -59.9987 & -62.9183 & -62.0609 & -53.2154 & -62.0667 \\ -52.5740 & -52.8020 & -68.3940 & -62.3140 & -51.4940 & -61.0280 \end{bmatrix}
$$

$$(6)$$

Through the K-mean clustering algorithm, the clustering fingerprint database is established, so that the positioning system does not need to traverse all the fingerprint points in the fingerprint database and only need to calculate the Euclidean distances between fingerprints and cluster head signal intensities to selected fingerprint points from subsets and estimate distances. The clustering fingerprint database can reduce the operation time of the algorithm in real-time positioning, so that the location can be quickly obtained.

3.2   Positioning Experiment Analysis of Different Fingerprint Databases

Twenty five locations were selected randomly and the Wi-Fi signals collected at the locations are made into the test sequence. The traditional location fingerprint database, probability estimation fingerprint database and improved clustering algorithm fingerprint database are used in simulation experiments. The positioning results are shown in Fig. 2.

As can be seen from the simulation map, the positioning accuracy of the traditional location fingerprint database is lower than that of the Bayesian-Gaussian probability algorithm fingerprint database and the clustering algorithm fingerprint database. Bayesian-Gaussian probability fingerprint database is not suitable to be applied in indoor positioning because the fingerprint database needs more samples. From the positioning simulation in Fig. 2, clustering effect of K-mean clustering algorithm is obvious. In the sequence of the locations, the clustering effect can be achieved, and the positioning accuracy is high. Comparison of three kinds of fingerprint database positioning error is shown in Fig. 3. The average errors of three kinds of fingerprint positioning are 2.5355 m, 2.1423 m and 1.5821 m. It can be obtained that the traditional fingerprint location has the worst results.

Therefore, it can be found that the accuracy of Bayes-Gaussian probability fingerprint database is better, and the accuracy of the improved average clustering fingerprint database positioning is improved. Through the comparison of the positioning error sequence, the maximum error of the K-mean clustering fingerprint database is 3.28 m, and the maximum error of the traditional fingerprint database and the Bayes-Gaussian probability fingerprint database is 6.27 m and 5.51 m. The improved clustering algorithm fingerprint database based on traditional fingerprint database can greatly improve the positioning accuracy.

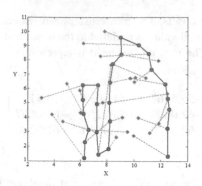

(a) traditional location fingerprint database

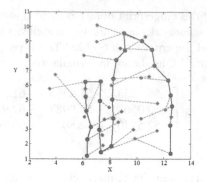

(b) probability estimation fingerprint database

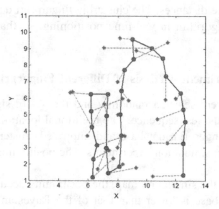

(c) improved clustering algorithm fingerprint
database

Fig. 2. Clustering positioning experiment

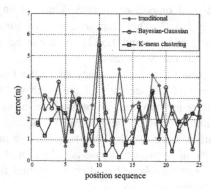

Fig. 3. Comparison of positioning erros

4 Experiment

In a real experimental environment, the Wi-Fi real-time positioning system is tested, and the performance of the positioning algorithm is analyzed. The impact of different terminals on clustering algorithm is investigated. Three kinds of Android mobile phone MiPhone, Samsung and ZTE are taken as the positioning terminals. The laboratories and the corridor are selected as experimental environment. Real-time positioning scene is shown in Fig. 4. Figure 5 shows the details of indoor positioning interface. The black cross is a symbol of positioning terminal, and left digitals represent Euclidean distance. The last column numbers indicate the selected region fingerprint database. Because of different terminal screen size, origin calibration is required at the initial stage of positioning. A laboratory corner is selected as the origin in this experiment.

(a) MiPhone

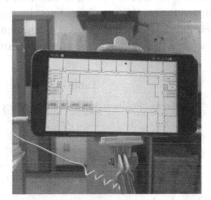
(b) Samsung

Fig. 4. Real-time positioning sence

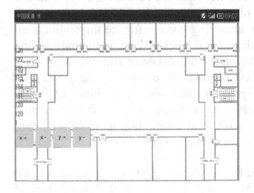

Fig. 5. The indoor positioning interface

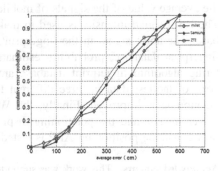

Fig. 6. The accumulative error of three kinds of different terminals

In the real-time positioning stage, a point in the fingerprint database is selected randomly. Three different mobile terminals are selected for testing, and the actual location information is recorded. The value of WKNN_X and WKNN_Y is extracted from APP, and the probability of accumulative error is obtained by calculating the positioning error. The accumulative error of three kinds of different terminals is shown in Fig. 6. It can be seen that the fingerprint database established by using MAC classification and signal intensity clustering keeps different terminals from producing large deviation in the actual experiment.

From Table 4, when different terminals are used to locate, the cluster fingerprint database can ensure that the locations are in the clustering subset to reduce the positioning range and improve the positioning accuracy. By matching of the collected Wi-Fi signal intensities and the clustering fingerprint database, the location clustering subsets are obtained and the most similar fingerprint points are selected. WKNN positioning algorithm is used to calculate the real-time positioning distances which are displayed on the UI interface. Experimental results show that the K-mean clustering fingerprint database has a lower positioning error in the positioning experiment, and can achieve the indoor positioning function.

Table 4. Accuracy of clustering subset

Terminals	Positioning times	Frequency of the same cluster	Correct probability
MiPhone	33	24	0.73
Samsung	33	26	0.79
ZTE	33	27	0.82

5 Conclusion

Wi-Fi indoor positioning technology based on location fingerprint and cluster analysis is studied. Specific locations are calculated by using RSSI nearest neighbor estimation method. The positioning accuracies of different terminals are compared. It is found that the average value of the signals of mobile phones is smaller than that of the notebook. The RSSI signal intensity is used to make clustering process for the fingerprint database. The noise signal in the fingerprint database is filtered. The traditional location fingerprint database, probability estimation fingerprint database and improved clustering algorithm fingerprint database are established. By comparing the positioning error of the test data in three different fingerprint databases, the accuracy of indoor positioning is improved. Finally, the Wi-Fi data receiving module, the positioning server module and the positioning display module of positioning terminal are established, and the positioning APP is tested in the actual environment.

Acknowledgements. This work was supported by the following funds: (1) Project of National Natural Science Foundation of China (51475107, 51605258); (2) Basic Research Plan of Shenzhen (JCYJ20150403161923526 and JCYJ20170413112645981); (3) Shenzhen Technology Innovation Program (JCYJ20150625142543473 and JSGG20150330103937411).

References

1. Bahl, P., Padmanabhan, V.N.: RADAR: an in-building RF-based user location and tracking system. In: Proceedings of IEEE 19th Joint Conference of the IEEE Computer and Communications Societies INFOCOM 2000, pp. 775–784. IEEE (2000)
2. Youssef, M.: The Horus WLAN location determination system. In: International Conference on Mobile Systems, Applications and Services, pp. 205–218. ACM (2005)
3. Want, R., Hopper, A., Gibbons, J.: The active badge location system. ACM Trans. Inf. Syst. 10(1), 91–102 (1992)
4. Patil, A.P., Kim, D.J., Ni, L.M.: A study of frequency interference and indoor location sensing with 802.11b and bluetooth technologies. Int. J. Mobile Commun. 4(6), 621–644 (2006)
5. Hatami, A., Pahlavan, K.: Performance comparison of RSS and TOA indoor geolocation based on UWB measurement of channel characteristics. In: IEEE International Symposium on Personal, Indoor and Mobile Radio Communications, pp. 1–6. IEEE (2006)
6. Schölkopf, B.: Gaussian processes for machine learning. Int. J. Neural Syst. 14(6), 311–315 (2006)
7. Mlakar, M., Petelin, D., Tušar, T., et al.: GP-DEMO: differential evolution for multiobjective optimization based on Gaussian process models. Eur. J. Oper. Res. 243(2), 347–361 (2015)
8. Patil, A.P., Kim, D.J., Ni, L.M.: A study of frequency interference and indoor location sensing with 802.11b and bluetooth technologies. Int. J. Mob. Commun. 4(6), 621–644 (2006)
9. Fontana, R.J., Gunderson, S.J.: Ultra-wideband precision asset location system. In: 2002 IEEE Conference on Ultra Wideband Systems and Technologies. Digest of Papers, pp. 147–150 (2002)
10. Madhuri, G., Bakal, J.: A Hybrid indoor positioning system based on WiFi hotspot and WiFi fixed nodes. In: IEEE International Conference on Engineering and Technology, pp. 56–60 (2016)
11. Sun, Y., et al.: WiFi signal strength-based robot indoor localization. In: IEEE International Conference on Information and Automation, ICIA (2014)

A Real-Time and Energy-Efficient Embedded System for Intelligent ADAS with RNN-Based Deep Risk Prediction using Stereo Camera

Kyuho Lee[1(✉)], Gyeongmin Choe[2], Kyeongryeol Bong[1],
Changhyeon Kim[1], In So Kweon[2], and Hoi-Jun Yoo[1]

[1] Semiconductor System Laboratory, KAIST, Daejeon, Korea
kyuho.jsn.lee@kaist.ac.kr
[2] Robotics and Computer Vision Laboratory, KAIST, Daejeon, Korea

Abstract. The advanced driver assistance system (ADAS) has been actively researched to enable adaptive cruise control and collision avoidance, however, conventional ADAS is not capable of more advanced functions due to the absence of intelligent decision making algorithms such as behavior analysis. Moreover, most algorithms in automotive applications are accelerated by GPUs where its power consumption exceeds the power requirement for practical usage. In this paper, we present a deep risk prediction algorithm, which predicts risky objects prior to collision by behavior prediction. Also, a real-time embedded system with high energy efficiency is proposed to provide practical application of our algorithm to the intelligent ADAS, consuming only ~ 1 W in average. For validation, we build the risky urban scene stereo (RUSS) database including 50 stereo video sequences captured under various risky road situations. The system is tested with various databases including the RUSS, and it can maximally achieve 30 frames/s throughput with 720p stereo images with 98.1% of risk prediction accuracy.

Keywords: Real-time · Energy-efficient · Deep risk prediction · ADAS · Embedded system · Risky urban scene stereo (RUSS)

1 Introduction and Related Works

As advanced driver assistance system (ADAS) and autonomous driving technology have been more emphasized in recent years, Deep Neural Network approaches have gained attention worldwide for robust object recognition such as traffic sign recognition [1], traffic light recognition [2], pedestrian detection [3], vehicle detection [4, 5], etc. However, conventional object detection or recognition are not enough solutions for the autonomous driving technology. Rather the system should be capable of behavior analysis to interpret the motion of the detected objects for intelligent vehicle control, as shown in Fig. 1(a). There were several attempts to the behavior analysis [6–9], but they suffered from their extensive computation.

The problem of realizing such an intelligence into vehicles is not only the matter of software, but also the matter of hardware because the system should not consume too much power while numbers of algorithms must be executed simultaneously. The

© Springer International Publishing AG 2017
M. Liu et al. (Eds.): ICVS 2017, LNCS 10528, pp. 346–356, 2017.
DOI: 10.1007/978-3-319-68345-4_31

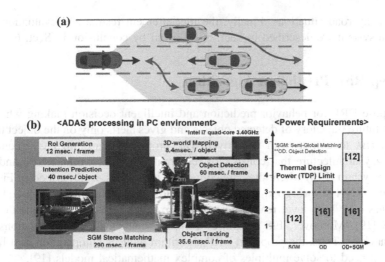

Fig. 1. (a). The needs of behavior analysis and behavior prediction, (b). Examples of ADAS algorithms and requirements.

computationally intensive ADAS algorithms require powerful GPUs or CPUs, however, the power consumption of those computers exceeds the order of 100 W, which is impractical for real applications. For feasible applications, the ADAS computer should consume < 3 W [10] due to the thermal design power limits [11] as well as the demands of increased fuel efficiency and battery efficiency. In addition to the power consumption, the algorithms must fulfill the real-time processing requirement (30 fps). Nevertheless, they failed to satisfy the throughput even with GPUs and CPUs as the examples in Fig. 1(b) shows. Therefore, hardware engineers are in rush to develop state-of-the-art computing engines to facilitate real-time processing with lower power consumption along with the successful development of Deep Neural Network algorithms.

Recently, ADAS processors for low-power and real-time operation have been proposed in the field of System-on-Chips (SoCs) [16–18], but they were only capable of object detection without Semi-Global Matching (SGM) that is essential for accurate depth estimation [12]. Several works on SGM implementation were reported [12–15], but they are not suitable for automotive applications because it exceeds 3 W when used with other functions with the state-of-the-art ADAS processor [16] as in Fig. 1(b). Therefore, a dedicated ADAS SoC and embedded system integrating the chip are necessary for feasible implementation of intelligent ADAS functions.

In this paper, we propose an intelligent behavior prediction algorithm for collision avoidance and a dedicated energy-efficient embedded system (*AUTOBRAIN_ES*) that integrates the proposed low-power and high-performance ADAS SoC (*AUTOBRAIN*) for realizing intelligent ADAS with ∼ 1 W.

The rest of this paper is organized as follows. In Sect. 2, the proposed deep risk prediction (DRP) algorithm which is based on recurrent neural network is described. Section 3 introduces overall ADAS algorithm flow and the *AUTOBRAIN* SoC in detail. In Sect. 4, we present the risky urban scene stereo (RUSS) database captured under various risky road situations. Finally, the measurement results and evaluation of the proposed system are described in Sect. 5, followed by conclusion in Sect. 6.

2   Deep Risk Prediction Algorithm

We propose DRP for behavior prediction and intelligent decision making which predicts the future trajectory of detected objects and gives alerts only on the object that has potential *risk* to collide with the driver. The proposed algorithm has a concurrent neuro-fuzzy architecture that consists of recurrent neural network (RNN) and fuzzy inference system (FIS) where they are connected in a series, as described in Fig. 2(a). By nature, RNN shows good performance in low-level computation while FIS has advantages over high-level reasoning; and neuro-fuzzy takes both strengths of RNN and FIS [19]. Moreover, FIS simplifies complex mathematical computations using fuzzy variables. Thus, the proposed DRP algorithm reduces computation cost because it does not need to solve multiples of complex mathematical models [19].

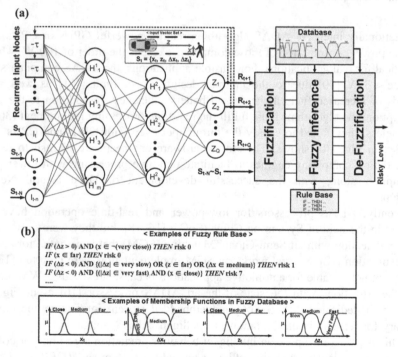

Fig. 2. (a). The proposed deep risk prediction (DRP) algorithm, (b). Examples of membership functions and rule base used for DRP.

The purpose of time-series prediction is to estimate future value in a data sequence by learning the tendency of previous data. DRP belongs to the time-series prediction, because motion state of each object changes with a tendency pertaining to time. We deploy RNN since it achieves robust accuracy in time-series prediction because of its feedback connection, which utilizes the temporal relationship by maintaining its internal state [20]. Moreover, real-time processing of video sequences explicitly involves with spatio-temporal coherency, which provides RNN with high time-series prediction accuracy, because the location and motion of an object between contiguous frames are continuous. In addition, RNN is capable of N-step-ahead predictions in trade of accuracy degradation. Thus, using RNN for DRP provides more future trajectories so that FIS can decide risk level with much information, resulting in high DRP accuracy.

The state of each object is obtained after performing depth estimation by stereo matching, object detection, and 3D-world mapping of which the details are described in Sect. 3. The state at current time t is defined as $S_t = \{x, z, \Delta x, \Delta z\}_t$ where x is lateral distance, z is longitudinal distance, Δx is lateral velocity, and Δz is longitudinal velocity of each object as shown in Fig. 2(a). To interpret the motion of each object, RNN takes a set of motion states of the object as input, (S_t-to-S_{t-N}), which can be interpreted as the history of trajectory and velocity of an object from N previous frames to the current frame. At each frame, RNN is trained on-line for each object using backpropagation [21]. Then, using the trained weight values, feed-forward operation of RNN predicts the estimated future motion states for next Q frames, (R_{t+1}-to-R_{t+Q}), where they become another input set to RNN.

After RNN prediction, FIS takes the whole sets of history and future motion information, (S_{t-N}-to-R_{t+Q}), as input. The computation of FIS begins with fuzzification stage where *crisp values* are converted into *fuzzy variables* by transferring membership functions that are stored in the fuzzy database, as depicted in Fig. 2(a). The membership function represents the degree of class to which a variable belongs. Unlike crisp values, fuzzy variables does not have to belong to a particular class (e.g. *close, far, slow, fast*, etc.), that is a value can be on the boundary of *close* and *medium* in the figure. Then, fuzzy inferencing is performed using fuzzy *IF-THEN* rules stored in the Rule Base. Finally, the result is defuzzified into the crisp variable representing the risky level of detected object by applying center-of-mass method.

Figure 2(b) shows some examples of fuzzy rule bases and membership functions used in DRP. Rule base is the core to decision making; for example, if an object is far from the driver in x direction, then it is not risky. If the object is getting closer to the car with very fast speed Δz and is close in x direction, then the object is risky.

The distances (x, z) and velocities $(\Delta x, \Delta z)$ have different membership functions according to the vehicle's speed, because the fuzzy metric changes when objects are getting closer with faster speed. For example, a driver would think that an object in front of 10 m ahead is "far away" if the speed is slow, but the same object is regarded as "too close" to the driver if he drives with 100 km/h speed. Therefore, membership function should be adapted to different environments. For example, "close" metric should become wider when the speed is high. This adaptation to different environment is done by simply adjusting membership functions. Thus, utilizing FIS in DRP can provide high-level intelligence by adapting membership function in different environments.

3   Overall Algorithm Flow and System Architecture

3.1   Overall ADAS Algorithm

Figure 3 shows the overall ADAS algorithm which runs on the *AUTOBARIN* processor. The system takes two input images from the stereo camera (CAM0, CAM1) and only SGM uses both inputs for depth estimation, while other blocks use the reference image (CAM0) as input. The optical flow features are extracted and tracked, and depth information indicating the longitudinal distance is extracted by SGM. The results are fed to ego-motion compensation block that compensates for self-motion of the vehicle.

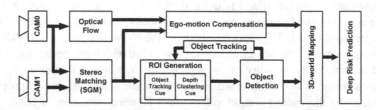

Fig. 3. Overall intelligent ADAS algorithm flow.

For faster processing, we utilize a high-accuracy Region-of-Interest (ROI) generation [22] to reduce the overall computation cost by selecting small portions of image. The object detection and object tracking are performed only within the selected ROIs. Then, the location of detected objects are transformed into the 3D-world coordinate, and DRP of each detected object is performed over every single object that gives alerts on risky objects, meaning they have potential risk to collide.

3.2   Low-Power and High-Performance ADAS Processor

Figure 4 shows the overall architecture of the *AUTOBRAIN* SoC [22]. It consists of 9 accelerators and each of them has dedicated architecture. The pipelined semi-global matching processor computes SGM with 64-disparity range with 30 fps. The optical flow processor extracts and tracks features, and the ROI generation processor accelerates object tracking as well as ROI generation. The object detection processor detects vehicles and pedestrians, and the ego-motion compensation processor compensates for the vehicle's self-motion and computes 3D-world mapping. The DRP processors decide the riskiness of each detected object, and only the risky objects are notified to the driver. The maximal performance of the *AUTOBRAIN* is 502 Giga-Operation-per-Second [GOPS], 30 fps throughput with 720 p stereo images. The average power consumption is only 330 mW at 250 MHz with 862 GOPS/W of energy efficiency.

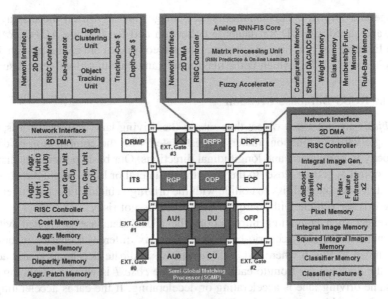

Fig. 4. Overall SoC architecture of the proposed *AUTOBRAIN*.

4 Test Environment and Database Collection

The proposed system is tested with various databases including KITTI [23] and Daimler Stereo Pedestrian Detection [24], which are famous benchmarks for automotive application. However, it is hard to show the effectiveness of the proposed DRP where severe cases show the best performance. Hence, we also created our own database.

4.1 Test Environment

We mounted the embedded system *AUTOBRAIN_ES* onto the test vehicle as indicated in Fig. 5. A laptop is used for data acquisition from the stereo camera, Bumblebee2, via Firewire (IEEE 1394) interface since the *AUTOBRAIN_ES* cannot support ~ 500 GB

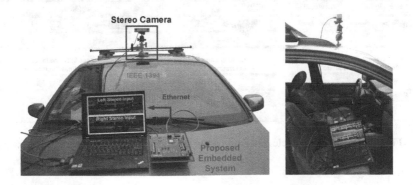

Fig. 5. System environment of the *AUTOBRAIN_ES* mounted to vehicle.

of storage and Firewire. The acquired stereo images are shown on the display while driving, and saved in HDD for database collection and fed into the *AUTOBRAIN_ES* through Ethernet for real-time evaluation. The stereo images are captured with 1024 x 768 resolution @ 20 fps, which is the maximum frame rate that Bumblebee2 supports.

4.2   The RUSS Database Creation

Risky objects are not every object that cuts in the driving lane. In other words, *risk* is not a single variable function; rather it is estimated with the combination of distance and velocity in both lateral and longitudinal directions. Our basic principle is that if the detected object is getting closer to the car either in lateral or longitudinal direction with fast speed, it has potential risk to collide with the driving vehicle. If the target gets away from the driving vehicle with marginal distance, it is not risky.

To reflect such contextual information, the RUSS database is created with two criteria: normal data and scenario-based data. The six different scenarios of our database is shown in Fig. 6 where red and blue arrows indicate deceleration and acceleration of the detected car from/to each position. The *case 1* is when a foregoing object on the same driving lane is accelerating or decelerating. If the car is accelerating, it is not risky. If the object decelerates and gets closer to the driver fast, it is risky because the driver is not decelerating with the ratio of the deceleration of leading object. The *case 2* is when the object is on side lane, and this is not a risky case. The *case 3* is when the object is changing its lane. In both cases of overtaking and undertaking, the *risk* depends on the distance and velocity of the object. If the object is changing its lane but either of longitudinal or lateral distance is too close to the driver, it is risky. If the object overtakes with marginal distance, it is not risky. The *case 4* is similar to the *case 3* but in the other direction. It is risky only when the object is getting closer in any direction with fast speed. Finally, the *case 5* and the *case 6* show fluctuation in lateral and longitudinal directions, respectively. Both cases can be classified as an abnormal driving which indicates drowsy driving or reckless driving. Such an object in these situations have potential risk to collide.

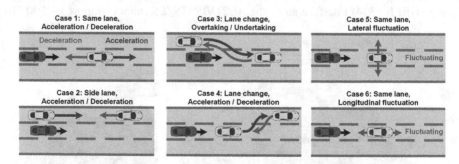

Fig. 6. The RUSS vehicle database depending on the scenarios for evaluation.

Figure 7 shows the subset of our collected database. The RUSS database includes 50 video sequences. For various verifications, the vehicle database includes normal scenes captured from rural, urban and highway environment, while the vehicle scenario database is taken according to the vehicle's speed from urban area (40 km/h and 80 km/h) and highway (100 km/h). For safety, only the normal database contains crowded regions. The pedestrian database is captured from both urban and university campus, and the scenario-based scenes from university campus.

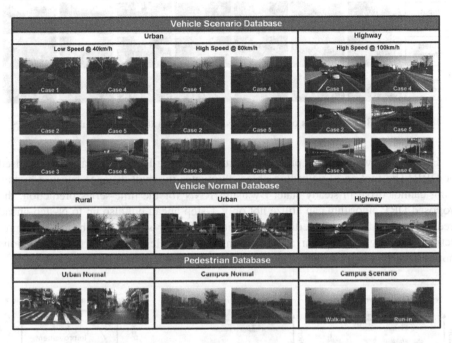

Fig. 7. Examples of the RUSS database. Note that red and blue arrows in the vehicle database indicate deceleration and acceleration of the object, and red arrows in pedestrian scenario database indicate the movement of pedestrian from curb.

5   Measurement Results and Evaluation

As mentioned in Sect. 4, the proposed system is tested with KITTI, Daimler Stereo Pedestrian Detection, and the RUSS databases. Figure 8 explains the example test scenes of object detection and DRP results with the RUSS dataset in different regions. The color of rectangles in the classical object detection indicates the object class: Pedestrian (green) and vehicle (yellow). Unlike conventional object detection returns every objects, only pedestrians and vehicles that pop out in front of the driver and getting closer with high speed are attended with red rectangle before collision in the proposed DRP.

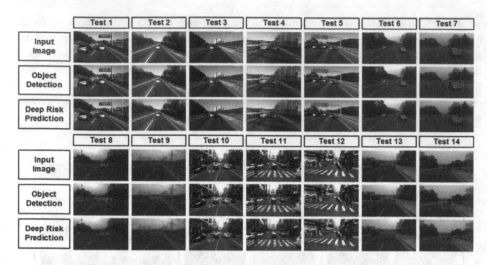

Fig. 8. Test results of the proposed system with the RUSS database

Figure 9 shows the RNN prediction results from the RUSS database that are used for DRP. The motion of preceding object fluctuates in small distance because human being cannot drive in steady state. By using RNN for the time-series prediction, the proposed DRP algorithm can utilize not only 1-step-ahead but also up to N-step-ahead predictions in advance. Nevertheless, predicting further steps ahead brings with prediction accuracy degradation as shown in Table 1. Hence, the further predictions should have less confidence for the final DRP decisions to have high accuracy.

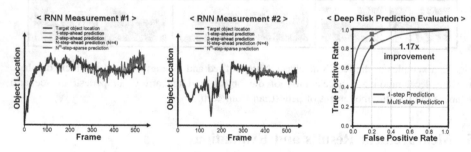

Fig. 9. The measurement results of RNN prediction and evaluation of DRP.

Table 1. Evaluation of error of RNN prediction according to the N-step-ahead prediction.

	Test 1	Test 2	Test 3	Test 4	Test 5	Test 6	Average
1-step-ahead	1.921	2.105	0.9125	1.96	5.015	3.858	2.629
2-step-ahead	2.257	4.197	1.571	4.006	7.619	5.422	4.179
3-step-ahead	3.374	5.450	2.895	5.123	9.879	7.510	5.705
4-step-ahead	4.182	6.298	4.007	6.158	10.58	8.826	6.675

Moreover, the N-step-ahead prediction of RNN only has local information while global motion of the target object must also be considered for robust risk prediction. As shown in Fig. 9, N-step-ahead predictions are sensitive to dynamic changes in motion. In order to enhance the DRP accuracy by employing global motion that is less sensitive to the local fluctuation, N^{th}-step sparse prediction is utilized, in which the on-line learning is taken by every N^{th} frame, together with multiple-step-ahead predictions. As a result, the final DRP accuracy is improved by 17%, achieving 98.1% accuracy.

6 Conclusion

In this paper, a deep risk prediction algorithm that predicts risky objects prior to collision as well as a real-time embedded system for practical application of the intelligent ADAS are proposed. The energy-efficient embedded system integrating a dedicated System-on-Chip consumes only $\sim$ 1 W of power in average when processing 720 p stereo images with 30 frames/s throughput. For validation, we built the risky urban scene stereo database including 50 stereo video sequences under versatile risky road situations and successfully tested with the database. As a result, the proposed deep risk prediction algorithm running on the embedded system achieved 98.1% of risk prediction accuracy.

References

1. Mao, X., et al.: Hierarchical CNN for traffic sign recognition. In: Proceedings of IEEE Intelligent Vehicles Symposium (IV), pp. 130–135, June 2016
2. Weber, M., Wolf, P., Zollner, J.M.: DeepTLR: a single deep convolutional network for detection and classification of traffic lights. In: Proceedings of IEEE Intelligent Vehicles Symposium (IV), pp. 342–348, June 2016
3. Yu, L., et al.: A monocular vision based pedestrian detection system for intelligent vehicles. In: Proceedings of IEEE Intelligent Vehicles Symposium (IV), pp. 524–259, June 2008
4. Fan, Q., Brown, L., Smith, J.: A closer look at faster R-CNN for vehicle detection. In: Proceedings of IEEE Intelligent Vehicles Symposium (IV), pp. 124–129, June 2016
5. Lange, S., et al.: Online vehicle detection using deep neural networks and lidar based preselected image patches. In: Proceedings of IEEE Intelligent Vehicles Symposium (IV), pp. 954–959, June 2016
6. Liebner, M., Klanner, F., Baumann, M., Ruhhammer, C., Stiller, C.: Velocity-based driver intent inference at urban intersections in the presence of preceding vehicles. IEEE Intell. Transp. Syst. Mag. 5(2), 10–21 (2013)
7. Kasper, D., et al.: Object-oriented Bayesian networks for detection of lane change maneuvers. IEEE Intell. Transp. Syst. Mag. 4(3), 19–31 (2012)
8. Barth, A., Franke, U.: Tracking oncoming and turning vehicles at intersections. In Proceedings of IEEE International Conference on Intelligent Transportation Systems, pp. 861–868, September 2010
9. Hermes, C., Wohler, C., Schenk, K., Kummert, F.: Long-term vehicle motion prediction. In: Proceedings of IEEE Intelligent Vehicles Symposium (IV), pp. 652–657, July 2009
10. Forster, F.: Heterogeneous processors for advanced driver assistance systems. Atz Elektronik Worldwide 9(1), 14–18 (2014)

11. Stein, F.: The challenge of putting vision algorithms into a car. In: Proceedings of IEEE Computer Society Conference on Computer Vision and Pattern Recognition Workshops (CVPRW), pp. 89–94, June 2012

12. Gehrig, S.K., Eberli, F., Meyer, T.: A Real-Time Low-Power Stereo Vision Engine Using Semi-Global Matching. In: Fritz, M., Schiele, B., Piater, J.H. (eds.) ICVS 2009. LNCS, vol. 5815, pp. 134–143. Springer, Heidelberg (2009). doi:10.1007/978-3-642-04667-4_14

13. Ernst, I., Hirschmüller, H.: Mutual Information Based Semi-Global Stereo Matching on the GPU. In: Bebis, G., Boyle, R., Parvin, B., Koracin, D., Remagnino, P., Porikli, F., Peters, J., Klosowski, J., Arns, L., Chun, Y.K., Rhyne, T.-M., Monroe, L. (eds.) ISVC 2008. LNCS, vol. 5358, pp. 228–239. Springer, Heidelberg (2008). doi:10.1007/978-3-540-89639-5_22

14. Gehrig, S.K., Rabe, C.: Real-time semiglobal matching on the CPU. In: Proceedings of IEEE Computer Society Conference on Computer Vision and Pattern Recognition Workshops (CVPRW), pp. 85–92, June 2010

15. Michael, M., et al.: Real-time stereo vision: optimizing semiglobal matching. In: Proceedings of IEEE Intelligent Vehicles Symposium (IV), pp. 1197–1202, June 2013

16. Tanabe, J., et al.: A 1.9TOPS and 564GOPS/W heterogeneous multi-core SoC with color-based object classification accelerator for image-recognition applications. In: IEEE International Solid-State Circuits Conference (ISSCC) Dig. Tech. Papers, pp. 328–329, February 2015

17. Tanabe, Y., et al.: A 464GOPS 620GOPS/W heterogeneous multicore SoC for image-recognition applications. In: IEEE ISSCC Digest, pp. 222–223, February 2012

18. Park, J., et al.: A 646GOPS/W multi-classifier many-core processor with cortex-like architecture for super-resolution recognition. In: IEEE ISSCC Digest, pp. 168–169, February 2013

19. Juang, C.-F., Lin, C.-T.: An online self-constructing neural fuzzy inference network and its applications. IEEE Trans. Fuzzy Syst. 6(1), 12–32 (1998)

20. Giles, C., et al.: Noisy time series prediction using recurrent neural network and grammatical inference. J. Mach. Learn. 44(1), 161–183 (2001)

21. Williams, R.J., Peng, J.: An efficient gradient-based algorithm for on line training of recurrent network trajectories. Neural Comput. 2, 490–501 (1990)

22. Lee, K.J., et al.: A 502GOPS and 0.984mW dual-mode ADAS SoC with RNN-FIS engine for intention prediction in automotive black-box system. In: IEEE ISSCC Digest, pp. 256–257, February 2016

23. Geiger, A., Lenz, P., Urtasun, R.: Are we ready for autonomous driving? The KITTI vision benchmark suit. In: Proceedings of IEEE CVPR, pp. 3354–3361, June 2012

24. Keller, C., Enzweiler, M., Gavrila, D.M.: A new benchmark for stereo-based pedestrian detection. In: Proceedings of IEEE Intelligent Vehicles Symposium (IV), pp. 691–696, June 2011

Open-Source Development of a Low-Cost Stereo-Endoscopy System for Natural Orifice Transluminal Endoscopic Surgery

Jia Xin Koh[ID] and Hongliang Ren[✉][ID]

Department of Biomedical Engineering,
National University of Singapore (NUS), Singapore, Singapore
ren@nus.edu.sg

Abstract. As a minimally invasive procedure, Natural Orifice Transluminal Endoscopic Surgery (NOTES) offers many significant benefits over traditional open surgery, including reduced risks of post-operative complication and a faster recovery rate. However, one major challenge commonly faced when performing such procedures is the lack of depth perception provided by standard monocular endoscopes, which can in turn pose a limitation on the effectiveness of such endoscopic surgery. To overcome this undesirable lack of depth perception during endoscopic imaging, stereoscopic vision can be introduced into current endoscopy technology to assist surgeons in performing safer and faster operations with better depth judgement. While there is already a vast range of highly advanced stereo-endoscopy systems commercially available in the market, practical implementation of these systems still remains to be largely minimal as a result of their high costs. This paper presents our approach for integrating affordability with functionality, through the development of a simple, low-cost stereo-endoscopy system. Constructed using commonly off-the-shelf materials, the system runs in real time to present stereoscopic images acquired from the stereo-endoscope cameras into the surgeon's eyes simultaneously, thereby equipping the surgeon with binocular vision for depth perception during endoscopic surgery.

Keywords: Stereoscopic vision · Stereo-endoscopy · Low-cost · Open-source · Depth perception · Matlab

1 Introduction

With the main feature of being minimally invasive, Natural Orifice Transluminal Endoscopic Surgery (NOTES) offers to patients many significant benefits, such as reduced risks of post-operative complication and a faster recovery rate [1, 2]. In NOTES, vision inside the confined spaces of the body is primarily achieved with the help of a single-lens endoscope, which provides the surgeon with a close-up view of the surgical target structure via an insertion through a natural orifice. However, as most endoscopes used in current endoscopy procedures are only capable of providing surgeons with monocular vision, the lack of depth perception in these two-dimensional endoscopic images acquired can pose a great challenge for surgeons.

© Springer International Publishing AG 2017
M. Liu et al. (Eds.): ICVS 2017, LNCS 10528, pp. 357–370, 2017.
DOI: 10.1007/978-3-319-68345-4_32

Depth perception is the visual ability to recognize the three-dimensional structures of scenes in the real world, as well as to understand spatial relationships between different objects. By interpreting a variety of monocular and binocular depth cues that are collected by our visual system, we can obtain useful depth information from the natural environment. Unlike in open surgery, the lack of binocular disparity provided by the monocular endoscopes greatly limits the amount of depth cues that are available for surgeons to perceive depth in the surgical site. Furthermore, with the lack of shadows in the narrow operative field of endoscopic surgery, this eliminates the possibility of using shadows as one of the monocular depth cues for depth perception [3]. Without sufficient depth information present in the endoscopic images, this makes it difficult for surgeons to accurately determine the spatial positions of the endoscope and other surgical instruments with respect to the surrounding anatomical structures [4]. As a result, surgeons must invest a great amount of time and intensive training to achieve the necessary experience required to overcome these limitations when performing endoscopic surgery [5].

To improve depth perception during NOTES, stereoscopic vision can be added into current endoscopic technology to provide surgeons with binocular disparity. With this additional binocular depth cue provided, the replacement of monocular 2D vision with binocular 3D vision clearly has potential in enabling both inexperienced and experienced surgeons to perform safer and faster operations, while minimizing performance errors at the same time [6–8]. Despite these significant benefits that stereoscopic endoscopy can present to both the surgeon and the patient, the actual usage of 3D endoscopes in hospitals still remains to be very minimal today due to the higher manufacturing and implementation costs of 3D endoscopic systems as compared to standard 2D endoscopic systems [8, 9].

In this paper, we will introduce the development of a simple, low-cost stereo-endoscopy system that creates depth perception in endoscopic imaging through the technique of stereoscopy. Using two regular endoscope cameras, a Matlab algorithm acquires simultaneous streams of images from these two cameras. A real-time stereo-video of the surgical scene is then generated and viewed through a head-mounted display, which provides the user with an immersive 3D environment for better depth judgement. Not only does this system not only focus on providing surgeons with better depth perception during endoscopic surgery; it also aims to encourage the use of 3D endoscopy in hospitals by offering to the market a more affordable and accessible version of a 3D endoscopic system.

2 Theoretical Background

In the human vision system, depth perception is achieved through stereoscopic vision, whereby horizontal separation of the two eyes causes the left and right eyes to perceive a real 3D scene from slightly different points of view. As a result of positional differences between the left and right retinal projections of a specific point in the scene [10], binocular disparity thus arises and this subsequently allows the brain to extract useful depth information about the scene.

In computer vision systems, stereo vision can be similarly stimulated through the technique of stereoscopy, whereby the two identical monocular cameras are typically utilized to replicate the binocular human vision system [11]. The cameras are horizontally separated by a baseline distance, thereby allowing them to capture slightly different images of a 3D scene. When the acquired stereo-images are presented to the left and right eyes respectively at the same time, resulting binocular disparities between the two images are then used to derive accurate depth information about objects in the scene [12, 13]. Therefore, the brain is eventually able to generate a complete 3D image of the scene for better depth perception.

Based on the simple principle of acquiring binocular stereo-images with a pair of horizontally separated cameras, this 3D imaging technique can thus be applied to easily convert monocular endoscopy into binocular stereo-endoscopy through the use of dual sensor chips. Replicating human vision system during endoscopic surgery, the dual sensor chips equips the surgeon with binocular vision, thereby providing the ability to perceive depth of anatomies in the surgical image.

3 Development of Stereo-Endoscopy System

3.1 Design of Stereo-Endoscope Rig

Adopting from the typical layout of a stereoscopic vision system, our proposed stereo-endoscope prototype consists of two identical USB video endoscope cameras that are mounted together side-by-side in a 3D-printed stereo rig.

Determining Baseline Separation
As mentioned in the previous section, the baseline distance, which separates the optical centers of the two cameras, is important in allowing the brain to perceive depth from binocular disparities between the left and right images. In order to determine the most effective baseline distance for our stereo-endoscope prototype, it is essential to first understand the geometric relationship between the two endoscope cameras and a target surface point [14], as well as its governing principle of triangulation. In the concept of triangulation, the centers of the two cameras are positioned in a fronto-parallel configuration and horizontally separated by the baseline distance B, as shown in Fig. 1. The baseline distance B and a surface point X on the target object are in turn perpendicularly related by a depth distance Z. Similar to this geometric relationship in a typical stereoscopic computer vision system, the concept of triangulation can be used to define a similar relationship for the human vision system as well.

In humans, binocular vision is influenced by our interpupillary distance or IPD, that is the horizontal distance between the centers of the pupils of our two eyes. Apart from receiving binocular vision from our eyes, humans' ability to perceive depth accurately is also naturally determined by the brain's perception of our arm length [15]. This implies that the optimal distance at which an individual is able to judge depth most accurately can actually be derived from the individual's arm length, as illustrated in Fig. 2. Connecting Figs. 1 and 2 together, we can therefore understand how triangulation can also be used to link the horizontal interpupillary distance between human eyes with the optimal depth perception distance of an arm length.

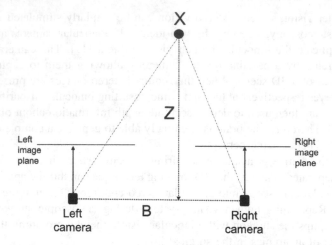

Fig. 1. Concept of stereo-triangulation to illustrate the relationship between two cameras and a target surface point X in real world

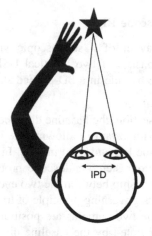

Fig. 2. Humans judge depth most accurately at a distance that corresponds with their arm length, as concluded in a study conducted by Robert Volcic and his team of researchers at the Istituto Italiano di Tecnologia (IIT) on depth perception.

Using the concept of similar triangles, the relationship between the stereoscopic computer vision system in Fig. 1 and the binocular human vision system in Fig. 2, can be defined:

$$\frac{B}{IPD} = \frac{Z}{Average\ arm\ length} \tag{1}$$

where B is the baseline distance between the centers of the camera lens, IPD is the interpupillary distance between the centers of the eyes, Z is the working distance of the stereo-endoscope to represent the distance between B and the target object.

This relationship in (1) provides a straightforward method for us to determine the baseline distance required to achieve effective depth perception with our stereo-endoscope prototype. As both of the USB endoscope cameras used in our stereo-endoscope prototype have a focal length range of 40–60 mm, the working distance of the prototype was thus set to the maximum value of 60 mm. Since a larger baseline will generally produce a better estimate of an object's depth information [16], setting the working distance to this maximum value will thereby allow us to derive a larger baseline distance value correspondingly. The working distance Z here refers to the perpendicular distance at which the stereo-endoscope cameras are able to accurately focus and perceive depth of objects in a scene. Taking the average human interpupillary distance and the average human arm length to be 62 mm and 635 mm respectively, the desirable baseline distance for our stereo-endoscope is calculated to be 5.9 mm according to the above relationship in (1).

Diameter of Stereo-Endoscope Rig

Another important aspect to consider in the design of a functional stereo-endoscope is the trade-off between the baseline distance and the diameter of the stereo-endoscope [15]. While the concept of triangulation relies on a sufficient baseline distance to ensure the accuracy of depth perception, the baseline distance is also limited by the miniature diameter of the stereo-endoscope as well. To accommodate both the baseline distance and the two endoscope cameras with a diameter of 5.5 mm each, the ideal diameter of our stereo-endoscope prototype is hence set to be 16 mm, which is reasonably small to allow the stereo-endoscope prototype to be inserted comfortably into the patient's orifice without inducing damage to the surrounding soft tissues. After determining the dimensions for both the baseline distance and the diameter, the stereo rig for our stereo-endoscope prototype is then 3D-printed. Figure 3 shows the completed product of our stereo-endoscope rig.

In addition to higher fabrication productivity and lower manufacturing costs, advancements in 3D printing technology has also enabled the possibility of designing and producing custom-made products [17]. Thus, by utilizing the method of 3D printing, this can potentially pave the way for the mass production of affordable stereo-endoscopes that can be customized to suit each user's needs. Following the completion of the manufactured stereo-rig, the two endoscope cameras are then fitted into the stereo-rig in the fronto-parallel orientation via manual alignment of the acquired stereo-images.

3.2   Stereo Camera Calibration

In computer vision, camera calibration is used to estimate the intrinsic and extrinsic parameters of a single camera, as well as to describe the geometric relationship between a pair of cameras in a stereoscopic vision system. This information is important for establishing a relationship between 3D coordinates of a world scene and 2D coordinates of the acquired images [18, 19]. Therefore, camera calibration is a pivotal process in

Fig. 3. Completed stereo-endoscope prototype consisting of a 3D-printed stereo rig and two standard USB endoscope cameras

developing a good stereoscopic vision system [20, 21], as it provides the foundation for the system to accurately reconstruct the 3D scene via the principle of triangulation. With proper calibration of the stereoscopic vision system, it can provide an accurate representation of the 3D scene, which in turn enables the user to accurately perceive depth of target objects using reliable point correspondences between the two images [22].

Calibration of our stereo-endoscope prototype is performed using the Stereo Camera Calibrator app that is available in Matlab's Computer Vision System Toolbox [23]. The app uses a checkerboard pattern as a calibration target to estimate camera parameters from correspondences between 3D world points and the acquired 2D image points. For the calibration of the stereo-endoscope prototype, a checkerboard pattern, comprising of black and white squares with dimensions of 0.3 cm by 0.3 cm each, is used as the calibration target, as shown in Fig. 4.

The accuracy of the stereo-camera calibration can be evaluated by analyzing the mean reprojection error, which represents the average distance in pixels between

Fig. 4. A stereo-pair of left and right images acquired from the stereo-endoscope prototype during calibration

detected points in the checkboard pattern and the corresponding reprojected points in the camera images. As the reprojection error quantifies the amount of correction required to adjust one of the two images in order to achieve perfect correspondences in a set of image points [24], a smaller mean reprojection error value will thereby indicate a higher accuracy of the calibration in establishing perfect point correspondences between the detected world points and the reprojected image points. From the stereo camera calibration results, a value of 0.5786 pixels is obtained as the mean reprojection error of the stereo-endoscope prototype.

Since the generally acceptable value range for reprojection errors is less than one pixel, this ensures that our stereo-endoscope prototype is able to acquire streams of stereo-images with reasonably good point correspondences between the left and right images, in turn ensuring the accuracy of depth estimation from these point correspondences.

3.3 User Interface with Matlab

After successful calibration, the stereo-endoscope prototype can then be connected to a laptop or computer, via an USB connection as shown in Fig. 5, to view the endoscopic images acquired from the cameras. With the aim of making the proposed system user-friendly, acquisition and display of the images are compiled into a simple Matlab program code that essentially creates a general user interface (GUI). With the help of Matlab's Image Acquisition Toolbox, the GUI features a split-screen window, on which real-time video previews from the left and right endoscope cameras are simultaneously displayed side-by-side as seen in Fig. 6. This thereby presents users with a real-time stereoscopic vision display of the scene on the computer screen. To enable the user to view the scene in 3D and perceive depth in the scene, this stereoscopic display

Fig. 5. Image acquisition and display is processed on a regular laptop, via Matlab and an USB connection between the laptop and the stereo-endoscope prototype.

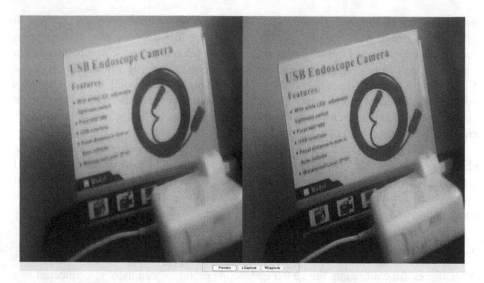

Fig. 6. The Matlab GUI features a real-time side-by-side (left and right) display of acquired endoscopic images.

on the computer has to be directly projected into the user's eyes, such that images captured by the left and right endoscope cameras are presented to the user's left and right eyes respectively.

Additionally, to ensure that surgeons can actually benefit significantly from the enhanced depth perception during endoscopic surgery, it is also crucial to minimize any time lag throughout the process of acquiring, mirroring and projecting of the stereo-scopic images into the surgeon's eyes. Thus, the program code was designed to run in real time, so as to present surgeons with an accurate and updated stereoscopic view of the surgical scene at all times.

With the aim of keeping our stereo-endoscope system as simple as possible, we chose to use a standard binocular head-mounted display for the projection of images from the stereoscopic display on the Matlab GUI to the user's eyes. With their ability to place stereoscopic images right before the user's eyes, the implementation of head-mounted displays thereby makes it possible for the stereo-endoscope cameras to replicate the binocular vision of human eyes even during minimally invasive endo-scopic surgery, where vision is typically limited by the small size of endoscope cameras. Prior to using the Silvertec VR Magic Virtual Reality Glasses (Fig. 7), the stereoscopic display on the computer is first paralleled onto a smartphone screen via a screen-mirroring app, such as Chrome Remote Desktop and MirrorOp. With the Matlab GUI display mirrored onto the smartphone screen, the smartphone then presents the acquired stereo-images to the user's eyes through the virtual reality glasses.

3.4   Creating an Open-Source Guide

Lastly, as part of our objective of encouraging greater understanding and use of stereo-endoscopy, we have created an open-source guide on developing our proposed

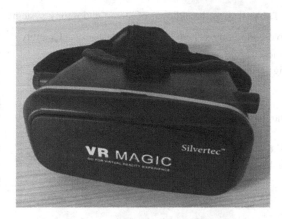

Fig. 7. Silvertec VR Magic Virtual Reality Glasses

low-cost stereo-endoscopy system, which is freely available in the following website: http://bioeng.nus.edu.sg/mm/fyp/opendostereo.htm. The guide consists a step-by-step tutorial on how to manufacture the system, from assembling the cameras and stereo-rig together to running the program code on Matlab for stereoscopic display of the acquired endoscopic images. With this open-source guide, not only does this help users to better appreciate and hence leverage the technique of stereo-endoscopy, they are also able to freely explore the benefits of stereo-endoscopy with minimal financial and legal restrictions as well.

4 Evaluation of Stereo-Endoscopy System

Keeping in mind our primary objective of developing a simple and low-cost stereo-endoscopy system, we focused principally on maintaining a balance between affordability and functionality by building our stereo-endoscopy system with standard medium-quality materials that are largely affordable and easily purchasable. As such, it is therefore not feasible to evaluate the efficacy of our stereo-endoscopy system based on comparison with commercially available stereo-endoscopy systems, since manufacturers of commercial endoscopic equipment usually prioritize quality and product advancement over cost in order to stay competitive in the market.

According to Table 1, the total cost of manufacturing our stereo-endoscopy system sums up to be approximately S$1364.72. With such relatively low material and manufacturing costs, our system is thus able to provide users with a basic and more affordable alternative to commercial stereo-endoscopy systems that can easily cost over a few hundred thousand dollars.

Next, to assess the functional capability of our stereo-endoscopy system in improving depth perception through stereoscopic vision, we performed a simple test by comparing a monocular 2D image (Fig. 10) and an anaglyphic 3D image (Fig. 9) that was created from a pair of stereo-images (Fig. 8). By visual comparison of Figs. 9 and 10, the presence of binocular disparities between the left and right images is clearly

Table 1. Cost breakdown of stereo-endoscopy system

Components of stereo-endoscopy system	Quantity	Unit price
USB endoscope camera	2	S$25
3D-printed stereo rig (printed with ABS material)	1	Approximately S$10
Basic laptop	1	S$1000
Matlab home software with image processing and computer vision toolbox	1	S$293.82
Chrome remote desktop app	1	Free
Silvertec VR Magic Virtual Reality Glasses	1	S$35.90
Total		S$1364.72

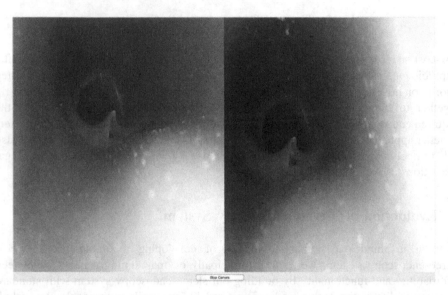

Fig. 8. A pair of stereo-images was acquired from the stereo-endoscope prototype and displayed stereoscopically on the Matlab GUI, depicting a scene taken inside the oesophagus of a medical dummy.

apparent in Fig. 9, as opposed to the lack of such disparities in a single 2D image in Fig. 10. This presence of binocular disparities is essential as a visual cue for understanding of depth in a scene, as the range of the disparities provides important information on the distance of a target object in the scene relative to the camera or observer [25–27]. Disparities of objects in a pair of stereo-images are larger when the objects are near as opposed to when the objects are further away in the scene, where disparities turn out to be smaller instead.

With this correlation between the range of disparity and the depth of an object in mind, we can then make use of the binocular disparities present in Fig. 9 to gain useful information about the spatial relationship of objects in the scene, particularly that of the

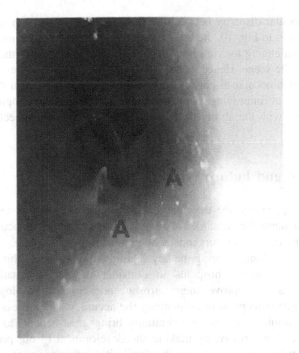

Fig. 9. An analgyph image was created from the pair of stereo-images acquired in Fig. 7 to highlight the presence of binocular disparities between the left and right images.

triangular flap and the bump whose top is denoted by the letter 'A' for easy identification. By observing the anaglyphic image in Fig. 9, viewers can easily deduce the fact that the bump is located in front of the flap, given that the letter clearly generated a

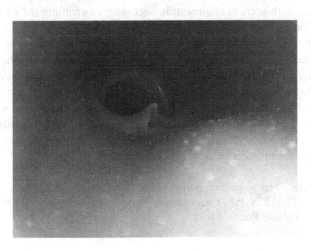

Fig. 10. A monocular 2D image of the same scene in Fig. 7 was acquired from a single endoscope camera.

much larger binocular disparity between the left and right images than the triangular flap. Comparing this to Fig. 10, the lack of binocular disparity in the monocular image makes it more challenging for viewers to judge the relative depths of the bump and the triangular flap in the scene. Hence, through the implementation of stereoscopic vision to generate useful binocular disparities, our stereo-endoscopy system thereby plays a fundamental role in improving depth perception during endoscopic surgery, by assisting surgeons with the ability to deduce depths of different objects in the endoscopic images.

5   Conclusion and Future Works

In this paper, we presented the development of a simple, low-cost stereo-endoscopy system that implements the principles of stereoscopic vision and binocular disparity to improve depth perception of surgeons when performing endoscopic surgery. With affordability and functionality being the key features of our system, this can serve as a form of encouragement for hospitals to consider the implementation of stereo-endoscopy systems to improve their current endoscopic technology. Given the importance of depth perception in influencing the accuracy and success of endoscopic surgery, such an implementation can eventually bring great benefits to both surgeons and patients alike. Furthermore, by making the development of our proposed system freely available online, users can enjoy the flexibility and freedom of customizing the system to better meet their needs, thereby optimizing the benefits of stereo-endoscopy.

To further refine our stereo-endoscopy system, we will examine the use of a standard servo motor for semi-automatic positioning of cameras into the fronto-parallel orientation that is ideal for triangulation. Currently, alignment of the stereo-endoscope cameras into the fronto-parallel orientation is performed by visually inspecting the real-time preview feeds from the pair of endoscope cameras, and then manually rotating the cameras so that both camera previews show upright, parallel images of the target scene. Although such an alignment is necessary in enabling the stereo-endoscope cameras to achieve accurate stereoscopic vision via triangulation, this method of camera positioning is both subjective and time-consuming, which can be an obstacle in producing practical stereo-endoscopes with precise stereoscopic vision. As such, this forms our motivation to automate the process of positioning the stereo-endoscope cameras, by using a standard servo motor to automatically rotate the cameras instead of the current method of doing it manually. Overall, our future works on the stereo-endoscope system will focus on making the system more versatile to meet the different needs of endoscopic surgery, as well as on automating the system to better assist users in performing endoscopic procedures.

Acknowledgements. This work is supported by the Singapore Academic Research Fund under Grant R-397-000-227-112, NUSRI China Jiangsu Provincial Grant BK20150386 & BE2016077 awarded to Dr. Hongliang Ren.

References

1. Zhou, Y., Ren, H., Meng, M.Q.-H., Tse, Z.T.H., Yu, H.: Robotics in natural orifice transluminal endoscopic surgery. J. Mech. Med. Biol. **13**(02), 1350044 (2013). doi:10.1142/S0219519413500449
2. Ren, H., Rank, D., Merdes, M., Stallkamp, J., Kazanzides, P.: Multisensor data fusion in an integrated tracking system for endoscopic surgery. IEEE Trans. Inf. Technol. Biomed. **16**(1), 106–111 (2012). doi:10.1109/titb.2011.2164088
3. Bogdanova, R., Boulanger, P., Zheng, B.: Depth perception of surgeons in minimally invasive surgery. Surg. Innov. **23**(5), 515–524 (2016). doi:10.1177/1553350616639141
4. Yu, H., Wu, L., Wu, K., Ren, H.: Development of a multi-channel concentric tube robotic system with active vision for transnasal nasopharyngeal carcinoma procedures. IEEE Rob. Autom. Lett. **1**(2), 1172–1178 (2016). doi:10.1109/lra.2016.2530794
5. Ohuchida, K.: New advances in three-dimensional endoscopic surgery. J. Gastrointest. Dig. Syst. **03**(04), 2 (2013). doi:10.4172/2161-069x.1000152
6. Van Bergen, P., Kunert, W., Bessell, J., Buess, G.F.: Comparative study of two-dimensional and three-dimensional vision systems for minimally invasive surgery. Surg. Endos. **12**(7), 948–954 (1998). doi:10.1007/s004649900754
7. Peitgen, K., Walz, M.V., Walz, M.V., Holtmann, G., Eigler, F.W.: A prospective randomized experimental evaluation of three-dimensional imaging in laparoscopy. Gastrointest. Endos. **44**(3), 262–267 (1996). doi:10.1016/s0016-5107(96)70162-1
8. Sørensen, S.M.D., Savran, M.M., Konge, L., Bjerrum, F.: Three-dimensional versus two-dimensional vision in laparoscopy: a systematic review. Surg. Endos. **30**(1), 11–23 (2015). doi:10.1007/s00464-015-4189-7
9. Currò, G., La Malfa, G., Caizzone, A., Rampulla, V., Navarra, G.: Three-dimensional (3D) versus two-dimensional (2D) laparoscopic bariatric surgery: a single-surgeon prospective randomized comparative study. Obes. Surg. **25**(11), 2120–2124 (2015). doi:10.1007/s11695-015-1674-y
10. Qian, N.: Binocular disparity and the perception of depth. Neuron **18**(3), 359–368 (1997). doi:10.1016/s0896-6273(00)81238-6
11. Park, S.-Y., Baek, S.-H.: Stereo vision. Series in Optics and Optoelectronics, pp. 1–32. (2013) doi:10.1201/b13856-2
12. Freeman, R.D.: Stereoscopic vision: which parts of the brain are involved? Curr. Biol. **9**(16), R610–R613 (1999)
13. Durrani, A.F., Preminger, G.M.: Three-dimensional video imaging for endoscopic surgery. Comput. Biol. Med. **25**(2), 237–247 (1995). doi:10.1016/0010-4825(95)00001-k
14. Geng, J.: Three-Dimensional Endoscopic Surface Imaging Techniques. Series in Optics and Optoelectronics, pp. 335–360. CRC Press, Boca Raton (2013). doi:10.1201/b13856-15
15. Volcic, R., Fantoni, C., Caudek, C., Assad, J.A., Domini, F.: Visuomotor adaptation changes stereoscopic depth perception and tactile discrimination. J. Neurosci. **33**(43), 17081–17088 (2013). doi:10.1523/jneurosci.2936-13.2013
16. Fanto, P.L.: Automatic positioning and design of a variable baseline stereo boom. Doctoral dissertation, Virginia Polytechnic Institute and State University (2012)
17. Ventola, C.L.: Medical applications for 3D printing current and projected uses. PT **39**(10), 704–711 (2014)
18. MathWorks.: What is camera calibration? (n.d.). https://www.mathworks.com/help/vision/ug/camera-calibration.html
19. Cuevas-Jiménez, E.V.: Intelligent robotic vision. Doctoral dissertation, Freie Universität, Berlin (2006)

20. Cui, Y., Zhou, F., Wang, Y., Liu, L., Gao, H.: Precise calibration of binocular vision system used for vision measurement. Opt. Express **22**(8), 9134 (2014). doi:10.1364/oe.22.009134

21. Liu, H., Dong, Y., Wang, F.: Study on camera calibration for binocular stereovision based on matlab. In: Jia, Y., Du, J., Zhang, W., Li, H. (eds.) Proceedings of 2016 Chinese Intelligent Systems Conference. LNEE, vol. 405, pp. 201–209. Springer, Singapore (2016). doi:10.1007/978-981-10-2335-4_20

22. Machacek, M., Sauter, M., Rösgen, T.: Two-step calibration of a stereo camera system for measurements in large volumes. Meas. Sci. Technol. **14**(9), 1631–1639 (2003). doi:10.1088/0957-0233/14/9/314

23. The MathWorks, Inc.: Stereo Calibration App (n.d.). https://www.mathworks.com/help/vision/ug/stereo-camera-calibrator-app.html

24. Hartley, R., Zisserman, A.: Multiple View Geometry in Computer Vision. Cambridge University Press, Cambridge (2004). doi:10.1017/cbo9780511811685

25. Glennerster, A., Rogers, B.J., Bradshaw, M.F.: Cues to viewing distance for stereoscopic depth constancy. Perception **27**(11), 1357–1365 (1998). doi:10.1068/p271357

26. Harris, J.M.: Binocular vision: moving closer to reality. Philos. Trans. R. Soc.: Math. Phys. Eng. Sci. **362**(1825), 2721–2739 (2004). doi:10.1098/rsta.2004.1464

27. Sousa, R., Brenner, E., Smeets, J.B.J.: A new binocular cue for absolute distance: disparity relative to the most distant structure. Vision. Res. **50**(18), 1786–1792 (2010). doi:10.1016/j.visres.2010.05.035

Image Retrieval

Self-adaptive Feature Fusion Method
for Improving LBP for Face Identification

Xin Wei[1(✉)], Hui Wang[1], Huan Wan[1], and Bryan Sctoney[2]

[1] School of Computing and Mathematics, Ulster University, Jordanstown, UK
wei-x@email.ulster.ac.uk
[2] School of Computing and Information Engineering,
Ulster University, Coleraine, UK

Abstract. In a recent paper, a multi-scale information fusion method
was presented to improve LBP for face identification. However, the additional parameters employed in that method cannot be automatically
optimised. In this paper, a novel self-adaptive feature fusion method
is proposed which extends the mLBP method by removing the need
to optimise these parameters. Our method involves four steps. Firstly,
a large number of initial features are generated. Then, we proposed a
Fisher criteria-based method for evaluating the discriminative capabilities of different feature groups. After that, we proposed a model based on
prism volume for selecting the optimal parameter combination. Finally,
the resulting multi-scale feature are fused by a extended Euclidean distance fusion. Extensive experiments on two face databases have shown
the proposed self-adaptive feature fusion method can find parameters
that are optimal to the data in question, and can produce excellent classification performance.

Keywords: Self-adaptive · Feature fusion · Face identification · LBP

1 Introduction

Face identification has drawn considerable interest in the research community
in recent years due to its wide use and huge potential. Image representation is
a vital process for face identification. Common image representation methods
include LBP [7], HOG [5], SIFT [9], Gabor [6] and so on. Their effectiveness has
been demonstrated through multiple image analysis tasks. However, there is substantial scope for improvement in order to achieve higher recognition accuracy
and better robustness. So researchers are still actively looking for new image
representations or new ways to use the existing methods. Information fusion is
one approach of the latter type.

Information fusion techniques have been applied at different levels of a pattern recognition task – the feature level [10], the decision level [11], and a mixture
of both such as the layered dynamic mixture model [12]. In general information
fusion considers multiple modes of input at different levels, thus it can effectively
alleviate the unreliability brought about by single mode of input [20].

© Springer International Publishing AG 2017
M. Liu et al. (Eds.): ICVS 2017, LNCS 10528, pp. 373–383, 2017.
DOI: 10.1007/978-3-319-68345-4_33

Nikan et al. [13] presented a face identification method using information fusion at the decision level. This method divides each face image into 4×6 regions, then uses *local phase quantisation* (LPQ) and multi-scale *local binary pattern* (LBP) for feature extraction. At the classification stage, a local k-NN classifier is built for each region. And the final classification decision is made by a fused classifier which consists of all the sub-classifiers. In [14], feature-level information fusion is used in a robust face identification algorithm, which extracts global features and local features by discrete cosine transform and Gabor wavelet transform. Then, all the features are fused together through a weighted product sum to build a larger feature vector. The linear regression classifier is used for recognition.

Instead of fusing information from different image descriptors, Wei et al. [2] explored a different way of fusing information for image analysis – fusing information from the same LBP image descriptors with different parameters. The base value in computing an LBP pattern is changed from the intensity of a pixel to the mean intensity of a neighbourhood of the pixel, thus the resulting LBP pattern is less sensitive to noise. This extension of LBP is called *mean-based LBP* or *mLBP* for short, thus an image is represented as an *mLBP feature vector* which is a histogram of *mLBP patterns*. At last, we can obtain mutiple mLBP feature vectors for one facial image, and fuse the resulting feature vectors into a similarity function.

However, this method introduces some additional parameters that need to be optimised explicitly, making it more difficult to use in practice. This paper aims to remove the need of explicitly optimising these parameters.

1.1   Our Contribution

The proposed method in this paper involves four steps. Firstly, a large number of initial multi-scale feature vectors are generated. Then, a novel scoring method is applied for evaluating the discriminative capabilities of different feature groups based on the Fisher criteria. After that, we proposed a model based on prism volume for selecting the optimal parameter combination. Finally, a distance function is designed and used for fusing the resulting multi-scale feature vectors under the automatically learned parameters. Figure 1 shows the pipeline of the proposed method. Extensive experiments on two face databases demonstrate the effectiveness of the proposed self-adaptive feature fusion method – the automatically learned parameters can produce good performance comparable to those optimal parameters obtained by a brute force method. The main contributions of this paper are summarised as follows:

1. A feature generation method is proposed, by which a large number of initial multi-scale features can be generated. This lays a solid foundation for later feature selection.
2. A novel scoring method based on Fisher criteria is proposed, which can be used to sort feature vectors extracted by different parameter combinations according to their discrimination ability.

3. A novel optimum set selection method based on prism volume model is proposed for parameters learning, which can be used to set parameters automatically without degrading much the image classification performance.

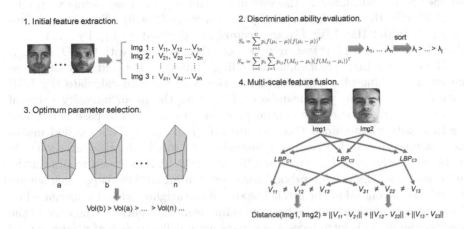

Fig. 1. Pipeline of the proposed self-adaptive feature fusion method.

The rest of the paper is organised as follows. In Sect. 2 the proposed method is presented. The experimental results are illustrated in Sect. 3. The paper concludes with a summary in Sect. 4.

2 Self-adaptive Feature Fusion Method

The proposed method involves four stages. This section will describes the details of each stage. The goal of our effort is to avoid manual selection of parameters during the process of extracting LBP feature vectors and ultimately to improve performance. To realize this goal, the multi-scale means-based LBP (mLBP) [4] is incorporated as it has excellent performance.

2.1 Initial Multi-scale Feature Extraction

LBP has a key parameter – *radius*, which determines the fineness of image texture in representation. The LBP descriptors with different radius can leads to different features. Thus they can also represent different fineness of image texture. However, among numerous LBP versions, some of them have only one radius parameter (e.g. Uniform LBP [7]), and others have more than one radius parameter (e.g. Hierarchical Multi-scale LBP [8]).

In the case of Uniform LBP, a number of LBP feature vectors are generated for each face image by setting different radius values – from its minimum (2 pixels) to a specified maximum. These feature vectors are denoted as $V_{2j}, V_{3j} \ldots V_{ij} \ldots$, where V_{ij} is the Uniform LBP feature vector of jth face image with the radius being i. In Hierarchical Multi-scale LBP (HM LBP), there are three radius parameters need to be set. Here, a base radius vector – $(1, 2, 3)$ and a new term – Fineness Factor (FF) are introduced. Then the final three radius parameters are calculated in the way of multiplying the base radius vector by FF. If FF is 2, the final three radius parameters are $(2, 4, 6)$. Given the jth face image, its initial HM LBP feature vectors are denoted as $V_{1j}, V_{2j}, \ldots V_{ij}, \ldots$, where V_{ij} is the HM LBP feature vector of jth face image with the FF being i.

The existing LBP algorithms, including Uniform LBP and HM LBP, use the intensity value of a central pixel as the base value to calculate the LBP patterns. By contrast, the mean-based LBP uses the mean intensity value of a neighbourhood around the central pixel in question as the base value, and the LBP patterns obtained this way are *mLBP patterns*. This method makes the image representation relatively insensitive to small intensity variations. So in this work, the modified Uniform LBP and HM LBP are used to obtain the initial features. The neighbourhood considered in mLBP is axis-parallel, square shaped, and is centred at the pixel. The size of the neighbourhood is measured by the number of pixels along the horizontal line from the centre to the edge of the neighbourhood. This introduces a new parameter called *radius of neighbourhood* (NR). For example, a neighbourhood of radius 1 has one pixel, and one of radius 2 has $3 * 3 = 9$ pixels, and one with radius 3 has $5 * 5 = 25$ pixels. Figure 2 is an illustration.

Fig. 2. Three neighbourhoods with radius of 1, 2 and 3 respectively.

The final initial features are obtained in the following way. In the case of Modified Uniform LBP, the initial LBP feature vectors are generated by varying the radius and the NR parameters – from a minimum of 2 pixels to a specified maximum. These feature vectors are denoted as $V_{22k}, V_{23k}, \ldots V_{ijk} \ldots$, where V_{ijk} is the Modified Uniform LBP feature vector of kth face image with the radius being i and NR being j. In Modified HM LBP, its initial LBP feature vectors are generated by varying the FF and the NR parameters. The initial Modified HM LBP feature vectors are denoted as $V_{12k}, V_{13k}, \ldots V_{ijk} \ldots$, where V_{ijk} is HM LBP feature vector of kth face image with the FF being i and NR being j.

2.2   Scoring Method Based on Fisher Criteria

In this section, a scoring method based on Fisher Criteria is presented. It is designed to measure the discrimination ability of a set of feature vectors extracted under a given combination of parameters and it gives each parameter combination a score. This score is used for selecting appropriate parameters.

In the first stage, a collection of initial feature vectors are extracted for each face image. We can then construct a matrix for each image, consisting of these feature vectors. The feature matrix for the jth face image in the ith class (i.e. ith person) is denoted as: $M_{ij} = (V_1, V_2, \cdots, V_n)$, where V_n, a column vector, is the feature vector extracted under the nth parameter combination.

Then, we use the between-class scatter matrix S_b to measure separability between different classes and within-class scatter matrix S_w to measure compactness of one class. S_b and S_w are defined as follows:

$$S_b = \sum_{i=1}^{C} p_i f(\mu_i - \mu)(f(\mu_i - \mu))^T \tag{1}$$

$$S_w = \sum_{i=1}^{C} p_i \sum_{j=1}^{N_i} p_{ij} f(M_{ij} - \mu_i)(f(M_{ij} - \mu_i))^T \tag{2}$$

$$f(X) = (||v_1||, ||v_2||, ..., ||v_n||), X = \begin{pmatrix} v_1 & v_2 ... & v_n \end{pmatrix} \tag{3}$$

where $p_i = \frac{N_i}{N}$, $p_{ij} = \frac{1}{N_i}$, N is the number of images, N_i is the number of images in class i, C is the number of classes, μ_i is the mean of instances in class i, μ is the mean of all instances, M_{ij} denotes the jth instance in class i and X is a matrix composed by column vectors $v_1, v_2, ..., v_n$. Here $f(X)$ is used to transfer matrix X into a row vector by computing the norm of each column vector in X.

We hope to find a projective matrix W that projects data from one data space to a new one such that the between-class scatter matrix S_b in the new space is maximised and simultaneously the within-class scatter matrix S_w is minimised.

Thus the Fisher objective function is defined as follows:

$$J(W) = \frac{|W^T S_b W|}{|W^T S_w W|} \tag{4}$$

This problem is equal to looking for a projective matrix W^*, which can maximises $J(W)$; that is

$$W^* = \arg \max_{W} J(W) \tag{5}$$

It turns out the sought-after projective matrix W^* is composed of the eigenvectors corresponding to the largest eigenvalues of $S_w^{-1} S_b$, based on the assumptions of normally distributed classes or equal class covariances. To obtain W^*, let $f = W^T S_b W$ and $g = W^T S_w W - \alpha = 0$, where $\alpha > 0$ can be any constant. The optimisation is thus equivalent to finding a projective matrix W to maximize f under the g constraint. For this we define $L = f - \lambda g$, where $\lambda \neq 0$ is Lagrange's multiplier. By setting the derivative of L with respect to W to zero, we get

$$\frac{\partial L}{\partial W} = 2S_b W - 2\lambda S_w W = 0 \implies S_b W = \lambda S_w W \tag{6}$$

If S_w is nonsingular, then $S_w^{-1} S_b W = \lambda W$. Therefore, the columns of the sought-after projective matrix W^* are the eigenvectors corresponding to the largest eigenvalues of $S_w^{-1} S_b$, i.e.

$$W^* = \left(w_1 \; w_2 \ldots w_n \right) \tag{7}$$

where $w_1, w_2, \ldots, w_n$ are the eigenvectors corresponding to eigenvalues $\lambda_1, \lambda_2, \ldots, \lambda_n (\lambda_1 > \lambda_2 > \ldots > \lambda_n)$.

By combining (4), (6) and (7), the Fisher objective function $J(W)$ becomes

$$J(W^*) = \frac{|\lambda W^{*T} S_w W^*|}{|W^{*T} S_w W^*|} = \lambda_1^2 + \lambda_2^2 + \ldots + \lambda_n^2 \tag{8}$$

This means the bigger the eigenvalue is, the more contribution is made by its corresponding column in M_{ij}. As each column of M_{ij} is a feature vector extracted under a certain parameter combination, we can use an eigenvalue as the score of the corresponding parameter combination. Higher score means stronger discrimination ability of a parameter combination under Fisher Criteria.

2.3   Optimum Set Selection Based on Prism Volume Model

In the first stage, we obtain a set of initial mLBP feature vectors for an image, each of which is obtained under one parameter combination. Then, we get a score for every initial feature vector at the second stage. In order to find the optimal set of feature vectors for an image, we use an optimum set selection method based on the *prism volume model*.

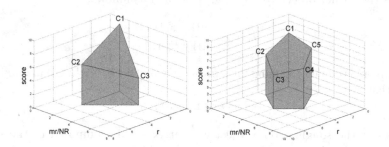

Fig. 3. Triangular prism volume model and pentagonal prism volume model.

In this method, two main factors are considered. The first one is the scores which are obtained in stage 2. The feature vector (corresponding to a combination of parameters) with high score should be considered preferentially, since higher score represents stronger discrimination ability as discussed previously.

The second one is the distribution of different parameter combinations. This distribution should be relatively even as only in this situation can different scales complement each other well. In this context, a Prism Volume Model is proposed, which has different forms under different numbers of scales (for simply, we use the term–'a scale' to represent a parameters combination).

The forming of a prism requires at least three scales (because a prism is a polyhedron made of a base, a translated copy, and at least 3 faces joining corresponding sides) and more time will be required if more scales are considered, so the cases of three scales and five scales are explored in this paper. When three scales are used to find the optimum set, a triangular prism is used. As shown in Fig. 3, z-axis and y-axis represent score and radius (r) respectively, and x-axis represents NR or FF (In the case of Uniform LBP, it represents NR; in the case of HM LBP, it denotes FF). Three vertexes – C_1, C_2 and C_3 – denote any one scale respectively, i.e. one parameter combination denoted by (NR/FF, r, score).

We consider that the optimum set, i.e. the best group of three scales, ought to maximise the volume of this triangular prism, as this goal can well balance the two factors in question. The scales with high scores are preferred, and they lead to an increase in the volume. On the other hand, if the distribution of different scales is more even (separated), the volume of this triangular prism will also be greater. So the goal is to search all initial scales obtained in the previous section, and find out a group of three scales which can maximise the volume of this triangular prism. We use the following way to calculate the volume of a triangular prism: $Vol = area(ABC) * 1/3(AC_1 + BC_2 + CC_3)$, where $area(ABC)$ denotes the area of triangle ABC, and $1/3(AC_1 + BC_2 + CC_3)$ denotes the average length of AC_1, BC_2 and CC_3. Because of the small amount of calculation, we calculate the volumes of every group of scales. All these scales are sorted by their volumes then, and the three greatest scales make up the optimum set. On another aspect, when five scales are used to constitute the optimum set, a pentagonal prism (see Fig. 3) is introduced and the solution is quite similar. The only difference is that we use the following way to calculate the volume of a pentagonal prism: $Vol = area(ABCDE) * 1/5(AC_1 + BC_2 + CC_3 + DC_4 + EC_5)$, where $area(ABCDE)$ denotes the area of pentagon $ABCDE$.

2.4 Multi-scale Feature Fusion

In this section, a feature fusion method is applied to fuse the multiple feature vectors from each face image, which was initially explored in [1,3]. Here, the focus is the distance function which is used for calculating the relationship of two face images. As shown in the previous stages, multiple mLBP feature vectors are generated with automatically learned parameters for each face image by different image descriptors. These *descriptor* can be single scale LBP (e.g. Uniform LBP) or multi-scale LBP (e.g. HM LBP).

Let m and m' be two images. Let $V_1, V_2, \cdots, V_n$ be the feature vectors for image m; and similarly $V_1', V_2', \cdots, V_n'$ be the feature vectors for image m'. Then the distance between the two images is defined as follows:

$$d(m, m') = ||V_1 - V_1'|| + ||V_2 - V_2'|| + ... + ||V_n - V_n'|| \qquad (9)$$

where $||V_i - V_i'||$ is the Euclidean distance of vectors V_i and V_i'. With Eq. 9, different distance function can be obtained for different number of scales.

3   Experiments

In this section, the proposed self-adaptive feature fusion method is evaluated through experiments on two publicly available face image databases – ORL face database [15] and AR face database [16]. Besides, two LBP variants are modified and used in the experiments, i.e., Uniform LBP and Hierarchical Multiscale LBP. In these experiments, we expect that the automatically found feature vectors are comparable with those optimal feature vectors.

In the first set of experiments, we use Uniform LBP and Hierarchical Multiscale LBP as the *base LBP algorithms*. Thus face images are represented as Uniform LBP feature vectors and Hierarchical Multiscale LBP feature vectors at 1, 3 and 5 scales, resulting in 1, 3 and 5 base LBP feature vectors for each image. In the second set of experiments, mLBP is applied on the Uniform LBP and Hierarchical Multiscale LBP at 1, 3 and 5 scales, resulting in multiple mLBP vectors for each image. In the third, final set of experiments we test our self-adaptive feature fusion method (i.e. add the parameters self-adaptive module compared with the second set of experiments). In all experiments, the image distance function in Eq. 9 is used to measure image distance, and then use 1-nearest neighbour classifier. It's important to note that, in the first and second sets of experiments, optimal parameter combination search is used (i.e., consider all possible parameter combinations and then select the combination that gives the best result) resulting in optimal feature vectors. For dimension reduction, we apply the popular PCA + LDA [17,18] combination to all LBP vectors in the experiments. As a benchmark, we also consider the well-known Principal Component Analysis as a face identification algorithm [17] and its variant 2D Principal Component Analysis (2DPCA) [19].

ORL database [15] contains 400 images of 40 people and each person has 10 images, where the face images were taken at different time, under different illumination, facial expression and facial details (wearing glasses or not). In the experiments, we use 5 images of each person for training while use the other 5 images for testing. AR face database [16] has more than 4000 images taken from 126 people, among which there are 70 men and 56 women. We use a subset of the images in our experiments, which contains 1400 face images from 100 people with 14 images for each person. After the pre-processing, the face portion of each image is cropped out and normalised to the size of 100 * 80 pixel. And seven images of each person are used for training while the other seven images are used for testing.

Table 1 lists the recognition accuracy of different methods on ORL database. It is clear that the recognition accuracy of Uniform LBP increased by up to 6.0% after multi-scale mLBP is applied, and the recognition accuracy of Hierarchical Multiscale LBP increased from the original 95.5% to the highest 99.0% after multi-scale mLBP is used. It is also clear that the proposed self-adaptive method

Table 1. Recognition accuracy of different methods on the ORL and AR database. (* represents the original methods.)

	Accuracy on ORL			Accuracy on AR		
	1 scale	3 scale	5 scale	1 scale	3 scale	5 scale
PCA		88.5%			67.4%	
2DPCA		90.5%			72.1%	
Uniform LBP*	91.5%	94.0%	94.0%	61.4%	75.9%	76.7%
Uniform mLBP	91.5%	97.5%	97.5%	61.4%	80.7%	81.3%
Self-adaptive Uniform mLBP		97.5%	97.5%		80.6%	81.1%
HM LBP*	95.5%	98.0%	97.0%	96.1%	97.1%	97.9%
HM mLBP	97.0%	99.0%	98.0%	97.1%	98.1%	99.0%
Self-adaptive HM mLBP		98.0%	98.0%		94.4%	97.6%

has no reduction in accuracy compared with when the optimal feature vectors are used, in all cases except that there is a 1% decrease in HM mLBP at 3 scales.

Table 1 also shows the recognition accuracy of different methods on the AR database. It is can be seen that the recognition accuracy of Uniform LBP increased by up to 19.9% after applying multi-scale mLBP, and the recognition accuracy of Hierarchical Multiscale LBP increased from the original 96.1% to the highest 99.0% after multi-scale mLBP is used. It is also clear that the proposed self-adaptive method has a negligible (0.2%) reduction in accuracy in the case of Uniform LBP. In the case of multi-scale HM LBP, the self-adaptive method has a reduction of 3.7% in accuracy at 3 scales due to a lack of multi-scale information and a reduction of 1.4% at 5 scales.

The experiments on both face databases have shown that the self-adaptive feature fusion method proposed in this paper can automatically select feature vectors that are comparable to those optimal feature vectors, which requires time and effort to find. In effect, the proposed method is able to learn parameters automatically.

4   Conclusion

This paper presents a novel self-adaptive feature fusion method, which can automatically select good mLBP feature vectors and then fuses them through an image distance function which can be used to classify images. This reduces the need to select the optimal feature vectors in a brute force fashion, which requires time and effort. The experimental results show that the proposed method can automatically select feature vectors that are comparable to those optimal feature vectors. In effect, the proposed method is able to learn parameters automatically.

References

1. Wei, X., Wang, H., Guo, G., Wan, H.: A general weighted multi-scale method for improving LBP for face recognition. In: Hervás, R., Lee, S., Nugent, C., Bravo, J. (eds.) UCAmI 2014. LNCS, vol. 8867, pp. 532–539. Springer, Cham (2014). doi:10.1007/978-3-319-13102-3_84
2. Wei, X., Wang, H., Guo, G., Wan, H.: Multiplex image representation for enhanced recognition. Int. J. Mach. Learn. Cybern. 1–10 (2015)
3. Wei, X., Guo, G., Wang, H., Wan, H.: A multiscale method for HOG-based face and palmprint recognition. Technical report, Ulster University. Accepted by 8th International Conference on Intelligent Robotics and Applications (2015)
4. Wei, X., Wang, H., Guo, G., Wan, H.: Multiscale feature fusion for face recognition. Accepted by the 3rd IEEE International Conference on Cybernetics (2017)
5. Dalal, N., Triggs, B.: Histograms of oriented gradients for human detection. In: IEEE Computer Society Conference on Computer Vision and Pattern Recognition, CVPR 2005, vol. 1, pp. 886–893. IEEE (2005)
6. Liu, C., Wechsler, H.: Gabor feature based classification using the enhanced fisher linear discriminant model for face identification. IEEE Trans. Image Process. 11(4), 467–476 (2002)
7. Ojala, T., Pietikainen, M., Maenpaa, T.: Multiresolution gray-scale and rotation invariant texture classification with local binary patterns. IEEE Trans. Pattern Anal. Mach. Intell. 24(7), 971–987 (2002)
8. Guo, Z., Zhang, D., Mou, X.: Hierarchical multiscale LBP for face and palmprint recognition. In: 2010 17th IEEE International Conference on Image Processing (ICIP), pp. 4521–4524. IEEE (2010)
9. Lowe, D.G.: Distinctive image features from scale-invariant keypoints. Int. J. Comput. Vis. 60(2), 91–110 (2004)
10. Hou, J., Pelillo, M.: A simple feature combination method based on dominant sets. Pattern Recogn. 46(11), 3129–3139 (2013)
11. Zhou, H., Yuan, Y., Sadka, A.H.: Application of semantic features in face recognition. Pattern Recogn. 41(10), 3251–3256 (2008)
12. Wu, Z., Cai, L., Meng, H.: Multi-level fusion of audio and visual features for speaker identification. In: Zhang, D., Jain, A.K. (eds.) ICB 2006. LNCS, vol. 3832, pp. 493–499. Springer, Heidelberg (2005). doi:10.1007/11608288_66
13. Nikan, S., Ahmadi, M.: Local gradient-based illumination invariant face recognition using local phase quantisation and multi-resolution local binary pattern fusion. IET Image Process. 9(1), 12–21 (2014)
14. Gao, Z., Ding, L., Xiong, C., Huang, B.: A robust face recognition method using multiple features fusion and linear regression. Wuhan Univ. J. Nat. Sci. 19(4), 323–327 (2014)
15. http://www.cl.cam.ac.uk/research/dtg/attarchive/facedatabase.html
16. Martinez, A., Benavente, R.: The AR face database. CVC Technical report 24, Report 24 (1998)
17. Turk, M.A., Pentland, A.P.: Face identification using eigenfaces. In: Proceedings IEEE Computer Society Conference on Computer Vision and Pattern Recognition, CVPR 1991, pp. 586–591. IEEE (1991)
18. Belhumeur, P.N., Hespanha, J.P., Kriegman, D.: Eigenfaces vs. fisherfaces: recognition using class specific linear projection. IEEE Trans. Pattern Anal. Mach. Intell. 19(7), 711–720 (1997)

19. Yang, J., Zhang, D., Frangi, A.F., Yang, J.: Two-dimensional PCA: a new approach to appearance-based face representation and recognition. IEEE Trans. Pattern Anal. Mach. Intell. **26**(1), 131–137 (2004)
20. Rogova, G.L., Nimier, V.: Reliability in information fusion: literature survey. In:
Proceedings of the Seventh International Conference on Information Fusion, pp.
1158–1165 (2004)

Bridging Between Computer and Robot Vision Through Data Augmentation: A Case Study on Object Recognition

Antonio D'Innocente[✉], Fabio Maria Carlucci, Mirco Colosi,
and Barbara Caputo

Sapienza University of Rome, Rome, Italy
ant.dinnocente@gmail.com

Abstract. Despite the impressive progress brought by deep network in visual object recognition, robot vision is still far from being a solved problem. The most successful convolutional architectures are developed starting from ImageNet, a large scale collection of images of object categories downloaded from the Web. This kind of images is very different from the situated and embodied visual experience of robots deployed in unconstrained settings. To reduce the gap between these two visual experiences, this paper proposes a simple yet effective data augmentation layer that zooms on the object of interest and simulates the object detection outcome of a robot vision system. The layer, that can be used with any convolutional deep architecture, brings to an increase in object recognition performance of up to 7%, in experiments performed over three different benchmark databases. An implementation of our robot data augmentation layer has been made publicly available.

1 Introduction

The ability to understand what they see is crucial for autonomous robots deployed in unconstrained settings, such as those shared with humans. Recent advances in visual recognition, induced by the deep learning tidal wave, has brought high hopes that the very same impressive progresses seen in the computer vision community would have been quickly shared by the robot vision community [1]. Experimental evaluations have repeatedly shown that this is not the case. Although the use of convolutional neural networks has brought important improvements in performance, compared to approaches based on shallow classifiers, several authors have shown that we are still far from the level of performance necessary to robots in the wild (we refer to Sect. 2 for a review of previous work on the topic).

An issue that has called considerable attention is the difference between web images and robot images (Fig. 1). Web images, that constitute the main training resource of modern deep networks, tend to show objects in the center of the scene,

B. Caputo—This work was partially supported by the ERC grant 637076 - RoboExNovo (B.C.), and the CHIST-ERA project ALOOF (B.C, F. M. C., A.D.).

M. Liu et al. (Eds.): ICVS 2017, LNCS 10528, pp. 384–393, 2017.
DOI: 10.1007/978-3-319-68345-4_34

in various contexts, from canonical view-points, i.e. view-points capturing the most informative parts of the object of interest (Fig. 1, left). As opposed to this, robots acquire snapshots of objects to be recognised based on the figure-ground segmentation algorithms they are equipped with. This often leads to objects imaged at unusual angles and scale, and only partially visible in the image (Fig. 1, right). This is a crucial issue, because the overwhelming majority of deep visual recognition networks are trained over ImageNet, a 1.4 M images database of 1000 object categories derived from the Web [2]. Hence, any visual object recognition system attempting to use such deep networks for robot vision, is attempting to recognise objects based on a very different type of visual information than what the robot perceives in its situated scenario.

The focus of this paper is on how to bridge among these two different visual domains, with the aim to increase the performance of deep visual object recognition networks when used on robotic data. We propose to enrich the original web images with rescaled and cropped version of the original view, so to simulate to a certain extent the visual experience of an autonomous agent. The procedure can be integrated into any deep architecture as a data augmentation layer (Fig. 2). Extensive experiments on 3 different databases and 2 different deep networks show that our approach leads to increases in absolute performance of up to 7%. A python implementation of our data augmentation strategy is available at https://sites.google.com/view/robocrop/.

Fig. 1. Images from classes *stapler, water bottle, cellphone, spray can* as seen in *Imagenet* (left) and *JHUIT-50, HelloiCubWorld* (right)

The rest of the paper is organized as follows: after a review of relevant literature (Sect. 2), we describe our strategy for generating robot-like object images starting from web images, and how the data augmentation layer works in practice. Section 4 reports our experimental setup and the results obtained over the Washington-RGBD [10], JHUIT-50 [8] and HelloiCubWorld [9] databases. We conclude with a summary and discussing future research directions.

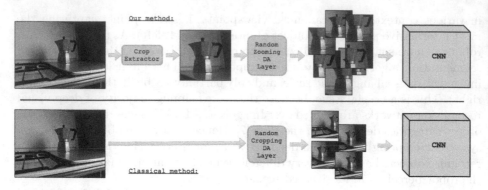

Fig. 2. Above, the proposed pipeline: from each image we extract one or more objects, using bounding box annotations. Each centered object goes then through our data augmentation layer which extracts a number of crops at varying zoom levels. Below, the classical [4] approach: each image is randomly cropped by a small amount, with no notion of objectness.

2   Related Work

State of the art work in computer vision reveals that deep convolutional models, when pre-trained on a large and diverse dataset like ImageNet [3], are able to extract general and high level information from images [7]. Exploiting this generalized knowledge for new tasks is common practice. In [11], the use of a pre-trained convolutional model, installed on a robot, was combined with context aware semantic web mining for object recognition. In [14], a pre-trained CNN model was used as feature extractor on the RGB-D Object dataset [10] for pose estimation. Large convolutional models pre-trained on RGB images have been used to extract rich features from depth images by representing depth with three channels [12,13] combined RGB and depth classification, parallelizing deep pre-trained models for each modality. Robot images are usually more prone to scaling and translation noise; [15] shows behaviours of features extracted from pre-trained deep models with different degrees of visual transformations. While the robot vision community is exploring several valid strategies, recent works in the field share the same specific step: they use an AlexNet [4] model pre-trained on the ImageNet 1000 object categories dataset [2] for classification or feature extraction on RGB images. We argue that features extracted from these models, while having shown generality [7], are still tied to the original representations, suffering from their own bias. Web images are directly downloaded from the web, and often they have been acquired by humans and subjected to manual cleaning and annotation. Hence, they are prone to heavy background noise. Robot acquired images are often taken in large quantities in the same setting instead, such as the same room or office, and are subject to a different kind of bias. The robot often walks around the office, taking pictures of various things of interest. In our approach we train deep convolutional models by artificially injecting robot images' bias on the training dataset. By applying bounding box cropping and random zooming transformations on web images, we make them more similar to robot images and subsequently test how our adapted models perform in robot vision task against models trained on original images. We are not aware of any previous work in this direction.

3   Robot Specific Data Augmentation

We propose a methodology for improving performances in robot vision tasks when pre-training deep convolutional models on web images (Fig. 2).

Very often CNN models pre-trained on the 1000 object categories dataset [2] are used for feature extraction on robotic tasks. Classification scores in these scenarios are good but not exceptional. The state of the art seems to suggest problems related to a domain gap between ImageNet's [3] web acquired images and robot images. Web images are often acquired by humans and the main source of noise is the background, which may vary significantly between pictures belonging to the same category. Robot acquired images are subject to a different kind of noise, objects are usually zoomed in or translated, while the background view is limited.

Since pre-trained models are trained on web pictures, we process the CNN's training dataset to make its images resemble robot-acquired images, so that our deep convolutional models learn features more resistant to robot vision noise. Instead of training directly on web images, we use off-line preprocessing to build a crop dataset by using bounding boxes annotation. We also enlarge original bounding boxes by 20% before cropping. At training time, we use random zooming on the object crops to make the network see randomly zoomed versions of the same object. The data-augmentation extracts patches at casual position, with a random zooming factor between 1.0x and 2.0x. After zooming, images got resized to fit the first convolutional layer's input size using bilinear interpolation.

Combinining our off-line and on-line processing methodologies we trained networks on patches containing zoomed-in or partially excluded objects, common properties for robot images, and results show that models pre-trained on these object parts significantly outperform models pre-trained on original images in every robot vision task we tested them for.

4   Experiments

We train two models for each of our training datasets, a model based on the "AlexNet" architecture [4] and a model based on the "Inception-v3" architecture [6], using the data-augmentation techniques described in previous section. We then select several robotic datasets with centered, non-centered, zoomed-in and artificially translated images, and use our pre-trained CNNs models as features extractors on these datasets [7]. Lastly, we run a linear classifier on the extracted features to evaluate how well our models have generalized to the robotic tasks.

4.1 Databases

CNN's Training Datasets. We collect 3 datasets from ImageNet [3] for training our models. We will refer to these datasets as Baseline, Clean Crops and Dirty Crops for the rest of the article. The Baseline dataset consists of a set of images, all having bounding boxes annotations, for which, like in the 1000 object categories dataset [2], there is no semantic overlap between the classes. Clean Crops is another dataset without semantic overlaps between the classes, it contains 930.000 images, obtained from Baseline by cropping objects outside original pictures using bounding boxes annotation. For the Dirty Crops dataset, we used every ImageNet's bounding box to crop objects, and as a result, this dataset contains many IS-A relationships between its classes, but, with approximately 1.2 million images, its also larger than the Clean Crops.

Robotic Datasets. We run our experiments on the JHUIT-50 [8], HelloiCub-World [9] and RGB-D Object [10] datasets. The JHUIT-50 dataset is focused on the task of fine-grained instance recognition and consists of 50 objects and hand tools, with images being acquired by rotating a camera around the objects at different heights - it contains almost 15.000 images. HelloiCubWorld contains a "human" and a "robot" dataset. Images in the datasets are obtained by using human or robot modes of acquisition. In the human mode acquisition, a human moves the object while the robot tracks it. In the robot mode acquisition, the robot moves the object in its own hand, tracking it. The HelloiCubWorld-human dataset is obtained by using human mode acquisition, and the HelloiCubWorld-robot dataset is obtained by using robot mode acquisition. Both datasets consist of objects organized in 7 classes and each of them contain 7.000 images. The RGB-D Object dataset has been obtained by collecting frames from objects spinning on a turntable, it consists of 300 objects organized into 51 categories; with around 50.000 images it's the largest we experiment on. We also created artificially translated versions of the RGB-D Object dataset to study translation invariance of features extracted by our models. We created 3 additional versions, RGB-D_tr_10%, RGB-D_tr_20% and RGB-D_tr_30% for which we have randomly translated original crops by 10%, 20% and 30% respectively (see Fig. 3).

4.2 Architectures

AlexNet. AlexNet [4] is the architecture behind the competition winning model for the ILSVRC 2012 competition [2], it consists of 5 convolutional layer, followed by 3 fully connected layer. The AlexNet is currently one of the most widely used architecture in the robotic community.

Inception-v3. The Inception-v3 [6] is an improved version of the original Inception architecture [5]. It consists of several inception modules stacked on top of each other. Compared to the AlexNet [4], the Inception-v3 is a more advanced architecture which achieved far better classification results on the ILSVRC competition.

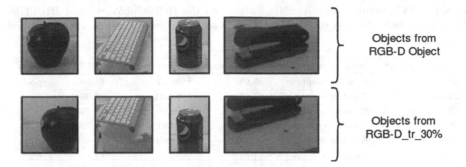

Fig. 3. Original crops from the RGB-D Object dataset (top) and the same crops after random translations (bottom)

4.3 Results

For each architecture, we trained one model on the Baseline dataset with random cropping, and two models for each of the crops datasets, one with random cropping and the other with random zooming. On AlexNet, random cropping was obtained by taking random 227×227 patches from the 256×256 input images; on Inception-v3, we took 299×299 patches on 384×384 input images. AlexNet models were trained by setting initial learning rate at 0.01 and dividing it by a factor of 3 each time validation loss didn't improve for 4 consecutive epochs; this procedure was repeated 6 times. Inception-v3 models were trained by setting learning rate at 0.01 and dividing it by a factor of 10 each time validation loss got worse, with this procedure being repeated 2 times. All models were also trained using random horizontal flipping.

After training, we extracted features of robotic images from different layers. On the AlexNet models, we extracted features from pool5, fc6 and fc7. On the Inception-v3 models, we extracted features from a max pooling layer and an average pooling layer we placed on top of the last convolution; for both of those layers we used kernel size 8 and stride 2.

Final classification occurred by running a linear SVM on extracted features. Hyperparameter for the SVM was chosen by running a 3-fold cross validation for the RGB-D Object dataset and its variations, while it was left at the default value for the other robotic datasets.

Model's results are summarized in the following tables and charts. Accuracy score refers to results obtained by running the linear classifiers on features extracted by a model trained on a specific dataset and with a corresponding data-augmentation technique. Each Table refers to features extracted from a certain architecture, which is indicated in the caption (Tables 1 and 2).

On Inception-v3 models, features extracted from the average pooling layer provided inferior results compared to features extracted from the max pooling layer for the JHUIT-50 and HelloiCubWorld datasets. For this reason we didn't test the average pooling's features on the RGB-D Object datasets and its variations.

Table 1. SVM results using AlexNet features on the HelloiCubWorld and JHUIT-50 datasets. In bold the best results for a given layer. Best overall results are highlighted in red.

Training dataset	Data augmentation	iCub (human)	iCub (robot)	JHUIT-50	Layer
Baseline	Random cropping	93.66	94.11	85.00	pool5
Clean crops	Random cropping	94.14	**96.31**	85.36	
Clean crops	Random zooming	93.49	96.09	85.79	
Dirty crops	Random cropping	93.66	94.11	85.00	
Dirty crops	Random zooming	**94.60**	95.60	87.05	
Baseline	Random cropping	91.91	92.91	84.53	fc6
Clean crops	Random cropping	93.09	94.00	84.13	
Clean crops	Random zooming	94.26	**97.54**	84.04	
Dirty crops	Random cropping	93.27	94.91	84.67	
Dirty crops	Random zooming	94.86	96.89	**85.41**	
Baseline	Random cropping	89.94	90.66	**81.82**	fc7
Clean crops	Random cropping	90.46	93.43	81.58	
Clean crops	Random zooming	92.86	97.89	81.18	
Dirty crops	Random cropping	**93.46**	95.17	81.62	
Dirty crops	Random zooming	93.23	96.11	81.09	

Table 2. SVM results using AlexNet features on the RGB-D Object dataset and it's artificially translated versions. In bold the best results for a given layer. Best overall results are highlighted in red.

Training dataset	Data augmentation	RGB-D Object	Tr_10%	Tr_20%	Tr_30%	Layer
Baseline	Random cropping	84.90 ± 1.02	82.92 ± 1.17	79.41 ± 1.30	76.74 ± 1.53	pool5
Clean crops	Random cropping	86.29 ± 1.83	84.85 ± 1.56	81.85 ± 1.81	79.68 ± 1.75	
Clean crops	Random zooming	88.38 ± 1.42	86.55 ± 1.63	83.64 ± 1.56	81.70 ± 1.62	
Dirty crops	Random cropping	87.53 ± 1.97	85.79 ± 1.97	82.88 ± 1.89	80.49 ± 1.76	
Dirty crops	Random zooming	88.67 ± 1.81	87.13 ± 2.07	84.71 ± 2.07	82.31 ± 2.07	
Baseline	Random cropping	81.99 ± 1.20	80.28 ± 1.36	77.66 ± 1.32	75.39 ± 1.43	fc6
Clean crops	Random cropping	84.38 ± 2.00	82.94 ± 2.01	80.36 ± 1.76	77.74 ± 1.70	
Clean crops	Random zooming	85.36 ± 1.59	83.21 ± 2.43	81.82 ± 2.03	80.41 ± 1.89	
Dirty crops	Random cropping	85.76 ± 2.22	84.11 ± 2.31	80.90 ± 2.10	79.02 ± 1.81	
Dirty crops	Random zooming	**86.05 ± 1.99**	**84.54 ± 2.29**	**82.75 ± 2.02**	80.93 ± 1.74	
Baseline	Random cropping	78.15 ± 1.40	76.62 ± 1.36	74.08 ± 1.31	71.13 ± 71.13	fc7
Clean crops	Random cropping	81.63 ± 2.39	80.07 ± 2.55	76.84 ± 2.29	73.68 ± 2.23	
Clean crops	Random zooming	81.80 ± 1.93	80.64 ± 2.16	78.90 ± 2.08	77.04 ± 2.12	
Dirty crops	Random cropping	**82.93 ± 2.32**	80.80 ± 2.25	77.53 ± 2.05	74.73 ± 1.97	
Dirty crops	Random zooming	82.58 ± 2.54	**81.57 ± 2.47**	**79.97 ± 2.56**	**77.63 ± 2.00**	

4.4   Discussion

Our results show that the best models are those trained on the crops datasets using random zooming. On the AlexNet architecture the best model has been the one trained on Dirty Crops, while the Inception-v3 models trained on Dirty Crops and Clean Crops had comparable results, suggesting that AlexNet generalized better features by using more training images, even in the presence of semantically overlapping labels.

Inception-v3 model trained on Clean Crops achieved a mean accuracy score of 91.76 on the RGB-D Object splits, compared to the Baseline model which scored 88.78, and also scored 92.50 points on the JHUIT-50 task, 4.5 points higher than the corresponding Baseline score. Inception-v3 model trained on Dirty Crops also surpassed the Baseline on the RGB-D Object and JHUIT-50 tasks, scoring 91.04 points and 93.13 points respectively. Models trained with our methodology and tested on the HelloiCubWorld-human dataset didn't improve the Baseline results, while they performed worse for the HelloiCubWorld-robot task, albeit the difference is lower than one point and the dataset is small.

We also test the models we trained on artificially translated versions of the RGB-D Object dataset. Features extracted from the models trained on Crop datasets with Random Zooming performed better than features extracted from models trained on the Baseline against increasing levels of artificial translations.

Since we employed Random Zooming to simulate the zooming and off-target detection phenomena we commonly see in robotic data-set, we used it only for models trained on object crops. Since we are comparing models trained with random zooming with a baseline model trained with random cropping, it could be argued that it is the random zooming itself giving better results, and not the crop dataset used for training. Also the Dirty Crops datasets contain crops extracted from images not in the Baseline dataset. However, by comparing results obtained with the Baseline models with results obtained with the models trained on Clean Crops with random cropping, we observe that using the crop dataset is also beneficial for the final classification task. Features extracted from the AlexNet models trained on Clean Crops with random cropping outperformed the corresponding Baseline features in every task. Features extracted from the Inception-v3 model trained on Clean Crops with random cropping outperformed Baseline features by 1.23 and 4.57 points on the RGB-D Object and JHUIT-50 tasks, while they got outperformed on the smaller HelloiCubWorld human and robot datasets by 0.08 and 0.5 points (Figs. 4 and 5).

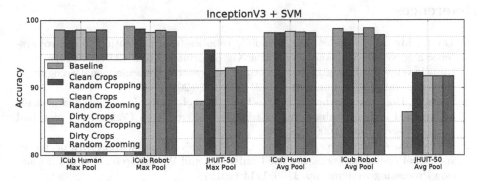

Fig. 4. Results on HelloiCubWorld and JHUIT-50 - InceptionV3. Notice how our proposed methods boosts extensively the accuracy on JHUIT-50; the same cannot be said about HelloiCubWorld but it must be kept in mind that it is a small dataset, the accuracy is already extremely high, and the differences are statistically insignificant.

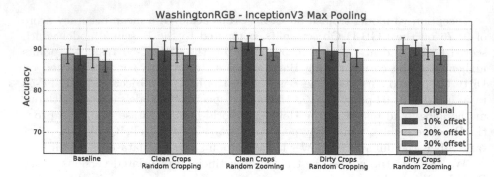

Fig. 5. Results on Washington RGB - InceptionV3 max pool.

5   Conclusions

This paper presented a simple yet effective approach for improving the object classification accuracy of any deep network trained over large scale databases collected from the Web and used in the robot vision context. Our idea is to increase the similarity between the data acquired in the two visual domains by randomly scaling, zooming and cropping each image in a data augmentation layer. Results over three different benchmark databases confirm the effectiveness of the method.

While this technique certainly give a small but consistent help in bridging between computer and robot vision, very many challenges remain open. In particular, we will dedicate future work attempting to close the gap between these two different perceptual tasks by leveraging over the domain adaptation literature, aiming for methods working in the unsupervised domain adaptation setting without heavy requirements about the deep architecture of choice.

References

1. Tai, L., Liu, M.: Deep-learning in mobile robotics-from perception to control systems: a survey on why and why not. arXiv preprint arXiv:1612.07139 (2016)
2. Russakovsky, O., Deng, J., Su, H., et al.: Imagenet large scale visual recognition challenge. Int. J. Comput. Vis. **115**(3), 211–252 (2015)
3. Deng, J., Dong, W., Socher, R., Li, L.-J., Li, K., Fei-Fei, L.: Imagenet: a large-scale hierarchical image database. In: The IEEE Conference on Computer Vision and Pattern Recognition (2009)
4. Krizhevsky, A., Sutskever, I., Hinton, G.E.: ImageNet classification with deep convolutional neural networks. In: The Conference and Workshop on Neural Information Processing Systems, pp. 1106–1114 (2012)
5. Szegedy, C., Liu, W., Jia, Y., Sermanet, P., Reed, S., Anguelov, D., Erhan, D., Vanhoucke, V., Rabinovich, A.: Going deeper with convolutions. In: The IEEE Conference on Computer Vision and Pattern Recognition, pp. 1–9 (2015)

6. Szegedy, C., Vanhoucke, V., Ioffe, S., Shlens, J., Wojna, Z.: Rethinking the inception architecture for computer vision. In: The IEEE Conference on Computer Vision and Pattern Recognition (2016)

7. Donahue, J., Jia, Y., Vinyals, O., Hoffman, J., Zhang, N., Tzeng, E., Darrell, T.: DeCAF: a deep convolutional activation feature for generic visual recognition. In: The International Conference on Machine Learning (2014)

8. Li, C., Reiter, A., Hager, G.D.: Beyond spatial pooling fine-grained representation learning in multiple domains. In: The IEEE Conference on Computer Vision and Pattern Recognition (2015)

9. Fanello, S.R., Ciliberto, C., Natale, L., Metta, G.: Weakly supervised strategies for natural object recognition in robotics. In: IEEE International Conference on Robotics and Automation, pp. 4223–4229 (2013)

10. Lai, K., Bo, L., Ren, X., Fox, D.: A large-scale hierarchical multi-view rgb-d object dataset. In: IEEE International Conference on Robotics and Automation (2011)

11. Young, J., Kunze, L., Basile, V., Cabrio, E., Hawes, N., Caputo, B.: Semantic web-mining and deep vision for lifelong object discovery. In: IEEE International Conference on Robotics and Automation (2017)

12. Eitel, A., Springenberg, J.T., Spinello, L., Riedmiller, M., Burgard, W.: Multimodal deep learning for robust RGB-D object recognition. In: IEEE/RSJ International Conference on Intelligent Robots and Systems (2015)

13. Gupta, S., Girshick, R., Arbelaez, P., Malik, J.: Learning rich features from RGB-D images for object detection and segmentation. In: European Conference on Computer Vision (2014)

14. Schwarz, M., Schulz, H., Behnke, S.: RGB-D object recognition and pose estimation based on pre-trained convolutional neural network features. In: IEEE International Conference on Robotics and Automation (2015)

15. Pasquale, G., et al.: Object identification from few examples by improving the invariance of a deep convolutional neural network. In: IEEE/RSJ International Conference on Intelligent Robots and Systems (2016)

Design and Optimization of the Model for Traffic Signs Classification Based on Convolutional Neural Networks

Jiarong Song, Zhong Yang[✉], Tianyi Zhang, and Jiaming Han

Nanjing University of Aeronautics and Astronautics,
Nanjing 210016, People's Republic of China
jrsnuaa@163.com, {YangZhong,hjm}@nuaa.edu.cn,
ufozty@126.com

Abstract. Recently, convolutional neural networks (CNNs) demonstrate state-of-the-art performance in computer vision such as classification, recognition and detection. In this paper, a traffic signs classification system based on CNNs is proposed. Generally, a convolutional network usually has a large number of parameters which need millions of data and a great deal of time to train. To solve this problem, the strategy of transfer learning is utilized in this paper. Besides, further improvement is implemented on the chosen model to improve the performance of the network by changing some fully connected layers into convolutional connection. This is because that the weight shared feature of convolutional layers is able to reduce the number of parameters contained in a network. In addition, these convolutional kernels are decomposed into multi-layer and smaller convolutional kernels to get a better performance. Finally, the performance of the final optimized network is compared with unoptimized networks. Experimental results demonstrate that the final optimized network presents the best performance.

Keywords: CNNs · Transfer learning · Optimization

1 Introduction

In recent years, with the improvement of calculation speed of computers, convolutional neural networks (CNNs) are applied more and more and present remarkable performance especially in computer vision. As a result, there is an increasing number of researchers begin to apply CNNs in their work to solve vision problems which are difficult for traditional vision methods.

A CNN with excellent performance generally contains a large number of parameters which need millions of data to train. However, data available to us are usually limited. In this case, training a CNN usually containing millions of parameters is possible to produce over fitting problem [1]. In order to solve this problem, paper [2] proposes feature extraction algorithms to reduce the dimensionality of data to avoid over fitting. But handmade feature extraction easily abandons some useful features, which indicates methods in [2] may weaken the performance of a network. A network that is restricted to work on a small labelled region is presented in [3]. Undeniably, this

© Springer International Publishing AG 2017
M. Liu et al. (Eds.): ICVS 2017, LNCS 10528, pp. 394–403, 2017.
DOI: 10.1007/978-3-319-68345-4_35

method may also limit the application of the network in practice. Paper [4] develops an approach which learns to get effective filter sets based on the fixed filter sets to overcome the problem of limited data. Nevertheless, it probably limits the learning ability of feature extraction of a network. A noisy CNN algorithm is described in [5] which assists a network to give better performance on small data. Paper [6] investigates data augmentation complementary approaches to deal with limited training data. However, these two methods are not able to essentially optimize the structure of a network. Yu et al. propose a method of 1 x 1 convolutional layers to reduce the parameters to get a CNN model with better performance on hyperspectral image classification in [7]. However, the model is still large when it contains a great number of features. All of the above articles put forward their respective methods which are instructive to get an excellent model based on small data, even though they have a few disadvantages.

In this paper, based on small data, the strategy of transfer learning is utilized by employing a well-trained feature extractor and further optimization is implemented on the chosen CNN model to design a new model. Compared with above approaches, the method in this paper enables to reduce the amount of parameters and alleviate the over fitting problem without data preprocessing. Besides, this method will not restrict the application of the network in practice. Based on AlexNet [8], the first step is changing some fully connected layers into convolutional layers. In addition, these convolutional kernels are furtherly decomposed into multi-layer and smaller convolutional kernels to decrease the amount of parameters. Finally, experimental results demonstrate that the new model achieves excellent classification ability on our data and presents strong robustness.

2 Classification Network

In this section, as one of the most famous classification networks, AlexNet [8] which achieves an excellent performance of the 1000 class classification is introduced. Its structure can be divided into two parts. The first part is a feature extractor and the second part is a classifier.

2.1 The Feature Extractor

The feature extractor in AlexNet mainly consists of convolutional layers, activation function units and pooling layers. Convolutional kernels are similar to filters used in traditional vision systems. However, convolutional kernels, which are more advantageous than filters used in traditional vision systems, are able to not only extract low-level features of images such as edge information, direction information but also extract high-level features such as class information, etc.

The Eq. (1) illustrates the output size of an image after the convolution operation. The Eq. (1) shows that the size of output is generally smaller than the size of input after convolution operation. In this case, increase of convolutional layers easily leads to the shrinkage of data dimension propagating forward in a CNN. It means features of data that can be used in a network are greatly reduced, which is a restriction on the depth of a CNN. In order to solve this problem, padding which means to resize an input into a larger size is introduced. It is realized by boundary filling according to the size of the convolutional kernels. After padding, the size of output after the convolution operation is illustrated in (2). The Eq. (3) presents the size of output after an operation consisting of two steps. The first step is padding and the second step is convolution operation. The convolutional kernel is supposed to be in $N \times N$ size and its stride is supposed to be 1. As a result, the size of output is able to keep as the same as the input, which efficiently solves the shrinkage of data problem.

At the same time, in order to reduce the data dimension propagating forward in a network, pooling layers acting as the role of sampling are introduced. The main function of pooling layers is to simplify the output of their upper convolutional layers [9, 10]. Activation function used in AlexNet, which introduces nonlinear factors into a network, is ReLU function rather than tanh function [8]. Since data saturation which will induce gradient vanishing will never occur in ReLU function. Additionally, computing the derivative of ReLU function is faster than tanh [11, 12]. For ReLU function, if the input value is larger than 0, the gradient is set to be one. Otherwise, the gradient is zero.

$$size_{output} = \left(\frac{H_{input} - N}{str} + 1\right)\left(\frac{W_{input} - N}{str} + 1\right) \tag{1}$$

$$size_{output\_p} = \left(\frac{H_{input} + 2P - N}{str} + 1\right)\left(\frac{W_{input} + 2P - N}{str} + 1\right) \tag{2}$$

$$size_{output\_} = \left[\left(H_{input} + 2 \times \frac{N-1}{2} - N\right) + 1\right]\left[\left(W_{input} + 2 \times \frac{N-1}{2} - N\right) + 1\right]$$
$$= H_{input} \times W_{input}$$

$$\tag{3}$$

where $H_{input} \times W_{input}$ presents the size of the original input, P presents the boundary filling, $size_{output}$ presents the size of output without padding, $size_{output\_p}$ and $size_{output\_}$ present the size of output with padding, the convolutional kernel is in $N \times N$ size and its stride is str. Besides, all of the above formulas represent operations on a single channel.

2.2   The Classifier

The classifier in AlexNet mainly consists of fully connected layers and output layers. Outputs of the classifier are inputs of the feature extractor. Fully connected layers learn to combine features from the feature extractor in a reasonable way to get the most likely class of inputs of the whole network, which is similar to a function mapping [13, 14]. In order to alleviate over fitting [1, 15] and improve robustness and accuracy of a convolutional neural network, dropout layers are introduced [8, 15].

The principle of dropout is randomly selecting activated neurons according to a certain probability and setting their outputs to be zero. In this case, a whole network is divided into many subnetworks since only a part of neurons work every time [8]. During the training phase, our purpose is to improve the performance of each sub-network as far as possible. Hence, each subnetwork finally inclines to give correct classification. Additionally, because that only one subnetwork works every time. As a result, all these subnetworks work independently rather than in a certain combination [8, 15], which is able to efficiently avoid over fitting. Meanwhile, with dropout layers, fewer features are used at every turn during the training phase. This is also capable of avoiding over fitting. During the test phase, local noises may lead some subnetworks to output bad scores. However, most subnetworks still have good performances, which helps the whole network to show a remarkable performance. This character leads the whole network to demonstrate excellent robustness.

Besides, in order to use more information of data, dropout layers will be cancelled sometimes during the test phase, which needs additional data processing. In this case, the value of inputs should be reduced according to the drop ratio. Otherwise, inputs for neurons are larger than expected, which is showed in Eqs. (4) and (5). This may cause some mistakes because of the change in data distribution.

$$input_{withdropout} = p \sum w_i x_i + b \tag{4}$$

$$input_{withoutdropout} = \sum w_i x_i + b \tag{5}$$

where $input_{withdropout}$ and $input_{withoutdropout}$ present the total input of a neuron, p presents the value of the drop ratio and p is in region [0, 1], w_i presents the value of a weight, x_i presents an input of this neuron, b presents the value of the bias.

3 Transfer Learning and Optimization

3.1 Transfer Learning and Its Reason and Reasonability

Training a convolutional network is greedy for data. However, our samples are limited. In order to alleviate the over fitting problem and gain an excellent performance, transfer learning [16–19] is introduced here. This is because that data used in our network and used in AlexNet are both image data, which implies that the feature extractor trained on AlexNet is suitable for our network. Transfer learning is achieved by fine tuning the feature extractor of AlexNet and designing a new classifier in this paper.

3.2 Network Structure and Optimization

The simplest transfer learning method is just changing the output number of AlexNet into our class number, which is marked as network 1. The classifier of network1 contains nearly 5×10^7 parameters which are large for our data sets. Thus, changing fully connected layers into convolutional layers is considered. This is because that the weight shared feature of convolutional layers [20, 21] is able to reduce the amount of parameters. In this paper, the first fully connected layer of AlexNet is changed into a convolutional layer which consists of $5 \times 5 \times 256$ sized convolutional kernels. After this step, network 2 is constructed and the classifier of network 2 contains nearly 4×10^7 parameters that are still large. Thus, further optimization is needed.

Before doing further optimization, two combinations of convolutional kernels are compared with each other in Table 1. In Table 1, the input is supposed to be in size of $H \times W \times C$ and all kernels are in $N \times N \times C$ size. Table 1 shows that the $3 \times 3 \times C$ and $3 \times 3 \times C$ combination structure includes fewer parameters. It implies that a network which consists of multi-layer and smaller convolutional kernels contains fewer parameters. According to this conclusion, based on the preliminary improvement, further optimization is implemented on network 2. Further optimization is decomposing $5 \times 5 \times C$ convolutional kernels into multi-layer and smaller $3 \times 3 \times C$ and $3 \times 3 \times C$ sized convolutional kernels. After this step, network 3 which is our final model is obtained. The classifier of network 3 contains around 1×10^7 parameters and N presents class number. The structure of network 3 is showed in Fig. 1.

Table 1. Comparison of two different combinations of convolutional kernels.

The combinational of convolutional kernels	Perception size	Number of weights	Number of multiply-adds
$5 \times 5 \times C$	25	$25C$	$25\,HWC^2$
$3 \times 3 \times C$ and $3 \times 3 \times C$	25	$18C$	$18\,HWC^2$

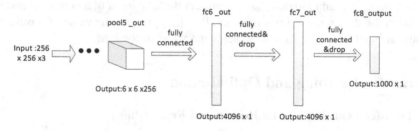

Fig. 1. The structure of network 3

4 Experiment and Analysis

4.1 Experimental Data

The purpose of this paper is to classify traffic signs. Training sets consist of samples from other places and testing sets consist of samples from campus. Both of them are divided into three categories. Because of data limitation, data amount is augmented by rotating, cropping and mirroring. Details are given in Table 2.

4.2 The Influence of Drop Ratio

According to Sect. 2, dropout layers are introduced into CNNs to prevent over fitting [1]. Generally, the higher the drop ratio is, more independent subnetworks will be [8], more excellent performance a network presents. Since our data sets are small, in order

Table 2. Data statistics.

Samples	Training set	Testing set
No parking sign	398	55
Speed limit sign	386	50
Crosswalk	358	47
total	1142	152

to obtain a remarkable performance, a little higher drop ratio is chosen. However, too much high drop ratio will have bad influence on a network. Figure 2 shows loss values of different drop ratios based on network 3. Figure 3 is the local enlarged image of Fig. 2. Drop ratio1, drop ratio2, drop ratio3, drop ratio4 are respectively equal to 0.4, 0.9, 0.8, 0.6. Interval [130, 138] is in the region in which all loss values are stable.

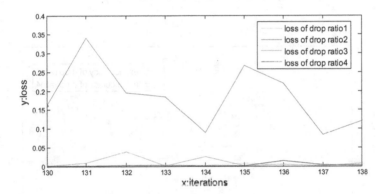

Fig. 2. Loss values on training sets

Evidently, according to Figs. 2 and 3, drop ratio4 and drop ratio1 have the best loss values. Drop ratio2 has the worst loss value when compared with others. This is because that too many features are dropped during the training phase with drop ratio2, which easily generates under fitting [1]. Under the condition of drop ratio3, many useful features are still dropped when compared with drop ratio1 and drop ratio4. Obviously, if the drop ratio is set to be 1, the network will stop updating.

In addition, accuracy values of drop ratio1 and drop ratio4 are compared with each other in Fig. 4. Interval [76, 87] is in the region in which both accuracy values are stable. Figure 4 illustrates that drop ratio4 has a higher accuracy value on the testing set than drop ratio1 even though they have nearly same loss values on the training set. It implies that network 3 with drop ratio4 has better robustness than this network with drop ratio1. On the basis of this section, drop ratio4 is chosen as the value of the drop ratio in the next section.

4.3 Training and Testing of Networks

According to session 4.2, all drop ratios in network 1, in network 2 and in network 3 are set to be 0.6. Classifiers of these three networks have the same learning rate 0.01 for

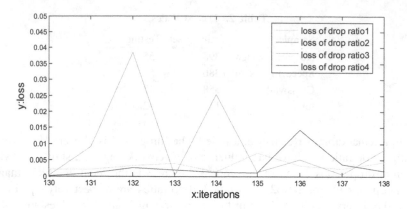

Fig. 3. Local enlarged image of Fig. 2

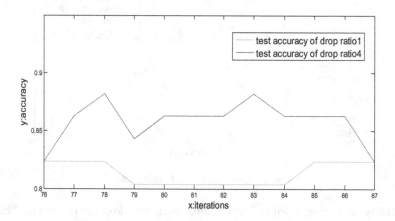

Fig. 4. Accuracy values on testing sets

weights and 0.02 for biases. The learning rate of feature extractors of these three networks is almost equal to 0. Experimental results are shown in Figs. 5 and 6, which respectively present loss values on training sets and accuracy values on testing sets. Interval [112, 128] is in the region in which all loss values are stable and interval [126, 135] is in the region in which all accuracy values are stable. Figures 5 and 6 present that these three networks all have good loss values which are not more than 0.04 and accuracy values which are not less than 88%. Since that transfer learning method is used and data sets are not large. In this case, these three networks are likely to show excellent performance in training loss and testing accuracy.

In order to furtherly analyze these results, we calculate average values of accuracy in region [126, 135] of these three networks according to Fig. 5. Results are presented in Table 3. Evidently, network 3 has the best result in test accuracy. This is because that network 3 has the fewest parameters when compared with other networks. Thus, under the condition of the same amount of data, network 3 relatively has the most

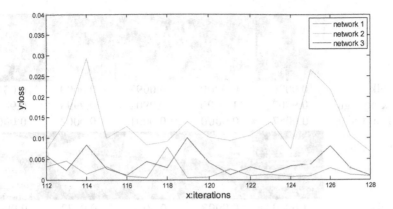

Fig. 5. Loss values on training sets

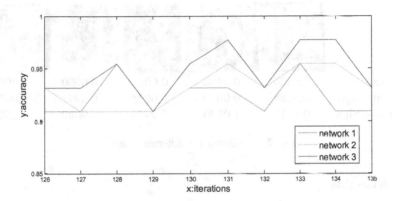

Fig. 6. Accuracy values on testing sets

Table 3. Test accuracy of three networks

Model	Test accuracy
Network 1	92.3%
Network 2	92.6%
Network 3	94.9%

sufficient samples to get a more superior performance. From the experiment, it comes to a conclusion that network 3 has the best performance on our data.

Finally, some prediction experiments of single inputs are conducted based on network 3 and results are presented in Fig. 7. In Fig. 7, results represent the probability that every image belongs to each class. Figure 7 shows that some pictures are rotated and fuzzy. However, network 3 still shows excellent performance on the accuracy of classification, which proves network 3 has a high accuracy of classification and strong robustness.

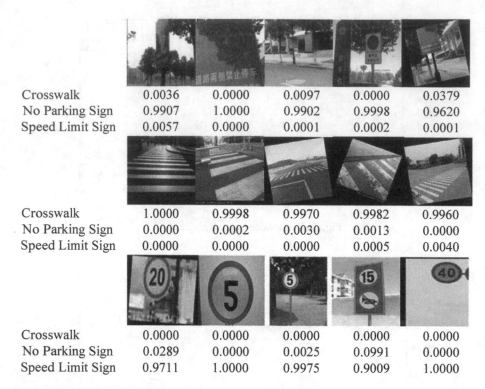

Crosswalk	0.0036	0.0000	0.0097	0.0000	0.0379
No Parking Sign	0.9907	1.0000	0.9902	0.9998	0.9620
Speed Limit Sign	0.0057	0.0000	0.0001	0.0002	0.0001
Crosswalk	1.0000	0.9998	0.9970	0.9982	0.9960
No Parking Sign	0.0000	0.0002	0.0030	0.0013	0.0000
Speed Limit Sign	0.0000	0.0000	0.0000	0.0005	0.0040
Crosswalk	0.0000	0.0000	0.0000	0.0000	0.0000
No Parking Sign	0.0289	0.0000	0.0025	0.0991	0.0000
Speed Limit Sign	0.9711	1.0000	0.9975	0.9009	1.0000

Fig. 7. Prediction for different inputs

5   Conclusions

This paper utilizes the strategy of transfer learning to construct a CNN model to alleviate over fitting problem on small data. An excellently well-trained feature extractor that is difficult to achieve just on small data sets is obtained by using the strategy of transfer learning. In this case, our data are mainly used to train the classifier, which is more likely to generate a satisfying model. Meanwhile, in order to reduce the amount of parameters and get a network with more superior performance. In this paper, the first step is changing some fully connected layers into convolutional connection according to the weight shared feature of convolutional layers. Next, these convolutional kernels are decomposed into multi-layer and smaller convolutional kernels, which further cuts down the number of parameters contained in the network. Finally, the experimental result proves the final optimized network has the best performance.

Acknowledgement. This work was supported by the National Natural Science Foundation of China (No. 61473144), Aviation Science Foundation (Key Laboratory, No. 20162852031) and Major Scientific Instruments and Equipment Development of the Ministry of Science and Technology (No. 2016YFF0103702).

References

1. Gu, Y., et al.: An optimal sample data usage strategy to minimize over fitting and under fitting effects in regression tree models based on remotely-sensed data. Remote sens. **8**(11) pp. 1–13, Article 943 (2016)
2. Kumar, S., Ghosh, J., Crawford, M.M.: Best-bases feature extraction algorithms for classification of hyperspectral data. IEEE Trans. Geosci. Remote Sens. **39**(7), 1368–1379 (2001)
3. Windrim, L., et al.: Hyperspectral CNN classification with limited training samples (2016)
4. Jacobsen, J.H., et al.: Structured receptive fields in CNNs, pp. 2610–2619 (2016)
5. Audhkhasi, K., Osoba, O., Kosko, B.: Noise-enhanced convolutional neural networks. Neural Netw. Off. J. Int. Neural Netw. Soc. **78**, 15–23 (2015)
6. Cui, X., Goel, V., Kingsbury, B.: Data augmentation for deep neural network acoustic modeling. In: 2014 IEEE International Conference on Acoustics, Speech and Signal Processing, ICASSP 2014, pp. 5582–5586. IEEE (2014)
7. Yu, S., Jia, S., Xu, C.: Convolutional neural networks for hyperspectral image classification. Neurocomputing **219**, 88–98 (2016)
8. Krizhevsky, A., Sutskever, I., Hinton, G.E.: ImageNet classification with deep convolutional neural networks. In: International Conference on Neural Information Processing Systems, pp. 1097–1105. Curran Associates Inc. (2012)
9. Lecun, Y., Bengio, Y., Hinton, G.: Deep learning. Nature **521**(7553), 436–444 (2015)
10. Sun, M., et al.: Learning pooling for convolutional neural network. Neurocomputing (2016)
11. Glorot, X., Bordes, A., Bengio, Y.: Deep sparse rectifier networks. Learn. Stat. Optim. (2010)
12. Jarrett, K., et al.: What is the best multi-stage architecture for object recognition? In: Proceedings of International Conference on Computer Vision, pp. 2146–2153 (2009)
13. Li, H.X., Chen, C.P.: The equivalence between fuzzy logic systems and feedforward neural networks. IEEE Trans. Neural Netw. **11**(2), 356–365 (2000)
14. Wilamowski, B.M.: Neural network architectures and learning algorithms. Ind. Electron. Mag. IEEE **3**(4), 56–63 (2010)
15. Srivastava, N., et al.: Dropout: a simple way to prevent neural networks from over fitting. J. Mach. Learn. Res. **15**(1), 1929–1958 (2014)
16. Tajbakhsh, N., et al.: Convolutional neural networks for medical image analysis: full training or fine tuning? IEEE Trans. Med. Imaging **35**(5), 1299–1312 (2016)
17. Krizhevsky, A.: Convolutional deep belief networks on CIFAR-10 (2012)
18. Shin, H.C., et al.: Deep convolutional neural networks for computer-aided detection: CNN architectures, dataset characteristics and transfer learning. IEEE Trans. Med. Imaging **35**(5), 1285 (2016)
19. Marmanis, D., et al.: Deep learning earth observation classification using ImageNet pretrained networks. IEEE Geosci. Remote Sens. Lett. **13**(1), 105–109 (2016)
20. Kim, J.K., Lee, M.Y., Kim, J.Y.: An efficient pruning and weight sharing method for neural network. In: IEEE International Conference on Consumer Electronics, p. 2 (2016)
21. Bouvrie, J.: Notes on convolutional neural networks. Neural Nets (2006)

Selection and Execution of Simple Actions via Visual Attention and Direct Parameter Specification

Jan Tünnermann[✉], Steffen Grüne, and Bärbel Mertsching

GET Lab, University of Paderborn, Pohlweg 47-49, 33098 Paderborn, Germany
{tuennermann,gruene,mertsching}@get.uni-paderborn.de

Abstract. Can early visual attention processes facilitate the selection and execution of simple robotic actions? We believe that this is the case. Following the selection–for–action agenda known from human attention, we show that central perceptual processing can be avoided or at least relieved from managing simple motor processes. In an attention–classification–action cycle, salient pre-attentive structures are used to provide features to a set of classifiers. Their action proposals are coordinated, parametrized (via direct parameter specification), and executed. We evaluate the system with a simulated mobile robot.

1 Introduction

Artificial visual attention is a very active research domain in the field of computer vision. Even though earlier attempts have been made at computationally modeling human visual attention, the work by Itti et al. [11] has triggered the visual attention boom of the last twenty years. The motivation behind the many artificial attention approaches is to make the impressive capacities of early human vision in selecting relevant from irrelevant information available for technical applications. With an upstream visual attention mechanism that rapidly generates regions of potential interest, subsequent visual processing, such as object recognition, can be highly facilitated. Especially autonomous robots in dynamic environments benefit from filtering the impeding—and at least to some degree unpredictable—visual information. In this sense, attention is in service of visual perception; it is the doorkeeper of higher visual cognition.

But is a filter for subsequent perception really the only job in which attention can be beneficially employed? This paper (among others, e.g., [5]) argues "no", artificial attention can be effectively used in the selection and execution of actions, too. In a novel framework, we show how an "attend–classify–perform" cycle facilitates the selection of appropriate robot actions in dynamic environments.

In earlier work, the role of attention in selecting among alternative actions and providing information about potential targets has been neglected by the artificial attention community. One can even say that it is effectively ignored, given the explosion of artificial attention methods that purely focus on visual

© Springer International Publishing AG 2017
M. Liu et al. (Eds.): ICVS 2017, LNCS 10528, pp. 404–414, 2017.
DOI: 10.1007/978-3-319-68345-4_36

perception. Especially research on "salient object detection" (see [6]) has contributed massively to the growth of the artificial attention literature that ignores attentional selection for action.

Intriguingly, the neglect of actions in the early study of attention as well as the later conclusion that both attention and action should not be studied in isolation is also present in human psychological research [16]. After starting on separate paths in the 19th century, the study of attention and action in psychology has been joined by the observation that both involve the selection of targets. In this context, the term selection–for–action (as opposed to selection–for–perception) was coined by Allport in the eighties [2]. Furthermore, the close link between eye movements (which are actions) and attention has substantiated the view that attention and action influence each other [7,18]. Pratt and colleagues write: "The interaction of attention and action in the prioritization of visual information and the planning of actions is so ubiquitous, so efficient, and typically so successful that it guides our behaviors despite being in the very deep background of awareness" [16]. Hence, the trajectory of the importance of selection–for–action and similar concepts in psychology is mirrored (maybe with some decades delay) in the technical domain of artificial attention systems. The present paper contributes to the emerging action-oriented perspective on attention (extending on preliminary work presented in [10]). Whereas the usual focus on selection–for–perception often leads to "images in, images out" approaches, in which an (image-based) priority map is provided for consumption by subsequent perception processes, the present paper aims at establishing an "images in, actions performed" version of attention, which directly results in robot behavior.

2   Attention, Actions, and Direct Parameter Specification

The proposed selection–for–action architecture is based on a cycle that buffers the input, calculates attention to select low-level image structures, feeds these into a set of classifiers, and uses their output to select and trigger predefined actions. In addition, the attention system provides information about the targets to parametrize the selected actions. A system overview is provided in Fig. 1, and the data flow and processing stages are described in the following sections.

2.1   Gathering Images and Calculating Attention

In step ① (see Fig. 1) sensors collect data from the environment. In the visual context of this work, cameras are used to gather color images. A chunk of 20 subsequent images is considered as spatiotemporal processing volume for the attention calculation. Hence, in step ② (see Fig. 1), low-level pre-attentional structures are constructed within the processing volume by applying a modified "Growing Neural Gas"-algorithm (GNG, [8,21]), which is listed below as Algorithm 1 in Sect. 2.1 The structures are connected groups of "neurons" that approximate the topology of the objects (more precisely, homogeneously colored elements) in the scene and they are used to calculate attention. The results of

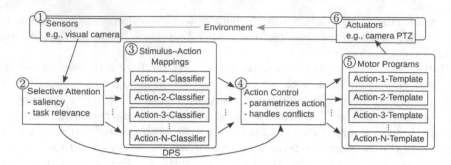

Fig. 1. Overview of the proposed selection–for–action architecture. Arrows indicate the flow of data between the components. Details are provided in the main text.

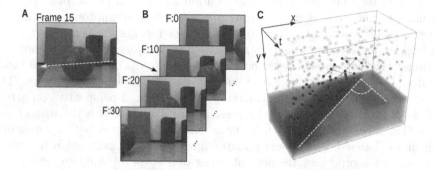

Fig. 2. A Frame from the middle of a short sequence. A ball rolls from right to left as indicated by the white arrow. **B** Exemplary frames of the sequence illustrate how the frames are stacked to form a spatiotemporal processing volume. **C** The GNG-based graph structures within the pixel volume (pixels in the upper part hidden for better visibility of the graphs). The orange neurons represent the ball and its motion. Faint neurons belong to background objects. The angle between the white lines highlights how moving objects differ from static ones in spatiotemporal volumes. (color figure online)

these computations can then be used even without forming an image-based priority map, which motivates their use in the present action-centered paper. Similar methods have been used in [23–25], where image segmentation instead of the GNG approach was used. The advantage of GNG over image segmentation is the convenient (and possibly task-depending) control of the computation time investment, which is of particular importance in the present dynamic scenario: Depending on the termination criteria (e.g., number of iterations), quick rough results or more time-demanding accurate results can be generated. Figure 2 shows a result which is sufficiently fine-grained but which was also generated sufficiently fast for the tasks in the present study (the tasks are described below).

The attention components that are calculated are saliency (low-level image contrasts in different feature dimensions; e.g., see [11]) and top-down activation (knowledge- and task-dependent components, such as biases toward specific

Algorithm 1. Pre-attentional structures via "Growing Neural Gas" in spatiotemporal image volumes. Distance measure δ adds Euclidean distances in (x,y), (t) and (L, a, b), each normalized by maximum possible distance

1: Place two neurons at random (x,y,t) positions.
2: **repeat**
3:     Draw sample σ at random (x,y,t) position.
4:     $n_1 \leftarrow$ neuron closest to σ according to $\delta(n, \sigma)$.
5:     $n_2 \leftarrow$ neuron second closest to σ according to $\delta(n, \sigma)$ with $n \neq n_1$.
6:     Increase age counters a of all edges e connected to n_1
7:     Update properties p (x,y,t,L,a,b) of neuron n_1, moving it closer to the sample σ:
8:     $p = p + \epsilon_\beta(\sigma - p)$
9:     Similarly for the properties p of n_2, $p = p + \epsilon_\beta(\sigma - p)$
10:    If edge exists between n_1 and n_2, set edge age a to zero. Otherwise, create edge.
11:    **if** iteration is a multiple of λ **then**
12:        $n_{emax} \leftarrow$ node with maximum local error.
13:        $n_{nemax} \leftarrow$ neighbor of n_{emax} with maximum local error.
14:        Insert new node n_n halfway between n_{emax} and n_{nemax} (connect with edges).
15:        n_n's properties p are averages of those from n_{emax} and n_{nemax}.
16:        The local errors E of n_{emax} and n_{nemax} are reduced by multiplying them with a parameter $\alpha < 1$. The error of n_n is set to the reduced value as well.
17:    **end if**
18:    Reduce local errors E of all nodes by multiplying their error with a para. $\beta < 1$.
19: **until** Maximum number of iterations (or other termination criteria) reached.

locations, features, objects, etc.; e.g. see [20,22]). For the tasks performed in the present study, bottom-up motion saliency and top-down color biases are of interest. Hence, the calculations of these attentional components and feature dimensions are described here. In principle, however, further feature dimensions can be considered in bottom-up and top-down contexts. The reader is referred to the segmentation-based calculations in [3,4,20,24] for bottom-up and top-down attention of motion, color, orientation, elongation, symmetry, and size, which can be performed analogously on the GNG-based pre-attentional structures (cf. [21]).

The horizontal **bottom-up motion saliency** component $\uparrow MS_i^{xt}$ of pre-attentional structure PS_i is calculated as

$$\uparrow MS_{xt}^i = \sum_{j=1}^{|PS|} \frac{min(|\phi_{xt}(PS_j) - \phi_{xt}(PS_i)|, |\phi_{xt}(PS_i) - \phi_{xt}(PS_j)|)}{90^\circ} \cdot \frac{1}{|PS|}, \quad (1)$$

where the subscript xt indicates the spatiotemporal domain with the spatial x- and the temporal t-axis. Hence, $\phi_{xt}(PS_i)$ is the spatiotemporal angle of pre-attentional structure PS_i in the xt-domain which is calculated as

$$\phi_{xt}(PS_i) = (-1) \cdot \text{atan2}(1, m_{xt}), \quad (2)$$

where m_{xt} is the slope of a regression line fitted to the positions (x, t) of all neurons in PS_i. Then, the atan2 function is used to obtain the angle between the regression line and the x-axis. These spatiotemporal angles enter Eq. 1, in which differences between them are calculated. The differences are normalized via division by the maximum possible angle difference of 90°.

The vertical bottom-up motion saliency component $\uparrow MS_{yt}^i$ is calculated similarly, only exchanging the spatial x-axis with the y-axis.

A third component is $\uparrow MS_e^i$, saliency due to spatiotemporal expansion. That is, objects are considered salient if their projection in the visual field expands (typically, when they move toward the observer). To calculate this motion saliency component, the GNG neurons are distributed into temporal bins (we use 4 bins for the 20 frame volumes). A linear regression is fitted to estimate the slope of the increase in neuron number over time. The saliency component $\uparrow MS_e^i$ is then calculated analogously to Eq. 1. Overall motion saliency $\uparrow MS^i$ is then obtained as the average $\frac{1}{3}(\uparrow MS_{xt}^i + \uparrow MS_{yt}^i + \uparrow MS_e^i)$.

The **top-down color activation** is calculated as the relative similarity of the color of a pre-attentional structure, $c(PS_i)$, and a predefined target color, $c(T)$. For this calculation, the CIELAB color space is used. This color space has the dimensions L, luminance, a, the red–green axis, and b, the blue–yellow axis, mimicking the opponent-color organization of human vision. Furthermore, equal distances in the color space are approximately equal to color differences experienced by human observers. Due to these properties, CIELAB is a good basis to compute the top-down color activation (it is also frequently used in popular color-based bottom-up saliency methods, e.g. [1]).

We obtain top-down color activation $\downarrow C_i$ of pre-attentional structure PS_i as

$$\downarrow C_i = 1 - \frac{|c(PS_i) - c(T)|}{\Delta_m}, \tag{3}$$

where the numerator is the Euclidean distance between the L * a * b color vectors of pre-attentional structure PS_i and target T. Term Δ_m represents the maximum possible color distance. Hence, the highest activation is assigned to the structure with the smallest L * a * b color distance.

Elements which are salient according to these measures provide the input for the action classifiers. Different attention dimensions feed into different action classifiers as explained in the next section.

2.2   Action Classification, Selection and Execution

In this step (Fig. 1③), an ensemble of classifiers receives the output of the attention system and each classifier decides whether or not to propose the execution of its associated action. This is best explained with examples matching the test cases in our evaluation below, which uses a wheel-based autonomous robot in a dynamic world: The "Dodge-Classifier" receives from the attention system features of saliently moving objects. Based on these features, the classifier proposes whether or not it is required to execute motor commands to avoid being hit by the moving object. Similarly the "Pass-through-Doorway-Classifier" receives information from the attention system about candidate door frames via the top-down stream. The top-down bias is tuned to favor elements that resemble a predefined door frame template. The classifier decides whether the attended visual information supports the action of driving straight ahead through a door frame. In this work we used k-nearest-neighbors (and other methods, see Fig. 3) to implement the classifiers. Table 1 shows the associated attention outputs, classification features, action types with parameters, and motor commands.

Why are several separate binary "go or no-go" classifiers used instead of a single multi-class one? Ensembles of classifiers are sometimes used to optimize the classification performance (e.g., see [9]). However, in the present paper, several practical points motivate the discreteness:

1. Separate classifiers can be trained individually for specific actions. Whereas the immediate success of individual actions (e.g., dodge or approach potential doorway) can be evaluated (a requirement for classifier training) easily, the longterm success (e.g., survival, well-being, etc.) of conjoined actions is much harder to quantify and evaluate.
2. New actions can be easily added to a system. Re-training the existing classifiers is unnecessary.
3. Several actions may be possible in parallel to each other. Hence a single multi-class solution would have to consider the relevant combinations, which harms the efficiency when the number of actions increases.
4. Based on prior knowledge of the system designer, the relevant features for the individual decisions are fed to the respective classifiers. A "Dodge-Classifier" does not have to bother with uninformative static features, which may be relevant for other actions (see Table 1).

Table 1. Stimulus–action mappings. The entries marked with * are hypothetical and not implemented in the present paper.

Action type	Attention	Classification features	Parameters (for DPS)	Motor commands
Dodge	Bottom-up motion saliency	Spatial x-pos., Sp. temp. orient., Sp. temp. expansion	Sp. temp. orient. $\sim$ *direction*	Back off left or right (depend. on *direction*)
Drive-through-doorway	Top-down color influence (with template "red")	Aspect ratio, Spatial x-pos	Move towards $\sim$ *point ahead*	Forward motion (toward *point ahead*)
Collect power-up*	Top-down color and symmetry influence	Symmetry, Size, Spatial x-pos	Move towards $\sim$ *point ahead*	Forward motion (toward *point ahead*)
Take picture*	Bottom-up overall saliency	All spatial features	Zoom in at $\sim$ *focus point*	Zoom in (at *focus point*), trigger snapshot

The cost of this flexibility is the requirement of a unit that resolves conflicts between different actions proposed by the classifiers. This component is called "Action Control" in step ④ of Fig. 1. At this point, the component adheres to the designer's decisions, such as to give the dodge action priority over a drive-through-doorway action. Similarly it prevents conflicting motor commands (such as turn left vs. turn right) from simultaneous execution. In future work, the component could use machine learning, too, to acquire prioritization rules dynamically. The action control unit has a further task: It performs the direct parameter specification (DPS) procedure to parametrize the action before execution.

The concept of DPS was introduced in cognitive psychology by Neumann [14]. In the traditional view, a stimulus is first perceived before a reaction to it can occur. However, as Neumann writes, it was already recognized by 19th-century psychophysicists in Wundt's laboratory that the perceptual stage is sometimes not included. Neumann summarizes these insights: "With simple, well-practiced actions there is, however, the alternative possibility that the stimulus triggers the motor response directly in a kind of short circuit" ([14], p. 211). In this view, the action is prepared and ready to be executed, only awaiting its target parameters, or again in Neumann's words, "sensory information can be used for the control of action without perception as a mediating stage". This directly parametrized motor response for well-practiced actions is what he calls DPS.

Above we described a system that is trained to select actions based on cues from the earliest stages of visual attention. These stages precede perceptual stages at which object recognition and other high-level processes take place. Hence, all that is needed now to execute the action in step ⑤ (see Fig. 1) is to provide target information for the predefined motor commands: Where to move to for dodging the object? In which direction to drive when specific attentional cues occur? After avoiding a central perception stage when selecting the actions to be performed, there is little incentive to include it now for producing the target parameters. Instead, we follow Neumann's concept of DPS and provide parameters directly to the motor commands. The parameters are extracted from the salient pre-attentional structures. Which of their features are useful parameters for an action depends on the action and is predefined by the designer of the system (see Table 1 for DPS features). For example, the spatiotemporal orientation (see Eq. 2) describes the speed and direction of motion. Therefore, it can be used as a DPS for the dodge action, which depending on the parameter quickly moves the robot out of danger backwards to the left or to the right. Note, that the features that are used as parameters for the actions are not necessarily the same as for the classification when selecting the action. For example, even though a hypothetical "Look-at-Person's-Face-Classifier" may propose its action based on high symmetry and skin color, it would still be the location of the stimulus which is required to turn the robot head toward the face.

To sum up, the steps in this section classify, prioritize, and initialize actions, which are then performed by the actuators (Fig. 1⑥). The actions can change the environment or the robot position, providing fresh inputs to the sensors for subsequent cycles.

3 Training, Evaluation and Results

The training of the action-classifiers (implemented via [15]) and the evaluation of the system was conducted in a simulated dynamic environment (established with Gazebo [12] and the Robot Operating System [17]). Two actions which already have been mentioned, "dodge" and "drive-through-doorway", were trained independently as motivated above.

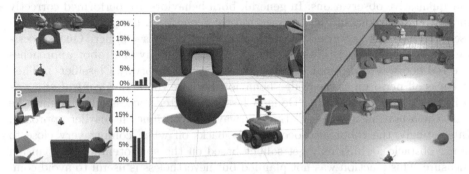

Fig. 3. (**A**)—Exemplary training environment and classification performance for the dodge action and (**B**)—for the drive-through-doorway action. The bar plots show the observed classification errors for different classifiers. From left to right: kNN(3), Random Forest, AdaBoost (see [15]). (**C**)—Simulated robot executing the dodge action. (**D**)—Prototype of a continuous world to be used in future work.

In the **dodge** behavior, the robot backs off in a curve away from the incoming object (cf. Table 1). To train this action, the robot is placed in a room with ramp and some random distractor objects (see Fig. 3A). From the ramp, balls are released that roll roughly toward the robot. In each of 200 learning steps, the ramp is placed at a random position and angle so that some balls will hit the robot and some will not. Hits and misses are recorded. The features for the classification are the spatial position and the spatiotemporal angle of element with the highest motion saliency (see Sect. 2.1).

The **drive-through-doorway** behavior is to be executed when a door frame is centrally in front of the robot. To train this behavior, random distractor objects or target door frames are placed in front of the robot. If the object was a doorway that is successfully passed on approach, a positive outcome is recorded and otherwise a negative one. The features for classification are the L*a*b color values, the spatial position, and the ratio of width to height of the element which is most important according to the top-down color activation (see Sect. 2.1).

The performance is evaluated on new data (200 trials) individually for each action. Both behaviors performed their actions successfully (see Figs. 3A and B). The error rates of three classifiers (from [15]) that performed well are shown in the figure. For the dodge task, the error frequency is below 3% (average precision/recall: 92%/93%). For passing the doorway, more false classifications (error rate: ∼10%; average precision/recall: 89%/96%) occurred. These are mainly driven by false positives. When the actions are executed in a dynamic environment, falsely recognizing the doorway is often unproblematic: While approaching it, further input is gathered and further classifications are performed, often correcting the false alarm before the object is reached.

The case in which both types of stimuli, moving balls and doorways, occur in one dynamic environment is especially interesting. However, the overall success in such a world is hard to quantify at this point. Therefore, we briefly report our qualitative observations: In general, both behaviors are performed correctly in such an environment. The success mostly depends on the *action control unit* (see Fig. 1④) that coordinates the actions in case of a conflict. One successful conflict resolution is illustrated in Fig. 3C: Originally the robot approaches the red doorway (triggered by the "Drive-through-Doorway-Classifier"). Then it backs off performing the dodge behavior, because the *action control unit* prioritizes the proposal of the "Dodge-Classifier". After successfully dodging the ball, the robot "re-recognizes" the doorway and continues its earlier approach. Interestingly, the robot also occasionally backs off when coming very close to static obstacles, which may get salient based on the spatiotemporal expansion measure. This reaction was not planned but nevertheless is useful to avoid coming to close to obstacles. To quantify the success of combined behavior in future work, we developed a world with several stages connected through doorways. At this point a good set of evaluation scores for this scenario is lacking. Furthermore, the longterm success in such a world also depends on the default behavior which the robot performs when neither a doorway not a rolling ball is in the visual field. Our preliminary tests indicate that a well tuned mixture between broad exploration (e.g., turning the camera head) and stout forward motion in the direction of the next stage must be found for a useful default behavior.

4   Discussion and Conclusion

It is probably unusual to start a discussion by pointing out what the work is *not* about and what has *not* been presented in the paper. However, in the present context, just this is required because there is some danger of taking a misleading perspective. This work is neither about robot navigation nor about reflexive obstacle avoidance, despite our prototypical implementation and test scenarios may make it look like it was. Instead, we explored a framework that links selective visual attention to simple actions, avoiding a central perceptual stage that first integrates (different) low-level features to a focus of attention, orients processes—such as object recognition or scene interpretation—toward it, and maybe then initiates some deliberate actions. In addition to showing that the perception-free approach is useful in general to solve basic tasks, several interesting and beneficial aspects emerged: Because the contingency between the visual signal and the action initialization is not explicitly defined but learned, it automatically takes the embodiment of the system into account. Neither the dimensions of the robot, its camera parameters, nor its driving speed need to be modeled explicitly. Attentional selection ensures that relevant features in the scene are

learned, leading to a good transferability of the training. In preliminary tests of
the dodge behavior with a real robot (see Fig. 2), the actions were successfully
initiated. The attentional selection constitutes a main difference to work such
as [19], which also uses machine learning for action decisions but considers the
whole scene as input.

If the goal of the presented work is not to demonstrate the specific avoidance
and target-approaching behaviors, why have these been chosen for the tests?
The reason is that these behaviors can be supported by attentional selection,
providing an action-oriented default mode as starting point for more deliberate
behaviors. More than a century ago, Münsterberg wrote concerning the human
action–perception link that "[w]hen we apperceive the stimulus, we have as a
rule already started responding to it. Our motor apparatus does not wait for our
conscious awareness, but does restlessly its duty, and our consciousness watches
it and has no right to give it orders" ([13], p. 173, Neumann's translation [14]).
As Neumann points out, this is an extreme view. It is probably limited to simple actions and often perception follows the immediate action. Similarly in our
technical scenario, perceptual processes can call in, suppressing, taking over, or
modifying the action-triggered behaviors. For instance, if an object is thrown at a
humanoid robot, a "Dodge-Classifier" triggered by the salient motion may initiate to move out of the way. This is a good response for many objects approaching
at high speeds. However, if a trailing perceptual process recognizes the object as
a light-wight ball (or and expensive vase), the robot may decide to rather catch
it by explicitly triggering the appropriate actions. If someone alarmed the robot
in advance about airborne ming porcelain, the *action control unit* could have
prepared an early (perception-free) catching behavior.

It remains for future work to show that this link with trailing perceptual
processes is feasible. Furthermore, situations where many competing simple
actions are available must be tested. Admittedly, using only two actions, as
in the present experiments, demonstrates only the minimum possible selectivity.
Given the flexible architecture, the encouraging results reported here, and further preliminary tests (e.g., in natural scenarios), we see great potential in this
concept.

References

1. Achanta, R., Hemami, S., Estrada, F., Susstrunk, S.: Frequency-tuned salient
   region detection. In: IEEE Proceedings of CVPR (2009)
2. Allport, D.A.: Attention and performance. In: Cognitive Psychology: New directions (1980)
3. Aziz, M.Z., Mertsching, B.: Fast and robust generation of feature maps for region-
   based visual attention. IEEE Trans. Image Process. **17**(5), 633–644 (2008)
4. Aziz, M.Z., Mertsching, B.: Visual search in static and dynamic scenes using fine-
   grain top-down visual attention. In: Gasteratos, A., Vincze, M., Tsotsos, J.K. (eds.)
   ICVS 2008. LNCS, vol. 5008, pp. 3–12. Springer, Heidelberg (2008). doi:10.1007/
   978-3-540-79547-6_1
5. Balkenius, C., Hulth, N.: Attention as selection-for-action: a scheme for active perception. In: IEEE Third European Workshop on Advanced Mobile Robots (1999)

6. Borji, A., Cheng, M.M., Jiang, H., Li, J.: Salient object detection: a benchmark. IEEE Trans. Image Process. **24**(12), 5706–5722 (2015)
7. Deubel, H., Schneider, W.X.: Saccade target selection and object recognition: evidence for a common attentional mechanism. Vis. Res. **36**(12), 1827–1837 (1996)
8. Fritzke, B., et al.: A growing neural gas network learns topologies. In: NIPS, vol. 7 (1995)
9. Galar, M., Fernández, A., Barrenechea, E., Bustince, H., Herrera, F.: An overview of ensemble methods for binary classifiers in multi-class problems: experimental study on one-vs-one and one-vs-all schemes. Pattern Recogn. **44**(8), 1761–1776 (2011)
10. Grüne, S.: Vorbereitung und Ausführung von einfachen Handlungen autonomer Roboter basierend auf raumzeitlichen Aufmerksamkeitsprozessen [Preparation and execution of simple actions in autonomous robots based on spatiotemporal attention processes]. Bachelor's thesis, Paderborn University (2017)
11. Itti, L., Koch, C., Niebur, E.: A model of saliency-based visual attention for rapid scene analysis. IEEE Trans. PAMI **20**(11), 1254–1259 (1998)
12. Koenig, N., Howard, A.: Design and use paradigms for Gazebo, an open-source multi-robot simulator. In: IEEE/RSJ Proceedings of IROS (2004)
13. Münsterberg, H.: Beiträge zur experimentellen Psychologie [Contributions to Experimental Psychology], no. 1. JCB Mohr, Heidelberg (1889)
14. Neumann, O.: Direct parameter specification and the concept of perception. Psychol. Res. **52**(2–3), 207–215 (1990)
15. Pedregosa, F., Varoquaux, G., Gramfort, A., Michel, V., Thirion, B., Grisel, O., Blondel, M., Prettenhofer, P., Weiss, R., Dubourg, V., Vanderplas, J., Passos, A., Cournapeau, D., Brucher, M., Perrot, M., Duchesnay, E.: Scikit-learn: machine learning in Python. J. Mach. Learn. Res. **12**, 2825–2830 (2011)
16. Pratt, J., Taylor, J.E.T., Gozli, D.G.: Action and attention. In: The Handbook of Attention (2015)
17. Quigley, M., Conley, K., Gerkey, B., Faust, J., Foote, T., Leibs, J., Wheeler, R., Ng, A.Y.: ROS: an open-source Robot Operating System. In: ICRA Workshop on Open Source Software (2009)
18. Rizzolatti, G., Riggio, L., Dascola, I., Umiltá, C.: Reorienting attention across the horizontal and vertical meridians: evidence in favor of a premotor theory of attention. Neuropsychologia **25**(1), 31 (1987)
19. Tai, L., Li, S., Liu, M.: A deep-network solution towards model-less obstacle avoidance. In: IEEE/RSJ Proceedings of IROS (2016)
20. Tünnermann, J., Born, C., Mertsching, B.: Top-down visual attention with complex templates. In: Proceedings of VISAPP, no. 1 (2013)
21. Tünnermann, J., Born, C., Mertsching, B.: Saliency from growing neural gas: learning pre-attentional structures for a flexible attention system (in preparation)
22. Tünnermann, J., Krüger, N., Mertsching, B., Mustafa, W.: Affordance estimation enhances artificial visual attention: evidence from a change-blindness study. Cogn. Comput. **7**(5), 526–538 (2015)
23. Tünnermann, J., Mertsching, B.: Continuous region-based processing of spatiotemporal saliency. In: Proceedings of VISAPP, no. 1 (2012)
24. Tünnermann, J., Mertsching, B.: Region-based artificial visual attention in space and time. Cogn. Comput. **6**(1), 125–143 (2014)
25. Wischnewski, M., Belardinelli, A., Schneider, W.X., Steil, J.J.: Where to look next? Combining static and dynamic proto-objects in a TVA-based model of visual attention. Cogn. Comput. **2**(4), 326–343 (2010)

Visual Detection

Fully Convolutional Networks for Surface Defect Inspection in Industrial Environment

Zhiyang Yu[1], Xiaojun Wu[1,2(✉)], and Xiaodong Gu[1]

[1] Harbin Institute of Technology, Shenzhen 518055, Guangdong, China
wuxj@hit.edu.cn
[2] Shenzhen Key Laboratory for Advanced Motion Control and Modern
Automation Equipment, Shenzhen, Guangdong, China

Abstract. In this paper, we propose a reusable and high-efficiency two-stage deep learning based method for surface defect inspection in industrial environment. Aiming to achieve trade-offs between efficiency and accuracy simultaneously, our method makes a novel combination of a segmentation stage (stage1) and a detection stage (stage2), which are consisted of two fully convolutional networks (FCN) separately. In the segmentation stage we use a lightweight FCN to make a spatially dense pixel-wise prediction to inference the area of defect coarsely and quickly. Those predicted defect areas act as the initialization of stage2, guiding the process of detection to refine the segmentation results. We also use an unusual training strategy: training with the patches cropped from the images. Such strategy has greatly utility in industrial inspection where training data may be scarce. We will validate our findings by analyzing the performance obtained on the dataset of DAGM 2007.

Keywords: Fully convolutional networks · Surface defect inspection · Segmentation

1 Introduction

Defect inspection plays an important role in guaranteing the quality of produces. The type of defect is various such as blur, scratch, spot, etc. (show in Fig. 1.).

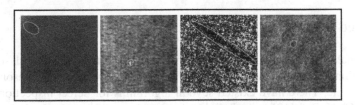

Fig. 1. Different types of defect in industrial environment

Most of the state-of-the-art computer vision based defect inspection algorithms are pattern-based approaches [1] that involve feature extraction or modeling and classifier

© Springer International Publishing AG 2017
M. Liu et al. (Eds.): ICVS 2017, LNCS 10528, pp. 417–426, 2017.
DOI: 10.1007/978-3-319-68345-4_37

design (support vector machine, nearest neighbor classifier, etc.). Feature extraction is the crucial step. It describes the correlation between an input image containing millions of pixels and an information-rich feature vector, which can be used for classification stage [2]. The feature extractor is commonly well designed manually by experienced algorithm designer case-by-case.

A number of recent papers have made efforts in this step. Ref. [3] uses Proposed IFCM method based on a histogram for segmentation of defect area on mobile phone screen glass. Ref. [4] uses AGLR method to monitor grayscale images. Those feature extractor designing requires designers to have rich prior knowledge, and the challenge is that such methods can hardly be generalized or reused and may be inapplicable to the image conditions found in real runnel images [1]. The special pre- and post-processing and the case-by-case feature extractor-designing make the development cycle relative complex and time-consuming. Therefore, the goal of this paper is to design a general and reusable algorithm framework for surface defect inspection in industrial environment. The general and reusable algorithm aims to help us process various types of defect in a similar framework end-to-end without any prior knowledge for pre-/post-process or case-by-case designing. This framework can shorten the deployment cycles and make the development process more automatic and user friendly.

Deep learning, particularly Convolutional Neural Network (CNN), whose feature extractor and classifier can be trained end-to-end automatically from the input images themselves [5], can cover those shortages of the traditional manual approaches. Besides that, the highly nonlinear reflecting capability of CNN makes it very effective solving real problems of surface defect inspection, which are mostly highly nonlinear problems. However, due to the individual requirements for specific application in industrial environment, we should take accuracy, efficiency, exploitativeness and ease of use totally into consideration. In this paper, we introduce a two-stage Fully Convolutional Networks based algorithm framework to specialize the implementation of CNN for the issue of surface defect inspection in industrial environment.

The paper is organized as follows: Section 2 Reviews related works of CNN in various visual task, and reify the issue of surface defect inspection. Section 3 Introduces our two-stage FCN for the implement of industrial inspection. Section 4 Validates our approach experimentally. Section 5 Draws conclusion.

2 Related Work

Convolutional neutral networks have been proved effective end-to-end solution to various vision tasks such as detection [6], segmentation [7], super-resolution [8], tracking [9], etc. There have existed several algorithms for defect inspection with the method of CNN. Ref. [10] trains individual networks at different scales independently, and then combines networks of different scales into a new network. The method of combination is just the concat of top-layer feature maps of different networks where computation is not amortized. This means the computation increases approximately linearly with the number of combined networks. Besides that, VIDI–a commercial software [11] developed by a Swiss company is the first ready-to-use deep learning vision software dedicated to automated aesthetic inspection and classification. Its red tool is used for anomaly detection. No detail information can be achieved about the underlying algorithm of this software, so we just assess this software from the inspection results. More details will be found in Sect. 4.

3 Two-Stage Fully Convolutional Networks

Convolutional networks have shown compelling quality and efficiency in various visual tasks. How to take full advantage of CNNs in our task depends on how we define the issue of surface defect inspection. The issue of defect inspection is more like a semantic segmentation task, which requires us making a prediction at every pixel. So, we choose fully convolutional networks as our basic network structure, which has been demonstrated to outperform other approaches in image segmentation. The networks can thus be trained end-to-end, pixel-to-pixel, given the category-wise semantic segmentation annotation. Besides that, FCN has the property to allow arbitrary size of image as the input of the networks. This property facilitates the processing of images in different size.

Ahead of the introduction of our algorithm framework, we propose a hypothesis based on the observion of the datasets: local information or the patch of defect area is rich enough to represent the existence of defect, and the inspection process has little relation with the geometric shape of the whole defect area. This hypothesis means that defect area is not a common object whose geometric shape or global information is important in inspection process. Visualization can be found in Fig. 2.

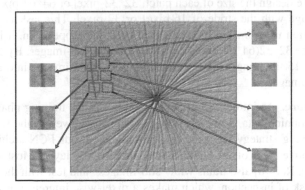

Fig. 2. A schematic diagram of patches cropped from images. The red-solid-line rectangles illustrate patches cropped from defect areas and the green-dotted-line rectangles illustrate patches cropped from non-defect areas (Color figure online)

3.1 Stage 1—Coarse Segmentation of Defect Area

This stage aims to giving a quick but coarse inference of defect area which is also called the region of interest (ROI). The predicted ROIs will be the initialization of stage 2 to limit the search range of stage 2. The ultimate goal is to improve inspection efficiency. However, using an off-the-shelf FCN like [7] in this task is not so proper, as the model designed for general segmentation is always deep, complex and computationally expensive in order to classify various objects of different classes, but the training dataset coming from industrial environment is scarce which may cause over-fitting. And the images of defect surface are quite different from that in nature, so the availability of annotated datasets such as ImageNet [12] can hardly be assumed in many applications, particularly industrial inspection, and the pre-training for classification and then transfer-learning the feature by fine-tuning from classification to segmentation in [7] may not work, as datasets for training classification is quite different from defect datasets. Therefore, we need to find a proper convolutional network structure and a proper training strategy to avoid over-fitting.

Dataset Extension. We choose the dataset of DAGM 2007 [13] as our development and validation dataset. The data is artificially generated, but similar to real world problems. The first six out of ten datasets, denoted as development datasets, are supposed to be used for algorithm. Each development dataset consists of 150 'defective' images saved in grayscale 8-bit PNG format. Each dataset is generated by a different texture model and defect model. Therefore, for each texture model or defect model we only have 150 images for both training and testing which is too scarce to train a FCN for segmentation. Due to the hypothesis we proposed in Sect 3, for patches cropped from a certain statistically textured surface image illustrated in Fig. 2, we can tell easily whether the patches have the defect areas and which pixel belongs to defect area in each patch.

Therefore, we can extend the dataset by cropping patches in the original images. Each patch can act as a training data instead of only using the whole image as one training data. We design the size of each patch 32*32-pixel or 64*64-pixel, and crop in the original image with the stride of 16-pixel or 32-pixel. This task is just like computing convolution in an image. However, unlike a linear operation, it just copies the patches under the 32*32(64*64) window as the training sub-images. By this means, we can decompose 150 training images of one type of defect images into approximately 16000 training images.

FCN Architecture. As introduced in above section, in the training phase, we sample patches as the training data, however, in the testing phase we use the whole image as input. This training strategy has special requirement on our FCN architecture, especially the receptive field of the units located on the top-layer. Most related to our training strategy, Ref. [8] also trains with "sub-images" and test with the whole image. Although the task of inspection, which makes a pixel-wise inference, is quite different from super-resolution where each output pixel is a real-number regressor of intensity values, the architecture design has something to learn from each other—the receptive field should not be too large. If the receptive field is small, the network can focus on rich local spatial information rather than global object-level information. To interpret what influences the receptive field, we assume a network, the kernel size of the i-th layer (layer i) is K_i, s_i is the stride of layer i and S_i is the integral stride before layer i. We denote R_i as the receptive field of each neuron located on the i-th layer (noted as layer-i). Then the recurrence relation of R_i and S_i can be calculated as follows:

$$R_i = R_{i-1} + S_{i-1}(K_i - 1) \tag{1}$$

$$S_i = s_i \times S_{i-1} \tag{2}$$

It can be concluded from the recursion formula that the receptive field is influenced by K_i, s_i and the depth of network layer-i. We pick Zeiler and Fergus model trained for RPN in [14] as our basic architecture. We use only the first 4 layers as our feature extractor layer and append a score layer at the end of feature layers, and we change the strides of all convolutional layers from s_i to 1 (s_i is the original stride of layer i in ZF). Overlap pooling used in RPN controls model capacity and increases receptive field size, resulting in a coarse, highly-semantic feature representation. While effective and necessary for extracting object-level information, this general architecture results in low resolution features that are invariant to pixel-level variations. This is beneficial for classification and identifying object instances but poses challenge for pixel-labeling tasks. So we change overlap pooling to non-overlap pooling as the former cause lager R_i in the following layers. To maintain the resolution of feature map used for classification, we insert a deconvolutional layer [15] before the score layer. We use logistic regression as the loss function for segmentation. More details about the network structure are shown in Fig. 3.

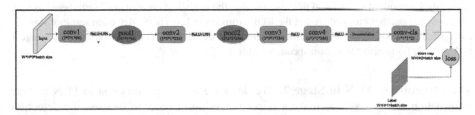

Fig. 3. Structure of FCN in stage 1. (W*H*C*N) is on behalf of width, height, channels and number respectively.

3.2 Stage 2—Segmentation Refinement with Instance-Sensitive Patches

An Overview of Stage 2. This stage is to refine the segmentation result of stage 1 with a method of detection. In stage 1, we focus too much on local information. However, due to the 4th principle, the object-level information is also necessary to segment a defect area. That means "If this piece of area is a defect area or not" is also important information in defect inspection. Therefore, stage 2 is a detection task to refine stage 1 with object-level information. We still use the patches cropped in stage 1 as our training datasets, however, stage 2 is a task of detection not segmentation. Therefore, we should not use the manual annotated segmentation mask of the training data. In this paper, we label the patches whose defect area covers over $n\%$ of the total area as the defect patches (n can be changed for different accuracy requirement, in our experiment in this paper, we design $n = 40$), and others as the non-defect ones. Ref. [16] also uses a patch-based method. Quite different from their work, in this paper we do not sample patches in the completely input image, we only get the samples around the ROI output by stage 1, which raises the inspection speed significantly.

The Fusion of Stage 1 and Stage 2. The segmentation result (ROI) is the initialization of stage 2. We crop patches around ROIs and classify each patch into 2 class—defect patch or not. Then we retain the intersection of the two stages. More details are shown in Fig. 4.

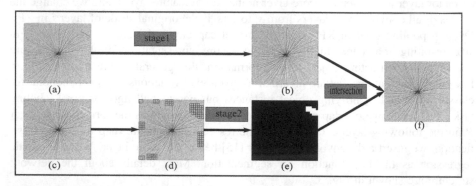

Fig. 4. Fusion of stage 1 and stage 2. (a) is the original image to be inspected, (b) is the coarse segmentation result of stage 1 and this result is also the initialization of stage 2 (numbered as (c)), (d) shows the patches cropped around the ROIs from stage 1. (e) is the detection result of stage 2, each patch is classified into either defect patch or non-defect one. (f) is the intersection of stage 1 and stage 2, (f) is also the final inspection result.

The Structure of FCN in Stage 2. We design a multi-loss-function in FCN to fuse information across layers to make a skip connection in order to increase the detection accuracy. All the loss function is logistic regression. As we still use FCN in a detection task, we label the patch with a label map that has the same resolution as output layer and its values are all the same—0 for defect patches and 1 for non-defect patches (illustrated in Fig. 5).

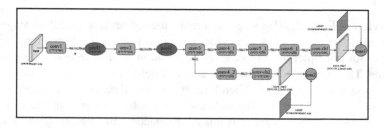

Fig. 5. Multi-loss-function structure of FCN in stage 2. ReLU is the activation function and LRN is short for local response normalization layer.

During the inspection process, similarly to [17] we vote the score map of one single softmax layer and then average the results from different softmax layers. This approach can be view as two merging propose: (1). Average the results of certain-size receptive fields under one patch. (2). Average the results of different-size receptive field under one patch. More details is illustrated in Fig. 6. Besides that, hard negative mining method [18] is applied during the training phrase.

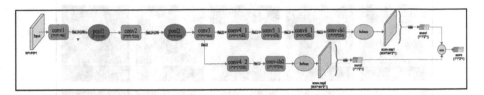

Fig. 6. Illustration of inspection process. Score1 and score2 is the mean value of each corresponding score map and score is the average number of score 1 and score 2.

4 Experiments

4.1 Experimental Framework

We train by SGD with momentum. We use a minibatch size of 128 patches and fixed learning rates of 10-3 for both stage 1 and stage 2. In stage 2, the ratio of training defect patches and non-defect patches is 4:1. We use momentum 0.9, weight decay of 5*10-4 and doubled learning rate for biases. We initialize the retained ZF's feature layer with the ZF's weights trained as a RPN (done in [14]) and randomly initialize the modified layer. Local Response Normalization is included where used in the RPN net. ReLu is used as activation function. We train and test our framework on the dataset of DAGM 2007 [13] and extension the dataset as mentioned in Sect. 3.

4.2 Metrics

We use mean accuracy mentioned in [7] to evaluate the performance of our system. The ground truth is obtained from manual annotation and is used to train our model. This approach is a reasonable one as it is to train a human-like model in defect inspection. We expect that this framework can give an inspection results the same as artificial detection results. Therefore, we also use manual annotation ground truth to assess algorithm performance.

4.3 Results

We test our framework on the dataset of DAGM 2007 [13] which provides six types of defect area, each type contains 150 images for develop and test. We train the framework with 120 images of each type of defect, and test the framework with the rest 30 images per type. Overall, 720 images are used for training and 180 for testing. The develop environment is as follows: CPU: i5-6500, GPU: GTX1080, memory: 16G, develop environment: matlab R2015a and caffe. It takes about 0.04 s for stage1 and 0.05 s for stage2 with the size of input image 512*512.

In Fig. 7 we show a few qualitative segmentation results comparison of ours, and we show the overall performance in Table 1. While our results are visually more consistent with ground truth and achieve higher mean accuracy in quantitative analysis.

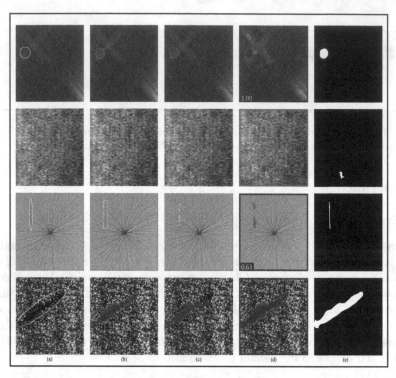

Fig. 7. Results comparison: (a) Initial input images. (b) Results of ours. (c) Results of FCN (d) Results of ViDi. (e) Ground truth.

Table 1. Overall performance of segmentation

Inspector	Mean accuracy	Time for inspection (512*512 input)
FCN(voc-fcn32s) [7]	79.3547%	71 ms
FCN(voc-fcn16s) [7]	90.0371%	75 ms
FCN(voc-fcn8s) [7]	92.2488%	78 ms
ViDi [11]	93.7488%	20 ms
Ours(stage 1)	95.9830%	48 ms
Ours(stage 2)	**95.9934%**	20–50 ms

4.4 Experiment of the Receptive Field of Stage 1

As mentioned in Sect. 3 the inconsistence between the training data and testing data requires the receptive fields of the unit located on the last layer of FCN should not be too large. In this experiment, we change the receptive field of the FCN in Fig. 2 by changing the strides of conv1 and conv2 from 1 to 2. The testing result is shown as follows (Fig. 8). It is obvious that, in this training and testing strategy, the receptive field of network should better not be too large.

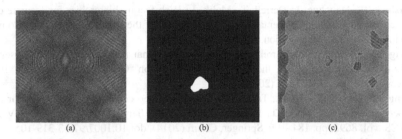

Fig. 8. Results of experiment: (a) Initial input image. (b) Ground truth. (c) Results of stage 1.

In another CNN based surface defect detection paper, we utilize the sliding windows based scheme to locate the defect position. Although the detection rate is higher than the method in this paper, it uses blocks to denote the position of the defects and cannot achieve the pixel-wise segmentation accuracy.

5 Conclusion

In this paper, we have presented a novel 2-stage FCN framework for surface defect inspection in industrial environment. Our framework achieves meaningful results in terms of performance and speed. Different from the recent method based on sliding window, we design a combination of a segmentation task and a detection task. The segmentation stage provides coarse ROIs and the detection stage refines the ROIs. This framework is more general and reusable than traditional ones. Besides that, it can provide pixel-wise inference of defect area and is computed efficiently. We also introduce an unusual training strategy for the scarce training data in industrial environment and investigate its special requirement on our FCN architecture. Since we provide a framework to treat the defect inspection as an object segmentation problem, more advanced algorithm for refining the segmentation might be applied to achieve better results. We leave this for future studies.

References

1. Koch, C., Georgieva, K., Kasireddy, V., Akinci, B., Fieguth, P.: A review on computer vision based defect detection and condition assessment of concrete and asphalt civil infrastructure. Adv. Eng. Inf. **29**(2), 196–210 (2015)
2. Duda, R.O., Hart, P.E., Stork, D.G.: Pattern Classification. Wiley, Hoboken (2001)
3. Jian, C., Gao, J., Ao, Y.: Automatic surface defect detection for mobile phone screen glass based on machine vision. Appl. Soft Comput. **52**, 348–358 (2017)

4. Wells, L.J., Shafae, M.S., Camelio, J.A.: Automated surface defect detection using high-density data. J. Manuf. Sci. Eng. **138**(7), 071001 (2016)
5. Krizhevsky, A., Sutskever, I., Hinton, G.E.: Imagenet classification with deep convolutional neural networks. In: Advances in Neural Information Processing Systems, pp. 1097–1105 (2012)
6. Girshick, R., Donahue, J., Darrell, T., Malik, J.: Rich feature hierarchies for accurate object detection and semantic segmentation. In: Proceedings of the IEEE Conference on Computer Vision and Pattern Recognition, pp. 580–587 (2014)
7. Long, J., Shelhamer, E., Darrell, T.: Fully convolutional networks for semantic segmentation. In: Proceedings of the IEEE Conference on Computer Vision and Pattern Recognition, pp. 3431–3440 (2015)
8. Dong, C., Loy, C.C., He, K., Tang, X.: Learning a deep convolutional network for image super-resolution. In: Fleet, D., Pajdla, T., Schiele, B., Tuytelaars, T. (eds.) ECCV 2014. LNCS, vol. 8692, pp. 184–199. Springer, Cham (2014). doi:10.1007/978-3-319-10593-2_13
9. Nam, H., Han, B.: Learning multi-domain convolutional neural networks for visual tracking. In: Proceedings of the IEEE Conference on Computer Vision and Pattern Recognition, pp. 4293–4302 (2016)
10. Bian, X., Lim, S.N., Zhou, N.: Multiscale fully convolutional network with application to industrial inspection. In: 2016 IEEE Winter Conference on Applications of Computer Vision (WACV) pp. 1–8. IEEE (2016)
11. https://www.vidi-systems.com. Accessed 10 Apr 2017
12. Deng, J., Dong, W., Socher, R., Li, L.J., Li, K., Fei-Fei, L.: Imagenet: a large-scale hierarchical image database. In: IEEE Conference on Computer Vision and Pattern Recognition, CVPR 2009, pp. 248–255. IEEE (2009)
13. https://hci.iwr.uni-heidelberg.de/node/3616. Accessed 10 Apr 2017
14. Ren, S., He, K., Girshick, R., Sun, J.: Faster R-CNN: towards real-time object detection with region proposal networks. In: Advances in Neural Information Processing Systems, pp. 91–99 (2015)
15. Zeiler, M.D., Krishnan, D., Taylor, G.W., Fergus, R.: Deconvolutional networks. In: 2010 IEEE Conference on Computer Vision and Pattern Recognition (CVPR), pp. 2528–2535. IEEE (2010)
16. Hou, L., Samaras, D., Kurc, T.M., Gao, Y., Davis, J.E., Saltz, J.H.: Patch-based convolutional neural network for whole slide tissue image classification. In: Proceedings of the IEEE Conference on Computer Vision and Pattern Recognition, pp. 2424–2433 (2016)
17. Li, Y., He, K., Sun, J.: R-FCN: object detection via region-based fully convolutional networks. In: Advances in Neural Information Processing Systems, pp. 379–387 (2016)
18. Felzenszwalb, P.F., Girshick, R.B., McAllester, D., Ramanan, D.: Object detection with discriminatively trained part-based models. IEEE Trans. Pattern Anal. Mach. Intell. **32**(9), 1627–1645 (2010)

The New Detection Algorithm for an Obstacle's Information in Low Speed Vehicles

Sinjae Lee and Seok-Cheol Kee[✉]

Smart Car Research Center, Chungbuk National University,
B324 Yangcheong 4-gil, Ochang-eup, Cheongwon-gu,
Cheongju, Chungbuk 28116, South Korea
{sinjaelee,sckee}@chungbuk.ac.kr

Abstract. MOD (Moving Object Detection) development methods were used motion region detection methods in image, but it is necessary to detect the position and the size of obstacles in a warning area for collision avoidance in a low speed vehicle. Therefore, this paper proposed the new obstacle detection algorithm. First, the proposed algorithm detects the motion region using MHI (Motion History Image) algorithm, which is based on motion information between image frames. After the algorithm is processed by a high-speed and real-time image processing of a moving obstacle, a warning logic system receives the information of the position and the size of the obstacle nearest to a car. Finally, it determines warning signal send to the control part or not. The proposed algorithm recognizes both fixed and moving obstacles such as cars and buildings using 4 - channel AVM camera images and has a fast calculation speed. After we simulated with the image DBs and the simulation tool, we have 80.07% with the average detection rate.

Keywords: Moving Object Detection · Low speed driving · Image calibration · Collision warning

1 Introduction

1.1 Background

A 4-channel AVM (Around View Monitoring) camera usually used for parking, narrow-road driving and it only provides the function of displaying only an image to a driver. However, by analyzing the image of each input channel, it is possible to recognize objects that are expected to collide while driving, and then to provide new safety functions. Therefore, carmakers are developing Advanced Driver Assistance System (ADAS) are trying to commercialize an AVM system with a Moving Object Detection (MOD) function that recognizes and alerts to a warning logic for avoiding a collision.

Moreover, MOD algorithm based on MHI (Motion History Image) [1, 2] algorithm that implements high-speed and real-time image processing of short-distance obstacles (parking vehicles, etc.) with motion and detects them as a warning area. There are many object detection algorithms which are the deep neural networks for OD (Object

© Springer International Publishing AG 2017
M. Liu et al. (Eds.): ICVS 2017, LNCS 10528, pp. 427–436, 2017.
DOI: 10.1007/978-3-319-68345-4_38

Detection), SFM-based DC/OD for AVM [3], the machine vision software for OD, and the online calibration and the image stitching [4].

The MOD function development method uses motion area detection method in image, but it is difficult to recognize wall or pillar of single color or simple pattern, which is difficult to detect as motion object. On the other hand, there is also a problem that a lane existing in a free space, or an object such as a lid of a manhole is a wrong recognition as a moving object, thereby causing a recognition error. Therefore, this paper proposes a new MOD method that can solve the above problems.

1.2   The Basic Approaches

There are various types of obstacles around the vehicle so we attempt to detect obstacles to be protected from the risk of having a possible collision. Generally, a vehicle access obstacle sensing system includes an ultrasonic sensor and Lidar. The sensors recognize the nearest object from the vehicle to inform about the information of object to the driver. However, we need a different approach using a 4-channel AVM camera installed in the vehicle instead of ultrasonic and laser sensors to detect an obstacle by using the image captured through the sensors.

Camera-based MOD is different from ultrasonic or laser sensors. Specifically, if the system is an Around View Monitoring (AVM) system, it is common to use a wide-angle camera with a wide-angle image. However, a radial distortion in which the degree of distortion is determined by the refractive index of the convex lens is inevitably. Thus, not only the visual distortion of the display image but also the image distortion of the image processing apparatus. It can cause serious errors in the recognition of unknowns. As the above reasons, we introduce a new algorithm with many advantages will be proved by the following sections.

2   The MOD Algorithm

2.1   Description

The algorithm estimates a risk of collision based on the distance between the detected obstacle location and the vehicle using the front camera. The way to get the information is to calculate the coordinate values using the distance transformation matrix (row, column order) then in the same column, it searches from the nearest line.

Since the camera uses a fisheye lens, the image distortion is occurred, so a calibration process is momentary. The calibration process must have a distance value from the vehicle to the obstacle is calculated by a matrix of the obstacle in the top view image. In case of low-speed driving, the collision scenario between a vehicle and an obstacle can be determined by calculating the position, direction and speed of the nearest obstacle and calculating the time to collision (TTC). Therefore, by using the above algorithm, it is possible to predict the probability from time of collision of the obstacles in the warning zone and to avoid the collision when the driver is careless.

For measuring the distance between the vehicle and the obstacle, the position of the obstacle can be calculated in the top view by inserting the distortion correction formula and inputting the parameter value. For example, if the coordinates before distortion correction are (195, 155) and the coordinates after distortion correction are calculated as (238,109), then we can know the position in the region of interest (ROI) by using the internal parameters. In this case, since the output value of the collision warning logic is green (safe), the vehicle can be driven without control (braking). The homomorphic (H) matrix given in the distortion correction is as

$$H = \begin{bmatrix} 7.23823306322797, & -0.540772651280243, & -2482.63262928865 \\ -0.558113443689797, & 12.52997421347332 & 78.874861185145 \\ 0.000137102291708695, & -0.00700525466611019, & 1 \end{bmatrix} \quad (1)$$

The value of the world coordinate can be obtained by using the H matrix (1). The following chapter will mention about the matrix precisely. The value of this coordinate is the position of the obstacle in the top view and its position is treated as the basic value when the vehicle's is stopping for the warning zone in the vehicle's direction. The warning logic is detected in the 8 regions (Fig. 1) in four directions in front, back, left and right by the three levels of warning. Performance evaluation of this area will be the most important measure in a specific zone.

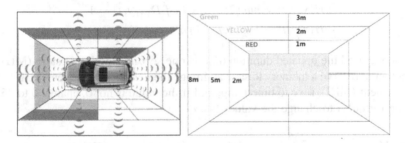

Fig. 1. The warning logic

In Fig. 2, there are obstacles in the current state, multiple obstacles are detected, and the closest obstacle values are calculated and transmitted to the warning logic. The warning logic allows the vehicle to proceed without passing on to the control part since

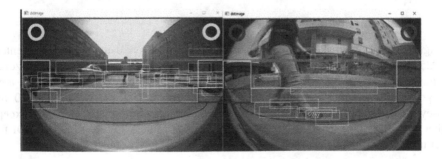

Fig. 2. The images of our system (Color figure online)

the position of the obstacle is not the warning zone. It includes the ROI and warning signals like red, yellow and green.

2.2 The Main Idea for the MHI

First, MHI is extracted from the input image that expressing the degree of change of motion, the brightness of the image becomes bright from dark and it is proportional to time for motion. By expressing MHI where the action occurred, we can calculate how much time in which direction. It is possible to obtain the temporal and spatial information whether the motion is occurred in Fig. 2 [5, 6].

$$H\tau(x, y, t) = \tau \; if \; D(x, y, t) = 1$$
$$H\tau(x, y, t) = max\,(0, H\tau(x, y, t - 1) - 1)\; otherwise, \tag{2}$$

Equation (2) is defined by Bobick and Davis [4] of MHI. H means MHI, D means a binary image from difference images between frames and τ is a continue time for motion. In this paper, the Eq. (2) is modified as shown in the following Eq. (3) with k is a constant.

$$H(x, y, t) = min(255, \tau \times k) \; if \; D(x, y, t) = 1$$
$$H(x, y, t) = H(x, y, t - 1) \; otherwise \tag{3}$$

In Fig. 4, we used the updated duration time is one second, Motion History (MH), and the function to reserve a memory to save an image then check any movement. If there is any movement (MHI), save to timestamp, and if the value is not 0, change 0 to 255 for using the formulas to change the values (4).

$$mask(x, y) = \frac{255}{MHI\_Duration} [mhi(x, y) - (timestamp - MHI\_Duration)]$$
$$= (scale \times mhj(x, y)) + (scale \times t),$$
$$scale = \frac{255}{MHI\_Duration} \tag{4}$$
$$t = MHI\_Duration - timestamp$$

2.3 The Region of Interest

In Figs. 2 and 3, we make an area with a direct collision risk using a code like center. y > 250 and it means the area is excluded of safety and caution area. Like the red zone, we make green and yellow areas. Yellow areas are 150 < center.y < 250 and the area has possibility to enter the red zone except center.x < 100 and center.x > 620 for fish-eye lenses. The last one is a green area which has building, and mountain except center.x < 50, and center.x > 670. We excluded the vehicle's body from the ROI for deleting the error detection.

```
if (cy1 > 300)
{ cvCircle(dstImage, cvPoint(100, 100), 50, CV_RGB(255, 0, 0),10,8,1);
cvCircle(dstImage, cvPoint(1350, 100), 50, CV_RGB(255, 0, 0),10,8,1); }
```

Fig. 3. The ROI code for the red (Warning zone) (Color figure online)

3   Experiments and Results

3.1   Correction for Distortion

For the warning logic to prevent obstacle collision, it is aimed to measure the coordinates and distance of the closest obstacle among the obstacles approaching in the direction of the vehicle in advance and transmit it to the integrated safety control system. Therefore, we precisely calculated the position of object then get the TTC. For fish-eye cameras, we must change from image to world coordinate using the formulas. Figure 4 are a processing steps to change world coordinates from image coordinates. In Fig. 5, from the black box to 400 pixels are 8 meters and we can get the ROI for the warning logic after the processing steps are images of distortion corrections, top-view images, then images for the ROI. The results of this steps are in Fig. 5.

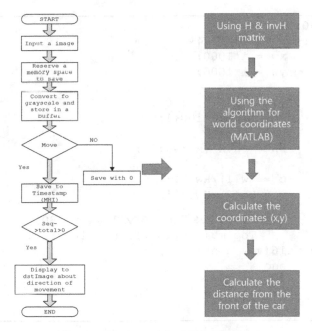

Fig. 4. The flow of the MHI algorithm

The equations in Fig. 4, the first one of the above is to get a normalized coordinate and the second one is to get the distance of the center for an object and the next one is

<original>   <undistorted>   <top-view>

Fig. 5. The images of distortion correction and the top-view image

the pixel coordinate. Finally, we can get the coordinate in the distortion image. As we already mentioned, H matrix is a intrinsic parameter for camera calibration.

After an object enters in the warning zone (Fig. 2), we can calculate a coordinate and the distance from the object to the front or the side of the vehicle. The first step is using H matrix (1) and/or inverse H matrix (5) to get world coordinates. The next is to use the algorithm in Fig. 6 for changing coordinates by MATLAB. Then we should get the object's location in the top-view image and calculate the distance from the center of the car. We can calculate the distance in 2 cm by 1 pixel in Fig. 5.

```
for(i=0:-0.01:-8)
  for(j=4:-0.01:-4) % -4~4m 10cm
            xw = j*1000;
            yw = i*1000;

            y = (-1*i+0)*100+1;
            x = (-j+4)*100+1;

            Hw = invH*[xw;yw;1];

            u = Hw(1)/Hw(3);
            v = Hw(2)/Hw(3);

            if(u>1 && u< 720 && v>1 && v<480)
                 TopImg(uint16(y), uint16(x), :) =
OutImg2(uint16(v), uint16(u), :);
            end

        end
    end
```

Fig. 6. The algorithm to get world coordinates

$$invH = \begin{bmatrix} 0.117004387911269, \ 0.198380785365152, \ 345.802325178971 \\ 0.00575131602499519, \ 0.0838405911917846, \ 37.6594380552932 \\ 2.42478636977637e-05, \ 0.000560126232351153, \ 1 \end{bmatrix} \quad (5)$$

3.2 Performance Evaluation

For the evaluation, we used the 4-ch AVM camera with our autonomous driving car. There are many specifications of the camera. The specifications are outputs are NTSC_CVBS (1Vpp_Typ), the average frame rate is 30 fps, the angle of view is 195° for horizontal and 148° for vertical, and the dimension is 21.0 × 21.0 × 24.5(H). Also, we recorded as many as the video files to save and collect the image DBs that have many different weather conditions, speed and environments.

Before we use the DBs, we must detach and make one channel file such as a front camera for MOD because this research uses 4-channel AVM. Also, we recorded the MOD videos as many as in parking spaces, narrow roads, and exit areas. For evaluating the performance of the system, GT (Ground Truth) value can be obtained and compared with the value of the obstacle in the warning zone in the evaluation tool (Fig. 7). The GT values was compared with the objects in the warning zone. In this study, the performance of the front camera image database was evaluated and its performance was confirmed to be 80.07% with the average detection rate in Fig. 8.

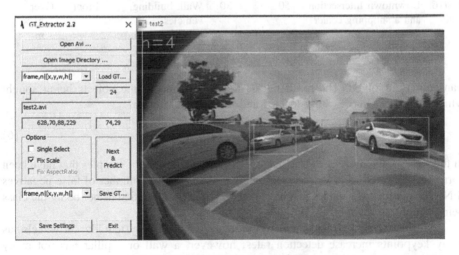

Fig. 7. The evaluation tool [7]

For the performance evaluation of this research, we used the image DBs in Table 1 with the simulation tool then we calculated coordinates for the detection areas and GT values to compare the two datasets and get the detection rates. Also, we used the front camera and the fps is 30 in Table 1. The size of the sample DB is 2314 frames and the below figure shows the detection rate by decreasing order. The vertical axes represent the percentage of detection rates, and the horizontal axes represent the number of

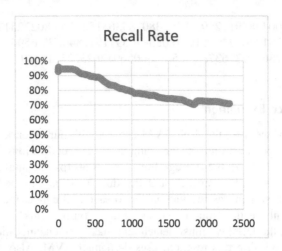

Fig. 8. The detection rate

Table 1. The image DB

File	Driving environment	Duration time (about)	FPS	Objects	Camera	The size of object (s)
test16. avi	Downtown Intersection and a shopping center area	50 s	30	Wall, building, vehicles, pedestrians, curb	Front	Over 1 m × 1 m

transactions involved. The recall rate is the percentage of the objects being sought which have been successfully located and the formula is like

$$\text{Recall} = tp/(tp + fn) \tag{6}$$

In the Eq. (6), the number of true positives (TP): the number of samples that have been correctly identified as being the class being sought, and the number of false negatives (FN): the number of samples that have been incorrectly identified as not being the class being sought.

As the above result, there are many characteristics in this system like car wheels has many keypoints increase detection rates; however, a wall or a pillar has not many keypoints decrease detection rates so we will advance the disadvantage. Also, we can increase the detection rate while the ROI is changed, it means that remove an error detection like a mountain or a building include a body of a test car. If the system considers to detect a movement with vector and a same color that has a high possibility with one object, the detection rates can be increased. We missed 19.93% from the detection rate because there were very different environments in the places like a basement parking space, a dark side of the building and many directions or warning signals on the road.

4 Conclusion

It can improve image processing speed based on MHI algorithm enables real-time processing over 24 fps with the detection rate (80.07%). Obstacle detection functions can be implemented in the Mirrorless Camera System (MCS), which is expected to be applied to a commercial product in the future. The contribution of this paper is to develop a warning logic to prevent obstacle collision, it is aimed to measure the coordinates and distance of the closest obstacle approaching in the direction of the vehicle and transmit the information to the integrated safety control system. The advantages of this system are that recognition availability for fixed and moving objects and fast calculation speed. We will research that remove a center lane and shadows which are not detected in the images, and too many detections occur on unpaved roads. Also, we will research a method to detect a motion area detected in a square unit in a motion object such as vehicle, wall, and pedestrians and to reduce false alarm and shorten image processing speed by restricting only the area can collide with the car. Moreover, we can optimize to reduce sensitivity to a far-field motion and increase sensitivity to a near-field motion by tuning. This system can detect only an object has direct possibility to collide a vehicle so we will consider not to detect a leaf or a napkin which are no risk to the vehicle.

Acknowledgement. This work was supported by Institute for Information & communications Technology Promotion (IITP) grant funded by the Korea government (MSIP) (No. R7117-16-0164, Development of wide area driving environment awareness and cooperative driving technology which are based on V2X wireless communication).

References

1. Kim, S.-K.: Gesture recognition using MHI shape information. Korea Comput. Inform. Soc. **16**(4), 1–13 (2011)
2. Davis, J.W.: Hierarchical motion history image for recognizing human motion. In: Proceedings of IEEE Workshop on Detection and Recognition of Events in Video (2001)
3. Carnegie Mellon University, and Mando Corporation, The Robotics Institute "SFM-based DC/OD for AVM", Research Project (2014)
4. Mando and Adasens Esow, "Machine Vision Software for OD, Online Calibration and Image Stitching" Engineering Statement of Work (2012)
5. Bobick, A.F., Davis, J.W.: The recognition of human movement using temporal templates. IEEE Trans. Pattern Anal. Mach. Intell. **23**(3), 257–267 (2001)
6. Ahad, A.R.: Motion history image: its variants and applications. Mach. Vis. Appl. **23**(2), 255–281 (2010)
7. Blog. http://darkpgmr.tistory.com/16
8. Szegedy, C., Toshev, A., Erhan, D.: Deep neural networks for object detection. In: NIPS (2013)
9. Jung, H.G., Kim, D.S., Yoon, P.J., Kim, J.: Parking slot marking recognition for automatic parking assist system. In: Intelligent Vehicles Symposium, Tokyo, Japan, 13–15 June 2006 (2006)

10. Lee, S., Hyeon, D., Park, G., Back, I.-J., Kim, S.-W., Seo, S.-W.: Directional-DBSCAN: parking-slot detection using a clustering method in around-view monitoring system. In: 2016 IEEE Intelligent Vehicles Symposium (IV) (2016)
11. Suh, J.K., Jung, H.G.: High-level sensor fusion-based parking space detection. In: KSAE (2014)
12. Dalal, N., Triggs, B.: Histograms of oriented gradients for human detection. In: CVPR (2005)
13. Viola, P., Jones, M.J.: Rapid object detection using a boosted cascade of simple features. In: CVPR (2001)
14. Wagner, D., Reitmayr, G., Mulloni, A., Drummond, T., Schmalstieg, D.: Pose tracking from natural features on mobile phones. In: International Symposium on Mixed and Augmented Reality, Cambridge, UK, September 2008
15. Lowe, D.G.: Distinctive image features from scale-invariant keypoints. In: IJCV (2004)

Trajectory-Pooled Deep Convolutional Networks for Violence Detection in Videos

Zihan Meng[✉], Jiabin Yuan, and Zhen Li

College of Computer Science and Technology,
Nanjing University of Aeronautics and Astronautics, Nanjing, China
{zihan,jbyuan,cristianlee}@nuaa.edu.cn

Abstract. Violence detection in videos is of great importance in many applications, ranging from teenagers protection to online media filtering and searching to surveillance systems. Typical methods mostly rely on hand-crafted features, which may lack enough discriminative capacity for the specific task of violent action recognition. Inspired by the good performance of deep models for human action recognition, we propose a novel method for detecting human violent behaviour in videos by integrating trajectory and deep convolutional neural networks, which takes advantage of hand-crafted features [21] and deep-learned features [23]. To evaluate this method, we carry out experiments on two different violence datasets: Hockey Fights dataset and Crowd Violence dataset. The results demonstrate the advantage of our method over state-of-the art methods on these datasets.

Keywords: Violence detection · ConvNets · Trajectory

1 Introduction

Violence detection in videos is of great importance due to its potential usefulness in many applications. Currently, massive video materials have become ubiquitous online, its very necessary to protect children against the aggressive videos. Surveillance systems deployed in scenes such as prisons, schools and streets need to alert people to dangerous situations in real-time. For these practical considerations, we focus on the detection of human violent behavior by using computer vision techniques. The purpose of violence detection is to judge if the video sequence involves the violent behavior. However, this brings a huge challenge to the computer vision community due to its intense action, the crowed scene and the different distance between the camera and the person.

In the last few years, we have paid a lot of attention to human action recognition. Based on the approach of extracting features, currently, human action recognition in videos has two mainly types: hand-crafted features and deeplearned features [23].

The first type is local hand-crafted descriptors, and conventional approaches include Space Time Interests Points [20], 3D-SIFT [15], HOG3D [14] and

© Springer International Publishing AG 2017
M. Liu et al. (Eds.): ICVS 2017, LNCS 10528, pp. 437–447, 2017.
DOI: 10.1007/978-3-319-68345-4_39

Improved Trajectories [21]. Generally, these conventional approaches first extract feature descriptors around the interest points, such as trajectories, gradients, orientations, flow intensities and other features. These local features are less affected by illumination, rotation and poster. Then, they usually choose the bag-of-words [25] to get the various feature words, and make the words into histograms using k-means clustering. Finally, they use a classifier like SVM to classify the human actions. However, these traditional hand-crafted may lack enough high discriminate information facing human action recognition.

The second type is deep-learned features, which has got excellent performance in many tasks based on vision, such as scene classification, image classification and detection, semantic segmentation. The well known methods include 3D convolutional networks [9], Two-stream ConvNets [1], and VGG ConvNets [22] and recurrent neural networks [13]. These deep learning models learn features from the raw video through the Convolutional Neural Networks, which is trained from a large amount of labeled data. These learned feature maps can well represent the semantic information and can be visual.

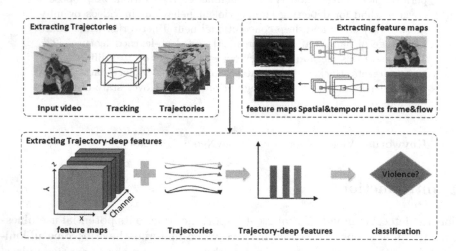

Fig. 1. The whole framework of our proposed trajectory-deep method: (1) extracting trajectories, (2) extracting convolutional feature maps, (3) extracting 3D volume trajectories through feature maps, (4) judging whether the video is violent or not.

A lot of former works about human action recognition concentrate on general actions like jumping, walking or chasing [20,21]. In our paper, we face the challenge of detecting violence in videos. Inspired by the above analysis, we propose a novel method for violence detection in videos by integrating trajectory and deep neural networks. As shown in Fig. 1, the proposed method contains two streams to capture the violent features. First, we extract trajectories from the input videos. Then we treat two deep ConvNet models trained on the specific violent dataset as an extractor to extract the convolutional feature maps. Next, we get the 3D volume trajectories from these feature maps. Finally, Fisher vector are chosen to encode the feature vectors and use a liner SVM to determine if the video is a violent video.

The rest of this paper is organized as follows: the related work is introduced in Sect. 2, then our method is proposed, and experiments are presented in the fourth part. Finally, the conclusion is presented in Sect. 5.

2   Related Work

Violence detection as a specific task in human action recognition domain has been less studied. A lot of the former works are based on audio and color features [3,16,19]. As the first proposal in violence detection, Nam et al. [16] used blood and flame in the video scene to capture the situation of the motion, and the special sounds of the violent behavior. Cheng et al. [3] proposed using a hierarchical method to detect explosions, gunshots, and car braking. However, this method leads to low detection rate. Datta et al. [4] captured human body information, such as motion and orientation to detect. This approach needs foreground segmentation to get the information, which is complicated.

Actually some surveillance videos in public scenes, such as squares, hospitals, schools lack audio information for reasons of privacy protection. In recent years, Bermejo et al. [18] proposed detect violent information based on spatiotemporal interest-point, such as STIP [20], MoSIFT [2]. Hassner et al. [11] presented a simple method to address the difficulty of the crowded scenes. However, the performance of this method is not good in other scenarios. Deniz et al. [5] used the Radon transform to process the energy spectrum of two continuous frames to detect the motion change in violent videos. A Gaussian Model of Optical Flow (GMOF) [26] is established to find some violence regions as the candidate, then they detect violence on the video in the candidate regions. In addition, there are a few methods based on the deep learning. Ding et al. [6] proposed a 3D ConvNet method to detect violence. However, this method ignored the time dimension information. Dong et al. [7] took advantage of acceleration for detecting, and this method performs best on Hockey Fights dataset for now. However, this method consists of six deep neural networks, which relied on large training datasets.

Considering the above problems, a simple and robust method for violence detection are proposed in this paper. These following three are our mainly contributions:

- Our trajectory-deep features contain enough high discriminative information compared to those hand-crafted features for violent action recognition.
- We propose a novel method for violence detection by integrating trajectory and deep neural networks, which takes advantage of the method of improved trajectory to capture long-term action information.
- Experimental results on two different violence datasets demonstrate that our proposed method performs better than the state-of-the-art methods.

3 The Proposed Method

In this section, we first elaborate two ConvNet streams respectively and then introduce extracting 3D volume trajectory-deep feature strategy in details.

3.1 Spatial Stream

Discriminative frames in videos carry a lot of information about scenes and objects detected in the video. Some violence always occurs with specific scenes. For instance, supposing someone holding a big stick is fighting with the other one, this violence is close to the scenes, such as the stick. This deep ConvNet which operates on the still frames has effectively performed in many visual tasks such as object detection [10] and image classification [12].

In this paper, We pre-train our network using the public convNets model [24], which is trained by RGB frames ($224 \times 224 \times 3$) on the UCF101 dataset. This ConvNet model is developed from VGG-19 net, which contains 17 convolution-pool-norm layers and two fully connected layers. This implementation steps and training parameters can be seen in Sect. 4.2.

As shown in Fig. 1, once the spatial ConvNet is trained, we take it as the feature extractor to get the spatial feature maps. Therefore, we make a modification about the net for feature extraction. We choose to remain the layers from conv1 to conv5 and remove the layers full7 and full8. Then, we can obtain any convolutional layer feature maps. Given a video V, we get its convolution feature maps:

$$\mathbf{C}\left(V\right) = \{C_1^s, C_2^s, \cdots, C_M^s\} \tag{1}$$

where $C_m^s \in \mathbb{R}^{H_m \times W_m \times L \times N_m}$ is the mth spatial net's feature map, H_m is the height, W_m is the width, L is the video frames, and N_m is the amount of channels.

3.2 Temporal Stream

We model the temporal stream to describe the dynamic violent motion information like the kick or hit on purpose. The temporal stream aims to learn the effective motion features and has got excellent performance in action classification [1]. Optical Flow is a successful method to capture the short motion information between any consecutive frames. In this paper, we follow the idea in the two stream convNets.

We use the Farneback [8] method to compute the dense optical flow, which is implemented in the OpenCV library3 due to its efficiency and accuracy. For each frame in videos, we first obtain its horizontal (x) and vertical (y) optical flow values. Then, we stack horizontal (x) and horizontal (y) optical flow fields as the input of the temporal net ($224 \times 224 \times 2L$, L is the length of stacking flows). We finetune our temporal model on the pre-trained model as mentioned above. This ConvNet architecture is the same as the spatial net. This implementation steps and training parameters can also be seen in Sect. 4.2. Similar to the spatial stream, we need to obtain the temporal feature maps. Given a video V, we get its convolution feature maps:

$$\mathbf{C}(V) = \{C_1^t, C_2^t, \cdots, C_M^t\} \tag{2}$$

where $C_m^t \in \mathbb{R}^{H_m \times W_m \times L \times N_m}$ is the mth temporal net's feature map, H_m is the height,W_m is the width, L is the video frames, and N_m is the amount of channels.

3.3 Modeling Long-Term Information with Improved Trajectories

Optical Flow fields can only model short motion information between two frames, therefore, the temporal network still lacks video-level action information. As mentioned in Sect. 1, Improved trajectories have shown good performance for representing video-level information. We then integrate deep neural networks and trajectory-based methods. We use improved trajectories to extract 3D volume trajectories from deep-convolutional feature maps to capture long-term action information.

Improved Trajectories. This method has been successfully employed in video action recognition such as TDDs, which is extended from dense trajectories. To get dense trajectories, it samples dense points from each frame on 8 spatial scales on a grid spaced by 5 pixels and then track them by median filtering in a dense optical flow field.

$$P_{t+1}(x_{t+1}, y_{t+1}) = (x_t, y_t) + (\varepsilon * \omega_t) \,|\, (\overline{x_t}, \overline{y_t}). \tag{3}$$

where ε is the median filtering kernel, $(\overline{x_t}, \overline{y_t})$ is the neighbor point of (x_t, y_t), $\omega_t = (u_t, v_t)$ is the dense optical flow field, $*$ is the operation of the convolution. Setting the length of each trajectory to 15 can avoid the useless drifting information. Improved trajectories take account of camera motion to improve the performance. To remove camera motion, it estimates a homography matrix with RANSAC, which can be obtained by comparing dense points between dense optical flow and frames. There is a video V, and we can get some trajectories:

$$\mathbf{T}(V) = \{T_1, T_2, \cdots, T_k\} \tag{4}$$

where K represents the amount of trajectories, and T_k represents the kth trajectory:

$$T_k = \{(x_1^k, y_1^k, z_1^k), (x_2^k, y_2^k, z_2^k), \cdots, (x_L^k, y_L^k, z_L^k)\} \tag{5}$$

where (x_l^k, y_l^k, z_l^k) is the lth point position on the kth trajectory,and L is trajectory's length (L = 15).

Modeling 3D Volume Trajectories. After the step of extracting feature maps, we will model 3D volume trajectories by using trajectory pooling method. There are a trajectory T_k and a feature map C_m^n, which is m^{th} spatial or temporal feature map $n \in (s, t)$, we conduct the deep-trajectory feature by the following equation:

$$F(T_k, C_m^n) = \sum_{l=1}^{L} C_m^n \left(\tilde{x}_l^k, \tilde{x}_l^k, z_l^k\right). \tag{6}$$

$F(T_k, C_m^n)$ is the final feature combining the advantages of both improved trajectories and two-stream ConvNets.

4   Experiments

In this section, we describe the two typical violence datasets firstly. Then we show the specific experimental steps. Finally, the results and analysis for our method compared with other approaches are given.

4.1   Datasets

To verify the performance of our proposed violence detection method, we conducted our experiments on two typical violence datasets: Hockey Fights dataset [18] and Crowd Violence dataset [11].

Crowd Violence Dataset. This set is a collection of realistic videos for fighting behavior. These videos are collected from YouTube, real-world and crowd scenes. The dataset has 140 videos with a resolution of 320×240 pixels. There are 75 violence videos and 65 non-violence videos.

Hockey Fights Dataset. This set was collected from the National Hockey League matches and was designed to judge videos as violent or normal. Specifically, Hockey Fights contains 1,000 videos with a resolution of 360×228 pixels, which are divided into five splits for each category. As Hockey Fights dataset is larger than Crowd violence dataset, we use Hockey Fights dataset to train the model and evaluate our method on these two datasets.

4.2   Implementation Details

In the Sect. 4.2, we present the specific experimental steps, including two ConvNet models training and results, feature encoding, dimension reduction and different layers.

Training and Results About Spatial ConvNets. We choose the dataset of Hockey Fights as the training data. The ConvNets training tool is Caffe toolbox. We set the training batch size as 50 and set SGD with momentum as 0.9. We first reshape the video frames as 340×256, and then a 224×224 region is randomly extracted from the frames. We pre-train our network using the public convNets model. At last, we choose the Hockey Fights dataset as the training set and fine tune the model with multi GPUs, in which the learning rate is set to 0.001 and training stopped at 500 iterations after 10 epochs. To test this trained model, we use 200 hockey videos and we obtain 91.5% recognition accuracy.

Training and Results About Temporal ConvNets. Its input is optical flow fields, and we choose the Farneback algorithm using the Opencv-3.0 Implementation. The input data is 10 stacked flow fields. The training network structure is almost the same as the spatial stream and we randomly croped a $224 \times 224 \times 20$

sub-region from the input data. This learning rate is set to 0.005 and training stopped at 100 iterations. To test this trained model, we use 200 hockey videos and we obtain 87% recognition accuracy. We also evaluate the above two nets by fusion and the best performance is 93%.

Feature Encoding. o encode final features, we choose to use Fisher vector which has shown an good performance for both image and action classification [17]. To train GMMs, we first reduce the dimension to D using PCA, as in [17]. Then, we choose the Gaussian component K as 256, training 768000 features from the training set and the video can be represented by a 2KD dimensional Fisher vector. A linear SVM is used as a classifier $(C = 2)$.

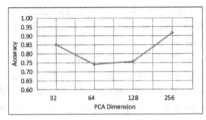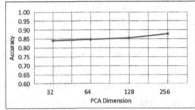

Fig. 2. Left: Performance curve with different PCA dimension on spatial conv4. Right: Performance curve with different PCA dimension on temporal conv4.

Table 1. The result of 5 layers of two nets on the Crowd Violence dataset

	conv1	conv2	conv3	conv4	conv5	conv1	conv2	conv3	conv4	conv5
Acc	78.1%	82.5%	84.1%	**91.2%**	75.9%	70.1%	79.8%	84.4%	**87.7%**	82.1%

Dimension Reduction. To determine the dimension using for training GMMs, we choose different dimensions for PCA in the Crowd Violence dataset. We vary the dimension from 32 to 256 with spatial conv4 and temporal conv4 feature maps and the results are shown in Fig. 2. The results show that dimension 256 achieves the high performance. Thus, we use this method to specify the PCA dimension in the following experiments.

Different Layers. The result of every layer of these two nets on the Crowd Violence dataset are shown in Table 1. During the 17 convolutional layers, we choose the outputs of conv1-2, conv2-2, conv3-3, conv4-2 and conv5-3 layers. We see that for spatial net and temporal net, conv4-2 achieves highest performance. Therefore, in the following experiments, we use conv4-2 feature maps to extract trajectories. In order to express simply, we replace the layers with conv1, conv2, conv3, conv4, and conv5.

4.3   Experimental Results and Analysis

In Sect. 4.3, we compared the performance of our method to the state-of-the-art techniques on the Hockey Fights and Crowd Violence dataset, and the experimental results are reported in Tables 2 and 3.

Analysis on the Crowd Violence Dataset. This dataset is very challenging because the scenes are very crowded. In order to prove our the better performance of the proposed method, we compared it with other existing methods, including HOG, HOF [18], MoSIFT [2], ViF [11], and OHOF [26]. For the spatiotemporal features (HOF, HOG, MoSIFT), we set the dictionary size as 100 in this experiment.

According to the results in Table 2, while the deep network model was trained from the Hockey Fights dataset, our proposed method outperforms the others, especially for those spatiotemporal features (HOF, HOG, MoSIFT). Spatiotemporal descriptors perform bad because crowded scenes seriously affect their needed scene and motion information. Two Convnets perform much better than HOF and HOG features, which proves that deep-learned features learn more discriminative information than hand-crafted features and more robust even in crowded scenes. We also compare our method with original two-stream ConvNets. As the results shown, we see that both our spatial and temporal streams combined with improved trajectories perform well than spatial and temporal nets. These results indicate that trajectory sampling is a good method to model video-level descriptors and improve the recognition accuracy.

Table 2. Classification results on the Crowd Violence dataset

Algorithm	Accuracy
STIP(HOG)vac100 [18]	55.4%
STIP(HOF)vac100 [18]	56.0%
MoSIFT Vac100 [2]	56.4%
ViF [11]	81.3%
OHOF [26]	82.7%
Spatial net [1]	66.4%
Temporal net [1]	69.2%
Spatial + IDT stream (ours)	91.6%
Temporal + IDT stream (ours)	87.7%
Two-stream + IDT (our best result)	92.5%

Analysis on the Hockey Fights Dataset. In the final step of classification, 270 videos in this dataset to train. HOG, HOF [18], MoSIFT [2], ViF [11], 3D CNN [6], Improved dense trajectory [21] and multi streams + LSTM [7] are compared. According to Table 3, the proposed method performs much better

Table 3. Classification results on the Hockey Fights dataset

Algorithm	Accuracy
STIP(HOG)vac100 [18]	81.0%
STIP(HOF)vac100 [18]	79.0%
MoSTIP Vac100 [2]	89.5%
3D CNN [6]	91.0%
ViF [11]	71.2%
IDT [21]	91.1%
Mulit streams + LSTM [7]	93.7%
Spatian net [1]	91.5%
Temporal net [1]	89%
Two-streams [1]	93%
Spatial + IDT stream (ours)	97.3%
Temporal + IDT stream (ours)	95.7%
Two-stream + IDT (our best result)	98.6%

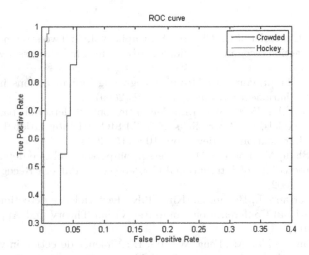

Fig. 3. ROC curves with our method on two datasets

than the state-of-the-art approaches and our best result achieves 98.6%. The performance of spatiotemporal descriptors (HOG, HOF, MoSIFT) turns out to be better than ViF. That is because this dataset contains people violence behaviors at a comparatively short distance. Additionally, our trajectory-pooled deep networks perform better than [6, 7, 21], which indicates our advantage over the trajectory based or other deep networks based methods.

Figure 3 gives the ROC curve obtained by our method on two datasets. These results show that its very effective for our method to detect violence in videos, even in crowd scenes.

5   Conclusion and Future Work

In this paper, we propose a novel method for violence detection in videos by integrating trajectory and deep neural networks, which takes advantage of the method of improved trajectory to capture long-term action information. We overcome the difficulty of detecting specific violent action. In addition, the advantage is that our method also applies to crowd scene videos. Analysis on two different violent datasets was given in the end and the results show the advantage of our method over state-of-the art methods. In the future we will take detecting violence regions into consideration.

Acknowledgments. This work was supported by the "Application platform and Industrialization for efficient cloud computing for Big data" of the Science and Technology Supported Program of Jiangsu Province (BA2015052) and "Research and Industrialization for Intelligent video processing Technology based on GPUs Parallel Computing" of the Science and Technology Supported Program of Jiangsu Province (BY2016003-11).

References

1. Annane, D., Chevrolet, J.C., Chevret, S., Raphael, J.C.: Two-stream convolutional networks for action recognition in videos. Adv. Neural Inf. Process. Syst. **1**(4), 568–576 (2014)
2. Chen, M.Y., Hauptmann, A.: Mosift: recognizing human actions in surveillance videos. Ann. Pharmacother. **39**(1), 150–152 (2009)
3. Cheng, W.H., Chu, W.T., Wu, J.L.: Semantic context detection based on hierarchical audio models. In: Proceedings of ACM SIGMM International Workshop on Multimedia Information Retrieval, pp. 109–115 (2003)
4. Datta, A., Shah, M., Lobo, N.D.V.: Person-on-person violence detection in video data. In: Proceedings of International Conference on Pattern Recognition, vol. 1, pp. 433–438 (2002)
5. Deniz, O., Serrano, I., Bueno, G., Kim, T.K.: Fast violence detection in video. In: The International Conference on Computer Vision Theory and Applications, pp. 478–485 (2014)
6. Ding, C., Fan, S., Zhu, M., Feng, W., Jia, B.: Violence detection in video by using 3D convolutional neural networks. In: Bebis, G., et al. (eds.) ISVC 2014. LNCS, vol. 8888, pp. 551–558. Springer, Cham (2014). doi:10.1007/978-3-319-14364-4_53
7. Dong, Z., Qin, J., Wang, Y.: Multi-stream deep networks for person to person violence detection in videos. In: Tan, T., Li, X., Chen, X., Zhou, J., Yang, J., Cheng, H. (eds.) CCPR 2016. CCIS, vol. 662, pp. 517–531. Springer, Singapore (2016). doi:10.1007/978-981-10-3002-4_43
8. Farnebäck, G.: Two-frame motion estimation based on polynomial expansion. In: Bigun, J., Gustavsson, T. (eds.) SCIA 2003. LNCS, vol. 2749, pp. 363–370. Springer, Heidelberg (2003). doi:10.1007/3-540-45103-X_50
9. Garcia-Garcia, A., Gomez-Donoso, F., Garcia-Rodriguez, J., Orts-Escolano, S., Cazorla, M., Azorin-Lopez, J.: PointNet: a 3D convolutional neural network for real-time object class recognition. In: International Joint Conference on Neural Networks, pp. 1578–1584 (2016)

10. Girshick, R., Donahue, J., Darrell, T., Malik, J.: Rich feature hierarchies for accurate object detection and semantic segmentation. In: Computer Vision and Pattern Recognition, pp. 580–587 (2014)
11. Hassner, T., Itcher, Y., Kliper-Gross, O.: Violent flows: real-time detection of violent crowd behavior. In: Computer Vision and Pattern Recognition Workshops, pp. 1–6 (2012)
12. Krizhevsky, A., Sutskever, I., Hinton, G.E.: Imagenet classification with deep convolutional neural networks. In: International Conference on Neural Information Processing Systems, pp. 1097–1105 (2012)
13. Lev, G., Sadeh, G., Klein, B., Wolf, L.: RNN fisher vectors for action recognition and image annotation. In: Leibe, B., Matas, J., Sebe, N., Welling, M. (eds.) ECCV 2016. LNCS, vol. 9910, pp. 833–850. Springer, Cham (2016). doi:10.1007/978-3-319-46466-4_50
14. Li, W., Li, X., Qiu, J.: Human action recognition based on dense of spatio-temporal interest points and HOG-3D descriptor. In: International Conference on Internet Multimedia Computing and Service, p. 44 (2015)
15. Liu, P., Wang, J., She, M., Liu, H.: Human action recognition based on 3D SIFT and LDA model. In: Robotic Intelligence in Informationally Structured Space, pp. 12–17 (2011)
16. Nam, J., Alghoniemy, M., Tewfik, A.H.: Audio-visual content-based violent scene characterization. In: Proceedings of International Conference on Image Processing, ICIP 1998, pp. 353–357 (1998)
17. Nchez, J., Perronnin, F., Mensink, T., Verbeek, J.: Image classification with the fisher vector: theory and practice. Int. J. Comput. Vis. **105**(3), 222–245 (2013)
18. Nievas, E.B., Suarez, O.D., García, G.B., Sukthankar, R.: Violence detection in video using computer vision techniques. In: Real, P., Diaz-Pernil, D., Molina-Abril, H., Berciano, A., Kropatsch, W. (eds.) CAIP 2011. LNCS, vol. 6855, pp. 332–339. Springer, Heidelberg (2011). doi:10.1007/978-3-642-23678-5_39
19. Sadlier, D.A., O'Connor, N.E.: Event detection in field sports video using audio-visual features and a support vector machine. IEEE Trans. Circ. Syst. Video Technol. **15**(10), 1225–1233 (2005)
20. Samanta, S., Chanda, B.: FaSTIP: a new method for detection and description of space-time interest points for human activity classification. In: Eighth Indian Conference on Computer Vision, Graphics and Image Processing, p. 8 (2012)
21. Wang, H., Schmid, C.: Action recognition with improved trajectories. In: IEEE International Conference on Computer Vision, pp. 3551–3558 (2013)
22. Wang, L., Guo, S., Huang, W., Qiao, Y.: Places205-vggnet models for scene recognition. Comput. Sci. (2015). arXiv preprint arXiv:1508.01667
23. Wang, L., Qiao, Y., Tang, X.: Action recognition with trajectory-pooled deep-convolutional descriptors. In: IEEE Conference on Computer Vision and Pattern Recognition, pp. 4305–4314 (2015)
24. Wang, L., Xiong, Y., Wang, Z., Qiao, Y., Lin, D., Tang, X., Gool, L.: Temporal segment networks: towards good practices for deep action recognition. In: Leibe, B., Matas, J., Sebe, N., Welling, M. (eds.) ECCV 2016. LNCS, vol. 9912, pp. 20–36. Springer, Cham (2016). doi:10.1007/978-3-319-46484-8_2
25. Yue, H., Chen, W., Wu, X., Wang, J.: Visualizing bag-of-words for high-resolution remote sensing image classification. J. Appl. Remote Sens. **10**(1), 015022 (2016)
26. Zhang, T., Yang, Z., Jia, W., Yang, B., Yang, J., He, X.: A new method for violence detection in surveillance scenes. Multimedia Tools Appl. **75**(12), 7327–7349 (2016)

Hybrid Distance Metric Learning for Real-Time Pedestrian Detection and Re-identification

Xinyu Huang$^{(\boxtimes)}$, Jiaolong Xu, Gang Guo, and Ergong Zheng

Aviation University of Airforce, Changchun 130022, China
xinyu_huang121@126.com

Abstract. Cross-camera pedestrian re-identification (re-ID) is of paramount importance for surveillance tasks. Although considerable progress has been made to improve the re-ID accuracy, real-time pedestrian detection and re-ID remains a challeging problem. In this work, first, we proposed an enhanced aggregated channel features (ACF+) based on the ACF pedestrian detector [1] for real-time pedestrian detection and re-ID; Second, to further improve the representation power of the combined multiple channel features, we proposed a novel hybrid distance metric learning method. Extensive experiments have been carried on two public datasets, including VIPeR, and PRID2011. The experimental results show that our proposed method can achieve state-of-the-art accuracy while being computational efficient for real-time applications. The proposed hybrid distance metric learning is general, thus can be applied to any metric learning approaches.

Keywords: Pedestrian re-identification · Aggregated channel features · Hybrid distance metric learning

1 Introduction

Surveillance systems use the network of cameras to cover large public spaces (*i.e.* airport terminals, train stations, *etc.*). Cross-camera pedestrian re-identification (re-ID) is crucial for visual surveillance tasks. Due to the large variations in camera viewpoints, different background, human poses, illumination changes, partial occlusion, low resolution and motion-blur *etc.*, pedestrian re-ID is a challenging task.

Pedestrian re-ID can be divided into two steps: (1) feature extraction, *i.e.*, extracting features from detected pedestrian candidates; (2) matching, *i.e.*, matching a given *prob* pedestrian against a *gallery* of candidate ones. For feature representation, many delicate handcrafted features have been proposed, *e.g.* Hist-Moment feature [5], LOMO [11]. Recently, deep convolutional neural networks are used to learn robust feature representation [2,3]. Regarding to the matching, various metric learning methods have been proposed to improve matching accuracy, Liao *et al.* [12] proposed a weighting positive and negative samples differently with a positive semidefinite constraint. In [15], the differences

© Springer International Publishing AG 2017
M. Liu et al. (Eds.): ICVS 2017, LNCS 10528, pp. 448–458, 2017.
DOI: 10.1007/978-3-319-68345-4_40

and commonness between image pairs are both considered and presented that the covariance matrices of dissimilar pairs can be inferred from similar pairs. Besides that, kLFDA [5] and XQDA [11] are very popular ones. Although continuous progress has been made in recent years, little focus has been paid on real-time re-ID. In this work, the re-ID computation cost is one of our major concerns.

For re-ID applications, pedestrian detection is usually regarded as a separate task or pre-processing step, or assuming the pedestrian bounding boxes have been provided. In this work, we consider the detection and re-ID in the joint pipeline and take advantages of detection to extract features for re-ID. As ACF pedestrian detector is known to be both fast and accurate [1], we build our re-ID framework based on it. Though features can be automatically extracted during detection, the obtained feature representations might be suboptimal for re-ID tasks. This is because the features are originally designed for classifying pedestrians and background. For example, the aggregated channel features extracted by ACF detector is consist of LUV channels (3 channels), gradient magnitude channel (1 channel) and histogram of oriented gradient channels (6 channels). These features are very discriminative for classifying pedestrians and background, but not for distinguishing different pedestrian instances.

In this paper, our contributions are threefolds: (1) We proposed an enhanced ACF (ACF+) by integrating HSV histogram and SILTP [11] features as additional channels, and it has already achieved comparable accuracy to the state-of-the-art LOMO feature; (2) We further explored better distance metric learning methods to leverage the representation power of different feature subspaces and then proposed a hybrid distance metric learning method which can find the best combination of distance metric for the aforementioned channel features; (3) We build a real-time pedestrian re-ID framework based on the proposed method. The experimental results on multiple public datasets show the efficacy and low computational cost of the proposed method. As the hybrid distance metric learning is general, it can be applied to any metric learning algorithm.

2   Related Work

For pedestrian Re-ID, many works focus on how to construct effective feature representation and numerous features are proposed. The most effective features can be categoried into two groups: color-based and texture-based features [3]. Among them, HSV color histogram [4], LAB color histogram [16], LBP histogram [9] and their fusion are the most popular ones. Recently, LOMO is proposed to combine HSV histogram and SILTP [11], which acheives state-of-the-art re-ID accuracy. Other methods consider combining other cues of pedestrians. For example, [14] proposed to incoporate human part-based features and [4] proposed to use silhouette and symmertry structure of person. Salience based features is used in [16] which can deal with large pose variations. Notably, none of these work consider resuing the features extracted from prior detection process. As feature extraction are normally computational expensive, reusing the features extracted from detection step can save a lot of computation time and thus facilitate real-time re-ID. In this work, we build our re-ID framework based on ACF detector [1]. Using ACF features alone is not sufficient for effective re-ID representation. Inspired from the LOMO feature, we proposed an enhanced ACF features (ACF+) by combining HSV histogram and SILTP to form robust features.

Based on the extracted features, metric learning are commonly used for measuring the similarity of two samples due to its flexibility. Most researches used holistic metric for feature matching, others took part information into account and divide samples into several groups [3]. In [5], various kernel-based metric learning methods have been evaluated. Among them, kLFDA with linear or RBF kernel has shown robust performance. Recently, [11] proposed XQDA based on Mahalanobis distance and achieved state-of-the-art results. These metric learning algorithms handle the extracted features as a single vector without considering the underlying components. In this work, we argue that instead of combining the ACF+ as a single vector, we can learn different distance functions according to the type of channels. After that, we combine all these distances by a hybrid distance metric. Our experimental results show that the hybrid distance metric obtained significantly better results than simple concatenation.

3   Proposed Methods

In this section, we first give an overview of the detection and re-identification framework, then we introduce the novel feature representation ACF+. Finally, we illustrate the proposed hybrid distance metric learning method.

3.1   Pedestrian Detection and Re-identification Framework

The re-identification framework is as follows. We first apply the ACF detector to detect pedestrian candidates. The bounding boxes of pedestrians and the corresponding ACF features are obtained at this stage. Then HSV histogram and SILTP features are extracted from the bounding box locations and integrated with ACF to form ACF+. As the dimension of ACF+ is large and there might be redundant information among the channels, we make use of hybrid distance metric learning to reduce dimensions of ACF+ and improve its discriminative power.

3.2   Enhanced Aggregated Channel Features (ACF+)

As we will see from the experiments, the ACF extracted by detector has limited representation capability for re-ID task, thus we consider to enhance it with other discriminative features. HSV histogram and SILTP (Scale Invariant Local Ternary Pattern) [10] descriptors are known to be effective for re-ID task from the previous literatures. HSV histogram feature can improve performance with color information and SILTP contains texture information. In this work, we extract

HSV histogram and SILTP features as additional channels to the ACF. For HSV color feature, we compute histograms on each channel with bin size of 8, and there are 24 channels in total for the final feature map. SILTP is computed with two scales with radius [3,5], neighbour points of 4, and scale factor of 0.3, which constructs a 2-channel feature map. All these feature maps are concatenated with ACF and forms the enhanced ACF, which we call it ACF+. The final feature representation contains following feature channels: 3 LUV channels, 1 normalized gradient magnitude channels, 6 histogram of oriented gradient channels, 24 HSV histogram channels, and 2 SILTP channels. The entire feature has dimensions of 21642. The advantages of ACF+ are twofold: (1) saving the computation time of features for re-identification; (2) improving re-ID performance by fusing different types of features.

3.3 Metric Learning

In this work, we apply a subspace metric learning method called Cross-view Quadratic Discriminant Analysis (XQDA) to the extracted features for pedestrian re-ID. XQDA has shown superior performance with LOMO feature. So we first investigate its application to the proposed ACF+. Next, we propose a hybrid distance metric learning to the split ACF+ feature spaces to further boost its matching accuracy.

Cross-View Quadratic Discriminant Analysis. In this section, we first briefly review the XQDA method. The XQDA algorithm is inspired from the Bayesian face recognition and the KISSME algorithm. These methods define the intra-class variation and inter-class variation as two classes of zero-mean Gaussian distribution, which can be formulated as the following:

$$p_s\left(\mathbf{x}_i, \mathbf{x}_j\right) = \frac{1}{(2\pi)^{n/2}|\mathbf{\Sigma}_s|^{1/2}} e^{-\frac{1}{2}(\mathbf{x}_i - \mathbf{x}_j)^\top \mathbf{\Sigma}_s^{-1}(\mathbf{x}_i - \mathbf{x}_j)}$$
$$p_d\left(\mathbf{x}_i, \mathbf{x}_j\right) = \frac{1}{(2\pi)^{n/2}|\mathbf{\Sigma}_d|^{1/2}} e^{-\frac{1}{2}(\mathbf{x}_i - \mathbf{x}_j)^\top \mathbf{\Sigma}_d^{-1}(\mathbf{x}_i - \mathbf{x}_j)}, \tag{1}$$

where $\mathbf{x}_i - \mathbf{x}_j$ is the difference of two samples, p_s is the intra-class distribution, *i.e.* the probability of *same* individual, p_d is the inter-class distribution, *i.e.* the probability of *different* individual. $\mathbf{\Sigma}_s$ and $\mathbf{\Sigma}_d$ are the covariance matrices of intra-class and inter-class respectively. The log likelihood ratio is used to estimate the two Gaussian distributions:

$$d\left(\mathbf{x}_i, \mathbf{x}_j\right) = log\left(\frac{p_d(\mathbf{x}_i, \mathbf{x}_j)}{p_s(\mathbf{x}_i, \mathbf{x}_j)}\right)$$
$$= (\mathbf{x}_i - \mathbf{x}_j)^\top \left(\mathbf{\Sigma}_s^{-1} - \mathbf{\Sigma}_d^{-1}\right)(\mathbf{x}_i - \mathbf{x}_j). \tag{2}$$

In theory, the distance function of (2) can be directly used for pedestrian re-ID. However, the original feature dimension of $\mathbf{x}$ is usually large, and a lower dimension space is preferred for classification. XQDA extends the Bayesian face recognition and KISSME algorithm and proposes to learn a subspace and at the same time a distance function. So the distance function of (2) in the reduced subspace can be written as:

$$d_Q\left(\mathbf{x}_i, \mathbf{x}_j\right) = \left(\mathbf{x}_i - \mathbf{x}_j\right)^\top \mathbf{Q}\left(\mathbf{\Sigma}_s^{'-1} - \mathbf{\Sigma}_d^{'-1}\right)\mathbf{Q}^\top\left(\mathbf{x}_i - \mathbf{x}_j\right), \tag{3}$$

where $\mathbf{Q}$ is the projection matrix which projects the $\mathbf{x}$ to a lower subspace, $\mathbf{\Sigma}_s^{'} = \mathbf{Q}^\top\mathbf{\Sigma}_s\mathbf{Q}$ and $\mathbf{\Sigma}_d^{'} = \mathbf{Q}^\top\mathbf{\Sigma}_d\mathbf{Q}$. In [11], it is shown that optimizing the projection matrix $\mathbf{Q}$ is equivalent to solve the following optimization problem:

$$\max_Q \mathbf{Q}^\top\mathbf{\Sigma}_d\mathbf{Q}, \quad s.t.\, \mathbf{Q}^\top\mathbf{\Sigma}_s\mathbf{Q} = 1, \tag{4}$$

which can be solved by the generalized eigenvalue decomposition method.

Hybrid Distance Metric Learning. In this section, we explain our hybrid distance metric learning based on ACF+ and XQDA. As ACF+ is a concatenation of different types of features, each of them may have different representation abilities. We propose to split the ACF+ into separate feature space according to the feature type and learn individual distance metric for each type. Each individual metric may have its specific discriminative ability, our goal is to find the optimal combination of them to boost the overall re-ID performance.

The straightforward way is to apply ensemble learning methods, *i.e.* combining multiple hypothesis to form a (hopefully) better hypothesis. For example, voting mechanism can be used to choose the best distance metric among the individual distances. We denote it by $\mathbf{d}_{ij}^k, i \in M, j \in N$ the distance of sample $\mathbf{x}_i$ and $\mathbf{x}_j$, where $k \in K$ is the kth feature type in ACF+ and K is the number of types, M is the size of gallery set and N is the size of probe set. The maximum voting can be expressed as: $\mathbf{d}_{ij}^* = \max_k \mathbf{d}_{ij}^k$, where $\mathbf{d}_{ij}^*$ is the final distance for re-ID. Similarly, we can calculate minimum and average voting $\mathbf{d}_{ij}^* = \min_k \mathbf{d}_{ij}^k$ and $\mathbf{d}_{ij}^* = \frac{1}{K}\sum_{k=1}^K \mathbf{d}_{ij}^k$. These three methods are denoted by MAX, MIN and MEAN respectively.

However, such methods might be suboptimal as they are not able to learn hybrid distance from the training data. To address this problem, we propose to learn the combination weights of individual distance function from the training data. We denote $\mathbf{D}^k = \{\mathbf{d}_{ij}^k | i \in M, j \in N, k \in K\}$ the distance matrix of individual feature. Our goal is to learn parameters $\mathbf{w} = \{\omega_k | k \in K\}$ to obtain final distance matrix $\mathbf{D}^*$:

$$\mathbf{D}^* = \sum_k \omega_k * \mathbf{D}^k, \tag{5}$$

which can be explicitly written as:

$$\begin{bmatrix} \omega_1 d_{11}^1 + \omega_2 d_{11}^2 + \cdots + \omega_K d_{11}^K & \cdots & \omega_1 d_{1N}^1 + \omega_2 d_{1N}^2 + \cdots + \omega_K d_{1N}^K \\ \vdots & \ddots & \vdots \\ \omega_1 d_{M1}^1 + \omega_2 d_{M1}^2 + \cdots + \omega_K d_{M1}^K & \cdots & \omega_1 d_{MN}^1 + \omega_2 d_{MN}^2 + \cdots + \omega_K d_{MN}^K \end{bmatrix}. \tag{6}$$

Because in the training set, we can obtain the ground truth identities of the pedestrian, and thus define the perfect matching distances of $\mathbf{D}^*$. In this practice, we let $\mathbf{d}_{ij}^* = 0$ if sample i and sample j are from the same identity, otherwise

$\mathbf{d}_{ij}^* = 1$. Note that $\mathbf{D}^*$ and $\mathbf{D}^k$ are matrices of size $M \times N$. We can flatten $\mathbf{D}^*$ and $\mathbf{D}^k$ into column vectors, denoted by $\mathbf{d}^*$ and $\mathbf{d}^k$ respectively. Equation (5) then can be written as:

$$\mathbf{d}^* = \mathbf{w}^\top \mathbf{z}, \tag{7}$$

where $\mathbf{z} = [\mathbf{d}^1, \mathbf{d}^2 \ldots \mathbf{d}^K]$. As we have already known the perfect distance matching values of $\mathbf{d}^*$, (7) can be converted into to a linear regression problem, where $\mathbf{z}$ is the input variables, $\mathbf{d}^*$ is the measured variables, and $\mathbf{w}$ is the K-dimension parameter vector. Equation (7) can be easily solved by off-the-shelf linear regression solvers. At testing time, we can apply the learned parameters $\mathbf{w}$ to the input $\bar{\mathbf{d}} = \mathbf{w}^\top \mathbf{z}$, where $\bar{\mathbf{d}}$ is the predicted final distances. Compare to the simple ensemble methods, the hybrid distance learning method can learn optimal parameters from the training data. This is verified in the experiment section.

4   Experiments and Analysis

In this section we describe the set of experiments used to evaluate efficiency of the proposed feature representations as well as the hybrid distance metric learning method.

4.1   Datasets and Experimental Protocol

Our methods were evaluated on two public datasets which are commonly used throughout the literatures. We repeat the experimental process 10 times and average the performance for the final report.

The **VIPeR** [13] dataset is a challenging test bed for person re-id. It contains 632 identities and each has two images captured outdoor from two cameras with different views and illumination intensity. Meanwhile the whole images are scaled to 128×48 pixels. The 632 image-pairs are randomly divided into two parts, one is used as training set and the other for testing.

The **PRID2011** [6] dataset consists of person images captured from two cameras. We use the singleshot version of this dataset in our experiments. Specifically, Camera A captures 385 persons and camera B captures 749 persons. Only 200 people appear in both of them. We follow the data splitting of [7]. For training set, we randomly choose 100 identities from camera A and their counterparts from camera B, while the remaining 100 identities of camera A are used as the probe set, and the remaining 649 samples of camera B are used as the gallery set.

Evaluation Protocol. Our experiments follow the protocol in [11]. The dataset is divided into training set and test set, and test set further divided into two parts, one is the gallery set, and another is the probe set. Then we match each probe image with every image in the gallery set and rank the similarity scores. The experimental results is evaluated by *CMC* (Cumulative Matching Characteristic) curves [11], which is an estimation of the expectation of finding the correct match in the top n matches.

4.2   Performance of the ACF+ Feature

First we conduct experiments to evaluate the performance of the proposed ACF+ feature representation. We compared ACF+ to four different feature representations, namely ACF, Hist-HSV, HistMoment-6Patch and LOMO, where ACF is the original features extracted from ACF detector, Hist-HSV is the channel feature of HSV histograms, HistMoment-6Path is the patch based features in [5], and LOMO is the state-of-the-art feature proposed in [11]. Table 1 shows the matching scores on top 1 to top 20, and Fig. 1 depicts the CMC curves. It can be seen that using ACF only results in poorest performance as ACF is not discriminative for intra-class variations of the pedestrians. Hist-HSV alone shows much better results and even outperforms a patch based feature representation HistMoment-6Path, which integrates LBP, RGB and HSV histograms. From this comparison we can see that channel-feature based representation like Hist-HSV is competitive to the path-based ones, while being much faster as can be seen from the following experiments. When integrating Hist-HSV and SILTP with ACF to generate ACF+, we achieved comparable accuracy with the state-of-the-art LOMO feature.

Table 1. CMC scores on VIPeR (higher the better)

Method	Rank1	Rank5	Rank10	Rank15	Rank20
ACF	2.88	8.70	14.27	18.92	22.91
Hist-HSV	20.25	42.37	55.89	64.87	71.80
HistMomet-6Patch [8]	19.37	41.39	53.35	61.08	66.46
LOMO [11]	40.28	68.32	80.89	87.12	91.20
ACF+	36.39	66.68	79.34	86.04	90.60

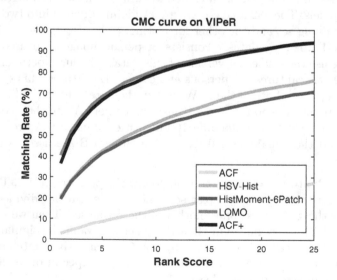

Fig. 1. CMC curves of different features on VIPeR

Next we compare the feature computation time of different features. Table 2 summarizes the feature dimension and frame rate on 128 × 48 size images. As we can see from the results, ACF is the fastest due to the simplicity of channel feature computation. Hist-HSV is slower than ACF but the discriminative capability is excellent, so we integrate it into the ACF+. Moreover, ACF+ can share some computation with ACF detector and achieves frame rate of 20 fps, which can be used for real-time applications. Note that all these experiments are conducted on laptop with Intel core i5 CPU. The code are written in MATLAB and thus speed can be further improved by optimizing the implementation.

Table 2. Feature computation time on 128 × 48 size images.

Feature type	ACF	Hist-HSV	HistMoment-6Path	LOMO	ACF+
Dimension	3840	9216	6966	26960	21642
FPS	131	25	<1	17	20

4.3   Evaluation of the Hybrid Distance Metric Learning

In this section, we evaluate the proposed hybrid distance metric learning method. Our *baseline* method is built on XQDA [11] metric learning method using ACF+ as feature representation. Three ingredients of ACF+, namely ACF, HSV-Hist and SILTP are used to learn different distance metrics using XQDA, and then get a jointed distance metric. To evaluate the performance of the proposed hybrid distance metric learning method, we compared different ensemble methods. Table 3 describes the details of the compared methods in our experiments.

$$PUR = \frac{log\,(G) - \sum_{r=1}^{C} M\,(r)\,log\,(M\,(r))}{log\,(G)} \tag{8}$$

The Proportion of Uncertainty Removed (PUR) score is defined in (8), where G is the size of the gallery set, $M\,(r)$ is the accumulated match characteristic

Table 3. The compared methods

Method	Description
Baseline	ACF+ with XQDA without hybrid distance metric
MIN	Take the minimum value among different distance metric
MAX	Take the maximum value among different distance metric
MEAN	Take the mean value among different distance metric
PUR-weight	The weight factors are computed by PUR score (Eq. 8)
FIT-weight	The weight factors are learned from training set

matrix at rank $r(r \leq 20)$. $r = 1$ is preferred in the literatures and also used in our experiments.

As PUR has been widely used in Re-ID literature as an performance indicator because of its invariant quality for the size of the gallery set, we use it to rank the different distance metrics and compute the weight factors. The weight factors are computed as following: $\omega_i = \frac{PUR_i}{PUR_1+\cdots+PUR_i+\cdots PUR_n}, i \in (1, 2, \cdots n)$, where ω_i is the weight of distance metric i. The larger score of PUR, the better accuracy of the distance metric. Thus the weight of distance metric ω_i should be counted more, if its PUR score is larger.

Table 4. CMC scores on VIPeR (%)

Method	Rank1	Rank5	Rank10	Rank15	Rank20
XQDA	36.39	66.68	79.34	86.04	90.60
MIN	2.53	11.30	19.91	26.30	32.53
MAX	34.02	62.66	76.30	83.13	87.59
MEAN	32.22	61.33	73.61	80.76	86.20
PUR-weight	34.78	63.64	76.23	83.01	87.41
FIT-weight	**37.88**	**67.56**	**80.44**	**87.22**	**91.42**

Table 5. CMC scores on PRID2011(%)

Method	Rank1	Rank5	Rank10	Rank15	Rank20
XQDA	19.00	38.60	49.60	55.80	60.90
MIN	1.20	6.60	11.10	14.40	18.50
MAX	19.90	39.60	50.10	57.70	62.40
MEAN	19.40	37.40	47.20	52.90	57.10
PUR-weight	18.90	37.00	46.70	53.20	58.00
FIT-weight	**22.60**	**43.70**	**53.00**	**59.40**	**63.60**

We conduct experiments on two public datasets. Tables 4 and 5 show the results on VIPeR and PRID2011 respectively. Figure 2 depicts the CMC curves on VIPeR and PRID2011. From the results, we can see that FIT-weight achieves the best performance on both datasets. Especially on PRID2011, it outperforms the baseline by a large margin (up to 5 percentage points). Among all these methods, PUR-weight obtains second best results. However, it still gets lower accuracy than the baseline. Other methods obtained worse results than baseline, showing that simple ensemble methods fail to improve the ACF+. This further verified the efficacy of the proposed hybrid distance metric learning method, which learns optimal weight factors from the training data.

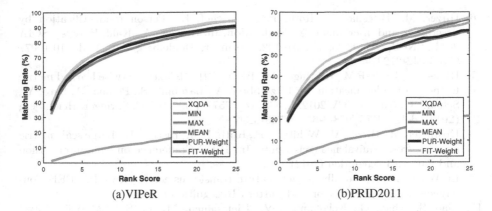

Fig. 2. CMC curves on different datasets.

5 Conclusion

In this work, we proposed a novel feature representation called ACF+ for pedestrian re-identification. ACF+ can share feature computation with ACF detector, and perform pedestrian detection and re-identification in real-time. To further boost the accuracy of the ACF+, we proposed a hybrid distance metric learning method which learns optimal weight factors for different metrics and outperforms the simple feature concatenation of ACF+. In the future work, we would like to explore the proposed method with other metric learning algorithms and further improve the computation time.

Acknowledgments. This work is supported by National Natural Science Foundation of China (project no. 6160011396).

References

1. Appel, R., Belongie, S., Perona, P., Doll, P.: Fast feature pyramids for object detection. IEEE Trans. Pattern Anal. Mach. Intell. **36**(8), 1532–1545 (2014)
2. Chen, S.Z., Guo, C.C., Lai, J.H.: Deep ranking for person re-identification via joint representation learning. IEEE Trans. Image Process. **25**(5), 2353–2367 (2016)
3. Yi, D., Lei, Z., Liao, S., Li, S.Z.: Deep metric learning for person re-identification. In: International Conference on Pattern Recognition (2014)
4. Farenzena, M., Bazzani, L., Perina, A., Murino, V., Cristani, M.: Person re-identification by symmetry-driven accumulation of local features. In: IEEE Conference on Computer Vision and Pattern Recognition (2010)
5. Xiong, F., Gou, M., Camps, O., Sznaier, M.: Person re-identification using kernel-based metric learning methods. In: Fleet, D., Pajdla, T., Schiele, B., Tuytelaars, T. (eds.) ECCV 2014. LNCS, vol. 8695, pp. 1–16. Springer, Cham (2014). doi:10.1007/978-3-319-10584-0_1

6. Hirzer, M., Beleznai, C., Roth, P.M., Bischof, H.: Person re-identification by descriptive and discriminative classification. In: Heyden, A., Kahl, F. (eds.) SCIA 2011. LNCS, vol. 6688, pp. 91–102. Springer, Heidelberg (2011). doi:10.1007/978-3-642-21227-7_9

7. Hirzer, M., Roth, P.M., Köstinger, M., Bischof, H.: Relaxed pairwise learned metric for person re-identification. In: Fitzgibbon, A., Lazebnik, S., Perona, P., Sato, Y., Schmid, C. (eds.) ECCV 2012. LNCS, vol. 7577, pp. 780–793. Springer, Heidelberg (2012). doi:10.1007/978-3-642-33783-3_56

8. Kostinger, M., Hirzer, M., Wohlhart, P., Roth, P.M., Bischof, H.: Large scale metric learning from equivalence constraints. In: IEEE Conference on Computer Vision and Pattern Recognition (2012)

9. Li, W., Wang, X.: Locally aligned feature transforms across views. In: IEEE Conference on Computer Vision and Pattern Recognition (2013)

10. Liao, S., Zhao, G., Kellokumpu, V., Pietikainen, M., Li, S.Z.: Modeling pixel process with scale invariant local patterns for background subtraction in complex scenes. In: IEEE Conference on Computer Vision and Pattern Recognition (2010)

11. Liao, S., Hu, Y., Zhu, X., Li, S.Z.: Person re-identification by local maximal occurrence representation and metric learning. In: IEEE Conference on Computer Vision and Pattern Recognition (2015)

12. Liao, S., Li, S.Z.: Efficient PSD constrained asymmetric metric learning for person re-identification. In: International Conference on Computer Vision (2015)

13. Gray, D., Brennan, S., Tao, H.: Evaluating appearance models for recognition, reacquisition, and tracking. In: Proceedings of IEEE International Workshop on PETS (2007)

14. Xu, Y., Lin, L., Zheng, W.S., Liu, X.: Human re-identification by matching compositional template with cluster sampling. In: International Conference on Computer Vision (2013)

15. Yang, Y., Liao, S., Lei, Z., Li, S.Z.: Large scale similarity learning using similar pairs for person verification. In: AAAI (2016)

16. Zhao, R., Ouyang, W., Wang, X.: Unsupervised salience learning for person re-identification. In: IEEE Conference on Computer Vision and Pattern Recognition (2013)

RGB-D Saliency Detection by Multi-stream Late Fusion Network

Hao Chen[1], Youfu Li[1,2(✉)], and Dan Su[1]

[1] Department of Mechanical and Biomedical Engineering,
City University of Hong Kong, Tat Chee Avenue,
Kowloon Tong, Hong Kong SAR
meyfli@cityu.edu.hk
[2] City University of Hong Kong, Shenzhen Research Institute, Shenzhen, China

Abstract. In this paper we aim to address the problem of saliency detection on RGB-D image pairs based on a multi-stream late fusion network. With the prevalence of RGB-D sensors, leveraging additional depth information to facilitate saliency detection task has drawn increasing attention. However, the key challenge that how to fuse RGB data and depth data in an optimum manner is still under-studied. Conventional wisdom simply regards depth information as an undifferentiated channel and models RGB-D saliency detection by using existing RGB saliency detection models directly. However, this paradigm is incapable of capturing specific representations in depth modality and also powerless in fusing multi-modal information. In this paper, we address this problem by proposing a simple yet principled late fusion strategy carried out in conjunction with convolutional neural networks (CNNs). The proposed network is able to learn discriminant representations and explore the complementarity between RGB and depth modalities. Comprehensive experiments on two public datasets witness the benefits of the proposed RGB-D saliency detection network.

Keywords: RGB-D · Saliency detection · Convolutional neural networks

1 Introduction

Saliency detection, which targets at highlighting objects attracting human beings most in a scene [1], has been a fundamental task for its wide range of applications in computer vision and robotic vision such as image compression [2] and video classification [3]. With the availability of RGB-D sensors such as Kinect and RealSense, the depth information has gradually been adopted as additional information to boost performance on saliency detection recently. Compared to RGB data, which supply appearance and texture information and are sensitive to light variations, depth data provide more shape information, clear edges and are robust against changing lighting condition. The complementary relationship between the paired RGB and depth images for saliency detection is shown in Fig. 1. It is easy for us to reason that on a large body of challenging scenes that the appearance of salient object and background regions are too similar to distinguish, the paired depth information is able to assist RGB data on saliency detection effectively. To conduct RGB-D saliency detection, the additional

© Springer International Publishing AG 2017
M. Liu et al. (Eds.): ICVS 2017, LNCS 10528, pp. 459–468, 2017.
DOI: 10.1007/978-3-319-68345-4_41

RGB   Depth   HHA   Groundtruth

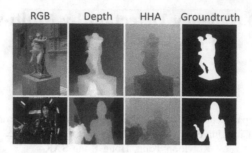

Fig. 1. Examples to show the complementarity between RGB and depth data

depth data give rise to two fundamental questions: on the one hand, how to model depth-induced saliency detection reasonably with considering the hallmark of depth data; on the other hand, how to combine RGB and depth modalities in an optimal approach.

Typically, saliency detection methods can be generally categorized into top-down methods [4] and bottom-up methods [5, 6]. Top-down methods rely on high-level saliency priors to identify the saliency regions, while bottom-up methods are data-driven and task-independent, which aim to measure saliency values by contrasting the distinctiveness of each region in a local or global context with low-level features.

To leverage depth data for saliency detection, traditional methods typically use original depth values directly or further explore handcrafted features from depth values, which does not go beyond the reliance on low-level features. Indeed, the low-level features are unable to capture high-level reasoning towards saliency detection and lack generalization ability when adopted to variant scenes.

Besides, most previous RGB-D saliency detection models [7–14] are based on the RGB saliency detection frameworks, in spite of their difference in using depth data. To be more specific, depth values are either simply regarded as an undifferentiated additional channel together with RGB channels [10, 12], or referred as weights to regularize RGB-induced saliency values [15]. However, both these two solutions are too simple to model the specialties of depth modality in terms of data distribution and structure and also fail to capture the complementary correlations between RGB and depth data.

Recently, we witness the success of deep learning techniques [16] in a large range of computer vision and robotic vision tasks [16–19] due to their powerful representation ability and feature-correlations modeling capacity. It has been widely acknowledged that deep learning is advantageous in terms of capturing high-level representations such as uniqueness and objectness. The high-level representations are of radical importance for saliency detection to mitigate the background interference on locating the salient objects. Besides, another reason for the success of deep learning is that each layer in a deep learning architecture has strong ability to select and fuse the features in the former layer. Motivated by these priorities of deep learning, we reason that it is a promising and reasonable choice by adopting deep learning, especially convolutional neural networks (CNNs) [16], in RGB-D saliency detection, not only for its strength in learning representative features in both RGB and depth modalities, but also for its potential in fusing RGB and depth features.

To conduct RGB-D saliency detection with CNNs, two key issues should be taken into account: (1) how to design the network for saliency detection. (2) How to design the fusion architecture to efficiently capture the complementary information between RGB and depth modalities.

In this paper, we solve these two problems by proposing a multi-modal late fusion network, in which the deep representations of each modality is firstly extracted separately and then fused at a late point. Then the complementary relationships between RGB and depth modalities are learnt in the fusion layer and final saliency predictions are made based on the joint RGB-D high-level representations.

In summary, our contributions in this papers are three-fold:

(1) To the best of our knowledge, this work is among the earliest ones that adopt deep learning for RGB-D saliency detection in a end-to-end manner.
(2) We design a late fusion CNN architecture to capture the correlationship of high-level features from two modalities, since the higher layers are closer to the same groundtruth and consequently more task-specific and modal-agnostic.
(3) Comprehensive experiments demonstrate the priorities of our proposed model compared to state-of-the-art methods.

2 Related Work

Most previous RGB-D saliency detection models follow the basic framework of traditional RGB saliency detection veins, including local-contrast methods or global-contrast methods. In [15], depth values are utilized as saliency cues in a global-contrast manner to measure saliency values directly and meanwhile weight the RGB-induced saliency. Peng et al. [8] generate the depth-induced saliency by combining the saliency results generated by local-contrast, global-contrast and background priors, while the RGB-induced saliency is computed by existing methods and the final RGB-D saliency is then gained by simple multiplication of saliency values obtained from RGB and depth data. In [10], depth values are directly contrast to measure the difference between two regions and the final saliency map is generated by multiplying saliency cues from RGB and depth modalities. To mitigate the drawbacks of directly adopting depth values to infer saliency values, [13] introduce a handcrafted feature in depth modality based on the anisotropic center-surround difference to measure saliency. Similarly in [20], a new RGB-D feature is designed based on the assumption that salient object should be distinctive in its local context. Ren et al. [9] introduce two priors from depth values and surface orientations and fuse the saliency cues in a stage-wise manner. Although these methods demonstrate progress on RGB-D saliency detection, they do not go beyond the vein of resorting to hand-crafted low-level features and traditional bottom-up contrast-based saliency cues, which lack high-level representations and generalization ability. [21] introduce deep learning on RGB-D saliency detection. However, this work rely on extracting low-level features firstly and then inputting these extracted features to a CNN, rather than directly predicting saliency in an end-to-end manner with original images as inputs. Besides, as donated in their experiments, the performance of this method highly relies on the adopted

Laplacian propagation as post-processing. In contrast, our method generate the saliency map in an end-to-end pipeline with a CNN, without extracting any handcrafted features firstly and any post-processing to further boost the performance.

3   Proposed Method

In this paper, to relieve the reliance on handcrafted features and capture high-level representations for RGB-D saliency detection, we propose to leverage convolutional neural networks (CNNs) to model depth-induced saliency and fuse the complementary features from RGB and depth data. Specifically, we formulate our RGB-D saliency detection framework in a stage-wise manner. We firstly train the saliency detection networks for RGB and depth modalities separately and then train a multi-modal network by fusing their deep representations in a late point. Considering the characteristics of saliency detection task, which needs global understanding to localize the salient object and meanwhile local details to further obtain accurate boundaries for the highlighted salient object, we adopt dilated convolutional filters [22] to replace the traditional convolutional filters in the higher layers. The dilated convolutional filters is able to enlarge receptive filed exponentially while the computational consumption only increase linearly. In the final layer, we adopt a fully convolutional layer as the prediction layer to reserve the spatial correspondence in feature maps and simultaneously reduce parameters. Besides, we use the AlexNet [16] as our basic architecture, which contains 5 convolutional layers and several fully connected layers. Here we only retain the convolutional layers. The specific-designed networks based on AlexNet has less parameters, which reduce the possibility of overfitting due to the fact that the RGB-D saliency detection datasets only contains a small number of training samples compared to the ImageNet [16].

3.1   RGB Stream for Saliency Detection

For the RGB stream in Fig. 2, the input RGB image is firstly resized to 224×224 pixels and then feed into the first convolutional layer, which is inherited from the original AlexNet, while the following four convolutional layers are replaced with dilated convolutional layers to reserve the resolution of feature maps with the dilation factor as 2,4,4,4, respectively. Then the feature maps of the fifth dilated convolutional layer after activation with a ReLU layer is fed into a fully convolutional layer with 1×1 convolutional kernels, the output of which is just the predicted 50×50 saliency map.

3.2   Depth Stream for Saliency Detection

For the depth stream in Fig. 2, we firstly encode the original depth values into three-channel HHA representations [23] (i.e., the horizontal disparity, height above ground, and the angle of the local surface normal with the inferred gravity direction) to enable the use of pre-trained models in RGB modality, e.g. the AlexNet. Also, the encoded HHA representations is capable of presenting more information than depth

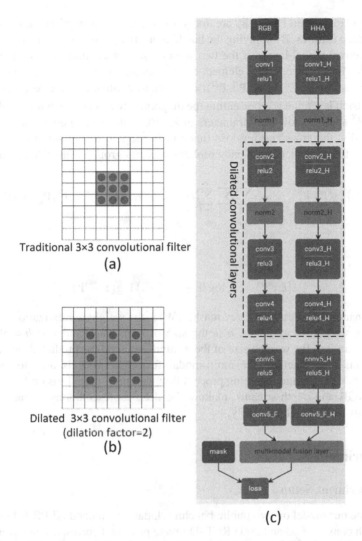

Fig. 2. The traditional convolutional module (a) and dilated convolutional module (b) and the network architecture of the proposed model (c).

values, which, as a result, will enable the CNN for depth modality learn more representative features. The network architecture and practice details for depth stream follows the ones in the RGB stream. Note that the mean values for HHA is set by computing the mean values of training HHA samples.

3.3 Multi-modal Fusion Network

After we have trained the RGB and depth saliency detection streams, the multi-modal fusion stage will be conducted by truncating the prediction layers and connect the high layers of each stream at a late point.

The input image pair $\mathbf{F}_i^R$ and $\mathbf{F}_i^D$ are firstly fed into RGB and depth stream respectively to extract deep features. By applying the late fusion strategy, the activation outputs of the last fully convolutional layers of the two streams are concatenated and combined by a multi-modal fusion layer in an element-wise summation manner, which produce the saliency prediction $\Psi(\mathbf{F}_i^R, \mathbf{F}_i^D | \theta, \mathbf{P}^R, \mathbf{P}^D)(x, y)$ with θ donating the parameters of the multi-modal fusion layer and ψ representing the mapping function of the whole multi-modal network. $\mathbf{P}^R$ and $\mathbf{P}^D$ show the parameters in the RGB stream and depth stream, respectively. Finally, the cross-entropy loss function is adopted to measure the discrepancy between the fused prediction saliency probabilities and ground truth saliency masks:

$$
L(\{\mathbf{F}_i^R, \mathbf{F}_i^D, L_i\}_N | (\mathbf{P}^R, \mathbf{P}^D)) = -\frac{1}{n} \sum_{i=1}^{n} \sum_{x=1}^{w} \sum_{y=1}^{h} \ell(L_i(x, y), + \Psi(\mathbf{F}_i^R, \mathbf{F}_i^D | \theta, \mathbf{P}^R, \mathbf{P}^D)(x, y)) + \lambda r(\mathbf{W}),
$$

(1)

where

$$
\ell(L_i, \Psi) = L_i \log \Psi + (1 - L_i) \log(1 - \Psi)
$$

(2)

L_i is the binary ground truth saliency mask, $r(\mathbf{W})$ is the weight regularization term and λ denotes the weight decay factor. n is the size of mini-batch and $w = h = 50$ are the width and height of the warped size of the ground truth and the predicted saliency map.

With this loss function, the multi-modal fusion network is able to enable the gradients back-propagation learning process flow the multi-modal fusion layer and then both the RGB and depth streams, making the deep representations of each modality learnt jointly and complementarily.

4   Experiments

4.1   Experiment Setup

We evaluate our model on two public benchmark datasets named NLPR [8] and NJUD [13], which consist 1000 and 2003 RGB-D image pairs and corresponding ground truth saliency masks. We combine 650 image pairs picked from the NLPR dataset and 1400 image pairs from the NJUD dataset randomly as the training set. Meanwhile, we pick 50 image pairs from the NLPR dataset and 100 image pairs from the NJUD dataset randomly as the validation set.

We adopt Precision-Recall (PR) curve, AP (average precision) score and F-measure scores as evaluation metrics. The precision-recall curves are plotted by comparing with the ground truth with setting a group of thresholds on the saliency maps to achieve binary masks. F-measure is computed by

$$
F_\beta = \frac{(1 + \beta^2) \cdot Precision \cdot Recall}{\beta^2 \cdot Precision + Recall},
$$

(3)

where we follow the practice in [24] to set $\beta^2 = 1$.

4.2 Implementation Details

We augment the training dataset by horizontally-flipping and image cropping on boundaries of image pairs and corresponding ground truth masks locally. By which, we augment the training set 12 times.

The mini-batch size is set as 8 and the training rate is set as 0.0000001, which is accumulated from 2500 nodes. Besides, the weight decay, and momentum are set to 0.0002, and 0.9, respectively. The experiments are implemented on a workstation with one GTX 1070 GPU.

4.3 Experimental Results

In this part, we compare our results with other state-of-the-art RGB-D saliency detection methods quantitatively and qualitatively. The compared models include LBE [20], NLPR [8], SRDS [15], EGP [9] and ACSD [13]. The quantitative metrics including the PR curves shown in Fig. 3 and the AP and F-measure scores shown in Table 1 showcase the effectiveness of our model.

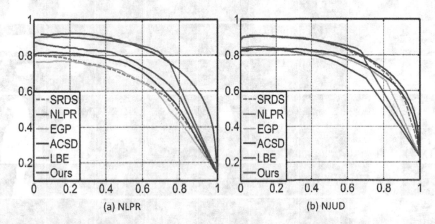

Fig. 3. The Precision-Recall (PR) curves on NLPR dataset (a) and NJUD dataset (b) of our model (denoted as 'Ours') and other state-of-the-art methods

As shown in Fig. 4, on the most challenging cases including small distinctiveness between the salient object and background (e.g., the 1st row), intra-inconsistent salient object (e.g., the 2nd row), the salient object is scattered (e.g., the 3th row), large depth variance (e.g., the 4th row), the scene is complex and confusing (e.g., the 5th–6th row), multiple objects (e.g., the 7th row), our model is able to leverage different properties of RGB and depth data and the complementary information between them to identify the salient object accurately. By contrast, other models, limited by low-level handcrafted features or heuristic and simple fusion strategies for RGB and depth data, are intractable on these challenging conditions.

Table 1. Average precision (AP) values and F-measure scores on NLPR and NJUD datasets of our model (denoted as 'Ours') and other state-of-the-art methods

Methods	AP		F-measure	
	NLPR	NJUD	NLPR	NJUD
SRDS	0.796	0.494	0.580	0.671
NLPR	0.688	0.631	0.573	0.454
EGP	0.733	0.600	0.515	0.491
ACSD	0.754	0.820	0.592	0.652
LBE	0.768	0.766	0.709	0.664
Ours	**0.813**	**0.812**	**0.729**	**0.701**

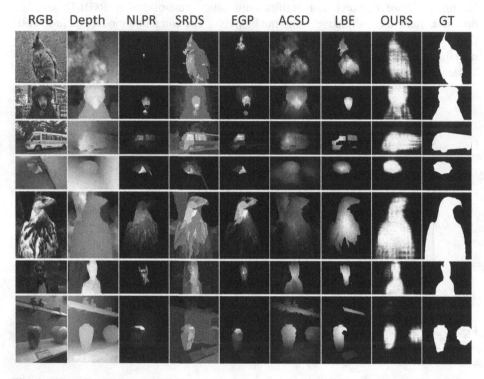

Fig. 4. The comparison of RGB-D saliency maps of our model (denoted as 'OURS') and other state-of-the-art methods

5 Conclusion

In this work, we propose to leverage CNN to learn high-level representations for depth modality and introduce a multi-modal late fusion network for RGB-D salient object detection. The proposed network is able to learn more generalizable and high-level features for depth data compared to conventional methods based on hand-crafted features. Besides, the late fusion strategy is more capable of capturing commentary correlations between RGB and depth data than existing simple fusion ideas. Comprehensive experiments demonstrate the advantages of the proposed RGB-D saliency detection model and the effectiveness of the adopted late fusion strategy. Besides, we reason that the proposed multi-modal network can be applied to other RGBD-induced tasks readily and further extended to fuse other modalities, such as RGB and LiDAR, temporal and spatial information and so on.

Acknowledgments. This work is funded by the Research Grants Council of Hong Kong (CityU 11205015) and the National Natural Science Foundation of China (NSFC) (61673329).

References

1. Cheng, M., Mitra, N.J., Huang, X., Torr, P.H., Hu, S.: Global contrast based salient region detection. IEEE Trans. Pattern Anal. Mach. Intell. **37**(3), 569–582 (2015)
2. Guo, C., Zhang, L.: A novel multiresolution spatiotemporal saliency detection model and its applications in image and video compression. IEEE Trans. Image Process. **19**(1), 185–198 (2010)
3. Itti, L.: Automatic foveation for video compression using a neurobiological model of visual attention. IEEE Trans. Image Process. **13**(10), 1304–1318 (2004)
4. Yang, J., Yang, M.-H.: Top-down visual saliency via joint CRF and dictionary learning. In: CVPR 2012, pp. 2296–2303 (2012)
5. Harel, J., Koch, C., Perona, P.: Graph-based visual saliency. In: NIPS 2007, pp. 545–552 (2007)
6. Zhang, Y., Han, J., Guo, L.: Saliency detection by combining spatial and spectral information. Opt. Lett. **38**(11), 1987–1989 (2013)
7. Niu, Y., Geng, Y., Li, X., Liu, F.: Leveraging stereopsis for saliency analysis. In: CVPR 2012, pp. 454–461 (2012)
8. Peng, H., Li, B., Xiong, W., Hu, W., Ji, R.: RGBD salient object detection: a benchmark and algorithms. In: Fleet, D., Pajdla, T., Schiele, B., Tuytelaars, T. (eds.) ECCV 2014. LNCS, vol. 8691, pp. 92–109. Springer, Cham (2014). doi:10.1007/978-3-319-10578-9_7
9. Ren, J., Gong, X., Yu, L., Zhou, W., Yang, M.Y.: Exploiting global priors for RGB-D saliency detection. In: CVPR Workshop 2015, pp. 25–32 (2015)
10. Cheng, Y., Fu, H., Wei, X., Xiao, J., Cao, X.: Depth enhanced saliency detection method. In: ICIMCS 2014, p. 23 (2014)
11. Ciptadi, A., Hermans, T., Rehg, J.M.: An in depth view of saliency. In: BMVC 2013, pp. 9–13 (2013)
12. Desingh, K., Krishna, K.M., Rajan, D., Jawahar, C.V.: Depth really matters: improving visual salient region detection with depth. In: BMVC 2013 (2013)
13. Ju, R., Ge, L., Geng, W., Ren, T., Wu, G.: Depth saliency based on anisotropic center-surround difference. In: ICIP 2014, pp. 1115–1119 (2014)
14. Lang, C., Nguyen, T.V., Katti, H., Yadati, K., Kankanhalli, M., Yan, S.: Depth matters: influence of depth cues on visual saliency. In: Fitzgibbon, A., Lazebnik, S., Perona, P., Sato, Y., Schmid, C. (eds.) ECCV 2012. LNCS, pp. 101–115. Springer, Heidelberg (2012). doi:10.1007/978-3-642-33709-3_8
15. Fan, X., Liu, Z., Sun, G.: Salient region detection for stereoscopic images. In: DSP 2014, pp. 454–458 (2014)
16. Krizhevsky, A., Sutskever, I., Hinton, G.E.: ImageNet classification with deep convolutional neural networks. In: NIPS 2012, pp. 1097–1105 (2012)

17. Jia, Y., Shelhamer, E., Donahue, J., Karayev, S., Long, J., Girshick, R., Guadarrama, S., Darrell, T.: Caffe: convolutional architecture for fast feature embedding. In: ACM MM 2014, pp. 675–678 (2014)
18. Long, J., Shelhamer, E., Darrell, T.: Fully convolutional networks for semantic segmentation. In: CVPR 2015, pp. 3431–440 (2015)
19. Simonyan, K., Zisserman, A.: Very deep convolutional networks for large-scale image recognition. arXiv preprint arXiv:1409.1556 (2014)
20. Feng, D., Barnes, N., You, S., McCarthy, C.: Local background enclosure for RGB-D salient object detection. In: CVPR 2016, pp. 2343–2350 (2016)
21. Qu, L., He, S., Zhang, J., Tian, J., Tang, Y., Yang, Q.: RGBD salient object detection via deep fusion. IEEE Trans. Image Process. **26**(5), 2274–2285 (2017)
22. Yu, F., Koltun, V.: Multi-scale context aggregation by dilated convolutions. arXiv preprint arXiv:1511.07122 (2015)
23. Gupta, S., Girshick, R., Arbeláez, P., Malik, J.: Learning rich features from RGB-D images for object detection and segmentation. In: Fleet, D., Pajdla, T., Schiele, B., Tuytelaars, T. (eds.) ECCV 2014. LNCS, vol. 8695, pp. 345–360. Springer, Cham (2014). doi:10.1007/978-3-319-10584-0_23
24. Martin, D.R., Fowlkes, C.C., Malik, J.: Learning to detect natural image boundaries using local brightness, color, and texture cues. IEEE Trans. Pattern Anal. Mach. Intell. **26**(5), 530–549 (2004)

Visual Recognition

A Cloud-Based Visual SLAM Framework for Low-Cost Agents

Jianhao Jiao[✉], Peng Yun, and Ming Liu

Robotics and Multi-perception Lab (RAM-LAB), Robotics Institute,
The Hong Kong University of Science and Technology, Hong Kong, China
jjiao@ust.hk

Abstract. Constrained by on-board resource, most of the low-cost robots could not autonomously navigate in unknown environments. In the latest years, cloud computing and storage has been developing rapidly, making it possible to offload parts of visual SLAM processing to a server. However, most of the cloud-based vSLAM frameworks are not suitable or fully tested for the applications of poor-equipped agents. In this paper, we describe an online localization service on a novel cloud-based framework, where the expensive map storage and global feature matching are provided as a service to agents. It enables a scenario that only sensor data collection is executed on agents, while the cloud aids the agents to localize and navigate. At the end, we evaluate the localization service quantitatively and qualitatively. The results indicate that the proposed cloud framework can fit the requirement of real-time applications.

Keywords: Cloud robotics · Mobile robot · Visual SLAM

1 Introduction

1.1 Motivation

Simultaneous Localization and Mapping (SLAM) jointly estimates the state of the robot and the map of environments. In the past few decades, SLAM, especially visual SLAM (vSLAM), has been an active research domain and many vSLAM algorithms have been presented to achieved great accuracy and robustness, such as [1–3]. However, vSLAM is both data intensive and computation intensive. In practical applications, the on-board resource is limited for service robots. For the applications such as augmented and virtual reality, it is hard to meet the computation and memory requirements.

This work was sponsored by the Research Grant Council of Hong Kong SAR Government, China, under project Nos. 16212815, 21202816 and National Natural Science Foundation of China Nos. 6140021318 and 61640305; Shenzhen Science, Technology and Innovation Comission (SZSTI) JCYJ20160428154842603 and JCYJ20160401100022706; partially supported by the HKUST Project IGN16EG12. All rewarded to Prof. Ming Liu.

© Springer International Publishing AG 2017
M. Liu et al. (Eds.): ICVS 2017, LNCS 10528, pp. 471–484, 2017.
DOI: 10.1007/978-3-319-68345-4_42

The rapid development of network technology and the availability of commercial Internet servers make the solution to this dilemma envisaged. The cloud provides high-bandwidth connections, massive storage, data management, and computation. Regarding vSLAM, a cloud is able to process the steps such as local or global bundle adjustment, map fusion, and loop detection. Besides, the cloud can be understood as a center for knowledge sharing, giving robots the access to infrastructure, platform, software and data. For example, traditionally, each robot would have to explore and build its own map in large environments. But now, we use the cloud to save a live, global map of the large environment. If a new robot is introduced to the same environment, it will reuse the existing map without exploration effort.

There are few works with a lightweight and low-cost approach targeting complete SLAM applications. Therefore, it is worthwhile to investigate a proper solution for lightweight, low-cost robots navigation. To this end, we design a robot with a simple visual-inertial sensor, an ARM7 processor, and WiFi connection.

1.2   Contribution

In this paper, we build on the ORB-SLAM2 system (monocular part) [3], the place recognition work of DBoW2 [4] and $OpenResty^{TM}$ platform[1], to design a cloud-based framework providing a localization service for low-cost robots. This service enables a robot with a smartphone-class processor to reuse maps and locate itself in environments. Compared with standard SLAM, it reduces much computation complexity. The contributions of this paper are:

1. We proposed a novel cloud-based framework which is able to provide different services and has two important features:
   (a) *Secure:* only authorized robots with right IP and password are allowed to connect to the cloud.
   (b) *Extensibility:* services are implemented with C/CPP and Lua scripts. Researchers are allowed to develop new applications freely.
2. We developed a lightweight localization service for the low-cost robots aided by the cloud. This service could reach real-time rate even though the bandwidth is limited.

1.3   Organization

This paper is organized into the following sections. Related work is described in Sect. 2. An overview of the system is introduced in Sect. 3, and details of our online localization service and framework are presented in Sect. 4, followed by the experiments shown in Sect. 5. Conclusion and future work are presented in Sect. 6.

---

[1] OpenResty: a registered trademark owned by OpenResty Inc. https://openresty.org.

2   Related Work

2.1   Low-Cost Localization Approaches

VSLAM is the primary approach for localization with low-cost sensors. An overview of SLAM was given by [5]. The most successful vSLAM systems currently in use are DSO [1] and ORB-SLAM [3,6]. DSO is a sparse and direct approach to monocular visual odometry, jointly optimizing the full likelihood for all involved model parameters to minimize the photometric error. OBB-SLAM is a feature-based monocular SLAM, which is able to close loops and reuse its map to achieve zero-drift localization in already mapped areas. However, ubiquitous optimization in these systems results in a high requirement for computational cost, which exceeds the capability of many mobile robots' processors.

Visible light communication (VLC) is a type of wireless communication technique and has many advantages such as low-cost and meeting the requirements of both illumination and communication. Researchers have tried to use VLC to deal with low-cost localization problem from a different perspective. In [7], Liu et al. discussed the feasibility of achieving accurate localization and preliminarily introduced a Gaussian Process to model the environmental light. By fusing the previous works [8,9], they demonstrated a low-cost VLC-based localization system in [10]. However, compared with vision version, VLC-based localization is only available in known places and limited by DoF. Fusing these techniques might overcome the limitations of each other [11].

2.2   Place Recognition Techniques

A survey by Williams et al. [12] compared the performance of appearance-based, map to map, and image to image methods for place recognition. Within appearance based approaches, a typical one is the FAB-MAP system [13]. It detects loops with an omnidirectional camera, obtaining great accuracy in long distance, but its robustness decreases when the images depict very similar structures for a long time. In contrast to the FAB-MAP, DBoW2 [4] uses bags of binary words obtained from BRIEF descriptors along with the efficient FAST feature detector to build a vocabulary tree offline. The work of Raulmur in [14] demonstrated DBoW2 to be very accurate and efficient.

2.3   Cloud-Based Framework

Based on Hadoop with ROS [18] as the master that manages all communications, DAvinCi was proposed in [19]. The goal of this architecture is to offload data- and computation-intensive tasks from the on-board resources on the robots to a backend cluster system. For proving its effectiveness, a parallel implementation on DAvinCi of Fast-SLAM was presented. However, the authors did not consider the data compression in any environment. They might face difficulties in transferring ROS message involving large data between the server and the robots.

The RoboEarth project [20] aims to develop a worldwide, open-source platform that allows any robot with a network connection to generate, share and reuse data. Later Rapyuta, an open source Platform-as-a-Service (PaaS) framework designed specifically for scalable robotic applications, was presented as the RoboEarth Cloud Engine in [21]. As a part of the RoboEarth project, it provides access to RoboEarth's knowledge repository, enabling the sharing of data and skills among robots. Based on Rapyuta, the author of [22] developed a parallel and dense visual odometry algorithm for collaborative 3D mapping on low-cost robots. Although many benefits of these frameworks are mentioned previously, there will be some potential drawbacks and challenges. In order to simplify the problem, most of the frameworks assumed that the online resource is unlimited. Actually, most resources in the cloud such as network bandwidth and CPU occupancy are limited.

Considering the real constraints, in [23], Riazuelo et al. presented the C2TAM framework for collaborative mapping in on multi-agents and discussed a solution about how to use the cloud's storage and computation resources properly. Furthermore, the RTAB-Map memory management approach [24] might be a good method to handle larger map's size in long-term and large-scale online mapping. In addition, fierce resource competition in multi-agents systems usually makes the bandwidth limited. Resource allocations strategies like [25] should be introduced to cope with this problem.

3   System Design

An overview of the cloud robotics system is illustrated in Fig. 1. The system consists of two components: a server (runs a cloud-based framework) and multiple robots. Generally, the simple processes like sensor data collection and data compression run on the robots. The computation- or memory-intensive tasks run on the server, which can concurrently handle a series of requests from different robots at the same time.

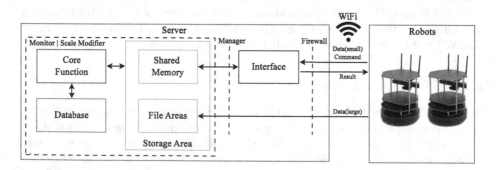

Fig. 1. An overview of the cloud robotics system

Considering hardware cost, real-time limitation, data I/O, network bandwidth, and computational requirements, a specific instance of our framework is described as following:

3.1 Robot (Client)

The low-cost robot is shown in Fig. 2. It equips with a single board computer (OrangePi Plus2[2]), a visual-inertial sensor($Loitor^{TM}$), and a WiFi module, uploading image features to the server to request its position. The details are shown in Fig. 3.

Fig. 2. The low-cost robot consists of a single board computer (<\$40) OrangePi Plus2 and a visual-inertial sensor (<\$90) $Loitor^{TM}$

OrangePi Plus2		Loitor	
CPU	Quad-core H3 Coretex-A7 processor	Camera	Global shutter I 24-65fps
Memory	2GB DDR3	Resolution	320x240 I 640x480 I 752x480
OS	Lubuntu	IMU	MPU-6050 I 200fps
Size	108mm x 67mm	Size	118mm x 30mm
Weight	83g		

Fig. 3. Details of OrangePi Plus2 and Loitor

3.2 Server

The server is a high-performance computer, running a cloud-based framework. It should have 5 main components: Interface, Shared Memory, File Areas, Core Function, and Database. If the size of some messages exceeds 100 Kbytes (called large messages), they will be uploaded from the robots through HTTP directly and then saved in the File Areas part. Other messages (called small messages) are sent through WebSocket by robots, decoded by the Interface part and then saved in the Shared Memory part.

---

[2] OrangePi Plus2: http://www.orangepi.org/orangepiplus2.

1. *Interface:* It sets WebSocket (small messages) and HTTP (large messages) as the communication protocol and decodes the small messages from String into JavaScript Object Notation (JSON)[3] format. It is also responsible for the connection to the robots.
2. *Shared Memory:* They are blocks of RAM that store messages (small) and can be accessed by the Interface part and Core Function part.
3. *File Areas:* They are areas in the hard disks that store image features posted from robots and can be accessed by Core Function part.
4. *Core Function:* They are mutually independent processes, providing localization services for robots. Their input is the image features and output is robots' position.
5. *Database:* It stores a feature database based on DBoW2 module and a trajectory database.

In order to ensure that the server could provide secure, stable and elastic compute services, we design the server with 4 additional parts: a firewall, a manager, a monitor and a scale modifier. The main function of each part is described below:

1. *Firewall:* It protects the server according to the secure rules, including open ports, access control lists and packet filter, etc.
2. *Manager:* It distributes data and tasks to Storage Areas and Core Functions according to different requests.
3. *Monitor:* It monitors and visualizes the server's states including CPUs and usage of the Storage Areas, the Core Functions and bandwidth, etc. Once some events get detected, the monitor will inform the scale modifier.
4. *Scale Modifier:* It scales the capacity of CPUs and memory up or down based on the online application's real-time demands.

After requests pass through the firewall, the manager distributes the requests to the proper Storage Areas and Core Functions. For example, it will distribute more resources to a complex request than normal ones. When the monitor detects errors, it will alter the scale modifier. Finally, the scale modifier will modify the scale of the abnormal parts.

4   Online Localization Service and Framework

In this section, we will describe the details of executing the localization service (Sects. 4.1 and 4.2) and building up the framework (Sect. 4.3).

---

[3] JSON: a lightweight data-interchange that is easy for humans to read and write. http://www.json.org.

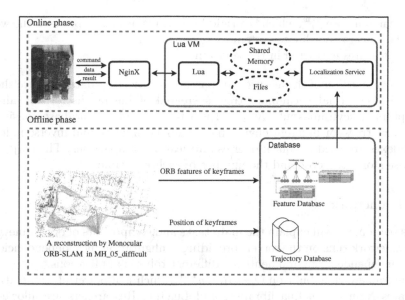

Fig. 4. Pipeline of the online localization service (top) and the off-line database creation (bottom)

4.1   Online Phase

Figure 4 introduces the pipeline of the online localization service and building process of the database. In the initialization step, the robot should firstly connect to the server. Once this connection is established, the robot starts capturing images and then uploading them to the server.

After receiving the new message, Lua virtual machine on the server will decode the command-type messages into JSON and save them in the Shared Memory.

The other part, called Core Function, runs simultaneously and provides localization service for the robot. Assuming that if some images captured by different cameras are matching with high scores, these cameras can be considered at the same place roughly. This assumption is used in the relocalization and loop detection step of some vSLAM systems. Each image is extracted ORB features and then searched its similarity in the feature database by using the bags of words place recognition module based on DBoW2 [4]. Finally, the robot's global localization will be retrieved in the trajectory databased and returned.

4.2   Offline Phase

Maps of large environments can be created by the Visual Monocular ORB-SLAM system. But different from [3], we only save the keyframes and disregard the 3D map points, co-visibility graphs, and essential graphs. The main reason is that after optimization, keyframes could reconstruct an environment in some extent. For each keyframe K_i, it stores:

1. The camera pose T_i^w, which is a rigid body transformation between the world to the camera coordinate system.
2. ORB features extracted in the keyframe.

The composition of the feature databases and trajectory databases are shown in Fig. 4. The visual vocabulary tree is created offline by discretizing all the descriptors of keyframes into K visual words. The feature database consists of vocabulary trees for different environments, direct indexes, and inverse indexes. The indexes are used for quick queries and feature comparisons. The trajectory database stores the pose and the number of each keyframe.

4.3   Framework

In this section, we will explain the main tasks and components of our framework. The framework runs on the server, providing configuration files, dependencies as well as independent environments for different robotic applications.

The framework is built on $OpenResty^{TM}$, which is a powerful web platform integrates Nginx core, Lua libraries, and LuaJIT. Researchers are allowed to implement web services on it with Lua scripts, Nginx C modules, and C/CPP programming languages. Compared with huge overhead of ROS, $OpenResty^{TM}$ is capable of handling 10K to 1000K connections on a single server.

Communication Protocol. The protocol defines the specification for message transmitting behaviors. Shown in Fig. 4, messages transmitted between robots and server could be classified into three types: command, data, and result. In every round, the robot sends command and data to the server and waits for the results. After establishing the connection, a Lua virtual machine is created by the server. The following computation tasks are completely processed in the Lua VM.

The command-type and result-type messages should be firstly encoded into JSON-type string format. JSON is a common communication format in web server, and many libraries available for JSON have been developed for various programming languages. We use the $RapidJSON^4$ to encode or decode the messages. But these JSON-type strings might be a burden to network bandwidth, so they will be further compressed before sending.

WebSocket is used to send command-type and result-type messages, which provides a full duplex, constant communication between robots and cloud in the framework. Compared with HTTP, WebSocket-based transmission helps save bandwidth resources hundreds of times under high concurrent connection. It also helps reduce 70% network delay compared with the HTTP long polling [26]. So it is efficient to send small messages through WebSocket.

Large messages will potentially consume plenty of bandwidth resources. Some results in [21] demonstrated that the delay and packet loss will increase if the

---

[4] RapidJSON: a fast JSON parser/generator for C++. http://rapidjson.org.

payload length of messages increases. At this point, the WebSocket protocol is not suitable for large messages transmission.

For instance, in the localization service or other complex services, robots need to offload some data like features or point clouds for storage or computation. These data might be larger than 100 Kbytes. Converting these data to JSON-type string format would result in an even larger message size because a float number might be transformed into multiple chars. As discussed above, the increasing pay length will limit the transmission of the messages. Therefore, we use HTTP to post files to the server instead of encoding them into String so that this limitation is avoided.

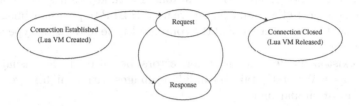

Fig. 5. The life of a Lua VM. When the connection is established, the Lua VM is created. The robotic service will be provided in a request-response way. Once the connection is closed, the Lua VM will be released

Isolated Computing Environment. When the connection between a robot and the server is established, a Lua VM is created to be used as an isolated environment. An isolated environment means that both memory and services are only provided for this robot and will not interfered with by other robots.

After creating a Lua VM, the service starts providing. In the next step, the robot will continuously send messages to the server and wait for the results. If the robot does not need services anymore (after sending a quit-type command), this connection will be closed and the Lua VM will be released simultaneously. The life length of Lua VM is as the same to the connection, which is shown in Fig. 5.

5 Experiment

In this section, we implemented the online localization service based on the cloud-based framework on the robot and ran the monocular ORB-SLAM system [3] on the same platform (called on-board ORB-SLAM). We compared the computational and memory cost of these two algorithms to demonstrate the feasibility and features of our proposed service.

5.1   Experiment Process

The cloud-based framework runs on a laptop (Intel Core i5, 2.5 GHz, 4 GB RAM). Both the laptop and the robot have a wireless connection to the campus Local Area Network. In this experiment, the server only handles a single request at the same time.

EuRoC dataset [27] contains 11 sequences recorded from a micro aerial vehicle (MAV), flying around two different rooms and an industrial environment. The sequences are classified as $easy, medium, difficult$ depending on MAV's speed, illumination, and scene texture. All the images were captured at 640×480.

In the offline phase, we ran the monocular ORB-SLAM in MH_01_easy to MH_05_difficult and then built up the databases with keyframes. Databases were saved on the server. In the online phase, we used HTTP to post new images to the server and used WebSocket to send the command-type and result-type messages (defined in Fig. 6).

There exist some feature matching errors because of the visual overlap between images. We firstly take 5 candidate images with a high score and then choose the most similar one.

What's more, we compared our localization service with the Monocular ORB-SLAM system [3]. We ran the ORB-SLAM system on the robot without connecting to the server and recorded the cost.

Command

```
{
    "type": "command"
    "id": "x"
    "content": "localization"
}
```

Result

```
{
    "type": "result"
    "id": "x"
    "content": "position($p_x, p_y, p_z, q_x, q_y, q_z, q_w$)"
}
```

Fig. 6. Definitions of command-type and result-type messages in the localization service

5.2   Results

Cost and Bandwidth Analysis. Figure 7 shows the bandwidth required by the algorithm in MH_05_difficult. The red lines show the required bandwidth for the data from the client to the server, which are recorded every 0.5 s. Images are dominant in the data transmission so the command-type and result-type messages are not displayed. Note that the size of images determines the height of redlines.

The average bandwidth required was around 1.80 MB/s, which is less than the maximum available in a wireless connection (6 MB/s). The data transmission did not exceed the capacity of the current network.

Figure 8 shows a double-axis figure which compares the computational cost per frame of two algorithms (the localization service and the on-board ORB-SLAM) in MH_05_difficult. The average computational time of the on-board ORB-SLAM is around 332 ms/frame, while the time of our localization service

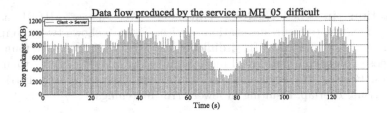

Fig. 7. Data flow produced by the localization service in MH_05_difficult of 2273 frames. Redline stands for images uploaded from client to the server. Compared with images, the command-type and result-type messages are small so they are not displayed. Each peak is recorded every 0.5 s. The average data flow for this localization service was 1.80 MB/s, below the usual wireless bandwidth which is 6 MB/s (Color figure online)

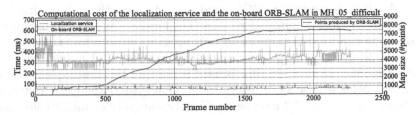

Fig. 8. A comparison of computational cost between the localization service and the on-board ORB-SLAM. The purple curve stands for the increasing map size caused by the ORB-SLAM, bringing memory burden to the robot (Color figure online)

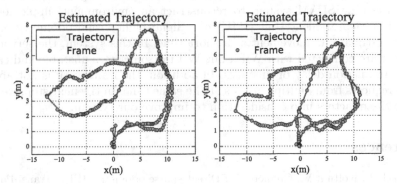

Fig. 9. Estimated trajectory in MH_04_difficult and MH_05_difficult. Note that the estimated trajectory in MH_04_difficult has less error matching

is around 57 ms/frame. Loading the vocabulary tree and saving the map are required by the ORB-SLAM, bringing extra memory and computational cost to the robot. Especially in long-term exploration, the increasing map size and optimization may exceed the robot's capability. So we consider that our proposed system is more suitable for low-cost robots.

Localization in the EuRoC Dataset. We choose MH_01_easy to MH_05_difficult to test our localization service. Figure 9 shows two examples of the estimated trajectory in MH_04_difficult and MH_05_difficult. We found that our proposed algorithm performed more accurate in MH_04_difficult than other sequences. Because the keyframes in MH_04_difficult have sparse distribution and less visual overlap, resulting in fewer error matchings.

6   Conclusion and Future Work

In this paper, we have presented a novel cloud-based framework that is built on WebSocket and $OpenResty^{TM}$, introduced its key components, and implemented an online localization service on it. Compared with other cloud robotics frameworks, it does not rely on ROS, send messages directly and is suitable for computation- and memory-intensive tasks. The localization service enables low-cost robots to relocalize themselves by reusing maps created by SLAM system. This service is able to handle each request within 60 ms. But influenced by the transmission delay, most of the time is used to wait for the new requests. So the transmission delay will be a bottleneck to our cloud-based application. Furthermore, based on the DBoW2 module, our localization service might cause some feature matching errors, which might limit the accuracy of our service. Finally, we ran a monocular ORB-SLAM on the robot (Cortex-A7 processor) and showed that our system is more suitable for low-cost robots.

The accuracy of the location service can be improved by using a dense- or semi-dense type SLAM system to reconstruct an environment, implementing an Inertial Measurement Unit (IMU) or a lightweight visual odometry on the robot to estimate its movement at a short time. In this system, the server and the robot are connected with WiFi, but WiFi is sometimes unstable and causes some transmission delay or mistakes. In addition, the framework is not able to handle requests from multiple robots at the same time. In the next step, we plan to take these factors into consideration to improve our system.

References

1. Engel, J., Koltun, V., Cremers, D.: Direct sparse odometry. IEEE Trans. Pattern Anal. Mach. Intell. (2017)
2. Engel, J., Schöps, T., Cremers, D.: LSD-SLAM: large-scale direct monocular SLAM. In: Fleet, D., Pajdla, T., Schiele, B., Tuytelaars, T. (eds.) ECCV 2014. LNCS, vol. 8690, pp. 834–849. Springer, Cham (2014). doi:10.1007/978-3-319-10605-2_54
3. Mur-Artal, R., Tardos, J.D.: ORB-SLAM2: an open-source SLAM system for monocular, stereo and RGB-D cameras. arXiv preprint arXiv:1610.06475 (2016)
4. Gálvez-López, D., Tardos, J.D.: Bags of binary words for fast place recognition in image sequences. IEEE Trans. Rob. **28**(5), 1188–1197 (2012)
5. Cadena, C., Carlone, L., Carrillo, H., Latif, Y., Scaramuzza, D., Neira, J., Reid, I.D., Leonard, J.J.: Simultaneous localization and mapping: present, future, and the robust-perception age. arXiv preprint arXiv:1606.05830 (2016)

6. Mur-Artal, R., Montiel, J.M.M., Tardos, J.D.: ORB-SLAM: a versatile and accurate monocular slam system. IEEE Trans. Rob. **31**(5), 1147–1163 (2015)
7. Liu, M., Qiu, K., Che, F., Li, S., Hussain, B., Wu, L., Yue, C.P.: Towards indoor localization using visible light communication for consumer electronic devices. In: 2014 IEEE/RSJ International Conference on Intelligent Robots and Systems (IROS 2014), pp. 143–148. IEEE (2014)
8. Zhang, F., Qiu, K., Liu, M.: Asynchronous blind signal decomposition using tiny-length code for visible light communication-based indoor localization, pp. 2800–2805 (2015)
9. Qiu, K., Zhang, F., Liu, M.: Visible light communication-based indoor localization using gaussian process, pp. 3125–3130 (2015)
10. Qiu, K., Zhang, F., Liu, M.: Let the light guide us: VLC-based localization. IEEE Robot. Autom. Mag. **23**(4), 174–183 (2016)
11. Vadeny, D., Chen, M., Huang, E., Elgala, H.: VSLAM and VLC based localization
12. Williams, B., Cummins, M., Neira, J., Newman, P., Reid, I., Tardós, J.: A comparison of loop closing techniques in monocular SLAM. Robot. Auton. Syst. **57**(12), 1188–1197 (2009)
13. Cummins, M., Newman, P.: FAB-MAP: probabilistic localization and mapping in the space of appearance. Int. J. Robot. Res. **27**(6), 647–665 (2008)
14. Mur-Artal, R., Tardós, J.D.: Fast relocalisation and loop closing in keyframe-based SLAM. In: 2014 IEEE International Conference on Robotics and Automation (ICRA), pp. 846–853. IEEE (2014)
15. Liu, M., Siegwart, R.: Topological mapping and scene recognition with lightweight color descriptors for an omnidirectional camera. IEEE Trans. Rob. **30**(2), 310–324 (2014)
16. Whelan, T., Kaess, M., Leonard, J.J., McDonald, J.: Deformation-based loop closure for large scale dense RGB-D SLAM. In: 2013 IEEE/RSJ International Conference on Intelligent Robots and Systems (IROS), pp. 548–555. IEEE (2013)
17. Glover, A.J., Maddern, W.P., Milford, M.J., Wyeth, G.F.: FAB-MAP + RAT-SLAM: appearance-based SLAM for multiple times of day. In: 2010 IEEE International Conference on Robotics and Automation (ICRA), pp. 3507–3512. IEEE (2010)
18. Quigley, M., Conley, K., Gerkey, B., Faust, J., Foote, T., Leibs, J., Wheeler, R., Ng, A.Y.: ROS: an open-source robot operating system. In: ICRA Workshop on Open Source Software, Kobe, vol. 3, p. 5 (2009)
19. Arumugam, R., Enti, V.R., Bingbing, L., Xiaojun, W., Baskaran, K., Kong, F.F., Senthil Kumar, A., Meng, K.D., Kit, G.W.: DAvinCi: a cloud computing framework for service robots. In: 2010 IEEE International Conference on Robotics and Automation (ICRA), pp. 3084–3089. IEEE (2010)
20. Markus, W., Michael, B., Javier, C., d'Andrea, R., Elfring, J., Galvez-Lopez, D., Häussermann, K., Janssen, R., Montiel, J.M.M., Perzylo, A., et al.: RoboEarth. IEEE Robot. Autom. Mag. **18**(2), 69–82 (2011)
21. Hunziker, D., Gajamohan, M., Waibel, M., D'Andrea, R.: Rapyuta: the RoboEarth cloud engine. In: 2013 IEEE International Conference on Robotics and Automation (ICRA), pp. 438–444. IEEE (2013)
22. Mohanarajah, G., Usenko, V., Singh, M., D'Andrea, R., Waibel, M.: Cloud-based collaborative 3D mapping in real-time with low-cost robots. IEEE Trans. Autom. Sci. Eng. **12**(2), 423–431 (2015)
23. Riazuelo, L., Civera, J., Montiel, J.M.M.: C2TAM: a first approach to a cloud framework for cooperative tracking and mapping

24. Labbe, M., Michaud, F.: Appearance-based loop closure detection for online large-scale and long-term operation. IEEE Trans. Robot. **29**(3), 734–745 (2013)
25. Wang, L., Liu, M., Meng, M.Q.H.: A hierarchical auction-based mechanism for real-time resource allocation in cloud robotic systems. IEEE Trans. Syst. Man Cybern. 1–12 (2016)
26. Lubbers, P., Albers, B., Smith, R., Salim, F.: Pro HTML5 Programming: Powerful APIs for Richer Internet Application Development. Apress, Berkely (2010)
27. Burri, M., Nikolic, J., Gohl, P., Schneider, T., Rehder, J., Omari, S., Achtelik, M.W., Siegwart, R.: The EUROC micro aerial vehicle datasets. Int. J. Robot. Res. **35**(10), 1157–1163 (2016)

Vision System for Robotized Weed Recognition in Crops and Grasslands

Tsampikos Kounalakis[1]([✉]), Georgios A. Triantafyllidis[2],
and Lazaros Nalpantidis[1]

[1] Department of Materials and Production, Aalborg University, Copenhagen,
Denmark
{tkoun,lanalpa}@make.aau.dk
[2] Department of Architecture, Design and Media Technology, Aalborg University,
Copenhagen, Denmark
gt@create.aau.dk

Abstract. In this paper, we introduce a novel vision system for robotized weed control on various weed recognition tasks. Initially, we present
a robotic platform and its camera setup, that can be used in crop-based
and grassland-based weed control tasks. Then, we develop our proposed
vision system for robotic application, using a weed recognition framework. The resulting system derives from a sequence of state-of-the-art
processes including image preprocessing, feature extraction and detection, codebook learning, feature encoding, image representation and classification. Our novel system is optimized using a dataset which represents
a crop-based weed control problem of thistles in sugar beet plantation.
Moreover, we apply the proposed vision system to a grassland-based
weed recognition problem, the control of the Broad-leaved Dock (Rumex
obtusifolius L.). It is experimentally shown that our proposed visual system yields state-of-the-art recognition in both examined datasets, while
presenting advantages in terms of autonomy and precision over competing methodologies.

1 Introduction

Precision agriculture systems are becoming increasingly important for the sus-
tainability of modern agriculture. Great efforts have been made towards the
development of robotics systems for weed control [1–5]. An efficient weed control
leads to the use of less pesticides, thus favoring quality, quantity and cost of the
produced agricultural and dairy products. Our DockWeeder robot [6] is a precision agriculture system designed for the autonomous control of the Broad-leaved
dock (Rumex obtusifolius L.) on dairy organic farms. With the use of GPS-based
navigation, our robot scans the grasslands using a combination of 2D and 3D
sensor information in order to detect and recognize weed plants. Weed control is
then performed by treating weed plant by applying steam directly to the upper
root region (hypocotyl).

Despite the proliferation of weed recognition systems and algorithms
[1–5,7–9], systems and methods are still designed with a specific weed recognition task in mind. This results to either crop-based or grassland-based weed

© Springer International Publishing AG 2017
M. Liu et al. (Eds.): ICVS 2017, LNCS 10528, pp. 485–498, 2017.
DOI: 10.1007/978-3-319-68345-4_43

recognition systems, that due to the nature of operational environment require different aspects of preprocessing. Although, all the aforementioned systems converge to a common structure and sequence of individual processes.

In this paper, we propose a vision recognition system that is able to cope with various weed recognition robotic applications. The *contribution* of this paper is twofold. First, a major extension for the weed recognition framework in [9] is proposed. The extension includes a great variety of preprocessing and individual processes, i.e., feature detection and extraction, codebook learning, feature encoding, image representation methodologies and classifiers. This allows the development and implementation of visual recognition systems in different weed control tasks, i.e., weed recognition both in crops and grasslands. Using an optimization sequence for each of the methodologies included in the proposed extended framework, we conlcude to our novel vision system. The proposed vision system can be used for the weed recognition task of thistle in sugar beet crops, as well as, the recognition of the Broad-leaved dock in grasslands. We experimentally show that the resulting weed recognition vision system yields state-of-the-art results in both examined datasets. Furthermore, we experimentally show that the proposed weed recognition vision system is developed considering further robotic applications, in robots such as the one shown in Fig. 1a. The weed recognition performance of our state-of-the-art system is measured in terms of autonomy and weed identification efficiency. All the above, result in a weed recognition system that can be the core of many robotics systems for weed control.

2   Related Work

As described in the introductory part, weed recognition systems are designed to provide specific solutions to either crop-based or grassland-based weed recognition tasks.

In [7], authors propose a weed recognition system for the identification of thistles in sugar beet plantations. That method is using plant/soil segmentation, a common preprocessing technique when using data from crops or fields with good visual separation. The segmentation process results to a binary mask highlighting the examined plan and treating it as a Region-Of-Interest (ROI). As a result, that system is able to disregard background information. Then, authors evaluate various feature detection and recognition algorithms using a common codebook learning, feature encoding and image representation architecture. Moreover, they propose a color-based feature, termed Color Vegetation Index (CVI), a combination between Shape Context [10] and the Twin Leaf Regions (TLR) detector [11] providing state-of-the-art results for the examined dataset in [11].

However, that system's performance is related to the efficiency of segmentation, which is a process not always guaranteed in realistic illumination and environmental conditions. Moreover, that system architecture can not be adopted by other weed recognition tasks, such as weed recognition in grasslands where segmentation is no longer applicable.

Authors in [9], propose a framework which facilitates the development of weed recognition systems for identifying Broad-leaved docks in dairy grasslands. That framework allows combinations between the comprising processes of weed recognition systems. These processes include feature detection and extraction, codebook learning, feature encoding, image representation methodologies and various classifiers. Using that framework, authors concluded in a weed recognition system for the examined RUMEX 100 [9] dataset.

However, the true potential of that framework were never examined since it was only limited to some process combinations, i.e., Scale-Invariant Feature Transform (SIFT) feature [12] in combination with feature detection methods, as well as, some feature encoding and image representation architectures. Moreover, the aspects of applying the same framework to other weed recognition tasks was not properly examined. That framework was lacking preprocessing capabilities, required by crop-based weed recognition tasks.

3   Robot and Vision Setup

Designing a visual recognition system for various weed control tasks, also requires the consideration of dedicated robot for such implementation. To suit the requirements of the Dockweeder project, a robot must implement a visual system robust to illumination and environmental conditions. Moreover, the camera setup should also facilitate the required space for end-effector used for weed control. All the aforementioned requirements, resulted to a prototype unmanned ground vehicle (UGV), shown in Fig. 1a.

 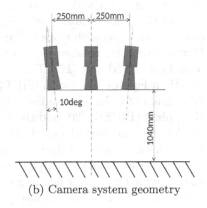

(a) Prototype robotic platform   (b) Camera system geometry

Fig. 1. The platform (a) is carrying the camera system of the DockWeeder robot, shown in sketch (b).

The UGV is equipped with a three cameras system mounted on a common rigid rig. The camera setup design specifications can be seen in Fig. 1b. The central camera provides a top-view, i.e., most used view in all weed recognition systems [1–5, 7–9]. As a result, the proposed camera setup is extremely compatible with all aforementioned methodologies and their examined weed recognition tasks respectively. Furthermore, the proposed camera system consists of two side cameras with a ten degree inclination towards the central view. This camera setup feature will allow future research towards multi-view recognition or stereo correspondence [13]. Moreover, the proposed camera setup guarantees the robust acquisition of 3D information in both crops and grasslands, while under realistic illumination and environmental conditions [14].

4   Developing the Proposed Weed Recognition System

Our proposed system is developed using a major extension of the framework presented in [9]. The addition of preprocessing techniques, i.e., plant/soil segmentation, facilitates the development and implementation of visual systems for different weed recognition tasks. The proposed framework constitutes a major extension of individual processes such as feature detection and extraction, codebook learning, image representation and classifiers.

For preprocessing the crop-based image data, we use the segmentation process proposed in [7]. The plant/soil segmentation is performed using the ExG vegetation index [15], thus highlighting each examined plant a Region-Of-Interest (ROI). As a result, we are able to develop a common system for both crop and grassland-based image, disregarding background if it is required by the examined weed recognition task.

For feature detection we extend the framework of [9] by including the feature extraction over dense grids [9], the Pyramid Histogram Of visual Words (PHOW) proposed in [16], the determinant of the Hessian detector (detHess) [17], difference of Gaussian in multi-scale regions (DoG) [12], Determinant of Hessian for space localization with trace of Laplacian for scale detection (HessLapl) [17] and Harris cornerness measure for space localization with trace of Laplacian for scale detection (HarrLapl) [17]. Then, feature extraction is performed using Scale-Invariant Feature Transform (SIFT) [12], Speed-Up Robust Feature (SURF) [18], Histogram of Oriented Gradients (HOG) [19], Binary Robust Invariant Scalable Keypoints (BRISK) [20] and the Fast Retina Keypoints (FREAK) [21].

All the aforementioned features are described with codebooks learning methodologies such as Elkan k-means [22], Lloyd k-means [23], K-Singular Value Decomposition (K-SVD) [24] and Gaussian Mixture Models (GMM) [25]. Each of the examined codebook learning methods are combined feature encoding methods, such as Vector Quantization (VQ), k-d tree [26], Locality-constrained Linear Coding (LLC) [27], Fisher feature encoding [28] and Vectors of Linearly Aggregated Descriptors (VLAD) [29].

Feature encoded features are then combined using image representation such as the Bag of Features (BoF) model [30] and the Spatial Pyramid Matching (SPM) [31] including various one-level, two-level and three-level image pyramid architectures.

Finally, for the classification our proposed framework includes a non-linear Support Vector Machine (SVM)[32] include a c-Support Vector Classification (c-SVC).

Through the implementation of an extensive optimization on the aforementioned process sequence, we develop our proposed weed recognition system. During our experimental evaluation, initial parameters and methodologies change according to the best performing results. The optimization sequence is performed on images without any preprocessing, i.e., images without segmentation. This allows the development of a very robust and adaptable system, that can be implemented both in crop and grassland-based image data.

In the ensuing Sect. 5.5, our proposed visual recognition system is experimentally shown to yield state-of-the-art results in all examined datasets representing crop and grassland weed recognition tasks. Furthermore, our system experimentally shows its capabilities in autonomy and weed identification, important factors when taking into consideration the implementation on robotic systems for weed control.

5 Experimental Assessment

5.1 Experimental Settings

For the experimental assessment, we are using two datasets describing different weed control problems. First, we have the dataset presented in [11] describing the problem of controlling thistles in sugar beet crops. This dataset consists of 474 images depict sugar beets and thistle plants in various states of plant growth, representing the 7th, 10th and 12th week of plantation. Images consisting this dataset can be seen in Fig. 2a.

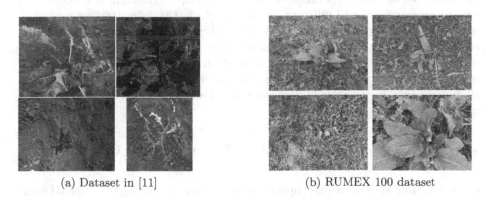

(a) Dataset in [11]   (b) RUMEX 100 dataset

Fig. 2. Example images from the weed recognition dataset presented in [11] and the *RUMEX 100* weed recognition dataset [9].

In [9], the dataset is compiled as a benchmark for the weed recognition task of the Broad-leaved dock (Rumex obtusifolius L.) in dairy grasslands. The RUMEX

100 weed recognition dataset consists of 100 images depicting the weed plant in its natural environment, i.e., grass and soil. For the purpose of recognition and detection, authors in [9] also provide the dataset in annotated form. Each image, is segmented in 3×3 spatial regions which are then described by two labels denoting their content, i.e., weed or grass. The resulting dataset has 900 images. Images describing the contents of RUMEX 100 weed recognition dataset can be seen in Fig. 2b.

The experimental evaluation of the proposed framework is separated in two parts. Using the proposed framework, we follow an optimization process to construct a weed recognition system for thistles in sugar beet plantations using the dataset in [11]. Then, we are assessing the resulting system to other weed recognition task such as the one described in the RUMEX 100 dataset [9].

For the experimental assessment of our novel framework, we establish a common experimental process across all experiments. We follow the experimental process proposed in [7] also followed in [9] for both examined datasets. All the ensuing tables include recognition accuracy calculated using $ACC = (TP + TN)/(TP + FP + TN + FN)$, calculated from true-positive (TP), true-negative (TN), false-positive (FP) and false-negative (FN) rates. In order to efficiently evaluate the performance of the resulting system we also introduce the mean False-Negative rates (FNR), mean False-Positive values rates (FPR), as well as, Recall and Precision evaluation terms. The aforementioned metrics are calculated using the following equations $FNR = FN/(TP + FN)$, $FPR = FP/N$, $Recall = TP/(TP + FN)$ and $Precision = TP/(TP + FP)$.

For the training process of all examined codebooks, we use randomly selected features derived from the training set of images, which are also used to train all classifiers. The number of training features per image are initially kept to 20, as defined in [7]. However, in Sect. 5.3 that number is set according to optimize performance. So, for each experiment we are computing 10 different codebooks. All experiments are using 10 different randomly selected training/testing sets, that remain constant for every experiment. In combination with the aforementioned 10 codebook training sets per experiment, that results to 100 combinations per experiment. Training sets consists of 50% of all available image data, with the remaining used for testing. All classifier-based parameters are kept stable across all experiments and examined datasets with classifier cost set to 10 during our experimental evaluation.

5.2 Combinations Between Feature Extraction and Detection Methods

We initiate our aforementioned optimization process by finding the optimal combinations between feature description and detection methodologies for the examined dataset [11].

We are using our proposed framework with the experimental settings presented in [7]. Thus, codebook learning is performed using a codebook with 100 codewords, computed using the Elkan k-means methodology. Features are encoded using the k-d tree methodology, and then combined with a two-level

SPM pyramid with 20 spatial region histograms. In detail, the first pyramid level consists of 2×2 spatial regions and the second is defined by 4×4 spatial regions. The resulting 2000-dimensional image representation vector are then used for classification using the c-SVC classifier, with the parameters denoted in Sect. 5.1.

Table 1. Recognition rates (%) from the comparison between various feature extraction and feature detection methods.

Feature	Feature detection methodology					
	PHOW	Dense	DoG	det(Hes)	HessLapl	HarrLapl
SIFT	82.11 ± 1.71	84.04 ± 1.86	80.44 ± 1.84	82.64 ± 1.77	83.69 ± 1.84	81.60 ± 1.98
SURF	-	83.85 ± 2.22	-	$\mathbf{87.22 \pm 1.78}$	-	-
HOG	-	83.35 ± 2.00	-	83.22 ± 1.85	-	-
BRISK	-	76.84 ± 1.90	-	78.39 ± 2.16	-	-
FREAK	-	78.71 ± 2.17	-	79.86 ± 2.26	-	-

Recognition results between combinations of feature extraction and detection methods are presented in Table 1. The work in [7], shows that several combinations between feature extraction and detection methods occur due to the implementation of specific features. SIFT is the most compatible feature descriptor, thus providing results for all the examined feature detection methods. The top-performing combination using SIFT, is the one with the dense feature extraction presented in [9] yielding the second best recognition accuracy among feature descriptor methodologies.

For rest of the examined feature descriptors, we exclude the incompatible PHOW, DoG, HessLapl and HarrLapl feature detectors. As a result, we end up using the remaining methodologies of dense feature extraction and det(Hes). The experimental results show that the det(Hes) is the top-performing feature detection method for most combinations with feature descriptors. The best overall combination in the examined dataset is yielded by the SURF feature descriptor and det(Hes) feature detection, i.e., the default feature detection method of SURF descriptors [18].

5.3 Combinations Between Codebook Learning and Encoding Methodologies

The next optimization step consists of finding the top-performing combination between codebook learning and feature encoding methodologies.

In Table 2, we present the mean accuracy of each examined combination, as well as, the optimized dictionary parameters. As a result, the dictionary training parameters of [7] presented in Sect. 5.2 no longer apply. The optimized parameter for each dictionary method, as presented in the second part of Table 2.

Table 2. Recognition rates (%) from the comparison between various codebook learning and feature encoding methodologies. The second part of the table describes number of training features per image/number of codewords/and maximum computation iterations

	Feature encoding methods				
	VQ	K-d tree	LLC	Fisher	VLAD
K-means Elkan	87.58 ± 1.92	87.50 ± 2.03	80.10 ± 1.90	-	86.67 ± 1.80
K-means Lloyd	87.56 ± 1.90	87.46 ± 1.94	80.39 ± 2.10	-	86.51 ± 1.84
K-SVD	87.52 ± 1.79	$\mathbf{88.33 \pm 1.33}$	80.90 ± 1.86	-	85.61 ± 1.84
GMM	87.71 ± 1.82	88.17 ± 1.64	83.96 ± 1.82	86.20 ± 1.62	86.41 ± 1.83
	Dictionary parameters				
K-means Elkan	30/110/50	30/100/50	20/110/30	-	20/100/60
K-means Lloyd	30/110/50	30/100/50	30/130/40	-	20/100/50
K-SVD	30/110/40	**10/120/60**	30/110/60	-	40/150/50
GMM	30/100/10	40/100/10	30/110/50	50/90/10	30/100/10

By examining the codebook learning methodologies, one can observe that our current weed recognition system is favored from codebooks computed using the GMM methodology. This method provides the best overall improvements regardless the examined feature encoding methodologies. Furthermore, K-SVD computed codebooks generally outperform those computed by k-means. However, K-SVD based codebooks combined with the appropriate feature encoding methodology yield improved recognition results.

When comparing feature encoding methodologies, the experimental comparison shows that LLC provides the least favorable results. Furthermore, VLAD and Fisher feature encoding methodologies provide similar results when using GMM. However, VLAD is slightly outperforming Fisher encoding when combined with other codebooks. It should be noted that, Fisher feature encoding is only examined in combination with the GMM since it constitutes part of its implementation. When comparing the two top performing feature encoding methods, results suggest that VQ is outperforming k-d tree when using k-mean based codebooks. However, k-d tree yields its two top-performing combination when using K-SVD and GMM generated codebooks. In conclusion, k-d tree with K-SVD using less features for training but provides encoded features with greater dimensionality that yield the top-performing combination for this experiment.

5.4　Comparison of Image Representation Architectures

The next optimization step for our proposed weed recognition system, is to choose appropriate image representation architecture. As described earlier, for our experimental evaluation we are using the BoW and the SPM model, the two most known image representations. Moreover, we use metrics that can assist further the evaluation of examined architectures.

The recognition performance of BoW is represented in the first row of Table 3. This image representation technique is only using one histogram, thus denoted with 1, to describe all encoded image features in an unordered manner. Compared to other image representation architectures, BoW outperforms only those represent with four spatial regions.

Table 3. Recognition accuracy, FNR, FPR, Recall, Precision rates (%) from the comparison between various image representation architectures. For FNR and FPR rates less is better.

Pyramid	Accuracy	FNR	FPR	Recall	Precision
1	85.00 ± 1.97	11.00 ± 2.99	21.56 ± 4.71	89.00	87.11
4	83.54 ± 1.66	11.24 ± 2.76	25.00 ± 3.94	88.76	85.32
9	89.10 ± 1.56	6.28 ± 2.09	18.46 ± 3.78	93.72	89.26
16	88.12 ± 1.47	5.61 ± 1.92	22.14 ± 3.83	94.39	87.47
1 4	84.87 ± 1.61	10.27 ± 2.65	23.09 ± 3.80	89.73	86.42
1 9	89.69 ± 1.34	6.07 ± 1.73	17.25 ± 3.61	93.93	89.92
1 16	89.05 ± 1.32	5.13 ± 1.68	20.49 ± 3.63	94.87	88.35
4 9	88.47 ± 1.55	6.84 ± 2.01	19.21 ± 3.74	93.16	88.81
4 16	88.33 ± 1.33	5.79 ± 1.78	21.30 ± 3.80	94.21	87.87
9 16	89.47 ± 1.48	4.70 ± 1.90	20.08 ± 3.72	95.30	88.60
1 4 9	88.99 ± 1.49	6.55 ± 1.88	18.32 ± 3.77	93.45	89.31
1 4 16	88.84 ± 1.31	5.67 ± 1.82	20.14 ± 3.54	94.33	88.46
1 9 16	$\mathbf{89.90 \pm 1.50}$	$\mathbf{4.48 \pm 1.74}$	$\mathbf{19.31 \pm 3.61}$	**95.52**	**89.01**

However, top-performing results are provided when using the SPM image representation model. The recognition accuracy is generally favored when using 3×3, i.e., 9 spatial regions to compute the image representation vector. That trend is also evident when considering more pyramid levels for system image representations.

When using a three-level 1×1, 3×3 and 4×4 image representation pyramid there is a balance between autonomy and weed recognition. The system is able to identify thistles with high accuracy, thus making it very efficient for weed control. Its FNR rates, i.e., when the system does not recognize a weed plant, are the lowest in our comparison thus leading to increased Recall percentage. The low FPR rates, i.e., when the system decides for a weed where a sugar beet exists, also leads to one of the best Precision percentage in this comparison. These two rates indicate a system with high autonomy, i.e., a system that does not initiate treatment when none is needed.

Overall, the concluding weed recognition system on the examined task consists of SURF features, with detected keypoints using the det(Hes), K-SVD codebook learning combined with k-d tree feature encoding, and a three-level pyramid image representation of 1×1, 3×3 and 4×4 spatial regions classified using the C-SVC classifier. The system was experimentally shown to yield state-of-the-art recognition results on unsegmented images for the examined dataset [11].

5.5 Transferring the System to Other Weed Recognition Problems

The conclude our experimental assessment we apply the aforementioned optimized state-of-the-art weed recognition system, using segmented images from the same dataset [11]. Furthermore, the proposed system is tested in a different weed recognition task using the dataset for Broad-leaved dock [9]. In Table 4, we present the comparison between our proposed system and the top-performing systems of [9,11] for each of the examined datasets.

Table 4. Recognition accuracy, FNR, FPR, Recall, Precision rates (%) from the comparison between top-performing methods in the examined datasets. For FNR and FPR rates less is better.

	Accuracy	FNR	FPR	Recall	Precision
[11] dataset, segmented					
SC – CVI9 + TLR4 [7]	**99.04 ± 0.44**	2	1	98	99.38
SURF – det(Hes) [7]	93.68 ± 1.62	1.03 ± 0.81	14.98 ± 4.25	98.97	91.54
SIFT – Heslap [7]	96.98 ± 1.02	1.58 ± 0.97	7.93 ± 2.92	98.42	95.31
Proposed system	97.53 ± 0.92	**1.19 ± 0.84**	4.56 ± 2.02	**98.81**	97.26
[11] dataset, non-segmented					
SC – CVI9 + TLR4 [7]	-	-	-	-	-
SURF – det(Hes) [7]	86.56 ± 1.86	5.67 ± 1.84	26.15 ± 4.15	94.33	85.52
SIFT – Heslap [7]	83.25 ± 2.00	10.96 ± 3.01	26.22 ± 4.16	89.04	84.76
Proposed system	**89.90 ± 1.50**	**4.48 ± 1.74**	**19.31 ± 3.61**	**95.52**	**89.01**
RUMEX 100 dataset [9]					
SC – CVI9 + TLR4 [7]	-	-	-	-	-
SURF – det(Hes) [7]	80.11 ± 1.41	70.90 ± 4.88	1.55 ± 0.74	29.1	96.85
SIFT – Heslap [7]	78.61 ± 1.80	51.61 ± 6.08	10.52 ± 1.81	48.39	62.32
SIFT – PHOW	84.96 ± 1.14	41.01 ± 6.21	4.02 ± 0.90	59.00	84.07
Proposed system	**86.11 ± 1.15**	**38.91 ± 4.45**	4.89 ± 1.71	**61.09**	81.79

First, we examine the recognition performance of our proposed system using a plant/soil segmentation preprocess on images from the dataset in [11], also described in Sect. 4. It should be noted, that all systems in [7] are optimized in this weed recognition scenario, i.e., where visual data are visually separable. The experimental results indicate that our optimized system on unsegmented images is outperforming some of the systems in [7]. Even when compared to a system using the same feature detection and extraction algorithms, the proposed system is still better in every metric. However, when compared to the state-of-the-art system on segmented data the proposed system lacks both in accuracy and FPR. So, the system can still provide high accuracy in recognition but it is adversely affected in terms of autonomy. The top-performing system is using a combination of features, i.e., Shape context [10] and a Color Vegetation Index [7], extracted with the use of the binary mask. But, due to the nature of its feature extraction technique, is dependent on segmentation quality between the plant and the background. This generally constitutes a problem for environments with no controlled illumination conditions such as fields and crops. Moreover, the fact that feature extraction requires a segmentation makes this system directly applicable only to the examined weed recognition problem.

For our second comparison, we are using the same dataset as before [11], but with no segmentation preprocessing. The second part of Table 4, presents the effects in terms of performance from the lack of segmentation preprocessing in all competing systems. The weed recognition systems of [7] are adversely affected with the SIFT-Heslap system reporting the biggest performance drop. Our proposed system derives from an optimization on non-segmented images. As a result, it outperforms all competing systems, indicating state-of-the-art performance in every metric.

Finally we examine the performance of all systems in a dataset representing the weed control problem of the Broad-leaved dock in grasslands [9]. For this examined dataset, no segmentation preprocessing is available.

The SIFT-based system of [7] fail to adapt to the needs of the new dataset, thus resulting to decreased recognition accuracy and increased FNR and FPR rates. In the other hand, the SURF-based system of [7] may not yield a good accuracy but it provides the lowest FPR rate. As reported in [9], it is preferable that recognition accuracy to be accompanied by low FPR rates, since in that weed recognition scenario, autonomy is more important than the miss recognition of some weed plants. Focusing at the FNR rates, we can conclude that the SURF-based system of [7] may recognize grass very efficiently, however when it comes to the identification of weeds it does not yield the same performance. The system in [9], was proposed and optimized using the examined dataset. However, as shown in Table 4, the accuracy of that system is outperformed by the proposed system. Moreover, that system is adversely affected in terms of FNR rates, but yields slightly improved FPR rates than the proposed system. The system of [9] can achieve better recognition of weed plants, but lacks in term of autonomy thus providing decreased Recall rates. In the other hand, our proposed system yields increased accuracy and a very balanced recall and precision rates.

From all the above, we can conclude that our proposed system not only provides state-of-the-art results in the dataset for which was optimized, but also yields state-of-the-art results in datasets presenting different weed recognition problems.

6   Conclusions

In this work, we introduce a novel vision system for robotized weed control on various weed recognition tasks. We present a robotic platform and its camera setup, which can be used both in crop-based and grassland-based weed control tasks. Then, we develop our proposed vision system for robotic application, using our extended weed recognition framework and an exhaustive optimization. The resulting system derives from a sequence of individual system processes optimized using unsegmented image data from the dataset in [11], thus achieving state-of-the-art recognition results. Moreover, we apply the proposed vision system to a grassland-based weed recognition problem represented by the dataset in [9]. We experimentally show that our proposed visual system yields state-of-the-art recognition in both examined datasets. Moreover, our novel vision system has the advantage in terms of autonomy and precision over competing methodologies when considering its implementation in weed control robotic applications, as shown by the state-of-the-art precision and recall rates.

Acknowledgements. This work has been supported by the DockWeeder project (project ID: 30079), administered through the European Union's Seventh Framework Programme for research, technological development and demonstration under grant agreement no. 618123 [ICT-AGRI 2]. The project has received funding from the Ministry of Economic Affairs (The Netherlands), from the Federal Office for Agriculture (Switzerland), and from Innovation Fund Denmark, the Ministry of Science, Innovation and Higher Education (Denmark).

References

1. Kargar, A.H.B., Shirzadifar, A.M.: Automatic weed detection system and smart herbicide sprayer robot for corn fields. In: 2013 1st RSI/ISM International Conference on Robotics and Mechatronics (ICRoM), pp. 468–473. IEEE, February 2013
2. Wong, W., Chekima, A., Mariappan, M., Khoo, B., Nadarajan, M.: Probabilistic multi SVM weed species classification for weed scouting and selective spot weeding. In: 2014 IEEE International Symposium on Robotics and Manufacturing Automation (ROMA), pp. 63–68. IEEE, December 2014
3. Pérez-Ortiz, M., Peña, J., Gutiérrez, P., Torres-Sánchez, J., Hervás-Martínez, C., López-Granados, F.: A semi-supervised system for weed mapping in sunflower crops using unmanned aerial vehicles and a crop row detection method. Appl. Soft Comput. **37**, 533–544 (2015)
4. Pérez-Ortiz, M., Peña, J.M., Gutiérrez, P.A., Torres-Sánchez, J., Hervás-Martínez, C., López-Granados, F.: Selecting patterns and features for between- and within-crop-row weed mapping using UAV-imagery. Expert Syst. Appl. **47**(C), 85–94 (2016)
5. Michaels, A., Haug, S., Albert, A.: Vision-based high-speed manipulation for robotic ultra-precise weed control. In: 2015 IEEE/RSJ International Conference on Intelligent Robots and Systems (IROS), pp. 5498–5505. IEEE, September 2015
6. DockWeeder: The DockWeeder robot enables organic dairy farming by controlling grassland. In: European Unions Seventh Framework Programme for Research, Technological Development and Demonstration Under Grant Agreement no. 618123 [ICT-AGRI 2] (2015)

7. Kazmi, W., Garcia-Ruiz, F., Nielsen, J., Rasmussen, J., Andersen, H.J.: Exploiting affine invariant regions and leaf edge shapes for weed detection. Comput. Electron. Agricult. **118**(C), 290–299 (2015)
8. Lottes, P., Hoeferlin, M., Sander, S., Muter, M., Schulze, P., Stachniss, L.C.: An effective classification system for separating sugar beets and weeds for precision farming applications. In: 2016 IEEE International Conference on Robotics and Automation (ICRA), pp. 5157–5163. IEEE (2016)
9. Kounalakis, T., Triantafyllidis, G.A., Nalpantidis, L.: Weed recognition framework for robotic precision farming. In: 2016 IEEE International Conference on Imaging Systems and Techniques (IST), pp. 466–471. IEEE, October 2016
10. Belongie, S., Malik, J., Puzicha, J.: Shape Context: a new descriptor for shape matching and object recognition. IN: NIPS, pp. 831–837 (2000)
11. Kazmi, W., Garcia-Ruiz, F.J., Nielsen, J., Rasmussen, J., Jørgen Andersen, H.: Detecting creeping thistle in sugar beet fields using vegetation indices. Comput. Electron. Agricult. **112**(C), 10–19 (2015)
12. Lowe, D.G.: Distinctive image features from scale-invariant keypoints. Int. J. Comput. Vis. **60**(2), 91–110 (2004)
13. Nalpantidis, L., Sirakoulis, G.C., Gasteratos, A.: Review of stereo vision algorithms: from software to hardware. Int. J. Optomech. **2**(4), 435–462 (2008)
14. Nalpantidis, L., Gasteratos, A.: Stereo vision for robotic applications in the presence of non-ideal lighting conditions. Image Vis. Comput. **28**(6), 940–951 (2010)
15. Woebbecke, D., Meyer, G., Von Bargen, K., Mortensen, D.: Color indices for weed identification under various soil, residue, and lighting conditions. Trans. ASAE **38**(1), 259–269 (1995)
16. Bosch, A., Zisserman, A., Munoz, X.: Image classification using random forests and ferns. In: 2007 IEEE 11th International Conference on Computer Vision, pp. 1–8. IEEE (2007)
17. Mikolajczyk, K., Schmid, C.: An affine invariant interest point detector. In: Heyden, A., Sparr, G., Nielsen, M., Johansen, P. (eds.) ECCV 2002. LNCS, vol. 2350, pp. 128–142. Springer, Heidelberg (2002). doi:10.1007/3-540-47969-4_9
18. Bay, H., Ess, A., Tuytelaars, T., Van Gool, L.: Speeded-up robust features (SURF). Comput. Vis. Image Underst. **110**(3), 346–359 (2008)
19. Dalal, N., Triggs, B.: Histograms of oriented gradients for human detection. In: Proceedings - 2005 IEEE Computer Society Conference on Computer Vision and Pattern Recognition, CVPR 2005, vol. I, pp. 886–893. IEEE (2005)
20. Leutenegger, S., Chli, M., Siegwart, R.Y.: BRISK: binary robust invariant scalable keypoints. In: Proceedings of IEEE International Conference on Computer Vision, pp. 2548–2555. IEEE, November 2011
21. Alahi, A., Ortiz, R., Vandergheynst, P.: FREAK: fast retina keypoint. In: Proceedings of IEEE Computer Society Conference on Computer Vision and Pattern Recognition, pp. 510–517. IEEE, June 2012
22. Hamerly, G., Elkan, C.: Alternatives to the k-means algorithm that find better clusterings. In: Proceedings of 11th International Conference on Information and Knowledge Management, vol. 4, no, 09, pp. 600–607 (2002)
23. Kanungo, T., Mount, D., Netanyahu, N., Piatko, C., Silverman, R., Wu, A.: An efficient k-means clustering algorithm: analysis and implementation. IEEE Trans. Pattern Anal. Mach. Intell. **24**(7), 881–892 (2002)
24. Aharon, M., Elad, M., Bruckstein, A.: K-SVD: An algorithm for designing over-complete dictionaries for sparse representation. IEEE Trans. Sig. Process. **54**(11), 4311–4322 (2006)

25. Dempster, A.P., Laird, N.M., Rubin, D.B.: Maximum likelihood from incomplete data via the EM algorithm. J. Roy. Stat. Soc. Ser. B **39**(1), 1–38 (1977)
26. Silpa-Anan, C., Hartley, R.: Optimised KD-trees for fast image descriptor matching. In: 26th IEEE Conference on Computer Vision and Pattern Recognition, CVPR, pp. 1–8. IEEE, June 2008
27. Wang, J., Yang, J., Yu, K., Lv, F., Huang, T., Gong, Y.: Locality-constrained linear coding for image classification. In: Proceedings of IEEE Computer Society Conference on Computer Vision and Pattern Recognition, pp. 3360–3367. IEEE, June 2010
28. Perronnin, F., Sánchez, J., Mensink, T.: Improving the fisher kernel for large-scale image classification. In: Daniilidis, K., Maragos, P., Paragios, N. (eds.) ECCV 2010. LNCS, vol. 6314, pp. 143–156. Springer, Heidelberg (2010). doi:10.1007/978-3-642-15561-1_11
29. Jégou, H., Perronnin, F., Douze, M., Sánchez, J., Pérez, P., Schmid, C.: Aggregating local image descriptors into compact codes. IEEE Trans. Pattern Anal. Mach. Intell. **34**(9), 1704–1716 (2012)
30. Li, F.-F., Perona, P.: A Bayesian hierarchical model for learning natural scene categories. In: 2005 IEEE Computer Society Conference on Computer Vision and Pattern Recognition (CVPR 2005), vol. 2, pp. 524–531. IEEE (2005)
31. Lazebnik, S., Schmid, C., Ponce, J.: Beyond bags of features: spatial pyramid matching for recognizing natural scene categories. In: Proceedings of IEEE Computer Society Conference on Computer Vision and Pattern Recognition, vol. 2, pp. 2169–2178. IEEE (2006)
32. Fan, R.E., Chen, P.H., Lin, C.J.: Working set selection using second order information for training support vector machines. J. Mach. Learn. Res. **6**, 1889–1918 (2005)

Pedestrian Detection Over 100 fps with C4 Algorithm

Fei Wang[1(⊠)], Caifang Lin[1], and Qian Huang[2]

[1] Harbin Institute of Technology Shenzhen Graduate School, Shenzhen 518000,
People's Republic of China
1392135844@qq.com
[2] Wright State University, Dayton, OH 45324, USA

Abstract. In this paper a novel pedestrian detection algorithm on GPU is presented, which takes advantage of features of census transform histogram (CENTRIST), rather than common HOG feature. The proposed algorithm uses NVIDIA CUDA framework, and can process VGA images at a speed of 108 fps on a low cost notebook computer with a GPU, while without using any other auxiliary technique. Our Implementation enables a factor 17 speedup over original CENTRIST detector while without compromising any accuracy.

Keywords: Pedestrian detection · GPU · CENTRIST · CUDA · Real-time

1 Introduction

Pedestrian detection plays an important role in many applications, for example video surveillance, mobile robots, driving assistance systems and so on. In some applications like robot, real-time detection is critical [1]. There are many popular descriptors for pedestrian detection, for example HOG [2], LBP [3], ChnFtrs [4] and so on, but algorithms based on these descriptors are generally slow for real time applications.

Graphics Processing Units (GPUs) can run massive threads in parallel, and can accelerate a variety of image processing tasks. Quite some works have been conducted on pedestrian detection. There have been many studies of using the GPU to accelerate HOG-based pedestrian detection. Wojek et al. [5] achieved 30 times speedup on INRIA person test set. Prisacariu and Reid [6] achieved a 67 speedup in color mode and a 95 speedup in grayscale mode. Lillywhite et al. [7] presented a real-time implementation which can process VGA images at 38 fps. Benenson et al. [8] presented a very fast pedestrian detection algorithm which can run at 100 fps. This work was the fastest algorithm before our work described in this paper. Big differences between our proposed algorithm and Benenson's algorithm are: (1) Benenson's algorithm is based on ChnFtrs descriptors [4], ours is based on CENTRIST descriptors (2) Besides GPU parallel computing, Benenson's algorithm takes advantage of other auxiliary algorithms like stixel and ground plane estimation, therefore detections are conducted on reduced area, our algorithm explores GPU's parallel computing capability only. Most of all, our detection speed outperforms Benenson's using the same hardware. More detail analysis can be seen in Sect. 4.

© Springer International Publishing AG 2017
M. Liu et al. (Eds.): ICVS 2017, LNCS 10528, pp. 499–506, 2017.
DOI: 10.1007/978-3-319-68345-4_44

The critical information in features can lead to efficient detection architecture. Wu et al. propose Census Transform Histogram (CENTRIST) descriptors, which can characterize critical contour information for pedestrian detection [9]. It is remarkable that the algorithm (C4) can detect pedestrians in real time with high accuracy. As an example, human detection based on C4 is illustrated in Fig. 1.

Fig. 1. An example of C4 for pedestrians

In this paper a GPU version of C4 algorithm is presented, which can detect pedestrians at 108 fps for VGA images. Section 1 gives a survey on similar works now days. Section 2 briefly describes the CENTRIST visual descriptor. Section 3 introduces the parallel version of the C4 algorithm in detail. Section 4 summarizes the performance of the parallel C4 algorithm, and Sect. 5 concludes this paper.

2   CENTRIST Descriptor

Global contour is believed to be the most useful information to characterize a pedestrian [9], and signs of comparisons among neighboring pixels represent this information. CENTRIST visual descriptor encodes this sign information, and does not require pre-processing (padding image and gamma normalization).

Building CENTRIST visual descriptors begins from computing Sobel gradient image. Sobel image can smooth high frequency local texture information, and can hold the contour information. And then Census Transform (CT) is conducted, which can be illustrated as Eq. 1. The pixel in the center is compared with its eight neighboring pixels. A neighbor pixel value will be replaced by a bit 1 (0) if the gray level of the central pixel is bigger (smaller) than that of the neighbor pixel. The resulting eight bits are collected from left to right and from top to bottom. The eight bits are converted to a radix-10 number in [0 255].

$$
\begin{matrix} 32 & 32 & 90 \\ 82 & 82 & 96 \\ 64 & 64 & 98 \end{matrix} \Rightarrow \begin{matrix} 1 & 1 & 0 \\ 1 & & 0 \\ 1 & 1 & 0 \end{matrix} \Rightarrow (11010110)_2 \Rightarrow CT = 214 \tag{1}
$$

This number is named as the CT value of the central pixel. Histogram based on CT values is named as CENTRIST descriptor [10] (Fig. 2).

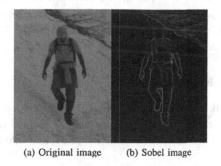

(a) Original image   (b) Sobel image

Fig. 2. An example of C4 for pedestrians

A window is slid over the image, and CENTRIST features are evaluated at the current window position for pedestrian detection. The detection window size is 108×36. The window is split into 9×4 cells, so each cell contains $12 \times 9 = 108$ pixels. Any adjacent 2×2 cells can be combined into a block, so the number of blocks in a window is $8 \times 3 = 24$. As the feature vector for each block has 256 dimensions, a window has a feature vector with a size of $256 \times 24 = 6144$ dimensions. Then this feature vector is fed into a two stage cascaded classifier to decide whether current window contains any pedestrian. The linear classifier guarantees fast testing speed, and HIK SVM classifier achieves high detection accuracy [11, 12].

3 Parallel C4 Algorithm

Only a small portion of our parallel implementation is performed on the host processor. The image and cascade classifier are loaded from the host. Final results, i.e., window locations on all image scales containing a pedestrian, are returned to the host for non-maximal suppression (NMS). While all the other computations are performed on the GPU.

3.1 Calculating CENTRIST Features

As a pedestrian in the image may be bigger than the window size, the pedestrian can be detected after the image is shrunk until the pedestrian can fit into the window. In our implementation, the image is shrunk seven times, and a pyramid with seven levels is created, which is stored in the global memory. At each level, CENTRIST features are calculated at every sliding detection window location.

Sobel is an edge detection operator, which can be created after two successive 3×3 convolutions are applied on the gray level image. An example code named Sobel Filter from the NVIDIA CUDA SDK is utilized. On the Sobel gradient image, CT transform is conducted except those boundary pixels, as no padding is applied. Signs of comparisons between neighbor pixels are encoded. All above computation take the same execution configuration: the thread block dimensions is set as 16×16, and the thread grid dimensions is set $\frac{h_r}{16} \times \frac{w_r}{16}$ (h_r and w_r mean the height and width of the image at current scale after being shrunk), with each thread computing one pixel. As long as all CENTRIST features are available, they are fed into the linear classifier, where windows which do not contain any pedestrian are dropped.

3.2   Linear Classifier Evaluation

In traditional approach like SVM, to judge whether a window contains a pedestrian, the following formulation is evaluated, where f denotes the feature vector, and ω denotes a linear classifier trained offline. Both of them may be broken into chunks to fit the block size:

$$\omega^T f = \sum_{i=1}^{8} \sum_{j=1}^{3} \omega_{i,j}^T f_{i,j}. \tag{2}$$

If $\omega^T f \geq 0$, then a pedestrian is detected, otherwise not. Unlike single SVM, Wu et al. proposed a two-stage classifier [9], i.e., a linear classifier followed by a HIK SVM classifier. Using the linear classifier, windows which do not contain any pedestrian, i.e. $\omega^T f < 0$, can be excluded quickly. However, any feature vector which can pass the first-stage linear classifier, i.e. $\omega^T f \geq 0$, does not guarantee the existence of any pedestrian in current window. Further evaluation is conducted at the second-stage classifier, i.e., the HIK SVM classifier.

Suppose a cell has a size of $h_s \times w_s$, and a block has a size of $2h_s \times 2w_s$, and (t, l) is the coordinate of the upper left corner of the detection window, $\omega_{i,j}^k$ is the k-th component of $\omega_{i,j}^k$, and $C(x, y)$ means a pixel in CT image, then $\omega^T f$ in Eq. 2 can be converted into the following form:

$$\sum_{i=1}^{8} \sum_{j=1}^{3} \sum_{x=2}^{2h_s-1} \sum_{y=2}^{2w_s-1} \omega_{i,j}^{C(t+(i-1)h_s+x,l+(j-1)w_s+y)} \tag{3}$$

To accelerate the computation of Eq. 3, Wu et al. calculate an auxiliary image A instead.

$$A(x, y) = \sum_{i=1}^{8} \sum_{j=1}^{3} \omega_{i,j}^{C((i-1)h_s+x,(j-1)w_s+y)} \tag{4}$$

Then Eq. 3 can be computed as

$$\omega^T f = \sum_{x=2}^{2h_s-1} \sum_{y=2}^{2w_s-1} A(t+x, l+y) \tag{5}$$

Therefore an integral image can be build to calculate $\omega^T f$ while without explicit acquiring f or ω. A CUDA kernel function is dedicated to compute the auxiliary image A. Again each thread block is set as 16×16 threads, with each thread processing one pixel.

Building an integral image on GPU can be decomposed into three steps, (1) conduct inclusive scan along the horizontal direction (2) transpose the scan results (3) conduct the inclusive scan along the horizontal direction, and then transpose results again. Taking advantage shared memory, both scan and matrix transpose (therefore integral image) can be computed efficiently [14, 15].

When conducting inclusive scan, each row of the image is broken into several segments, with 256 pixels contained in each segment, and with 128 threads in one thread block. The thread grid size is $n \times h$, where n is the number of segments in each row, and h is the height (or width) of the image.

When doing transpose, results are dumped into the global memory, and un-coalesced memory accessing may happen, which may degrade computing efficiency. Special attentions have to be paid to avoid this. Again shared memory is utilized. By dedicated organizing, data in non-contiguous locations in shared memory are dumped into contiguous locations in the global memory. In addition, in order to avoid bank conflicts in the shared memory, one column is padded [15].

When the integral image is ready, the score for each detection window (contain 108×36 pixels) can be calculated efficiently. Execution configuration is taken as that described in the Sobel gradient computation section.

If the score of a detection window is than less 0, then this window does not contain any pedestrian; otherwise this window possibly contains a pedestrian, and following HIK SVM classifier is applied to make for sure.

3.3 HIK SVM Classifier Evaluation

Suppose the sliding step size of the detection window is 2 pixels, for a VGA resolution (640×480) image, there are more than ten million windows. Out of these windows, only a small portion of them have non-negative scores. Using an approach known as stream reduction [16], these windows can be picked out quickly, while other windows will be dropped off.

In the HOG-based detection algorithm by Prisacariu and Reid [6], the sliding step size of detection window is exactly equal to the width or height of cell (four pixels), so histogram over each cell can be calculated once, and can be reused by each related block. In contrast, in our implementation of CENTRIST-based detection algorithm, the sliding step size of the detection window is usually smaller than the width or height of a cell, e.g., 2 pixels. Therefore histogram over a cell or block cannot be reused again when the detection window moves to the next position.

A kernel is designed for computing block histograms for those windows, which can pass the first-stage linear classifier. In terms of CUDA execution configuration, the gird size is equal to the number of blocks in all detection windows, with each thread block containing Nwarp number of warps in charge of computing the histogram of a block in the detection window. Following sample code from NVIDIA CUDA SDK, histogram calculation kernel function is designed. After trying different values, in each thread block, shared memory with a size of $256 \times 2 \times 4$ bytes is allocated. Two sub-histograms are produced in a block. The sub-histogram arrays are then combined to form the histogram over a block.

Two kernels are constructed to compute the score of the detection window. The first kernel is used to compute the score of each block in the detection window, with each thread block computing the score of a block. Using this histogram value as an index, corresponding score can be looked up from HIK SVM classifier which stays in the texture memory. Summarizing scores corresponding to those pixels which have valid census transform, the score corresponding to the block can be gotten, where parallel reduction is conducted. To maximize efficiency, shared memory is utilized, where branch divergence and bank conflict are avoided [18]. The second kernel function is in charge of computing the final score of the window. As each window contains 24 blocks, the final score can be gotten by summarizing scores of these 24 blocks. If the final score of any window is greater than 0, i.e., this window does contain a pedestrian, the coordinates of the window is stored in the global memory. As coordinates of these windows in global memory are not close each other, stream reduction is conducted again, coordinates of windows containing any pedestrian are compacted together in the global memory, and then transferred back to host PC. At the host PC, non-maximal suppression is conducted, because the same pedestrian may be detected multiple times in separated but closely nearby windows at different image scale.

4 Experiment Results

To verify the efficiency of our design, experiments are conducted using INRIA dataset [2] and BAHNHOF video sequence [19]. INRIA data set is composed of the training set and test set. Our implementation is run on a notebook machine with Intel Core i5-4200H CPU and NVIDIA GeForce GTX 950 M GPU. As our implementation exactly repeats Wu's code in terms of calculating accuracy, therefore we take over all Wu's analysis about detection accuracy of C4 algorithm, while emphasizing speed comparison. Currently C4's accuracy is slightly lower than some methods,while comparable or higher than many other methods [9].

For the purpose of comparison, the original serial version C4 code is run on the same platform. Speed comparisons over different image size are summarized in Table 1. Further tests are conducted using the BAHNHOF video sequence. The algorithm by Benenson et al. is the fastest algorithm before ours [8], so it is used as a benchmark for comparison. Benenson uses a combination of variety of techniques. One of the key features of his algorithm is the Very Fast detector. N/κ classifiers trained offline can be transferred into N classifiers by dedicated approximation technique, while image resizing computation is saved. In our implementation, images are rescaled 7 levels with a ratio of 1.25 on 640×480 image.

Table 1. Example running times for three image sizes

Implementation	320 × 240	640 × 480	1280 × 960
C4 on CPU	31.6 ms	133.4 ms	642.4 ms
C4 on GPU	2.3 ms	8.4 ms	39.0 ms

In addition, Benenson's algorithm uses scene geometry information like ground plane [20] and stixel world model (stixel ≈ sticks above the ground in the image) [21] as prior knowledge for object detection. By assuming pedestrian always stands on the ground, window searching area is largely reduced [20, 22].

Benenson's algorithm is re-run on our machine platform, and results are summarized in Table 2. Without using any prior knowledge, our implementation search pedestrians with brute force, and can reach a speed of 108 fps. Furthermore our implementation is 17 times faster than original CENTRIST implementation.

Table 2. Processing speed for BAHNHOF sequence

Implementation	Speed
ChnFtrs (baseline)	20 fps
VeryFast + ground plane	38 fps
VeryFast + stixels	98 fps
CPU C4	6 fps
Our GPU C4	108 fps

5 Conclusions

A parallel implementation of pedestrian detection algorithm is presented, which is based on census transform histogram algorithm. Our implementation achieves 17 times speedup over the original C4 implementation, i.e., 108 fps speed on 640 × 480 images. To our knowledge, our implementation outperforms Benenson's implementation in speed, therefore is the most efficient one by far. Further improvement and rigorous test of our C4 implementation are undergoing.

References

1. Gerónimo, D., López, A.M., Sappa, A.D., Graf, T.: Survey of pedestrian detection for advanced driver assistance systems. IEEE Trans. Pattern Anal. Mach. Intell. **32**(7), 1239–1258 (2010)
2. Dalal, N., Triggs, B.: Histograms of oriented gradients for human detection. In: Proceedings of the Conference on Computer Vision and Pattern Recognition, CVPR 2005, San Diego, CA, vol. 1, pp. 886–893, June 2005
3. Wang, X., Han, T.X., Yan, S.: An HOG-LBP human detector with partial occlusion handling. In: Proceedings of the International Conference on Computer Vision, ICCV 2009, Kyoto, Japan, pp. 32–39 (2009)
4. Dollár, P., Tu, Z., Perona, P., Belongie, S.: Integral channel features. In: Proceedings of the British Machine Vision Conference, BMVC 2009, London, United Kingdom, pp. 1–11 (2009)

5. Wojek, C., Dorko, G., Schulz, A., Schiele, B.: Sliding-windows for rapid object class localization: a parallel technique. In: Proceedings of 30st Annual Symposium of the Deutsche Arbeitsgemeinschaft fur Mustererkennung, DAGM 2008, Munich, Germany, pp. 71–81 (2008)
6. Prisacariu, V., Reid, I.: Fast HOG- a real-time GPU implementation of HOG. Technical report 2310/09, Department of Engineering Science, Oxford University (2009)
7. Lillywhite, K., Dah-Jye, L., Dong, Z.: Real-time human detection using histograms of oriented gradients on a GPU. In: Proceedings of the Workshop on Applications of Computer Vision, WACV 2009, Snowbird, Utah, pp. 1–6, December 2009
8. Benenson, R., Mathias, M., Timofte, R., Van Gool, L.: Pedestrian detection at 100 frames per second. In: Proceedings of the Conference on Computer Vision and Pattern Recognition, CVPR 2012, Rhode Island, USA, pp. 2903–2910 (2012)
9. Wu, J., Geyer, C., Rehg, J.M.: Real-time human detection using contour cues. In: Proceedings of the International Conference on Robotics and Automation, ICRA 2011, Shanghai, China, pp. 860–867 (2011)
10. Wu, J., Rehg, J.M.: CENTRIST: a visual descriptor for scene categorization. IEEE Trans. Pattern Anal. Mach. Intell. 33(8), 1489–1501 (2011)
11. Wu, J., Rehg, J.M.: Beyond the Euclidean distance: creating effective visual codebooks using the histogram intersection kernel. In: Proceedings of the IEEE International Conference on Computer Vision, ICCV 2009, Kyoto, Japan, pp. 630–637 (2009). doi:10. 1109/ICCV.2009.5459178
12. Maji, S., Berg, A.: Max-margin additive classifiers for detection. In: Proceedings of the IEEE International Conference on Computer Vision, ICCV 2009, Kyoto, Japan, pp. 40–47 (2009). doi:10.1109/ICCV.2009.5459203
13. Bilgic, B., Horn, B.K.P., Masaki, I.: Efficient integral image computation on the GPU. In: Proceedings of the 2010 IEEE Intelligent Vehicles Symposium, IV 2010, La Jolla, CA, USA, pp. 528–533 (2010). doi:10.1109/IVS.2010.5548142
14. Harris, M., Sengupta, S., Owens, J.D.: Parallel prefix sum (scan) with CUDA. GPU Gems 3 (39), 851–876 (2007)
15. Ruetsch, G., Micikevicius, P.: Optimizing matrix transpose in CUDA. NVIDIA GPU Computing SDK (2009)
16. Horn, D.: Stream reduction operations for GPGPU applications. GPU Gems 2(36), 573–589 (2005)
17. Billeter, M., Olsson, O., Assarsson, U.: Efficient stream compaction on wide SIMD many-core architectures. In: High Performance Graphics, pp. 159–166 (2009)
18. Harris, M.: Optimizing parallel reduction in CUDA (2010). http://developer.download. nvidia.com/compute/cuda/sdk/website/projects/reduction/doc/reduction.pdf
19. Ess, A., Leibe, B., Schindler, K., Gool, L.V.: Robust multiperson tracking from a mobile platform. IEEE Trans. Pattern Anal. Mach. Intell. 31(10), 1831–1846 (2009)
20. Sudowe, P., Leibe, B.: Efficient use of geometric constraints for sliding-window object detection in video. In: Proceedings of the 8th International Conference on Computer Vision Systems, ICVS 2011, Sophia Antipolis, France, pp. 11–20 (2011). doi:10.1007/978-3-642-23968-7_2
21. Badino, H., Franke, U., Pfeiffer, D.: The stixel world - a compact medium level representation of the 3D-world. In: Proceedings of the 31st Annual Symposium of the Deutsche Arbeitsgemeinschaft fur Mustererkennung, DAGM 2009, Jena, Germany, pp. 51–60 (2009). doi:10.1007/978-3-642-03798-6_6
22. Benenson, R., Timofte, R., Gool, L.V.: Stixels estimation without depth map computation. In: Proceedings of the 2011 IEEE International Conference on Computer Vision, ICCV 2011, Barcelona, Spain, pp. 2010–2017 (2011). doi:10.1109/ICCVW.2011.6130495

Fire and Smoke Dynamic Textures Characterization by Applying Periodicity Index Based on Motion Features

Kanoksak Wattanachote[✉], Zehang Lin, Mingchao Jiang, Liuwu Li,
Gongliang Wang, and Wenyin Liu

School of Computer Science and Technology, Guangdong University of
Technology, Guangzhou, Guangdong, China
kanoksak.wattanachote@gmail.com, gdutlin@outlook.com,
13246876815@163.com, itrues@163.com, wglcoco@gmail.com,
liuwy@gdut.edu.cn

Abstract. Dynamic texture has been described as images sequence that demonstrates continuous movement of pixels intensity change patterns in time. We consider the motion features of smoke and fire dynamic textures, which are important for fire calamity surveillance system to analyze the fire situation. We propose a method to understand the motion of intensity change. The objective is not only for classification purpose but also to characterize the motion pattern of fire and smoke dynamic texture. The radius of vector usually describes how fast the intensity change. The motion coherence index has been developed to assess the motion coherency between observed vector and its neighborhoods. We implement strategic motion coherence analysis to determine the motion coherence index of motion vector field in each video frame. In practical, both covariance stationarity of average radius and motion coherence index are efficiently used to investigate fire and smoke characteristics by applying periodicity index for analysis.

Keywords: Periodicity index · Dynamic texture · Motion coherence index · Singular value ratio · Covariance stationary series

1 Introduction

Over the last decade, dynamic texture has ever been described as images sequence that continuously demonstrates movement of pixels intensity change patterns in time. Dynamic textures such fire and smoke have been emphasized for several study purposes, for instance, dynamic texture synthesis, video motion inpainting, and dynamic texture transformation, especially for visual artifact in video editing [1–3]. However, the periodic pattern of dynamic motion has seldom been studied for visual artifact purposes. Besides, characterization on fire and smoke dynamic texture for fire calamity surveillance system becomes important cognition to analyze the situation of fire. We propose a new cognition model aimed to fulfill the dynamic texture synthesis purpose and useful for fire situation awareness. The periodicity of motion in time-varying becomes an attribute of dynamic texture in video [4, 5]. For a sequence of images with

© Springer International Publishing AG 2017
M. Liu et al. (Eds.): ICVS 2017, LNCS 10528, pp. 507–517, 2017.
DOI: 10.1007/978-3-319-68345-4_45

time-varying, the images in sequence are independent realizations from a stationary distribution, [6]. Doretto et al. [6] used a temporal coherence intrinsic in the process that has been captured as a graylevel sequence for dynamic texture synthesis. Doretto et al. [6] applied the noisy version for video synthesis, by adapting Singular Value Decomposition (SVD) based algorithm and using optical flow to periodic estimation for dynamic texture recognition purpose. With an aim to address the challenge in measuring temporal periodicity of dynamic texture, Dmitry and Sandor [4] used warping error as an indicator of a dynamic texture, with its frequent discontinuities and occlusions. The idea shows that the appearance component was less important and possible to be added for further need. However, the warping error technique [4] was aimed solely at classification purpose. Our proposed method intentionally ignores appearance components, such as color and shape, in order to understand the information of motion that can also be implemented for dynamic texture analysis as well. Moreover, we propose a method to understand the motion of intensity change. The objective is not only for classification purpose but also for characterizing the behavior of dynamic texture. For instance, the motion of vector presented by optical flow can lead us to aware the happening situation of fire and smoke. We propose simply periodicity gained from optical flow vectors to analyze the latent information of dynamic textures. We extract the ordinary features of motion vector, for instance, the motion direction, the series of average radius, motion coherence index series, covariance stationary series, and the periodicity for analysis. The radius of vector usually describes how fast the intensity change. The motion coherence index has been developed to assess motion coherency between observed vector and its neighborhoods. Number of vector is observed to estimate the magnitude of vector field. We hence study the series of vector attributes, aimed to find a theoretical description of dynamic texture analysis. The periodical motion pattern analysis is observed through the motion vector fields on Texture of Interest (TOI) [3].

Dynamic textures in moving scenes, usually exhibit certain stationarity properties in time [1, 7]. The motion series has been proposed as an important metrics that was commonly aimed to evaluate statistical dependence between non-stationary series in several disciplines [8–10]. Generally, time-varying covariance is conventionally estimated from short-time data segments within a range having a certain bandwidth [10, 11]. Saisan et al. [12] have presented the stationary processes as an output of a stochastic dynamical model. However, their study could not define the description of the stationarity property of dynamic textures. Our investigation proposes a different discipline by implementing covariance stationary series model to present the stationarity of dynamic texture. We conduct an experiment to observe the dynamic textures by selecting the video scenes that demonstrate the continuity of motion to analyze the motion pattern on TOIs. However, it is not easy to discover an appropriate bandwidth to estimate the covariance with different degrees of non-stationarity. Therefore, we develop a prototype system that allows user to adjust different ranges of observed bandwidth for experiment. The system allows user to determine the radius threshold (T_r), and surface block (SB) size that impacts to the amount of vectors. User can also define the range of video to choose the interested motion scene. Our investigation shows that there exists significant difference among motion characteristics of fire and smoke observed by the series of motion features and periodicity index. This article introduces to motion series analysis model, which is effectively utilized to characterize fire and smoke. We expected that our proposed concept can also be leveraged to develop and optimize existing calamity surveillance video systems and technologies [13, 14], since the dynamic texture analysis is definitely involved.

In this article, all related works are educated in Sect. 2. Strategic motion coherence index and analysis are introduced in Sect. 3. Singular value decomposition and singular value ratio are devoted in Sect. 4. We then investigate stationarity analysis and periodicity index, and demonstrate the experimental results in Sect. 5. Conclusions are summarized in Sect. 6.

2 Related Works

2.1 Motion Estimation

In this article, we implement Farneback method. Farneback [15, 16], proposed an algorithm to estimate dense optical flow based on modeling the neighbors of observed pixel by quadratic polynomial basis, for example, $(1, x^2, y^2, x, y, xy)$. Farneback represents motion estimation in the neighborhood of each pixel or SB of pixels by a 3D surface. Here, the 3D surface represents the motion of SB in time. The idea is to determine the optical flow by finding where the SB was moving on the next frame. The optimization is to show that it is not done on a pixel-level, but rather is done on neighborhood-level. Therefore, the optimum displacement can be found on both the pixels and their neighbors. For example, the quadratic polynomials assigned the local signal model expressed in a local coordinate system [16], as described in (1),

$$f(x) \sim x^T A x + b^T x + e, \tag{1}$$

where A is a symmetric matrix, b is a vector and e is a scalar. The coefficients are estimated from a weighted least-squares fit to the signal values in the neighborhood. The weighting composes of two components namely, the certainty and the applicability. The certainty will be coupled to the signal values in the neighborhood. In our study, the value of certainty outside the TOI will be set as zero. Since the pixels outside TOI will never have been considered, to avoid the impact of coefficient estimation. Besides, the applicability is applied to determine the relative weight of points in the neighborhoods based on their positions. Hence, the high weight will be assigned to the center and decreased radially. Regarding to the weighting and neighborhood relationship, we will evaluate the motion coherence index on observed vector and its three adjacent neighborhoods on East, Southeast, and South connected.

2.2 Covariance Stationary Series

In the theory of stationary time series, if the random variable x is indexed to a series, denoted by t, the observations $\{x_t, t \in T\}$ can be called a time series, where T is a time index set, $T \in \mathbb{Z}$. The traditional stationarity means covariance stationarity [5, 17, 18].

If the covariance function in expectation form denoted as $\gamma(t, t+\tau) = E\{[x_t - \mu(t)][x_{t+\tau} - \mu(t+\tau)]\}$ for series x_t, and $t = 1, 2, \ldots, S$, is an univariate function of time interval τ, it means

$$\gamma(t, t+\tau) = \gamma(\tau). \tag{2}$$

The series x_t is a correlation coefficient stationary series if $y_t = [x_t - \mu(t)]/\sigma(t)$. We usually find a covariance stationary series, when $\mu(x_t) = \mu(t)$ and $\sigma^2(x_t) = \sigma^2(t)$, since $\mu(x_t)$ and $\sigma^2(x_t)$ are the mean and variance functions of data series set y_t respectively, where $\mu(x_t) \to 0$ and $\sigma^2(x_t) \to 1$. We implement this module in our system by passing 30 first frames as a series model for automatically covariance stationary series estimation of the upcoming next 300 consecutive video frames [5].

2.3   Singular Value Decomposition (SVD)

In the past decade, SVD related to a matrix, which had some applications in the field of signal processing. The SVD of $m \times n$ matrix M can be defined as (3) [4, 19]. Assume that the period is N and place the successive n-interval of x_k into the rows of $m \times n$ data matrix, where $m \times n = N$.

$$M_N = \begin{bmatrix} x_1 & x_2 & \cdots & x_n \\ x_{n+1} & x_{n+2} & \cdots & x_{2n} \\ \vdots & \vdots & \vdots & \vdots \\ x_{(m-1)n+1} & x_{(m-1)n+2} & \cdots & x_{mn} \end{bmatrix} \tag{3}$$

Suppose that, m rows with same length of n nodes are cut out consecutively from a series. The SVD of M is defined as

$$M = UDV^T, \tag{4}$$

where U is $m \times m$ matrix and its columns are orthonormal vectors, V is $n \times n$ matrix and its columns are orthonormal vectors and D is $m \times n$ diagonal matrix and its diagonal elements are called "singular values of matrix M". The singular values are usually denoted by $\sigma_1, \sigma_2, \ldots, \sigma_n$ respectively. The columns of U are eigenvectors of MM^T, the columns of V are the eigenvectors of M^TM, and the squares of the diagonal elements of D are the eigenvalues of MM^T and M^TM.

3   Strategic Motion Coherence

We apply an efficient coherence metric proposed in [3], to find the average motion coherence index c in a video frame. The geometry for angular distance metric is in the Cartesian coordinate system. An axis coincides with a rotation and an angle is measured in radians. The radian in this article is measured by using z-axis as the rotation axis. We demonstrate the angle length on system user-interface in degrees to present the proper results for human perception. Theoretically, the degrees are in range between $0°$ and $360°$ used to represent the radians in range between 0 and 2π. In this manner, the beginning point is at $(x, 0)$. The radians are drawn in the clockwise direction, and represented by θ. Our proposed method shows that the motion coherence index is proper used to evaluate the coherency of two vectors, and resulted in a decimal range [0, 1]. Our technique demonstrates that the coherence index of motion radians 0 and 2π is 1, whereas that of 0 and π is incoherent motion, which is close to human perception.

3.1 TOI Segmentation

In temporal analysis, we implement 3D surface blocks derived from Farneback motion estimation method to do automatic segmentation. Our prototype system initially starts to choose only the 3D surface block whose vector radius (r) length is greater than a given threshold (T_r), as demonstrated in (5).

$$SB = \begin{cases} 1, & r > T_r \\ 0, & otherwise \end{cases} \tag{5}$$

Suppose, SB represents a 3D surface block and r represents the radius of vector of that block. Here, SB will be examined by a given radius threshold, T_r. If r is less than T_r, the system will not consider that SB for the next calculation steps. The examples of motion vector field after thresholding are demonstrated in Fig. 1(a) and (b). However, this segmentation technique is proper only for the stationary video scene, where the background of the video scene is static with less annoying signal [3, 5].

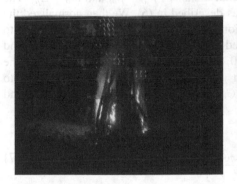 

(a) Fire situation with large smoke region, the *PI* of Cov. of $r = 0.5758$ and the *PI* of Cov. of $c = 0.4846$.

(b) Fire situation with less smoke, the *PI* of Cov. of $r = 0.2610$ and the *PI* of Cov. of $c = 0.2242$.

Fig. 1. Demonstration of the smoke and fire situations in a video scene, shows that the motion features could impact the periodicity index.

3.2   Motion Coherence Index

The strategic motion coherence index is applied to evaluate the motion coherence index of every four adjacent vectors. The average index will be assigned as an attribute of an observed vector located on the top-left corner among those four vectors. We iterate this operation on every four adjacent vectors in scan line approach from top to bottom until end of TOI. This process will estimate the motion coherence index as an attribute for each observed vector on TOI. An example of finding the aforesaid attribute will be described in this section.

Suppose $\theta_{(x,y)}$ denotes the radian of observed vector on xy-coordinate. There are three adjacent vectors on East, Southeast, and South of the observed vector, where the radians are denoted by $\theta_{(x+1,y)}$, $\theta_{(x+1,y+1)}$, and $\theta_{(x,y+1)}$ respectively. Here, $x = 0$ and $y = 0$ represent the coordinate of the most top-left observed vector on TOI. We then calculate the average radian of any couples among four of vectors based on the observed vector, θ_o. Hence, we have got three mean values denoted by μ_1, μ_2, and μ_3 as the average radians between the radian $\theta_{(x,y)}$ of observed vector and the radians of its neighbors, $\theta_{(x+1,y)}$, $\theta_{(x+1,y+1)}$, $\theta_{(x,y+1)}$ respectively. They are calculated by using a simple arithmetic of mean calculation approach, for example, $\mu_p = (\theta_o + \theta_p)/2$, where $p = 1, 2, 3$, $\{\theta_p | \theta_1 = \theta_{(x+1,y)}, \theta_2 = \theta_{(x+1,y+1)}, \theta_3 = \theta_{(x,y+1)}\}$, and $\theta_o = \theta_{(x,y)}$.

$$C_p = \left| 100.0 - 2 \left(\frac{100.0 \times \text{argmin}\left(|\theta_o - \mu_p|, |\theta_o - \Delta_p|\right)}{\pi} \right) \right| \tag{6}$$

We then find the difference between each μ_p and π, which is denoted by Δ_p, where $\Delta_p = \pi - \mu_p$. After that, we find the Euclidian distances $|\theta_o - \mu_p|$ and $|\theta_o - \Delta_p|$. The minimal distance is chosen for calculation as described in (6). We then normalized the motion coherence C_p in (6) to gain the motion coherence index (C_{np}), which is close to human eye perception [3, 5], as demonstrated in (7). That means, for instance, if θ_o and θ_1 is coherent, the C_{np} will equal to 100, and if two vectors are incoherent, the coherence index will be 0.00. For system user-interface, we redistributed [0, 1] to percentile unit. Hence, the coherence index C_{np} varies in a floating range between 0 and 100.

$$C_{np} = \begin{cases} 0; \ C_p \le 70 \\ \left[3\left(\frac{C_p - 70}{30}\right)^2 - 2\left(\frac{C_p - 70}{30}\right)^3 \right] \times 100; \ 70 < C_p \le 100 \end{cases} \tag{7}$$

Suppose the motion coherence index calculated between θ_o and any θ_i on TOI is C_{ni}. We then calculate the motion coherence index of motion vector field by (7), (8) and (9), denoted by c,

$$C_{ni} = \frac{\sum_{p=1}^{3} C_{npi}}{3}, \tag{8}$$

$$c = \frac{\sum_{ni=1}^{k} C_{ni}}{k}, \tag{9}$$

where, $ni = 1, 2, \ldots, k$, and k represents the total amount of vector in TOI.

4 Singular Value Ratio and Periodicity Index

In our experiment, we implement the SVD technique [4, 19, 20], to evaluate four features series namely, average radius, motion coherence index, and their covariance stationary series as described in Subsect. 2.2 [5, 17, 18]. We designed the experiment to test on 300 consecutive video frames. Suppose the video frame rate is approximate 30 fps. Therefore the elapsed time used for each time investigation is around 10 s. Suppose the series of average radius is denoted by r_i, and the coherence index period is denoted by c_i, where $i = 1, 2, \ldots, 300$. The data matrix of the average radius is demonstrated by matrix $R_{10 \times 30}$. The data matrix of the motion coherence index is demonstrated by matrix $C_{10 \times 30}$. For example, the matrix $C_{10 \times 30}$ is illustrated in (10).

$$C_{10 \times 30} = \begin{bmatrix} c_1 & c_2 & \cdots & c_{30} \\ c_{31} & c_{32} & \cdots & c_{60} \\ \vdots & \vdots & \vdots & \vdots \\ c_{271} & c_{272} & \cdots & c_{300} \end{bmatrix} \tag{10}$$

Kahjilal and Palit [20] defined a spectrum to search the period of a periodic series, named Singular Value Ratio (SVR) spectrum. The SVR spectrum has been defined as a spectrum of singular value ratio σ_1/σ_2 values against the different positive integer of n. The periodicity index (PI) is normalized to be in floating range [0, 1], calculated by $(\sigma_1 - \sigma_2)/\sigma_1$ [4, 20]. We applied SVD to find out the diagonal element of D, for calculating our adapted SVR. The elements consist of $\sigma_1, \sigma_2, \ldots, \sigma_n$. Our proposed periodicity index is calculated by $(\sigma_1 - \sigma_3)/\sigma_1$. Since we found that the σ_1 and σ_2 in the periodicity analysis based on covariance stationary series, are not significantly different for some sample data, as demonstrated in Fig. 2(b-1) and (b-2). The periodicity analysis based on covariance stationary series of average radius calculated by σ_1 (illustrated by magenta line) and σ_2 (illustrated by orange line) are quite not different. We implement the new periodicity index analysis to investigate fire and smoke characterization in our experiment. The results are demonstrated in Sect. 5.

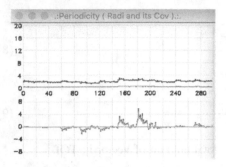

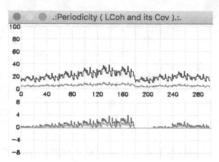

(a-1). The periodicity of covariance of average radius (magenta(σ_1), orange(σ_2)), where the *PI* is 0.5758.

(a-2). The periodicity of covariance series of coherence index (magenta(σ_1), orange(σ_2)), where the *PI* is 0.4846.

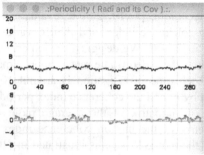

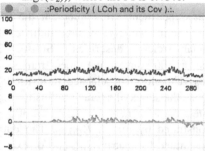

(b-1). The periodicity of covariance of average radius (magenta(σ_1), orange (σ_2)), where the *PI* is 0.2610.

(b-2). The periodicity of covariance series of coherence index (magenta(σ_1), orange (σ_2)), where the *PI* is 0.2242.

Fig. 2. Regarding to Fig. 1, this figure demonstrates the periodicity of covariance stationary series of average radius and motion coherence index of two states of fire. Row (a), (a-1) and (a-2) present the periodicity of fire state, where the smoke region is larger than fire. Row (b), (b-1) and (b-2) present the periodicity of fire state with less smoke region.

5 Experiments

Our prototype system was developed using C++, OpenCV and QT libraries. We experimented on ten samples of fire and eleven samples of smoke dynamic textures from different video sources, including onsite-collecting data, to evaluate the periodicity index, *PI*. The example results of *PI* of fire and smoke are showed in Table 1.

The results in Table 1 demonstrate that periodicity index of the covariance stationary series of smoke and fire based on radius and motion coherence index, are significant difference. Since the *PI* of covariance stationary series of fires based on radius and motion coherence index, are lower than 0.5 (*PI* < 0.5), lower than the *PI* of smokes. Moreover, our experimental results show that in the beginning of fire situation when the smoke region is larger than fire region (Smoke sample 11, Table 1), the periodicity index could be recognized as smoke. For example, the *PI* of covariance stationary series of radius has been equal to 0.5758 (Smoke sample 11, Table 1) in

Table 1. The *PI* of covariance stationary series based on average radius (Cov. of *r*) and motion coherence index (Cov. of *c*) on TOI.

Smokes			Fires		
Sample	PI of Cov. of r	PI of Cov. of c	Sample	PI of Cov. of r	PI of Cov. of c
1	0.7597	0.8846	1	0.4087	0.2533
2	0.7577	0.7983	2	0.1505	0.1328
3	0.9482	0.8235	3	0.3798	0.1845
4	0.8155	0.8079	4	0.1732	0.3605
5	0.9076	0.8730	5	0.3273	0.2914
6	0.8704	0.8706	6	0.1831	0.2206
7	0.8185	0.8928	7	0.1909	0.1538
8	0.9089	0.8887	8	0.2350	0.1977
9	0.9319	0.8407	9	0.3056	0.2113
10	0.6827	0.6962	10*	**0.2610**	**0.2242**
11*	**0.5758**	**0.4846**			

Fig. 1(a), was reduced to be 0.2610 (Fire sample 10, Table 1) in Fig. 1(b). Additionally, the *PI* of covariance stationary series of motion coherence index that has been equal to 0.4846 (Smoke sample 11, Table 1) in Fig. 1(a), was reduced to be 0.2242 (Fire sample 10, Table 1) in Fig. 1(b). The smoke sample 11 and the fire sample 10 were derived from the same video source to observe the fire situation in time varying. These mathematical results are used to explain that the covariance stationary series on fire with large smoke area could be considered as smoke texture.

Aforementioned, to improve fire calamity surveillance system development, we expected that our proposed method can be integrated to computer vision system development. The purpose is aimed to leverage fire situation detection and analysis from begin to end. We are currently emphasized on finding a model, which can describe fire situation from begin to end, by implementing motion features analysis on dynamic textures.

6 Conclusions

We proposed a new technique for fire and smoke characterization. The new periodicity index analysis was proposed to investigate the covariance stationary series based on two motion features namely, average radius and motion coherence index. We introduced a new attribute of motion vector field for analysis. However, there are some limitations need to be improved and some features need to be integrated for further investigation. For example, the total number of vectors occurred on TOI that will be derived from adjusting the radius threshold (T_r) and SB size. Our proposed method emphasized on motion analysis rather than the appearance analysis of components on dynamic textures. We are continuously studying to develop fire calamity surveillance system model to leverage this contribution for our future work. There are some features and configuration need to be integrated and configured for automatically detecting, which expected to be leveraged, for fire calamity surveillance system.

Acknowledgments. This work was partially supported by the Guangdong Innovative Research Team Program (No. 2014ZT05G157).

References

1. Doretto, G.: Dynamic textures: modeling, learning, synthesis, animation, segmentation, and recognition. Thesis, University of California (2005)
2. Tsai, J.C., Shih, T.K., Wattanachote, K., Li, K.C.: Video editing using motion inpainting. In: 26th IEEE International Conference on Advanced Information Networking and Applications, pp. 649–654 (2012)
3. Wattanachote, K., Shih, T.K.: Automatic dynamic texture transformation based on a new motion coherence metric. IEEE Trans. Circuits Syst. Video Technol. **26**(10), 1805–1820 (2016)
4. Dmitry, C., Sandor, F.: On motion periodicity of dynamic textures. In: British Machine Vision Conference, vol. 1, pp. 167–176 (2006)
5. Wattanachote, K., Li, K., Wang, Y., Shih, T.K., Liu, W.Y.: Preliminary investigation on stationarity of dynamic smoke texture and dynamic fire texture based on motion coherent metric. In: International Conference on Machine Vision and Information Technology, pp. 99–104 (2017)
6. Deretto, G., Chiuso, A., Wu, Y.N., Soatto, S.: Dynamic textures. Int. J. Comput. Vis. **51**(2), 91–109 (2003)
7. Soatto, S., Doretto, G., Wu, Y.N.: Dynamic textures. In: IEEE International Conference on Computer Vision, vol. 2, pp. 439–446 (2001)
8. Chan, S.C., Zhang, Z.G.: Local polynomial modeling and variable bandwidth selection for time-varying linear systems. IEEE Trans. Instrum. Measur. **60**(3), 1102–1117 (2011)
9. Zhang, Z.G., Hung, Y.S., Chan, S.C.: Local polynomial modelling of time-varying autoregressive models with application to time-frequency analysis of event-related EEG. IEEE Trans. Biomed. Eng. **58**(3), 557–566 (2011)
10. Chen, C.I., Chen, Y.C.: Comparative study of harmonic and interharmonic estimation methods for stationary and time-varying signals. IEEE Trans. Industr. Electron. **61**(1), 397–404 (2014)
11. Zhang, Z.G., Chan, S.C., Wang, C.: A new regularized adaptive windowed lomb-periodogram for time-frequency analysis of non-stationary signals with impulsive components. IEEE Trans. Instrum. Measur. **61**(8), 2283–2304 (2012)
12. Saisan, P., Doretto, G., Wu, Y., Soatto, S.: Dynamic texture recognition. In: IEEE International Conference on Computer Vision and Pattern Recognition, vol. 2, pp. 58–63 (2001)
13. Chen, T., Kao, C., Chang, S.: An intelligent real-time fire-detection method based on video processing. In: The International Carnahan Conference on Security Technology, pp. 104–111 (2003)
14. Ha, C., Jeon, G., Jeon, J.: Vision-based smoke detection algorithm for early fire recognition in digital video recording system. In: 7th International Conference on Signal Image Technology and Internet-Based Systems, pp. 209–212 (2011)

15. Farneback, G.: Fast and accurate motion estimation using orientation tensors and parametric motion models. In: 15th International Conference on Pattern Recognition, vol. 1, pp. 135–139 (2000)
16. Farnebäck, G.: Two-frame motion estimation based on polynomial expansion. In: Bigun, J., Gustavsson, T. (eds.) SCIA 2003. LNCS, vol. 2749, pp. 363–370. Springer, Heidelberg (2003). doi:10.1007/3-540-45103-X_50
17. Rasmussen, C.E., Williams, C.K.I.: Gaussian Processes for Machine Learning. MIT Press, Cambridge (2006). Chapter 4
18. Franses, P.H.: Time Series Models for Business and Economic Forecasting. Cambridge University Press, Cambridge (1998)
19. Liu, H.X., Li, J., Zhao, Y., Qu, L.S.: Improved singular value decomposition technique for detecting and extracting periodic impulse component in a vibration signal. Chin. J. Mech. Eng. 17(3), 340–345 (2004)
20. Kanjilal, P.P., Palit, S.: The singular value decomposition-applied in modelling and prediction of quasiperiodic processes. IEEE Trans. Sig. Process. 43(6), 1536–1540 (1995)

A Novel Real-Time Gesture Recognition Algorithm for Human-Robot Interaction on the UAV

Bo Chen, Chunsheng Hua[✉], Jianda Han, and Yuqing He

Shenyang Institute of Automation Chinese Academy of Sciences,
Shenyang, China
{chenbo,huachunsheng,jdhan,heyuqing}@sia.cn

Abstract. This paper provides a new real-time gesture recognition technology for Unmanned Aerial Vehicle (UAV) Control. Despite of the tradition robot controlling system that uses the pre-defined program to control the UAV, this system allows the users to on-line design and control the UAV to finish the abrupt urgent task with different gestures. The system is composed of three parts: On-line personal feature training system, Gesture recognition system and UAV motion control system. In the first part, we collect and analyze user gestures, extract features data and train the recognition program in real time. In the second part, a multi-feature hierarchical filtering algorithm is applied to guarantee both the accuracy and real-time processing speed of our gesture recognition method. In the last part, the gesture recognition result is translated to a UAV through a data transmitter based on Mavlink protocol to achieve the human on-line control for the UAV. Through two extensive experiments, the effectiveness and efficiency of our method has been confirmed.

Keywords: Gesture recognition · Multi-feature filtering · On-line training · UAV control

1 Introduction

In recent years, gesture recognition has drawn the attentions from many researchers and been proved to play important role in many field such as gaming console, VR device, computer smart controls, automobile driving and even in human-machine cooperation industry [1, 3, 4]. Following the rapid progress of modern industry, more and more robots are applied to cooperate with human, which leads to the request for smarter robot that can cooperate with people by recognizing and understanding human gesture. Different from the traditional gesture recognition methods that usually request pure-color background and infrared motion capture devices to recognize human gesture, vision-based gesture recognition method could be applied outdoors or in the factory conditions [2, 5].

According to their working mechanism, gesture recognition can be categorized into two kinds of identification methods: model-based or appearance-based recognition. The model-based methods use hand's 3D model whose projection fits the obtained hand images to be recognized. In order to make sure that the best match between 3D model

© Springer International Publishing AG 2017
M. Liu et al. (Eds.): ICVS 2017, LNCS 10528, pp. 518–526, 2017.
DOI: 10.1007/978-3-319-68345-4_46

and 2D image is obtained, optimization methods are generally used, which requires a large amount of computation [6, 7]. On the other hand, appearance-based methods make use of a set of image features that represent the hand or fingers without building a hand model [8, 9]. The appearance-based recognition methods are usually has a higher computational efficiency than the model-based methods, though this depends on how complex the feature matching algorithms are used [10].

However, vision-based gesture recognition still has many problems such as real-time problems, sub-optimal detection success rate and so on. [11] in this paper, we proposed a novel real-time gesture recognition method based on multiple features including the convexity and shape information of a hand. In order to demonstrate the accuracy and real-time of the recognition, we designed an experiment to control the UAV based on our hand gestures recognition system. For such purpose, three steps have been taken. Firstly, we developed a new real-time and hand gesture recognition algorithm based on appearance features. We choose three discriminative gesture features, which are essential to ensure its accuracy. Secondly, before the user's operation for the first time, the gesture feature information will be collected by the user interface as the user's personal recognition features and on-line training this recognition system rely on these features. Thirdly, in order to ensure the stability of the command sending by our recognition system, it will be executed by the UAV only if the two consecutive frames are the same.

1.1 On-line Personal Feature Training System

As shown in Fig. 1, it is difficult for a gesture recognition system to cover all the variation of human hands which could be caused by illumination, age, sex and so on. So we believe that personalized gesture recognition is an important means to ensure human-computer interaction.

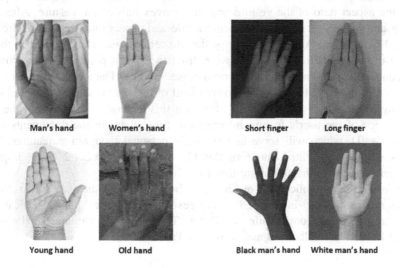

Man's hand   Women's hand   Short finger   Long finger

Young hand   Old hand   Black man's hand   White man's hand

Fig. 1. Huge variations of human hand.

In this experiment, we let the user wear a pair of gloves whose color is different from the background and other people's hand to ensure that the environment won't interfere our recognition. Secondly, the first time before the user do the operation, the gesture feature information will be collected by the user interface, as his personal feature for the recognition process next (Fig. 2).

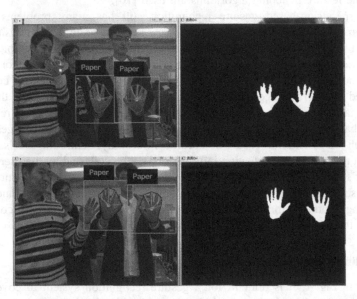

Fig. 2. Complex background and interfere may occurred during the experiment

The hand gestures feature information are separated into three parts: the gesture angle, the aspect ratio of the gesture and the convex hull of the gesture. After color filtering and MeanShift clustering, gesture angle and aspect ratio can be get from the Principal Component Analysis (PCA) of the clustering area. The last part is the calculation of convex hull. In this step, we extract the salient points of the region first. Then connect these points in turn to form a closed outline. The area of gray area is S1, The area of hand is S2 (Fig. 3). The convex hull of the gesture can be obtained by the following formula: $x_1 = S2/(S1 + S2)$. Rely on this method, we can obtain the mean and variance of the user's feature information. Store them in the documents named after user's ID, which will serve as the user's personal recognition features. These features will be substituted into formulas (1) and (2) in Sect. 1.2 as an important parameter of the Identification algorithm to train this system.

For example, we collected five different short videos of the user's five different gestures rely on the user interface. The five gestures are Vertical palm, Vertical knife, Horizontal palm, Horizontal knife and Paper. The mean and variance of these three types of features are calculated and shown in Table 1.

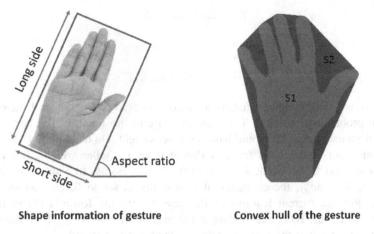

Shape information of gesture   Convex hull of the gesture

Fig. 3. Gesture feature illustration

Table 1. Mean and variance of hand features

Gesture name	Mean of convex hull	Mean of aspect ratio	Mean of gesture angle	Variance of convex hull	Variance of aspect ratio	Variance of gesture angle
Vertical palm	μ_{11}	μ_{12}	μ_{13}	δ_{11}	δ_{12}	δ_{13}
Vertical knife	μ_{21}	μ_{22}	μ_{23}	δ_{21}	δ_{22}	δ_{23}
Horizontal palm	μ_{31}	μ_{32}	μ_{33}	δ_{31}	δ_{32}	δ_{33}
Horizontal knife	μ_{41}	μ_{42}	μ_{43}	δ_{41}	δ_{42}	δ_{43}
Paper	μ_{51}	μ_{52}	μ_{53}	δ_{51}	δ_{52}	δ_{53}

1.2 Gesture Recognition Algorithm

Gesture recognition using a single feature always cause ambiguity. Especially when we want to recognize complex gestures, it is difficult to distinguish different gestures based on a single feature. In order to solve this problem, we design a multi-feature hierarchical filtering algorithm. This algorithm can greatly improve the recognition success rate and robustness while guaranteeing the real-time performance.

The best distinguishing feature should be chosen first. We consider a number of optional features, such as the number of fingers, palm area ratio, etc. But these features have big fluctuations in the actual test. Therefore, we choose the three features mentioned in Sect. 1.1 finally. For example, the convex hull is a feature of high discrimination between different gestures. The convex hull of gesture "paper" is generally between 60%–65%, while the "palm" and "knife" generally between 90%–96%. Based on the same principle, the conclusion can be draw that aspect ratio and angle are good distinguishing features also.

At the time of recognition. The camera collects the gesture image and calculates the three features of each gesture in real time, and brings the features of the current gesture into the following formula:

$$\gamma_n = \gamma_{n1} \times \gamma_{n2} \times \gamma_{n3} \tag{1}$$

$$\gamma_{ni} = \begin{cases} exp^{\frac{-(x_i - \mu_{ni})^2}{(k_n \delta_{ni})^2}} & |x_n - \mu_{ni}| < |N_n + 3\delta_{ni}| \\ 0 & |x_n - \mu_{ni}| \geq |N_n + 3\delta_{ni}| \end{cases} \tag{2}$$

Here we use the Normal Distribution function instead of Euclidean distance as the maximum probability criterion. The features close to the mean of the basis features obtained from user interface should have a greater weight. On the contrary, the features away from mean of the basis features should have a smaller weight. But even so, ambiguity still exists. So we deal with it in "0–1" processing. In addition to the range $(-N_n - 3\delta_n, N_n + 3\delta_n)$, the character of probability is set to 0. So gamma γ_n is 0 inevitable. Put the current features of the gesture into the formula (2) in turn and calculating, select the ID corresponding to the maximum value of γ_n. If all the value of γ_n is 0, it indicates that the current gesture is "unknown gesture".

1.3   UAV Motion Control System

If people want to operate UAV nowadays, they have no choice but using the remote control to control it. But for ordinary users, they needs a lot of practice to be proficient in using the remote control, or they'll have to practice the flight simulator for a long time before controlling the real UAV. But if people can control UAV by gestures, the user's experience will be more intuitive and comfortable.

Because of the high speed and flexibility of UAV flight, the difficulty of using visual recognition technology to control UAV's motion is mainly in two aspects: reliability and real-time.

The algorithm we choose to control the UAV is "H infinite". "H infinite" techniques have the advantage over classical control techniques in that they are readily applicable to problems involving multivariate systems with cross-coupling between channels.

Gesture information is collected by a camera on the ground. After the computer recognized and analyzed the gesture, the command is sent to the UAV through the data transmission device. UAV completes the corresponding action when the flight controller received the correct signals of command. The UAV's flight speed is proportional to the relative distance between the two hands.

2   Experiment

We set up two experiments to evaluate the performance of our algorithm as: (1) the gesture recognition experiment from the static camera; (2) combining the gesture recognition algorithm with UAV controlling system to control the UAV movement by the on-line human gesture comments.

2.1   Experiment of Recognition Rate Testing

Under the same conditions, it is obviously that the distance between the camera and operator will greatly affect the performance of the gesture recognition method. That is because gesture recognition results highly depend on the resolution of a hand in the image, the higher resolution usually leads to better recognition result.

In the first experiment, we collected four groups of samples in which the distance between user and camera are set to be 1 m, 1.5 m, 2 m and 2.5 m (Fig. 4). CPU of the computer we used in this experiment is Intel Core i7-4720HQ, whose frequency is 2.60 GHz. The camera capturing images is Basler acA640 whose resolution rate is 640 × 480. The recall rate and precision of recognition obtained by analyzing the experimental results are shown in Table 2.

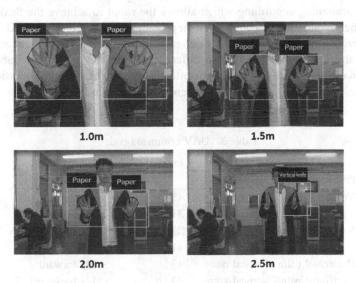

Fig. 4. Recognition rate test at different distances

Table 2. Experimental results of recognition rate

Distance (m)	Number of ground truth gestures (G)	Number of all recognized gestures (R)	Number of correctly recognized gestures (C)	Recall rate of gestures (C/G)	Precision of recognition (C/R)
1 m	1000	958	939	95.8%	98.01%
1.5 m	1000	1000	1000	100%	100%
2.0 m	1000	1000	1000	100%	100%
2.5 m	1000	864	821	86.4%	95.02%

When the distance is less than 1.5 m, hands always occasionally beyond the edge of the vision, which can lead to false recognition result easily. When the distance is more than 2.5 m, it is easy to lead the false recognition and misdetection as the gesture area is too small. Therefore, conclusion can be draw from the experiment result that the optimum operating range is the distance from 1.5 to 2.0 m, in which the precision of recognition reaches 100%.

2.2   Experiment of UAV Control Based on Gesture Recognition

To evaluate the performance of our method in real human-robot cooperation system, we combine our gesture recognition method with the UAV controlling system to control the UAV movement. Compared with the traditional pre-programmed UAV controlling system, such human-robot cooperative system could be considered as the on-line programming controlling which allows the robot to achieve the flexible task.

So in the second experiment, the first step is digital coding the two hands' gestures we recognized. Different combinations correspond to different UAV flight action. The actions of the UAV corresponding to different gestures are shown in Table 3. The control signal is transmitted to the flight control system by the data transmission device in real time. Pictures of the experiment scene are shown in Fig. 5.

Table 3. UAV command code

Gesture combination		Instruction code	UAV action
Left hand	Right hand		
Vertical palm	Horizontal knife	41	Fly towards left
Vertical palm	Horizontal palm	31	Fly towards right
Vertical palm	Vertical knife	21	Fly upward
Vertical palm	Vertical palm	11	Fly down
Horizontal palm	Vertical palm	13	Fly forward
Horizontal palm	Vertical knife	23	Fly backward
Horizontal palm	Horizontal knife	43	Rotate left
Horizontal palm	Horizontal palm	33	Rotate right

The computer and camera we used in this experiment is same to Sect. 2.1. If the system successfully recognized the gesture command, it will send one command to the UAV every 0.2 s. The experiment results show that the average UAV control delay time is within 0.35 s, which represents that this system has high real-time performance. Unstable situation of UAV control has not occurred in the course of the experiment (Table 4). If the UAV has not received the correct control command within 0.2 s, it will be in hover and waiting for the arrival of a new correct command.

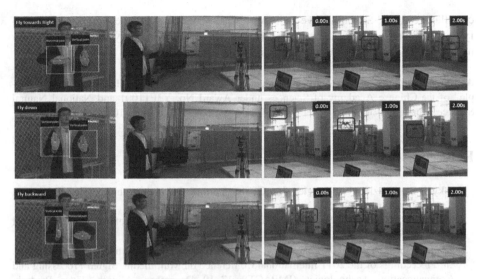

Fig. 5. Actual flight experiment results

Table 4. Response of the UAV

Command corresponding to UAV action	Number of recognized command (G)	Number of UAV's received commands (R)	Precision of UAV's responding action (C/R)	Average delay time (s)
Fly towards left	86	86	100%	0.31
Fly towards right	84	84	100%	0.33
Fly upwards	129	129	100%	0.31
Fly down	135	135	100%	0.35
Fly forward	54	54	100%	0.34
Fly backward	57	57	100%	0.31
Rotate left	178	178	100%	0.32
Rotate right	126	126	100%	0.35

3   Conclusion

In this paper, we build a new on-line programming gesture recognition system and a new application direction. The system is composed of three parts: On-line personal feature training system, Gesture recognition system and UAV motion control system. We proposed a multi-feature hierarchical filtering algorithm to guarantee both the accuracy and real-time processing speed of our gesture recognition method. And we designed a user interface which can extract the user characteristics and train the recognition system on-line in order to improve the accuracy of gesture recognition.

In the future, we need to put more effort into optimize the algorithm first. Find more identifying features to make the recognition system has the ability of recognizing more complex gestures. Secondly, we will improve the system with the function of identifying different dynamic actions. Thirdly, we will improve the system's adaptability under different light conditions as the light has a great impact on color extraction.

Acknowledgements. This work is supported by the Program of "One Hundred Talented People" of the Chinese Academy of Sciences under Award No. Y3F11001 and National Natural Science Foundation of China under Award No. 61573338, No. U1609210.

References

1. Akyol, S., Canzler, U., Bengler, K.: Gesture control for use in automobiles. In: MVA, Tokyo, Japan, pp. 349–352 (2000)
2. Wachs, J.P., Kolsch, M., Stern, H.: Vision-based hand-gesture applications. Commun. ACM **54**, 60–71 (2011)
3. Rautaray, S.S., Agrawal, A.: Interaction with virtual game through hand gesture recognition. In: Proceedings of the 2011 International Conference on Multimedia, Signal Processing and Communication Technologies (IMPACT), 17–19 December, Aligarh, Uttar Pradesh, pp. 244–247 (2011)
4. Walter, R., Bailly, G., Muller, J.: StrikeAPose: revealing mid-air gestures on public displays. In: Proceedings of the SIGCHI Conference on Human Factors in Computing Systems, Paris, France, pp. 841–850 (2013)
5. Hackenberg, G., McCall, R., Broll, W.: Lightweight palm and finger tracking for real-time 3D gesture control. In: Proceedings of the 2011 IEEE Virtual Reality Conference (VR), Singapore, pp. 19–26 (2011)
6. Stenger, B., Mendoncca, P.R., Cipolla, R.: Model-based 3D tracking of an articulated hand. In: Proceedings of the 2001 IEEE Computer Society Conference on Computer Vision and Pattern Recognition, CVPR 2001, Kauai, HI, USA, vol. 2, pp. 310–315 (2001)
7. Rehg, J.M., Kanade, T.: Model-based tracking of self-occluding articulated objects. In: Proceedings of the Fifth International Conference on Computer Vision, Cambridge, MA, USA, pp. 612–617 (1995)
8. Chang, W.Y., Chen, C.S., Hung, Y.P.: Appearance-guided particle filtering for articulated hand tracking. In: Proceedings of the IEEE Computer Society Conference on Computer Vision and Pattern Recognition, San Diego, CA, USA, vol. 1, pp. 235–242 (2005)
9. Wu, Y., Huang, T.S.: View-independent recognition of hand postures. In: Proceedings of the IEEE Conference on Computer Vision and Pattern Recognition, Hilton Head Island, SC, USA, vol. 2, pp. 88–94 (2000)
10. Minnen, D., Zafrulla, Z.: Towards robust cross-user hand tracking and shape recognition. In: Proceedings of the 2011 IEEE International Conference on Computer Vision Workshops (ICCV Workshops), Barcelona, pp. 1235–1241 (2011)
11. Hincapie-Ramos, J.D., Guo, X., Moghadasian, P.: Consumed endurance: a metric to quantify arm fatigue of mid-air interactions. In: Proceedings of the 32nd Annual ACM Conference on Human Factors in Computing Systems, Toronto, ON, Canada, pp. 1063–1072 (2014)

Unsupervised Local Linear Preserving Manifold Reduction with Uncertainty Pretraining for Image Recognition

Qianwen Yang[✉] and Fuchun Sun

State Key Lab of Intelligent Technology and Systems, Department of Computer Science and Technology, Tsinghua National Laboratory for Information Science and Technology, Beijing 10084, China
yangqw11@mails.tsinghua.edu.cn

Abstract. Manifold learning is an efficient dimensionalilty reduction algorithm. But in real applications, difficulty lies in learning the parameters with limited supervised samples. Our proposed algorithm focuses on sparse representation of local linear preserving manifold dimensionality reduction algorithm and can solve the problem of unsupervised clustering. The manifold preserving methods take use of labeled data in manifold reduction except for the final classifier which produces unsupervised manifold reduction algorithm. Another solution for limited data is a novel proposed pretraining using Bayesian nets to construct the initial parameters for manifold learning, which is also robust to data w.r.t. uncertain perturbations. Then we show its validation in experiments and finally apply the algorithm for real world data. The algorithm performs better in noisy input with limited labeled data.

Keywords: Manifold dimensionality reduction · Local linearity preserving · Sparsity coefficient · Bayesian pretraining

1 Introduction

Since the advent of "data explosion", more and more machine learning algorithms now focus on natural data and now called big data and massive data, or real valued data. In image processing, researchers now highly focused on different algorithms and test whether they are applicable for real world image database. Among them, manifold learning is a successful dimensionality reduction and feature extractor in high dimensional data. For example, in object recognition problems, manifold learning tends to be a representation of real valued data, which for large image databases is their extracted feature embedded in a manifold.

Before we focus on the recognition and classification problem in natural images, traditional manifold learning can do dimensionality reduction in unsupervised mapping and their input labels are nonetheless less informative except

© Springer International Publishing AG 2017
M. Liu et al. (Eds.): ICVS 2017, LNCS 10528, pp. 527–539, 2017.
DOI: 10.1007/978-3-319-68345-4_47

for discriminative manifolds. Similar to this problem, we proposed a new pre-training algorithm in which only limited labeled samples are needed, with less training needed. However the above pretraining methods are not always applicable in traditional manifold learning, because the developed mapping is no other than parameters of extracted features in common learning process. Thus we proposed the unsupervised local linear preserving manifold reduction algorithm. In this problem only limited supervised samples should be used. However the problem of learning the parameters with limited samples is still challenging, and our theory is applying graph model and inference from noisy data for manifold pretraining.

This paper is organized as following structure: Sect. 2 provides a brief review on manifold learning algorithms and the recent evolves in manifold data processing; section Sect. 3 proposes the LLP algorithm with its sparsity factor, and also the Bayesian uncertainty pretraining algorithm. Then section Sect. 4, we validate the method via some data examples. And section Sect. 5 we display the experiments on common databases. And lastly section Sect. 6 shows some perspectives on the algorithm and its future usage.

2   A Brief Review on Manifold Learning

In 2000, Tenebaum [1] and Rewis [2] and raised Isomap and LLE for manifold dimensionality reduction. The idea relies on the manifold embedding theory. Then in 2004, Zhang et al. [3] proposed the LTSA (Local Tangent Space Alignment) for tangent space of manifold data. Then manifold learning came to a new era. Researchers proposed LPP [4] and 2D-LPP [5] in order to accelerate the learning process. But for large dimensions, manifold learning is still limited to an off-line difficult problem. In [6] they proposed sparse coding manifold, and also many other researchers proposed many online versions of manifold learning [7]. Online manifold learning provided advantages over off-line learning and can solve the problem of new-coming examples but the problem of speed still exist.

In recent years, people discuss the statistic nature of manifold data. And scientists indicate that manifold can be learned through a construction of a general framework called graph embedding [8], in combination with other techniques e.g. linearization, kernelization and tensorization. This framework offered a unified view for explaining many popular manifold learning algorithms. However, manifold learning comes to another research direction which emphasizes its usage other than learning itself. In 2010, multiple examples of high dimensional data is reduced via manifold learning [9], extending the usage of manifold learning. Lately some deep learning scientists re-discover [10] manifold hypothesis in realistic data, and scientists developed the algorithm in [11,12]. However, these manifold learning algorithms were analytical models, but they still have many disadvantage of deterministic valued model that may be affected greatly with noise and also the input perturbations.

Yet still, a new direction emerged using non-deterministic methods for manifold learning via probabilistic view. Since 2012 [13], deep architecture emerged which claimed to be better representative for manifold. van der Matten and Hinton [14] developed a new parametric version of non-parametric manifold embedding algorithm and then applied it to represent the input. Yu et al. [15] devised a Local Coordinate Coding algorithm that describes a new global linear function to represent the local linearity of a manifold via a Lipshitz-smooth function, and then they applied it on local tangent space [16], then used in multiple layered manifold embedding.

In general, there are two types of research, generalization of embedding theory by using manifold properties and another is combination of the manifold learning with other types of machine learning techniques. Our research is in the light of the second theory and also it embedded with the generalization theory of manifold learning.

3   Our Method and Discussion

3.1   Local Linear Preserving with Sparse Coefficient

In LLE, embedding function:

$$\Psi : Y = mappedX = arg\Phi(Y) \equiv \sum_i |Y_i - \sum_j w_{ij}Y_j|^2 \qquad (1)$$

This is a linear transform of manifold data, and embedding locality property to the mapping space. Now, we represent and extract the mapping from a local preserving theory.

Suppose we have a set of observed input $X_1, X_2, \cdots, X_n$, n samples for which $n \leftarrow N$, where N is sufficient for D-dimensional data input space. As for the ith input X_i, we can devise the local graph from the view of local constraint graph:

$$X_i = \sum w_{ij}X_j \qquad s.t. \; L1(W_t) < C \qquad (2)$$

where w_{ij} is still a local linear coefficient, but the trick is we subscribe W_t to constraint $L1$, where C is a constant value for variable i, which is consistent to i. We call it the sparse coefficient; if chosen as 1, the very sparse state will come to exist in the simple weight problem. Yet still the local constraint is the projected to a manifold $\mathcal{M}$, embedding in the original D-dimensional input with $dim(\mathcal{M}) = d \ll D$, we need to caution that the different valued w_{ij} of each sample they will be a very crucial part for manifold structure.

Then the constraint C is a crucial parameter for sparse representation of each point i.

Given the input samples, our goal is to find a near sample embedding.

$$\phi(X_i) = dist(W_{local}X_{sample}, X_i) = arg\; min \left(\left(\sum_{j\neq i} w_{ij}X_j + L1(W) \right) - X_j \right)$$
$$(3)$$

Transformed to another none-singular problem of finding different solution of $min\ \varepsilon(W_i) = |X_i - \sum w_{ij}X_j + L1(W) - C|^2$, which is easy in local space. But globally, the mapping is then patched with no illustration of their global form.

In this problem, smoothing is easy to be formed, we apply a similarly sum-average pooling according to max-pooling algorithm and the result is easy to be constructed (Fig. 1).

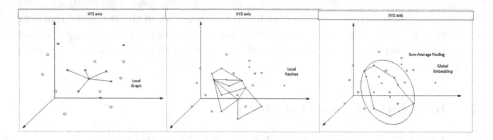

Fig. 1. With local patches P_{local}, we extend the local to global construction of a manifold $\mathcal{M}$, via sum-average pooling algorithm

The last step of the algorithm is mapping X to Y output space, also called embedding.

$$Y = sum - average\ Pooling(X + \phi(X)) \doteq average(mappedX) \qquad (4)$$

Reconstruction error is

$$\Phi(Y) = \sum_i |Y_i - \sum_j w_{ij}Y_j|^2 \qquad (5)$$

To estimate the algorithm value, it came to the calculation error of $\Phi(Y)$. The input X number and sparse factor C are involved. And as the sparse factor also affects the overlapping of local patches, we devise that the over-lapping rate as 0.5, if so, the calculation of manifold graph construction will be doubled to former manifold learning algorithms. This is a precision-speed or sparsity-speed compromise, which we will explore later.

Though in complexity it shows some property of lagging off than other tangent space algorithms, but we will gain a unique global construct from the local patches. We take the construction as the input space R^D, then embedded them in $\mathcal{M}$.

3.2 Pre-training with Uncertainty Inference

Machine learning algorithms, however, have certain characteristics that distinguish from other black-box optimization problems, such as parameters and their model. Manifold learning is also a well-structured learning, and can be refined

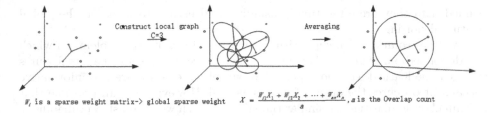

Fig. 2. The local linear preserving construction with sparse parameter

using tuning optimization [17]. In this theory, our proposed manifold algorithm with some input sensitive parameters, can also be fine tuned to become a very successful common image feature extractor (Fig. 2).

Tuning parameters in a probabilistic way is complicated, since many factors may affect the final output of manifold learning machine, such as initial state, noise etc. Nonetheless, we focus on a probabilistic way to the uncertain state of training. Similarly as probabilistic models, we develop the connections between the different parameters and then use a Bayesian nets to model them. And the pretraining processed by adapting the network as pretraining for our proposed manifold algorithm. Then a so-called "shallow" network structure is learned using EM algorithm via Gaussian priors.

In this work, we could not identify the network, due to the certain generative model of Bayesian inference against very limited known factors. We use the EM adaptive method for training each parameter of the networks, both structure and global probability. Then we will propose the network as a tentative pretraining to the above manifold method.

This idea provides more tolerance with noise and small perturbations in input as well as the parameter training process.

Analyze the Theoretical Advantage over the Current Manifold Learning Algorithms. One can consider the input subspace with degeneration g^*, with this transform the observed factors becomes x^* in the subspace, then the traditional problem will be solving the degenerated matrix form of a new problem.

This calls for the same problem of solving general plane form of eigen mapping:

$$min \ \varepsilon^*(W_t) = |X_i^* - \sum w_{ij}X_j|^2, \ transform \ locally \ from \ X \ to \ X^* \qquad (6)$$

Therefore, the problem will render W dispersive since local embedding will not be reliable. The result is solution to embedding map will become degenerated to manifold away from the actual subspace.

One formal idea of solving this problem is denoising, but with an unknown noise, e.g. the motion degeneration of a photo, the idea is useless. Of course one can recover the paper using information context as well, but the usually in real valued data they are often time-consuming and useless to focus on the global feature denoising.

Another solution is to cope with degenerated form of the problem, on which we developed our own idea. For images, each objective category has its features that can be learned with no supervision, yet obscured data are less informative because it obscures the output features as well. However, we can presume that within class similarities are similar though, for which we establish a probabilistic model for parameter setting and the results are used in local linear preserving distance will also presents a close neighbors within one class.

This idea can be tested via random sampling in data as we will latterly show, but in probabilistic theory, the noise(within a certain level) can be removed by steady Markov Chain Monte Carlo, by Markov property (Fig. 3).

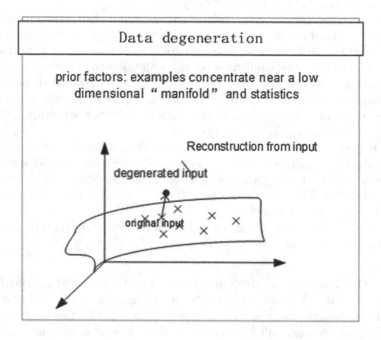

Fig. 3. Data degeneration and the reconstruction of degenerated input

Focus on Pretraining Method and the Bayesian Pretraining Strategy. As a matter of fact, too many training on learning machine will produce over-fit problems, we do pretraining in prevention of over-fitting. Still another reason for pre-training is the training cost. To start the idea of training the Bayesian inference network, we have to use the EM method to reach its maximum belief rates. But it cost too much time in an unsupervised classification. Otherwise, if the data degenerates, e.g. images with too much obscured, uncertainty of too many parameters will lead to recognition failure, then the learning will fail.

Some researchers also point out that the idea of pretraining in networks also helps get better priors, in our problem it helps to prefit parameters in manifold learning. Yet the idea that pretraining advantaged greatly in learning features is proposed by deep learning researchers, while their usage focused on pretraining priors, we do pretrain in the following steps:

a. Identify the input layer and its relation with output params (full-connected);
b. Initialize the parameters and put a learning rate on each weight matrix;
c. Train with initial data params and make possible manifold embedding of input;
d. Test similarity distance and the output labels and modify using backpropagation EM algorithm of the matrix parameter;
e. Check the above precision, end pretraining when meet requirements. Step (d) costs much more time and also produces good results when the pretrained data is enough to represent the distribution.

4   Validation of Locality Sparsity and Pretraining

4.1   Locality Sparsity

We use the random variable of a three dimensional sampler as an input space, and then test the efficient C in sparse constraint. In Fig. 4 (a) is the input space and (b) shows the dimensionality reduction result of sparse constrained LLP, and then the locality graph is devised in $C = 4$, $C = 10$ graph.

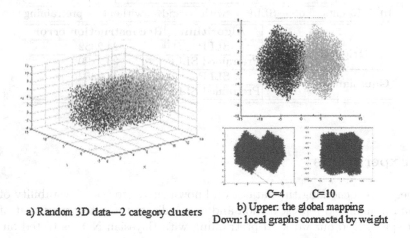

a) Random 3D data—2 category clusters

b) Upper: the global mapping
Down: local graphs connected by weight

Fig. 4. Random 3D-samples and their manifold reduction results. (a) The input data samples; (b) the dimension reduction of SLLP with $C = 4$ and $C = 10$ graph

And also with C grows, the Table 1 shows our best trade-off value of C values and latterly we will fix the value in certain experiments.

Table 1. The C value against final result of manifold dimensionality reduction

C	Local graph	No. of local graph	Overlap count	Total RE
2	2-link maximum	40000	4–10 average	4590.32
7	7-link maximum	7500	5–9 average	4700.43
13	10–13-link maximum	3000	4–7 average	4687.98
24	13–24-link maximum	1200	2–3 average	4932.32

4.2 Pretraining Effect

Pretraining in our experiments aims at eliminate the effect of degenerated input, we devise the last input with several very "diverged" points. The output parameter of C and weight is compared with non-pretraining as standard deviation in Table 2.

Table 2. Result of pretraining steps and maximum belief and paramters

Result of pretraining steps and maximum belief and paramters

a) Training results at and sample results of belief and parameters

	Parameters		Results		
Steps	Learning rate	MaxScore	C	sparse W
100		0.7982	12	$[W_1, \cdots, W_n]$
400	0.03	0.8354	14	$[W_1, \cdots, W_n]$

b) Results of SLLP with and without pretraining

Data	Algorithm	Reconstruction error
Original Data	SLLP	24.2352
	Pretrained SLLP	23.2120
Gaussian noisy Data	SLLP	44.2352
	Pretrained SLLP	27.3712

5 Experiments

We begin with checking the dataset on known curves to test the stability of the method in manifold representation and also indicate the category output of the input space. And our work on pretraining with Bayesian Nets is tested on real data via using pretrained parameters to tune the SLLP algorithm we proposed. In real world applications, we do experiments on the MNIST and also CIFAR-10 dataset to examine its advantage and disadvantage over other manifold learning algorithms.

5.1   SLLP on Simulated Data

In order to test the manifold algorithm, common curves such as swiss roll, twin peaks are usually used to test its visualization effect. In our experiment, the validation of SLLP is shown in Fig. 5.

In the above simulated data experiments, we can see that our method similar as LLE and LPP, which also preserve the local linearity property. But our method

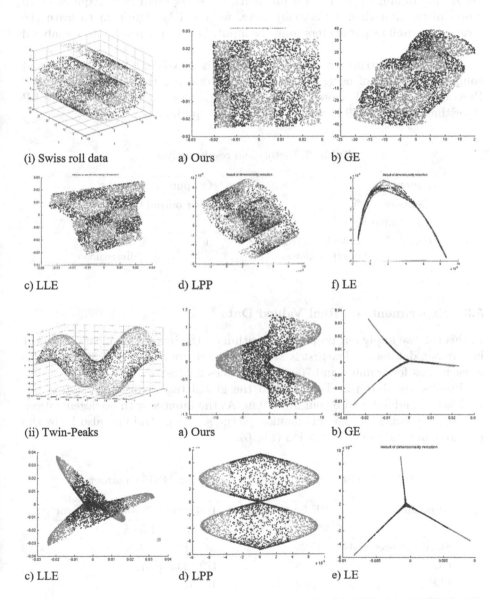

(i) Swiss roll data a) Ours b) GE

c) LLE d) LPP f) LE

(ii) Twin-Peaks a) Ours b) GE

c) LLE d) LPP e) LE

Fig. 5. Results of SLLP (a) GE with Gaussian kernel (b), LLE (c), LPP (d), LE (e) on swissroll (i) and twin-peaks (ii)

show improve in margin area where data density varies greatly than the center area. As for the graph embedding algorithm, it can explore the intrinsic structure via Gaussian kernel, but limited in simple examples.

5.2   SLLP with Pretrainin

We do pretraining on real world problems, since Bayesian Nets requires much more information than we actually have, we use EM algorithm to learn the structure as well as parameters from the input. Our factor-result effect analyzed in Table 3.

The common structure of each local area is 10N-500MP and 100 steps of computing instead of using error rate to approximate the optimal paramters. Pretraining in MNIST show a decrease of 11.7% in error rate w.r.t. the SLLP algorithm which we will show in the following experiments.

Table 3. Factors and result analyze

Factors			Output	
Category	N	$\longrightarrow \searrow$	layer output	
Noisy input	$\widetilde{x}$	$\longrightarrow \searrow$	C	
$\mathbf{f(x)}, \mathbf{f}^{\prime(\mathbf{x})}$	Calculated from interpolation	$\nearrow$	d	Intrinsic dimensions

5.3   Experiments on Real Valued Data

In this part we apply our proposed algorithm on the image classification project in common databases. The first is MNIST dataset, we apply 2000–3000 samples in each class for training and 700–1000 samples for test.

Results are shown in Table 4. And the global test error show best in GE with kernel and followed by our algorithm. As the input is with no degeneration, we carefully conclude that in common pictures, the pretraining also helps the picture refinement in classification (Fig. 6).

Table 4. The result of manifold learning on MNIST dataset

Algorithms	RE for training set	Test error	Classification error
SLLP	367.36	278.9532	1.53%
SLLP (+uncertainty)	345.23	232.1143	1.35%
GE	216.78	472.1233	1.12%
LLE	327.32	375.5748	3.32%
LPP	359.12	451.6237	2.01%

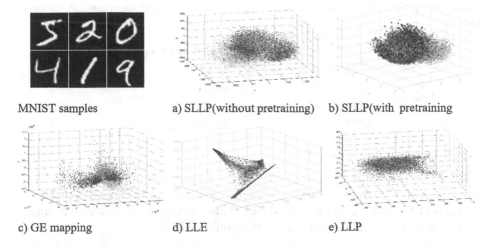

MNIST samples   a) SLLP(without pretraining)   b) SLLP(with pretraining

c) GE mapping   d) LLE   e) LLP

Fig. 6. Manifold reduction of MNIST dataset

Fig. 7. Sample images from ten category of CIFAR-10 database (Color figure online)

Another experiments is tested on CIFAR-10, Fig. 7 show some samples in CIFAR-10 image database. It is a set of natural color images of 32×32 pixels [18] it contains 10 classes, each with 5000 training samples and 1000 test samples. The CIFAR images vary from one class to the other, but some of the object are not centered and also some show only partial object. This is still a challenging

Table 5. Results of classification using representive manifold learning and its error rate

Algorithms	Classification error
SLLP (with pretraining)	27.32%
GE	33.94%
LLE	44.56%
LPP	42.37%

problem in classification. We apply the same procedure to the dataset. Our algorithm showed some improvement in classification esp. for "diverged" samples. In this aspect the training of pretrained SLLP also show a great tolerance in image centering and incomplete object classification (Table 5).

6   Conclusion

In our research, we combine the manifold learning and probabilistic model methods and proposed a novel view on sparse manifold via local generative graph with uncertainty pretraining of parameters. In the problem of automatic image recognition or classification, the algorithm shows better performance on real-valued databases as well as noisy datasets. In our projects, the algorithm still can be generalized to everyday recognition tasks via online training process. Although the algorithm performed better in manifold learning algorithms, it is also disadvantaged in computation complexity and also initialization of the weights in pretraining is still a difficult problem. In sum, we addresses the feasibility and complexity of the algorithm, and also experiments on real-valued database show it is applicable to real world problems. We will also try to improve the method in complexity and precision of pretraining.

References

1. Tenebaum, J.B., Silvam, V.D., Longford, J.C.: A global geometric framework for nonlinear dimensionality reduction. Science **290**, 2319–2323 (2000)
2. Rowels, S.T., Saul, L.K.: Nonlinear dimensionality reduction by locally linear embedding. Science **290**, 2323–2326 (2000)
3. Zhang, Z., Zha, H.: Principal manifolds and nonlinear dimension reduction via local tangent space alignment. SIAM J. Sci. Comput. **26**, 313–338 (2004)
4. He, X., Niyongi, P.: Locality preserving projection. Proc. Neural Inf. Process. Syst. **14**, 153 (2004)
5. Chen, S., Zhao, H., Kong, M., Luo, B.: 2D-LPP: a two-dimensional extension of locality pre-serving projections. Neurocomputing **70**(4–6), 912–921 (2007)
6. Silva, J., Marques, J., Lemos, J.: Selecting landmark points for sparse manifold learning. In: Advances in neural information processing systems, pp. 1241–1248 (2005)

7. Law, M.H.C., Jain, A.K.: Incremental nonlinear dimensionality reduction by man-ifold learning. IEEE Trans. Pattern Anal. Mach. Intell. **28**(3), 377–391 (2006)
8. Yan, S., Xu, D., Zhang, B., et al.: Graph embedding and extensions: a general framework for dimensionality reduction. IEEE Trans. Pattern Anal. Mach. Intell. **29**(1), 40–51 (2007)
9. Zhang, J., Huang, H., Wang, J.: Manifold learning for visualizing and analyzing high-dimensional data. IEEE Intell. Syst. **25**(4), 54–61 (2010)
10. Bengio, Y., Courville, A., Vincent, P.: Representation learning: a review and new perspectives. IEEE Trans. Pattern Anal. Mach. Intell. **35**(8), 1798–1828 (2013)
11. Hinton, G.E., Roweis, S.T.: Stochastic neighbor embedding. In: Advances in Neural Information Processing Systems, vol. 15, pp. 833–840, Cambridge, MA, USA, The MIT Press (2002)
12. Usman, M., Vaillant, G., Atkinson, D., et al.: Compressive manifold learning: esti-mating one-dimensional respiratory motion directly from undersampled k-space data. Megnetic Reson. Med. **72**(4), 1130–1140 (2014)
13. van der Maaten, L., Hinton, G.E.: Visualizing high-dimensional data using t-SNE. J. Mach. Learn. Res. **9**, 2579–2605 (2008)
14. van der Maaten, L.: Learning a parametric embedding by preserving local struc-ture. In: Proceedings of the Conference on Artificial Intelligence and Statistics (2009)
15. Yu, K., Zhang, T., Gong, Y.: Nonlinear learning using local coordinate coding. In: Proceedings of the Neural Information and Processing Systems (2009)
16. Yu, K., Zhang, T.: Improved local coordinate coding using local tangents. In: Pro-ceedings of the International Conference on Machine Learning (2010)
17. Snoek, J., Larochelle, H., Adams, R.P.: Practical Bayesian optimization of machine learning algorithms. In: Proceedings of the Neural Information and Processing Systems (2012)
18. Krizhevsky, A.: Learning multiple layers of features from tiny images. Technical report, University of Toronto (2009)

System Design

Visual Tracking and Servoing System for Experiment of Optogenetic Control of Brain Activity

Qinghai Liao[1]([✉]), Ming Liu[1], Wenchong Zhang[2], and Peng Shi[2]

[1] Hong Kong University of Science and Technology, Hong Kong, China
{qhliao,eelium}@ust.hk
[2] Department of Mechanical and Biomedical Engineering,
City University of Hong Kong, Hong Kong, China
chong1986@hotmail.com,pengshi@cityu.edu.hk
http://ram-lab.com/

Abstract. To study the wireless optogenetic control of neural activity using fully implantable devices, we designed experiments that we make laser emit 980-nm light on the experiment mice brain where the upconversion nanoparticles which works as transducer to convert near-infrared energy to visible lights is implanted, observe the mice activity and record its trajectories. Hence, we propose and implement a automatic visual tracking and servoing system to aid and speed up the experiment. Usually, people drives PTZ for active surveillance tracking which aims to keep the object in the middle of the field of view. In this work, we utilize a PTZ to cast laser beam on the target object as the actuator (PTZ) and the sensor (camera) decoupled that they can be arbitrarily installed. And we also present the automatic parameters calibration method and mathematical modeling for this system to keep high accuracy.

Keywords: Visual tracking · Servoing · Calibration

1 Introduction

Optogenetics is a transformative tool for targeted control of neural circuits by using photo-sensitive proteins, and usually requires delivery of light with tethered fiber optics. In our another experiment, we present an all-optical alternative for wireless optogenetic control of neural activity using fully implantable devices based on upconversion technology which acts as a transducer to convert near-infrared (NIR) energy to visible lights for stimulating neurons expressing channelrhodopsin (ChR) proteins. As shown in Fig. 1, to achieve this target we have to cast the laser beam on the surgical wound where the device is implanted. While in order to observe the mice's reaction we have to allow the mice to freely move and record the mouse activity pattern which makes it impossible to

© Springer International Publishing AG 2017
M. Liu et al. (Eds.): ICVS 2017, LNCS 10528, pp. 543–552, 2017.
DOI: 10.1007/978-3-319-68345-4_48

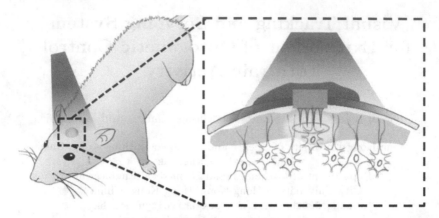

(a) Alternative optogenetic control experiment

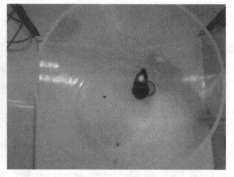

(b) Mouse with device implanted at brain   (c) Experiment with one mouse

Fig. 1. Effect of tracking system. Illuminate the surgical wound of lab rat head by laser beam

manually do the job. Hence, we propose and implement the automatic tracking and servoing system which address both casting laser beam task and position recording task.

Visual tracking and servoing are challenging research topics which involves lots of field such as computer vision, control, automation and pattern recognition and so on. Lots of works have been done on these topics [2,13,14], and also some algorithms and applications have been proposed and presented like [3,20]. Nonetheless, even the state-of-art algorithm can not satisfy the requests of our designed system. Even the learning-based method [7,10] seems be the universal key to most of research fields. Since most approaches focus on the pure tracking, detection or servoing algorithm, our need is the user friendly and accurate system. In this paper, we present one tracking and servoing system which is third-person view instead of traditional camera-in-hand. What's more, we give out the accurate parameter calibration method and full system model to keep the accuracy.

The surveillance task is similar to ours. In order to cover wide area or get large field of view (FOV), it usually use the large FOV lens which introduce the image distortion or utilize the camera with PTZ [11]. Guha et al. [6] proposed a method to keep the target always in the middle of the field of view of the camera through adjusting the camera pose via PTZ. It uses mean-shift algorithm for visual tracking. Jain et al. [9] present a stationary-dynamic (or master-slave) camera assemblies to achieve wide-area surveillance and selective focus-of-attention. Their approach features the technique to calibrates all degrees-of-freedom (DOF) of both stationary and dynamic cameras, using a closed-form solution that is both efficient and accurate. There are many state-of-the-art algorithms or approaches available for surveillance systems indeed, but as mentioned before, our system has negligible difference with them that the sensor and actuator are soft or arbitrarily linked which involves the extra parameters. And due to the mice's intense reaction our system is required to have high precision and dynamic performance.

In this work, based on the design request we integrate the visual tracking, servoing and automatic calibration in the proposed system. The change of structure makes our system different from the camera-PTZ control case which most are self-adjusting and involved extra calibration problem. Our proposed tracking and servoing system successfully solves above difficulties via system structure modeling and automatic calibration approach. Our contributions in this work are listed as follow:

- We propose and implement a automatic tracking and servoing system which has been successfully applied on the real biological experiments.
- We present full parameters mathematical model which is able to give a close-form solution. It greatly reduces the complexity of our tracking system since we don't have to utilize complicated control systems.
- Based on the model we introduce the automatic parameter calibration strategy and it is the foundation of arbitrary deployment.

The rest of the paper is organized as follows. Section 2 gives the overview of the tracking and servoing system. The visual object detection, model and parameter calibration are given in Sects. 3 and 4, respectively. Section 5 contains the experiments. Finally, Sect. 6 summarizes the paper.

2 System Overview

Figure 2 gives the overview of our system deployment. The tracking and servoing system mainly includes the camera, laser collimator with Pan-Tilt, holders, embedded controller board and PC. In Fig. 2, ④ is the IoT control board called ATOM which is small but powerful core, comprised of DUAL high performance processors (STM32 MCU and Linux-in CPU). It works as the lower level controller of the Pan-Tilt and makes it act according to the command from the PC [5,15–19]. The camera and Pan-Tilt are arbitrarily mounted whose only requirement is that their workspace or FOV can cover the target plane ③. Our system features friendly-usage, automatic calibration, low coupling of modules

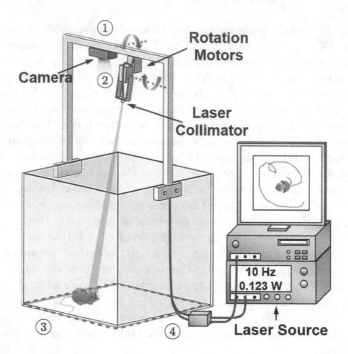

Fig. 2. Framework overview. ① Arbitrarily mounted camera ② Laser with Pan-Tilt ③ Target plane ④ IoT ATOM board

and extensibility. It can be taken as a tracking and servoing framework since its decoupled modules are easily replaced by other algorithms or approaches.

The workflow of our system is shown in Fig. 3 which contains two phases, calibration phase and execution phase. During the calibration phase, the primary work is to calibrate the system parameters: Pan-Tilt offsets. As shown in Fig. 2, it's not practical to directly accurately measure the system parameters. Hence, we propose the automatic calibration procedure to get these parameters by driving the Pan-Tilt to zigzag scan the plane. With the structure model and derived calibration formulas we know the minimum number of sample data is 7. The execution phase is a common detection-servo loop which keeps the laser spot on the brain of mice. We apply the visual methods on the image captured by the camera to locate the mice brain and laser spot and then calculate the commands α, β of the Pan-Tilt with the calibrated parameters. The dashed border block in Fig. 3 represents one optional module that offers feedback to the Pan-Tilt controller. We don't implement this module in our system but it won't be hard to implement and integrate.

3   Visual Detection

Object detection and tracking are very challenging problems that have been drawing lots of interests for couples of yeas. And many powerful algorithms or

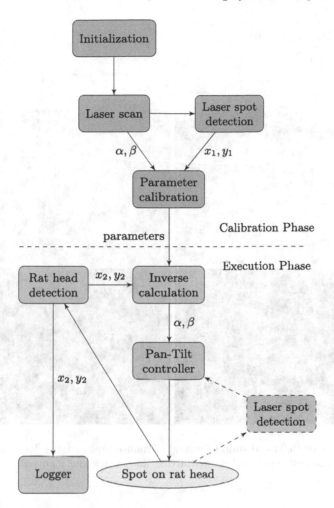

Fig. 3. System work flow. x_1, y_1 are laser spot position, x_2, y_2 are mice brain position. α, β are the pan and tilt angle

approaches such as Kalman filter-based algorithms [4] and CONDENSATION algorithm [8] have been proposed [21,22]. Especially, with the popular of neural network, the new learning-base approaches can handle much more complex environment and give out more accurate output information.

Considering the static and controllable environment of our case, the tracking problem of our system can be simplified and replaced by detection problem. The state-of-art learning-based detection approaches are very sophisticated and able to output accurate position but at the cost of speed which is an old truism. In this work, the laser stimulation will lead to the strenuous activity of mice and, accordingly, we prefer the high processing speed by applying color and geometry based detection methods.

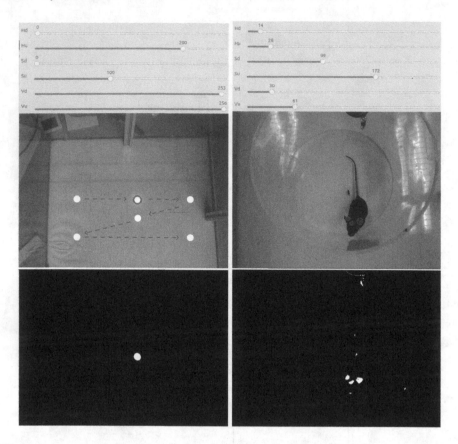

Fig. 4. Laser spot (left) and surgical wound of mouse brain (right) detection. Left: red circle marks the laser spot, red dashed arrow lines mark the scan path (Color figure online)

Visual detection approach serves in both parameter calibration phase and execution phase in this work. For parameter calibration, we detect the laser spot on the target plane and the location serves as the input of calibration algorithm with the control command. And for execution phase, we detect the surgical wound on the brain of the mouse which the is target position laser spot should be. As shown in Fig. 4, the laser spot has pure color, high light intensity and typical blob shape. In consideration of these characteristic of the detection target, we utilize the blob detection under HSV color space to locate the target position. We use the blob detector from OpenCV [1] which provides various and out-of-the-box algorithm implementations. As shown in Fig. 4, we first convert the image to HSV color space and get the threshold which the key parameter for blob detector. We manually set the filter parameters of the detector for different target and take the average of the blobs location as the rat head location for the surgical wound case.

4   Model and Parameter Calibration

The detailed structure of Pan-Tilt is shown in Figs. 5 and 2 shows the big picture of the deployment. We have two servo marked as ① and ② respectively and one laser emitter. First, we define the world frame as $O_0x_0y_0z_0$ which is the initial pose of first servo frame $O_1x_1y_1z_1$ and second servo frame as $O_2x_2y_2z_2$. z_0 and z_1 are the rotation axis of first servo and y_2 are the rotation axis of second servo. y_1 is parallel to y_2 and then we have only two offsets a_1, a_2 along x, z axis. We also assume that z_2 is the laser direction and the laser emitter has two offsets a_3, a_4 along x, y axis with respect to second servo. Let α, β represent the rotation angle of two servos. Finally, we have four parameters a_1, a_2, a_3, a_4.

Fig. 5. Actuator overview. ① First servo ② Second servo ③ Laser emitter ④ Rotation axis of first servo ⑤ Rotation axis of second servo

Let $\boldsymbol{a} = \begin{bmatrix} a_1 \ a_2 \ a_3 \ a_4 \end{bmatrix}^T$. With the help of our previous work [12] it's easy to know the laser direction $\boldsymbol{v}$

$$\boldsymbol{v} = \begin{bmatrix} \cos\alpha\sin\beta \\ \sin\alpha\cos\beta \\ -\sin\alpha \end{bmatrix}$$

and laser emitter position E:

$$E = \begin{bmatrix} a_1 + a_3 \sin\alpha + a_4 \cos\alpha \sin\beta \\ a_3 \cos\alpha + a_4 \sin\alpha \cos\beta \\ a_2 + a_4 \cos\beta \end{bmatrix}$$

$$= \begin{bmatrix} \cos\alpha & 0 & -\sin\alpha & \cos\alpha\sin\beta \\ \sin\alpha & 0 & \cos\alpha & \sin\alpha\sin\beta \\ 0 & 1 & 0 & \cos\beta \end{bmatrix} \begin{bmatrix} a_1 \\ a_2 \\ a_3 \\ a_4 \end{bmatrix}$$

$$= Ca$$

Then any point P_i on the target plane can be present as:

$$P_i = C_i a + r_i v_i = x P_0 P_x + y P_0 P_y + P_0 \tag{1}$$

where P_0, P_x, P_y are three selected base points on the target plane. Let's reorganize the Eq. 1 and get:

$$[x_i(C_1 - C_0) + y_i(C_2 - C_0) - (C_i - C_0)]a$$
$$+(1 - x_i - y_i)r_0 v_0 + x_i r_1 v_1 + y_i r_2 v_2 - r_i v_i = 0 \tag{2}$$

By driving the laser zigzag scan the target plane we can collect enough sample data P_i for calibration. Equation 2 can be represented as the homogeneous system of liner equations in shape of $Bx = 0$ and $x = \begin{bmatrix} a_1 & a_2 & a_3 & a_4 & r_1 & \dots & r_n \end{bmatrix}^T$. With the input $\begin{bmatrix} \alpha_i & \beta_i & x_i & y_i \end{bmatrix}$ $(i >= 7)$ we can solve it by SVD to get the parameters $\begin{bmatrix} a_1 & a_3 & a_4 & r_0 & r_1 & r_2 \end{bmatrix}$ (a_2 cannot be solved but doesn't affect the system).

For the execution phase we need the inverse kinematic to calculate the command $[\alpha, \beta]$ as given the $[x, y]$. With the simple constraint that EP_i should be parallel to the laser direction v we can get:

$$0 = EP_i \times v$$
$$= (EP_0 + P_0 P_i) \times v \tag{3}$$
$$= (C_0 a + r_0 v_0 + x_i P_0 P_2 + y_i P_0 P_3 - C_i a) \times v$$

By solving the Eq. 3 we can get exact solutions $[\alpha_i, \beta_i]$ for a detected point P_i.

5   Experiments

Our proposed system has been successfully applied to our optogenetic control experiments which got expected outcome. The system largely reduces the experiment time, increases the level of automation and shows high performance during the experiments. Figure 6 shows our field test and the laser beam sticks to the surgical wound on the mouse brain. Although laser spot is not perfectly coincident with the camera detected position, the laser spot is a dot with certain size instead of ideal point which compensate the position error. Considering the limited resolution of Pan-Tilt, the system has met our requirement. In the third figure of Fig. 6, we see the mouse stands up which doesn't satisfy our plane object assumption and this is the main point of our future work to extend our system to 3D space.

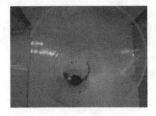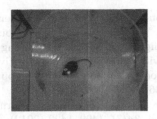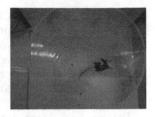

Fig. 6. Field test. Circles are the position detected by camera and purple spot is laser spot (Color figure online)

6   Conclusion

In this paper, we present a visual tracking and servo system which features low coupling, easy deployment and automatic parameter calibration. The proposed system has been successfully applied to our biological experiments and speeded up the process of experiments. With the help of automatic calibration approach, the camera and Pan-Tilt can be arbitrarily set up that traditional approaches don't have this capability. Moreover, as mentioned above our model is based on the 2D plane and objects usually are 3D or move in 3D space (last one in Fig. 6). Hence, Extending the system to 3D space is one of our future work. And we also will integrate better visual tracking and detection methods in the future.

References

1. Bradski, G.: OpenCV. Dr. Dobb's Journal of Software Tools (2000)
2. Collins, R.T., Lipton, A.J., Kanade, T., Fujiyoshi, H., Duggins, D., Tsin, Y., Tolliver, D., Enomoto, N., Hasegawa, O., Burt, P., Wixson, L.: A System for Video Surveillance and Monitoring, vol. 823 (2000). http://ieeexplore.ieee.org/lpdocs/epic03/wrapper.htm?arnumber=868676
3. Cucchiara, R., Prati, A., Vezzani, R.: Advanced video surveillance with pan tilt zoom cameras. In: In: Proceedings of the 6th IEEE International Workshop on Visual Surveillance, pp. 334–352 (2006). https://pdfs.semanticscholar.org/dfdb/9850aed7071c39e15090f7ad4649c60091e2.pdf
4. Ferryman, J., Maybank, S., Worrall, A.: Visual surveillance for moving vehicles. In: Proceedings of 1998 IEEE Workshop on Visual Surveillance, pp. 73–80, January 1998
5. Gianni, M., Papadakis, P., Pirri, F., Liu, M., Pomerleau, F., Colas, F., Zimmermann, K., Svoboda, T., Petricek, T., Kruijff, G.J.M., et al.: A unified framework for planning and execution-monitoring of mobile robots. Autom. Action Plan. Auton. Mob. Robots **11**, 09 (2011)
6. Guha, P., Palai, D., Goswami, D., Mukerjee, A.: DynaTracker: target tracking in active video surveillance systems. In: ICAR 2005 Proceedings of the 12th International Conference on Advanced Robotics 2005, pp. 621–627 (2005). http://ieeexplore.ieee.org/lpdocs/epic03/wrapper.htm?arnumber=1507473
7. He, K., Zhang, X., Ren, S., Sun, J.: Delving deep into rectifiers: surpassing human-level performance on imagenet classification. In: Proceedings of the IEEE International Conference on Computer Vision, pp. 1026–1034 (2015)

8. Isard, M., Blake, A.: Condensation - conditional density propagation for visual tracking. Int. J. Comput. Vis. **29**(1), 5–28 (1998). doi:10.1023/A:1008078328650

9. Jain, A., Kopell, D., Kakligian, K., Wang, Y.F.: Using stationary-dynamic camera assemblies for wide-area video surveillance and selective attention. In: Proceedings of the IEEE Computer Society Conference on Computer Vision Pattern Recognition, vol. 1, 537–544 (2006)

10. Kalal, Z., Mikolajczyk, K., Matas, J.: Tracking-learning-detection. IEEE Trans. Pattern Anal. Mach. Intell. **34**(7), 1409–1422 (2012)

11. Lalonde, M., Foucher, S., Gagnon, L., Pronovost, E., Derenne, M., Janelle, A., West, S.S.: A system to automatically track humans and vehicles with a PTZ camera. In: Proceedings of SPIE, vol. 6575 (2007). http://www.crim.ca/perso/langis.gagnon/articles/6575-1_final.pdf

12. Liao, Q., Zhang, W., Shi, P., Liu, M.: A flexible object tracking system for planary motion. In: IEEE International Conference on Real-Time Computing and Robotics (RCAR), pp. 362–367. IEEE (2016)

13. Pérez, P., Hue, C., Vermaak, J., Gangnet, M.: Color-based probabilistic tracking. In: Heyden, A., Sparr, G., Nielsen, M., Johansen, P. (eds.) ECCV 2002. LNCS, vol. 2350, pp. 661–675. Springer, Heidelberg (2002). doi:10.1007/3-540-47969-4_44

14. Smeulders, A.W., Chu, D.M., Cucchiara, R., Calderara, S., Dehghan, A., Shah, M.: Visual tracking: an experimental survey. IEEE Trans. Pattern Anal. Mach. Intell. **36**(7), 1442–1468 (2014)

15. Sun, Y., Liu, M., Meng, M.Q.H.: WiFi signal strength-based robot indoor localization. In: 2014 IEEE International Conference on Information and Automation (ICIA), pp. 250–256, July 2014

16. Tan, M., Wang, L., Tardioli, D., Liu, M.: A resource allocation strategy in a robotic ad-hoc network. In: 2014 IEEE International Conference on Autonomous Robot Systems and Competitions (ICARSC), pp. 122–127, May 2014

17. Wang, L., Liu, M., Meng, M.Q.H.: Towards cloud robotic system: a case study of online co-localization for fair resource competence. In: 2012 IEEE International Conference on Robotics and Biomimetics (ROBIO), pp. 2132–2137, December 2012

18. Wang, L., Liu, M., Meng, M.Q.H.: Real-time multisensor data retrieval for cloud robotic systems. IEEE Trans. Autom. Sci. Eng. **12**(2), 507–518 (2015)

19. Wang, L., Liu, M., Meng, M.Q.H., Siegwart, R.: Towards real-time multi-sensor information retrieval in cloud robotic system. In: 2012 IEEE Conference on Multisensor Fusion and Integration for Intelligent Systems (MFI), pp. 21–26, September 2012

20. Yang, C.S.: PTZ camera based position tracking in IP-surveillance system. In: 2008 3rd International Conference on Sensing Technology, pp. 142–146 (2008). http://ieeexplore.ieee.org/lpdocs/epic03/wrapper.htm?arnumber=4757089

21. Yilmaz, A., Javed, O., Shah, M.: Object tracking: a survey. ACM Comput. Surv. (CSUR) **38**(4), 13 (2006)

22. Zhao, Y., Shi, H., Chen, X., Li, X., Wang, C.: An overview of object detection and tracking. In: 2015 IEEE International Conference on Information and Automation, pp. 280–286, August 2015

Design and Implementation
of the Three-Dimensional Observation System
for Adult Zebrafish

Teng Li, Xuefeng Wang, Mingzhu Sun$^{(\boxtimes)}$, and Xin Zhao

Institute of Robotics and Automatic Information System (IRAIS)
and the Tianjin Key Laboratory of Intelligent Robotic (tjKLIR),
Nankai University, Tianjin 300071, China
sunmz@nankai.edu.cn

Abstract. In recent years, researchers have paid more attention to the neurobehavioral study of the adult zebrafish. It is very helpful to use a convenient observation system for the zebrafish experiments. However, the existing commercial observation systems are very expensive and the homemade systems are not flexible for different experiments. In this paper, we provide an observation system that has uniform illumination, multi-function, better flexibility and lower cost. Firstly, we designed a lighting system that has the uniform illumination through the optical simulation and polynomial fitting. Secondly, we designed the observation system, which includes tank modules and fixed bracket, so that the system can meet the requirements of many experiments. Finally, we chose white LEDs as light source and the aluminum profiles to implement the system, which make the system cheap and lightweight. In this paper, the observation system we designed achieves good result in the adult zebrafish experiments.

Keywords: Multifunctional observation system · The surface light source · Simulation and polynomial fitting

1 Introduction

Recently, increasing studies have demonstrated the utility of zebrafish in neurobehavioral research, such as drug screening [1, 2], neurotoxicology [3, 4] and so on. Behavioral assays monitoring the zebrafish are widely used for genetic research and drug discovery [5–7]. And adult zebrafish perform complex behaviors (e.g., social [8, 9], learning [10, 11] and affective responses [12–14]), which provide an opportunity for researchers to study further.

In the study of adult zebrafish, an observation system is convenient for researchers. Many types of zebrafish behavior observation systems have been developed. The most famous commercial systems for adult zebrafish include ZebraCube cockpit of ViewPoint company and EthoVision series products of Noldus company [15, 16]. ZebraCube

---

T. Li and X. Wang contributed equally to this work.

provides a controlled experimental environment, e.g., the light, sound and vibration. EthoVision XT system can analyze the data information. But these systems are very expensive. In biological laboratories, many researchers used homemade observation systems [17]. These systems are usually lack of stability and flexibility because they are designed for only one type of experiment.

Now, the technology of using computer vision for single-target tracking is very mature, and multi-target tracking has also made great progress. Most of the researches focused on the data association algorithm. One of the most classic frameworks for multi-target tracking is the multi-level tracking framework proposed by Nevatia et al. [18]. Furthermore, Yu Xiang proposed a multi-target tracking method using markov decision based on this framework [19]. These methods have achieved very good results in tracking multiple targets. But these methods cannot be applied to zebrafish tracking directly because of the randomness and variability of the zebrafish movement. Alfonso Pérez-Escudero et al. proposed a method for detecting zebrafish individuals based on zebrafish back texture features [20]. It points out that the back texture of zebrafish is similar to human fingerprints, so that the back texture can be applied to data association. In order to extract the back texture, it is essential for the observation system to provide the face illumination. However, most of the observation systems use only the backlight source to eliminate the zebrafish shadows.

Actually, zebrafish swim in the three-dimensional (3D) space. The occluded zebrafish in the images, which are captured by the overhead camera, may be not contact with each other in most cases, that is to say, zebrafish may be in the upper and lower positions in the side view. Therefore, a 3D observation system can be used to reduce the image occlusions, so that the tracking performance can be improved.

In this paper, we try to design a multi-functional observation system for adult zebrafish tracking, which has the following functions:

(1) Observing the zebrafish in 3D;
(2) Acquiring the zebrafish back-texture clearly, and ensuring the uniform distribution of the light brightness inside the water tank;
(3) The system is suitable for various experiments (e.g. T-tank experiment, Cross-tank experiment), and we can do multiple groups of experiments at the same time.

In order to meet the above requirements, we first added a camera to the side of the tank in order to observe the zebrafish in 3D. Secondly, we designed the LED lighting system that provides uniform illumination based on modeling and simulation method. Thirdly, the positions of the light sources and cameras can be adjusted as we need, which improve the efficiency and reduce the cost of the experiment.

The paper is organized as follows. The theoretical modeling of the LED surface light sources was analyzed, and a parameter calculation method based on optical simulation was proposed in Sect. 2. Based on the simulation method, the lighting system was designed and simulated in Sect. 3. Then we designed and realized the multi-functional observation system according to the calculation results and the experimental requirements in Sect. 4. The paper is concluded in Sect. 5.

2 Modelling of the Lighting System

2.1 Theoretical Model of Multiple LED Surface Light Sources

Generally, the radiation intensity distribution of a LED lamp is considered to be the distribution of the Lambertian cosine [21–23]. As shown in Fig. 1, the rays that a LED emits in space reach the receiving surface, h is the vertical distance from the receiving surface to the light source. The coordinate origin, x axis and y axis are located in the receiving surface, z axis is perpendicular to the surface. (x_0, y_0, h) is set to the spatial coordinate of the LED lamp, so the irradiance for any point (x, y) in the receiving surface is:

$$E(x,y) = \frac{I_0 \cos \theta h^m}{\left((x - x_0)^2 + (y - y_0)^2 + h^2\right)^{\frac{m+2}{2}}} \tag{1}$$

where I_0 is the intensity of the LED normal, θ is the light emitting angle of the LED, m is the radiation mode of the light source, which is related to θ.

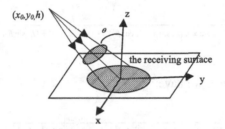

Fig. 1. The irradiance of a LED

For a LED light source array, its irradiance in the receiving surface is the super-position of the irradiance of all LEDs. Therefore, the irradiance of any point (x, y) in the receiving surface can be further deduced from the optical model of two LEDs. For an LED array with N-row and M- column, we set the coordinate origin in the center of the surface light source. Equation (2) shows the irradiance of the LDE array when N and M are odd.

$$E(x,y) = \sum_{i=-\frac{N-1}{2}}^{\frac{N-1}{2}} \sum_{j=-\frac{M-1}{2}}^{\frac{M-1}{2}} \frac{I_{LED}h^m}{\left((x - id \cos \theta)^2 + (y - jd \sin \theta)^2 + h^2\right)^{\frac{m+2}{2}}} \tag{2}$$

when N and M are even, the irradiance E is:

$$E(x,y) = \sum_{i=-\frac{N}{2}}^{\frac{N}{2}} \sum_{j=-\frac{M}{2}}^{\frac{M}{2}} \frac{I_{LED}h^m}{\left((x - (i - \frac{d}{2}) \cos \theta)^2 + (y - (j - \frac{d}{2}) \sin \theta)^2 + h^2\right)^{\frac{m+2}{2}}} \tag{3}$$

where θ is the angle between the light surface and z axis, $I_{LED} = I_0 cos\theta$ is the radiation intensity of the LED.

When considering a lighting system with multiple surface light sources, as shown in Fig. 2, the coordinate origin is located in the center of the receiving surface. The irradiance can be derived from Eqs. (2) and (3).

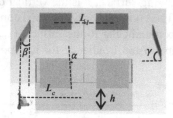

Fig. 2. The distribution of multiple surface light sources

When N and M are odd, we have:

$$E(x,y) = \sum_n \left(\sum_{i=-\frac{N-1}{2}}^{\frac{N-1}{2}} \sum_{j=-\frac{M-1}{2}}^{\frac{M-1}{2}} \frac{I_{LED} h^m}{((x - id \sin\alpha \pm (L_1 \sin\beta + L_c \cos\beta))^2 + (y - jd \sin\beta \pm (L_1 \sin\beta + L_c \cos\beta))^2 + (h - id \sin\gamma)^2)^{\frac{m+2}{2}}} \right) \tag{4}$$

when N and M are even, we have:

$$E(x,y) = \sum_n \left(\sum_{i=-\frac{N}{2}}^{\frac{N}{2}} \sum_{j=-\frac{M}{2}}^{\frac{M}{2}} \frac{I_{LED} h^m}{((x - id \sin\alpha \pm (L_1 \sin\beta + L_c \cos\beta))^2 + (y - jd \sin\beta \pm (L_1 \sin\beta + L_c \cos\beta)))^2 + (h - id \sin\gamma)^2)^{\frac{m+2}{2}}} \right) \tag{5}$$

where α, β, γ are the angles between the light emitting surface and yz, xz, xy surface respectively. L_1 is the distance between two surface light sources, L_c is the horizontal distance between the edge of the surface light source and the center of the receiving surface. n is the number of surface light sources.

2.2   Optimal Parameter Calculation Method Based on Optical Simulation

In order to get the uniform distribution of the irradiance, we defined an evaluation function for the uniformity of the irradiance in the lighting system. We used the variance as the evaluation function, as shown in Eq. (6).

$$\sigma^2 = \iint_\Sigma (E - \bar{E})^2 ds \tag{6}$$

where E is the irradiance of the point in the receiving surface in Eqs. (4) and (5), $\bar{E}$ is the average value of the irradiance, and S represents the area of the receiving surface.

In order to obtain the maximum value of the uniformity in the receiving surface, we need to get the minimum value of σ^2. Theoretically, we should make $\frac{\partial^2 E}{\partial x^2} = 0$. However, Eq. (6) contains multiple unknown parameters, including L_1, L_c, h, α, β, γ. The calculation is very complex and it is difficult to find the right solution in the case of optimal uniformity.

In this paper, we get the polynomial form of the function and calculate the optimal parameters by simulation and fitting. The specific method is listed as follows:

(1) Set L_1, L_c, h, α, β, γ as the parameters. With the increase of the parameter values, we simulate the irradiance in the receiving surface and get the corresponding Es;
(2) Import the relational data of the position parameters and the corresponding irradiance values into MATLAB, Using Eq. (6) to calculate the value of σ^2;
(3) Obtain the relationship between the position parameters and the value of evaluation function by using multiple nonlinear regression method in MATLAB.
(4) Get the optimal parameters of the function under multiple constraints, the bottom of the tank has the maximum uniformity and the side has better brightness.

3 Design and Simulation of the Lighting System

3.1 Design of the LED Surface Light Source

In this paper, we used a small water tank embedded in a big water tank to eliminate the projection of the fish. The size of the big water tank is set to $60\,\text{cm} \times 45\,\text{cm} \times 15\,\text{cm}$, so we can do 2 to 3 groups of the experiments in the tank. Furthermore, the size of the small water tank can be adjusted according to the number of the fish.

In order to adjust the position of the light source easily and improve the flexibility of the system, we set the size of the surface light source to $25\,\text{cm} \times 20\,\text{cm}$. we set $d_{max} = 2\,\text{cm}$ taking into account the utilization of the circuit boards and other factors. The number of the LEDs is set to 7×5 removing the space of other electronic devices occupied. In order to acquire the good luminance of the image and save costs, we selected six identical surface light sources arranged regularly as the lighting system.

3.2 Evaluation Function Analysis of the Lighting System

As shown in Fig. 3, the green structures represent the surface light sources, the gray structure represents the tank and the blue part represents the water. Then, we get $\alpha = 0$, $\beta = 0$, $\gamma = 90°$ in Fig. 2. Moreover, we use L_2 to replace L_c in Fig. 3 in order to make the equation more intuitive.

We put the parameters $m = 1$, $d = 2$ $\alpha = 0$, $\beta = 0$, $\gamma = 90°$ into Eq. (4) when N and M are 7 and 5 respectively. We obtained the irradiance $E(x, y)$ of the six surface light sources as show in Eq. (7).

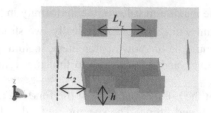

Fig. 3. The structure of the Lighting system.

$$E(x,y) = I_{LED}h^m \sum_{i=-2}^{2} \sum_{j=-3}^{3} \left((x - L_2)^2 \right)^{-\frac{3}{2}} + \left((x - L_2)^2 + (y + L_1 - 2j)^2 + (h - 2i)^2 \right)^{-\frac{3}{2}}$$

$$+ \left((x - 2j)^2 + (y - L_2)^2 + (h - 2i)^2 \right)^{-\frac{3}{2}} + \left((x + L_2)^2 + (y - 2j)^2 + (h - 2i)^2 \right)^{-\frac{3}{2}}$$

$$+ \left((x + L_2)^2 + (y + L_1 - 2j)^2 + (h - 2i)^2 \right)^{-\frac{3}{2}} + \left((x - 2j)^2 + (y + L_2)^2 + (h - 2i)^2 \right)^{-\frac{3}{2}}$$

$$\tag{7}$$

Then we put Eqs. (7) into (6), and obtained the polynomial form of the evaluation function for system uniformity, as shown in the Eq. (8).

$$\sigma^2 = \iint_{\Sigma} (E - \bar{E})^2 ds \Rightarrow \sigma^2 \approx a + b_1 L_1^{-3} + b_2 L_2^{-3} + b_3 h^{-3} + b_4 L_1^{-2} + b_5 L_2^{-2} + b_6 h^{-3} + b_7 L_1^{-1} + b_8 L_2^{-1} + b_9 h^{-3}$$

$$\tag{8}$$

where σ^2 is the variance of the irradiance of the bottom of the tank, L_1, L_2, h are the three parameters adjustable in the system, and a, b_i are the regression coefficients to be determined.

3.3   Lighting System Design Based on Optical Simulation

Instead of solving the evaluation function directly, we got the polynomial form of the evaluation function. Then we obtained the optimal parameters by the following steps:

(1)   we established the models of tank and surface light source in TracePro.
(2)   we set the parameters of the material, light source, receiving surface and other properties in TracePro before the light tracing.
(3)   we set L_1, L_2, h as the parameters and with the increase of the parameter values, we simulated the irradiance of the receiving surface and calculate σ^2. In this step, we set the parameters in the range of $20 \leq L_1 \leq 60, 0 \leq L_2 \leq 30, 25 \leq h \leq 60$ and selected 90 groups of the parameters for simulation.
(4)   we imported the parameters and σ^2 into Eq. (8) and obtained the relationship between L_1, L_2, h and σ^2 by using multiple nonlinear regression method in MATLAB. σ_1^2 is evaluation function of the uniformity on the tank bottom, and σ_1^2 is evaluation function of the brightness of the tank side, as show in Eqs. (9) and (10).

$$\sigma_1^2 = (0.0007 - 3.0605L_1^{-3} + 0.0084L_2^{-3} - 9.7254h^{-3} + 0.3764L_1^{-2}$$
$$- 0.001L_2^{-2} + 1.207h^{-2} - 0.0139L_1^{-1} - 0.0452h^{-1}) \times 10^3 \qquad (9)$$

$$\sigma_2^2 = (-0.0001 + 0.1254L_1^{-3} + 0.0065L_2^{-3} + 1.1964h^{-3} - 0.018L_1^{-2}$$
$$- 0.0025L_2^{-2} - 0.1367h^{-2} + 0.0009L_1^{-1} + 0.0003L_2^{-1} + 0.0054h^{-1}) \times 10^5$$
$$(10)$$

(5) we got the optimal position parameters by using the Sequence Quadratic Programming (SQP) method under the above constraints. The optimal values of the position parameters are $L_1 = 39$, $L_2 = 21$, $h = 34.92$. The bottom of the tank has the maximum uniformity and the side has better brightness at this time.

We put the three optimal parameters to simulation in TracePro. The simulated result of the irradiance distribution of the tank bottom is shown in Fig. 4. The irradiance distribution is uniform in the irradiance map. Furthermore, we calculated the variance of the irradiance on the tank bottom $\sigma_1^2 = 0.0056$, the difference is very small.

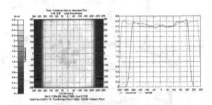

Fig. 4. The irradiance distribution map on the bottom of water tank

In order to further verify the correctness of the calculation results, we set one of the three parameters as fixed value, and changed the other two parameters. Figure 5 shows the uniformity with different parameters, Fig. 5(a) shows the uniformity with different L_2 and h when $L_1 = 39$. Figure 5(b) shows the uniformity with different L_1 and h when $L_2 = 21$. Figure 5(c) shows the uniformity with different L_1 and L_2 when $h = 34.92$. We get the maximum value of the uniformity when $L_1 = 39$, $L_2 = 21$, $h = 34.92$. We can conclude that the parameters we obtained by this method are optimal.

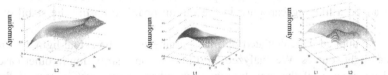

(a)The uniformity in the case of changing L_2 and h;(b) The uniformity in the case of changing L_1 and h; (c) The uniformity in the case of changing L_1 and L_2

Fig. 5. The uniformity with different parameters

4 Design and Implementation of Observation System

4.1 Design of the Observation System

We designed the observation system as shown in Fig. 6. The design details are listed as follows:

(1) we set the size of the system to 1.2 m × 1.1 m × 1.7 m (length × width × height) according to the size of the big tank and the optimal position parameters.
(2) we designed a cuboid structure as the frame of the observation system to ensure the stability of the system. At the same time, the big tank can be placed in the system.
(3) we used the 90° and 135° corner pieces to fix the cameras and used beams to sandwich each light board.
(4) we changed the positions of the camera and the light boards in any directions by adjusting the tightness of the bolts between the connectors.

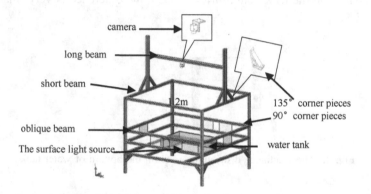

Fig. 6. Design of the observation system

4.2 Implementation of the Lighting System

Figure 7 shows the circuit design picture and the practicality picture of the surface light source. In the circuit board, the distance between two LEDs is 2 cm and each row has a potentiometer for the brightness adjustment. Meanwhile, a potentiometer in the total branch adjusts the brightness of the entire surface light source. There are two powers on both sides of the circuit board to make parallel connection between the circuit boards. We also added a filtering capacitor in the circuit board to ensure the stability of the circuit.

Then we applied the calculated optimal parameters to the actual light system with six surface light sources. We analyzed the illumination distribution in other cases. We captured the images of the tank bottom with other position parameters of the light source. Figure 8 shows the brightness distribution of the optimal parameters (Fig. 8(a)) and other parameters. We can safely conclude that the uniformity and the brightness is the best in the case of the optimal parameters we calculated.

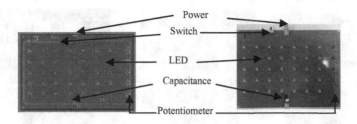

Fig. 7. Design of the light source

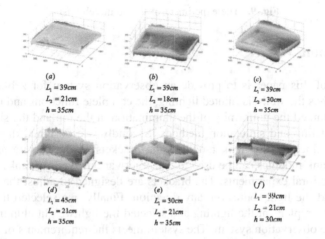

Fig. 8. Three-dimensional luminance map of the tank in actual system

4.3 Implementation of the Observation System

The implementation of the observation system is shown in Fig. 9(a). In the observation system, the six surface light sources are assembled on the iron plates, which are sandwiched between beams. Each beam of the fixed iron piece can be moved up and down by loosening the nut and bolt. The distance between the iron plate and the light source can be adjusted and the position of the light source can also be changed with the iron plate. The long slides and short slides that fixed the camera can be moved in all directions by loosening the nut and bolt, which ensured that the camera can be adjusted according to the photographed area.

We can get different types of the small water tanks by the combination of the water tank modules. Figure 9(b) (c) (d) show three kinds of classical behavioral experiments of the adult zebrafish in the proposed observation system. These prove that the observation system we designed has high flexibility and multiple functions.

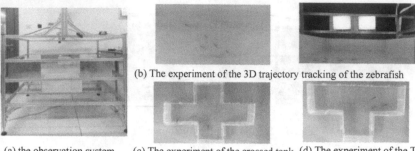

(a) the observation system   (c) The experiment of the crossed tank   (d) The experiment of the T font tank

(b) The experiment of the 3D trajectory tracking of the zebrafish

Fig. 9. The experiment of the adult zebrafish

5   Conclusion

The purpose of this paper is to provide an observation system for zebrafish experiments, which has the well-distributed lighting, the complete functions and the low cost. Firstly, we obtained the uniformity of the illumination in the top and the side views by using the modeling and simulation methods. Secondly, we designed the observation system, which includes the tank modules, the brackets of the camera and the light sources. The tank modules can be used to construct various types of tanks for different zebrafish behavioral experiments. The brackets are designed to adjust the positions of the camera and the light sources in any direction. Finally, we selected the cheap but bright LEDs to implement the lighting and selected the lightweight aluminum profiles to make up the observation system. The system meets the requirements of high quality image in computer vision technology, saves the expenses and improves the experimental efficiency.

Acknowledgement. This work is supported by the National Natural Science Foundation of China (NSFC: 61327802, U1613220), Major Science and Technology Project of Tianjin (14ZCDZGX00801), the Key Program of Science Foundation of Tianjin (14JCZDJC31800).

References

1. Burne, T., et al.: Big ideas for small brains: what can psychiatry learn from worms, flies, bees and fish? Mol. Psychiatr. **16**(1), 7 (2011)
2. Norton, W., et al.: Adult zebrafish as a model organism for behavioural genetics. BMC Neurosci. **11**, 90 (2010)
3. Gerlai, R.: Zebrafish antipredatory responses: a future for translational research? Behav. Brain Res. **207**, 223–231 (2010)
4. Champagne, D.L., et al.: Translating rodent behavioral repertoire to zebrafish (Danio rerio): relevance for stress research. Behav. Brain Res. **214**, 332–342 (2010)
5. Fan, C.Y., et al.: Gene expression changes in developing zebrafish as potential markers for rapid developmental neurotoxicity screening. Neurotoxicol. Teratol. **32**, 91–98 (2010)

6. Rihel, J., et al.: Zebrafish behavioral profiling links drugs to biological targets and rest/wake regulation. Science **327**, 348–351 (2010)
7. Xi, Y., et al.: Impaired dopaminergic neuron development and locomotor function in zebrafish with loss of pink1 function. Eur. J. Neurosci. **31**, 623–633 (2010)
8. Darrow, K.O., et al.: Characterization and development of courtship in zebrafish Danio rerio. Zebrafish **1**, 40–45 (2004)
9. Saverino, C., et al.: The social zebrafish: behavioral responses to conspecific, heterospecific, and computer animated fish. Behav. Brain Res. **191**, 77–87 (2008)
10. Salas, C., et al.: Neuropsychology of learning and memory in teleost fish. Zebrafish **3**, 157–171 (2006)
11. Gomez-Laplaza, L.M., et al.: Latent learning in zebrafish (Danio rerio). Behav. Brain Res. **208**, 509–515 (2010)
12. Cachat, J., et al.: Modeling withdrawal syndrome in zebrafish. Behav. Brain Res. **208**, 371–376 (2010)
13. Egan, R.J., et al.: Understanding behavioral and physiological phenotypes of stress and anxiety in zebrafish. Behav. Brain Res. **205**, 38–44 (2009)
14. Maximino, C., et al.: Scototaxis as anxiety-like behavior in fish. Nat. Protoc. **5**, 209–216 (2010)
15. http://www.viewpoint.fr/en/home, http://www.viewpoint.fr/en/p/equipment. Accessed 21 Mar 2017
16. http://www.noldus.com/animal-behavior-reasearch/products/ethovision-xt. Accessed 21 Mar 2017
17. Cachat, J., et al.: Three-dimensional neurophenotyping of adult zebrafish behavior. Plos One **6**(3), e17597 (2011)
18. Huang, C., Wu, B., Nevatia, R.: Robust object tracking by hierarchical association of detection responses. In: Forsyth, D., Torr, P., Zisserman, A. (eds.) ECCV 2008 Part II. LNCS, vol. 5303, pp. 788–801. Springer, Heidelberg (2008). doi:10.1007/978-3-540-88688-4_58
19. Xiang, Y., et al.: Learning to track: online multi-object tracking by decision making In: 15th International Conference on Computer Vision, Santiago, pp. 4705–4713. IEEE (2015)
20. Pérezescudero, A., et al.: idTracker: tracking individuals in a group by automatic identification of unmarked animals. Nat. Methods **11**, 743–748 (2014)
21. Bhattacharya, P., et al.: Semiconductor optoelectronic devices. Phys. Today **47**(12), 64 (1994)
22. Narukawa, Y.: White-light LEDS. Opt. Photonics News **15**(4), 24–29 (2004)
23. Moreno, I.: Effects on illumination uniformity due to dilution on arrays of LEDs. In: Proceedings of SPIE, vol. 5529 (2004)

A Novel Visual Detecting and Positioning Method for Screw Holes

Yuntao Wang[1,2,3,5], Guoyuan Liang[1,2(✉)], Sheng Huang[1,2,3,5], Can Wang[1,2], and Xinyu Wu[1,2,4]

[1] Key Laboratory of Human-Machine-Intelligence Synergic Systems, Shenzhen Institutes of Advanced Technology, Chinese Academy of Sciences, Shenzhen, China
{yt.wang, gy.liang}@siat.ac.cn
[2] Guangdong Provincial Key Lab of Robotics and Intelligent System, Shenzhen Institutes of Advanced Technology, Chinese Academy of Sciences, Shenzhen, China
[3] Shenzhen College of Advanced Technology, University of Chinese Academy of Sciences, Beijing, China
[4] Guangdong Provincial Key Laboratory of Computer Vision and Virtual Reality Technology, Shenzhen Institutes of Advanced Technology, Chinese Academy of Sciences, Shenzhen, China
[5] Shenzhen Institutes of Advanced Technology, Chinese Academy of Sciences, Shenzhen, China

Abstract. A new visual detecting and positioning method was proposed to solve the positioning problem of screw holes in dark-colored workpieces. Firstly, a red LED lighting system was designed and built to make the screw holes distinct even under dark background of workpieces. Then an improved Hough transform was applied to detect screw holes and a template matching method based on the features of gradation histogram was used for precise positioning of screw holes. After that, a sub-pixel positioning method was adopted in order to achieve the sub-pixel accuracy of screw holes. Further, the image coordinates of screw holes were transformed to the coordinates in world coordinates system according to the camera model. Finally, the experiment results demonstrated the effectiveness, accuracy as well as robustness of the proposed method.

Keywords: Visual positioning · Screwing manipulator · Template matching · Sub-pixel positioning

1 Introduction

With the development of information technology and artificial intelligence, intelligent manufacturing assembling is more and more widely used in manufacturing industries. Machine vision system, as one of the most important intelligent technologies, can greatly improve the flexibility and automation level of production line for its property of ease of integration [1]. At present, machine vision has been widely used in the field of automation assembling, defect detection and electronic packaging in place of the work of human eyes.

© Springer International Publishing AG 2017
M. Liu et al. (Eds.): ICVS 2017, LNCS 10528, pp. 564–575, 2017.
DOI: 10.1007/978-3-319-68345-4_50

A great amount of research has been carried out for the application of machine vision in industrial equipment for object recognition and grasping by many scholars. [3] used a method of edge detection and centroid detection to position a workpiece, which has high accuracy and was easy to modified. [4] built an active visual positioning system, which used the method of region based approach and shape characteristic detection to detect and position the boundary and centroid of the workpiece. Based on the analysis on the features of different screwing manipulators, [5] adopted Harris corner detection method and Hough transform to design a visual positioning system with high accuracy for screwing manipulator with three degrees of freedom. [6] applied a method of minimum enclosing rectangle to find the centroid of residual plastic film. Then target matching based on centroid feature was completed to position residual plastic film. [7] used a template matching approach based on gradation and sub-pixel positioning technique to position the lens of mobile phone and finish assembling. [8] adopted a bidirectional template matching method based on eight neighborhoods to detect the defect of punched paper tape holes and used BP neural network to classify the defect of holes. [9] introduced an iterative thresholding segmentation method based on PCNN, which had a better performance in intensity image compared with traditional thresholding methods.

At present, there is few research on using machine vision positioning for screwing manipulator in industry. There is usually a big difference between screw holes' color and the background of workpiece in most researches which aimed at vision positioning of screw holes [5]. It is an ideal situation for detecting and positioning of screw holes because the workpieces are usually metallic materials with light colors, so screw holes could be showed clearly under normal lighting system. But for dark-colored workpieces, like black and brown, whose surface is lumpy and background color is same as screw holes' color, normal fill light couldn't bring screw holes out and may appear many shadows which would block the holes. On the other hand, strong light will make the edge of screw hole fuzzy, so normal light and the methods mentioned above can't solve these problems well and their robustness is not enough to deal with the complex situation. This paper designed a light system and proposed a novel visual detection and positioning method for screw holes to overcome above problems.

The rest of the paper is organized as follows. Section 2 introduces the hardware setup of screwing manipulator and a new designed vision system platform. Section 3 introduces an improved Hough transform to detect circle holes and a template matching method based on the characteristics of gradation histogram to position screw holes. A sub-pixel positioning method is used to improve the accuracy of positioning results. Next, a coordinate transformation method is introduced according to the camera model. Finally, experiments are designed to evaluate the performance of proposed method in Sect. 4. Section 5 concludes the research.

2   A New Designed Vision System Platform

In this project, an automatic screwing manipulator is used, whose processes of screw feeding, screw transmission, screw hole positioning and screw locking can be carried out automatically and don't need the help of workers.

Usually, the camera is mounted on the arm of screwing manipulator and circle lighting source is mounted on the lens of the camera in previous vision system [5] where the camera could capture the screw holes in current vision with the movement of the arm. This strategy doesn't need complex circle detecting method and coordinates transform technique because the distance between the camera and screw holes is close and the distance between the camera target and screwing drill is fixed. But this strategy has two defects: (1) the camera can't capture the all positions of screw holes in the workpiece. (2) for dark workpieces, the fill light can't make the screw holes distinguished from background. The effect of normal lighting system for a dark-colored workpiece is showed as Fig. 1(a), it is obvious that the screw holes are not easy to clearly identified from the black background.

(a) The effect of normal lighting system   (b) The effect of proposed lighting system

Fig. 1. The effect of lighting system

In order to overcome the problems above, a new pattern is applied, which camera separates with the arm and light source separates with the camera. Then an oblique shining strategy based on double red annular LEDs is proposed to make screw holes distinguished from the dark-colored background. The main reason is that dark object will reflect the red light while screw holes can't. So, the surface would be bright and screw holes would appear dark color. The LEDs should be mounted by a certain degree to achieve that effect. The integration of the screwing manipulator and proposed lighting

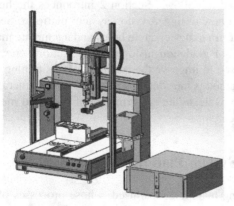
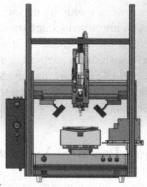

Fig. 2. Visual lighting system (the left is the overall view of lighting system; the right is the front view of lighting system)

system is showed as Fig. 2. The effect of proposed lighting system for the same workpiece is showed as Fig. 1(b), it's obvious that proposed strategy has better effect.

3 A New Vision Detection and Positioning Method

This section firstly introduces an improved Hough transform to detect the circle screw holes, then uses a template matching method based on the characteristics of gradation histogram. After that, a sub-pixel positioning method is applied to improve the positioning precision for screw holes. Finally, a coordinate transformation method is introduced according to the camera model.

3.1 An Improved Hough Transform

In classical Hough transform, the parameter space is discretized into many small cells, then discrete parameter values are brought into the cell in order. After that, the calculation result is put into the certain cell whose value is corresponding to calculation value and a "1" is added to the cell's accumulator. Finally, the parameter which has the most votes is the final result of Hough transform. But when parameter space is more than 2-dimension, it couldn't be tolerated that the sharp increase of the consumed time and storage space of parameters. So many improved Hough transform for circle detection need firstly reduce the dimensionality of the parameter space.

Shape Angle
shape angle [14] D_θ is a geometric invariant which can initially classify closed contours into different classes. D_θ is defined as follow:

$$D_\theta = \frac{1}{n}\sum\nolimits_{i=0}^{n-1} \theta_i = \frac{1}{n}\sum\nolimits_{i=0}^{n-1} arc\,cos(n_i, c_i) \tag{1}$$

where c_i is the line between point i at the contour and the centroid of the shape, n is the number of point at the contour, n_i is the normal vector at the point i, θ_i is the angle between c_i and n_i, which is shown in Fig. 3. The average value of all θ_i in the contour is the shape angle D_θ of the closed contour.

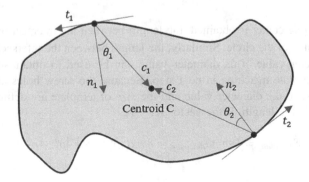

Fig. 3. Computing of the shape angle D_θ

D_θ can be used to classify the different closed contours because its value is only associated with the geometric shape of the contour and wouldn't be influenced by its location and orientation. D_θ of the ideal circle equals 0 [14]. According to this property, we can choose a specific shape after edge detection which could avoid to voting blindly to other object or region belonging to the background and make detecting process faster.

Rough Positioning of the Circle Center

Once the contour shape is determined correctly, the only thing to do is that to position the center of circle instead of determine its radius value. Then the contour lines should be scanned in two directions: horizontal and vertical [10]. To this way, the midpoint of the two intersections of each scan line and contour line can be obtained. After that, the linear Hough transform is used to get the line of all midpoints. For example, vertical diameter L_v can be obtained if contour is scanned by the red horizontal dotted lines (as H_1 and H_2 in Fig. 4). Similarly, horizontal diameter L_h can be obtained when contour is scanned by the orange horizontal dotted lines (V_1 and V_2 in Fig. 4). The center (x_c, y_c) of the circle is the intersection of L_v and L_h, which is shown as Fig. 4.

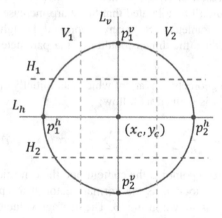

Fig. 4. Locating the center of a circle by cross-line scanning

After the circle center is obtained, the length between the intersection p_1^v and p_2^v is the diameter value of the circle. Similarly, the length between the intersection p_1^h and p_2^h is also a diameter value. This diameter value can be used to obtain the size of the template for template matching in next step. Because the screw holes are usually not standard circles, so the diameter value and the size of template are defined as formula (2), where $|X|$ is the length of the vector X.

$$S_{Template} = Length_{diameter} = max(|p_1^v - p_2^v|, |p_1^h - p_2^h|) \tag{2}$$

3.2   A Template Matching Method Based on the Features of Gradation Histogram

As a basic descriptor of the distribution of color and intensity, the statistical characteristics of histogram is used to evaluate the similarity between two regions. Based on the statistical characteristics of histogram including mean, the variance and the Kolmogorov-Smirnov variable, [11] proposed a template matching method to improve the accuracy of object matching. In order to enhance the robustness and accuracy of matching results further, this paper uses an improved template matching method based on the statistical characteristics including the mean, the variance, the skewness and the Kolmogorov-Smirnov variable of histogram, to position the screw hole center. The similarity between two histograms is measured by the weighted sum of the four characteristics above.

The k order origin moments M_k and the k order central moments η_k of the histogram are defined as follows:

$$M_k = \sum_{i=0}^{L-1} i^k p(r_i) \tag{3}$$

$$\eta_k = \sum_{i=0}^{L-1} (i - \mu)^k p(r_i) \tag{4}$$

where i is a certain intensity value, r_i is the number of pixels whose gray value is i. $p(r_i)$ is the probability density function of r_i, L is the upper bound of intensity scale, equals to 256 in this paper, k is the order, when $k = 1$, the mean value $\mu = M_k$, when $k = 2$, the variance $\sigma^2 = \eta_k$.

The skewness of histogram is a measurement for the deviation from the intensity symmetrical distribution. The definition of the skewness of histogram is as follow:

$$S = \frac{1}{\sigma^3} \sum_{i=0}^{L-1} (i - \mu)^3 p(r_i) \tag{5}$$

where σ is the standard deviation of the intensity histogram.

In addition, Kolmogorov-Smirnov method uses probability distribution function of histogram to compute the similarity between each other, the indexes of KS and SD are defined as follows:

$$KS = \max_k |P_1(r_k) - P_2(r_k)| \tag{6}$$

$$SD = \sum_k |P_1(r_k) - P_2(r_k)| \tag{7}$$

where, $P(r_k) = \sum_{i=0}^{k} \frac{n_i}{n}$ is probability distribution function, n is the total number of pixels, n_i is the number of pixels whose intensity value is i. If $|KS-SD|$ is less than a certain threshold, then the two histograms are similar with each other.

The correlation between two histograms is defined as $D_{Cov}(H_1, H_2)$. An algorithm for comprehensively utilizing various statistical features of histogram is designed as follow:

Algorithm: Compute_Similarity_between _Two_Histograms

Input: H_1, H_2 are histograms

Output: The value of $D_{Cov}(H_1, H_2)$

Begin:

   Computing μ_1 and μ_2, Let $\Delta\mu = \frac{|\mu_1 - \mu_2|}{255}$

   If $\Delta\mu > t_\mu$

   $D_{Cov}(H_1, H_2) = NULL$, return

   Computing σ_1^2 and σ_2^2, Let $\Delta\sigma^2 = \frac{|\sigma_1^2 - \sigma_2^2|}{255^2}$

   If $\Delta\sigma^2 > t_{\sigma^2}$

   $D_{Cov}(H_1, H_2) = NULL$, return

   Computing S_1 and S_2, Let $\Delta S = |S_1 - S_2|$

   If $\Delta S > t_S$

   $D_{Cov}(H_1, H_2) = NULL$, return

   Computing KS and SD

   If $|KS - SD| > t_{KS}$

   $D_{Cov}(H_1, H_2) = NULL$, return

   ELSE

   $D_{Cov}(H_1, H_2) = \omega_\mu \Delta\mu + \omega_{\sigma^2}\Delta\sigma^2 + \omega_S \Delta S + \omega_{KS}|KS - SD|$

End

where t_μ, t_{σ^2}, t_S and t_{KS} are the threshold of each statistical various, ω_μ, $\omega_{\sigma^2}, \omega_S$ and ω_{KS} are weights of each statistical various respectively. When D_{Cov} is less than a certain threshold, then the two histograms match successfully.

3.3   Subpixel Location Algorithm Based on Quadratic Spline Interpolation

With good robustness and high accuracy, quadratic spline interpolation not only solves the problem that first derivative or second derivative becomes the corner at the terminal, but also overcomes the defects for great calculation and inconsistent convergence of high-order spline. Therefore, this paper adopts the method of quadratic spline interpolation to achieve positioning for sub-pixel level precision.

After obtaining the matching point of the pixel level precision, the coordinates of the eight adjacent points and the corresponding intensity values can be easily obtained. The peak position of the center of the neighborhood is divided into four directions: vertical, horizontal, left oblique and right oblique, as Fig. 5 shows. Then the vertex positions in the four directions are obtained by the method of the quadratic spline interpolation, denoting as (x_1, y_1), (x_2, y_2), (x_3, y_3) and (x_4, y_4) respectively. The final position with sub-pixel precision is the point which has minimum sum of distances to each vertex.

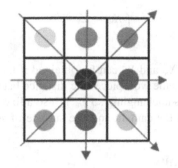

Fig. 5. Calculating direction

3.4 Image Coordinates to World Coordinates

After the coordinates of screw holes are obtained, they are demanded to convert to the 3D coordinates in world coordinates system. According to the principle of pinhole imaging, the camera model [13] is showed as follow:

$$z \begin{bmatrix} u \\ v \\ 1 \end{bmatrix} = \begin{bmatrix} f_u & 0 & u_0 & 0 \\ 0 & f_v & v_0 & 0 \\ 0 & 0 & 1 & 0 \end{bmatrix} \begin{bmatrix} R & T \\ 0^T & 1 \end{bmatrix} \begin{bmatrix} X_w \\ Y_w \\ Z_w \\ 1 \end{bmatrix} = M_1 M_2 P \tag{8}$$

where (u, v) is the coordinate on the image, f_u is the scale factor of u axis, f_v is the scale factor of v axis, (u_0, v_0) is the pixel coordinate of the intersection of the camera optical axis and the image plane, R is the rotation matrix of 3×3, T is the translation matrix of 3×1, M_1 is the intrinsic matrix of camera, M_2 is the extrinsic matrix of camera, P is the homogeneous coordinate in world coordinates system. The parameters above can be obtained by the camera calibration method [12].

From one camera, we can't obtain the 3D coordinate of a certain point on the image directly. Therefore, we make the camera coordinates system coincide with the world coordinates system, then M_2 is as follow:

$$M_2 = \begin{bmatrix} 1 & 0 & 0 & 0 \\ 0 & 1 & 0 & 0 \\ 0 & 0 & 1 & 0 \\ 0 & 0 & 0 & 1 \end{bmatrix} \tag{9}$$

Through the derivation, Eq. (8) is changed as follow:

$$\begin{cases} zu = f_u X_w + u_0 Z_w \\ zv = f_v Y_w + v_0 Z_w \\ z = Z_w \end{cases} \tag{10}$$

Then, X_w and Y_w are as follow:

$$\begin{cases} X_w = Z_w \frac{u-u_0}{f_u} \\ Y_w = Z_w \frac{v-v_0}{f_v} \end{cases} \tag{11}$$

According to Eq. (11), X_w and Y_w can be obtained if the value of Z_w and the value of (u, v) is known. For the same workpiece, the distance between the camera target and the surface of screw holes is unchanging, so Z_w is also a fixed value and its value equals the distance value between the camera and the surface of screw holes.

4   Experimental Results

Basler aca1600-gc camera with 1624×1234 pixels and Coputar-M3520-MPW2 lens are used to capture images. In order to reduce the influence of noise, preprocessing for the image is demanded. Median filter is adopted with 7×7 adjacences which could avoid the image to be excessively fuzzy. Then Canny edge detection is used to find the edge of the target.

The accuracy of proposed method is evaluated by a standard visual calibration board which is made of glass and consists of 7×7 solid circles. The diameter of each circle is 1.875 mm, the distance between any two centers of circles is 3.750 mm and the tolerance is 0.001 mm, as Fig. 6 shows. Firstly, the circles are detected and positioned by proposed method, then the length between any two centers among circles are calculated. In order to demonstrate the robustness of proposed method, the distances are computed by horizontal and oblique 45 degree. A part of results are showed in Tables 1 and 2, where (i, j) denotes the position of the circle of column j in line i. The distance line between circle (1, 1) and circle (7, 7) is showed in Fig. 6.

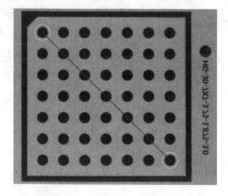

Fig. 6. Recognition and positioning result

From the Tables 1 and 2, in the horizontal position, the average positioning error is less than 0.01 mm, while in the case of 45-degree obliqueness, the error is not more than 0.02 mm. It is demonstrated that proposed method has high accuracy. At the same time, it's easy to find that the horizontal positioning error is smaller than the error in oblique direction, the reason is that the oblique length is longer than horizontal direction, so more and more errors are accumulated. On the other hand, although the

Table 1. Visual positioning results and errors by horizon

Starting point (4, 1)	End point						Average error (mm)
	(4, 2)	(4, 3)	(4, 4)	(4, 5)	(4, 6)	(4, 7)	
True distance/mm	3.750	7.500	11.250	15.000	18.750	22.500	−0.006
Detection distance/mm	3.755	7.510	11.262	15.010	18.7529	22.496	
Absolute error/mm	−0.005	−0.010	−0.012	−0.010	−0.003	0.004	

Table 2. Visual positioning results and errors by oblique 45 degree

Starting point (1, 1)	End point						Average error (mm)
	(2, 2)	(3, 3)	(4, 4)	(5, 5)	(6, 6)	(7, 7)	
True distance/mm	5.3033	10.6066	15.9099	21.2132	26.5165	31.8198	−0.0149
Detection distance/mm	5.3135	10.6205	15.9268	21.2319	26.5343	31.8317	
Absolute error/mm	−0.0102	−0.01387	−0.01695	−0.01868	−0.01778	−0.01189	

error induced by distortion of lens has been rectified, there is still some inaccuracy because the camera model and the distortion model is theoretically approximate.

In the application, the proposed method also has high robustness. Classical Hough transform is applied here to compare with the proposed method. In Fig. 7, it's obvious that using Hough transform directly would not obtained accurate detecting results and there is error detection which are not expected for the screw holes whose boundary is

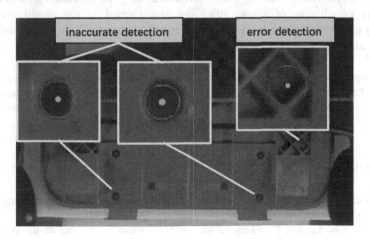

Fig. 7. The positioning results of Hough transform

fuzzy and is not a standard circle by red lighting. As Fig. 8 shows, the proposed method has obtained better results and can correctly position the screw holes in higher accuracy. At the same time, error detection is not happened in complex environment. But proposed method need the distance between camera target and the surface of the workpiece is fixed and unchanging, otherwise the parameters of camera need to be calculated again.

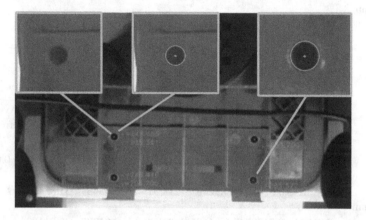

Fig. 8. The positioning results of proposed method

5 Conclusion

In order to solve the confusion and shadow blocking problem of screw holes in the workpieces whose surface is complex, a new vision system is designed in this paper. Then a novel visual detecting and positioning method was proposed to position screw holes accurately based on an improved Hough transform, a template matching method based on the features of intensity histogram and a sub-pixel positioning method. Next, the image coordinates of screw holes are transformed to the world coordinates according to the camera model. Experiment results demonstrate that proposed method has high accuracy and robustness.

Acknowledgement. This work was supported by Shenzhen technology development project of science and technology plan (CXZZ20150929140642779), Shenzhen technology research project of science and technology plan (JSGG20160301160558713), Guangdong commonweal research and capacity building special project (2015A010103011).

References

1. Bianconi, F., Ceccarelli, L., Fernández, A., et al.: A sequential machine vision procedure for assessing paper impurities. Comput. Ind. **65**(2), 325–332 (2014)
2. Guo, B., Zhu, G., Lu, Y., Zhao, J.: Research on visual positioning of the workpiece in intelligent feeding system. Comput. Measur. Control **24**(2), 232–238 (2016)

3. Zhu, L., Lin, H., Wu, W.-J.: Workpiece positioning of industrial robot based on machine vision. J. Chin. Comput. Syst. **37**(8), 1873–1877 (2016)
4. Liao, W.-H., Li, L.: Stereo vision for tracking and location system working on industrial robot. Microcomput. Inf. **25**(8), 242–244 (2009)
5. Li, Z.-W.: Research on the application of workpiece positioning vision system in coordinate robot system. Chongqing University (2016)
6. Jiang, S.-Q., Zhang, H.-D., Hua, Y.-J.: Research on location of residual plastic film based on computer vision. J. Chin. Agric. Mech. **37**(11), 150–154 (2016)
7. Zhang, J.-Z., He, Y.-Y., Li, J.: Application research of vision-location in robotic assembly equipment. J. Mech. Electr. Eng. **28**(8), 934–937 (2011)
8. Han, T. A study on punched paper tape holes defect detection based on machine vision computer. Hangzhou Dianzi university (2015)
9. Gao, C., Zhou, D., Guo, Y.: An iterative thresholding segmentation model using a modified pulse coupled neural network. Neural Process. Lett. **39**(1), 81–95 (2014)
10. Qin, K.-H., Wang, H.-Y., Zheng, J.-T.: A unified approach based on hough transform for quick detection of circles and rectangles. J. Image Graph. **15**(1), 109–115 (2010)
11. Zhu, L.: The Application of digital library technology in the integrated management platform for military information. Comput. Technol. Autom. **23**(2), 48–51 (2004)
12. Zhang, Z.: A flexible new technique for camera calibration. IEEE Trans. Pattern Anal. Mach. Intell. **22**(11), 1330–1334 (2000)
13. Zhu, Z.-T.: Research on key technology of precision measurement based on computer vision image. South China University of Technology (2004)
14. Teutsch, C.: Real-time detection of elliptic shapes for automated object recognition and object tracking. SPIE **6070**, 1–9 (2006)

Learning the Floor Type for Automated Detection of Dirt Spots for Robotic Floor Cleaning Using Gaussian Mixture Models

Andreas Grünauer, Georg Halmetschlager-Funek, Johann Prankl,
and Markus Vincze[✉]

Vision for Robotics Laboratory, Automation and Control Institute,
Vienna University of Technology, 1040 Vienna, Austria
{ag,gh,jp,vm}@acin.tuwien.ac.at

Abstract. While small floor cleaning robots rather cover area than detect actual dirt, larger floor cleaning robots in commercial settings need to actively detect and clean dirt spots. Floor types that have a single colour or simple texture could be tackled with an approach based on a fixed pattern. However, this restricts the use of the robots considerably. It terms of ease-of-use it is desirable to automatically adapt to a new floor type while still detecting dirt spots. We approach this problem as a one class classification problem and exploit the capability of the Gaussian Mixture Model (GMM) for learning the floor pattern. The advantage of the method is that it operates in an unsupervised way, which allows to adapt to new floor types while moving. An extensive evaluation shows that our method detects dirt spots on different floor types and that it outperforms state-of-the-art approaches especially for floor types with a high-frequency texture.

1 Introduction

While small cleaning robots entered our homes, more and more professional floor cleaning machines enter factory buildings, hospitals, supermarkets, train stations, airports and other large public areas such as malls. Flat surfaces, a clearly defined working space, and a simple task made it possible to narrow the robot's functional requirements down to the essentials: wander around with an activated cleaning system and drive back to the docking station as soon the energy drops under a predefined level. Different to domestic vacuum cleaning, industrial cleaning rather demands for scrubbers and similar wet floor cleaning technology. The challenge is to deal with large scale areas, daily and infra-daily cleaning missions, different pollution patterns, and challenging environments with many different types of floors. Pollution and dirt patterns should be detected to optimise cleaning patterns. Due to the limitation of the robot's mobile resources and the growing awareness for the need of more efficient and ecological machines, the robotic solution asks for strategies to deploy robots to those areas where needs is immediate.

© Springer International Publishing AG 2017
M. Liu et al. (Eds.): ICVS 2017, LNCS 10528, pp. 576–589, 2017.
DOI: 10.1007/978-3-319-68345-4_51

Fig. 1. Summary of the main concept: learning of the floor structure and determination of dirt probabilities. Left: original image. Right: extracted probabilities for detecting cigarette stumps.

The contribution of this paper sets out to enable a more efficient operation to extend the operational radius of industrial cleaning robots. The goal is to add a method for recognizing polluted areas such that the mobile cleaning robot is able to adapt the amount of used cleaning suspension and energy to achieve a more efficient cleaning procedure. The underlying main task simplifies to the classification of clean and dirty areas (see Fig. 1). This detection of dirt on the floor or polluted areas has hardly been tackled in robotics so far. An exception is the method proposed in [5], which assumes different image frequencies of the background and the polluted areas. This assumption limits applications to floors of single color or texture patterns much larger than the particle that shall be detected.

The contribution of this paper is a solution that adapts online to novel floor types and does not need to learn the clean target appearance of the floor. To achieve this we propose an unsupervised novelty detection algorithm that learns a Guassian Mixture Model (GMM) of the present floor type. The algorithm learns a background model of the floor and identifies dirt spots on the fly for each image. For the evaluation of our algorithms we extract 850 ground truth annotated images from the framework provided by [5] and added 240 challenging real life images with new floor patterns. For the evaluation we created an evaluation framework that is independent of the Robot Operation System (ROS). We used this framework for the evaluation of the proposed method against the algorithm published in [5] and results indicate a significant improvement of the performance.

In summary, the contributions are

– a dirt detection method that takes advantage of an unsupervised on-line learning algorithm and uses GMMs to distinguish between the floor and dirt spots,
– an approach using this method for adapting to new floors types during the time of robot operation, and
– the extension of the database in [5] to also contain more challenging cases. The dataset now contains 1090 high quality annotated ground truth images that can be utilized by the community for further research.

The full dataset will be published on our web page after acceptance of the paper.

The paper is structured as follows. After reviewing the related work in Sect. 2, we present the dirt detection method in Sect. 3 and proceed with the description of the dirt databases used for our experiments in Sect. 4. Then we discuss the experiments and the results in Sect. 5, followed by a conclusion and outlook in Sect. 6.

2   Related Work

Visual dirt detection for autonomous cleaning devices is a recent research field. Various manufacturers released commercial robotic vacuum cleaners as the iRobot Roomba[1] or the Dyson 360 Eye[2]. These devices are designed to clean the whole floor several times a week. Typically optical and piezo-electronic sensors inside the vacuum bin inform the robot about the degree of pollution for the adaption of the cleaning process. These sensors are not capable of detecting certain kind of dirt, e.g. stains on a carpet. Another drawback is that each location needs to be treated at least once to detect its cleanliness. In industry, first cleaning robots are operating such as the robots from Intellibot[3] or Cyberdyne[4]. However, they are programmed to clean a certain area rather than check cleanliness and operate depending on it.

The visual detection of dirt spots on floors closely relates to the problem of the identification and removal of film defects as dirt particles and scratches for digital movie restoration. Works in this field [14,15] incorporate spatial-temporal segmentation methods which are based on the fact that noise appears only in a single or a few consecutive frames. Nevertheless, this temporal filtering methods are not directly applicable to the visual floor inspection task, because here the dirt spots do not appear and disappear from the floor in consecutive camera frames.

Another approach would be to train an object detection system either on all possible appearances of dirt, or the appearance of the clean floors, similar to the approach of learning a background model in static scenes [2]. While the first is not feasible due to the various different appearances of dirt, the latter has the disadvantage that the system needs to be learned in prior on each new floor pattern individually.

A naive approach of detecting dirt would be the interpretation of dirt as all objects sticking out of an estimated ground plane, which would not work for extremely flat objects as paper or liquids. 3D saliency methods [12,13] detect objects based on color, depth and curvature to segment objects. These approaches involve analysis of point cloud data and are therefore not applicable on our problem, as the dimensions of small dirt particles are smaller than the spatial resolution of current RGB-D sensors.

---

[1] www.irobot.com.
[2] www.dyson360eye.com.
[3] www.intellibotrobotics.com.
[4] www.cyberdyne.jp.

Recently approaches using multi-layer or convolutional neural networks (CNNs) gained a lot of attention. Several works attempted to use these networks on texture detection tasks. For example, [8] represent textures by the correlations between feature maps in several layers of the network. They show that across layers the texture representations increasingly capture the statistical properties of natural images while making object information more and more explicit, with the goal to provide insight into the deep representations learned by convolutional neural networks. The work by [6] have evaluated a number of state-of-the-art texture descriptors on different benchmarks derived from the OpenSurfaces dataset and all regarding texture analysis and detection. The main finding is that orderless pooling of convolutional neural network features is a remarkably good texture descriptor, versatile enough to capture scene and object descriptors. Another approach is the work in [1], where the authors introduce an energy measure that enables to discard the overall shape information analyzed by classic CNNs. They show that with their T-CNN architecture performance in texture recognition is increased while largely reducing the complexity, memory requirements and computation time. However, a problem of all these approaches is that they require a rather large data set (rather a million than several thousand annotated images). This is not feasible for the cleaning scenario, where floor types may change rapidly and deployment in new areas requires to automatically adapt to a new floor type.

Regarding related work in detecting dirt on floors, Bormann et al. [3,5] introduce a learning-free 2D saliency method, which identifies dirt as the salient parts in the scene using the algorithm of Hou and Zhang [9]. Hou and Zhang found that most images roughly share the shape of their log amplitude spectra. Assuming that this common shape corresponds to the background in the images, the difference of the original and the smoothed logarithmic amplitude spectrum represents the prominent parts of the image. Bormann et al. calibrate the saliency filter response against the response of a modified scene image containing artificially added standard pollution. The parts of the calibrated filter response which are above a empirically depicted threshold are subsequently considered as dirt. In a successive work [4] the algorithm was enhanced to reduce the high false-positive rate by matching potential false-positive image patches against a database of known false-positive floor templates (e.g. power plugs in the floor).

Another possible solution is the application of novelty detection, which is the task of identifying data that differ from the vast majority of available training data. An overview of the state-of-the-art novelty detection approaches is given in [11]. In [7] novelty detection based on GMMs is used for face detection. Inspired by this work, our contribution is a patch-wise color gradient feature that turns this initially supervised classification problem into a novelty detection task, which enables an unsupervised solution of the dirt detection task using GMMs and pure RGB data. The selected feature and the robust unsupervised learning method makes the use of geometric information and a sufficient camera calibration obsolete. I.e., the presented method does not need any warping of the camera image into the bird's eye perspective as in [5].

3   Unsupervised Dirt Detection

The presented dirt detection algorithm is based on the extraction of a patch-wise texture feature vector followed by a novelty detection using GMMs. An overview of the processing pipeline is displayed in Fig. 2. The individual steps are explained in detail in the following subsections.

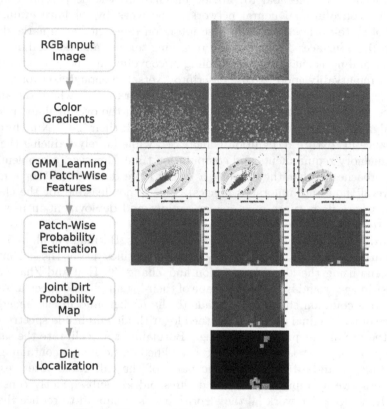

Fig. 2. Pipeline of the dirt detection system.

3.1   Color Gradient Feature

Novelty detection requires the extraction of a set of feature vectors to obtain a model that has the power to discriminate between *one* class (the clean floor) and all other possibilities (dirt). Therefore, we introduce a color gradient feature. When it comes to color, RGB images of real world scenarios often exhibit unbalanced lighting conditions, which introduce a high variation in color appearance of the same floor texture appearing for different parts of the image. A classification task of feature vectors based on this color space would therefore not generalize well in such conditions. Therefore, we first decompose the RGB input image into the lightness channel L^*, the color channel along the red-green axis a^*, and the color channel along the yellow-to-blue axis b^* of the CIE $L^*a^*b^*$ color space [10], which allows for the separation of color information from the illumination in a scene. For each color channel we extract feature vectors in the following way: We compute the gradient magnitude image and split the image into patches using a sliding window with fixed dimensions and step sizes as depicted in Fig. 3. For each patch we compute a 2D feature vector holding mean and standard deviation of its gradient magnitude values. More formally, we define $X^{(c)}$ to be a feature representation of patch $\mathcal{P}$ computed on channel $c \in \{L^*, a^*, b^*\}$. Each image $\mathcal{I}$ is therefore, described by the first and second statistical moments of its gradient magnitudes for each color channel.

3.2   Novelty Detection Using GMMs

The proposed dirt detection reformulated as novelty detection problem assumes that the vast majority of samples represent clean floor, and polluted regions will appear as outliers. The previous calculation of the texture feature yields a sample in two dimensions for each patch in the color channels that shows the polluted floor. We separately train for each input image three GMMs (one per color channel) with a number of K mixture components on the samples. We denote the set of all estimated parameters of a GMM by $\theta^{(c)}$. Therefore, the likelihood of a sample X under the floor model is calculated as

$$p(X|\theta) = \prod_{c \in \{a,b,L\}} p(X^{(c)}|\theta^{(c)})$$

where statistical independence between the channels is assumed. The probability of a patch considered as dirt is consequently defined as $1 - p(X|\theta)$. A patch is labelled as dirt, if its dirt probability exhibits a fixed dirt probability threshold T_p.

As the quality of the floor model depends strongly on the pureness of the training set a filtering (masking) may be crucial to avoid the model fitting on structures that do not belong to the floor (ref. Sect. 5). This can be realized i.e. by using a method similar to [5] where a mask is generated using RGB-D data and ground plane detection.

4   Dirt Database

The following section gives a short overview of the evaluation database, which combines the reference data from Bormann et al. [5] (IPA Dirt Database) and adds data recordings inspired by the targeted industrial cleaning task.

4.1   IPA Dataset

In order to evaluate the dirt detection method described in Sect. 3 we adapted the office dirt database published in [5], which contains various dirt scenarios

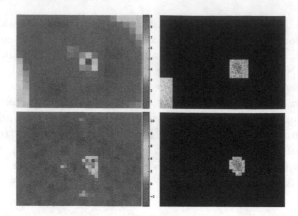

Fig. 3. Influence of two different patch sizes $\mathbf{p_n} = [p_x, p_y]^T$ and step widths $\mathbf{w_n} = [w_x, w_y]^T$ on the joint dirt probability map (left) and the masked output image (right). Starting from top: $\mathbf{p_0} = [64, 64]$, $\mathbf{w_0} = [32, 32]$ and $\mathbf{p_1} = [32, 32]$, $\mathbf{w_1} = [16, 16]$. (Color figure online)

recorded on three different surfaces (*carpet, tiles, linoleum*) at five different locations. The original evaluation framework makes use of a transformation step that projects the detected dirt into an occupancy grid to enable spatial filtering over several frames. In addition, ground truth (GT) annotation is provided in the 3D space. The projection and the annotation makes the framework depending on odometry and RGB-D data and hardens it to add new data. Since we aim to open up the data for a broad community, we extended the framework with interface classes, extracted the original bird's-eye RGB image of the floor, projected the GT annotation to the image frame, stored the 2D GT image, and saved the not thresholded result of the framework's core detection algorithm of each image for a later evaluation. Due to the error prone nature of the odometry, the originally used annotation is only sufficiently precise for the first few frames of the recorded sequences. Hence, we manually interrupted the extraction of the images as soon as the projection of the annotation showed a misalignment between the RGB and the GT image. With this, we were able to extract 850 precisely annotated image sets, each consisting of the masked floor image, the GT image, and the saliency image generated with the algorithm described in [5] (ref. Fig. 4).

Fig. 4. Image set extracted from [5] (from left to right): bird's-eye RGB image, GT image, saliency image.

4.2   Our Dataset

We recorded an additional dataset focused on imbalanced lighting conditions, high-frequent floor textures, and motion blur to cover more realistic and challenging industrial cleaning scenarios.

For our recording set-up we used the Pioneer P3-DX mobile robot platform, with a Asus Xtion Pro Live RGB-D camera mounted 1.10 m above the ground and tilted 40° downwards. The platform was steered remotely by an operator at a speed of 0.5–1.0 m/s, imitating an industrial cleaning robot during operation.

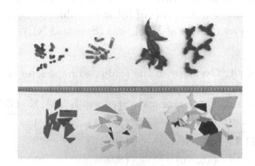

Fig. 5. Types of dirt used in the database (from left to right): small stones, cigarette stumps, leaves, plastics, different cardboards. We also used liquid stains for testing.

We have recorded two types of floor: single-colored *linoleum* as found in laboratories and hospitals, and a *hallway* with granular texture. For each of the floor types we used three different kinds of dirt: *cardboard* snippets, *cigarette* ends and spilled *liquid* stains, as shown in Fig. 5. The dirt was uniformly distributed along the path of the robot in distances of 0.20–0.50 m between each other. Instead of annotating the GT of the dirt locations in a reconstructed 3D scene, we have labelled the dirt pixel-wise in 40 consecutive color images of each scene, resulting in a total number of 240 images of ground truth data. The advantage of this time-consuming annotation is that the precision of the ground truth is independent from the accuracy of the 3D localization and mapping system. Together with the data we publish an evaluation script which other developers can easily adapt to execute their algorithms on each data set. The script also saves the evaluation scores and generates the scoring plots shown in Sect. 5.

5   Evaluation

For the evaluation we compare our unsupervized dirt detection algorithm using optimized parameter configurations with the only available state-of-the-art algorithm published in [5]. As performance measure we use the Receiver Operating Characteristic (ROC) curve, which shows the performance of a binary classifier under variation of its cut-off threshold. The ROC curve is created by plotting the fraction of true positives out of positives (true-positive rate) versus the fraction of false positives out of the negatives (false-positive rate), in which the positive class represents dirt. In the presented approach the parameter under variation is the dirt probability threshold T_p as defined in Sect. 3.2. For the evaluation of the method of [5] the parameter under variation is the threshold T_d applied on the rescaled filter response image.

The three different parameters (number of K mixture components, patch size and step width) have been assessed using grid search. Table 1 shows the selection of four parameter configurations that demonstrate the performance of the presented algorithm under variation of the parameters. For a comparison with the state of the art, the method of [5] was evaluated both *with* and *without* line removal, denoted as (Spectral-WL) and (Spectral-NL).

Table 1. Overview of the evaluated parameter sets.

Param. set	Patch size [px]	Step width [px]	K (GMM)
GMM1-32	(32, 32)	(16, 16)	1
GMM3-32	(32, 32)	(16, 16)	3
GMM1-16	(16, 16)	(8, 8)	1
GMM3-16	(16, 16)	(8, 8)	3

In our first experiment we evaluated these six methods on our dataset as reported in Sect. 4 to assess their performance under realistic conditions that an industrial cleaning robot would encounter in the field. The ROC curves in Fig. 7 show that the proposed method outperforms the state of the art. In Fig. 8 each box plot summarizes the distribution of area under the ROC curves (AUC) over all frames belonging to the same floor type, computed for each method. The largest performance gains have been achieved for scenes of hallway floor. The AUC scores grouped by type of dirt in Fig. 8 demonstrate that our method delivers more stable results with less variation and works exceptionally well on liquids.

Figure 6 shows the masked RGB input image of the ground plane, the scaled filter response by the state-of-the-art method [5], the dirt probability map of the proposed method, and the labelled ground truth image with dirt represented by white color. The examples show coffee stains both on linoleum and hallway (columns 1 and 2) as well as cigarette ends on hallway (column 3). The dirt probability maps computed by our method yield high values at the location of the liquid stain and the cigarettes, whereas the spectral filter response of the state-of-the-art method (Spectral-WL) exhibits high responses at the heterogeneous, fine grained floor pattern, but not at the dirt locations. This is due to the fact, that the state-of-the-art method is based on the method of spectral image saliency of [9], which is based on the assumption that foreground objects are represented by high frequencies and background objects are represented by low frequencies

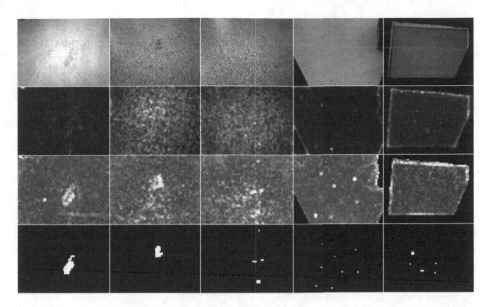

Fig. 6. Examples of input and output images computed on various scenes of the dataset. The *rows* show (from top to bottom): (1) the masked RGB input image of the ground plane, (2) the scaled filter response by the state-of-the-art method of Bormann et al. [5] with no line removal (SPECTRAL-NL), (3) the dirt probability map of our method using a patch size of 16 by 16 pixel (GMM1-16) and (4) the labeled ground truth image. The *columns* show the following combinations of floors and dirt type (from left to right): (1) linoleum & liquid, (2) hallway & liquid and (3) hallway & cigarettes, (4) linoleum & paper, and (5) kitchen & fuzz. The first two scenes are taken from the office dataset of [5] and the second three scenes have been recorded as described in Sect. 4.2.

in the frequency domain. For heterogeneous, highly textured floor types as in the given example, this assumption does not hold, hence the state-of-the-art method cannot distinguish dirt from floor in these cases.

In a second experiment the same six methods have been evaluated on the adapted office dataset as described in Sect. 4. The resulting ROC curves in Fig. 9 show that the presented method yields comparable results to the method of [5]. The AUC scores grouped by floor type in Fig. 10 show some limitations of our proposed method in detecting dirt in the kitchen scenes. An example of a kitchen scene is shown in Fig. 6 (column 5), where the dirt probability map exhibits high dirt probabilities for visible parts, but low probabilities for the actual dirt regions in the image. The limited performance in this particular scenes can be derived from tainted input data that include parts of the wall surface which are detected by our algorithm but not marked as dirt spots in the GT data. These wall patches are – from the novelty detection point of view – correctly detected as outliers, as their features differ clearly from the floor. At the same time the GMM adapts to these isolated points in the feature space. Compared to these outliers, the features of true dirt are much more similar to the features of the floor and therefore yield a low dirt probability. As mentioned in Sect. 3.2 a sufficient pre-filtering of the input data could guarantee for the pureness of the input data.

This image is a very good example to demonstrate that an accurate ground plane extraction (and camera calibration) is a crucial precondition for the proposed novelty-based dirt detection method and will be addressed in future by incorporating the camera pose and the localization map.

Another interesting finding is the performance loss of the state-of-the-art method with line removal (Spectral-WL) on the corridor of the office dataset and the hallway in our dataset, as depicted in Fig. 8. The removal of high responses along the straight joints between the tiles in the corridor scene wrongly suppresses valid dirt responses close to the joints. For the hallway case, the high responses of the coarse floor texture led to a high amount of randomly detected lines, which mask out the spectral filter response almost completely, including dirt peaks.

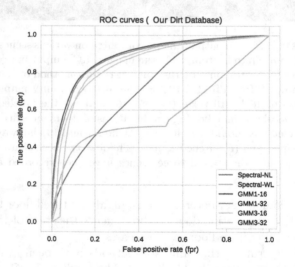

Fig. 7. ROC curves of the assessed methods evaluated for our dataset.

Figure 7 demonstrates, that the configuration of a GMM of one component in combination with a patch size of 16 by 16 pixels and a step size of 8 by 8 pixels achieves the best results on our data. A visual comparison of the influence of different patch sizes on the probability map and dirt mask is presented in Fig. 3. The same figure shows that the presented algorithm is capable of detecting dirty regions that spread over several adjoining patches, as they differ from the far more patches of clean floor on which the floor model was trained on. The similarity of the ROC curves in Fig. 7 indicates that the proposed algorithm performs robust against the change of patch size and number of GMM components. This shows that the descriptiveness power of the introduced color gradient feature

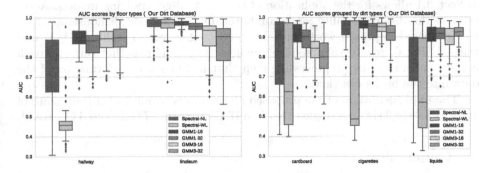

Fig. 8. Box plots showing the variation of frame-wise AUC scores evaluated our dataset, grouped by floor type (left) and by dirt type (right).

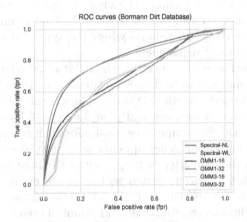

Fig. 9. ROC curves of the assessed methods evaluated on the office dataset.

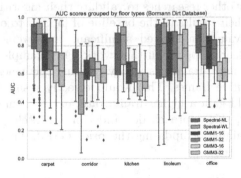

Fig. 10. Box plots showing the variation of frame-wise AUC scores evaluated on the office dataset, grouped by floor type.

in Sect. 3.1 allows for the application of simple, well-generalizing models. Additionally the dirt probability maps computed by our method demonstrate, that the presented approach works on unwarped (Fig. 6, row 3, columns 1–3) and warped (Fig. 6, row 3, columns 4–5) images. This confirms that our approach is independent of any preprocessing step that includes a transformation of the data into the bird's eye view.

The implementation of the proposed algorithm is running at a frame rate of approximately 3 Hz on a single core of an i7 CPU with 2.7 GHz and 4 GB RAM.

6   Conclusion

In this paper we presented an unsupervised learning approach based on GMMs to learn floor patterns and to detect dirt for the purpose of targeted robotic cleaning. The algorithm is designed to cope with unknown floor types and does not need a separate step of learning the clean target appearance. With these characteristics the method sets out to solve industrial cleaning tasks in large areas such as supermarkets and airports where the type of floor may change and initial learning may hinder deployment.

The proposed method reveals its strength on data that offer low image quality (e.g. motion blur), inhomogeneous floor structures, or high-frequent floor texture. The evaluation confirmed that the 2D saliency approach [5] offers good performance within strict boundaries, especially on floors with low-frequent patterns, while our approach achieves competitive results for such scenarios. Nevertheless, the combination of both approaches appears as a promising way to detect dirt independently from the regularity or frequency of the floor pattern.

The database that has been created will be made public to initiate further improvements for this industrial use case. The base contains 1090 image sets, including the input images showing clear and polluted areas, ground truth annotated images, saliency images that have been extracted with the baseline algorithm of [5], and an image showing dirt probabilities generated with our GMM approach outlined in Sect. 3. In addition, we provide an easy to use evaluation script that will allow other researches to validate their algorithms with our database and compare their results to the baseline of [5] and to our approach.

Although the evaluation showed significant improvements over previous methods, there is clear scope for further work. For example, the system could be developed into a multi-frame system by re-using the generated GMM model as prior for consecutive frames. This would directly result in lower computational cost and could gain a higher frame rate and real-time capability of the algorithm. However, this approach demands for an intelligent algorithm that is capable of maintaining or updating the prior GMM. This might be worth a future investigation.

Acknowledgements. This work was partially supported by the European Commission through the Horizon 2020 Programme, call H2020-ICT-2014-1, Grant agreement no. 645376.

References

1. Andrearczyk, V., Whelan, P.F.: Using filter banks in convolutional neural networks for texture classification. Pattern Recognition Letters, abs/1601.02919 (2016). http://arxiv.org/abs/1601.02919
2. Bischof, H., Grabner, H., Rot, P.M., Grabner, M.: Autonomous learning of a robust background model for change detection. In: Ferryman, J.M. (ed.) IEEE International Workshop on Performance Evaluation of Tracking and Surveillance (PETS 2006), pp. 39–46. IEEE (2006)
3. Bormann, R., Fischer, J., Arbeiter, G., Weisshardt, F., Verl, A.: A visual dirt detection system for mobile service robots. In: 7th German Conference on Robotics, Proceedings of ROBOTIK 2012, pp. 1–6 (2012)
4. Bormann, R., Hampp, J., Hägele, M.: New brooms sweep clean-an autonomous robotic cleaning assistant for professional office cleaning. In: 2015 IEEE International Conference on Robotics and Automation (ICRA), pp. 4470–4477 (2015)
5. Bormann, R., Weisshardt, F., Arbeiter, G., Fischer, J.: Autonomous dirt detection for cleaning in office environments. In: Proceedings - IEEE International Conference on Robotics and Automation, pp. 1260–1267 (2013)
6. Cimpoi, M., Maji, S., Vedaldi, A.: Deep filter banks for texture recognition and segmentation. In: Proceedings of the IEEE Conference on Computer Vision and Pattern Recognition CVPR (2015)
7. Drews, P., Núñez, P., Rocha, R.P., Campos, M., Dias, J.: Novelty detection and segmentation based on Gaussian mixture models: a case study in 3D robotic laser mapping. Robot. Auton. Syst. 61, 1696–1709 (2013)
8. Gatys, L.A., Ecker, A.S., Bethge, M.: Texture synthesis and the controlled generation of natural stimuli using convolutional neural networks. CoRR abs/1505.07376 (2015). http://arxiv.org/abs/1505.07376
9. Hou, X., Zhang, L.: Saliency detection: a spectral residual approach. In: Proceedings of the IEEE Computer Society Conference on Computer Vision and Pattern Recognition, pp. 1–8 (2007)
10. Jain, A.K.: Fundamentals of Digital Image Processing. Prentice-Hall Inc., Upper Saddle River (1989)
11. Pimentel, M.A.F., Clifton, D.A., Clifton, L., Tarassenko, L.: A review of novelty detection. Sig. Process. 99, 215–249 (2014)
12. Potapova, E., Zillich, M., Vincze, M.: Attention-driven segmentation of cluttered 3D scenes. In: 2012 21st International Conference on Pattern Recognition (ICPR), pp. 3610–3613 (2012)
13. Potapova, E., Zillich, M., Vincze, M.: Local 3D symmetry for visual saliency in 2.5D point clouds. In: Asian Conference on Computer Vision, pp. 434–445 (2013)
14. Ren, J., Vlachos, T.: Detection and recovery of film dirt for archive restoration applications. In: 2007 IEEE International Conference on Image Processing, pp. IV–21. IEEE (2007)
15. Wechtitsch, S., Schallauer, P.: Robust detection of single-frame defects in archived film. In: International Conference on Pattern Recognition (ICPR), pp. 2647–2650 (2012)

Wind Disturbance Rejection in Position Control of Unmanned Helicopter by Nonlinear Damping

Xiaorui Zhu$^{(\boxtimes)}$ (iD), Lu Yin (iD), and Fucheng Deng (iD)

Harbin Institute of Technology (Shenzhen),
Shenzhen, Guangdong 518055, China
xiaoruizhu@hit.edu.cn

Abstract. This paper presents a new design of a Lyapunov-redesigned control system for large horizontal wind disturbance rejection on a small-scale unmanned autonomous helicopter (UAH). In this paper, the wind disturbance cannot be treated as small perturbations around the equilibrium state any more. Instead, wind disturbances are considered as force/moment disturbances in the state equation. The force/moment caused by the wind can be estimated by the experimental data obtained in the wind tunnel. The whole control system consists of a nominal system controller and a wind disturbance controller. The nominal system controller is designed with back-stepping algorithm while the wind disturbance controller is designed with nonlinear damping algorithm. The nonlinear damping is introduced to ensure that the whole system has a uniformly bounded solution under uncertain large horizontal wind disturbances. Both longitudinal and lateral wind disturbances are considered in the simulation. The simulation results show the wind disturbances are well rejected and the proposed method can be effective for the position control of UAH in windy environment.

Keywords: UAH · Position control · Wind disturbance rejection · Backstepping algorithm · Nonlinear damping

1 Introduction

Unmanned autonomous helicopter (UAH) has been widely used in variety of areas [1]. In the last decades, there is a growing worldwide attention in the field of small-scale UAHs. Autonomous flight control of UAH is essential for the applications in complex environments. This topic has been constantly active both in industry and academia.

Numerous controller design methods have been proposed in last decades. Generally, most of the controller designs are based on model-based-control techniques. Advanced linear control methods like LQG-based controller [2], PD-PID controller [3] are proposed in recent years. However, the stability and robustness of linear methods are not satisfying in complex environments due to the inherent approximate linearization in these methods. Based on nonlinear helicopter system model, many nonlinear control methods have also been reported, such as sliding mode [4], fuzzy gain-scheduling [5], nonlinear model predictive control [6] and backstepping method [7]. The backstepping method could effectively enable systematic and structured

© Springer International Publishing AG 2017
M. Liu et al. (Eds.): ICVS 2017, LNCS 10528, pp. 590–599, 2017.
DOI: 10.1007/978-3-319-68345-4_52

controller design, especially for the UAH with upper triangle form characteristics of state equation. Furthermore, A few research groups have tried non-model-based control strategies. A neural network-based tracking controller [8] was developed for an unmanned helicopter system with guaranteed global stability in the presence of uncertain system dynamics. Similarly, a reinforcement learning algorithm [9] was proposed for autonomous flight control system, which did not require an exact model of the system. However, these methods all depend on plenty of data from pilot experience, which is not applicable for many scenarios such as windy environments.

Practically, large wind disturbances have become one of the main challenges especially for outdoor applications. Only a few literatures have focused on this subject so far. A sensor was applied to estimate the wind disturbance and the nonlinear feedforward controller was designed to attenuate the vertical and horizontal wind disturbance [10]. An constrained finite time optimal controller (CFTOC) was used to operate an unmanned quadrotor helicopter under severe wind conditions [11]. Some researchers use the active wind gust disturbance compensation method to attenuate large wind disturbance [12–14]. The information of disturbance is obtained by different disturbance observers such as high gain state observer [12], extended state observer [13], Kalman state estimator [14]. However, the observation-based approaches sometimes may introduce inaccurate observations. A new hybrid control architecture [15] was proposed taking advantage of the direct force/moment compensation based on the wind-tunnel experimental data. But the force and moment may not be computed correctly due to the variety of the real condition. Therefore, in this paper, a new control system is designed considering uncertain and large wind disturbances based on the hybrid architecture. Firstly, we design a backstepping controller for the nominal system. And then we adopt nonlinear damping technique to design the wind-rejection part.

The organization of this paper is arranged as follows. Section 2 illustrates the control system design. Section 3 shows the simulation results, and Sect. 4 concludes this paper.

2 Control System Design

2.1 Nonlinear System Model

The six-freedom degree rigid body dynamics [16, 17] are presented as,

$$\dot{\xi}^I = V^I \tag{1}$$

$$V^I = RV^B \tag{2}$$

$$\dot{V}^B = V^B \times \Omega^B + F^B/m + \hat{g} \tag{3}$$

$$J\dot{\Omega}^B = -\Omega^B \times J\Omega^B + M^B \tag{4}$$

where $V^B = (u, v, w)^T$ and $\Omega^B = (p, q, r)^T$ are linear velocity vector and angular velocity vector of the helicopter in the body frame, respectively. J is the inertial matrix; m is the mass of the helicopter; $F^B = [F_x, F_y, F_z]$ is the vector of the external forces and $M^B = [L_m, R_m, N_m]$ is the vector of the external moments. The external forces and moments are assumed acting on the center of gravity of the helicopter. R is the rotation with respect to the attitude angle, and $\hat{g}$ is gravitational vector in the body frame.

The main rotor and fly-bar flapping dynamics represents the relationships between the servo actuator outputs δ_{lon}, δ_{lat}, δ_{ped}, δ_{col} and main rotor flapping angles a_1, b_1, rotor flapping angles c, d. Servo actuator dynamics [18] show the relationships between servo actuator inputs u_{lon}, u_{lat}, u_{col}, u_{ped} and servo actuator outputs.

2.2 Hybrid Control Architecture

The hybrid control architecture proposed by our group previously is applied to achieve attenuation of uncertain large horizontal wind disturbances, Fig. 1 [15].

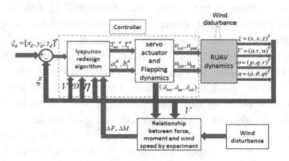

Fig. 1. The block diagram of the proposed control architecture

The nonlinear model of UAH presented in Sect. 2.1 is defined as the nominal system. The force/moment vector $(\Delta F, \Delta M)$ is assumed as the disturbance term including uncertain variables caused by wind disturbances which can be used as an extra input, rather than a small perturbation under a small horizontal wind disturbances. In this case, the disturbance term satisfies the matching condition of Lyapunov redesign. The nominal desired force/moment vector (F^d, M^d) is designed using backstepping algorithm without considering the wind disturbance. A nonlinear damping term (f_c, m_c) is designed to attenuate the wind disturbance term (F^d, M^d). The nonlinear damping term is then fed into the backstepping algorithm to guarantee that the small-scale UAH can be bounded around the desired position in finite time.

2.3 Force/Moment Vector of Wind Disturbances

The force/moment caused by wind can be estimated as follows [15]:

$$F_x = a_{333}\delta_{lat}^3\delta_{lon}^3\delta_{wind}^3 + a_{332}\delta_{lat}^3\delta_{lon}^3\delta_{wind}^2 + \cdots + a_{330}\delta_{lat}^3\delta_{lon}^3\delta_{wind}^0$$
$$+ a_{323}\delta_{lat}^3\delta_{lon}^2\delta_{wind}^3 + a_{322}\delta_{lat}^3\delta_{lon}^2\delta_{wind}^2 + \cdots + a_{320}\delta_{lat}^3\delta_{lon}^2\delta_{wind}^0 \cdots \tag{5}$$
$$+ a_{003}\delta_{lat}^0\delta_{lon}^0\delta_{wind}^3 + a_{002}\delta_{lat}^0\delta_{lon}^0\delta_{wind}^2 + \cdots + a_{000}\delta_{lat}^0\delta_{lon}^0\delta_{wind}^0$$

$$F_y = b_{333}\delta_{lat}^3\delta_{lon}^3\delta_{wind}^3 + b_{332}\delta_{lat}^3\delta_{lon}^3\delta_{wind}^2 + \cdots + b_{330}\delta_{lat}^3\delta_{lon}^3\delta_{wind}^0$$
$$+ b_{323}\delta_{lat}^3\delta_{lon}^2\delta_{wind}^3 + b_{322}\delta_{lat}^3\delta_{lon}^2\delta_{wind}^2 + \cdots + b_{320}\delta_{lat}^3\delta_{lon}^2\delta_{wind}^0 \cdots \tag{6}$$
$$+ b_{003}\delta_{lat}^0\delta_{lon}^0\delta_{wind}^3 + b_{002}\delta_{lat}^0\delta_{lon}^0\delta_{wind}^2 + \cdots + b_{000}\delta_{lat}^0\delta_{lon}^0\delta_{wind}^0$$

$$F_z = p_{66}\cdot\delta_{col}^6\delta_{wind}^6 + p_{65}\cdot\delta_{col}^6\delta_{wind}^5 + \cdots + p_{60}\cdot\delta_{col}^6\delta_{wind}^0\cdots$$
$$+ p_{06}\cdot\delta_{col}^0\delta_{wind}^6 + p_{05}\cdot\delta_{col}^0\delta_{wind}^5 + \cdots + p_{00}\cdot\delta_{col}^0\delta_{wind}^0 \tag{7}$$

where F_x, F_z, F_z are the forces in different axes, the inputs are cyclic pith input δ_{lon}, lateral cyclic pitch input δ_{lat} and wind velocity δ_{wind}.

The wind tunnel experiment we did before [15] can provide the necessary input data such as δ_{lon}, δ_{lat}, δ_{col} and δ_{wind}, and the resulting force F_x, F_y, F_z. Then we can use means of least squares to identify all the parameters above. The moment on the three axis orientations can be also obtained using the same techniques.

The changes of these forces caused by wind disturbance can be represented as,

$$\Delta F = [\, Fx_w - Fx \quad Fy_w - Fy \quad Fz_w - Fz\,]^T \tag{8}$$

where Fz_w Fy_w Fz_w denotes the force under wind disturbance, F_x, F_y, F_z denote the forces without wind disturbance which means $\delta_{wind} = 0$.

Since the coefficients are known constant, we can treat the wind velocity input δ_{wind} as unknown terms.

$$\Delta F_x = \vec{\Gamma}_{Fx}\cdot\vec{\delta}_x \tag{9}$$

where $\vec{\Gamma}_{Fx} = \left[\, a_{333}\delta_{lon}^3\delta_{lat}^3 \quad \cdots \quad a_{ijk}\delta_{lon}^i\delta_{lat}^j \quad \cdots \quad a_{001}\delta_{lon}^0\delta_{lat}^0 \,\right]_{1\times48}, \vec{\delta}_x = [\,\vec{\delta}_{wind} \quad \cdots$

$\vec{\delta}_{wind}]_{1\times16}^T$ and $\vec{\delta}_{wind} = \left[\, \delta_{wind}^3 \quad \delta_{wind}^2 \quad \delta_{wind}^1 \,\right]$. The force disturbances in y and z axes can be denoted similarly. In this way, we can get:

$$\Delta F = [\Delta F_x \quad \Delta F_y \quad \Delta F_z]^T = \left[\, \vec{\Gamma}_{Fx}\cdot\vec{\delta}_x \quad \vec{\Gamma}_{Fy}\cdot\vec{\delta}_y \quad \vec{\Gamma}_{Fz}\cdot\vec{\delta}_z \,\right]^T = \vec{\Gamma}_F\vec{\delta}_F \tag{10}$$

In the objective system of this paper, a gyroscope fixed on the tail of the helicopter can attenuate the moment on the z axis. Therefore, with respect to the moment part, we only consider the moment attenuation on the x and y axes. In a similar way, the moment disturbance can be represented as,

$$\Delta M = [\Delta M_x \quad \Delta M_y \quad 0]^T = \left[\, \vec{\Gamma}_{Mx}\cdot\vec{\delta}_x \quad \vec{\Gamma}_{My}\cdot\vec{\delta}_y \quad 0 \,\right]^T = \vec{\Gamma}_M\vec{\delta}_M \tag{11}$$

2.4   Backstepping Control with Nonlinear Damping

In this part, the backstepping algorithm is designed to incorporate the nominal control law and the nonlinear damping term for the helicopter to attenuate uncertain large horizontal wind disturbances, Fig. 1.

First, the nominal control law via backstepping algorithm without considering $(\Delta F, \Delta M)$ is designed [18]. The first Lyapunov function can be chosen as,

$$W_1 = 1/2(\xi^I - \xi_d^I)^T(\xi^I - \xi_d^I). \tag{12}$$

Denote $z_0 = \xi^I - \xi_d^I$ and if the desired velocity V_d^I satisfies the following equation:

$$V_d^I = -\alpha z_0 = R V_d^B \tag{13}$$

where α is a controller parameter and $\alpha > 0$, the derivative of the first Lyapunov function is negative definite.

Denote the error between the actual velocity and the desired velocity as $z_1 = V^I - V_d^I = R(V^B - V_d^B)$, we can get the actual derivative of the first Lyapunov function as,

$$\dot{W}_1 = -\alpha z_0^T z_0 + z_0^T z_1 \tag{14}$$

The second Lyapunov function is introduced as,

$$W_2 = 1/2 z_1^T z_1 \tag{15}$$

The time derivative of Eq. (15) can be derived as,

$$\dot{W}_2 = z_1^T R(F^B/m + \hat{g} + V^B \times \Omega^B + \alpha V^B) \tag{16}$$

In order to make $\dot{W}_1 + \dot{W}_2 \leq 0$, we can introduce another controller parameter β and construct an equation satisfies,

$$V^B \times \Omega^B = -\alpha V^B - \beta \Omega^B \tag{17}$$

According to Eq. (17), we get the desired angular velocity Ω_d^B:

$$\Omega_d^B = -\alpha(S(V^B) + \beta I)^{-1} V^B \tag{18}$$

Denote the error between the actual angular velocity and the desired angular velocity as $z_2 = \Omega^B - \Omega_d^B$, and we can obtain the actual derivative of the second Lyapunov function as,

$$\dot{W}_2 = -z_1^T z_0 - z_1^T z_1 + z_1^T R S(V_d^B) z_2 \tag{19}$$

Then, F^d is chosen such that:

$$\begin{cases} z_1^T F^d / m = z_1^T (\beta \Omega^B - \hat{g} - R^T(\xi^I - \xi_d^I) - (V^B - V_d^B))(z_1 \neq 0) \\ F^d / m = -\hat{g}(z_1 = 0) \end{cases} \tag{20}$$

Substituting Eqs. (18) and (20) into Eq. (19), when the angular velocity achieves the desired value, the derivative of the Lyapunov function becomes:

$$\dot{W}_1 + \dot{W}_2 = -\alpha z_0^T z_0 - z_1^T z_1 \leq 0 \tag{21}$$

Next, we choose the third Lyapunov function:

$$W_3 = 1/2 z_2^T z_2 \tag{22}$$

Take the time derivative:

$$\dot{W}_3 = z_2^T (J^{-1}(-\dot{\Omega}^B \times J\dot{\Omega}^B + M) - \dot{\Omega}_d^B) \tag{23}$$

In order to make the overall Lyapunov function $W = W_1 + W_2 + W_3$ satisfies $\dot{W} \leq 0$, the desired moment should be:

$$M^d = J(\dot{\Omega}_d^B - S^T(V_d^B)V^B - z_2) + \Omega^B \times J\Omega^B \tag{24}$$

Then we can verify that:

$$\dot{W} = \dot{W}_1 + \dot{W}_2 + \dot{W}_3 = -\alpha z_0^T z_0 - z_1^T z_1 - z_2^T z_2 \leq 0 \tag{25}$$

For the overall system, since we already obtain the nominal desired force/moment (F^d, M^d) that can stabilize the nominal system. For the next step, we will design a control component (f_c, m_c) according to nonlinear damping to ensure the boundness of the overall system.

The overall control law can be described as,

$$F^B = F^d + f_c, \quad M^B = M^d + m_c \tag{26}$$

Then the derivative of the overall Lyapunov function W satisfies:

$$\begin{aligned} \dot{W} &= (-\alpha z_0^T z_0 + z_0^T z_1) \\ &+ z_1^T R(F^d / m + \hat{g} + V^B \times \Omega^B + \alpha V^B) + z_1^T R(f_c + \Delta F / m) \\ &+ z_2^T [J^{-1}(-\dot{\Omega}^B \times J\dot{\Omega}^B + M^d) - \dot{\Omega}_d^B] + z_2^T J^{-1}(m_c + \Delta M) \end{aligned} \tag{27}$$

Defining $w_1^T = z_1^T R/m, w_2^T = z_2^T J^{-1}$, and substituting Eq. (20), Eq. (24) into Eq. (27) result in:

$$\dot{W} = -az_0^T z_0 - z_1^T z_1 - z_2^T z_2 + w_1^T (f_c + \Delta F) + w_2^T (m_c + \Delta M) \tag{28}$$

Substituting Eq. (10)–(11) into Eq. (28), we can get:

$$\dot{W} = -az_0^T z_0 - z_1^T z_1 - z_2^T z_2 + w_1^T (f_c + \vec{\Gamma}_F \vec{\delta}_F) + w_2^T (m_c + \vec{\Gamma}_M \vec{\delta}_M) \tag{29}$$

where $f_c = -k_{fc} w_1 \left\| \vec{\Gamma}_F \right\|_2^2, k_{fc} > 0; m_c = -k_{mc} w_2 \left\| \vec{\Gamma}_M \right\|_2^2, k_{mc} > 0$, we can obtain:

$$\dot{W} \leq -az_0^T z_0 - z_1^T z_1 - z_2^T z_2 - (k_{fc} \|w_1\|_2^2 \left\| \vec{\Gamma}_F \right\|_2^2 - \|w_1\|_2 \left\| \vec{\Gamma}_F \right\|_2 K_F)$$
$$- (k_{mc} \|w_2\|_2^2 \left\| \vec{\Gamma}_M \right\|_2^2 - \|w_2\|_2 \left\| \vec{\Gamma}_M \right\|_2 K_M) \tag{30}$$

where K_F, K_M are unknown upper bound on $\left\| \vec{\delta}_F \right\|, \left\| \vec{\delta}_M \right\|$. It is obviously:

$$\dot{W} \leq -(a-1)z_0^T z_0 - \|X\|_2^2 + \frac{K_F^2}{4k_{fc}} + \frac{K_M^2}{4k_{mc}} \leq -(a-1)z_0^T z_0, \tag{31}$$

where $X = [z_0 \ z_1 \ z_2]^T$, $a > 1$, Since $\|X\|_2^2 \geq \frac{K_F^2}{4k_{fc}} + \frac{K_M^2}{4k_{mc}}$

This shows that the solutions of the state z_0, z_1, z_2 are uniformly bounded around the origin point. So it is clear that in finite time, the position, linear velocity and angular velocity of the UAH can approach a bounded set around the desired ones.

After deriving the reference force and moment (F^B, M^B), we can get the control inputs through main rotor, fly-bar flapping dynamics function and servo actuator dynamics function.

3   Simulation and Discussion

In this section, the proposed control system was simulated in MATALAB/ SIMULINK@. Both longitude and lateral wind disturbances are simulated. The initial position is set at (−0.5 m, 0.5 m, 0.5 m) while the desired position is the origin. Gust wind from 0 (longitude) and 270 (lateral) degree directions are simulated respectively.

Case A: There is no wind disturbance at the beginning of 10 s and the last 10 s, and there is a constant wind velocity (varying from 2 m/s to 8 m/s) during 10 s and 20 s.

Figure 2 shows the position regulation of the helicopter under the longitude wind disturbance. The chosen parameters are $\alpha = 2.5$, $\beta = 3$. Figure 3 shows the position regulation of the helicopter under the lateral wind disturbance with the controller parameters are $\alpha = 2.5$, $\beta = 3$. Figure 4 shows the control inputs when the longitude velocity of short-period wind is 6 m/s.

Case B: Wind disturbances exist during the whole simulation period (30 s), and the wind velocity is 2 m/s, 4 m/s, 6 m/s, 8 m/s respectively. Figure 6 shows the position regulation of the helicopter under the longitude wind disturbance. The chosen parameters are $\alpha = 2.5$, $\beta = 3$. Figure 5 shows the position regulation of the helicopter under the lateral wind disturbance where the chosen parameters are $\alpha = 2.5$, $\beta = 3$. Figure 7 shows the control inputs when the lateral velocity of long-lasting wind is 6 m/s.

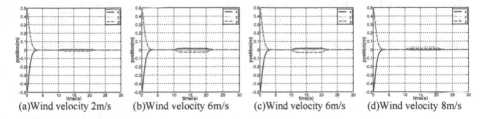

(a)Wind velocity 2m/s (b)Wind velocity 6m/s (c)Wind velocity 6m/s (d)Wind velocity 8m/s

Fig. 2. Performance of the position control in Case A with longitude wind disturbance

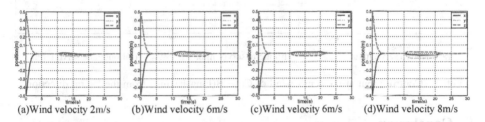

(a)Wind velocity 2m/s (b)Wind velocity 6m/s (c)Wind velocity 6m/s (d)Wind velocity 8m/s

Fig. 3. Performance of the position control in Case A with lateral wind disturbance

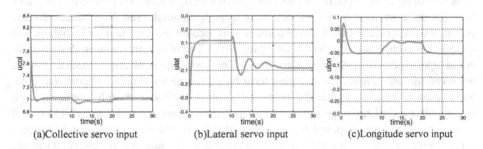

(a)Collective servo input (b)Lateral servo input (c)Longitude servo input

Fig. 4. Control input at the 6 m/s wind of Case A (Gust) from the longitude direction

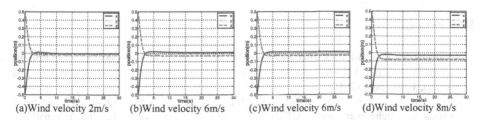

(a)Wind velocity 2m/s (b)Wind velocity 6m/s (c)Wind velocity 6m/s (d)Wind velocity 8m/s

Fig. 5. Performance of the position control in Case B with lateral wind disturbance

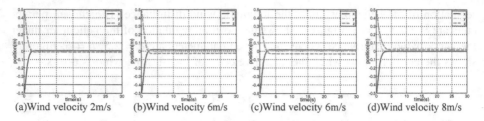

(a)Wind velocity 2m/s   (b)Wind velocity 6m/s   (c)Wind velocity 6m/s   (d)Wind velocity 8m/s

Fig. 6. Performance of the position control in Case B with longitude wind disturbance

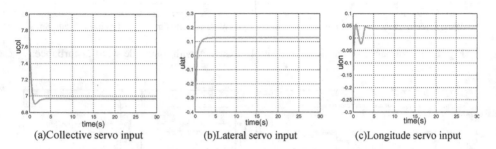

(a)Collective servo input   (b)Lateral servo input   (c)Longitude servo input

Fig. 7. Control input at the 6 m/s wind of Case B(long-lasting) from the lateral direction

4   Conclusion

This architecture incorporates a theoretic control design and experiment-based force/moment compensation in order to attenuate large horizontal wind disturbances. In this paper, the experiment-based force/moment was treated as uncertain perturbation and cannot be compensated directly and precisely. The theoretic control design took advantage of the backstepping algorithms. The force/moment compensation can be achieved through a nonlinear damping term based on the wind tunnel experiment data. Simulation results show that the proposed control method can well attenuate large horizontal wind disturbance to the desired position. Compare with the hybrid control architecture [15] we proposed before, when the force and moment may not be computed correctly due to the variety of the real condition, the new control system designed in this paper can still work on well. In the future, the authors will deal with the practical flight trial with proposed controller on a small scaled unmanned helicopter.

References

1. Nonami, K., Kendoul, F., Suzuki, S., Wang, W., Nakazawa, D.: Autonomous Flying Robots: Unmanned Aerial Vehicles and Micro Aerial Vehicles. Springer Science and Business Media, Heidelberg (2010)
2. El Ferik, S., Omar, H.M., Koesdwiady, A.B., Al-Yazidi, N.M.: LQG-based control of unmanned helicopter using OKID-based identification approach. In: International Multi-Conference on Systems, Signals and Devices, pp. 1–6 (2013)

3. Pounds, P.E.I., Dollar, A.M.: Stability of helicopters in compliant contact under PD-PID control. IEEE Trans. Robot. **30**, 1472–1486 (2014)
4. Zeghlache, S., Saigaa, D., Kara, K., Harrag, A., Bouguerra, A.: Fuzzy sliding mode control with chattering elimination for a quadrotor helicopter in vertical flight. In: Corchado, E., Snášel, V., Abraham, A., Woźniak, M., Graña, M., Cho, S.-B. (eds.) HAIS 2012. LNCS, vol. 7208, pp. 125–136. Springer, Heidelberg (2012). doi:10.1007/978-3-642-28942-2_12
5. Kadmiry, B., Bergsten, P., Driankov, D.: Autonomous helicopter control using fuzzy gain scheduling. In: 2001 Proceedings IEEE International Conference on Robotics and Automation, vol. 2983, pp. 2980–2985 (2001)
6. Zhang, J.: Fast model predictive control of 3-DOF helicopter. Inf. Control **38**, 5924–5929 (2014)
7. Roy, T.K.: Position control of a small helicopter using robust backstepping. In: International Conference on Electrical and Computer Engineering, pp. 787–790 (2012)
8. Jiang, Y., Yang, C., Dai, S.-l., Ren, B.: Deterministic learning enhanced neutral network control of unmanned helicopter. Int. J. Adv. Rob. Syst. **13** (2016). doi:10.1177/1729881416671118
9. Lee, D.J., Bang, H.: Model-free LQ control for unmanned helicopters using reinforcement learning. In: International Conference on Control, Automation and Systems, pp. 117–120 (2011)
10. Bisgaard, M., Cour-Harbo, A.L., Danapalasingam, K.A.: Nonlinear feedforward control for wind disturbance rejection on autonomous helicopter. In: IEEE/RSJ International Conference on Intelligent Robots and Systems, pp. 1078–1083 (2010)
11. Alexis, K., Nikolakopoulos, G., Tzes, A.: Constrained optimal attitude control of a quadrotor helicopter subject to wind-gusts: experimental studies. In: American Control Conference, pp. 4451–4455 (2010)
12. Zhang, H., Huang, J., Meng, Z., Xu, W.: An active wind gust rejection controller for an autonomous helicopter. In: Proceedings of 2013 2nd International Conference on Measurement, Information and Control, pp. 742–746 (2013)
13. Martini, A., Leonard, F., Abba, G.: Robust nonlinear control and stability analysis of a 7DOF model-scale helicopter under vertical wind gust. In: IEEE/RSJ International Conference on Intelligent Robots and Systems, pp. 354–359 (2008)
14. Cheviron, T., Chriette, A., Plestan, F.: Robust control of an Autonomous reduced scale helicopter in presence of wind gusts. In: AIAA Guidance, Navigation, and Control Conference and Exhibit (2006)
15. Zhu, X., Zeng, W., Li, Z., Zheng, C.: A new hybrid control architecture to attenuate large horizontal wind disturbance for a small-scale unmanned helicopter. Int. J. Adv. Robot. Syst. **9**, 1 (2012)
16. Nelson, R.C.: Flight Stability and Automatic Control. WCB/McGraw-Hill, New York (1989)
17. Prouty, R.W.: Helicopter Performance, Stability, and Control. Krieger Publishing Company, Malabar (1995)
18. Ahmed, B., Pota, H.R.: Flight control of a rotary wing UAV using adaptive backstepping. In: IEEE International Conference on Control and Automation, pp. 1780–1785 (2010)

3D Vision/Fusion

Calibration of a Structured Light Measurement System Using Binary Shape Coding

Hai Zeng[1,2], Suming Tang[1(✉)], Zhan Song[1], Feifei Gu[1], and Ziyu Huang[2]

[1] Guangdong Provincial Key Laboratory of Robotics and Intelligent System, Shenzhen Institutes of Advanced Technology, Chinese Academy of Sciences, Shenzhen 518055, China
{hai.zeng,sm.tang,zhan.song,ff.gu}@siat.ac.cn
[2] School of Electrical Engineering and Information, Southwest Petroleum University, Chengdu 610500, China

Abstract. In this paper, a calibration method for structured light system is proposed, which is based on pseudo-random coding theory to generate binary shape-coded pattern. In this method, the checkerboard and binary shape-coded patterns are captured by the camera of the structured light system method. Based on the geometric feature of binary shape-coded pattern, a feature point detector is designed. Then, the feature points in the binary geometric image are extracted, and the topological structure is constructed. After that, the pattern elements are extracted with the affine transformation theory and bilinear interpolation algorithm. The identification of pattern elements is modeled as a supervised classification problem, and the convolutional neural network technique is adopted to recognize the pattern elements by collecting a large number of training samples. Thus, the code-words of the feature points are confirmed. According to the projective transformation principle, the correspondence between the camera image plane and projector image plane is determined. Then, the corner points in the camera image plane are transformed into the projector image plane with the correspondence. Thereby the camera and projector are calibrated with Zhang's calibration method, and the system calibration is achieved. The experimental results show that the calibration accuracy can reach about 0.2 pixels with the proposed method and the quality of reconstructed surface is great.

Keywords: Binary shape coding · Structured light system · Calibration · Projective transformation

1 Introduction

3D measurement technique based on structured light has many advantages, such as non-contact, flexibility, high precision and long working distance, which is widely used in the fields of industrial inspection, machine manufacturing, entertainment, human body scanning, medical surgery [1, 2]. A basic structured light system is composed of a camera and a projector, which can be seen as a reverse camera. Thus, a structured light

© Springer International Publishing AG 2017
M. Liu et al. (Eds.): ICVS 2017, LNCS 10528, pp. 603–614, 2017.
DOI: 10.1007/978-3-319-68345-4_53

system can be seen as a binocular stereo vision system. However, the system must be calibrated before the measurement, and the calibration accuracy can affect the measurement precision. The purpose of system calibration is to obtain the intrinsic parameters of the camera and projector and the relative position between them. After system calibration, the correspondences obtained by decoding the coded patterns can be transformed into 3D information with the calibrated parameters and triangulation principle, thereby 3D reconstruction is realized.

Since a projector has the same imaging model as a camera and there are many accurate and flexible camera calibration methods [3, 4], the projector can be directly calibrated as a camera. However, it is a programmable illuminant but not an imaging device, which makes it difficult to obtain the image of calibration points from the view of the projector. Normally it projects particular patterns to establish the correspondence of the calibration points and their images in projector, such as a checkerboard, circle and phase patterns. But the coordinates of the projection patterns are obtained with errors, which make the correspondence between calibration points and their imaging points imprecise, and the imprecise correspondence between the calibration points and their projector images makes it difficult to obtain accurate projector calibration. Thus, it requires calibration methods able to minimize the influence of the imprecise correspondence [5]. At present, there are many research studies conducted to calibrate the structured light measurement system. The calibration methods can be mainly classified into two categories. The first category is to calculating the object world coordinates of projection points by the calibrated camera or other approaches, and then the projection points are used to calibrate the projector [6–9]. In the second category, the phase mapping or active adjustment method is used to obtain the image coordinates of the calibration points in the projector from the camera images, and then the projector can be calibrated in the same way as the camera by using the calibration points and their corresponding projector image points [10–13]. The first category is simple and convenient, but the calibration accuracy of the projector relies on that of camera. The worst projector calibration accuracy is a single order of magnitude lower than the camera. On the contrary, the second category depends less on camera calibration and can achieve higher accuracy, yet its process is complex because it needs to project multiple phase images each time, and phase unwrapping or identification is vulnerable to environment [13].

In this paper, a novel calibration method for structured light system is proposed. Unlike the above two categories of calibration methods, the coordinates of 3-D calibration points in the projector image plane are calculated through establishing the corresponding relation between the camera image plane and projector image plane by projecting a robust binary shape-coded pattern which is generated based on the pseudo-random coding theory. After that, the camera and projector are calibrated simultaneously, and the extrinsic parameters of the structured light system are computed. Based on the reverse projection principle of camera calibration, the calibrated parameters are integrally optimized with the help of pseudo-random coded pattern, and the calibration of the structured light system is accomplished. The rest of the paper is organized as follows. Section 2 describes the calibration model of structured light system. Section 3 introduces the proposed calibration method. Section 4 provides some experimental results to verify the calibration accuracy. Finally, the conclusions are drawn in Sect. 4.

2 System Model

In general, the structured light system can be modeled as camera imaging and projector projection. And based on the stereo vision model, both are simplified as ideal perspective projection transformation, as shown in Fig. 1. The relationship between a 3-D space point and its image points in the camera image plane can be expressed as

$$
s_c \begin{bmatrix} u_c \\ v_c \\ 1 \end{bmatrix} \begin{bmatrix} f_x & \gamma & u_0 \\ 0 & f_y & v_0 \\ 0 & 0 & 1 \end{bmatrix} \begin{bmatrix} r_{11} & r_{12} & r_{13} & t_1 \\ r_{21} & r_{22} & r_{23} & t_2 \\ r_{31} & r_{32} & r_{33} & t_3 \end{bmatrix} \begin{bmatrix} x_w \\ y_w \\ z_w \\ 1 \end{bmatrix} = K_c [R_c \quad T_c] \begin{bmatrix} x_w \\ y_w \\ z_w \\ 1 \end{bmatrix} \tag{1}
$$

where (x_w, y_w, z_w) are the world coordinates of 3-D space point p_w, (u_c, v_c) are the camera image coordinates of p_w, s_c is the scale factor, K_c is the intrinsic parameters matrix of camera, it includes the coordinates of the principal point (u_0, v_0), the focal lengths f_x and f_y along the u and v axes of the image plane, and the parameter γ describing the skewness of two image axes, $[R_c \quad T_c]$ is the extrinsic parameters matrix of camera.

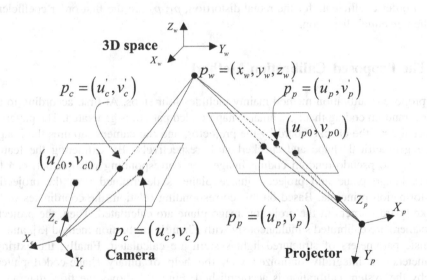

Fig. 1. Schematic diagram of the structured light system model.

Similarly, the projector projection is regarded as the inverse camera imaging, thus can be expressed as

$$
s_p \begin{bmatrix} u_p \\ v_p \\ 1 \end{bmatrix} = K_p [R_p \quad T_p] \begin{bmatrix} x_w \\ y_w \\ z_w \\ 1 \end{bmatrix} \tag{2}
$$

where (u_p, v_p) are the projector image coordinates of 3-D space point p_w, s_p is scale factor, K_p is the intrinsic parameters matrix, $[R_p \quad T_p]$ is extrinsic parameters matrix of projector.

In fact, the actual camera imaging or projector projection is not ideal. It needs to consider the lens distortion on the imaging and projection. Commonly, only first- or second-order distortion model is adopted to correct the radial distortion [7]. Then the relationship between the ideal image points and the actual image points are shown as follows:

$$
\begin{bmatrix} \hat{u} \\ \hat{v} \end{bmatrix} = \begin{bmatrix} u_d + \delta_u \\ v_d + \delta_v \end{bmatrix} = \begin{bmatrix} u_d \\ v_d \end{bmatrix} + \begin{bmatrix} u_r r^2 & u_r r^4 \\ v_r r^2 & v_r r^4 \end{bmatrix} \begin{bmatrix} k_1 \\ k_2 \end{bmatrix} + \begin{bmatrix} 3u_r^2 + v_r^2 & 2u_r v_r \\ 2u_r v_r & u_r^2 + 3v_r^2 \end{bmatrix} \begin{bmatrix} p_1 \\ p_2 \end{bmatrix}
$$

(3)

where $(\hat{u}, \hat{v})$ are the ideal image coordinates, (u_d, v_d) are the actual image coordinates which contain lens distortion, (u_r, v_r) are the relative image coordinates, that is $u_r = u_d - u_0$, $v_r = v_d - v_0$, and $r^2 = u_r^2 + v_r^2$, $\theta = [k_1 \; k_2 \; p_1 \; p_2]$ denotes the radial distortion and tangential distortion, where the coefficients k_1, k_2 are the first- and second-order coefficients for the radial distortion, p_1, p_2 are the first-order coefficients for the tangential distortion.

3   The Proposed Calibration Method

Our proposed calibration method mainly includes four steps. At first, according to the pseudo-random coding theory, a binary shape-coded pattern is generated. The pattern is projected onto the checkerboard by the projector, and the camera captures the images of the geometrical shape and checkerboard, respectively. By extracting the feature points in the pseudo-random coding image, the corresponding relation between the camera image plane and projector image plane is determined with the projective transformation principle. Based on this corresponding relation, the coordinates of the checkerboard corners in the projector image plane are calculated. Then, the projector and camera are calibrated simultaneously with Zhang's calibration method [3], and the extrinsic parameters of structured light system are calculated. Finally, the extrinsic parameters are integrally optimized with the help of binary shape-coded pattern, thereby the system calibration is accomplished. Figure 2 shows the flow diagram of system calibration.

3.1   Pattern Generation and Grid-Point Detection

The binary geometrical pattern is usually based on the pseudo-random array with unique window property. The code-words in the array are represented by geometric primitives. Following the array generating method as described in [14], a pseudorandom array of size 65×63 can be obtained with the window size of 2×2. As shown in Fig. 2, eight geometric primitives are designed to embed into the grid shape with black background. The intersection points of any two orthogonal grid-lines, namely

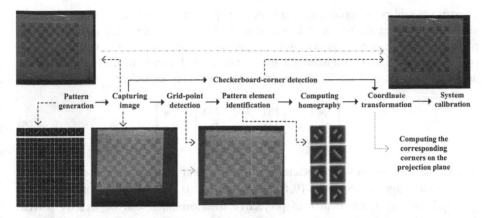

Fig. 2. Flow diagram of the structured light system calibration.

grid-points, are defined as the feature points. The code-word combination of four geometric primitives around one grid-point is viewed as its code-word.

The binary geometrical pattern is projected onto the calibration board with gray-white checkerboard by the projector, and the camera captures the images of geometrical shape and checkerboard respectively by changing the projected pattern into the all-white light. Because the checkerboard and geometrical shape patterns are easily overlapped with each other, as shown in Fig. 2, it is hard to extract the grid-points for traditional corner detection algorithms [15–18]. To solve this problem, an effective grid-point detector is proposed. The captured image is transformed into a grey image. Then, a cross template is designed to conduct the convolution operation with the grey image for the recognition of candidate grid-points. The operation can be expressed as:

$$
H = \sum_{\alpha=-w}^{w} \sum_{\beta=-w}^{w} I(i+\alpha, j+\beta) \\
- \sum_{\gamma=0}^{l} \sum_{\eta=0}^{l} \left(\begin{array}{l} I(i-w+\gamma, j-w+\eta) + I(i-w+\gamma, j+w-\eta) \\ + I(i+w-\gamma, j-w+\eta) + I(i+w-\gamma, j+w-\eta) \end{array} \right) \tag{4}
$$

where I denote the image intensity, w is the radius of cross template and l is set as $w/3$, H measure indicates the sum of image intensity accumulations along the i and j directions at the position. With an empirical threshold value of H, the candidate grid-points with self-centered property can be detected around the true grid-point positions. Since the perfect rotation symmetry is shown at the positions of true grid-points, the false points can be removed with this property. The detail can be found in Ref. [14]. Thus, the true grid-points can be extracted accurately, as shown in Fig. 2.

3.2 Identification of the Pattern Elements

After extracting the grid-points, the coordinates of grid-points can be acquired. Thereby the topological network of all the grid-points can be established. Based on the constructed grid-point topological network, each pattern element can be detected. Then, suppose the object surface is relatively smooth, i.e. the surface patch covered by one pattern element can be approximately viewed as a planar patch. On this the blurred pattern element can be transformed into a normalized image using four grid-points around it. The process can be expressed as the following equation:

$$
\begin{bmatrix} u_{pt} \\ v_{pt} \\ 1 \end{bmatrix} = \begin{bmatrix} p_{11} & p_{12} & p_{13} \\ p_{21} & p_{22} & p_{23} \\ p_{31} & p_{32} & p_{33} \end{bmatrix} \begin{bmatrix} v_{im} \\ u_{im} \\ \mu \end{bmatrix}
\tag{5}
$$

where (u_{pt}, v_{pt}) denotes the detected grid-points, and (u_{im}, v_{im}) represents the four normalized image corner points $(0,0)$, $(a,0)$, (a,b), $(0,b)$. Given four pairs of points (u_{pt}, v_{pt}), (u_{im}, v_{im}), the matrix of projective transformation can be exactly solved. Then, the distorted pattern elements can be projected to the normalized image via bilinear interpolation.

The pattern elements are usually blurred because of the gray-white checkerboard as shown in Fig. 2. To recognize the pattern elements accurately, pattern element recognition is regarded as a supervised classification problem. Because the deep learning technique has excellent performance in deal with such a problem, the convolutional neural networks is adopted to classify the pattern elements. Collecting sufficient pattern element samples is very vital for the training of convolutional neural networks. However, the geometric primitive numbers within one projected pattern are still limited, the database should be expanded to achieve higher discriminating power. The main operation is described as follows: (1) Add Gaussian noise into high-contrast samples; (2) Add random white/black lines into the samples; (3) Conduct small affine transformation; (4) Filter the samples with Gaussian filter.

According to the above operations, a database including sufficient pattern elements can be established. Since the pattern element recognition is similar with handwritten digit recognition problem, and the Lenet-5 [19] is a multi-layer feed-forward neural network with a deep supervised learning architecture, it has excellent performance in deal with such a problem. Therefore, the Lenet-5 is adopted to classify the pattern elements. With the convolutional neural networks, high recognition rate can be obtained in the pattern element identification algorithm.

3.3 System Calibration

Based on the multi-view geometry theory, the process from the projected pattern to calibration board to captured image can be viewed as projective transformation between the projector image plane and camera image plane, which can be expressed as

$$
m_p = \sigma H m_c, \text{ and } H = \begin{bmatrix} h_{11} & h_{12} & h_{13} \\ h_{21} & h_{22} & h_{23} \\ h_{31} & h_{32} & 1 \end{bmatrix}
\tag{6}
$$

where m_p and m_c are the homogeneous coordinates of the grid-points in the projector image plane and camera image plane respectively, σ is a non-zero scale factor, H is the homography matrix, it can be calculated with the coordinates of $l(l \geq 4)$ pairs of non-collinear grid-points between two image planes.

With the homography matrix H, the coordinates of the checkerboard corners in projector image plane are determined. Then, the projector and camera can be calibrated simultaneously with Zhang's calibration method. Thereby the intrinsic and extrinsic parameters of the camera and projector are obtained. Using the extrinsic parameters of the camera and projector, the extrinsic parameters of the structured light system, i.e., the rotation matrix R_s and transformation matrix T_s, can be calculated according to the following equation.

$$\begin{cases} R_s = R_c R_p^{-1} \\ T_s = T_c - R_s T_p \end{cases} \tag{7}$$

where (R_c, T_c) and (R_p, T_p) represent the extrinsic parameters of the camera and projector respectively.

Because the results calculated from Eq. (7) has large error, it is necessary to optimize the parameters with the inverse projection principle of the camera calibration, which can be expressed as follows

$$e_c = m_c - g^{-1}\left(m'_p, K_c, \theta_c, R_c, T_c, K_p, \theta_p\right) \tag{8}$$

where m_c is the real coordinates of the grid-points in the camera image plane, $g^{-1}()$ denotes the transformation from the projector image plane to camera image plane, m'_p is the ideal coordinates of the grid-points in the projector image plane, K_c and θ_c denotes the intrinsic parameters and distortion coefficients of the camera respectively, R_c and T_c are the rotation matrix and transformation matrix of the camera, and $R_c = R_s R_p^{-T}$, $T_c = T_s + R_s T_p$, K_p and θ_p express the intrinsic parameters and distortion coefficients of the projector, respectively.

According to Eq. (8), the following objective function for optimization can be obtained

$$f(R_s, T_s) = \frac{1}{2} \sum_{i,j} e_c^T e_c \tag{9}$$

The optimization of Eq. (9) is a non-linear least square problem, which can be solved with the Levenberg-Marquart algorithm by setting the results of R_s and T_s calculated from Eq. (7) as the initial values. Therefore, the optimization of the intrinsic and extrinsic parameters of the structured light system can be achieved.

4 Experimental Results

The experimental setup is consisted of one projector with 1920×1080 pixels resolution and one digital camera with 5184×3456 pixels resolution, as shown in Fig. 3. To obtained high calibration accuracy with the proposed calibration method, the

Fig. 3. The experimental setup.

calibration board with checkers, and the size of each checker is 20×20 mm^2. Besides, the size of each geometric primitive in the projected pattern is 16×16 pixels. The working distance of the system is about 800 mm. The binary shape-coded pattern is projected onto the calibration board with gray-white checkerboard by the projector, and the camera captures the images of the geometrical shape and checkerboard respectively by changing the projected pattern into the all-white light. By capturing 15 groups of calibration images, the system can be calibrated with the proposed calibration method. Tables 1 and 2 show the calibration results of the system.

Table 1. Calibration results of intrinsic parameters of the structured light system

Device	Intrinsic parameters							
	f_u	f_v	u_0	v_0	k_1	k_2	p_1	p_2
Camera	11997.68	12043.56	2551.71	1534.49	0.78925	−25.101	−0.0156	−0.0027
Projector	4386.26	4387.67	914.91	893.91	0.01589	11.702	−0.0052	−0.0230

Table 2. Calibration results of extrinsic parameters of the structured light system

Extrinsic parameters					
omc_1	omc_2	omc_3	t_1	t_2	t_3
−0.02665	−0.30583	0.02461	299.8595	−74.4135	65.7907

In order to analyze the accuracy of system calibration, the reverse projection error of the camera and projector are calculated, as shown in Fig. 5(a) and (b), respectively. From these two pictures, it can be seen that the reverse projection error of the camera and projector are about less than 0.2 pixels. To further analyze the calibration error, the mean error and standard deviation of the camera and projector are computed. The results for the camera are 0.25 pixels and 0.16 pixels separately, those for the projector are 0.28 pixels and 0.19 pixels respectively. From these results, we can see that our calibration method has great performance in the calibration accuracy (Fig. 4).

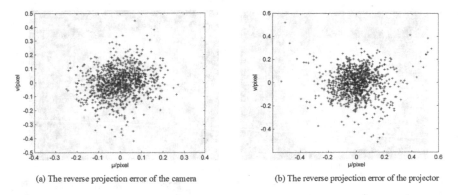

(a) The reverse projection error of the camera   (b) The reverse projection error of the projector

Fig. 4. The reverse projection error of system calibration.

There are two important indexes for evaluating the accuracy of system calibration, planeness error and depth error. Thus, to achieve the evaluation of calibration accuracy, two objects are chosen in the experiment. The first object is a standard plane as shown in Fig. 5(a). The second object is a standard sphere as shown in Fig. 6(a). The binary shape-coded pattern in this paper can be used to calibrating the system, it can also be used as the projected pattern of one-shot shape acquisition. Therefore, the pattern is projected onto surfaces of these two targets respectively, and the reflected light are captured by the camera separately. Then, with the proposed grid-point detection

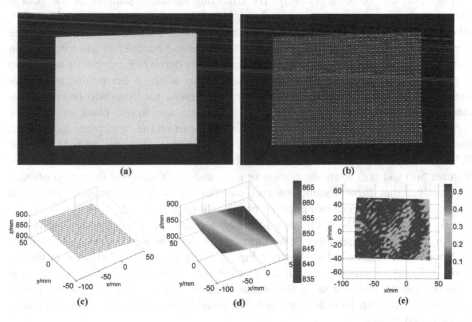

Fig. 5. 3-D reconstruction of a standard plane: (a) the target, (b) grid-detection result, (c) 3-D points, (d) depth reconstruction result, and (e) map of depth error.

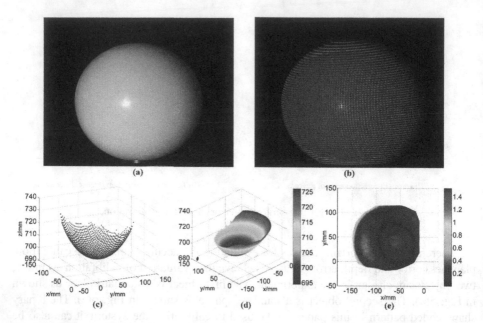

Fig. 6. 3-D reconstruction of a standard sphere: (a) the target, (b) grid-detection result, (c) 3-D points, (d) depth reconstruction result, and (e) map of depth error.

algorithm, the grid-points in the images for these two targets can be detected, as shown in Figs. 5(b) and 6(b), respectively. By collecting sufficient samples of the pattern elements, the decoding task can be achieved, and the correspondences can be found. Thereby the 3-D points for these two objects can be obtained by transforming the correspondences into 3-D information with the calibrated parameters and triangulation principle, as shown in Figs. 5(c) and 6(c). Because the density of 3-D points are not too high, the bilinear interpolation method is applied to obtain dense point-clouds. Figures 5(d) and 6(d) show the depth reconstruction results for these two objects, separately. Then, the point-clouds for these two targets are used to fit a plane and a sphere with the least square fitting method, respectively. Based on the fitted plane and sphere, the mean error can be calculated, the results for the plane and sphere are 0.11 mm and 0.18 mm respectively when the working distance of the system is about 800 mm. Figures 5(e) and 6(e) show the planeness error and depth error for these two objects, separately. From these results, we can see that the system calibration with high accuracy can be achieved using the proposed calibration method.

To further verify the calibration accuracy, a plaster bottle with rough surface as shown in Fig. 7(a) is selected as the target. With the proposed decoding method, its 3-D points can be acquired as shown in Fig. 7(c). Figure 7(d) shows the reconstructed surface. From this picture, we can see that not only the system calibration with high accuracy can be achieved using the proposed calibration method, but also the reconstructed surface with high quality can be obtained by projecting the proposed binary shape-coded pattern.

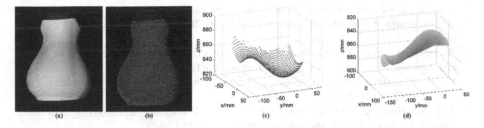

Fig. 7. 3-D reconstruction of a plaster bottle: (a) the target, (b) grid-detection result, (c) 3-D points, and (d) depth reconstruction result.

5 Conclusions

This paper proposed a novel calibration method for the structured light system. The coordinates of 3-D calibration points in the projector image plane are calculated through establishing the corresponding relation between the camera image plane and projector image plane by projecting a robust binary shape-coded pattern which is generated based on the pseudo-random coding theory. After that, the camera and projector are calibrated simultaneously, and the extrinsic parameters of the structured light system are computed. Based on the reverse projection principle of camera calibration, the calibrated parameters are integrally optimized with the help of pseudo-random coded pattern, and the calibration of the structured light system is accomplished. The experimental results demonstrate that the system calibration with high accuracy can be achieved using the proposed calibration method. Besides, not only the proposed binary shape-coded pattern can be applied to calibrate the structured light system, but also it can be used as the projected pattern of one-shot shape acquisition.

Acknowledgments. This work was supported in part by the National Key Research and Development Program of China (2017YFB1103600), Shenzhen Science Plan (CXZZ20140417 113430730, JSGG20150925164740726), Shenzhen Technology Project under Grant (JCYJ2017 0413152535587), Shenzhen Key Laboratory of Acousto-Optic Detection Technology and Equipment (2015-74), and the National Natural Science Foundation of China (61375041, U1613213).

References

1. Zhang, S., Yau, S.: High-resolution, real-time 3D absolute coordinate measurement based on a phase-shifting method. Opt. Express **14**(7), 2644–2649 (2006)
2. Robert, S., Krzeslowski, J., Maczkowski, G.: Archiving shape and appearance of cultural heritage objects using structured light projection and multispectral imaging. Opt. Eng. **51**(2), 021115–021118 (2012)
3. Zhang, Z.: A flexible new technique for camera calibration. IEEE Trans. Pattern Anal. Mach. Intell. **22**(11), 1330–1334 (2000)

4. Tsai, R.: A versatile camera calibration technique for high-accuracy 3-D machine vision metrology using off-the-shelf TV cameras and lenses. IEEE J. Robot. Autom. **3**(4), 323–344 (1987)
5. Huang, J., Wang, Z., Xue, Q., et al.: Calibration of a camera-projector measurement system and error impact analysis. Measur. Sci. Technol. **23**(12), 125402 (2012)
6. Huang, J., et al.: A novel color coding method for structured light 3D measurement. Proc. SPIE **808512**, 1–10 (2011)
7. Tsai, M., Hung, C.: Development of a high-precision surface metrology system using structured light projection. Measurement **38**(3), 236–247 (2005)
8. Da, F., Gai, S.: Flexible three-dimensional measurement technique based on a digital light processing projector. Appl. Optics **47**(3), 377–385 (2008)
9. Chen, L., Liao, C.: Calibration of 3D surface profilometry using digital fringe projection. Measur. Sci. Technol. **16**(8), 1554–1566 (2005)
10. Zhang, S., Huang, P.: Novel method for structured light system calibration. Opt. Eng. **45**(8), 083601 (2006)
11. Cui, S., Zhu, X.: A generalized reference-plane-based calibration method in optical triangular profilometry. Opt. Express **17**(23), 20735–20746 (2009)
12. Yin, Y., et al.: Calibration of fringe projection profilometry with bundle adjustment strategy. Optics Lett. **37**(4), 542–544 (2012)
13. Chen, X., et al.: Accurate calibration for a camera-projector measurement system based on structured light projection. Optics Lasers Eng. **47**(3), 310–319 (2009)
14. Lin, H., Nie, L., Song, Z.: A single-shot structured light means by encoding both color and geometrical features. Pattern Recogn. **54**(2016), 178–189 (2016)
15. Chen, J., Huertas, A., Medioni, G.: Fast convolution with Laplacian-of-Gaussian masks. IEEE Trans. Pattern Anal. Mach. Intell. **4**, 584–590 (1987)
16. Harris, C., Stephens, M.: A combined corner and edge detector. In: Proceedings of the Alvey Vision Conference, vol. 15, pp. 147–152 (1988)
17. Lowe, D.: Distinctive image features from scale-invariant keypoints. Int. J. Comput. Vis. **60**(2), 91–110 (2004)
18. Bay, H., Ess, A., Tuytelaars, T., et al.: Speeded-up robust features (SURF). Comput. Vis. Image Underst. **110**(3), 346–359 (2008)
19. Yann, L., Léon, B., Yoshua, B., et al.: Gradient-based learning applied to document recognition. Proc. IEEE **86**(11), 2278–2324 (1998)

An Automatic 3D Textured Model Building Method Using Stripe Structured Light System

Hualie Jiang[1], Yuping Ye[1], Zhan Song[1,2], Suming Tang[1],
and Yuming Dong[1(✉)]

[1] Guangdong Provincial Key Laboratory of Computer Vision and Virtual
Reality Technology, Shenzhen Institutes of Advanced Technology,
Chinese Academy of Sciences, Shenzhen, China
{hl.jiang,yp.ye,zhan.song,sm.tang,ym.dong}@siat.ac.cn
[2] The Chinese University of Hong Kong, Hong Kong SAR, China

Abstract. This paper presents a novel textured model building method using stripe structured light system. It is implemented by automatic registration of multiple point clouds obtained by the structured light system. Firstly, point clouds captured from different viewpoints are pairwise coarsely registered by feature matching of their corresponding RGB images. Secondly, we use an appropriate function to evaluate the quality of every pairwise coarse registration, and construct a pairwise coarse registration graph which uses point clouds as nodes and the evaluation function between them to weight their corresponding edges. Thirdly, an optimal registration tree will be generated by finding the maximum weight spanning tree of the graph and selecting a node as the root to minimize the depth of the tree. Finally, global fine registration is performed by applying ICP algorithm along the optimal registration tree. Median filtering in luminance space is also applied in the color of the integrated point model to adjust the RGB values. Experiment shows that this approach can automatically build full models which are well-registered and compatible in color for textured objects even when those objects are not rich in geometrical information.

Keywords: Textured 3D modeling · Image feature point matching · Multiple point clouds · Automatic registration

1 Introduction

3D reconstruction is an important research topic in both computer vision and graphics domains. Structured light system is a usual means for 3D scanning of objects [1, 2]. To achieve a complete 3D model of the target or scenario, multiple scans are usually demanded. Therefore, registration and fusion of point clouds is necessary. The process of aligning multiple point clouds is usually called global registration. Besides 3D geometry information, appearance of an object needs to be acquired for rendering purpose. The appearance acquisition is usually implemented by capturing an additional RGB image using the camera in the scanner or an additional color camera.

The ICP algorithm is a classical method in automatic registration of pair point clouds [3]. There are many efficient variants of ICP, which adopt different strategies in six main steps like point selection, matching, weighting, rejecting, error metric assigning and minimizing [4]. The ICP-based algorithms demand a good initial

© Springer International Publishing AG 2017
M. Liu et al. (Eds.): ICVS 2017, LNCS 10528, pp. 615–625, 2017.
DOI: 10.1007/978-3-319-68345-4_54

alignment of two point clouds to ensure global minimum. Therefore, pair point clouds need to be coarsely aligned before applying ICP algorithm. The coarse alignment is usually realized by least-squares fitting of some corresponding points between point clouds, which can be achieved by SVD method [5] or quaternion method [6]. The corresponding points are usually obtained by manually assigning, geometry feature matching or image feature matching.

To register multiple point clouds is a more complex problem than pairwise registration. A simplest method is to align each scan to its prior one, but that does not ensure that contiguous scans share enough overlapping region and usually accumulates alignment errors. The target of global registration is to align multiple point clouds evenly without concentrating error. Conventional global registration methods usually use every pairwise alignment as constraints, and aim at spreading out alignment error. In this paper, a coarse registration graph for pairwise alignments is established and then an optimal registration tree will be constructed from the graph. The edges of the tree usually indicate that their corresponding two nodes have adequate overlapping region and have been aligned well. Next, the ICP algorithm will be applied along the edges of the optimal registration tree to register all scans more accurately.

Besides registration, the textured model building usually contains the procedure of color blending. The RGB values obtained from different viewpoints generally vary due to many factors. The color inconsistency largely suffers from unequal illumination in our scanning setting, so we adjust color of the integrated model by median filtering in illumination space.

This paper is structured as follows: Sect. 2 contains related work; Sect. 3 describes the proposed approach, which contains three procedures. Firstly, we will explain how pair scans are coarsely aligned by feature matching of their corresponding color images and introduce a function for evaluating the performance of pairwise coarse alignment. Then, the method to generate an optimal registration tree of the pairwise coarse alignment graph is outlined. Thirdly, we will demonstrate the approach to achieve global registration by using ICP along the optimal registration tree and color adjusting method. A presentation of experimental results is in Sect. 4. Conclusions and directions for future work are discussed in Sect. 5.

2   Related Work

There are many automatic methods of finding corresponding point pairs for pair scans to make them coarsely aligned before using ICP and those methods are largely based on geometry and color feature matching, or the combination of them. Which strategy should be used depends on whether the geometry or color of the object is sufficiently distinctive. Newest proposed 3D key points include PFH [7] and FPFH [8] and 3D SURF [9]. Those features are usually scale and orientation invariant to some extent, and appropriate for 3D registration and recognition. However, those features may not work when the object is not adequately geometrically distinctive. Therefore, in order to build 3D texture model for object that is rich in texture but simple in geometry, we have to use image features. SIFT is used in multi-view point cloud registration in [10, 11] for Lidar data and RGB-D data respectively. They are both for reconstruction of large scale scenes, such as outdoor or indoor environment, where is rich in image feature. Works that combine geometrical and color information in registration can be found in [12, 13], and they both incorporate color data into ICP framework, namely using RGB values in finding matching points apart from 3D distance. This paper will apply SIFT in additional RGB images to implement pairwise coarse alignment.

Conventional techniques for global registration optimize in pairwise registration graph [14–16]. In [14], cycles within the pairwise registration graph are detected and the mutual inconsistency between pairwise alignments will spread out equally among all pairs of scans within that cycle. In [15], pairwise alignments in the graph that make the most global inconsistency are removed and thus producing a connected and consistent sub-graph, a spanning tree for global registration. Similarly, a spanning tree that maximizes the sum of overlapping area of pairwise alignment is generated for global registration [16]. Our method also generates a spanning tree from the coarse pairwise alignment graph that maximizes the sum of a evaluating function for pairwise alignments and the function is proposed according to the performance of pair coarse alignment based on SIFT point matching.

3D modeling of objects usually demands a turntable [17–19]. A turntable that is well calibrated to structured light scanner is adopted to control the relative motion between the target object and the scanner [17]. The structured light scanner thus can capture the object using 12 scans. While KinectFusion [18, 19] scans hundreds of times evenly and there is huge overlap between two successive scans by which frame-to frame camera motion can be tracked by ICP method quickly. The proposed method needs just about 20 scans for objects modeling and it can also capture the bottom and head of the object, while the turntable-based method cannot.

3 Methodology

The proposed approach consists of three main procedures. The first is to coarsely align every pair scans based on feature point matching of their corresponding pair RGB images, which involves SIFT algorithm [20], RANSRC technique and epipolar geometry model [21], solving rigid transformation between two corresponding 3D point sets [5]. After the first procedure, any pair scans can be considered to have been coarsely aligned if the evaluating function is big enough and the bigger the function, the better the pair scans aligned, thus producing a coarse alignment graph. The second procedure is to generate an optimal registration tree from the coarse alignment graph, which will use Kruskal algorithm and Floyd algorithm in graph theory [22] for spanning maximum tree and finding the best node of the tree as the root, respectively. The third procedure is to perform global registration along the optimal registration tree and adjust the color of the obtained full point model.

3.1 Pairwise Alignment

Every recovery 3D point in range image can have a corresponding pixel in the RGB image. The matching 3D points between scans derive from SIFT matching points in RGB images, then rigid transformation between scans can be estimated by least squares fitting. However, the estimation may be bad due ill matching of feature points. Therefore a function is proposed to evaluate the estimation, and the next procedure will filter out poor estimations according to this function.

Given two scans $\mathbb{Q}$ and $\mathbb{P}$, the specific steps their coarse alignments are listed as following.

- **Feature Matching**: use SIFT algorithm in the corresponding images of these two point clouds and obtain a set of matching pixel points.
- **Epipolar Geometry Constraint**: apply RANSAC algorithm on epipolar geometry model to fit this set of matching points, after which a fundamental matrix as well as a set of robust matching points are obtained; if the number of robust matching points less than a predefined threshold T_1, it means the overlapping region between those two scans is too small, so set the evaluation function $W(\mathbb{Q},\mathbb{P})$ to zero and return.
- **Rigid Transformation Estimation**: find the corresponding 3D matching points for the above robust matching points and apply RANSAC algorithm on rigid transformation model to fit the 3D matching points to obtain the rigid transformation and inliers of 3D matching points; if the number of inliers is small than a predefined threshold T_2, it means the set of 3D matching points is too noisy and thus set the evaluation function $W(\mathbb{Q},\mathbb{P})$ to zero and return.
- **Evaluation Function Calculation**: if this is reached, the two scans can be considered to have been coarsely aligned and the evaluating function should be calculated; as suggested by [5], the performance of the estimation depends on the distribution of the 3D matching points and the wider the distribution, the better the performance; the distribution information in a matrix H computed as

$$H = \sum_{i=1}^{n} y_i y_i'^{\mathrm{T}} \tag{1}$$

where $\{y_i\}_{i=1}^n$ and $\{y_i'\}_{i=1}^n$ are results when the centers of the original 3D matching points move to the origin; apply SVD on the matrix H

$$H = U \operatorname{diag}(\lambda_1, \lambda_2, \lambda_3) V^{\mathrm{T}} \tag{2}$$

the three singular values λ_1, λ_2 and λ_3 (in descending order) represent the distribution range in three principal directions and the effectiveness of rigid transformation estimation requires that the 3D matching points should distributed at least on a plane, therefore the evaluating function is

$$W(\mathbb{Q},\mathbb{P}) = \ln\left(N_{inliers} \cdot \lambda_1(\lambda_2 + \lambda_3) + 1\right) \tag{3}$$

where $N_{inliers}$ is the number of inliers of 3D matching points and it can relatively devalue the possible situation that a few actually mismatching points pass the above procedures; the reason for using the logarithm is to make the evaluating values of the generating tree more balanced; the number 1 is added to function for making it equal to zero when the inliers of 3D matching points are accurately on the same straight line, namely λ_2 and λ_3 equal to zero; afterwards, return the evaluating function value and the rigid transformation matrix.

Using the above algorithm to every pair of scans, a number of pairwise rough registrations and the corresponding evaluation functions. Then we use all scans as nodes to construct a pairwise rough registration graph by linking pairs whose evaluation function is bigger than zero and using it as the weight of the corresponding edge.

3.2   Generation of Optimal Registration Tree

After the construction of the pairwise rough registration graph, the global registration should performed along a spanning tree of the graph to avoid confliction by loops. Precise global registration should utilize the connection information of the graph to achieve best registration, thus the spanning tree has to maximize the sum of the evaluation function in the graph. To generate the maximum spanning tree, the conventional Kruskal algorithm can be adopted, only if the edge with highest weight is selected instead of the one with lowest weight in each step.

After generating maximum spanning tree, a node should be selected as the root to minimize the depth of the tree and we call such tree as the optimal registration tree. At the global registration procedure, the corresponding point cloud of the root of the tree will be the target and other point clouds will align to this root point cloud. When a point cloud align to target point cloud, it will add to it immediately to create enough overlapping region in the target point cloud for the fine registration of its direct child nodes. Therefore, the shorter the depth of tree, the less the accumulated error and the optimal root should minimize the depth of the tree.

Obviously, the depth of the tree must not longer than half of the length of its longest route between two nodes. Therefore, the center node of the longest route should be the root of the tree to optimize the depth to half of the longest route's length. Now, the problem transforms into finding the longest route between node pairs in the tree. Note that the tree has no loop, so the route between every node pair is unique and it means that the longest route is the shortest route for every node pair. Therefore, Floyd algorithm can be use in this task because it finds shortest path for every node pair in a graph.

3.3   Global Registration and Texture Coordination

After the above two procedure, the optimal registration tree and good coarse alignments along edges of the tree are obtained. The global registration can perform ICP algorithm along the optimal tree. Note that we just record rigid transformation matrices for pairwise coarse alignments instead of making rigid transformation between original point clouds. Therefore, the global registration is expressed as following.

I. Push the root of the optimal registration to an empty queue and add its corre-
    sponding point cloud into target point cloud;
II. Pop a node from the queue, and for every son node of this node perform the fol-
    lowing operations until every point cloud has added to the target point cloud:
    i.   align the point cloud of son node to its father's original point cloud by ap-
         plying coarse alignment transformation T_s^f on it;

    ii. align the point cloud of son node to target point cloud by applying the
         original point cloud of its father's registration transformation to the target
         point cloud on it;

    iii. apply ICP algorithm to precisely register the transformed son point cloud
         to the target point cloud and obtain the rigid transformation T_{icp}

    iv. record the fine registration transformation that current son point cloud to
         the target point cloud as

$$T_s^g = T_{icp} \cdot T_f^g \cdot T_s^f$$

    v.   push the current son node to the queue and add the son point cloud to the
         target point cloud.

After this global registration procedure, a well-registered and integrated point
model of is obtained. However, the intensity confliction between scans from different
viewpoints will reduce the visual effect of the model. Our technique to adjust the
intensity of the texture of the model is to transform the color form RGB space into HSV
and then perform median filtering in intensity component, before return RGB space.

4 Experimental Evaluation

The structured light system used in experiment is shown in Fig. 1, which composes of
one projector, one camera and a control board to synchronize the projector and the
camera. This structured light system can recover dense and accurate 3D sampled
points, because it is coded with gray code stripe and phase shifting technique. To
evaluate our approach, we mainly experiment on a matryoshka doll as shown in Fig. 1.
The doll is complex in texture but simple in geometry. 20 scans of the doll are captured
from different viewpoints, and we name them as view0 to view19, respectively.

Table 1 gives data results of some representative coarse pairwise alignments,
including the number of eventual inliers of 3D matching points $N_{inliers}$, their three
distribution principal components λ_1, λ_2 and λ_3, the evaluation function W and the root
mean square before applying ICP algorithm (those whose distance is larger than twice
of median distance are rejected).

Fig. 1. The stripe structured light system for 3D textured modeling

Table 1. Data results of some representative coarse pairwise alignments

Scan pair	$N_{inliers}$	λ_1	λ_2	λ_3	W	RMS (mm)
view4–view5	388	288313.2	69786.9	3414.9	29.73	0.0717
view1–view13	169	178405.7	27658	1034.4	27.49	0.0918
view10–view12	99	55547.1	8237.8	237.9	24.57	0.0953
view9–view15	35	21458.2	3847.4	100.8	21.81	0.0983
view3–view13	20	9406.6	265.1	16.3	18.61	0.1431
view2–view11	7	8507.1	108.1	7.6	15.75	1.1888
view4–view10	7	753.3	148.8	1.9	13.59	0.5319
view3–view9	7	519.3	77.0	0.2	12.54	0.7833
view3–view12	4	206.8	13	0	9.28	2.5828
view2–view7	3	10.8	2.4	0	4.35	2.1722

As shown by Table 1, the former 5 scan pairs are adequately registered, while the later 5 scan pairs are poorly registered. The evaluation function W decreases when the RMS approximately increases, therefore the proposed evaluation function predicts the performance of pairwise alignment as was expected.

Figure 2 shows the eventual matching inliers in RGB images for view10–view12 and view3–view9, and the matching point pairs are lined by straight lines. As can been seen from Fig. 2, view10 and view12 share over half of area, so they have a great many matching points and the mismatching between view3 and view9 is due to the texture similarity of the doll. Actually, most mismatching in our experiment is caused by texture symmetry or similarity. However, the probability that mismatching happens is much lower than correct matching. The incorporation of the number of inliers into evaluation function can further weaken the weights of mismatching scan pairs in the pairwise coarse registration graph, in order to avoid their appearance in the optimal registration tree.

The generated optimal registration tree is shown by Fig. 3. Apparently, all the weights of edges are bigger than 20 and adjacent scan pairs share enough overlapping region. Figure 4(a) shows the integrated model result directly after global registration

Fig. 2. 3D matching point inliers shown in RGB images: (a) view10–view12; (b) view3–view9.

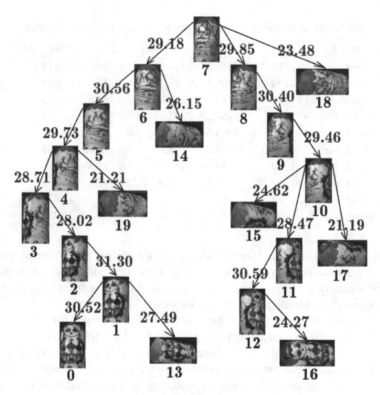

Fig. 3. The optimal registration tree

along the above optimal tree. From Fig. 4 we can see the texture of the model is coordinating, so the multiple scans have been well registered. Actually, the eventual RMS error between every son scan and the target point cloud after applying ICP is all smaller than 0.1 mm. However, the model has a poor visual effect due to illumination difference between different viewpoints. As shown by Fig. 4(b), the textured model after further color adjusting demonstrates much better visual effect.

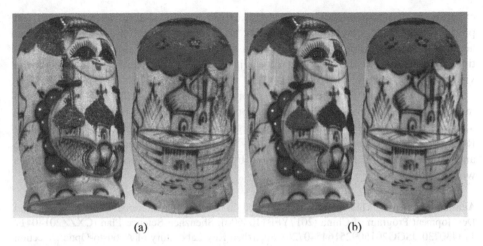

(a)   (b)

Fig. 4. The integrated model from two viewpoints: (a) the direct result of global registration; (b) the result after median filter in luminance space.

Another two 3D textured models of a mango and an apple built by the proposed approach is shown in Fig. 5. Both of them have been well precisely well reconstructed and registration and their texture is recovered correctly too, although there are some specular regions because they are non-lambertian surfaces.

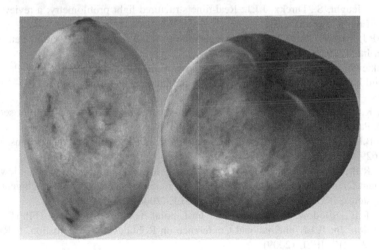

Fig. 5. The textured models of a mango and an apple.

5   Conclusions and Future Work

In this work we introduced an automatic registration approach of multiple scans for the purpose of building 3D textured models. There are three main procedures of the proposed approach, including pairwise alignments and the computation of the evaluation function, the generation of the optimal tree and the final global registration. We experiment on range images obtained by a tripe structured light system which can produce very dense point cloud. Experiment results show that the proposed method can accurately register point clouds, even when the target object is not geometrically distinctive. Additionally, the proposed color adjusting method can sufficiently enhance the visual effect of texture.

Future work will focus on further improving the texture effect of reconstructed models because texture from different viewpoints is not perfectly fused in this paper. In addition, the industrial camera in the structured light system cannot capture high quality RGB images. Therefore, a SLR camera may be used for generated high quality texture and how to mapping the texture obtained by SLR camera to point cloud is a future work direction too.

Acknowledgments. This work was supported in part by the National Key Research and Development Program of China (2017YFB1103600), Shenzhen Science Plan (CXZZ20140417 113430730, JSGG20150925164740726), Shenzhen Key Laboratory of Acousto-Optic Detection Technology and Equipment (2015-74), and the National Natural Science Foundation of China (61375041, U1613213).

References

1. Salvi, J., Fernandez, S., Pribanic, T., Llado, X.: A state of the art in structured light patterns for surface profilometry. Pattern Recogn. **43**(8), 2666–2680 (2010)
2. Van der Jeught, S., Dirckx, J.J.J.: Real-time structured light profilometry: a review. Optics Lasers Eng. **87**, 18–31 (2016)
3. Besl, P.J., Mckay, N.D.: Method for registration of 3-D shapes. IEEE Trans. Pattern Anal. Mach. Intell. **14**(2), 239–256 (1992)
4. Rusinkiewicz, S., Levoy, M.: Efficient variants of the ICP algorithm. In: 2001 Proceedings of Third International Conference on 3-D Digital Imaging and Modeling, pp. 145–152. IEEE (2001)
5. Arun, K.S., Huang, T.S., Blostein, S.D.: Least-squares fitting of two 3-D point sets. IEEE Trans. Pattern Anal. Mach. Intell. **5**, 698–700 (1987)
6. Horn, B.K.P.: Closed-form solution of absolute orientation using unit quaternions. JOSA A **4**(4), 629–642 (1987)
7. Rusu, R.B., Blodow, N., Marton, Z.C., Beetz, M.: Aligning point cloud views using persistent feature histograms. In: IEEE/RSJ International Conference on Intelligent Robots and Systems, IROS 2008, pp. 3384–3391. IEEE (2008)
8. Rusu, R.B., Blodow, N., Beetz, M.: Fast point feature histograms (FPFH) for 3D registration. In: IEEE International Conference on Robotics and Automation, ICRA 2009, pp. 3212–3217. IEEE (2009)
9. Knopp, J., Prasad, M., Willems, G., Timofte, R., Van Gool, L.: Hough transform and 3D SURF for robust three dimensional classification. In: Daniilidis, K., Maragos, P., Paragios, N. (eds.) ECCV 2010. LNCS, vol. 6316, pp. 589–602. Springer, Heidelberg (2010). doi:10.1007/978-3-642-15567-3_43
10. Zheng, Z., Li, Y., Jun, W.: Lidar point cloud registration based on improved ICP method and SIFT feature. In: 2015 IEEE International Conference on Progress in Informatics and Computing (PIC), pp. 588–592. IEEE (2015)

11. dos Santos, D.R., Basso, M.A., Khoshelham, K., de Oliveira, E., Pavan, N.L., Vosselman, G.: Mapping indoor spaces by adaptive coarse-to-fine registration of RGB-D data. IEEE Geosci. Remote Sens. Lett. **13**(2), 262–266 (2016)

12. Huhle, B., Magnusson, M., Straßer, W., Lilienthal, A.J.: Registration of colored 3D point clouds with a kernel-based extension to the normal distributions transform. In: IEEE International Conference on Robotics and Automation, ICRA 2008, pp. 4025–4030. IEEE (2008)

13. Men, H., Gebre, B., Pochiraju, K.: Color point cloud registration with 4D ICP algorithm. In: 2011 IEEE International Conference on Robotics and Automation (ICRA), pp. 1511–1516. IEEE (2011)

14. Sharp, G.C., Lee, S.W., Wehe, D.K.: Multiview registration of 3D scenes by minimizing error between coordinate frames. IEEE Trans. Pattern Anal. Mach. Intell. **26**(8), 1037–1050 (2004)

15. Huber, D.F., Hebert, M.: Fully automatic registration of multiple 3D data sets. Image Vis. Comput. **21**(7), 637–650 (2003)

16. Novatnack, J., Nishino, K.: Scale-dependent/invariant local 3D shape descriptors for fully automatic registration of multiple sets of range images. In: Forsyth, D., Torr, P., Zisserman, A. (eds.) ECCV 2008. LNCS, vol. 5304, pp. 440–453. Springer, Heidelberg (2008). doi:10. 1007/978-3-540-88690-7_33

17. Ye, Y., Song, Z.: An accurate 3D point cloud registration approach for the turntable-based 3D scanning system. In: 2015 IEEE International Conference on Information and Automation, pp. 982–986. IEEE (2015)

18. Newcombe, R.A., Izadi, S., Hilliges, O., Molyneaux, D., Kim, D., Davison, A.J., Kohi, P., Shotton, J., Hodges, S., Fitzgibbon, A.: Kinectfusion: real-time dense surface mapping and tracking. In: IEEE International Symposium on Mixed and Augmented Reality, pp. 127–136 (2012)

19. Heindl, C., Akkaladevi, S.C., Bauer, H.: Capturing photorealistic and printable 3D models using low-cost hardware. In: Bebis, G., et al. (eds.) ISVC 2016. LNCS, vol. 10072, pp. 507–518. Springer, Cham (2016). doi:10.1007/978-3-319-50835-1_46

20. Lowe, D.G.: Distinctive image features from scale-invariant keypoints. Int. J. Comput. Vis. **60**(2), 91–110 (2004)

21. Hartley, R., Zisserman, A.: Multiple View Geometry in Computer Vision. Cambridge University Press, Cambridge (2003)

22. Cormen, T.H.: Introduction to Algorithms. MIT Press, Cambridge (2009)

An Efficient Method to Find a Triangle with the Least Sum of Distances from Its Vertices to the Covered Point

Guoyi Chi[✉], KengLiang Loi, and Pongsak Lasang

Panasonic R&D Center Singapore, Singapore 469332, Singapore
chig0002@e.ntu.edu.sg, {kengliang.loi,pongsak.lasang}@sg.panasonic.com

Abstract. Depth sensors are used to acquire a scene from various viewpoints, with the resultant depth images integrated into a 3d model. Generally, due to surface reflectance properties, absorptions, occlusions and accessibility limitations, certain areas of scenes are not sampled, leading to holes and introducing undesirable artifacts. An efficient algorithm for filling holes on organized depth images is high significance. Points far away from a covered point, are usually low probability in the aspect of spatial information, due to contamination of outliers and distortion. The paper shows an algorithm to find a triangle whose vertices are nearest to the covered point.

Keywords: Filling-hole · Depth enhancement · Depth map · Filling the missing depth pixels

1 Nomenclature

ss The search size of a point.
$N = 4ss^2 + 4ss$ the total number of neighbour points.
$\mathcal{V} = \{v_1, v_2, \ldots, v_N\}$ The set of N points with ascending order.
$\mathcal{V}_x, \mathcal{V}' \subseteq \mathcal{V}$ a subset of $\mathcal{V}$;
    $x \in \{eg1, eg2, eg3, eg4, tri, t\}$.
$\mathcal{P}$ the set of point tags.
$\mathcal{P}(v_i)$ a tag of i-point.
$\mathcal{C}$ the set of complementary tags of each pair of points in $\mathcal{V}$.
$\mathcal{C}(v_i, v_j)$ a tag of (i, j)-pair of points.
$\mathcal{L}_{\mathcal{P}}(\mathcal{V}')$ the *bitwise or* sum of point tags in the set $\mathcal{V}'$.
$\mathcal{L}_{\mathcal{C}}(\mathcal{V}')$ the *bitwise or* sum of complementary tags in the set $\mathcal{V}'$.
$\mathcal{D}$ the value set for all $v_i's \in \mathcal{V}$, which is a matrix.

2 Introduction

Depth sensors are commonly used to acquire the scene from several viewpoints, with the resultant depth images integrated into a desired 3d model. In practice,

© Springer International Publishing AG 2017
M. Liu et al. (Eds.): ICVS 2017, LNCS 10528, pp. 626–639, 2017.
DOI: 10.1007/978-3-319-68345-4_55

due to surface reflectance properties, absorptions, occlusions, and accessibility limitations, certain parts of the scenes are frequently not sampled, leading to holes and introducing undesirable artifacts such as *poorly generated object bound- aries* and *missing depth pixels*. Moreover, depth images suffer from the poor accuracy problem caused by invalid pixels, noise and unmatched edges. Thus, hole-filling algorithms are employed in depth enhancement, reconstruction from point clouds and synthesis with high-quality depth map [1–6].

The literature reports many hole-filling approaches to enhance a depth and synthesize a high-quality depth map. Hybrid depth maps are fused to fill and refine the sparse or unsampled patches in [7]. Depth enhancement approach in [8] depends on an observation that similar RGB-D patches lie in a very low-dimensional subspace. The approach in [8] performs depth map completion as well as de-noising. The depth map correction in [9] utilizes a color-aware Gaussian-weighted averaging filter to refine low-cost depth sensors. In [10], the filling depth holes method is on the basis of 8-connectivity; and cross-bilateral filtering technique is used to refine the hole-filling result, leading to reduce false filling caused by incorrect depth-color fusion. In [11], the region growing method is used to accurately estimate the values of invalid pixels. Additionally, the adaptive bilateral filter is also employed in [11] to effectively reduce the noise of the depth image. All approaches depicted above utilize data from other sources like RGB images and other depth images, instead of itself data. Therefore, the paper considers data from the same depth to discuss the hole-filling problem. Generally, closest points of a missing depth pixel qualify high probability in the aspect of spatial information. Consequently, the paper focuses on finding a triangle with nearest points for triangulation interpolation.

The remainder of the paper is organized as follows. Section 3 introduces some fundamentals of bitwise description of points and edges and then gives a criterion of constructing a triangle. Section 4 describes a methodology to find an optimal triangle with the minimal summation of distances from its vertices to the covered point. Section 5 shows an experiment of the proposed method and compares the efficiency with *traditional method* and Sect. 6 is the conclusion of the paper.

3   Fundamentals

Hole-filling techniques are commonly used in enhancement of a surface where some patches are unsampled caused by reflectance, occlusions and accessibility limitations. Interpolation is a typically hole-filling method to enhance a surface according to the vicinity of observed points. In the paper, consider a relatively sample application situation where neighboured points are organized or griddable, instead of geometrically and topologically complex and unorganized surface. For example, a depth map resembles an organized image (or matrix) like structure, where the data is split into rows and columns. Thus, hole-filling becomes to find three nearest points and then use triangulation interpolation.

Proposition 1. *Consider a point o in an organized 2D image or matrix. Set Point o as the origin in a cartesian coordinate. If a triangle V_{tri} contains Point*

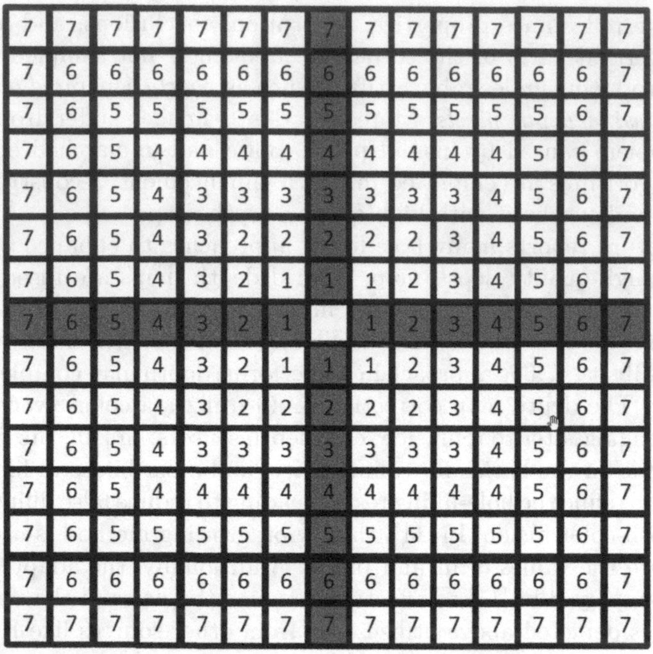

Fig. 1. The search zone $\mathcal{D}$ for Point o with the search size ($ss = 7$)

o, its area must cover four quadrants. Conversely, the area of a triangle $\mathcal{V}_{tri}$ covers four quadrants, the origin (i.e., Point o) must be in Triangle $\mathcal{V}_{tri}$.

In any cartesian coordinate, the origin can be regarded to belong to any quadrant. In other words, the origin covers four quadrants with the minimal area in a cartesian coordinate. Hence, any triangle $\mathcal{V}_{tri}$ covered four quadrants must cover the origin, and vice versa. According to Proposition 1, a new criterion is designed to find a triangle in the remaining of the paper.

3.1   Search Zone

When searching neighbours of Point o, it is not significant to search the whole organized 2D image or matrix because neighbours far away from Point o have a low probability for interpolation from the aspect of spatial analysis. Therefore, define ss as a proper search size and $\mathcal{D}$ as its corresponding search area. The search size ss is to trade off the computation cost and missing spatial information. The search zone is illustrated in Fig. 1. All points in the search area $\mathcal{D}$ are ranked by layers and distances from Point o. Due to the paper length limit, points in the first two layers are listed and ranked, showing Table 1.

3.2 Flag Interpretation

Note that a triangle containing how many quadrants is completely determined by its vertices and edges. An unified tag is introduced here for ease description of *the triangle-search algorithm*. Consider a 7-bit tag for each point and edge (see Fig. 2). The rightmost four bits are used to indicate which quadrant is occupied

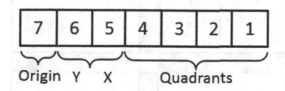

Fig. 2. An unified tag with 7-bit flags

or vacant. For more details, '1' represents the corresponding quadrant is occupied, otherwise '0' means the quadrant is vacant (i.e., no point and edge appears in the quadrant). The leftmost three bits are designed to prevent collinearity. It is worthy to mention that 'Origin' flag and 'Y-X' flags are independent. Next, flags are described in detail from point and complementary modes.

3.3 Point Mode

In point mode, 6-bit flags are used to indicate a point (see Fig. 3).

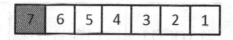

Fig. 3. Flags for a point tag

Condition 1. *if a point is on x-axis, 'Y-X' flags are set to* $(01)_2$ *and then quadrant flags depend on which quadrants are occupied, seeing axes V and VII in Fig. 4. In another case, if a point is on y-axis, 'Y-X' flags are assigned to* $(10)_2$ *and then quadrant flags depend on* bitwise occupation *of quadrants. Otherwise, if a point belongs to any quadrant, 'Y-X' flags are set into* $(11)_2$; *the corresponding quadrant is given by 1 and the other quadrants are assigned into 0.*

Example 1. In Fig. 5(a), consider a point set $\mathcal{V}_{eg1} = \{v_1, v_2, v_3\}$. Bitwise tags for each point in the set $\mathcal{V}_{eg1}$ are $\mathcal{P}(v_1) = (100011)_2$, $\mathcal{P}(v_2) = (011001)_2$ and $\mathcal{P}(v_3) = (010110)_2$. $\mathcal{L}_\mathcal{P}(\mathcal{V}_{eg1}) = \mathcal{P}(v_1)|\mathcal{P}(v_2)|\mathcal{P}(v_3) = (111111)_2$.

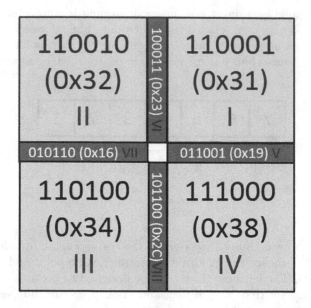

Fig. 4. Quadrants and axes

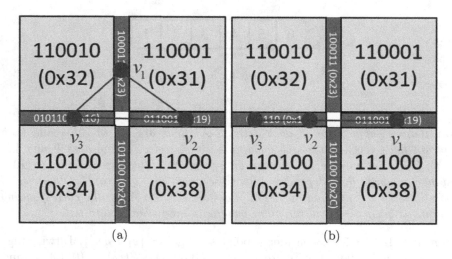

Fig. 5. Examples of the point mode

Example 2. In Fig. 5(b), consider a point set $\mathcal{V}_{eg2} = \{v_1, v_2, v_3\}$. Bitwise tags for each point in the set $\mathcal{V}_{eg2}$ describe $\mathcal{P}(v_1) = (011001)_2$, $\mathcal{P}(v_2) = (010110)_2$ and $\mathcal{P}(v_3) = (010110)_2$. $\mathcal{L}_\mathcal{P}(\mathcal{V}_{eg2}) = (011111)_2$. Note that points v_1, v_2, v_3 are collinear. Therefore, $\mathcal{L}_\mathcal{P}(\mathcal{V}_{eg2}) = 31$ means that it is impossible to construct a triangle to cover the origin.

Remark 1 (Geometry Meaning). The 'X' and 'Y' flags are introduced to prevent the collinearity of three points.

Therefore, the set of point tags $\mathcal{P}$ for the first two layers are shown in Table 1.

Table 1. The point set $\mathcal{V}$ and their tags $\mathcal{P}$ in first two layers

No.	Points $\mathcal{V}$	Tags $\mathcal{P}$ (hex)	Layer	Priority
1	$[-1, 0]$	16	1	1
2	$[0, 1]$	23	1	1
3	$[1, 0]$	19	1	1
4	$[0, -1]$	2c	1	1
5	$[-1, -1]$	34	1	2
6	$[-1, 1]$	32	1	2
7	$[1, 1]$	31	1	2
8	$[1, -1]$	38	1	2
9	$[-2, 0]$	16	2	3
10	$[0, 2]$	23	2	3
11	$[2, 0]$	19	2	3
12	$[0, -2]$	2c	2	3
13	$[-2, -1]$	34	2	4
14	$[-2, 1]$	32	2	4
15	$[-1, 2]$	32	2	4
16	$[1, 2]$	31	2	4
17	$[2, 1]$	31	2	4
18	$[2, -1]$	38	2	4
19	$[1, -2]$	38	2	4
20	$[-1, -2]$	34	2	4
21	$[-2, -2]$	34	2	5
22	$[-2, 2]$	32	2	5
23	$[2, 2]$	31	2	5
24	$[2, -2]$	38	2	5

3.4   Complementary Mode

In complementary mode, 5-bit flags are used to indicate a complement addition within a pair of points (see Fig. 6).

Fig. 6. Examples of the complementary mode

Condition 2. *The seventh flag is determined by*

(i) the segment of two points crosses the origin,
(ii) two points locate in the same quadrant or axis.

If either condition is satisfied, the 7th flag is set to 0. Otherwise, the 7th flag is assigned into 1. The quadrant flags is the bitwise subtraction between the segment and its two points.

Example 3. In Fig. 7(a), consider a point set $\mathcal{V}_{eg3} = \{v_1, v_2, v_3\}$. Its point tags are $\mathcal{P}(v_1) = (110001)_2$, $\mathcal{P}(v_2) = (110001)_2$ and $\mathcal{P}(v_3) = (110100)_2$. $\mathcal{L}_{\mathcal{P}}(\mathcal{V}_{eg3}) = (110101)_2$. The complementary tag of Segment $v_2 v_3$ is assigned as follows. The 7th flag is set to 1 because neither condition is satisfied. Segment $v_2 v_3$ covers three quadrants (i.e., $(1101)_2$). Point v_2 is in the first quadrant (i.e., $(0001)_2$) and Point v_3 locates in the third quadrant (i.e., $(0100)_2$). Thus, the bitwise subtraction between Segment $v_2 v_3$ and Points v_2, v_3 is $(1000)_2$. As a result, $\mathcal{C}(v_2, v_3) = (1001000)_2$. Similarly, $\mathcal{C}(v_1, v_2) = (0000000)_2$, and $\mathcal{C}(v_1, v_3) = (0001010)_2$. After *bitwise or* summation, $\mathcal{L}_{\mathcal{C}}(\mathcal{V}_{eg3}) = \mathcal{C}(v_1, v_2)|\mathcal{C}(v_2, v_3)|\mathcal{C}(v_1, v_3) = (1001010)_2$. $\mathcal{L}_{\mathcal{P}}(\mathcal{V}_{eg3})|\mathcal{L}_{\mathcal{C}}(\mathcal{V}_{eg3}) = (1111111)_2 = (127)_{10}$.

Example 4. In Fig. 7(b), consider a point set $\mathcal{V}_{eg4} = \{v_1, v_2, v_3\}$. Its point tags are $\mathcal{P}(v_1) = (110001)_2$, $\mathcal{P}(v_2) = (110001)_2$ and $\mathcal{P}(v_3) = (110100)_2$. $\mathcal{L}_{\mathcal{P}}(\mathcal{V}_{eg4}) = (110101)_2$. Looking upon Table 2, its complementary tags depict $\mathcal{C}(v_1, v_2) = (0000000)_2$, $\mathcal{C}(v_2, v_3) = (0001010)_2$ and $\mathcal{C}(v_1, v_3) = (0001010)_2$. $\mathcal{L}_{\mathcal{C}}(\mathcal{V}_{eg4}) = (0001010)_2$. Note that points v_1, v_2, v_3 are collinear. Hence, $\mathcal{L}_{\mathcal{P}}(\mathcal{V}_{eg4})|\mathcal{L}_{\mathcal{C}}(\mathcal{V}_{eg4}) = (0111111)_2 \neq (127)_{10}$.

Remark 2 (Geometry Meaning). The 'Origin' flag is utilized to avoid the collinearity of three points.

Table 2 shows complementary tags $\mathcal{C}$ of all segments in the first two layers.

Table 2. The complementary matrix $\mathcal{C}$ (hex) of the first two layers

	1	2	3	4	5	6	7	8	9	10	11	12	13	14	15	16	17	18	19	20	21	22	23	24
1	0	40	0	40	40	40	40	40	0	40	0	40	40	40	40	40	40	40	40	40	40	40	40	40
2	40	0	40	0	40	40	40	40	40	0	40	0	40	40	40	40	40	40	40	40	40	40	40	40
3	0	40	0	40	40	40	40	40	0	40	0	40	40	40	40	40	40	40	40	40	40	40	40	40
4	40	0	40	0	40	40	40	40	40	0	40	0	40	40	40	40	40	40	40	40	40	40	40	40
5	40	40	40	40	0	40	a	40	40	40	40	40	0	40	40	42	48	40	40	0	0	40	a	40
6	40	40	40	40	40	0	40	5	40	40	40	40	40	0	0	40	40	41	44	40	40	0	40	5
7	40	40	40	40	a	40	0	40	40	40	40	40	42	40	40	0	0	40	40	48	a	40	0	40
8	40	40	40	40	40	5	40	0	40	40	40	40	40	44	41	40	40	0	0	40	40	5	40	0
9	0	40	0	40	40	40	40	40	0	40	0	40	40	40	40	40	40	40	40	40	40	40	40	40
10	40	0	40	0	40	40	40	40	40	0	40	0	40	40	40	40	40	40	40	40	40	40	40	40
11	0	40	0	40	40	40	40	40	0	40	0	40	40	40	40	40	40	40	40	40	40	40	40	40
12	40	0	40	0	40	40	40	40	40	0	40	0	40	40	40	40	40	40	40	40	40	40	40	40
13	40	40	40	40	0	40	42	40	40	40	40	40	0	40	40	42	a	40	40	0	0	40	42	40
14	40	40	40	40	40	0	40	44	40	40	40	40	40	0	0	40	40	5	44	40	40	0	40	44
15	40	40	40	40	40	0	40	41	40	40	40	40	40	0	0	40	40	41	5	40	40	0	40	41
16	40	40	40	40	42	40	0	40	40	40	40	40	42	40	40	0	0	40	40	a	42	40	0	40
17	40	40	40	40	48	40	0	40	40	40	40	40	a	40	40	0	0	40	40	48	48	40	0	40
18	40	40	40	40	40	41	40	0	40	40	40	40	40	5	41	40	40	0	0	40	40	41	40	0
19	40	40	40	40	40	44	40	0	40	40	40	40	40	44	5	40	40	0	0	40	40	44	40	0
20	40	40	40	40	0	40	48	40	40	40	40	40	0	40	40	a	48	40	40	0	0	40	48	40
21	40	40	40	40	0	40	a	40	40	40	40	40	0	40	40	42	48	40	40	0	0	40	a	40
22	40	40	40	40	40	0	40	5	40	40	40	40	40	0	0	40	40	41	44	40	40	0	40	5
23	40	40	40	40	a	40	0	40	40	40	40	40	42	40	40	0	0	40	40	48	a	40	0	40
24	40	40	40	40	40	5	40	0	40	40	40	40	40	44	41	40	40	0	0	40	40	5	40	0

3.5 Triangle Criterion

According to Proposition 1, the criterion to construct a triangle is mathematically described in the following.

Criterion 1. *Given a point set $\mathcal{V}'$ with 3 points, a triangle can be constructed, which includes the origin (i.e., Point o). The following condition must be satisfied:*

$$\mathcal{L}_{\mathcal{P}}(\mathcal{V}')|\mathcal{L}_{\mathcal{C}}(\mathcal{V}') = (1111111)_2 = (127)_{10}. \tag{1}$$

The bitwise algorithm is introduced as follows. The point tags $\mathcal{P}$, complementary tags $\mathcal{C}$ and the set of vertices $\mathcal{V}'$ are inputs of Algorithm 1.

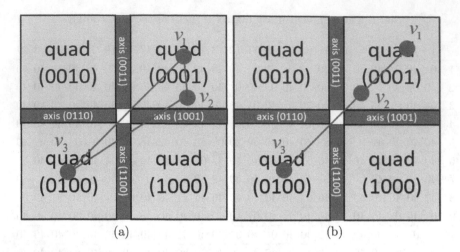

(a)   (b)

Fig. 7. Examples of the complementary mode

Algorithm 1. $\delta = includeTriangle(\mathcal{C}, \mathcal{P}, \mathcal{V}')$

1: $\mathcal{L}_\mathcal{P} := 0;$
2: $\mathcal{L}_\mathcal{C} := 0;$
3: $\delta :=$ false;
4: **for** $i := 1$ **to** $|\mathcal{V}'|$ **do**
5:     $\mathcal{L}_\mathcal{P} := \mathcal{L}_\mathcal{P}|\mathcal{P}(v_i);$
6:     **for** $j := i + 1$ **to** $|\mathcal{V}'|$ **do**
7:         $\mathcal{L}_\mathcal{C} := \mathcal{L}_\mathcal{C}|\mathcal{C}(v_i, v_j);$
8:     **end for**
9:     **if** $\mathcal{L}_\mathcal{P}|\mathcal{L}_\mathcal{C} = 127$ **then**
10:         $\delta :=$ true;
11:         break;
12:     **end if**
13: **end for**
14: return δ

Example 5. Consider the point set $\mathcal{V}_{eg1}$ again in Fig. 5(a). Its complementary tags are enumerated as $\mathcal{C}(v_1, v_2) = (1000000)_2$, $\mathcal{C}(v_2, v_3) = (0000000)_2$ and $\mathcal{C}(v_1, v_3) = (1000000)_2$. Thus, $\mathcal{L}_\mathcal{C}(\mathcal{V}_{eg1}) = (1000000)_2$. Verify $\mathcal{L}_\mathcal{P}(\mathcal{V}_{eg1})|\mathcal{L}_\mathcal{C}(\mathcal{V}_{eg1}) = (1111111)_2$. It can be concluded that the set $\mathcal{V}_{eg1}$ is a triangle covering the origin.

4   Methodology

This section introduces how to find a triangle with the least sum of distances from its vertices to Point o.

Theorem 1. *Consider a point o and its search area $\mathcal{D}$. Define a point set $\mathcal{V}'$ and a point v_t in the search area $\mathcal{D}$. Set $\mathcal{V}'$ contains all points which have higher priority than Point v_t, referring to Table 1. If the new set $\mathcal{V}_{new} = \mathcal{V}' \cup \{v_t\}$ satisfies Eq. (1) but Set $\mathcal{V}'$ does not satisfy Eq. (1), Point v_t is called as a target point. Then, define another point set $\mathcal{V}_t$ that contains all target points with the same priority. $\mathcal{V}' \cap \mathcal{V}_t = \varnothing$. Define N' as the cardinality of Set $\mathcal{V}'$ (i.e., $N' = |\mathcal{V}'|$). Consider that a triangle $\mathcal{V}_{tri}[v_t] = \{v_i, v_j, v_t\}$ regarding to a point $v_t \in \mathcal{V}_t$ has the least priority summation between two Points $v_i, v_j \in \mathcal{V}'(1 \leq i < j \leq N')$. If the triangle $\mathcal{V}_{tri}[v_t]$ covers Point o, the sum of distances from these three vertices to Point o is least.*

Proof. It is trivial to prove this theorem. Let $l_1 = |v_i o|, l_2 = |v_j o|, l_3 = |v_t o|$ and $c_{tri}[v_t] = l_1 + l_2 + l_3$. As described in the theorem, Point $v_t \in \mathcal{V}_t$ is a target point with the least priority. Hence, l_3 is the smallest distance when a triangle $\mathcal{V}_{tri}[v_t]$ is just constructed (which covers Point o). Note that two points v_i, v_j has the least summation of priority and thus $(l_1 + l_2)$ is minimal. Therefore, $c_{tri}[v_t]$ regarding to the target point v_t is least.

One may find that $c_{tri}[v_t]$ regarding to each target point $v_t \in \mathcal{V}_t$ has a different value. Consequently, define a set of triangles $\mathcal{H} = \{\mathcal{V}_{tri}[v_t] : v_t \in \mathcal{V}_t\}$. Mathematically, the optimization problem can be described as follows

$$\mathcal{V}_{tri}^* = \arg\min_{\mathcal{V}_{tri} \in \mathcal{H}} (l_1 + l_2 + l_3) \tag{2}$$

As summarized above, an algorithm is designed to search the triangle with the minimal sum of distances from its vertices to the covered point.

Algorithm 2. $\mathcal{V}_{tri}^* = FindTriangleWithLeastDistance(\mathcal{C}, \mathcal{P}, \mathcal{D})$

```
1:  V' := ∅; V_t := ∅;
2:  for all v_t ∈ V do
3:      if D(v_t) ≠ NA then
4:          δ := includeTriangle(C, P, V' ∪ {v_t});
5:          if δ then
6:              V_t := V_t ∪ {v_t};
7:              if no point as the same priority as v_t then
8:                  break;
9:              end if
10:         else
11:             V' := V' ∪ {v_t};
12:         end if
13:     end if
14: end for
15: if δ = false then
16:     return ∅;
17: end if
18: N' := |V'|; N_t := |V_t|; H := ∅
```

19: **for** $t := 1$ **to** N_t **do**
20:     **for** $k := 3$ **to** $2N' - 1$ **do**
21:         **for** $i := 1$ **to** $k/2$ **do**
22:             $j := k - i$;
23:             **if** $j \leq i \,||\, j > N'$ **then**
24:                 continue;
25:             **end if**
26:             $\mathcal{V}_{tri} := \{v_i, v_j, v_t\}$;
                 // $v_i, v_j \in \mathcal{V}'$ and $v_t \in \mathcal{V}_t$
27:             **if** includeTriangle($\mathcal{C}, \mathcal{P}, \mathcal{V}_{tri}$) **then**
28:                 **goto** *SKIP-LABEL*;
29:             **end if**
30:         **end for**
31:     **end for**
32:     *SKIP-LABEL*: $\mathcal{H} := \mathcal{H} \cup \{\mathcal{V}_{tri}\}$;
33: **end for**
34: $\mathcal{V}^*_{tri} :=$ find triangle with the least sum of distances in $\mathcal{H}$;

Table 3. Comparison of the time efficiency on Matrix $\mathcal{D}$ shown in Table 4

Method	Time (ms)
The paper	85
Traditional method	495

5   Case Study

This section verifies the paper proposed method. Simultaneously, a comparison between the paper proposed method and *traditional method* is conducted. *Traditional method* enumerates all triangle combinations with *ascending order of the priority summation* and then is terminated when finding the first triangle covering the desired point. Cross-product and dot-product are used in *traditional method* to judge whether a triangle is constructed as well as includes the origin. Figure 8 shows a 400×400 depth image, where *black* means no data, *cyan* indicates the height is below 0.1 m and *magenta* represents the height is more than 0.1 m. Consider Point o which locates at the pixel [200,200] of Fig. 8. The blue square in Fig. 8 shows the search size of Point o with $ss = 7$. Matrix $\mathcal{D}$ shows 224 neighbours of Point o in Table 4. Input Matrix $\mathcal{D}$ into Algorithm 2 and then execute Algorithm 2 on desktop computer with configuration of *Intel i7-6700K CPU and 32 GB RAM*. As a result, the set of target points is $\mathcal{V}_t = \{[-1, -2]\}$ and the set of all points ranked before Point $[-1, -2]$ is $\mathcal{V}' = \{[0, 1], [-1, 1], [1, 1], [0, 2], [-1, 2], [2, 1]\}$. Consequently, the optimal triangle

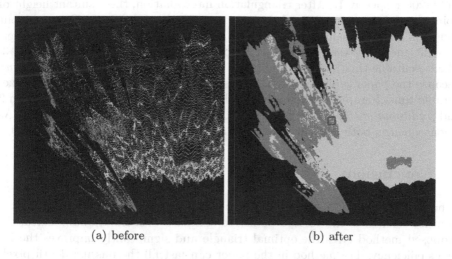

(a) before   (b) after

Fig. 8. Before and after hole-filling. Blue square zone indicates the search zone $\mathcal{D}$ shown in Table 4. (Color figure online)

Table 4. Matrix $\mathcal{D}$ at Point o (marked as $\triangle$) for search size ($ss = 7$).

	1	2	3	4	5	6	7	8	9	10	11	12	13	14	15
1	NA	0.812	NA	NA	NA	NA	0.359	0.000	0.000	NA	0.000	0.000	NA	NA	NA
2	0.803	NA	NA	0.214	NA	0.167	NA	NA	0.475	NA	NA	NA	NA	0.143	0.200
3	NA	0.814	NA	NA	NA	NA	0.000	0.465	NA	NA	NA	0.259	0.000	0.000	0.000
4	0.816	0.826	0.826	NA	NA	NA	0.000	NA	NA	NA	NA	NA	NA	0.000	0.229
5	0.313	NA	0.000	0.000	NA	0.000	NA	NA	NA	NA	NA	NA	0.000	NA	0.000
6	0.563	0.552	NA	NA	0.247	NA	0.200	NA	NA	NA	NA	NA	NA	0.152	NA
7	NA	NA	NA	0.284	NA	NA	NA	NA	NA	NA	NA	NA	0.156	0.000	0.169
8	0.000	0.000	NA	NA	NA	NA	$\triangle$	NA	NA	NA	NA	NA	NA	NA	NA
9	NA	NA	0.335	NA	NA	NA	0.150	0.000	0.400	0.367	0.000	0.000	0.308	0.287	NA
10	NA	0.369	NA	NA	0.000	0.000	0.245	0.000	NA	0.000	0.000	0.511	0.000	NA	NA
11	0.429	0.406	NA	0.316	NA	0.283	0.000	NA	0.448	0.203	0.179	NA	NA	NA	0.000
12	NA	NA	NA	NA	NA	NA	NA	NA	0.440	0.000	0.494	NA	NA	NA	NA
13	NA	NA	NA	0.000	NA	NA	0.530	0.529	0.000	0.000	NA	0.000	NA	0.330	NA
14	0.522	0.534	NA	0.389	0.356	0.543	0.000	NA	0.000	0.531	0.000	0.000	0.188	NA	0.000
15	0.666	0.612	0.590	0.578	0.568	0.556	0.314	NA	0.281	0.000	0.468	NA	0.000	0.346	0.193

is $\mathcal{V}_{tri}^* = \{[0,1],[1,1],[-1,-2]\}$. Heights of three points in $\mathcal{V}_{tri}^*$ are 0.000, 0.400 and 0.200 respectively. After triangulation interpolation, the resultant height of Point o is 0.200 m. *Traditional method* is executed using Matrix $\mathcal{D}$ as an input and thus gives the same triangle (i.e., $\mathcal{V}_{tri}^* = \{[0,1],[1,1],[-1,-2]\}$). However, it's efficiency is lower than the paper proposed method, referring to Table 3. The executable time shown in Table 3 is repeatedly executed by *1 million times* because the paper proposed method consumes too short time to record the executable time. Figure 8(a) shows the depth image before hole-filling. Algorithm 2 and *traditional method* are employed to fill holes of all missing pixels in Fig. 8. As a consequence, both methods give the same hole-filled image shown in Fig. 8(b).

6 Conclusion

A novel method is proposed to find a triangle with the least sum of distances from its vertices to the covered point. To compare with *traditional method*, the proposed method gives the optimal triangle and significantly improves the 5.8 times efficiency. The method in the paper can fast fill the missing depth pixels using triangulation interpolation. This technology can be used in the field which requires a high-efficiency hole-filling algorithm, like reverse-engineering.

References

1. Sheng, L., Ngan, K.N.: Depth enhancement based on hybrid geometric hole filling strategy. In: 2013 IEEE International Conference on Image Processing, pp. 2173–2176, September 2013
2. Wang, J., Oliveira, M.M.: A hole-filling strategy for reconstruction of smooth surfaces in range images. In: 16th Brazilian Symposium on Computer Graphics and Image Processing (SIBGRAPI 2003), pp. 11–18, October 2003
3. Liepa, P.: Filling holes in meshes. In: Eurographics/ACM SIGGRAPH Symposium on Geometry Processing, pp. 200–205 (2003)
4. Smolic, A., Muller, K., Dix, K., Merkle, P., Kauff, P., Wiegand, T.: Intermediate view interpolation based on multiview video plus depth for advanced 3D video systems. In: 15th IEEE International Conference on Image Processing, pp. 2448–2451, October 2008
5. Lee, C., Song, H., Choi, B., Ho, Y.S.: 3D scene capturing using stereoscopic cameras and a time-of-flight camera. IEEE Trans. Consum. Electron. **57**(3), 1370–1376 (2011)
6. Po, L.M., Zhang, S., Xu, X., Zhu, Y.: A new multidirectional extrapolation hole-filling method for depth-image-based rendering. In: 18th IEEE International Conference on Image Processing, pp. 2589–2592, September 2011
7. Saygili, G., Maaten, L.V.D., Hendriks, E.A.: Hybrid kinect depth map refinement for transparent objects. In: 22nd International Conference on Pattern Recognition, pp. 2751–2756, August 2014
8. Lu, S., Ren, X., Liu, F.: Depth enhancement via low-rank matrix completion. In: The IEEE Conference on Computer Vision and Pattern Recognition (CVPR), June 2014

9. Vijayanagar, K.R., Loghman, M., Kim, J.: Refinement of depth maps generated by low-cost depth sensors. In: 2012 International SoC Design Conference (ISOCC), pp. 355–358, November 2012
10. Yang, N.E., Kim, Y.G., Park, R.H.: Depth hole filling using the depth distribution of neighboring regions of depth holes in the kinect sensor. In: 2012 IEEE International Conference on Signal Processing, Communication and Computing (ICSPCC 2012), pp. 658–661, August 2012
11. Chen, L., Lin, H., Li, S.: Depth image enhancement for kinect using region growing and bilateral filter. In: 21st International Conference on Pattern Recognition (ICPR2012), pp. 3070–3073, November 2012

An On-Line Calibration Technique for General Infrared Camera

Dianle Zhou[(⊠)], Xiangrong Zeng, Zhiwei Zhong, and Yan Liu

National University of Defense Technology, Changsha 410073, China
laffiche@163.com

Abstract. The infrared thermal imaging technology has been widely used in the industrial and military fields because of the strong anti-interference ability. One of problem of the infrared camera application is calibration processing, especially, for the long focal length infrared camera. In this paper, we propose an on-line calibration method for general infrared camera where the infrared camera installed on the PAN-Tilt Unit(PTU). The majority advantage of proposal method is no need calibration board. First, infrared image matching algorithm using edge oriented histogram (EOH) descriptor to find correspondence between frames by setting the PTU to variant angles. Then we demonstrate the Pan-Tilt (PT) image matching and calibration algorithm, which is used to calculate the infrared camera intrinsic matrix. The experiments are done on different wavelengths and focal length infrared camera. Infrared calibration board and our proposal method result were compared. The experiment results show that the proposed method is robust and efficient. And we used on-line calibration technique for long distance UAV (Unmanned Aerial Vehicle) detection and localization.

Keywords: Infrared calibration · Edge oriented histogram · Pan-Tilt

1 Introduction

Infrared thermal imaging technology has strong anti- interference ability and it can be exploit in all weather. The majoring limitation of the infrared camera application is the tedious calibration process. The traditional calibration board cannot be used conveniently as a calibration template for infrared camera calibration, especially in the complicated battlefield environment, such as, in runway for UAV detection and localization [1].

There are existing research works proposed to calibrate the infrared camera using calibration board. Figure 1(a) of the infrared thermal image is shown to capture the heating of the image board. Some research methods have been put forward. Vidas [2] is in A4 size cardboard cutout 20 mm * 20 mm of 24 square as shown in Fig. 1(b) show. Ursine and Calado [3] the checkerboard pattern printed on a special production of PCB board. St-Laurent et al. [4] design the circular markers of infrared camera calibration template as shown in Fig. 1(c). In addition, the traditional pattern of the board is a small calibration template, suitable for close range camera calibration work, in the large field of view calibration will be result in a huge error and the uneven distribution of the

© Springer International Publishing AG 2017
M. Liu et al. (Eds.): ICVS 2017, LNCS 10528, pp. 640–651, 2017.
DOI: 10.1007/978-3-319-68345-4_56

accuracy of the field of view. Kong et al. [5] design of 3M * 3M square wooden frame calibration structure, as shown in Fig. 1(d), insert in every wood corner light a lamp incandescent lamp.

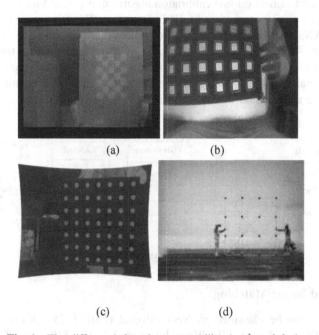

(a)   (b)

(c)   (d)

Fig. 1. The different infrared camera calibration board design

Other methods are also include using suspension electric wire network. Johnson and Bajcsy [6] open type flash light bulb line at both ends of a pole. Zheng et al. [7] patch near infrared luminescent tube arrangement for 8 * 8 arrays. Ellmauthaler et al. [8] use another calibration board. Cai and Yang [9] use nonlinear optimization estimating Near Infrared Camera intrinsic and external.

A summary of our lab previous work on infrared and visual calibration are listed as follow. Yu et al. [10] uses one calibration board for visual and infrared calibrate. Kong et al. [5] design of 3M * 3M square. Yan and Zhou [11] use differential GPS (DGPS) to calibrate large view camera external matrix. Li et al. [12] use DGPS to calibrate infrared, visual and distance model. All the above methods depend on complex calibration equipment, which make the calibration time consuming.

In this paper, we propose an on line calibration algorithm for general infrared camera, not depend on cardboard. First infrared image matching algorithm using edge oriented histogram (EOH) descriptor. Then we demonstrate the PT image matching and calibration algorithm, which is used to calculate the infrared camera intrinsic matrix. The experiments are done on different wavelengths and focal length infrared camera. Infrared calibration board and our proposal method result were compared. There also take full advantage of sequence image and rotation matrix to decrease intrinsic matrix error. And we used our method for long distance UAV detection and localization.

2 A On-Line Calibration Method for General Infrared Camera

A general infrared camera on-line calibration algorithm is divided into four parts. First, infrared feature point is matched using EOH from two PTU turn angle frames. Second we use the RANSAC to eliminate larger error points for estimation homography matrix between the pre-frame and current frame. Then there is structured the relationship image intrinsic matrix between with PTU rotation matrix and homograph matrix. There are using optimal to estimate image intrinsic matrix. Final it takes full advantage of sequence image and rotation matrix to decrease intrinsic matrix error (Fig. 2).

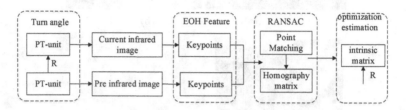

Fig. 2. The flow chart of our calibration algorithm

2.1 Infrared Image Matching

Infrared image can be classified as Near-Infrared (NIR: 0.75–1.4 μm), Short-Wave Infrared (SWIR: 1.4–3 μm), Mid-Wave Infrared (MWIR: 3–8 μm) and Long-Wave Infrared (LWIR: 8–15 μm) ones. Many research works have been done on infrared image matching, while they are most in LWIR, Li and Gu [13] use SIFT for IR image sequence mosaic, Aguilera and Barrera [14] use Edge-Oriented-Histogram (EOH) for visual and infrared registration. Many infrared cameras are 12-bit or 14-bit pixel image, while output is 8-bit pixel image. So using SIFT matching is not very well. Our paper use EOH for infrared and infrared image matching.

The feature points detection algorithm is described by using the EOH. EOH is similar as the scale-invariant feature transform descriptor. These EOHs corporate spatial information is the contours in the neighborhood of each feature point. The descriptor is based on the use of histograms of contours' orientations in the neighborhood of the given keypoints.

Firstly, this region is split up into 4 × 4 = 16 sub-regions. Then, each one of these sub-regions is represented by a histogram of contours operator. This histogram represents the spatial distribution of four directional edges and one non-directional edge (five bins in total), these bins correspond to contour orientations of 0, 45, 90, and 135 degrees. Additionally, a bin with no orientation is considered, which corresponds to those areas that do not contain a contour. Every pixel of each sub-region contributes to a bin of the histogram according to the five filters, of 3 × 3 pixels, shown in Fig. 3.

Infrared and visual image matching using EOH is show in Fig. 4. Figure 4 Left image is infrared, and right image is visual.

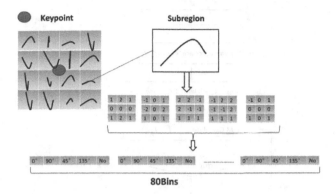

Fig. 3. EOH descriptor

Fig. 4. Infrared and visual image matching using EOH

2.2 Pan-Tilt Infrared Camera Calibrated

We assume the standard model for the intrinsic parameters of a camera without lens distortion at a same zoom scale, namely a 3 × 3 calibration matrix K given by

$$K = \begin{bmatrix} f_x & 0 & c_x \\ 0 & f_y & c_y \\ 0 & 0 & 1 \end{bmatrix} \tag{1}$$

Consider the feature correspondence $x_u \leftrightarrow x'_u$ between two matching feature points. The feature match is related by a homography, represented as a 3 × 3 matrix H that it acts on homogeneous image coordinates, $Hx_u \leftrightarrow x'_u$. This can also be expressed as

$$x'_u \times Hx_u = 0 \tag{2}$$

Infrared image matching has many error points, so it uses the RANSAC to eliminate larger error points.

Each such pair is related by a homography, which we can explicitly compute in terms of the intrinsic parameters [15]:

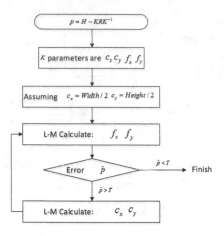

Fig. 5. Optimization solution

$$H = KRK^{-1} \tag{3}$$

where K is the calibration intrinsic matrix for the undistorted image, and R is the relative 3D rotation of the camera from PTU rotated. Note that all the image coordinates used to compute H are normalized with respect to the principal point.

Here is the analysis of the R matrix. As shown, the rotation angle of the three parameters of the PTU and the navigation coordinates are: a yaw angle θ around rotation X axis; Y axis of rotation about the pitch angle ψ; around Z axis roll angle ϕ. While PTU only contains yaw and pitch angle. According to the relationship between the three angles of rotation, we can see that the three angles of the direction cosine matrix, Yaw angle θ:

$$R_\psi = \begin{bmatrix} 1 & 0 & 0 \\ 0 & \cos(\theta) & \sin(\theta) \\ 0 & -\sin(\theta) & \cos(\theta) \end{bmatrix} \tag{4}$$

Pitch angle ψ:

$$R_\psi = \begin{bmatrix} \cos\psi & 0 & -\sin\psi \\ 0 & 1 & 0 \\ \sin\psi & 0 & \cos\psi \end{bmatrix} \tag{5}$$

Rotation matrix R can be expressed in three separate direction cosine transform matrix above. Therefore, the navigation coordinate system to PTU coordinate system transformation matrix R can be expressed as:

$$R = R_\theta \times R_\psi \tag{6}$$

2.3   Optimization Solution

There are at least 4 parameters in intrinsic parameters K, c_x and c_y are image center, f_x and f_y are scale factor of X axis and Y axis. It is difficult to directly solve the equation with four parameters. In this paper, we uses Levenberg-Marquardt (L-M) algorithm [16] to obtain camera intrinsic parameters K by iterative optimization for more accurate K.

The primary application of the L-M algorithm is in the least-squares curve fitting problem. Like other numeric minimization algorithms, the L-M algorithm is an iterative procedure. To start a minimization, the user has to provide an initial guess for the parameter vector. c_x and c_y can be as the center point of the image, f_x and f_y can be approximation estimation. In cases with multiple minima, the algorithm converges to the global minimum only if the initial guess is already somewhat close to the final solution. Nonlinear least square method is to solve $\hat{p}$, so $p = \hat{p}$ that at the time, the objective function is the minimum value.

$$p = H - KRK^{-1} \tag{7}$$

We can assume that c_x, c_y has be known, c_x and c_y are approximation considered as the center point of the image, Solving parameters f_x and f_y, and then assume f_x and f_y is right to solve the parameters c_x and c_y, and continue to solve f_x and f_y. Until the requirement errors is minimized.

A single PTU rotation accuracy may be not high, or sometimes PTU have gap that cause the rotation matrix accuracy is not high. This paper presents a real-time measurement intrinsic matrix K by a PTU rotation.

3   Experimental Results

In this paper, we compare NIR, SWIR and LWIR infrared, using different infrared camera and different focal length, and then compare with calibration of some classical methods. Verify the validity and feasibility of this method. The experimental process is show in Fig. 6. Signal calibration is to calibrate infrared intrinsic matrix, sequence calibration is also to calibrate infrared intrinsic matrix for improve accuracy, compared board-based and UAV localization is to show our method that is robust.

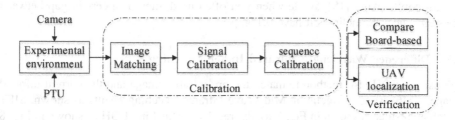

Fig. 6. Experimental process

3.1   Experimental Environment

The environment of the experiment includes the PTU and various infrared cameras, as shown in the Fig. 7.

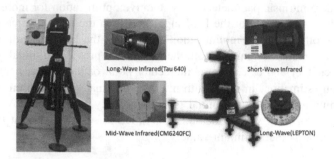

Fig. 7. Experimental environment

Tau 640 is FLIR Long-Wave Infrared. Pixel size is 640 × 512, wavelength is the 7.5–13.5 μm, focal length is 60 mm. CM6240FC refrigeration Mid-Wave Infrared. Pixel size is 640 × 480, wavelength is the 3.7–4.8 μm, focal length is 240 mm, field of view (FOV) is 2.3 × 1.8°, the camera do not good use general calibration table. The Short-Wave Infrared is near 2.5 μm, FOV is about 20°, LEPTON is FLIR Long-Wave infrared, pixel size is 80 × 60, wavelength is the 8–14 μm, FOV is about 120°, show in Table 1.

Table 1. Infrared cameral

Wave	Name	Pixel size	FOV/°
Long-wave	Tau 640	640 × 512	55 × 45
Long-wave	LEPTON	80 × 60	∼120
Mid-wave	CM6240FC	640 × 480	2.3 × 1.8
Short-wave	–	320 × 240	∼90

FLIR turret is America Foundation's selection biaxial gyro-stabilized turret, model PTU-D300. PTU-D300 is a stepper motor driver, able to meet the needs of the closed-loop tracking [18]. While when you often used, there is a certain gap between the gear wheel. Sometimes it have 0.1°gap.

3.2   Difference Wavelength Infrared Image Matching

We use the EOH [14] method to match the pre-infrared image and the current infrared image. CM6240FC refrigeration Mid-Wave infrared matching results as shown, SIFT matching results as shown in Fig. 8(a), the results of matching EOH as shown in Fig. 8 (b), EOH matching feature points and matching accuracy are greater than the matching SIFT. The camera intrinsic parameters detection error between different feature points matching will introduce next.

Fig. 8. Mid-Wave infrared matching. (a) SIFT matching, (b) EOH matching.

The Short-Wave infrared focal is near 2.5 μm. The matching results using SIFT are shown in Fig. 9(a), the results of matching EOH are shown in Fig. 9(b). From the figures we can see that the EOH matching method is more accurate than SIFT.

Fig. 9. Short-Wave infrared matching. (a) SIFT matching, (b) EOH matching.

Long-Wave infrared EHO matching results are shown in Fig. 10. Figure 10(a) is Tau-640 long-wave infrared EHO matching. Figure 10(b) is LEPTON long-wave infrared EHO matching. We also test the EHO matching algorithm in low resolution images, as show in Fig. 10(b). The result shows the applicability on the image resolution.

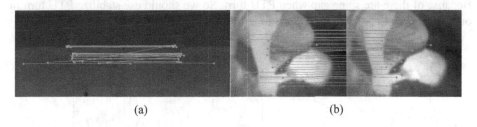

Fig. 10. Long-Wave infrared EHO matching. (a) Tau-640, (b) LEPTON using image amplification

3.3 Infrared Camera Calibration

Infrared image matching may be many error points, so it uses the RANSAC to eliminate larger error points. It uses formula (2) to solve H matrix.

$$H = \begin{bmatrix} 0.98 & 0.05 & 80.32 \\ -0.02 & 1.04 & -2.89 \\ 0 & 0 & 1 \end{bmatrix}$$

And then using the Fig. 5, the first step is to solve the equation, which error is $\|\hat{p}\| = 2.6e - 0.6$. Second step solution, error is $\|\hat{p}\| = 1.6e - 0.6$ and the last is $\|\hat{p}\| = 1.5e - 0.6$ when do fourth time.

$$K = \begin{bmatrix} 15604.33 & 0 & 320 \\ 0 & 15604.33 & 240 \\ 0 & 0 & 1 \end{bmatrix} \rightarrow \begin{bmatrix} 15604.33 & 0 & 319.72 \\ 0 & 15604.33 & 239.63 \\ 0 & 0 & 1 \end{bmatrix}$$
$$\cdots \rightarrow \begin{bmatrix} 15609.33 & 0 & 319.58 \\ 0 & 15609.33 & 239.51 \\ 0 & 0 & 1 \end{bmatrix}$$

CM6240FC refrigeration Mid-Wave Infrared FOV is $2.3 \times 1.8°$. The FOV $\operatorname{atan}(\frac{c_x}{f_x})$ is $2.35 \times 1.76°$, there are 2.1% errors. While SIFT matching FOV is $0.73 \times 0.57°$, the error is larger.

3.4 Solution of Rotation Process

A single PTU rotation may lead accuracy is not high, or sometimes PTU have gap that cause the rotation matrix is error. By using the real-time solution during the rotation of the turntable is useful. The continuous measurement method is adopted in the process of the rotation of the PTU. The results are shown in Fig. 11. In (a) green is PTU tile and blue is Pan. In (b) red is FOV. When Pan is increase in one direction as show the Time is less than 120, the FOV accurate is as well. When Pan is not increase in one direction or slower increase as show the Time is large than 120, the FOV accurate is not well. Because of there are some gap when PTU turn. So we should use stabilize PTU turn in one direction and list five times turn to calibrate, the last FOV is $2.32 \times 1.77°$.

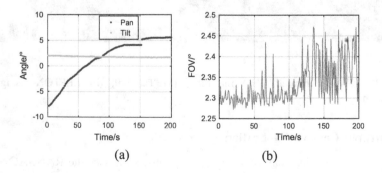

(a)   (b)

Fig. 11. Solution of rotation process (Color figure online)

3.5   Compare with Board-Based

We compare with the calibration board with literature [10]. That assume calibration board is accuracy. Parameter calibration experiment as shown in the Table 2, the error is about 1.5% (Fig. 12).

Table 2. The results of proposal and board-based calibration method

Tau-640	Proposal	Board [10]
f_x	630.319	639.119
f_y	629.144	639.119
c_x	315.704	319.100
c_y	255.710	255.629

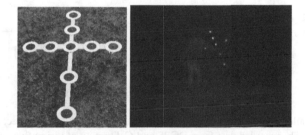

Fig. 12. Calibration board with literature 10

3.6   UAV Detection and Localization

We also used our on-line calibration technique for long distance UAV detection and localization. The FOV is $2.32 \times 1.77°$. It detect 2–4 km UAV target. The infrared camera shows in Fig. 13. That Fig. 13(a) is about 4 km UAV, (b) is about 2 km UAV. Top right corner is UAV amplifying image. We use Sobel to detect small infrared UAV and EKF to tracking small infrared UAV [17].

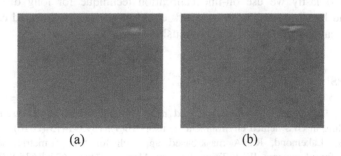

(a)   (b)

Fig. 13. Small infrared UAV Detection, (a) UAV is in 4 km, (b) UAV is in 2 km

3D coordinate localization [18] is show in Fig. 14. (a) The trajectory of the entire 2–4 km. (b)(c)(d) The recorded data from DGPS and Calibration of vision System is show in *X, Y* and *Z*–axis. (e)(f)(g) The absolute errors in *X, Y* and *Z* axis. *X* is horizontal direction, *Y* is depth direction, and *Z* is altitude direction. The *X-errors* is about 1 m, the *Y-errors* is about 4 m, the *Z-errors* is about 1 m.

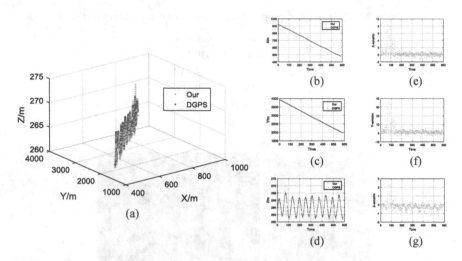

Fig. 14. The detailed presentation of 2–4 km UAV localization. (a) The trajectory of the entire 2–4 km. (b)(c)(d) The recorded data from DGPS and Calibration of vision System in *X, Y* and *Z*– axis. (e)(f)(g) The absolute errors in *X, Y* and *Z* axis.

4 Conclusion

In this paper, we propose an on-line calibration algorithm for universal infrared camera. The experiments are done by using Short-Wave Infrared, Mid-Wave Infrared, Long-Wave Infrared and different focal length, especially have lower resolution 80 × 60. Finally, the method using infrared calibration plate and the method of ours results were compared. The results show that the proposed method is robust and effective. And lastly we use on-line calibration technique for long distance UAV detection and localization. The future work could be combining infrared camera with visible light camera calibration synchronously.

References

1. Yang, T., Li, G., Li, J.: A ground-based near infrared camera array system for UAV auto-landing in GPS-denied environment. Sensors **16**(9), 1393–1413 (2016)
2. Vidas, S., Lakemond, R.: A mask-based approach for the geometric calibration of thermal-infrared cameras. IEEE Trans. Instrum. Measur. **61**(6), 1625–1635 (2012)

3. Ursine, W., Calado, F.: Thermal/visible autonomous stereo visio system calibration methodology for non-controlled environment. In: 11th International Conference on Quantitative Infrared Thermography (2012)

4. St-Laurent, L., Prévost, D., Maldague, X.: Fast and accurate calibration-based thermal/colour sensors registration. In: 10th International Conference on Quantitative InfraRed Thermo-graphy (2010)

5. Kong, W., Zhang, D., Wang, X., Xian, Z., Zhang, J.: Autonomous landing of an UAV with a ground-based actuated infrared stereo vision system. Int. Conf. Intell. Robot. Syst. **11**(3), 2963–2970 (2013)

6. Johnson, M.J., Bajcsy, P.: Integration of thermal and visible imagery for robust foreground detection in tele-immersive space. Inf. Fusion **44**(13), 1–8 (2008)

7. Zheng, B., Ji, J., Yang, R.: Calibration study of high-precesion near infrared camera. Med. Equip. J. **32**(12), 15–17 (2011)

8. Ellmauthaler, A., da Silva, E.A.B., Pagliari, C.L., Gois, J.N., Neves, S.R.: A novel iterative calibration approach for thermal infrared cameras. In: 20th IEEE International Conference on Image Processing, pp. 2182–2186 (2013)

9. Cai, K., Yang, R.: Near-infrared camera calibration for optical surgical navigation. J. Med. Syst. **40**(3), 67–79 (2016)

10. Yu, Z., Lincheng, S., Dianle, Z.: Camera calibration of thermal-infrared stereo vision system. Intell. Syst. Des. Eng. Appl. 197–201 (2013)

11. Yan, C., Zhou, D.: A new calibration method for vision system using differential GPS. In: 13th International Conference on Control, Automation, Robotics and Vision, pp. 1514–1517 (2014)

12. Li, H., Zhong, Z., Kong, W., Zhang, D.: A fast calibration method for autonomous landing of UAV with ground-based multisensory fusion system. In: International Conference on Information, pp. 3068–3072 (2015)

13. Li, L., Gu, G.: Infrared image sequence mosaic based on feature points and Poisson fusion. Infrared Laser Eng. **42**(9), 2584–2588 (2013)

14. Aguilcra, C., Barrera, F.: Multispectral image feature points. Sensors **12**, 12661–12672 (2012)

15. Ziyan, W., Radke, R.J.: Keeping a Pan-tilt-zoom camera calibrated. IEEE Trans. Pattern Anal. Mach. Intell. **35**(8), 1994–2007 (2013)

16. Manolis, L.A.: A brief description of the Levenberg-Marquardt algorithm implemented by Levmar. Inst. Comput. Sci. **3**, 1–6 (2005)

17. Tang, D., Tianjiang, H.: Ground stereo vision-based navigation for autonomous take-off and landing of UAVs: a Chan-Vese model approach. Int. J. Adv. Robot. Syst. **13**(2), 1–14 (2016)

18. Zhou, D., Zhong, Z., Zhang, D.: Autonomous landing of a helicopter UAV with a ground-based multisensory fusion system. In: 7th International Conference on Machine Vision, vol. 9445:94451R-94451R-6 (2015)

Author Index